BUSINESS ETHICS AND CORPORATE GOVERNANCE

BUSINESS ETHICS
AND
CORPORATE GOVERNANCE

Prof. K. Viyyanna Rao

Former Vice Chancellor
Acharya Nagarjuna University
Guntur (Andhra Pradesh)

Dr. G. Naga Raju

UGC-Post Doctoral Fellow
Department of Commerce & Business Administration
Acharya Nagarjuna University
Guntur (Andhra Pradesh)

TECHSAR™

NEW DELHI

Published and Printed by

Techsar Pvt. Ltd.
4435-36/7, Ansari Road, Daryaganj,
New Delhi–110 002 (India)
E-mail: tech_info@techsarworld.com
Website: www.techsarworld.com

ISBN: 978-93-85909-73-3

Reprint 2025

Dedicated to

Professor D. Dakshina Murthy

M.Com., Ph.D. (New York)

and

Madam Anuradha

With Unbounded Regards

Foreword

Though Ethics is integral to the human life to orient societies to a better order, it is only, of late, Business Schools have started taking interest in offering the same as a course of study. At least in India, the great mishap of Union Carbide occurred during December 2-3, 1984 has arisen debate on the conduct of business units. Even after the lapse of 32 years, victims were not able to forget the fateful day. It is also haunting the successive governments in terms of their involvement in handling or mishandling the situation. The sweep of the incident had been such that the death toll was put at a total of 3787 persons, besides 5,58,125 injuries and the loss of valuable biodiversity. Health hazards are occasionally reported even now. Thus, the whole mishap left a scar on the face of Business India.

Unfortunately, it was not the lone incident that occurred in India. World over, there are cases of misconduct being reported. Pollution of the air, water, high seas has remained a cause of worry. Clean air and potable water are emerging as the biggest challenges to the nations. That the Indian government had to earmark a fabulous amount of Rs. 20,000 crore for cleaning the River Ganga, which is considered sacred by Hindus, goes to highlight the severity of the situation. How much money needs to be spent for putting all other rivers of the country in order, remains anybody's guess.

Year after year, the planet earth is becoming quite unsafe for human and animal living. Tsunamis, tycoons, landslides, volcanoes, extremely high and low temperatures are emerging as the order of the day. Global warming and the consequent rise in the temperatures are frightening the world. The constant melting of ice at glaciers is causing floods at uneven times and also causing imbalance in biodiversity. Al Gore, as a matter of fact, sensitized the entire world with his much viewed film: An Inconvenient Truth.

Besides global warming, there are several other issues confronting the planet Earth; which include all kinds of pollution (air, water, soil, noise), climate changes, ozone depletion, deforestation, excessive urbanization, land use, public dumping and unclean environment, resulting in unwanted waste. In addition to the biodegradable waste, electronic refuse is challenging the world, suggesting to find ecofriendly ways and means of waste disposal and reuse. Overpopulation is also stated to be a menace to the environment on the planet, leading to scarcity of every resource, be it air, water, land, food and fuel. Intensive methods of agriculture are identified to be damaging the already strained environment, through the use of chemical fertilizers, pesticides and insecticides. It is for this reason, 'organic farming' is campaigned and advocated. Interestingly, genetic modification (via genetic engineering) is also said to contribute to the growth of toxins and diseases as genes from all allergic plants. Another serious problem emanating from these developments is that the insects are transforming resistant to antibiotics and thus cascading the use of more toxins and more damage to the environment.

Keeping aside the complex issues like the global warming and genetic engineering, even simple matters like waste disposal are also emerging as issues of serious nature to be looked into by the corporate and the governments as well. India is a great place for dumping the waste. As per one estimate, the Indian cities alone generate more than 100 million tons of solid waste a year. The common sight in India is that the street corners are piled with garbage and all public places are filled with filth and litter; making it necessary to launch major campaigns like 'Clean Ganga'. It is true not only with the River Ganges, it is an experience with every other river course in India. The 'Swatch Bharat Programme' unwieled by the Hon'ble Prime Minister, Shri Narendra Modi, is an indication of the problem at hand. Therefore, even a small step in this direction by the corporate world can change the face of the rural and urban India.

It is in this context, the present book is an attempt in the direction of sensitizing the people of the country towards business practices. Not only the faculty and students of the Business Schools, but also the captains of industry need to be aware of the ongoing development in the area of '**corporate governance**' and raise to the occasion beyond 'mere compliance' with the rules, regulations and guidelines. The businesses are, in my opinion, required to ingrain an ethical code into their veins and inculcate it as a 'philosophy' and not just as a business practice. I commend the effort of Prof. K. Viyyanna Rao and Dr. G. Naga Raju in bringing out a volume on the theme of great contemporary relevance as an useful addition to the existing literature.

V. Balamohandas

Preface

Businesses being integral parts of the society, are obliged to follow ethical principles in their conduct. Gone were the days when ethics was felt to be akin to individuals alone. When individuals are organizing themselves as groups, the latter are also subjected to the same code of ethics. Ethics shall be treated not as a charity, but as a bounded duty. For the very survival of the business entities is based on how faithful they are to the society. It is the society that permits them to operate as master. The servant is always under an obligation to obey the commands of the master. It is in this context, the '**Trusteeship Theory of Gandhiji**' is found aptly suited to the business organizations. Every business shall treat itself as a custodian and not as a owner of the resources of the society. By being ethical, one is justifying one's existence. As a matter of fact, human chains are said to survive only when societies are organized and subjected to a predefined '**code of ethics**'.

The obvious reasons that prompted us to write this book are : one, there are a spate of unethical practices that are coming to the notice of the people in the society that is leading to a kind of resentment against the business and industry. Deception is not the synonym of business. Promoters need to elevate themselves beyond the 'bottom lines' and anchor their vision in doing business on sound ethical principles. The cases cited in this book are a testimony to the contemporary practices. And unfortunately, big names like Volkswagen, Walmart, Maruti Suzuki, Coca-Cola, Reliance are involved and hitting the headlines of the print and electronic media. This is not the purpose for which they are supposed to have come to the fame. We feel that there is a great 'need of advocacy' to change the mindset of the business. The present attempt is a small step in that direction.

Secondly, there is every effort by the government to condition the behaviour of the business houses to comply with a code of conduct. Across the world, there has been an attempt to put in place '**a governance model**' beginning with the United Kingdom, following the appointment of Cadbury Committee. Many other countries in Europe, America and Canada are also seriously in the pursuit of imposing a kind of corporate discipline. The focus on corporate governance in India started with the constitution of Birla Committee. Even the industry association like the Confederation of Indian Industry (CII) also voluntarily expressed its concern to improve upon the governing practices. This was followed by the appointment of another committee under the Chairmanship of N.R. Narayana Murthy. Having considered the matter as a priority, the Government of India amended the Companies Act, 1956 and other relevant legislations. A final shape was given to the landmark legislation in the field of corporate management, by bringing out a comprehensive enactment in the name of 'Companies Act, 2013'. The effort is on and on with a recent amendment again in 2016.

In view of all these contemporary developments, it is felt desirable to bring out a new volume on the subject of '**Business Ethics and Corporate Governance**'. Hence, the present book. The authors will be grateful for comments to improve the next edition.

K. Viyyanna Rao
E-mail: kodativrao@gmail.com

G. Naga Raju
E-mail: nagaraju_7g@yahoo.com

Acknowledgements

We acknowledge the support extended by the colleagues in the department and for their helpful comments on the earlier drafts. Corporate governance is an issue much to do with the industry. We are given an opportunity by many industrialists to share their own feelings and experiences in the matter of compliance with the Governance Code. We are highly grateful to all of them and seek their excuse for not being able to acknowledge them by name. We feel obliged to place on record the useful services of research scholars and students of M.Com and M.B.A. in pooling up the learning resources and vibrant discussions in the classroom.

K. Viyyanna Rao

G. Naga Raju

Contents

1

CHAPTER

Ethics: Concept and Sources

1. INTRODUCTION

It is a common sense proposition that people urge to possess what they do not have. Ethics in the recent past has turned out to be a topic of hot debate. Human beings to be called 'civilized', need to follow certain principles of societal order. Lest, it should lead to anarchy or jungle raj; the phase which mankind has already passed through. With the fond hope that they do not revert to their 'stone age', there is a cry for establishing some kind of social order. The relations among people in the society to be conducted in an 'orderly manner', devised a 'code of conduct' to promote and proliferate them. Human beings do need a code to perform their duties to the satisfaction of every member of the society. A king (ruler) at the top needs a code and the man below the ladder down to the individual (as a member of the family and society) requires guidance. It is for this reason that 'ethics' occupies a prominent place in the society. To be ethical is to be responsible to one's fellow citizens.

2. MEANING OF ETHICS

The term 'Ethics' is said to have its origins in Greek. It is called 'Ethicos' in Greek and 'Ethicus' in Latin. It is also said that the word derives from 'ethos'; which means character or manners. *The Longman Dictionary of Contemporary English* (International Edition, 2004) defined Ethics (being the plural of ethic) as moral rules or principles of behaviour for deciding what is right and wrong. These may relate to a phenomenon or profession. The *Cambridge Advanced Learner's Dictionary* (Third Edition, 2010) defines 'ethics' as the study of what is morally right and what is not. A system of accepted beliefs which control behaviour, especially such a system is based on morals.

Adam Smith, an 18th century economist, who became popular through his work titled *An Enquiry into the Nature and Causes of Wealth of Nations* (1776); produced two other works, viz., *The Theory of Moral Sentiments* (1759) and *Lectures in Jurisprudence* (1762).

The first work appears more relevant to understand the meaning of 'ethics'; since ethics is understood as the study of morals. Adam Smith used the term 'sympathy' as equivalent of moral sentiments.[1] These were the feelings or passions of others. According to Smith, humans have a natural tendency to care about the well-being of others for no other reason than the pleasure one gets from seeing them happy. He states that this occurs under either of the flowing two conditions:

- We see first hand the fortune or misfortune of another person;
- The fortune or misfortune is vividly depicted to us.

Smith also proposes several variables that can moderate the extent of sympathy, as of the following:

- The vividness of the account of the condition of another person is proportional to the degree of vividness in our observation or the description of the event.
- Knowledge of the causes of the emotions.
- Whether other people are involved in the emotion.

Smith thus puts forth the argument that not only are the consequences of one's actions judged and used to determine whether one is just or unjust in committing them, but also whether one's sentiments justified the action that brought about consequences. Thus, 'sympathy' plays a role in determining judgements of the actions of others. Meaning thereby, if we sympathise with the affections that brought about the action, we are more likely to judge action as just and vice versa. Thus, it is the feeling or affection that shall coincide and tally with our own, leading to the suitable action and final approval of the same. If otherwise, we necessarily disapprove of them as extravagant and out of proportion. Smith's understanding of 'moral sentiments" is of most crucial value in judging what is right and what is wrong and what is ethical and what is unethical. After all, the 'code of ethics' developed and implemented by a society is based on the bundle of emotions or sentiments of the members of the group/society.

The efforts of Adam Smith got culminated and extended into the formulation of various theories on Ethics. Before going into this discussion, let us review a few definitions of various propositions on 'Ethics'.

- Ethics is the study of morals and moral choices. It focuses on standards, rules and codes of conduct that govern the behaviour of individuals and groups.
- Ethics is the science of morals. It is that branch of philosophy which is concerned with the human character and conduct.
- Ethics is a set of principles that guide behaviour of human beings to distinguish between right and wrong, or good and bad.
- Ethics is the study of what makes up good and bad conduct inclusive of related actions and values.

- Ethics is a branch of axiology, which together with metaphysics, logic and epistemology constitutes philosophy.
- It is the study of moral standards whose explicit purpose is to determine as far as possible whether a given moral standard is more or less correct.
- Ethics deals with things to be sought and things to be avoided with ways of life and telos; which means the chief aim or end in life.

We, being the authors, prefer to define the term Ethics 'as the social order', which enables human beings to evolve and thrive on the earth'. We intend to emphasize on the relationships that shall prevail among the people in the society. Those relationships need to be just and fair to be meaningful and promote order in the society. One thing that distinguishes 'man from beast' is the ethics or moral code. Stronger is the moral code, the more stronger would be the 'social fabric'. It is for the establishment of such society, we need to work for.

3. SOURCES OF ETHICS

It will be quite interesting to examine how does ethics germinate and take different forms. While we define ethics being a 'social order', there could be many ways by which the expected order can be brought about or put in place. The following are the major sources of Ethics in the opinion of the authors. It is believed that this view broadens the thinking and discussion on this topic.

1. Genetic inheritance
2. Religious scriptures
3. Philosophical discourses
4. Cultural experiences
5. Legal systems
6. Institutional practices

3.1 Genetic Inheritance

Dating back to the origins of mankind, we find that anarchy only prevailed. Survival of the fittest was the order of the day. Thriving on the weak is an accepted code of ethics. Anthrological explanation to the evolution of humans sets the tone for ethics. It is believed that behaviour is inherited, with limited understanding as to what do we inherit. With the advancement of the discipline of Genetics, scientists are trying to provide an explanation as to what do we inherit. Though research evidence is not conclusive as to what is exactly inherited; the impact of heredity is vastly recognized, particularly in the areas of biological and psychological disorders. The class of diseases called 'autoimmune disorders' has long been thought to be genetic in nature and inheritable from parent to offspring. These diseases arise from a failure by the body to distinguish between what is 'self' and what is 'foreign' or 'non-self. As a result, the body mounts immune response against its own molecules and cells, leading to extreme discomfort. Some of these autoimmune disorders can be mild such as psoriasis or scaling of the skin; while others are quite severe such as inflammation of connective tissues, type-1 or insulin dependent diabetes, and difficult to handle disease called Systematic Lupus Lrythematous (SLE). That these may be inheritable genetic disorders has been suggested from the observation that SLE is nine times more prevalent in women than in men and that it occurs far more frequently among the Chinese and Black population than others. To date, as many as 70 diverse diseases have been classified into the category of autoimmune disorders. Quite interestingly, there were a good number of cases of similarities cited in respect of twins and their behaviour. It is observed that identical twins have the same genetic endowment.

The following traits are generally said to be a part of inheritance:

1. Physical structure – tall or short; lean or stout; black or red, etc.
2. Reflexes indicating a direct response to a stimulus.
3. Innate drives consisting of sensitivity, aggressiveness, strength of sex drive, craving for alcohol, drugs, etc.
4. Intelligence in terms of verbal and mathematical abilities.
5. Temperament leading to emotional make-up.

Reverse Inheritance: So far it is believed that the child inherits from the mother. The so-called autoimmune disorders numbering around 70 are said to arise from two sources. One mode is through genetic inheritance or what you get from your parent. The other is the reverse of it, namely, what you end up getting from your child, even before the child is born. It has been reported by a group of scientists at the annual meeting of the American Association for the Advancement of Sciences held in San Francisco. In a study conducted by Dr. Deise Faustman of Mass General Hospital in Boston, it was revealed that autoimmunity disorders are caused by the heredity from the fetus to the carrying mother.

3.2 Religions Scriptures

These are said to be the dominant source of ethics in every society. Going by the world of religion, we have the most predominant forms like Christianity, Islam and Hinduism; though there are many other variants like Judaism, Jainism, Buddhism, Sikhism, etc. Each of these religions has ordained a code of conduct through their religious texts, considered sacrosanct. For instance, in the belief of Christianity, GOD has given the

Ten Commandments from Mount Sinai, accompanied by smoke, earthquakes and the blast of a trumpet to emphasize the importance of these laws. Moses recorded God's words in Exodus 20 and recounted the event again in Deuteronomy.[5] See both the versions below.

A. The Ten Commandments List in Exodus 20: 2-17

1. "I am the LORD, your God, who brought you out of the land of Egypt, out of the house of bondage. You shall have no other gods before Me.
2. "You shall not make for yourself a carved image—any likeness of anything that is in heaven above, or that is in the earth beneath, or that is in the water under the earth; you shall not bow down to them nor serve them. For I, the LORD, your God, am a jealous God, to those who love Me and keep My commandments.
3. "You shall not take the name of the LORD your God in vain, for the LORD will not hold him guiltless who takes His name in vain.
4. "Remember the Sabbath day, to keep it holy. Six days you shall labour and do all your work, but the seventh day is the Sabbath of the LORD your God. For in six days the LORD made the heavens and the earth, the sea, and all that is in them, and rested the seventh day. Therefore, the LORD blessed the Sabbath day and hallowed it.
5. "Honor your father and your mother, that your days may be long upon the land which the LORD your God is giving you.
6. "You shall not murder.
7. "You shall not commit adultery.
8. "You shall not steal.
9. "You shall not bear false witness against your neighbour.
10. "You shall not covet your neighbour's house; you shall not covet your neighbour's wife, nor his male servant, nor his female servant, nor his ox, nor his donkey, nor anything that is your neighbour's."

B. The Ten Commandments List in Deuteronomy 5: 6-21

1. "I am the LORD your God who brought you out of the land of Egypt, out of the house of bondage. You shall have no other gods before me.
2. "You shall not make for yourself a carved image. For I, the LORD your God, am a jealous God, visiting the iniquity of the fathers upon the children to the third and fourth generations of those who hate Me, but showing mercy to thousands, to those who love Me and keep My commandments.
3. "You shall not take the name of the LORD your God in vain, for the LORD will not hold him guiltless who takes His name in vain.

4. "Observe the Sabbath day, to keep it holy, as the LORD your God commanded you. Six days you shall labour and do all your work, but the seventh day is the Sabbath of the LORD your God. And remember that you were a slave in the land of Egypt, and the LORD your God brought you out from there by a mighty hand and by an outstretched arm; therefore the LORD your God commanded you to keep the Sabbath day.
5. "Honor your father and your mother, as the LORD your God has commanded you, that your days may be long, and that it may be well with you in the land which the LORD your God is giving you.
6. "You shall not murder.
7. "You shall not commit adultery.
8. "You shall not steal.
9. "You shall not bear false witness against your neighbour.
10. "You shall not covet your neighbour's wife; and you shall not desire your neighbour's house, his field, his male servant, his female servant, his ox, his donkey, or anything that is your neighbour's."

As we can see from the above, there are only slight variations in both the versions. It is not the question of variations, it is the question of belief.

Similarly, Islam defines ethics as 'good character'. The foundational source in the gradual codification of Islamic ethics was the Muslim understanding and interpretations of the Qur'an and practices of Muhammad. Its meaning has always been in context of active submission to God (Arabic: Allah), performed by the community in unison. The motive force in Islamic ethics is the notion that every human being is called to "command the good and forbid the evil" in all spheres of life. Muslims understand the role of Muhammad as attempting to facilitate this submission. Another key factor in the field of Islamic ethics is the belief that mankind has been granted the faculty to discern God's will and to abide by it. This faculty most crucially involves reflecting over the meaning of existence. Therefore, regardless of their environment, humans are believed to have a moral responsibility to submit to God's will and to follow Islam; as demonstrated in the Qur'an.

Like the Bible, the Qur'an also provides for a set of moral stipulations to guide the mankind. They can be read as follows:

1. **Worship only God:** Take not with Allah another object of worship; or thou (O man!) wilt sit in disgrace and destitution. (Quran 17:22)
2. **Be kind, honourable and humble to one's parents:** Thy Lord hath decreed that ye worship none but Him, and that ye be kind to parents. And, out of kindness, lower to them the wing of humility, and say: "My Lord! bestow on them thy Mercy even as they cherished me in childhood." (Quran 17:24)

3. **Be neither miserly, nor wasteful in one's expenditure:** And render to the kindred their due rights, as (also) to those in want, and to the wayfarer: But squander not (your wealth) in the manner of a spendthrift. (Quran 17:26) Verily spendthrifts are brothers of the Evil Ones; and the Evil One is to his Lord (himself) ungrateful. (Quran 17:27)
4. **Do not engage in 'mercy killings' for fear of starvation:** Kill not your children for fear of want: We shall provide sustenance for them as well as for you. Verily the killing of them is a great sin. (Quran 17:31)
5. **Do not commit adultery:** Nor come nigh to adultery: for it is a shameful (deed) and an evil, opening the road (to other evils). (Quran 17:32)
6. **Do not kill unjustly:** Nor take life – which Allah has made sacred – except for just cause; but let him not exceed bounds in the matter of taking life; for he is helped (by the Law). (Quran 17:33)
7. **Care for orphaned children:** Come not nigh to the orphan's property except to improve it, until he attains the age of full strength... (Quran 17:34)
8. **Keep one's promises:** ...fulfil (every) engagement [i.e., promise/covenant], for (every) engagement will be enquired into (on the Day of Reckoning). (Quran 17:34)
9. **Be honest and fair in one's interactions:** Give full measure when ye measure, and weigh with a balance that is straight: that is the most fitting and the most advantageous in the final determination. (Quran 17:35)
10. **Do not be arrogant in one's claims or beliefs:** And pursue not that of which thou hast no knowledge; for every act of hearing, or of seeing or of (feeling in) the heart will be enquired into (on the Day of Reckoning).

In Hinduism, Vedas, Upanishads, Epics prescribe codes of conduct. These principles are codified into two categories as:

A. Yamas (restrictions)

B. Niyamas (observances)

As if there is a broad agreement among diverse religions in declaring codes, the number of Yamas and Niyamas are also ten, as in the case of Christianity and Islam. Let us now look at the Commandments listed under both the above categories.

A. Yamas

These are don'ts that prevent an individual from doing something. In an orderly managed society, members are supposed to adhere to certain code of conduct to make life comfortable and meaningful. The list is as follows:

1. **Non-injury, Ahimsa:** Every individual shall practice ahimsa and cause no injury to any living being. The truth is that harm caused to others unfailingly returns to oneself. Hence, live peacefully with God's creation. Never be a source of dread, pain or injury. One should follow a vegetarian diet.

2. **Truthfulness, Satya:** Adherence to truth is the second and refraining from betraying promises and to speak only truth are inclusive. Knowing that deception creates distance, don't keep secrets from family or loved ones. Be fair, accurate and frank in discussions. Be a stranger to deceit. Admit your failings. Do not engage in slander, gossip or backbiting. Not to bear false witness against another.
3. **Non-stealing, Asteya:** Non-stealing is the third act which everyone shall observe. Everybody should learn to control desires and live within means. Not to use borrowed resources for unintended purposes or keep them past due. Also one should not gamble or defraud others and renege on promises. Do not use others' names, words, resources or rights without permission and acknowledgement.
4. **Divine Conduct, Brahmacharya:** Practicing brahmacharya is the divine conduct. Controlling lust by remaining celibate when single and faithful in marriage is the best policy. Before marriage, use vital energies in study, and after marriage in creating family success. One should also be restrained with the opposite sex and seek always holy company. Dress and speak modestly. One should also shun pornography, sexual humour and violence.
5. **Patience, Kshama:** Every human being shall exercise patience, and restrain with people. Let others behave according to their nature, without adjusting to you. Don't argue, and dominate conversations or interrupt others. Don't be in a hurry. Be patient with children and the elderly. Minimize stress by keeping worries at bay and remain poised in good and bad times.
6. **Steadfastness, Dhriti:** Overcoming non-perseverance, fear, indecision and changeableness is the most desired quality. To achieve one's goals, one should plan and pray with purpose. Be firm in your decisions. Avoid sloth and procrastination. Develop will power, courage and industriousness. Overcome obstacles. Not to carp or complain and also not to let opposition or fear of failure to result in changing strategies.
7. **Compassion, Daya:** This is the greatest quality one should practice. Conquering callous, cruel and insensitive feelings toward all beings is always welcome. One should see God everywhere. Be kind to people, animals, plants and the Earth itself. Forgive those who apologize and show true remorse. Foster sympathy for others' needs and suffering. Honour and assist those who are weak, impoverished, aged or in pain and oppose family abuse and other cruelties.
8. **Honesty, Arjava:** The saying 'honesty is the best policy', perhaps is drawn from this yama. Thus, one should maintain honesty, renouncing deception and wrong doing. Act honorably even in hard times. Obey the laws of your nation and locale. Pay your taxes. Be straightforward in business. Do an honest day's work. Do not bribe or accept bribes. The best is not to cheat, deceive or circumvent to achieve an end. One should also be frank with yourself and face and accept any faults without blaming others.

9. **Moderate Appetite, Mitahara:** To be moderate in appetite is always good enough. Eating too much, nor consuming meat, fish, shellfish, fowl or eggs leads to danger. Enjoy fresh, wholesome vegetarian foods that vitalize the body. Avoid junk food. Drink non-alcoholic beverages in moderation. Eat at regular times, only when hungry, at a moderate pace. Follow a simple diet, avoiding rich or fancy fare.
10. **Purity, Saucha:** One should also uphold the ethics of purity, and avoid impurity in mind, body and speech. Healthy mind in a healthy body. Keep a pure, uncluttered home and workplace. Act virtuously. Keep good company, never mixing with adulterers, thieves or other impure people. Keep away from pornography and violence. Not to use harsh, angered or indecent language.

B. Niyamas

These are observances, which one should perform to refine one's soul to elevate oneself into higher chakras of consciousness of love, compassion, selflessness, intelligence and bliss. They are:

1. **Remorse, Hri:** This principle underlies the expression of remorse, being modest and showing shame for misdeeds. Recognizing oneself to confess and make amends and sincerely apologizing to those hurt by the words or deeds. It also implies resolving all contentions before sleep. Connecting oneself of faults and bad habits is also the part of remorse. Welcoming correction as a means to bettering oneself and not to boost and pretend are inclusive.
2. **Contentment, Santosha:** One should always be contended with what one has. Being happy in life is the mantra. Living in constant gratitude for health, friends and belongings and not complaining about what we do not possess is the best part of the contentment. To keep the view that life is an opportunity for spiritual progress is the crux of the understanding.
3. **Giving, Dana:** This third principle centres around being generous to everyone. Giving liberally without thought of reward is the aim. Offering one tenth of your gross income (dashamamsha), as God's money, to temples, ashrams and spiritual organizations is also advised. Approaching temples with offerings; visiting gurus with gifts in hand; donating religious literature are all acts associated with this guna.
4. **Faith, Astikya:** Having an unshakable faith and believe firmly in the God is the fourth principle. In the process, it is also essential to have trust in the words of the masters, the scriptures and traditions. Practicing devotion and sadhana to inspire experiences that build advanced faith are also important. Maintaining lineage and satguru parampara are also essential.
5. **Worship, Ishvara-Pujana:** Worshipping the Lord every day is also advised. There shall not be any room for suspicion. It is necessary to have a shrine in the home. A systematic attempt in praying God with flowers or food is the practice to be

followed. Visiting temples at frequent intervals with heartfelt devotion, clearing the inner soul are the essential ingredients in the process of worship.

6. **Scriptural Listening, Siddhanta Shravana:** A devotee shall hear the scriptures, study the teachings and listen to the wisdom of gurus. Choosing a guru and flowing his path pays dividends in the life. To improve upon the wisdom, one should read, listen and follow the traditions. Continuous chanting is advised to keep oneself stay focused on the faith to God.
7. **Cognition, Mati:** Everybody should develop a spiritual will and intellect with satguru's guidance. Striving for knowledge of God, and to awakening the light within is the essence of devotion. Discovering the hidden lesson in each experience to develop a profound understanding of life lies at the heart of ethics. This can be achieved through meditation, and yoga and intuition by listening to the still, small voice within, and by understanding the subtle sciences, inner worlds and mystical texts.
8. **Sacred Vows, Vrata:** Every human being also shall embrace religious vows, rules and observances and never fail in fulfilling them. Spiritual contracts with the soul, community, guru are essential in religious life. To the extent possible, one should undertake the tour of religious places, monasteries to renew faith in religious traditions.
9. **Recitation, Japa:** This is the ninth principle in the Hindu scriptures. According to this principle, every individual should recite or chant mantras or rhymes.
10. **Austerity, Tapas:** This last principle is very important, as it suggests austerity and sacrifice. This should be attained through worship, meditation and pilgrimage. The Hindu scriptures talk about 108 prostrations or besting methods to practice penance. Some of them also go to the extent of self immolation, like the one practiced as 'Santhara in Jainism'. Similar dictates are given by many other religions, basing on the beliefs preached by their respective founders and gurus. In addition, there are also codes of moral conduct given by individual saints like Narada, Vidura, etc., in Hinduism.

3.3 Philosophical Discourses

Beginning with the Greek philosophers like Aristotle, there were several attempts made to describe and codify moral principles. They have defined these principles from the point of view of virtues; thus giving rise to 'virtue theory'. This theory argues that the aim of moral life is to develop those general dispositions called, moral virtues, and exercise and exhibit them in many situations that human life sets before us. According to this proposition, an action is morally right, if the action, exhibits or develops a morally virtuous character. It is morally wrong, if it promotes morally vicious character.

Ipso facto, wrongfulness of an action is determined by examining the kind of character, the action tends to produce or the kind of character that tends to produce the action. In either case, the ethics of the action depends on its relationship to the character of the agent. For example, it has been argued that the morality of abortion, adultery, or any other action is dubbed as morality by those who are engaged in such actions. If the decision to engage in such actions tends to develop a person's character and is treated as such then such actions are considered morally right. If the decision to engage in such actions tends to make people more self-centred, irresponsible, dishonest, careless, and selfish, then such actions are to be definitely treated as wrong. Actions are not only evaluated by the kinds of character they develop. We also condemn certain actions precisely because they are the outcome of a morally vicious character. For example, we condemn cruel actions because they exhibit a vicious character, and we condemn lies because they are products of a dishonest character.

Virtue theory not only provides a criterion for evaluating actions, it also provides a useful criterion for evaluating social institutions and practices. It has been argued that many a time that some economic institutions make people greedy, less responsible, and make them lazy and dependent. Whatever be the policies and actions of the Government, they need to be denounced forthwith.

3.3.1 Aristotle on the Theory of Moral Virtue

Aristotle is the first person to have used the term 'ethics' to name a field of study developed by his predecessors - Socrates and Plato. In the opinion of Aristotle, the purpose of ethics is to become good, not merely to know, but to act. And the right kind of action depends on the details of a particular situation, rather than being generated merely by applying a law. Aristotle argues that a moral virtue is a habit that enables a human being to live according to reason.

According to Aristotle, moral virtue is the disposition to act excellently, which a person develops partly as a result of his 'upbringing' and partly as a result of his 'habit of action'. He distinguishes the disposition to feel emotions of a certain kind from virtue and vice. But such emotional dispositions may also lie in the continuum of two extremes, viz., upbringing and habituation. The example he has provided for such dispositions is modesty, or a tendency to feel shame. It is a balanced feeling of sympathetic pain concerning the undeserved pleasures and pains of others. These dispositions finally culminate as virtues or vices depending on the emotions and feelings.

As a matter of fact, Aristotle is the one Greek Philosopher, who developed vast literature on the theory of Ethics. In the process, he feels that there are four cardinal virtues that are significant in deciding the moral virtue of an individual, as detailed below:

A. **Prudence:** This is also known as practical wisdom. This is the most important virtue for Aristotle. For instance in a war, soldiers must fight with prudence by making judgments through practical wisdom. This virtue is a must to obtain because courage requires judgment to be made on the spot.

B. **Temperance:** This implies self-control. Taking the above example of war, soldiers must display moderation with their enjoyment while at war in the midst of violent activities. Hence, it concerns courage and gives one moderation in private and public life.

C. **Courage:** This is the behaviour exhibited with respect to fear and confidence. Aristotle interpreted this notion as the means with regard to things that excite confidence or fear. This depends on circumstances that lead to the choice of action. Concerning warfare, Aristotle believes soldiers are morally significant and are military and political heroes. War is simply a stage for soldiers to display courage, and is the only way courage can be exemplified. Any other action is simply copying a soldier's ways; they may not be actually courageous.

D. **Justice:** This means giving the enemy what is due to them in the proper ways; being just towards them. In other words, one must recognize what is good for the community and also implies a good course of action.

The thinking of Aristotle had proved to be so influential that his foundations are being discussed even now in the schools of philosophy.

3.3.2 Discourses based on Hindu Philosophy

A major part of Indian Philosophy is guided by the Hindu religious scriptures and practices. According to Mimamsa, ethical action is the Supreme governing force of the universe. It is the belief that the universe is surviving because of the ethical actions of people only. Those that do good survive and those that do harm would peril. The following narration from one of the most revered epic (Ramayana) testifies the right kind of moral actions.

"Ravana, visiting the captive Sita, lays before her grand offers in the hope that she will be tempted to become his wife. He says that he has defeated both celestials and demons. He offers priceless gems to Sita. He offers to take care of Janaka's needs. He says Rama is in no way equal to him. He, Ravana, rules Lanka, but Rama is an exile. Ravana lives in an opulent palace, in his capital city, but Rama roams the forests. He says he is not one to suppress his desires, for he is a demon. It is the practice of demons to capture women they desire.

Sita points out to him that demons may not follow the same principles as others, yet to desire another man's wife cannot be justified. There are some values that are universal and no one can claim that there are exceptions to these principles and values, said Valayapet Ramachariar in a discourse. For example, we are urged to be honest, to do acts of charity, to treat elders with respect, etc. But sometimes there are exceptions to these rules. For example, it is not fair to ask a hunter or a fisherman to keep away from taking the life of an animal or fish, because his livelihood will then be lost. But there are some values which are applicable to all, not just to some.

These are not a matter of choice. It is not as if someone can say that he alone is exempt from these rules under some special provision. So even demons must adhere to certain basic principles, and even they cannot lay claim to another man's wife. And that is what Sita points out to Ravana. Nothing can be used as an excuse for his abduction of Sita."

Thus, according to the Hindu Philosophy, the entire universe functions on the 'keel of Dharma', which prescribes what is good, what is bad, what is right, what is wrong and finally what is ethical and what is unethical. As a matter of fact, it is believed that the following **two doctrines** guide the actions of people in the society.

A. Doctrine of Karma

B. Doctrine of Moksha

The doctrine of karma is said to be fundamental, not only to Hinduism, but also to Jainism and Buddhism. This doctrine lays emphasis on the actions of human beings. Karma means action; not only action, but also its result. It is felt that both are not separate. One follows the other. All the human actions are roped into the scope of karma, like thinking, breathing, seeing, hearing, eating, etc. The law of karma means the law of causation. As per the Hindu philosophy one can avoid but doing karma. The result depends on how good you are in performing these action. As is made clear, it is not alone action but thought also is the part of karma. Therefore, one has to be pure and honest in thought and action.

'As you sow, so you reap' is the adage of this doctrine. You sow a good thought and act accordingly, you reap the good fruits as crop. If you sow the seed of evil thought, you will reap the harvest of pain and suffering. Thus, happiness and suffering are said to germinate within you through your thinking and action. Karma is said to be of three kinds, viz., (1) Sanchita (accumulated works), (2) Prarabdha (fructifying works) and (3) Agami (current works). Sanchita is all the accumulated Karmas of the past. Part of it is seen in the character of man, in his tendencies and aptitudes, capacities, inclinations and desires, etc. Tendencies come from this. Prarabdha is that portion of the past Karma which is responsible for the present body. That portion of the Sanchita Karma which influences human life in the present incarnation is called Prarabdha. It is ripe for reaping. It cannot be avoided or changed. It is only exhausted by being experienced. You pay your past debts. Prarabdha Karma is that which has begun and is actually bearing fruit. It is selected out of the mass of the Sanchita Karma. Kriyamana is that Karma which is now being made for the future. It is also called Agami or Vartamana.

In Vedantic literature, there is a beautiful analogy. The bowman has already sent an arrow and it has left his hands. He cannot recall it. He is about to shoot another arrow. The bundle of arrows in the quiver on his back is the Sanchita; the arrow he has shot is Prarabdha; and the arrow which he is about to shoot from his bow is Agami. Of these, he has perfect control over the Sanchita and the Agami, but he must surely work out his Prarabdha. The past which has begun to take effect he has to experience.

There is another beautiful analogy also. The granary represents the Sanchita Karma; that portion taken from the granary and put in the shop for future daily sale corresponds to Agami; that which is sold daily represents Prarabdha. The whole lot of Sanchita Karma is destroyed by attaining Knowledge of Brahman or the Eternal. It can be greatly modified by entertaining lofty, divine thoughts, and doing virtuous actions. Agami Karma can be destroyed by expiatory rites or Prayaschitta; and by removing the idea of agency through *Nimitta Bhava* (attitude that one is an instrument in the hands of God) and *Sakshi Bhava* (attitude that one is silent witness of the actions of the senses and of the mind).

The pervasive influence of this doctrine on the believers of Hinduism is such that every action or even inaction is ascribed to this. As Lord Krishna declares through his 'Gita', people do not also have the sanction for not performing their duty. The verse reads that:

"karmanyevadhikaraste
ma phalesu kadacana
ma karma-phala-heturbhur
ma te sango'stvakarmani"

The meaning of this verse is that: "one has the right to perform the duty. He is not entitled to the result of the duty. One also cannot keep away from performing one's duty". Thus, people are destined to do their duty and there is no escape. Even if the act is harming the other (may be human being or animal), the ultimate does not count on the evil. The example quoted is of a butcher killing animals everyday for securing livelihood is of no sin; and so is the act of a hunter. Thus, goes the explanation of the doctrine of Karma.

The Doctrine of Moksha

This is the other highly valued doctrine, having profound influence on the actions of the people. It is believed in Hinduism that there is rebirth. Nobody knows how many rebirths one would take. It is said to be dependent on the good acts done by the individual. And there is no guarantee that what kind or form of rebirth one takes. By virtue of the good acts done in the past, one is born as human. Thus, it is an opportunity to put a stop to the process of this rebirth and get 'salvation' or Moksha. The term 'Moksha is interpreted in several ways to mean liberation, freedom and mukti, nirvana and kaivalya. In whatever manner, the soul liberates from the body. Some believe that it unites with the nature and some believe it to be uniting with the God. Therefore, all the worldly actions are to be performed or conducted with a view to attaining moksha in the ultimate.

There are different interpretations of this doctrine in terms of its meaning, belief and practice. The major schools of Hindu philosophy view Moksha in the following sense: the Nyaya, Vaisesika and Mimamsa schools of Hinduism consider moksha as possible only after death. Samkhya and Yoga schools consider moksha as possible in this life. In Vedanta school, the Advaita sub-school concludes moksha is possible in this life, while Dvaita and Visistadvaita sub-schools of Vedanta tradition believe that moksha is a continuous event, one assisted by loving devotion to God, that extends from this life to post-mortem.

Beyond these six orthodox schools, some heterodox schools of Hindu tradition, such as Charvaka, deny there is a soul or after-life or moksha. One among the Vedantic School suggests that the first step towards moksha begins with *mumuksutva*, that is desire of liberation. This takes the form of questions about self, what is true, why do things or events make us happy or cause suffering, and so on. This line of thinking about knowledge/creation is assisted by, claims of Adi Shankara in his Advaita Vedanta, which is the study of historical knowledge and viveka (critical thinking). Shankara cautions that the guru and historic knowledge may be distorted, so traditions and historical assumptions must be questioned by the individual seeking moksha. Those who are on their path to moksha (sanyasin), are quintessentially free individuals, without craving for anything in the worldly life, thus they are neither dominated by, nor dominating anyone else. It is for these wide variations, Hindu philosophy was not able to be deciphered by not only the common man, but also by experts to their satisfaction.

3.4 Cultural Experiences

Culture has a great influence on the ethics of an individual. Going by the ordinary meaning of the culture comprising values, beliefs, attitudes, habits influences the choice. Strong ethical and cultural standards set by an organization result in a positive ethical behaviour among employees. That is the reason why every company is deeply interested in developing a culture of its own. It is a fact that every culture is an integration of social and religious practices. Components of religion are meant to induce the desired behavioural patterns, lead to proper attitude formation for a healthy society. Hence, the corporate world is constantly engaged in providing ethical orientation to the employees of the organizations. So also the customs of the community amplifying the desired effect on the expected behaviour. A more detailed discussion on cultural values is made in the next chapter.

3.5 Legal System

Ethics is the source of law. What you believe in emerges as the code. Practices approved by the people in the society are given as law. In order to bring about order in the functioning of the society and avoiding anarchy, a set of behaviour is agreed upon. The same turns out to be the law of the land. What shall be the law is dictated by the ideology to which the people of the country are committed to. Basic tenets of life like freedom, liberty, fraternity, dignity, etc., decide the civil and procedural codes. The people of India have subscribed to the ideals of justice, liberty, equality and fraternity when they have solemnly resolved to constitute India into a Sovereign Socialist Secular Democratic Republic and thus they have given to themselves the constitution. The Preamble to the Constitution adequately explains the spirit behind the economic system of India. Thus follow all the kinds of rules, regulations and legislations.

For instance, Article 39 of the Constitution of India puts an obligation on the State that the "State shall, in particular, direct its policy towards securing:

(a) that the citizens, men and women equally, have the right to an adequate means of livelihood;
(b) that the ownership and control of the material resources of the community are so distributed as best to subserve the common good;
(c) that the operation of the economic system does not result in the concentration of wealth and means of production to the common detriment;
(d) that there is equal pay for equal work for both men and women;
(e) that the health and strength of workers, men and women, and the tender age of children are not abused and that citizens are not forced by economic necessity to enter avocations unsuited to their age or strength;
(f) that children are given opportunities and facilities to develop in a healthy manner and in conditions of freedom and dignity and that childhood and youth are protected against exploitation and against moral and material abandonment.

Similar would be the legal system in any country, since all the legal principles are to be derived from its own ethics.

3.6 Institutional Practices

It has now become common to the institutions, either they be companies or other organizations, to lay down their own work ethics, in the form of 'code of conduct'. In order to make employees act with integrity, companies are articulating their values, attitudes, beliefs, etc. These are taking the shape of vision, mission, objectives, targets, etc., in the management jargon. Company codes generally refer to general areas of business conduct or may apply to a specific area of the firm's business. These codes are expected to serve a variety of purposes right from 'image enhancing' to that of 'do the right thing' to help an employee to act in all fairness.

In a survey (1992) conducted by M.B.E. Clarkson and M. C. Deck on 200 enterprises using stakeholder model, it was revealed that most of the text in the corporate codes is concerned with the duty and responsibility of the employees to the company; as if to protect the firm from its employees. Instead, the right approach should have been to declare through code, the value system that the company believes in. Let us draw 'text' from a few codes developed by select companies:

3.6.1 Maruti Suzuki India Limited Code of Business Conduct and Ethics Introduction and Background

As a responsible corporate citizen, Maruti Suzuki India Limited ('Maruti' or "the Company") has always believed in following highest standards of corporate governance. Being a listed company, every act of the Company, its Board Members and its employees is the focus of public attention and accordingly, there is a need to reinforce Maruti's commitment towards maintaining highest standards of Corporate Governance. This Code of Business Conduct and Ethics ("Code of Conduct" or "Code") helps ensure compliance with the standards of business conduct and ethics and also with regulatory requirements. All Senior Management Personnel are expected to read and understand this Code of Business Conduct and Ethics to uphold these standards in day-to-day activities and also comply with all applicable standards, policies and procedures of the company.

The company expects that this Code of Conduct be read in conjunction with applicable regulations and procedures of the Company.

A. **Applicability:** MSIL has declared that the code is applicable to all Senior Management Personnel which would include its directors as well. All Senior Management Personnel are expected to comply with the code in letter and spirit. Management Personnel is also directed to comply with other applicable laws and regulations and the relevant policies, rules and procedures of the Company from time to time.

B. **Compliance with Applicable Laws and Regulations:** It is the wish of the company that the management personnel shall acquire appropriate knowledge of the requirements relating to their duties sufficient to enable them to recognize potential non-compliance issues and to know when to seek advice from the Legal Department on specific Company policies and procedures. It is also directed that no payment or transaction should be made to the Management Personnel, if the consequence of that transaction or payment would be in violation of any law in force.

C. **Honesty, Integrity and Ethical Conduct:** Senior Management Personnel shall act in accordance with the highest standards of integrity, honesty, fairness and ethical conduct. This means that the conduct that the actions of the mangers shall be free from fraud or deception. Ethical conduct includes ethical handling of actual or apparent conflicts of interest between personal and professional relationships. This is very important in case of senior managers. Senior Management Personnel should necessarily promote ethical behavior to prevail throughout company; so that employees can freely report violations of laws, rules, regulations or the Company's Code of Conduct to the appropriate authority. It is also important that the employees shall not make or accept facilitation payments or kickbacks of any kind. Facilitation payments are typically small, unofficial payments made to secure or expedite an action. Kickbacks are typically payments in return for a business favour/advantage such as payment made to secure the award of a contract. These things are needed to be avoided for a fair conduct in the company.

D. **Duties of Independent Directors:** The code of conduct declaration of the company is very particular, regarding the role of IDs. The code has made a mention the following duties:

1. Undertake appropriate induction and regularly update and refresh their skills, knowledge and familiarity with the Company.
2. Seek appropriate clarification or amplification of information and, where necessary, take and follow appropriate professional advice and opinion of outside experts at the expense of the Company.
3. Strive to attend all meetings of the Board and the committees thereof; of which they are members.
4. Participate constructively and actively in the committees of the Board.
5. Strive to attend the general meetings of the Company.
6. Where they have concerns about the running of the Company or a proposed action, ensure that these are addressed by the Board and, to the extent that they are not resolved, insist that their concerns are recorded in the minutes of the Board meeting.
7. Keep themselves well informed about the Company and the external environment in which it operates.
8. Not to unfairly obstruct the functioning of an otherwise proper Board or committee thereof.
9. Pay sufficient attention and ensure that adequate deliberations are held before approving related party transactions and assure themselves that the same are in the interest of the Company.

10. Ascertain and ensure that the Company has an adequate and functional vigil mechanism and to ensure that the interests of a person who uses such mechanism are not prejudicially affected on account of such use.
11. Report concerns about unethical behavior, actual or suspected fraud or violation of the Company's Code of Conduct or ethics policy.
12. Act within their authority, assist in protecting the legitimate interests of the Company, shareholders and its employees.
13. Not disclose confidential information, including commercial secrets, technologies, advertising and sales promotion plans, unpublished price sensitive information, unless such disclosure is expressly approved by the Board or required by law.
14. Subject to the provisions of the Companies Act, 2013 to act in accordance with the Articles of Association of the Company.
15. To act in good faith in order to promote the objects of the Company for the benefit of its members as a whole, and in the best interests of the Company, its employees, the shareholders, the community and for the protection of environment.
16. To exercise their duties with due and reasonable care, skill and diligence and exercise independent judgment.
17. Not to involve themselves in a situation in which they may have a direct or indirect interest that conflicts, or possibly may conflict, with the interest of the Company.
18. Not to achieve or attempt to achieve any undue gain or advantage either to themselves or to their relatives, partners, or associates.
19. Not to assign their office.

E. **Conflict of Interest:** It is the duty of every employee, including senior Management Personnel, to avoid and promptly disclose to the Company potential conflicts of interest regarding any matters pertaining to the Company. The code explains the conflict in the matters of individual interest and company's interest. They shall make disclosures to the board relating to all material (both financial and commercial) transactions, where they have personal interest. These interests may finally lead to conflict with the interests of the company at large. It is important to make a rule that staff shall not acquire assets for consideration other than cash from the Company and vice-versa.

F. **Business Interest:** This is a crucial condition to be followed by the employees. If any manager wants to invest in the business operations or activities of suppliers, competitors or any other stakeholder, the same must be disclosed to the company. Several factors become important in determining whether a conflict exists, including the size and nature of the investment; the Management Personnel's ability to influence the Company's decisions; his access to confidential information of the Company and the nature of the relationship between the Company and the other company or person. Accordingly, the Management Personnel make a disclosure to the Board before making such an investment and obtains a "pre-approval"/"no objection" from a committee comprised of Managing Director and all the Whole-time Directors where the amount of investment exceeds Rs. one million (Rs. 10 lac) including all the investments made earlier either individually or with his relatives.

G. **Related Party Transactions:** These transactions are viewed very important from the point of view of ethics. No manager is supposed to gain from the company though these activities by himself or through his relatives. As a general rule, Management Personnel should avoid conducting Company business with a relative, or dealing with a business in which a relative is associated in any significant role. Any dealings with a related party must be conducted in such a way that no preferential treatment is given and adequate disclosures are made as required by law and as per the applicable policies of the Company.

H. **Gifts:** Management Personnel shall not offer, give or receive gifts to or from persons or entities dealing with the Company. MSIL has put a monetary limit of Rs. 6000 in this case. Therefore, no person can accept gifts beyond this limit from any vendor, dealer, contractor, supplier and anyone having business dealings with the Company. These benefits may include free boarding, transport, lodging or other service or any other pecuniary advantage when provided by any person other than a near relative or a personal friend having no official dealings. It is suggested that the Management Personnel should also avoid accepting lavish or frequent hospitality from any individual or firm having official dealings with the Company.

I. **Business Opportunities:** Management Personnel should not exploit for their own benefit, opportunities that are discovered through the use of corporate property, information. It is also expected that the managers refrain from using the property of the company for personal gain or personal use. This would also help strengthen the relationships between the company and the managers.

J. **Confidentiality:** In the days of increasing competition, there will be a greater tendency to steal the secrets or confidential information relating to the company. Corporate espionage is growing and threatening their survival. Employees will have access to vital and confidential information about the Company. The disclosure of the same may destabilize the company. Hence, no Management Personnel shall provide any confidential or sensitive information either formally or informally, to the press or any other publicity media, unless specifically authorized to do so.

K. **Insider Trading:** It is also necessary that no Management Personnel or their relatives shall derive any benefit or assist others to derive any benefit from the access to and possession of information about the Company. All the Senior Management Personnel are required to comply with the Company's Code of Conduct on prevention of insider trading.

L. **Equal Opportunity and Anti-Harassment:** Maruti is committed to a policy of equal employment opportunity. It has put in measures to ensure that there shall be no discrimination or harassment against an employee or applicant on the grounds of race, colour, religion, sex, age, marital status, disability, national origin, or any other factor made unlawful by applicable laws and regulations. This policy shall relate to all phases of employment including recruitment, hiring, placement, promotion, transfer, compensation, benefits, and training. Employers are now-a-days trying to boast as 'equal employers'. Similarly, specific measures should be taken to avoid gender discrimination and cases of sexual harassment.

M. **Reporting:** This is an essential requirement to be followed by a company. Senior Management Personnel are required to report violations of the Code if any and also the cases of illegal or unethical behavior to the Compliance Officer. All reports will be treated in a confidential manner and it is Company's policy to not allow retaliation for reports made in good faith, of misconduct by others. If necessary company will get the matters investigated on the allegations and take appropriate action. Management Personnel are expected to cooperate in internal investigations of misconduct and violations of this Code.

N. **Disciplinary Actions:** Ethics are of the utmost important aspects to the Company, and its stockholders. Companies are supposed to conduct business in accordance with their stated values. MSIL expects all of its Senior Management Personnel to adhere to these rules in carrying out their duties for the Company.

   The Company will take appropriate action against any Management Personnel whose actions are found to violate these policies or any other policy of the Company. Disciplinary actions may include immediate termination of directorship, employment or business relationship at the Company's sole discretion.

3.6.2 Wipro Limited

This is yet another company that is seriously involved in implementing the ethical code. Therefore, it would be interesting to probe into the principles that were enshrined in the code by the company. The company titled the code as 'Code of Business Conduct and Ethics (COBCE)'. COBCE is designed to help employees recognize and deal with ethical issues in their work. Wipro's policy is to comply with all applicable laws and regulations. It is the objective of the company to conduct business in an ethical manner and acting with integrity in dealing with the customers, suppliers, partners, competitors, employees and other stakeholders.

A. **Applicability:** COBCE is applicable to all Wipro employees, including contract labour and other casual workers. The code is also equally applicable to members of the Board of Directors. Wipro requires its suppliers, service providers, agents, channel partners to conduct their businesses in a legal and ethical manner. To support the requirement for complete and accurate financial records and reporting, Wipro's Principal and Financial Officers have an additional Code of Conduct apart from the COBCE. The code is expected to guide employees on improved awareness of Wipro policies and procedures for ethical business conduct, and help them resolve concerns and report suspected violations. Basically, managers are responsible for supporting implementation of ethics and business conduct programmes and monitoring compliance of Wipro's values and ethical business conduct guidelines through such programmes. All employees must abide by the COBCE and take up annual certification. Employees are encouraged to ask questions, seek guidance, report suspected violations, and express concerns regarding compliance with the COBCE and the related procedures. They can also suggest improvements in the code.

B. **Duty to Speak Up:** It is also the policy of the company to make its employees to know the legal and ethical responsibilities that apply to a job. They are encouraged to speak up under the following situations:

- If they are unsure about the proper course of action and need advice.
- If they believe that someone acting on behalf of Wipro is doing — or may do — something that violates the law or Wipro's compliance and integrity standards.
- If they believe that they may have been involved in a possible misconduct.

C. **Overriding Fffect of COBCEE:** It is to be appreciated that the company is more restrictive than the applicable laws and regulations. Employees are required to abide by the COBCE even when it imposes requirements that go beyond legal obligations. If employees notice that the applicable legal requirements are in conflict with the code, they must bring the matter to the attention of the HR Manager or Compliance & Legal Team immediately.

4. THEORIES OF ETHICS

Ethics is the one subject that engages the attention of the intellectuals and rulers alike. It is nothing but natural to ponder over the existence of human being, the right way to promote and sustain mankind on the earth. Unlike animal kingdom, man needs certain discipline and rules to grow in number and power to conquer nature. Thus, the early thinkers paid much attention to codify the rules of existence and the mechanism by which social order can be brought about. In spite of the fact that there were several codes of ethics said to have been formulated and given since ages, the historical perspective dates back to about 5000 years only. While we speak of the Hindu codes or codes developed by the prophets of any other religion, the dating is an issue. Nevertheless, the literature is available in one or the other form. Leaving the discussion as to how old are these propositions aside, the western thought dates back to only 18th century with contributions of Immanuel Kant and Jeremy Bentham. The discussion, therefore, is limited to western thought only.

Accordingly, ethical theories are divided into the following two categories:

1. Teleological ethical systems
2. Deontological ethical systems

4.1 Teleological Ethical Systems

These are based on the principle that what is more important in deciding the question of ethics, ends (the outcome) are important. A decision or an act is judged ethical or unethical by measuring the probable outcome or consequences. The word 'teleological' derives from the Greek work 'Telos' which means 'end'. Hence, these theories focus more on the end results than the processes adopted to achieve those ends. The concept of 'goodness' is fundamental to these theories. The other concepts like rightness, obligation or duty are defined in terms of goodness only. The following three points of view can be considered integral to these theories.

A. Utilitarianism
B. Egoism
C. Distributive justice

4.1.1 Utilitarianism

This is one of the teleological theories which evaluates the morality of actions in terms of progress towards the goal. As indicated earlier, it is the outcome (i.e., the end result) that is more important. Utilitarianism defines morality in terms of maximization of net expectable utility for all parties affected by a decision or action. This is one of the age-old theories, whose concepts were first formulated by Jeremy Bentham (1748-1832) and later developed and consolidated by the British philosopher and economist, John Stuart Mill (1806-1873).

Utilitarianism operates on the simple basic principle that 'actions are right to the degree that they tend to promote the greatest good for the greatest number'. The question here is : what constitutes greatest good. J. Bentham interpreted it in the manner saying that it is the 'tendency to augment or diminish happiness or pleasure'.

While J.S. Mill has defined the 'good' in terms of 'well-being'. This is also dubbed as the '**greatest happiness**' principle. Happiness is the 'intended pleasure or the absence of pain'; and unhappiness means pain and the privation of pleasure. Since 'good' is defined by pleasure, it is also important to define pleasure itself. In utilitarianism, people can experience higher and lower pleasures. **Lower pleasures**, also called base pleasures, are the animalistic desires to eat, sleep, multiply; even kill. Humans can derive happiness from these, but they are not as good as the higher pleasures. **Higher pleasures** are those that can only be experienced by humans. We appreciate art and music, culture and society.

According to utilitarian theory, once people are aware of their higher pleasures, they can only be truly happy by cultivating this part of themselves. Therefore, an economic action that supports the arts would have a high utility because it creates a greater level of true happiness for lots of people. In the words of John Stuart Mill, one of the most influential contributors to utilitarianism, it's better to be a human being dissatisfied, than a pig satisfied. Humans are capable of having higher-level thinking, and therefore are morally obligated to their higher pleasures. This means that some happiness is better than other happiness in terms of utility.

According to the principle of 'greatest happiness', an act is right if and only if, it would give the greatest 'net good overall'. It is the principle as to how to act. It is an existence exempt as far as possible from pain, and as rich as possible in enjoyments, both in point of quantity and quality. The test of 'quality' and the rule for measuring it against quantity is the preference felt by those who experience self-consciousness and self observation. This is in fact the end of human action. This is the ultimate standard of morality. Morality being defined as the rules and precepts for human conduct.

It is also important to note that the purpose of morality is to bring about a particular state of the world. This is one framework to understand morality. It is important to think about whether this consequences-based understanding of morality is convincing. For example, consider something regarded as immoral, such as lying. Consider then a situation in which the telling of a lie could prevent five other people from having to lie. Is the first lie morally justified? The answer depends in part on whether one believes that morality's essential function is to bring about the "best," or whether its function is to govern individual acts independent of their more general consequences.

If one believes that the point of morality is to create a better world as a whole, and if you accept that lying is bad, then the fewer the lies in the world, the better the world is. Therefore, one may tell that first lie to prevent the other five from being told. However, one might argue that bringing about the best state of the world at large is not morality's concern. For example, one could argue that morality bears most strongly upon the conduct of a single person as an individual. As an individual, one should never lie, no matter what; to lie is to defile oneself morally. There are many variations of this argument, as well as completely different ways to potentially ground morality. It is in this context J.S. Mill has asserted that it is not enough simply to characterize actions as good or evil; rather, there must be something about these actions that gives them a moral nature.

In spite of the fact that the 'principle of greatest happiness' has got acclaimed by many, there are a few that took objection to the proposition as of the following:

1. It is not always clear what the outcome of an action will be, nor is it always possible to determine who will be affected by it. Judging an action by the outcome is therefore hard to do beforehand.
2. It is difficult to quantify pleasures for cost/benefit analysis (but since this only has to be done on a comparative scale, this may not be as serious an objection as it at first seems).
3. The calculation required to determine the right is both complicated and time consuming. Many occasions will not permit the time and many individuals may not even be capable of the calculations.
4. Since the greatest good for the greatest number is described in aggregate terms, that good may be achieved under conditions that are harmful to some, so long as that harm is balanced by a greater good.
5. The theory fails to acknowledge any individual rights that could not be violated for the sake of the greatest good. Indeed, even the murder of an innocent person would seem to be condoned if it served the greater number.

4.1.2 Egoism

As opposed to the principle of 'greatest happiness to all', egoism has emerged as the viewpoint of 'good' happening to one only. The pleasure or pain caused to oneself. In the dictionary meaning also, 'egoism' is termed the thinking only about oneself and considering oneself better and more important than others. In that sense, egoism can be dubbed as the 'self centred feeling or approach'. Critics view this feeling of selfishness as detrimental to 'social structure'; as such persons oppose or devoid of charity or parting something for the benefit of others. It is believed that societies cannot thrive on the basis of egoism. There are at least three different ways by which the theory of egoism is exhibited.

(i) Psychological Egoism

This is actually motivated by some selfish desire of the individual, which may include desire for reward, and avoidance. It is reported that *humans by nature are motivated only by self-interest*. Any act, no matter how of guilt, is carried out by the humans, if it benefits them. This is a **descriptive claim** about human nature. Hence, it is said that all acts are motivated by self interest.

It will be difficult to find an action that the psychological egoist will acknowledge as purely altruistic. There is almost always some benefit to ourselves in any action we choose. For example, if one helped his friend out of trouble, he may feel happy afterwards. But is that happiness, the motive for one's action or just a result of the action? The psychological egoist must demonstrate that the beneficial consequences of an action are actually the result of motivation of all of the actions. The question, however, remains that why would it make one happy to see one's friend out of trouble, if one didn't already *care* about his friend's best interest? It is this altruism is said to guide the human action.

(ii) Ethical Egoism

This is the claim that individuals *should* always act in their own best interest. It is a **normative claim**. If ethical egoism is to be true, we have to accept that psychological egoism is false. There would be no point to saying that we ought to do what we must do by nature.

But if altruism is possible, why should it be avoided? Some writers suggest that one should focus resources that satisfy his own interests, rather than those of others. Society will then be more efficient and this will better serve the interests of all. By referring to the interests of all, however, this approach reveals itself to be a version of utilitarianism, and not genuine egoism. It is merely a theory about how best to achieve the greatest good for the greatest number.

An alternative formulation of ethical egoism states that one ought to act in one's self-interest; even if this conflicts with the values and interests of others. Because that is what people value most. It is not clear how an altruist could argue with such an individualistic ethical egoist, but it is also not clear that such an egoist should choose to argue with the altruist. Since the *individualistic egoist* believes that whatever serves his own interests is (morally) right, he wants everyone *else* to be altruistic. Otherwise they would not serve the egoist's interests! It seems that anyone who truly believed in individualistic ethical egoism could not promote the theory without inconsistency. Indeed, the self-interest of the egoist is best served by publicly claiming to be an altruist and thereby keeping everyone's good favour.

(iii) Minimalist Egoism

When working with certain economic or sociological models, we may frequently assume that people will act in such a way as to promote their own interests. This is *not* a normative claim and usually not even a descriptive claim. Instead, it is a *minimalist assumption* used for certain calculations. If we assume only self-interest on the part of all agents, we can determine certain extreme-case (e.g., maximin) outcomes for the model. Implicit in this assumption is the idea that altruistic behavior on the part of the agents. Although it is not presupposed, it is expected that such action would yield outcomes at least as good and probably better.

4.1.3 Distributive Justice

This is a concept concerned with the fair distribution of society's benefits and burdens. The question of distributive justice arises when different people put forth conflicting claims on society's benefits and burdens. When the economies face shortages for food, housing, jobs, incomes and wealth, there would be a large number of claimants. Unfortunately, the reality is that every economy faces inadequacy in one or the other resource. Thus, there will be claims to devise a mechanism by which these resources (in short supply) are meaningfully and equitably distributed among the needy.

The fundamental principle involved in this approach is that equals should be treated equally and unequals treated unequally. More specifically, individuals who are similar in all respects relevant to the kind of treatment in question should be given similar benefits and burdens, even if they are dissimilar in other irrelevant aspects. And individuals who are dissimilar in a relevant aspect out ought to be treated dissimilarly, in proportion to their dissimilarity. A simple example could be: imagine that X and Y are doing the same work and there are no relevant differences between them or the work they are doing. Then the justice is that the wages paid to X and Y must be equal. If X is working for longer hours than Y (say twice longer than Y), X should be paid twice the wage paid to Y. Continuing the same example, if we wish to recognize differences in their productivity, and compensate them proportionately, work becomes the relevant aspect, but productivity levels may be dissimilar. Thus, the fundamental principle in the concept of 'distributive justice' is that there shall be equality and consistency in the treatment in the similar situations.

Nevertheless, there are many variations in the concept of distributive justice, as of the following:

(i) Justice as Equality: Egalitarianism: This is based on the notion that there are no relevant differences among people that can justify unequal treatment. Thus, every person should be given exactly equal shares of a society's or group's benefits and burdens. Equality has been proposed as a principle of justice not only for entire societies, but also within smaller groups and organizations. As a matter of fact, egalitarianism has a big appeal. This is dubbed as the 'ideal' that every society or government should aim at. Thus, there are many slogans such as: (1) men (including women) are born equal, (2) all are equal before law, (3) equal pay for equal work, (4) equality before religion, (5) equality of treatment in the social set up, etc. Thus, the demands arising in the society are for economic equality, social equality and cultural equality. Even in the present century, tensions are pent up on all these counts and thus many become the issues on the Agenda of the 'Political Parties'.

(ii) Justice, based on Contribution: Capitalist Justice: This is an argument based on the proposition that the distribution of benefits and burdens, based on their individual contribution to the society as a group. The more a person contributes to the society's pool of resources, the more that the person is entitled to take from that pool. This principle applies to the workers/labourers, in such a way that the worker gets the wages basing on his contribution to the work/project. Thus, justice in this context, is that the benefits people receive should be proportional to the value of their contribution. But the difficulty in this proposition pertains to the methodology applied to decide on the basis to assess the contribution that one is able to make to the pool. In the belief on 'puritan ethic', every individual has a religious obligation to work hard at his calling to his fullest capacity. However, justice has nothing to do with the religious sentiments, but only with the distribution of benefits and burden on an equitable basis.

(iii) Justice based on Needs and Abilities: Socialism: This is based on the principle that work burdens should be distributed according to people's abilities and benefits should be distributed according to their needs. This is widely opposed to the principle of individual initiative. Yet, based on the belief that individuals vary on their abilities in carrying out a given work. In spite of this fact, means are sought to be distributed according to the biological and health needs of the people. This is based on the analogy that just as the able family members willingly support the other family members, so also the able members of the society should contribute their full potential to the society taking up its burdens; while the needy should be allowed to share its benefits.

As we go by the experience the world over, the appreciation of this concept is on the wane. Even those countries that were considered replica of the socialism are not truly following this principle and the disintegration of USSR is an example of how inconsistent the very idea is.

5. DEONTOLOGICAL ETHICAL SYSTEMS

These ethical systems are based on the adherence to independent moral rules or duties fixed by the individuals. For this, first of all one has to determine one's own moral standards and compare his actions against the standards set. For, the very term 'deontology' derives from the Greek 'deon (means duty) and logos (means science)'. Thus, these theories place special emphasis on the relationship between duty and the morality of human actions. Under these ethical systems, an action is considered morally good, because of some characteristic of the action itself, not because the product of the action is good. It is hypothesized that at least some acts are morally obligatory regardless of their consequences for human welfare. It goes by the common adages that : 'duty for duty's sake', virtue has its own reward', let justice be done though the heavens fall'. Deontological theories have been termed formalistic, because of their central principle lying in conformity of an action to some rule or law.

5.1 Kant's Theory of Rightness of Rules

Immanuel Kant (1724-1804), a German Philosopher, was the first to define the deontological principles holding that 'nothing is good without qualification, except a goodwill. Kant views this as a 'categorical imperative', i.e., an unconditional command and that its content could be established by human reason alone.

In the opinion of Kant, any statement of moral obligation is based on the principle of action. In the context of a specific situation, it may constitute an "*imperative.*" The focus is on the choice to act on a statement of the form. For example, if one desires some specific end (e.g., happiness, maximum pleasure, power, etc.), then he *ought* to do such and such an action. In doing so, one would be acting on what Kant calls "a *hypothetical* imperative." However, Kant has already *ruled out ends* as the grounds for moral obligation. Therefore, ***hypothetical*** *imperatives cannot serve as the basis for determining moral duty*. If one acts on a principle which has the form, "in circumstances of such and such a character, *one ought to do a particular act*. Then one may be said to be acting on what Kant calls a "***categorical*** imperative".

In the opinion of Kant, *the* categorical imperative refers to the *principle* that ***all principles of our action (maxims) could consistently become universal laws***. The **categorical imperative** is a *principle about principles*, or a *"second order"* principle. "*First* order" principles would be the specific moral principles which determine one's ethical obligation, such as, for example the Ten Commandments; what the categorical imperative determines is the form of these first order principles. They must have the "form" that can be consistently "*universalized,*" i.e., held to apply as *universal moral laws* for all rational agents.

According to Kant *only rational beings can be said to act morally*. The general belief is that reasoning is the *same for all persons*. In other words, there isn't a poor man's reason versus a rich man's reason or a white man's reason versus a black man's reason. All persons are equal as *potentially rational beings*. Therefore, if reason dictates the action of a person in a particular situation. he has the moral *duty* to do a particular thing. Then ***any*** *person, in that same situation, would equally well have a duty to do that same thing*. In this sense Kant's reasoning parallels the way in which *stoicism* led Roman lawyers to the conclusion that all citizens are equal before the law. Thus, Kant is a moral "absolutist" in the sense that *all persons have the same moral duties*, for all persons are equal as rational beings. But this "absolutism" does not mean that Kant holds that our moral duties are not relative to the situation in which we find ourselves. Thus, it is quite possible for Kant to conclude that in *one* particular situation one may have a duty to *keep* the promise, but in *another* situation (in which, for example, keeping a promise conflicts with a higher duty) one may equally well be morally obligated to *break* a promise.

5.2 Agent-Centred Deontological Theories

According to these versions, we each have both permissions and obligations that give us agent-relative reasons for action. An agent-relative reason is an objective reason, just as are agent neutral reasons; neither is to be confused with the subjective reasons that form the nerve of psychological explanation of human action. An agent-relative reason is so-called because it is a reason relative to the agent whose reason it is. It need not constitute a reason for anyone else. Thus, an agent-relative *obligation* is an obligation for a particular agent to take or refrain from taking some action. The obligation does not necessarily give anyone else a reason to support that action. Each parent, for example, is commonly thought to have such special obligations to his/her child, obligations not shared by anyone else. Likewise, an agent-relative *permission* is a permission for some agent to do some act even though others may not be permitted to aid that agent in the doing of his permitted action. Each parent, is commonly thought to be permitted (at the least) to save his own child even at the cost of not saving two other children to whom he has no special relation. Agent-centred theories and the agent-relative reasons compel humans to do or not to do certain things.

At the heart of agent-centred theories is the idea of agency. The moral plausibility of agent-centred theories is rooted here. The idea is that morality is intensely personal. In the sense that human beings are enjoined to keep their moral houses in order. Our categorical obligations are not to focus on how our actions cause or enable other agents to do evil; the focus of our categorical obligations is to keep our own agency free of moral taint.

Each agent's distinctive moral concern with his/her own agency puts some pressure on agent-centred theories to clarify how and when our agency is or is not involved in various situations. Agent-centred theories famously divide between those that emphasize the role of intention or other mental states in constituting the morally important kind of agency, and those that emphasize the actions of agents as playing such a role. There are also agent-centered theories that emphasize both intentions and actions equally in constituting the morally relevant agency of persons.

5.3 Patient-Centred Deontological Theories

As distinguished from the agent-centred versions, these theories are based on rights of the individuals. All patient-centred deontological theories are properly characterized as theories promised on people's rights. An illustrative version posits, as its core right, the right against being used only as means for producing good consequences without one's consent. Such a core right is not to be confused with more discrete rights, such as the right against being killed, or being killed intentionally. It is a right against being used by another for the user's or others' benefit. More specifically, this version of patient-centred deontological theories prescribes *using* of another's body, labor, and talent without the latter's consent. One finds this notion expressed, albeit in different ways.

The oft-repeated example in explaining this theory is that of Trolley and Transplant. In Trolley, a runaway trolley will kill five workers unless diverted to a siding where it will kill one worker. Most people regard it as permissible and perhaps mandatory to switch the trolley to the siding. By contrast, in Transplant, where a surgeon can kill one healthy patient and transplant his organs to five dying patients, thereby saving their lives. The universal reaction is condemnation. The same is by and large true in case of a fat man, where the runaway trolley cannot be switched off the main track but can be stopped before reaching the five workers by pushing a fat man into its path, resulting in his death.

The injunction against using arguably accounts for these contrasting reactions is that after all, one life is sacrificed to save five. Yet there appears to be a difference in the means through which the net four lives are saved. In transplant (and fat man), the doomed person is used to benefit others. They could not be saved in the absence of his body. In trolley, on the other hand, the doomed victim is not used. The workers would be saved whether or not he is present on the second track.

The patient-centered version of deontology is aptly labeled libertarian in that it is not plausible to conceive of not being aided as being used by the one not aiding. Using is an action, not a failure to act. More generally, it is counter-intuitive to many to think that any of us have a *right* to be aided. For if there were a strong (that is, enforceable or coercible) duty to aid others, such that, for example, *A* had a duty to aid *X*, *Y*, and *Z*; and if *A* could more effectively aid *X*, *Y*, and *Z* by coercing *B* and *C* to aid them (as is *their* duty), then *A* would have a duty to "use" *B* and *C* in this way. For these reasons, any positive duties will not be rights-based ones on the view here considered; they will be consequentially-justified duties that can be trumped by the right not to be coerced to perform them.

Patient-centered deontologies are thus arguably better construed to be agent-relative in the reasons they give. Even so construed, such deontologies join agent-centered deontologies in facing the moral (rather than the conceptual) versions of the paradox of deontology. For a critic of either form of deontology might respond to the categorical prohibition about using others. If usings are bad, then are not more usings worse than fewer? And if so, then is it not odd to condemn acts that produce better states of affairs than would occur in their absence? Deontologists of either stripe can just deny that wrong acts on their account of wrongness can be translated into bad states of affairs. Two wrongings are not "worse" than one. Such wrongs cannot be summed into anything of normative significance.

Therefore, a deontologist might reject the comparability of states of affairs that involve violations and those that do not. Similarly, the deontologist may reject the comparability of states of affairs that involve more or fewer rights violations. They might attempt to back this assertion by relying upon the separateness of persons.

Wrongs are only wrongs to persons. A wrong to *Y* and a wrong to *Z* cannot be added to make some greater wrong because there is no person who suffers this greater wrong.

5.4 Contractualist Deontological Theories

Somewhat orthogonal to the distinction between agent-centred versus patient-centred deontological theories are contractualist deontological theories. Morally wrong acts are, on such accounts, those acts that would be forbidden by principles that people in a suitably described social contract would accept. Actions are termed contractual for the reason they are forbidden only by principles that such people could not "reasonably reject".

In deontology, as elsewhere in ethics, is not entirely clear whether a contractualist account is really normative as opposed to metaethical. If such account is a first order normative account, it is probably best construed as a patient-centred deontology. For the central obligation would be to do onto others; only that to which they have consented. But so construed, modern contractualist accounts would share the problems that have long bedeviled historical social contract theories. It is also to be decided as to how plausible is it that the "moral magic" of consent is the first principle of morality? And how much of what is commonly regarded as permissible to do to people can (in any realistic sense of the word) be said to be actually consented to by them, expressly or even implicitly?

6. OTHER CATEGORIES OF THEORIES

Ethics being such an important and interesting discipline, there are many other exponents that enriched the literature by their contributions. Though they cannot be termed comprehensive, a reasonable attempt has been made have to also peep into the theories of many other writers. Significant among them are discussed here.

6.1 Kohlherg's Theory of Moral Development

Lawrence Kohlberg, a moral philosopher and the director of Harvard's Centre for Moral Education, developed a theory based on the hypothesis that the process of moral development was principally concerned with justice and that it continues throughout the individual's lifetime. Kohlberg has identified six distinct stages in the moral development; grouped into three levels as shown below:

Level–I: (Pre-Conventional)

1. Obedience and punishment orientation (referring to how I can avoid punishment?)

2. Self-Interest orientation (referring to what is in it for? Implying payment for a benefit.)

Level–II: (Conventional)

3. Interpersonal accord and conformity (referring to social norms – say the good boy/girl attitude)
4. Authority and social order orientation (referring to law and order morality).

Level–III: (Post-Conventional)

5. Social contract orientation
6. Universal ethical principles

Kohlberg believes that the moral development evolves over a period of time and people learn by their experience; as if there is the possibility of upgradation and thus individual ethics transforms into universal ethics. According to Kohlberg: someone progressing to a higher stage of moral reasoning cannot skip stages. For example, an individual cannot jump from being concerned mostly with peer judgments (stage three) to being a proponent of social contracts (stage five). On encountering a moral dilemma and finding their current level of moral reasoning unsatisfactory, an individual may look to the next level. Realizing the limitations of the current stage of thinking is the driving force behind moral development, as each progressive stage is more adequate than the last. The process is therefore considered to be constructive, as it is initiated by the conscious construction of the individual, and is not in any meaningful sense a component of the individual's innate dispositions, or a result of past inductions.

Kohlberg states that preconventional level of moral reasoning is especially common in children, although adults can also exhibit this level of reasoning. Reasoners at this level judge the morality of an action by its direct consequences. The pre-conventional level consists of the first and second stages of moral development and is solely concerned with the '**self**' in an egocentric manner. A child with pre-conventional morality has not yet adopted or internalized society's conventions regarding what is right or wrong but instead focuses largely on external consequences that certain actions may bring.

In **stage one** (obedience and punishment driven), individuals focus on the direct consequences of their actions on themselves. For example, an action is perceived as morally wrong because the perpetrator is punished. "The last time I did that I got spanked, so I will not do it again." The worse the punishment for the act is, the more "bad" the act is perceived to be.

Stage two (self-interest driven) expresses the "what's in it for me" position, in which right behavior is defined by whatever the individual believes to be in their best interest but understood in a narrow way which does not consider one's reputation or relationships to groups of people. Stage two reasoning shows a limited interest in the needs of others, but only to a point where it might further the individual's own interests. As a result, concern for others is not based on loyalty or intrinsic respect, but rather a "you scratch my back, and I'll scratch yours" mentality. The lack of a societal perspective in the pre-conventional level is quite different from the social contract (stage five), as all actions at this stage have the purpose of serving the individual's own needs or interests. For the stage two theorist, the world's perspective is often seen as morally relative. The conventional level of moral reasoning is typical of adolescents and adults. To reason in a conventional way, is to judge the morality of actions by comparing them to society's views and expectations.

The conventional level consists of the third and fourth stages of moral development. Conventional morality is characterized by an acceptance of society's conventions concerning right and wrong. At this level, an individual obeys rules and follows society's norms even when there are no consequences for obedience or disobedience. Adherence to rules and conventions is somewhat rigid, however, and a rule's appropriateness or fairness is seldom questioned.

In **stage three** (good intentions as determined by social consensus), the self enters society by conforming to social standards. Individuals are receptive to approval or disapproval from others as it reflects society's views. They try to be a "good boy" or "good girl" to live up to these expectations; having learnt that being regarded as good benefits the self. Stage three reasoning may judge the morality of an action by evaluating its consequences in terms of a person's relationships, which now begin to include things like respect, gratitude, and the "golden rule". "I want to be liked and thought well of; apparently, not being naughty makes people like me." Conforming to the rules for one's social role is not yet fully understood. The intentions of individuals play a more significant role in reasoning at this stage. One may feel more forgiving, if one thinks that "they mean well".

In **stage four** (authority and social order obedience driven), it is important to obey laws, dictums, and social conventions because of their importance in maintaining the functioning of a society. Moral reasoning in stage four is thus beyond the need for individual approval exhibited in stage three. The post-conventional level, also known as the principled level, is marked by a growing realization that individuals are separate entities from society, and that the individual's own perspective may take precedence over society's view. And individuals may disobey rules inconsistent with their own principles. People regard basic human rights such as life, liberty, and justice. People who exhibit post-conventional morality view rules as useful to maintain the general social order and protect human rights. Rules are not absolute dictates that must be obeyed without question. Because post-conventional individuals elevate their own moral evaluation of a situation over social conventions. Some theorists have even speculated that many people may never reach this level of abstract moral reasoning.

In **stage five** (social contract driven), the world is viewed as holding different opinions, rights, and values. Such perspectives should be mutually respected as unique to each person or community. Laws are regarded as social contracts rather than rigid edicts. Those that do not promote the general welfare should be changed when necessary to meet "the greatest good for the greatest number of people". This is achieved through majority decision and inevitable compromise. Democratic government is ostensibly based on stage five reasoning. In **stage six** (universal ethical principles driven), moral reasoning is based on abstract reasoning using universal ethical principles. Laws are valid only in so far as they are grounded in justice, and a commitment to justice carries with it an obligation to disobey unjust laws.

6.2 Gilligan's Care Theory of Ethics

Carol Gilligan focused her attention on the care based and justice based morality. Gilligan felt that Kohlberg's theory did not address the gender differences properly in moral development and thus, she proposed 'care based morality', with the following principles:

- Emphasizing interconnectedness and universality.
- Acting justly means avoiding violence and helping those in need.
- Care-based morality is thought to be more common in girls because of their connections to their mothers.
- Because girls remain connected to their mothers, they are less inclined to worry about issues of fairness.

Justice-based morality is based on the following principles:

- Views the world as being composed of autonomous individuals who interact with another.
- Acting justly means avoiding inequality.
- Is thought to be more common in boys because of their need to differentiate between themselves and their mothers.
- Because they are separated from their mothers, boys become more concerned with the concept of inequality.

The care-based perspective approaches the problem differently. Rather than seeing all the parties as separate individuals with their own valid or invalid claims, it sees them as already in a difficult situation together. If there is a conflict between them, that is part of the problem. The point is not to decide the conflict one way or the other, but to find a way to get around it or remove it. This perspective starts from the particular case and the actual people within it and hopes to find a solution that will not damage anyone. It will be ready to embrace, compromise and create solutions.

The following are the three states of moral development in the ethics of care theory proposed by Carol Gilligan.

Stage	State of Moral Development	Goal
Pre-conventional	I love me to I love you	Individual survival to responsibility to others.
Conventional	I love you more than me	Self sacrifice is goodness.
Post-conventional	I love myself and you	Non-violence.

According to Gilligan, women can gain personal independence after they forget about the idea that their proper role is to overcome their interests to the interests of their husbands, children, or other people they care about. Gilligan says that in our society women really like to help others, however they should care just as much about themselves as they do about others.

6.3 Consequentialism vs non-Consequentialism

There is a broad theorization of morality in terms of 'means' and 'ends'. We have examined different bases on which ethics will rely. Some authors have focused on the 'ends' and others have emphasized on 'means'. All of them are grouped together to form broad categories as consequentialism and non-consequentialism.

A consequentialist theory judges the rightness or wrongness of an action based on the consequences that action has. Accordingly, the best action is the one that produces the 'greatest good for the greatest number'. The theory of utilitarianism is based on this philosophy. Accordingly, each person must assess the situation he or she is involved in and try to figure out which act would bring about the greatest amount of good consequences with the least amount of bad consequences, not just for himself or herself, but for everyone involved in the situation. Therefore, a legislator must consider carefully the best resolution for everybody for now and in the future. The statement could be: "If I were a legislator and exercised impartiality during tough times when people needed to stick together, yet favoured my constituents and worked hard to bring home the bacon when times were prosperous, I believe I would win the support and faith of my district".

Whereas, the non-consequentialist theory attempts to judge the rightness or wrongness of an action based on properties intrinsic to the action, not on its consequences. These are also called 'rule theories'. For instance, capital punishment (death penalty) is not justified by a deterrent effect, but instead is upheld as a moral statement of the requirements of justice. Similarly, accidental or violent deaths resulting from gun ownership are not germane to the issue, but the right to bear the arms in principle; thus consequence is not the factor to decide, but the rule relating to having it or not. These non-consequential theories include variants like duty theories, rights theories and justice theories.

References

1. Adam Smith, "The Theory of Moral Sentiments', Strand, Edinburg, 1759 (Quoted from website).
2. K.V. Rao, "Biological Perspective of Human Behaviour", *The Executive – A Business Journal*, Vol. 1, Jan-June, 2002, pp. 65-66.
3. Mike Bennett, "10 Commandments List" (Like Hope and Truth.com)
4. Islamic Ethics: Foundational Motifs (http://en.wikipedia.org)
5. Hinduism's Code of Conduct – Brief Summary, 26 March 2013 (www.sahms.org.za).
6. Manuel G. Velasquez, "*Business Ethics: Concepts and Cases*", Prentice-Hall of India, New Delhi, 2006, p. 113.
7. Aristotelian ethics (http://en.wikipedi.org).
8. Hindu Tenets, Hindu Online: Preserve, Practice, Propagate. (www.hinduonline.com/HinduReligion)
9. Moksha, Hinduism (http://en.wikipedi.org).
10. Directive Principles of State Policy, The Constitution of India, p. 102.
11. http://marutistorage.blob.core.windows.net/marutisuzukipdf/Presentation-Q4-FY-12.pdf.
12. http://www.wipro.com/documents/investors/pdf-files/code_of_business_conduct_and_ethics_march_2011.pdf
13. http://study.com/academy/lesson/what-is-utilitarianism-definition-theory-quiz.html
14. John Stuart Mill, "Utilitarianism", Chapter-1, General Remarks (http://www.sparknotes.com/philosophy/utilitarianism/section1.rhtml)
15. Charles D. Kay, 'Notes on Utilitarianism'. (http://sites.wofford.edu/kaycd/utilitarianism/)
16. Charles D. Kay, "Varieties of Egoism'. (http://sites.wofford.edu/kaycd/egoism/)
17. Comments On Kant's Ethical Theory (http://www.loyno.edu/~folse/Kant.html)
18. Deontological Ethics, Stanford Encyclopedia of Philosophy. (www.plato.stanford.edu/.../ethics-deontological)
19. Lawrence Kohlberg's stages of moral development (https://en.wikipedia.org/.../Lawrence_Kohl.)
20. Carol Gilligan's Theory of Moral Development (http://study.com/academy/lesson/carol-gilligans-theory-of-moral-development.html)
21. Robert Wright, 'Consequentialism and Non-consequentialism Theories of Ethics'.(http://www.academia.edu/2146503/Consequentialism_and_Nonconsequentialism)

2

CHAPTER

Values

1. INTRODUCTION

Values are integral part of ethics. While ethics, if understood as the philosophy of life, decides the way one wants to live. The life of an individual is guided by one's value system. All philosophical and religious underpinnings speak about the values to be promoted among the subjects for an orderly growth of the society. Good and bad, right and wrong, legal and illegal are all judged on the basis of the values believed in. For instance taking alcohol is quite routine in the west, but the same is denounced in the Indian setting. Same is true in case of smoking. Even in this, there could be variations like smoking in private and smoking in public places. The former is legal and the latter is illegal.

For human beings, certain things always assume precedence over the others, and values allow the members of an organization to interact harmoniously. Values affect their formation and development as individuals and make it easier to reach goals that would be impossible to achieve individually. It is necessary to have shared values to guide the well-being of a community. Otherwise the community will not function to the satisfaction of the majority. In a company's organizational culture, values are the foundation of employee attitudes, motivations and expectations. In a way, values define the behaviour of employees/executives and all other stakeholders. The ten commandments of an organizational value system are said to be: honesty, responsibility, communication, sincerity, respect, comradeship, solidarity, tolerance, learning and self improvement. It is believed that those organizations that keep faith in these values would grow faster than others and provide members with their greater personal satisfaction.[1]

2. MEANING OF VALUES

In Sanskrit, value means 'Ishta', i.e., the object of liking. What do people like and why do they like a thing, a phenomenon, an incident are guided by their desires. Desire and its satisfaction are the forces behind one's actions. If there is no 'desire', nobody needs to take up any work. This can be said to be the foundation for the entire 'human action'. Economists interpret 'desire' as the basis for economic activity. In the context of unlimited wants (desires), 'Economics' is the discipline which suggests a mechanism by which scarce resources can be effectively allocated among competing uses. The famous definition of Lionel Robbins on Economics reads as 'Economics is a science that studies human bahaviour as a relationship between limited resources and unlimited wants; which have alternative uses'.[2]

In contrast, the philospical view of Buddha is based on the realization that 'desires are the root cause for sorrow'. If one can devise a method to wipe out desires, there will be no case for sorrow. Thus, Buddha tried to know the cause for sorrow and lead a life that leads to 'nirvana'.

Values in this context paraphrase the liking of one's life and thus characterize the personality of an individual. Desire and satisfaction of the desire are the two key elements in the interpretation of the meaning of values. Going deep into the explanation of desire, perhaps we may have to depend on the Buddhist interpretation. Desire is equated with the concept of 'Tanha'; which means thirst, craving, desire, etc. It is defined as the craving to hold on to pleasurable experiences, to be separated from painful or unpleasant experiences or for neutral experiences or feelings not to decline. Buddha identified this as the principal cause in the arising of *dukha* (suffering anxiety, dissatisfaction). At the next stage, satisfaction of the desire would come into the picture. The question here pertains to the 'means'. Means adopted to fulfill the desire decide the 'value'. It is here we have to draw a distinction between the current value and future value. Value is a 'to be' phenomenon and relates to 'future'. Value is what you believe in. That belief is the one that guides current actions of the people. Sometimes, what one believes in or what one wishes to be may not as clear as fact. But still the future will decide that present. For example, a person who is currently eating meat may wish to be vegetarian and hence slowly stop consuming meat. In a way, the distant goal guides the present actions. The concept of values can be better explained through the following continuum.

Continuum–1: Value Chain Focusing on Means

Continuum–2: Value Chain Focusing on Action

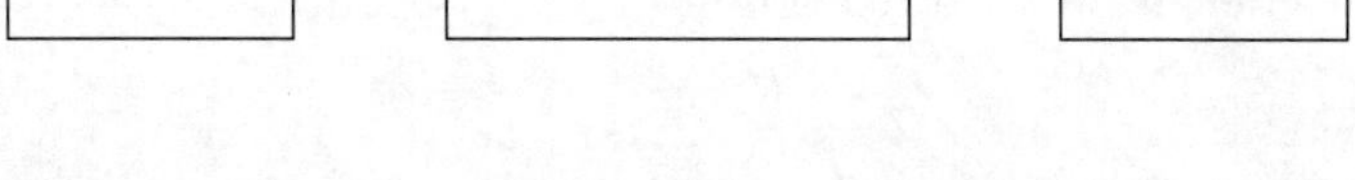

In the value system, means is as important as ends. As we have understood in the previous chapter, there are two schools of ethical thought. One that emphasizes on the ends or result and the other that focuses on the means. In the discussions on Ethics, both the schools of thought are important. The more factual situation is that people resort to action, if they like; avoid or keep away from acting, if they dislike. Thus likes and dislikes define the value system. Values are, thus, the attributes of the people.[3]

3. TYPES OF VALUES

Values are understood by many in diverse ways. This understanding is expected to broaden the concept of values. Literature on Ethics speaks of different kinds of values, as of the following:

3.1 Subjective vs Objective Values

Subjective values are those that depend on the changing likes and dislikes of the individuals. These may vary from individual to individual. For example, a person being an atheist at young age may turn out to be a theist at the later part of his life. Similarly, a non-vegetarian at the beginning may prefer to be a strict vegetarian in due course. They are subjective for the reason that they are akin to individuals. It is also difficult to measure the value compliance on a scale, since they may be varying at every point of time.

Objective values are those attributes that are akin to objects. Each object as a physical property, will have certain characteristics. Such attributes may change, when they are subjected to nature. This pertains to the animate things. Objective values may also pertain to certain things concerned with all the people or public at large. Generally, there could be no objection to such value statements like 'Education for All', 'Health for All' and 'Wealth for All' or 'Happiness for All'. There is a closing remark made at every congregation of people wishing them to be peaceful like 'Sarvejana Sukhino Bhavantu".

3.2 Instrumental vs Intrinsic Values

Instrumental value goes by the functional utility of an object or goods. All goods are expected to have some functional utility or performance value. We have a mobile, a communication device. The functional utility of the product is to the extent it enables us to talk to others, receive mails, send messages, photographs, etc. Therefore the value of the mobile depends on its functional capacity in terms of its uses/performance. Same would be true in case of an automobile, TV, refrigerator, etc. The instrument ceases to carry any value when it stops functioning or gets outdated or outmoded. To a great extent all these depend on the changes in the technology, preferences or attitudes of the consumers and new developments.

Whereas intrinsic value is the actual worth of the thing. It may be goods, individual or any other object. In addition to the physical features, like size, colour, model, etc., there may be certain other features, not seen or decided by apparent logic. These features, which are not visible, are also said to decide the value of goods or things. In that sense, these are treated as having intrinsic value. Intrinsic value is decided by certain basic characteristics of an individual or a thing. For instance, you need to decide on the intrinsic value of an individual, you may have to go by the honesty, integrity, compassion, etc; though it is difficult to measure such characteristics by any yardstick. Yet they are important for deciding the personality of an individual. In the valuation of shares in stock exchange, analysts take into consideration these intrinsic factors. In addition to the vision, mission and objectives, the general character of the promoters is also taken into account in company valuations. Besides quantitative factors such as sales, income, assets, capital, etc., qualitative aspects like the goodwill of the promoters, future prospects also influence the valuation of stocks. In the social setting, the parameters used to select a bride or a bridegroom would sufficiently explain the role of intrinsic value. All this speaks of the fact that what is not visible is as important as what is visible in deciding things.

3.3 Logical vs Ethical Values

Logic is the mother of legal education. Logic is a systematic attempt at explaining a situation/phenomenon; or drawing conclusions. Logic is said to be a science of discovery. In that context, logic is defined as the formal scientific method of examining or thinking about ideas. Logic is said to follow a sequence or a sequential application. Thus, logical values are derived from systematic examination of a given thing or phenomenon. They are used to establish facts about a thing or incident or a given situation. For this reason, logical value is also termed 'true value'; its worth. Logical values, thus, depend on the capacity of the interpreter. His perception, inference, comparison, postulation and finally his argumentative ability. Truth is sought to be established by reason, by argumentation and by acceptance or rejection of the postulations. Over a period of time, truths are established, reestablished by virtue of new findings. Till Copernicus proved that the Earth is round, people believed it to be flat. Similar is the truth about the creation of universe, and planets. We are counting today of nine planets. Tomorrow, scientists may prove the existence of the tenth.

Ethical values deal with the moral truth or morality. Morality is about one's way of life. What one wants to be or the way he wants to behave? Morality is the basis for social order. It is a fact that no person can live for oneself. Human beings are members of the society. One has to live within a group or society. Therefore, the conduct also shall keep pace with the members of the group. Whether he likes it or not, he has to condition his behaviour and follow the 'code of conduct' as agreed upon by the members forming part of the group or society. This affinity or association generates certain obligations too; like the obligation to the nature, to continue the race, to conserve/preserve its culture and so on. Ethical values define limits of operation to an individual. As a member of the group, one has to define himself (do good to him) and also help other members of the group (do good to other). Thus ethical behaviour as guided by ethical values is said to be influenced by such important factors as context, content, culture and time:

Ethical Behaviour = f[Context, content, culture and time]

3.4 Absolute vs Relative Values

An absolute value is the one that is ultimate. There could be no two opinions about such a value. Consider for instance the maxim that "justice be done though the heavens fall". The truth in the statement is absolute; which could never be violated under any circumstances. Similarly, Immanuel Kant has talked about 'good will'.[3A] There is no case for wishing otherwise. Absolute values are such on which there is a consensus. Even personal values may get elevated to the status of absolute values, provided the members of the group/society believe in them as the individual believes in.

Relative values are characterized by change. After all, the world is evolving. Old gives way to the new. Old traditions and beliefs are sidelined to establish new ones. 'change is the law of life', thus the saying goes. In such a context, there is nothing that is absolute or eternal. Origin and end are the two phases in the evolution. The universe itself is said to have come into existence by evolution. 'Big Bang Theory' of physics is now believed to be the origin of universe. In that view of things, substances are matters whose conception is atomic, time and space and they are characterized by mind and matter.

Perhaps, Albert Einstein's 'Theory of Special Relativity' would explain the concept of relativism better. In that, Einstein could prove that the laws of physics are the same for all non-accelerating observers, and showed that the speed of light within a vacuum is the same, no matter the speed at which an observer travels. As a matter of fact, Einstein could prove that our knowledge of reality is relative and thus declared that the Newton's three laws of motion were only approximately correct, breaking down when velocities approached that of light. He also proved that Newton's law of gravitation was only approximately correct, breaking down in the presence of very strong gravitational fields. After about 100 years of the postulation of the Theory of General Relativity (1918), scientists have detected the first gravitational wave signals, confirming Einstein's last unproven theory. Though the existence of gravitational waves is generally accepted within the scientific community, the same was not proved so far beyond doubt. This was done recently (dated 15-02-2016) with the declaration by the scientists at Laser Interferometer Gravitational – wave observatory (LIGO) that they picked up wave signals in September last year (2015) and said that the signal was coming from two distant black holes that merged about 1.3 billion years ago. When the black holes merged after spinning around one another several times per second, they created a massive explosion, therefore generating huge gravitational waves. Thus everything is relative, as long as the universe is evolving; so to say about moral values.

3.5 Aesthetic Values

Aesthetic values pertain to objects or an events having the capacity to create pleasure or displeasure. We cannot say it as hatred, but not happy in the negative connotation. They are generally related to beauty of an object; be it a painting or an art piece. These are mostly personal interpretations. What one believes in having aesthetics, the other may discard it saying it has no value. Generally, there are going to be wide variations in the perception of things. There had been scope for divergence of opinions on the painting of Leonardo da Vinci – Mona Lisa. People in this context, also speak about 'symmetry' or 'self similarity' present in the nature and thus feel that everything beautiful in the world is symmetrical; and that everything masculine is handsome!

3.6 Universal Human Values

Universal human values are those that are common to all human beings such as love, truth, and compassion. Though these may vary in different settings and contexts. Look at the following classification in diverse contexts.

Context	Examples of Values
Individual values	Self development, creativity, liberty, survival, freedom, etc.
Social values	Cooperation, tolerance, compassion, empathy, live and let live policy
Environmental values	Compassion to animals, no cruelty, vegetarianism, harmony with nature, no pollution.
Organisational values	Honesty, integrity, duty consciousness, sincerity, etc.
Constitutional values	Fundamental rights, duties, liberty, equality, justice, fraternity, etc.

Universal values of Human Rights are at the heart of UNESO's mandate that led to the adoption of Universal Declaration of Human Rights on 10-12-1948 in Paris with the motto that every individual has 'the right to live a life free from the haunting fear of poverty and insecurity'.[4]

The General Assembly of the United Nations proclaimed this Universal Declaration of Human Rights (UDHR) as a common standard for all peoples and all nations. The objective of the declaration is that every individual and every organ of society, keeping this Declaration constantly in mind, shall strive to promote respect for these rights and freedoms. Nations by their progressive measures shall attempt to secure their universal and effective recognition and observance, both among the peoples of Member States themselves and among the peoples of territories under their jurisdiction. The text in the articles runs as follows:

Article I

All human beings are born free and equal in dignity and rights. They are endowed with reason and conscience and should act towards one another in a spirit of brotherhood.

Article 2

Everyone is entitled to all the rights and freedoms set forth in the Declaration. There is no case for distinction of any kind, such as race, colour, sex, language, religion, political or other opinion, national or social origin, property, birth or other status. Furthermore, no distinction shall be made on the basis of the political, jurisdictional or international status of the country or territory to which a person belongs.

Article 3

Everyone has the right to life, liberty and security of person and property.

Article 4

No one shall be held in slavery or servitude. Slavery and the slave trade shall be prohibited in all their forms.

Article 5

No one shall be subjected to torture or to cruelty, or inhuman or degrading treatment or punishment.

Article 6

Everyone has the right to recognition everywhere as a person before the law.

Article 7

All are equal before the law and are entitled without any discrimination to equal protection of the law. All are entitled to equal protection against any discrimination. Violation of this principle is viewed as infringement of human rights.

Article 8

Everyone has the right to an effective remedy by the competent courts and national tribunals for acts violating the fundamental rights granted to him by the constitution or by law.

Article 9

No one shall be subjected to arbitrary arrest, detention or exile.

Article 10

Everyone is entitled in full equality to a fair and public hearing by an independent and impartial court or tribunal, in the determination of his rights and obligations and of any criminal charge against him.

Article 11

1. Everyone charged with a penal offence has the right to be presumed innocent until proved guilty. He has all the guarantees necessary for his defence in such trial.
2. No one shall be held guilty of any penal offence on account of any act or omission which did not constitute a penal offence, under national or international law, at the time when it was committed. Nor shall a heavier penalty be imposed than the one that was applicable at the time the offence was committed.

Article 12

No one shall be subjected to arbitrary interference with his privacy, family, home or correspondence. Nor one is permitted to attack upon his honour and reputation. Everyone has the right to the protection of the law against such interference or attacks.

Article 13

1. Everyone has the right to freedom of movement and residence within the borders of each State.
2. Everyone has the right to leave any country, including his own, and to return to his country.

Article 14

Everyone has the right to seek and to enjoy in other countries asylum from persecution. This right may not be invoked in the case of prosecutions genuinely arising from non-political crimes or from acts contrary to the purposes and principles of the United Nations.

Article 15

1. Everyone has the right to a nationality.
2. No one shall be arbitrarily deprived of his nationality nor denied the right to change his nationality.

Article 16

1. Men and women of full age, without any limitation due to race, nationality or religion, have the right to marry and to found a family. They are entitled to equal rights as to marriage, during marriage and at its dissolution.

2. Marriage shall be entered into only with the free and full consent of the intending spouses.
3. The family is the natural and fundamental group unit of society and is entitled to protection by society and the State.

Article 17

1. Everyone has the right to own property alone as well as in association with others.
2. No one shall be arbitrarily deprived of his property.

Article 18

Everyone has the right to freedom of thought, conscience and religion. This right also includes freedom to change his religion or belief, and freedom, either alone or in community with others and in public or private, to manifest his religion or belief in teaching, practice, worship observance.

Article 19

Everyone has the right to freedom of opinion and expression. This right includes freedom to hold opinions without interference and to seek, receive and impart information and ideas through any media regardless of frontiers.

Article 20

1. Everyone has the right to freedom of peaceful assembly and association.
2. No one may be compelled to belong to an association.

Article 21

1. Everyone has the right to take part in the government of his country, directly or through freely chosen representatives.
2. Everyone has the right to equal access to public services in his country.
3. The will of the people shall be the basis of the authority of government. This shall be expressed in periodic and genuine elections held by secret vote or by equivalent free voting procedures.

Article 22

Everyone, as a member of society, has the right to social security and is entitled to realization, through national effort and international cooperation and in accordance with the organization and resources of each State, of the economic, social and cultural rights indispensable for his dignity and the free development of his personality.

Article 23

1. Everyone has the right to work, to free choice of employment, to just and favourable conditions of work and to protection against unemployment.
2. Everyone, without any discrimination, has the right to equal pay for equal work.

3. Everyone has the right to just and favourable remuneration ensuring for himself and his family to lead an existence worthy of human dignity.
4. Everyone has the right to form and to join trade unions for the protection of his interests.

Article 24

Everyone has the right to rest and leisure, including reasonable limitation of working hours and periodic holidays with pay.

Article 25

1. Everyone has the right to a standard of living adequate for the health and well-being of himself and of his family, including food, clothing, housing and medical care and necessary social services, and the right to security in the event of unemployment, sickness, disability, widowhood, old age or other lack of livelihood in circumstances beyond his control.
2. Motherhood and childhood are entitled to special care and assistance. All children, whether born in or out of wedlock, shall enjoy the same social protection.

Article 26

1. Everyone has the right to education. Education shall be free, at least in the elementary and fundamental stages. Elementary education shall be compulsory. Technical and professional education shall be made generally available and higher education shall be equally accessible to all on the basis of merit.
2. Education shall be directed to the full development of the human personality and to the strengthening of respect for human rights and fundamental freedoms. It shall promote understanding, tolerance and friendship among all nations, racial or religious groups, and shall further the activities of the United Nations for the maintenance of peace.
3. Parents have a prior right to choose the kind of education that shall be given to their children.

Article 27

1. Everyone has the right freely to participate in the cultural life of the community, to enjoy the arts and to share scientific advancement and its benefits.
2. Everyone has the right to the protection of the moral and material interests resulting from any scientific, literary or artistic production of which he is the author.

Article 28

Everyone is entitled to a social and international order in which the rights and freedoms set forth in this Declaration can be fully realized.

Article 29

1. Everyone has duties to the community in which alone the free and full development of his personality is possible.
2. In the exercise of his rights and freedoms, everyone shall be subject only to such limitations as are determined by law solely for the purpose of securing due recognition and respect for the rights and freedoms of others and of meeting the just requirements of morality, public order and the general welfare in a democratic society.
3. These rights and freedoms may in no case be exercised contrary to the purposes and principles of the United Nations.

Article 30

Nothing in this Declaration may be interpreted as implying for any State, group or person any right to engage in any activity or to perform any act aimed at the destruction of any of the rights and freedoms set forth herein.

It is evident from the above, how United Nations has made an attempt to make rights of human beings universal. As a matter of fact, it is Thomas Paine who talked eloquently about the 'Rights of Man' (published in two parts in March 1791 and February, 1792).[5] Paine, being a strong supporter of French Revolution (which began in 1789) argued for the rights of the people under the French monarchy. He believed that human rights originate in nature. He has stated that it is a perversion of terms to say that a charter gives rights. It operates by a contrary effect and takes the rights away. Rights shall be inherent to all the inhabitants. One should not keep faith in the process that charters would ensure rights. It never happens. In effect, they are the instruments of injustice. Therefore, the individuals, by themselves, enter into a contract with each other to produce a government; that respects the rights of the individuals. It is no exaggeration to state that such works had served as the foundation for the drafting of the United Nations Declaration. Thus, it may be stated that universal human values are in built in nature, and they apply to all human beings alike.

3.7 Economic Values

These values pertain to the relations among diverse organs of the economy. A philosophy as to how economy shall operate. It is all about the mix of the 'factors of production', viz., land, labour, capital and organisation. This led to a great debate on the economic systems. The three ideologies that were discussed at length over a period of time include:

A. Capitalism
B. Communism/Socialism
C. Mixed Economy

Capitalism is such a kind of economic system that is based on the private initiative and freedom. The belief is that the welfare of the people in the economy will be best served only when the means of production are in the hands of private persons. The following are the chief features of this model.

(i) Absence of central planning
(ii) Free entry and free exit
(iii) Freedom of operation
(iv) Private ownership of resources
(v) Profit maximization
(vi) Capital accumulation
(vii) Market economy/free market

Akin to the philosophy of capitalism, many practices are considered consistent with the ethical setting or moral fabric. For example, markets decide everything like the production, distribution, prices, employment and wages. Markets are also made to operate on such a competitive note, finally those that withstand pressures would survive. Thus 'survival of the fittest', (the supposed to be the jungle law) would remain in force. It is considered ethical.

The thinking which started with the writings of Adam Smith on the Wealth of Nations, got reinforced with the contributions of David Ricardo (Theory of Value), J K Galbraith (Liberalism) and George Soros (laissez-faire). Adam Smith had held the view that value is a product of labour, taking a radical departure from the then dominant economic philosophy of 'mercantilism', which held sway in Europe for three centuries.[6] It is Smith who proposed during that time that individuals acting in their own self-interest would naturally seek out economic activities that provided the greatest financial rewards. He believed that this self-interest would, in turn, maximize the economic well-being of the society as a whole.

Whereas Ricardo (1772-1823) divided value into goods (value in use) and commodities (value in exchange). He hypothesized that only labour could create value and thus defined capital as a man made aid to production.[7] His great contribution is the recognition of three points of production, viz., land owners, capitalists and labourers is the key to economic activity. Ricardo stated that the value of a commodity or the quantity of any other commodity for which it will exchange depends on the relative quantity of labour which is necessary for its production, and not as the greater or lesser compensation which is paid for that labour. In that Ricardo sought to differentiate the quantity of labour necessary to produce a commodity from the wages paid to the labourers for its production.

J K Galbraith (1908-2006), a leading proponent of the 20th century American liberalism, pointed out that the American economy was managed by a triumvirate of big business, big labour and an activist government. Galbraith defined the actions of the industry lobby groups and unions as countervailing power. In his later writings (the New Industrial State), Galbraith expanded his analysis of the role of power in economic life, arguing that very few industries in the United States fit the model of perfect competition.[8]

George Soros, a well known supporter of progressive and liberal political thought, is credited for his role in the peaceful transition from communism to capitalism in Eastern Europe. He advocated the market fundamentalism by arguing in favour of removal of all kinds of regulations on the economic operation. He pleaded for the free movement of capital, entrepreneurship, and supported the idea of 'global financial markets' and equilibrium to take place only through the optimum allocation of resources.

As opposed to capitalism, communism is a philosophy that advocates common ownership of all the means of production. It is the 'State' that takes care of everything. State is the owner, producer, distributor and authority on the allocation of resources. The chief features of communism can be noted as below:

- ✓ State/social ownership of resources (means of production).
- ✓ Central planning through a State agency.
- ✓ Non-permission to hold private property.
- ✓ Distribution of income according to needs, not on the ability to contribute.
- ✓ State enterprising/entrepreneurship.
- ✓ No concept of profit or surplus value.

The basic thinking for this economic philosophy was contributed by Karl Max, Friedrich Engels, Vladimir Lenin, Stalin and later rulers of USSR, till it got disintegrated in 1991. Marxism is interpreted as a method of socio-economic philosophy originating from the mid-to-late 19th century works of German philosophers Karl Marx and Friedrich Engels. They analyzed class relations and societal conflict using a materialist interpretation of historical development and a dialectical view of social transformation.

Marxist methodology originally used economic and socio-political inquiry to analyze and critique the development of capitalism and the role of class struggle in systemic economic change. According to Marxist analysis, class conflict within capitalism arises due to intensifying contradictions between highly productive mechanized and socialized production performed by the proletariat, and private ownership and appropriation of the surplus product in the form of surplus value (profit) by a small minority of private owners called the bourgeoisie.[9] As the contradiction becomes apparent to the proletariat, social unrest between the two antagonistic classes intensifies, culminating in a social revolution. The eventual long-term outcome of this revolution would be the establishment of socialism – a socioeconomic system based on social ownership of the means of production, distribution based on one's contribution, and production organized directly for use. As the productive forces and technology continued to advance, Marx hypothesized that socialism would eventually give way to a communist stage of social development, which would be a classless, stateless, humane society erected on common ownership and the principle of "From each according to his ability, to each according to his needs".

Not leaning to either side of the philosophy, countries like India and some others in the Asian continent started trying a blend of the two, both capitalism and communism. India termed this philosophy in its constitution as the 'Sovereign, Socialist, Secular, Democratic Republic' also came to be known later as the '**Socialistic Pattern of Society**'. A peaceful coexistence of capital and labour and an optimum mix of private and public initiative were imagined. Thus we have in India, private property, private initiative as well as state property, state initiative. We have a large number of public enterprises operating in essential and non-essential (commercial) areas of activity. Government is willing to work with the private business; thus a new development model in the name of '**public-private-partnership**' is being experimented. To what extent this new experimental model of development meets with the success will be known only in the future. Thus the middle path is about taking into consideration the merits of both the systems and thus strike an 'optimum balance'.

Perhaps, the roots for this kind of thinking were in the political philosophy attempted to be promoted during that time (1950s) in the name of Non-Aligned Movement (NAM). Leaders of some countries who wanted to keep their economies away from the influence of both the 'isms', struck this policy.

Early in the nineteen sixties, India's first Prime Minister, Jawaharlal Nehru, Indonesia's first president Sukarno, Egypt's second President Camal Abdel Nasser, Ghana's first President Kwame Nkrumah and Yugoslavia's President, Josup Broz Tito (all five captains of their respective countries) thought that a middle course of economic thinking would be proper for the newly developing nations, thus, formed NAM at Belgrade in 1961.[10] It has a membership of 120 countries now (2012). The members of NAM are the believers in the struggle against imperialism, colonialism, racism and dominance of great powers, i.e., developed nations. The impact of these forces is to be felt in the relations between the haves and the have-nots; since New International Economic order is still elusive (in spite of the fact that the North-South Dialogue is continuing).

3.8 Socio-Cultural Values

In addition to economic values, socio-cultural values also decide the moral fabric of an individual. As sociologists believe, man is a 'social animal'. His behaviour is conditioned by the values and norms prescribed by the people/members within the group. They dare not challenge the standards fixed by the group. This is very much visible in the case of tribal societies. Their beliefs, customs, attitudes, practices are determined by the elders in the tribe. One has to simply follow them. In that context, social values are an important part of the culture of a society. In that the values account for the stability of the social order. They provide general guidelines for conduct. In doing so, they facilitate social control. Values in the context of societies perform certain functions; as of the following:

- ✓ Provide goals or ends for the members to aim for.
- ✓ Provide for stabilities and uniformities in group interaction.
- ✓ Hold the society together, because values are shared in common.
- ✓ Bring legitimacy to the rules that govern specific activities.
- ✓ Help to bring about some kind of adjustment between different sets of rules.

Culture has a profound influence on the value system of an individual. Culture of an individual or family decides the culture of the society and finally of the nation. The continuum can be depicted as below:

Continuum–3: Cultural Integration from Individual to Nation

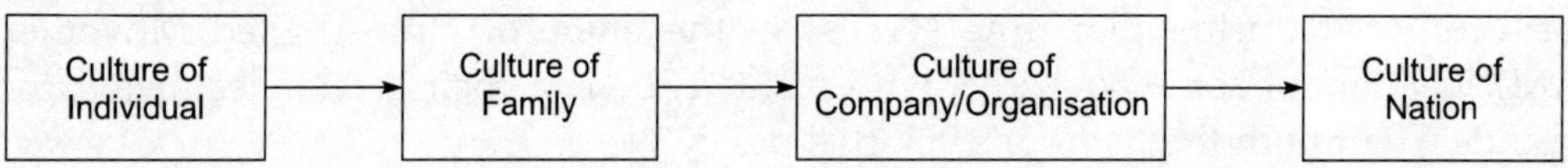

As a matter of fact, ethics is culture specific. It becomes much more relevant to the business enterprises. For, what is acceptable in one country, may not be approved in another country. Charging interest on money borrowed is common in non-Islamic countries. Whereas, collecting interest is treated as a sin in Islamic countries. Thus, the principles of Islamic banking are completely different from those accepted by others. Similarly, green is sacred to people in Pakistan, whereas saffron is preferred by Hindus in India. Such cultural differences have significant influence on business decisions. The subordinate position of women in the workforce and in business organisations is another culture issue, where normative standards of equality prevalent in most industrialized countries are not accepted in many Arab countries.[11] Similar are the cultural standards in many countries. While race is a factor of discrimination in the west, caste is the equivalent in segregating people of India. Triple 'Talaq' – a practice of divorce among Muslim community – has emerged a great social issue; whereupon the Government of India had to file an affidavit in the Supreme Court stating that the practice is violative of women's equality, and dignity. It also said that the practice is in gross violation of Quranic injunctions and values of justice and equality enshrined in the Indian Constitution. It also stated that the gender equality is non-negotiable. Similar is the practice of 'living together', without an approved/legal wedlock of male and female. Though accepted by the law, but denounced by the Hindu society.

In the discussions on culture, the distinction between Western and Indian culture is usually drawn. Let us therefore look into the foundations of both the cultures and also examine whether there is any real dichotomy.

3.8.1 Foundations of Western Culture

Culture, being interpreted in a broader context, may be understood as comprising social norms, ethical values, traditional customs, beliefs, artifacts, life styles and including technologies. It may be referred to include a host of artistic, philosophic, literacy, and legal themes to reflect upon the style of living.

Historical records of Western culture in Europe begin with Ancient Greece and Ancient Rome. Western culture continued to develop with Christianization during the Middle Ages, the reform and modernization triggered by Renaissance.[12] This was followed by globalization and consequent Industrial Revolution and reforms of the organisation of methods of production. The United States which is dominating the world is only a late entry into the Western model during 17th century, with the streaking in of European Colonists, mostly Britishers. As a whole, the Western culture is said to be symbolic of the following:

- Rationalism or rational thinking
- Individual initiative
- Humanism and human rights
- Free thought and expression
- Political pluralism
- Focus on science and technology
- Consumerism
- Market orientation and global connection
- Exploitation of the nature/conquering of the nature

After these countries came into prominence after industrial revolution, focus of the world shifted from the hither to civilizations/cultures to the West. After all, the ancient civilizations, including, Mesopotamian, Indus and Egyptian had occurred outside the areas (countries); which are now considered the epicenter of Western culture. Perhaps, the economic supremacy of those nations (in a neo-rich atmosphere) is stealing the sheen of the old cultures.

3.8.2 Foundations of Indian Culture

India has a rich cultural heritage descending from the times of Indus Valley Civilization, next only to Babylonian civilization. The culture of India combines both tradition and modernity. It is diverse in nature; thus '**unity in diversity**' is said to be most aptly suited to Indian culture. Indian culture is traditional in the sense that, it was handed down from generation to generation. There was a mix of wide variety of races and their cultures. As many philosophers have commented 'culture degenerates and becomes static, feeble, stagnant, if it does not have the contact with other cultures.[13] In that sense, Indian culture has grown rich over a period of centuries influencing and being influenced by the cultures of Dravidians, Aryans, Greeks, Persians, Arabs, Europeans and many others. Thus, it has emerged as a 'unique mix of diverse cultures', representing the richness of the tradition and modernity.

It is believed that at least six races in nine variations came from outside the country to make India.[14] The first race to move is the negroid race from Africa, made little contribution to Indian culture or language, but the later arrivals, the Austrics, whose descendants are to be found among the lower groups scattered in many parts of the country had a fairly advanced culture. They were agriculturists and fishermen. They cultivated rice and vegetables, tamed animals and knew the art of spinning and weaving. The Hindu idea of the incarnation of God in the form of tortoise and fish embodied in the Puranic mythology probably came from the Austrics. Far more decisive and pronounced was the influence of the Dravidians on Indian culture. The Dravidians had a highly developed culture of their own before they came into contact with the Aryans.

The Indus-Valley Civilization is a Dravidian Achievement

They had a highly developed language from which modern Dravidian languages grew. As distinguished from the fair complexioned Aryan invaders who were nomads and rural people, the Dravidians were town-dwellers, living in well laid-out cities; they were skilled craftsmen and agriculturists who had domesticated many animals. According to some historians, the Aryan social organization into castes and guilds owes its inspiration to the Dravidians. Dr. Suniti Kumar Chatterjee has pointed out how great was the cultural influence of the Dravidians on the Aryan mind. He observed that the Dravidian mind was profoundly moved by faith and a mystical sense, and the ideals of Yoga and personal mystical contact with the power behind the life. It was among the Dravidians that the great gods of post-Vedic Hinduism with both their cosmic and personal significance and appeal, like Siva and Uma, Vishnu and Sri, had their origin. The ideas of a great mother goddess, who was the source of all life, who was both nature and the conscious force behind nature, appear to have been brought in their germs to India from the original East Mediterranean homeland of the primitive Dravidians and then elaborated in the country. The *puja* as a mode of worship is said to be a Dravidian contribution.

The Aryans

The Aryans had a highly developed language, Sanskrit, in which poetry and drama, philosophy and religion, of the highest order have been expressed. It also stood for its richness in various forms of literature and music. As they settled down and established cultural contacts with the already settled people, they could produce religion and philosophy of the high order, which has the profound influence on the human behaviour. They speculated on the nature of Godhead, and the origin of the universe. They explained the relations between man, nature and god and the best way of realizing spiritual perfection. They developed a complex social organization based on caste and the four stages of life, both governed by well-defined moral codes, disciplines and duties. They had infinite intellectual curiosity. They welcomed all earnest seekers after the truth. Buddhism and Jainism were powerful reformist movements within Hinduism, which met with no intolerant opposition or persecution from the orthodox. Every other invadcr from the North made some contribution to indigenous culture and was absorbed in society, leaving no traces of foreign origin behind.

The most striking aspect of the Indian culture is that it has always been based on religious and moral values. Religion had a significant influence on the cultural foundations of Indians. In spite of the fact that there were many invasions by foreign rulers (particularly by Muslims), they could not obliterate the cultural tradition and the influence of religion on culture. India is a land of many religions. It is recognized as the birthplace for Hinduism, Jainism, Buddhism and Sikhism. While about 80 per cent of the people being the followers of Hinduism, there is the profound influence of Vedic culture.

Vedic Culture

The four vedas, their offshoots called Upanishads, epics like Ramanayana and Mahabharata guide the moral fabric of a vast majority of the Indians. The following are said to be the basic tenets of Vedic/Hindu culture:

- Hindu culture is not something fixed, static, unchanging, but is constantly developing, adapting itself to changing conditions, assimilating new ideas, responding to fresh challenges.
- An important feature of Hindu culture is its catholicity, its tolerance of doctrinal differences, its liberal approach to the problems of knowledge and truth. It regards all manifestations of the ultimate reality known by numerous names as equally entitled to worship. Brahmanism, Buddhism and Jainism have an equally honoured place in Hindu culture.
- Hindu culture is essentially spiritual and ethical. Man, according to it, is a spiritual being with a soul and a passionate awareness of the spiritual nature of the universe. Modern science and psychology do not understand that man has not only repressed desires and impulses which constitute his drives for action

but has also a soul, mind and consciousness. Through knowledge and discipline, he controls his desires and subordinates them to his will. Hindu culture attaches the highest importance to various kinds of discipline—physical, mental, moral and spiritual—through which man understands his own nature, the nature of the universe and the nature of Godhead. The nature of the ultimate reality, this limitless eternal being, can be apprehended not by a rational process or analysis but by meditation, contemplation and intuition.

- It is a profound belief that this universe is organized on the basis of justice. No evil remains unpunished, no good remains unrewarded. Death is no escape from punishment for a wrong done. The doctrine of Karma and transmigration of souls is not a doctrine of fatalism, but a doctrine of the ethical design of the universe.
- Hindu culture does not regard the acquisition of wealth or the enjoyment of senses as the principal aim of life. The real aims are righteousness and spiritual freedom. It does not condemn acquisition of wealth and pleasures of the senses, but it demands that, lest they should degenerate into greed and sensuality, they should be kept in restraint by moral and spiritual principles.
- The greatest aim of life is the achievement of spiritual perfection—a state in which man's ego is dissolved and he identifies himself with all beings of the universe regardless of sex, race, religion or nationality, a state in which he is neither elated by success nor depressed by failures.
- Man should always be guided in his actions by "Dharma" or moral principles and by duty. Hindu culture has no place for individual rights in its scheme of life but only for duties—duties towards parents, teachers, and others. Hinduism lays great stress on sacrifices which consist not in the performance of certain rites but in identifying our interests with the well-being of all others.
- Hinduism envisages organization of social life in four castes and four stages or ashrams. Originally, the caste system was based on a person's temperament, his acquisitions and his vocation. It assumed a hereditary character much later. Everyone is required to perform the duties of his office and leaving it to God to reward him for his actions. The duties of man in each period of life are laid down in the sacred books and commentaries. The first period is that of building up physical, mental and spiritual strength and discipline, the second that of a householder always animated by a sense of duty and sustaining people in other stages, the third that of renunciation, meditation, contemplation and the last that of giving mankind the benefit of intellectual and spiritual maturity.

Yet the impact of other cultures on the culture of Indians is no less insignificant. For instance, Islam and Islamic rulers like Akbar made an attempt to combine the divinity of both. Thus, Bhakti movement germinated on the Indian soil; culminating into the worship of saints like 'Shirdi Saibaba' and following the sayings of Kabir. In the process, the British brought a new philosophy of life based on freedom, liberalism, science and technology. Indians could as well invite and invoke the good, wherever it was available. But still, the people needed to be reformed against many a social evil such as child marriage, sati, adultery, sacrifices, etc. People like Dayanand Saraswathi, Raja Ram Mohan Roy led a crusade against these superstitious practices and achieved great success. Still it is becoming difficult to contain practices like caste system, dowry, discrimination and many other henious religious and non-religious practices.

Yet India has a great tradition in keeping faith in the broader issues like:

(a) Secularism
(b) Peace and non-violence
(c) Joint family system
(d) Art and architecture

India is rich in both the forms of performing and visual arts. Dance, drama, theatre, music, films are all popular. India is also a name in sculpture, painting and pottery. Thus a great responsibility is thrust on the present generation to maintain this great diversity and forge ahead to keep up the pride and prestige of the past and the present.

3.8.3 Dichotomy between Indian and Western Cultures

People often get curious to compare and contrast the Western culture against the Indian culture. People go to the extent of taking pride in their own cultures and discount others. After all, civilizations evolve over a period of time and they are not static. Time and space are the two major factors that influence the culture of any society. Without taking sides, one has to respect every way of life as acceptable and sacred and nothing to denounce or impaire. The apparent divergencies are summed up as follows:

Parameter	Indian Culture	Western Culture
Meaning	The culture which is followed in India, is Indian culture.	The culture which is followed in most western countries like USA, Spain, Canada, Europe, etc. is known as Western culture.
Religion	Hinduism, Islam, Christianity, Sikhism, Buddhism, Jainism.	Christianity, Judaism.
Family	Joint family	Nuclear family
Music	Folk, Classical, Sufi, Bollywood music is liked in Indian culture.	Hip-hop, Jazz, Blues, Rap, Heavy metal, Rock music is appreciated in western culture.

Contd.

Equality	Woman are considered inferior than man, however the thinking is changing with the impact of westernization.	Both man and woman are considered equal.
Languages	Hindi is the main spoken language, but however, there are other languages which are spoken in different areas like Telegu, Tamil, Marathi, Punjabi, Bengali, Bihari, Urdu, etc.	English is widely spoken in western countries, followed by French and Spanish.
Relation with family	Individuals are closely attached to their family, they respect and care about family more than themselves.	Individuals are not much attached to their family, they leave their parent's home by the age of 18.
Society	In India, people kill their own needs and desires because they assume in advance, what the society will think?	They are open minded and give priority to making themselves happy.
Marriages	Arranged marriages are preferred.	Love marriages are common.
Clothing	Traditional clothing depends on region and religion.	A person can wear whatever he/she likes.

Source: www.keydifferences.com

As a matter of fact Swami Vivekananda felt that there is no dichotomy between the two cultures and said that they are complimentary. He stated that the Western people have to learn much from Indian spirituality for their own well-being. In spite of her poverty – and backwardness, India had a great contribution to make to the world culture. Similarly, he advocated that India has to emulate west in terms of their great contributions in the fields of science, technology and humanism. He attempted to teach Indians to adopt Western humanism, especially the ideas of individual freedom, social equality and justice and respect for women.[15]

4. SWAMI VIVEKANANDA ON ETHICS

Swami Vivekananda (1863-1902) an Indian Hindu monk, and a chief disciple of the Indian mystic Ramakrishna Paramahamsa expressed valid and inspiring thoughts on ethics. They would perhaps guide the ethical thinking and life of the people, not only in India, but also in the West. Few important statements from his preachings are quoted here:

- Ethics always say 'Not I, but thou'. Its motto is 'not self, but non-self and put yourself last'.
- The laws of ethics say that one has to give up infinite pleasure through senses.

- All codes of ethics are based on renunciation.
- Utilitarian standards cannot explain the ethical relations of human beings.
- Utilitarian theories can only work under present social conditions. Beyond that they have no value. But an ethical code derived from religion and spirituality has the whole of infinite man for its scope
- Ethics itself is not the end, but the means to an end.
- That which is selfish is immoral, and that which is unselfish is moral.
- Virtue is that which tends to our improvement, and vice to our degeneration. Man is made up of three qualities – brutal, human and godly. That which tends to increase the divinity in you is virtue and that which tends to increase brutality in you is vice. You must kill the brutal nature and become human, i.e., loving and charitable.

References

1. Ferrell, O.C. et al., *'Business Ethics – A Case Perspective'*, Cengage Learning, New Delhi, 2007.
2. Lionel Robbins, 'An Essay on the Nature and Significance of Economic Science', 1932 (www.studylecturenotes.com)
3. Satish Modh, *'Ethical Management'*, MacMillan, Delhi, 2010.
4. 3A. Immanuel Kant, *'Fundamentals of the Metaphysics of Morals and What is Enlightenment'*, Trans, James Elligton, 1963.
5. Universal Declaration of Human Rights, United Nations (http://www.un.org/en/universal-declaration-human-rights)
6. Thomas Paine, *'Rights of Man'*, originally published in 1791 & 1972. Many publishers later printed copies of the same. Also available in the e-books store, like www.ebboks@adelaide.
7. Adam Smith, Capitalism's Founding Father, (http://www.vision.org/visionmedia/biography-adam-smith/868.aspx).
8. David Ricardo, History of economic thought, (https://en.wikipedia.org/wiki/History_of_economic_thought)
9. Galbraith, J.K., (https://en.wikipedia.org/wiki/John_Kenneth_Galbraith)
10. Marxism (https://en.wikipedia.org/wiki/Marxism)
11. www.nam.gov.za.
12. Hartman, Lawra P., *"Perspectives in Business Ethics'*, Tata McGraw Hill, New Delhi, 2003.
13. Western Culture (https://en.wikipedia.org/wiki/Western_culture)

14. Geert Hofstede, 'Cultural Dimension India', ITIM International, 2009. (http://geert-hofstede.com/india.html)
15. Vikash Mehra, 'Indian Culture', 2014 (http://www.importantindia.com/10518/indian-culture/)
16. Teachings and Philosophy of Swami Vivekananda (https://en.wikipedia.org/wiki/Teachings_and_philosophy_of_Swami_Vivekananda)

3

CHAPTER

Business Ethics

1. INTRODUCTION

We have observed in the previous two chapters that ethics is a 'way of life'. It is about a value system, and a commitment to morality. Societies thrive only on the foundation of moral principles or ethical codes. Civilization would not have survived thus for, if there had been no order or ethics involved. Even the animal kingdom appears to have survived on certain codes, except for a few incidents or behaviour of wild animals. Human interface with animals is also destined to be controlled to cover animal rights, animal welfare, law, cognition and conservation. There are laws in almost all countries preventing cruelty to animals. And even there has been an elaborate code in using animals for clinical research and it has become mandatory for the organizations to draw out a specific code of ethics for this purpose.

Whereas a human society is a group of people involved in persistent interpersonal relationships, sharing the same geographical or social territory; also subject to the same political authority and dominant cultural expectations. There are diverse viewpoints as to what constitutes the society. One notion is that there are five key elements that speak of a society, viz., (1) centralised government (2) organised religion (3) job specialization and social classes (4) arts, architecture and infrastructure and (5) writing.[1] According to another perspective, there are a number of elements of a society like similarity, difference, likeness, interdependence, cooperation, organization, social relationship, we-feeling, social grouping, social control and finally comprehensive culture that make up the society.[2] Each society is distinct from the other. Every society is unique because it has its own way of life and thus includes attitudes, judgements, morals, values, beliefs, ideas, ideologies and institutions. In a way, society decides the kind of living, thinking, behaving and acting as a member. Society has its own ways and means of controlling the behavior of its members. Co-operation exists in society. But side by side competition, conflicts, tensions, revolts and suppression are also there. They appear and re-appear off and on. The behaviour or the activities of people are to be controlled. Society has various formal and informal means of social control. It means society has customs, traditions, conventions and folkways, mores, norms and so on. All these are the informal means of social control. Society has also law, legislation, constitution, police, court, army and so on. All these are the formal means of social control to regulate the behaviour of the members of the society.

The Unique Collective Awareness of UCADIA a charitable foundation established by people of Greet Britain, USA and Australia, considers society as a living organism.[3] Just as a city may be defined by its components, a society may also be defined by its organic components. Thus the twelve laws of society are said to include the following:

- State creed (Goal law)
- Belief system (logos law)
- Constitution (creation law)
- Body politic (codependence law)
- Industry (specialization law)
- Infrastructure (geometry)
- Knowledge (awareness of position in dimension)
- Trade (immediate near neighbours)
- Sovereignty and defence (exclusiveness of position)
- Communication (conservation of effort)
- Gross production (change of position)

These laws of creation are said to be associated with the existence of a society as with the matter present in the society. This is also said to provide one with a basic framework for understanding the nature and behaviour of a society.

A pictorial representation in terms of diverse structures of the society may be shown as below (Fig. 3.1):

Viewed thus, a society is a combination of individuals and institutions. The interface among them decides the ethical foundations of the society. In the same manner, a company is constituted by various elements having continuous communication among them, known as stakeholders. In that context, beginning with the shareholders to that of people in the society are interested in the affairs of the corporate world. People consider them the contributors, beneficiaries and also victims as well. Therefore, the constituents of the corporate world may consist of promoters, shareholders, prospective investors, suppliers, customers, employees, competitors, government, and the general public. The same can be viewed in the following Figure 3.2.

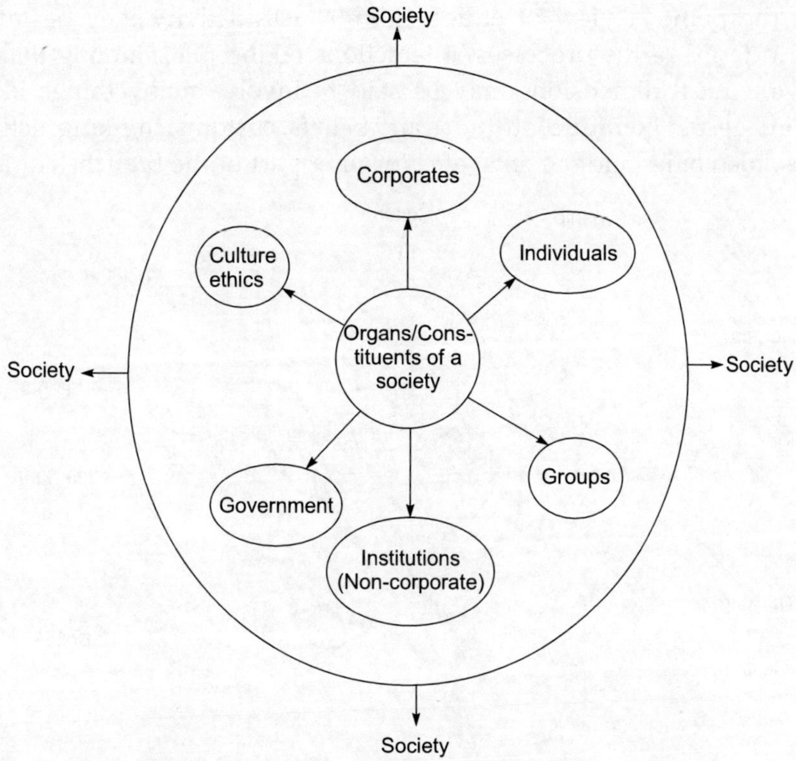

Figure 3.1: Structural Composition of the Society

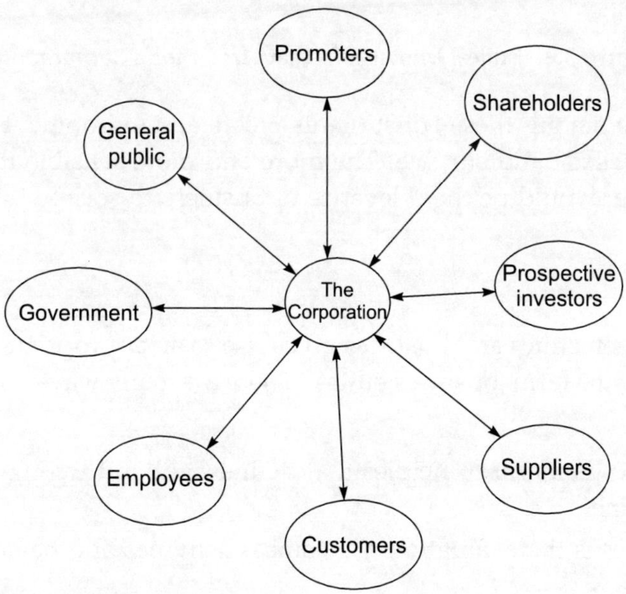

Figure 3.2: Stakeholders of a Corporation

But from the point of view of ethics, the business activity may be interpreted/understood in terms of the processes/interactions taking place among them. In such a perspective, ethical dimensions may be said to involve many things like culture, religion, language and literature, attitudes and beliefs, customs, thinking, actions, social relationships, ideologies, judgements, etc., forming part of the branches of a tree.

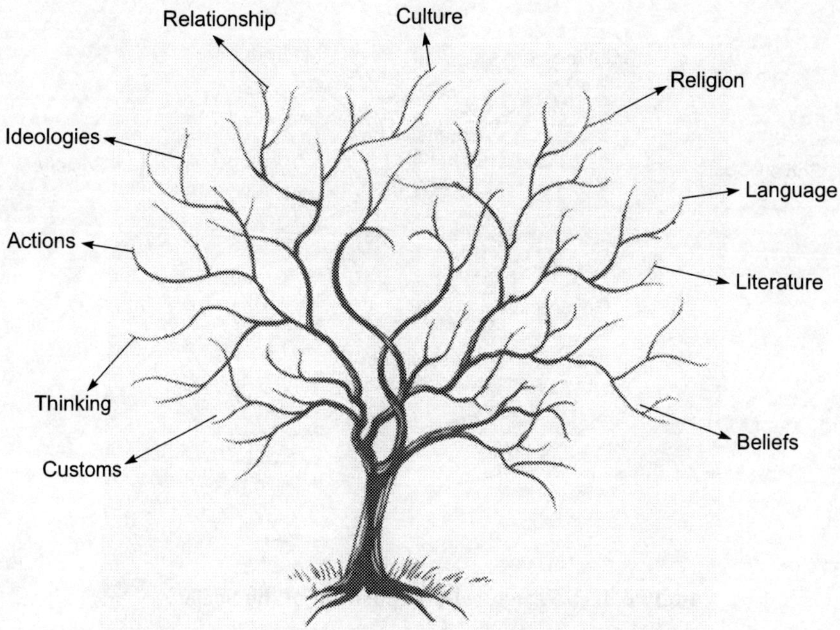

Figure 3.3: Ethical Dimensions that Matter for a Corporation.

The interactions among these constituents create an environment for corporations to come into being, exist and survive. The more and more sensible these interactions, the better and better would be the relevance of business to society.

2. MEANING

The interface between ethics and business gives rise to an appropriate interpretation of the true meaning of the term 'business ethics'. There are many ways for comprehending the phenomenon.

- Business ethics is moral principles that define right and wrong behaviour in the world of business.
- Business ethics is the evaluation of business activities and behaviour as right or wrong.

- A systematic study of moral matters pertaining to business, industry or related activities, institutions, or practices and beliefs.
- Business ethics is the systematic handling of values in business and industry.
- It is the application of general ethical rules to business behaviour.
- They are also called the rules of business conduct, by which the propriety of business activities may be judged.
- It is a specialized study of moral rights and wrongs. It is concerned with the moral standards as applied to business institutions, organizations and behaviour.

It is evident from the above interpretations that business ethics is the application of ethical principles to the business situations. As a matter of fact, business organizations are the primary economic institutions through which people in modern societies carry on the tasks of production and distribution of goods and services. They provide the fundamental structures within which the members of society combine their scarce resources – land, labour, capital and technology – into usable goods, and they provide the channels through which these goods are distributed in the form of consumer products. Mining, manufacturing, retailing, banking, marketing, transporting, insuring, constructing and advertising are all different facets of the productive and distributive processes of our modern business institutions. But it is the society which finally decides what is right and what is wrong. Businesses have to sail along with the changing moral contexts of the society. It is this 'art' that keeps certain businesses ahead of the others.

3. SIGNIFICANCE OF BUSINESS ETHICS

There is a general question that, do business need to be ethical either by consent or by force. Much has already been discussed in chapters 1 and 2 emphasizing that the foundations of ethics are universal in their application. The very survival of the mankind depends on the practice of ethics at every level. Same shall be applicable to the business world, since it being one of the constituents of the society. In a way, business and industry are the most influential institutions that decide the economy of a country. For, they are involved in the production and distribution of goods and services needed by the people. The resources of the country are to be exploited properly for achieving a better standard of living. Thus businesses become the crucial agents in deciding what resources to be used, to what extent to be used and how to be used. As a matter of fact, many of the resources are limited in their availability; once exhausted, cannot be replenished. Therefore, utmost care is required to be exercised while taking these decisions. In spite of the policy framing and decision making by the government, the optimum use of these resources rests with the business. Of the four factors of production (land, labour, capital and organization), it is the organizational ability of the business that promotes growth and development of the nation.

It is a fact that businesses wield tremendous influence in the society in terms of their sheer size. Forbes (an international magazine) compiled the list of Global 2000 world's largest, most powerful public companies, as measured by revenues, profits, assets and market value. The composite score of these four paramatres was used to list the top 25 largest companies of the world for the year 2015.[4] These 2000 Global companies (hailing from 60 countries) accounted for the combined revenues of $39 trillion, profits of 3 trillion with assets worth $162 trillion and market value of 48 trillion. Interestingly, the total market value of these global 2000 companies, grew by 9 per cent over the previous year. Whereas the position of the top 100 largest companies (of the 2000), reveals the fact that they are so mighty in terms of every conceivable parameter like the sales, profits, assets or market value. In terms of turnover (sales), all the 100 companies could muster $10,925.80 billion and in terms of market value, they account for $14,347.20 billion (see Appendix-1). In respect of predominance by ownership, United States has 37 companies out of 100 companies with a market value of $ $7,753.40 billion. Next in the order, the most envious aspect for India is that the neighbouring country, China has 15 companies figuring in the list; while no Indian company could make up to the list.

In a study conducted by *Business Insider,* 25 major American Corporations whose revenues surpass the 2010 GDP of the entire countries, often with a few billion dollars to spare. For instance, if Wal-Mart were a country, its revenue would make it on par with the GDP of the 25th largest economy in the world, by surpassing 157 smaller countries.[5] Similarly, a comparison of the revenue and GDPs of the countries, reveals that the revenues of certain companies are far greater than the GDPs of many nations.[6] For example, the revenue of Wal-Mart measures on par with the GDP of Norway. That of Exxon Mobil and Chevron exceeds the GDP of Romania. Even after the financial crisis, Bank of America, J P Morgan Chase, Citigroup and Wells Fargo remain in the top 20 of the world's largest corporations, each with revenues higher than Iraq's GDP. Costco's revenue was greater than the total GDP of Luxembourg. As per the latest survey (2014) of 'Make Wealth History' organization, 37 of the world's 100 largest economies are corporations. Of total companies, 8 of them are in the list of first 50.[7] Similarly, in a more recent study by Nicholas Freudenberg, it was revealed that there were 63 corporations in the list of top 100 largest governments and corporations by Revenue as per the data for 2014. The list is provided in Appendix-III, at the end of this chapter.

A cursory look at the Indian scenario also explains us, the dominance of Indian companies in terms of any of the significant parameters. The list of top 25 companies of India is provided on the basis of net profits made by them during 2015 in Appendix-III. As per the information available, Reliance could make a profit of Rs. 22,719 crore, followed by TCS (with Rs. 19,256 crore) and ONGC (Rs. 17,732 crore). Even the 25th company's (HUL) profit is around Rs. 4315 crore. This clearly shows the power of the corporate world.

Leaving aside the statistics part of the phenomenon, there are two kinds of argument, in favour of and against the proposition as to why companies need to be ethical.

3.1 Arguments in Favour of Ethics in Business

The need to bring in ethics into business is supported by the following aspects:

(i) Ethics should govern all voluntary human actions and because business is a voluntary human activity. Ethics thus should govern the business. There is nothing about business that would prevent us from applying the same standards of ethics to business activities that should be applied to all voluntary human activities.

(ii) Business is a cooperative activity, whose very existence requires ethical behaviour. This applies to all the managers, workers working in the organization. If their behaviour is unethical, there will be no company and no contribution by the company to the growth of the economy. It is for this reason, organizations are termed associations of people and not of structures.

(iii) No business can survive or conduct operations based on lying, theft, cheating, distrust and unrestrained self-interest.

(iv) Companies consistent with ethics only survive in the ultimate analysis. Though profit making is the objective of the company that should not result in exploitation, if the same is to be accepted by the society and thus become an integral part. Certain studies have shown that ethics does not detract from profit and seems to contribute to profits. It is also believed that firms that feel socially responsible could perform better on the stock market.[8]

(v) Much of the ethics is said to consist of rules that each constituent of the society shall choose to follow. Lest, every element of the society faces a kind of situation called prisoner's dilemma.[9] A prisoner's dilemma is the one relating to the confession by two thieves. Imagining that the penal code allows one to go free and punish the other who did not; both of them would be better if both of them agree to confess. Therefore, it is premised that the constituents of the society would be better off only when they cooperate with each other. Otherwise, every one of them receives punishment at the hands of the society.

(vi) By nature, people in the society value ethics in their acceptance or rejection of the businesses. Thus, following ethics has the chance of approval by the society and may contribute to the growth of the business in the long run.

(vii) Businesses have a bounded duty to be ethical to all the stakeholders such as the employees, customers, suppliers, investors, competitors and government. A fine balance among them only helps businesses to grow and become sustainable. Thus 'ethics can be understood as a balancing act' necessary for the orderly growth of the economy. Dishonesty or unethical behaviour leads to a less than optimum performance.

(viii) Among the rewards, for being more ethical and socially responsible in business, are increased efficiency in daily operations, greater employee commitment, increased investor willingness to entrust funds, improved customer trust and satisfaction and better financial performance. The reputation of the company has a major effect on its relationships with employees, investors, customers and many other parties.

3.2 Arguments Against Following Ethics by Business

There are also arguments against the case of bringing in ethics into the operation of business activities.

(i) Business exists for making profit. Profit making is consistent with the competition prevailing in the markets. The argument goes like this. In a perfectly competitive free market, the pursuit of profit will by itself ensure that the members of the society are served in the most socially beneficial ways. To be profitable, each firm has to produce only what the members of the society want and has to do this by the most efficient means available. The members of the society will benefit most, if the managers of the companies do not impose their own values on a business but instead devote themselves to the single minded pursuit of profit and thereby produce efficiently, what the members of the society value. Nevertheless, there are many arguments against this line of thinking. For, the existence of 'perfect markets' is based on many assumptions; which may turn out to be unrealistic and untrue.

(ii) There is what is called the 'loyal agent's argument' advanced by Alex C. Michaels.[10] He paraphrased his argument thus:

- As a loyal agent of his or her employer, the manager is duty-bound to serve the employer as he wishes.
- An employer would want to be served in whatever ways will advance his or her self-interests.
- Therefore, as a loyal agent of the employer, the manager has a duty to serve the employer in whatever ways he will advance the employer's self-interest.

  The argument can be, and often has been, used to justify a manager's unethical or illegal conduct; for example, the officer of a corporation may plead that, although he engaged in certain illegal or unethical conduct (e.g., price fixing), he should be excused because it was not for himself, but to protect the best interests of his company, its shareholders, or its workers. The loyal agent's argument underlies this kind of excuse.

A somewhat similar line of argument was put forth by Milton Friedman in his celebrated article titled 'The Social Responsibility of Business is to Increase its Profits', published in the New York Times magazine (September 13, 1970). In his opinion, the whole justification for permitting the corporate executive, to be selected by the stockholders, is that the executive is an agent serving the interests of his principal. This justification disappears when the corporate executive imposes taxes and spends the proceeds for "social" purposes. He becomes, in effect, a public employee, a civil servant, even though he remains in name as the employee of a private enterprise. On grounds of political principle, it is intolerable that such civil servants–in so far as their actions in the name of social responsibility are real and not just window-dressing–should be selected as they are now. If they are to be civil servants, then they must be elected through a political process. If they are to impose taxes and make expenditures to foster "social" objectives, then political machinery must be set up to make the assessment of taxes and to determine through a political process the objectives to be served. This is the basic reason why the doctrine of "social responsibility" involves the acceptance of the socialist view that political mechanisms, not market mechanisms, are appropriate to determine the allocation of scarce resources to alternative uses.[11]

(iii) The third kind of argument stems from the fact that businesses are only obliged to adhere to the laws of the land; nothing more, nothing less. This line of thinking is based on the analogy that business ethics is essentially obeying the law. In that sense of interpretation, law and ethics are to be treated identical. But that is not true. Law and morality do not always coincide. Social norms decide the moral standards of persons; whereas legal principles may view it in other point of view. For instance, law will not approve any transaction pertaining to superstition or certain customs. But members of the society may feel them good. Sometimes, law may be evolving and there may not be law for certain practices prevalent and approved by the society. In the course of events happening, 'living together' is accepted by the law in many countries, including India. But people in the society have to still accept or approve it as a norm. As discussed earlier, in the previous chapters, ethics goes beyond law.

4. APPROACHES TO UNDERSTAND BUSINESS ETHICS

Ethics, as such, is a multi-dimensional issue. When it is applied to the business operations, it acquires still further dimensions. As such, understanding business ethics is a complex issue. Yet, the subject can be approached under the following three ways:

1. Ethical reasoning.
2. Stakeholder management approach.
3. Issue-based understanding.

4.1 Ethical Reasoning

As applied to business, ethical reasoning is about principled decision making. It is also about applying moral principles in various phases of business activities such as creativity, negotiation, skill development and use them in solving real life business problems. There are at least three reasons that make ethical reasoning mandatory for businesses. First, many times laws do not cover all aspects or 'gray areas' of a problem. Questions are often raised regarding the trade in alcohol, tobacco, gutka, panparag, etc. It is legal to carry on business in many of these. But there is general resentment in the society about the consumption of these products. The grey areas in this trade include the extent to which law should regulate them. The question is: What sources of power or help can people expect in the situations of the law not being able to protect their interests. Suppose, an individual consuming gutka has acquired cancer, who would compensate him? In such cases, law may not be adequate; it is only moral persuasion that can help the people in the society.

There are laws in many countries discouraging the consumption of tobacco or smoking. Statutory warnings like the one present in India on the packs 'smoking is injurious to health' is a common phenomenon. Once there was a great controversy in India on the issue of printing the image of the 'skull' on the cigarette packs. This issue, in fact, rocked the Indian Parliament. Still in India and in many other countries, the sale of tobacco and products is permitted. Thus this can be taken as an example of attempting a balance between law and ethics.

Second, free-market and regulated-market mechanisms do not effectively inform owners and managers as to how to respond to complex issues that have far-reaching ethical consequences. Enron's former CEO Jeffrey Skilling believed that his new business model of Enron as an energy trading company was the next big breakthrough in a free-market economy. The idea was innovative and creative; the executive's implementation of the idea was illegal. Perhaps killing should have followed Enron's ethics code; it was one of the best available. But the model miserably failed after a few years; the greatest ever failure in the worldwide business.

A third argument holds that ethical reasoning is necessary because complex moral problems require 'an intuitive or learned understanding and concern for fairness, justice, and due process to people, groups, and of doing business. Judges have to use intuition and a kind of learn-as-you-go approach in many of their cases. In Microsoft's alleged monopoly case, for example, there were no clear precedents in the software industry – or with a company of Microsoft's size and global scope – to offer clear legal direction. Ethics, then, plays a role in business because laws are, many a time, insufficient to guide the action.

The question often addressed in the discipline of ethics pertains to whether this reasoning can be taught and managers trained to make themselves suit to this new kind of decision making process. It is strongly believed that ethical training can add value to the moral environment of a firm, as of the following:

- Provide people with rationale, ideas, and vocabulary to help them participate effectively in ethical decision-making processes.
- Help people 'make sense' of their environments by abstracting and selecting ethical priorities.
- Provide intellectual weapons to battle with advocates of economic fundamentalism and those who violate ethical standards.
- Enable employees to act as alarm systems for company practices that do not meet society's ethical standards.
- Enhance conscientiousness and sensitivity to moral issues, and commitment to finding moral solutions.
- Enhance moral reflectiveness and strengthen moral courage.
- Increase people's ability to become morally autonomous, ethical dissenters, and the conscience of a group.
- Improve the moral climate of firms by providing ethical concepts and tools for creating ethical codes and social audits.

4.2 Stakeholder Management Approach (SMA)

The Stakeholder Management Approach is based on an instrumental theory that argues 'a subset of ethical principles' (trust, trustworthiness, and cooperativeness) can result in significant competitive advantage'. At the same time, this approach includes analytical concepts and methods for identifying, mapping, and evaluating corporate strategy with stakeholders. Management Gurus refer to these methods as 'stakeholder analysis'. The stakeholder management approach, including frameworks for analyzing and evaluating a corporation's relationships (present and potential) with external groups, aims ideally at reaching 'win-win' collaborative outcomes. Here, 'win-win' means making moral decisions that benefit the common good of all constituencies within the constraints of justice, fairness, and economic interests. Unfortunately, this does not always happen. There are usually winners and losers in complex situations, where there is a perceived zero-sum game (i.e., a situation in which there are limited resources, and what is gained by one person is necessarily lost by the other).

Scholars and consultants, however, have used the stakeholder management approach as a means for planning and implementing collaborative relationships to achieve win-

win outcomes among stakeholders. Structured dialogue facilitated by consultants is a major focus in these collaborative communications. The aim of using the stakeholder approach as communication strategy is to change perceptions and 'rules of engagement' to create win-win outcomes.

The stakeholder approach does not have to result from a crisis, as so many examples from ethics literature and the news provide. It can also be used as a planning method to anticipate and facilitate business decisions, events, and policy outcomes. The stakeholder analysis is also not limited to large enterprises. Business units, teams, and groups can use this approach. This approach also begins, by asking what external forces in the general environment are affecting an organization. This context can often provide clues to responses by stakeholders to opportunities, crises, and extraordinary events. Corporate scandals that followed the Enron debacle suggest that there were several factors in the general environment that were at play in addition to certain corporate executives' greed. For example, the dot-com bubble created a financial environment where venture funds followed innovative ideas in exorbitant and exuberant ways. Investment banks loaned large amounts to Enron and other companies without due diligence. Stock analysts lied and encouraged deceptive investments from the public. Boards of directors abandoned their fiscal responsibilities, as did large accounting firms like Arthur Andersen. The general legal and enforcement environment during the 1990s appeared indifferent to monitoring corporate activities and protecting shareholders. This all changed after Enron.

As a matter of fact, Stakeholder Management Approach is a pragmatic way of identifying and understanding multiple (often competing) claims of many constituencies. As part of a general stakeholder approach, the stakeholder analysis is a method to help understand the relationships between an organization and the groups with which it must interact. Each situation is different and therefore requires a map to guide strategy for an organization dealing with groups, some of whom may not be supportive of issues such as outsourcing jobs. The aim here is to familiarize with the framework so that one can apply it in the classroom and in news events that appear in the press and electronic media. Even though one is not an executive or manager, the framework can enable him to see and understand more clearly complex corporate dealings.

The interface between the stakeholders and their moral responsibilities are well depicted in the following Matrix [see Figure 3.4]. Such a Matrix is expected to help the organization identify economic, legal, ethical and voluntary responsibilities for each group of stakeholders, so that one can develop strategies consistent with each stakeholder.

Stakeholders	Responsibilities: Legal	Economic	Ethical	Voluntary
Owners				
Customers				
Employees				
Community interest groups				
Public (citizens at large)				

Source: Weiss, Joseph, *'Business Ethics : Concepts and Cases'*, New Delhi, Cengage Learning, 2009.

Figure 3.4: Stakeholder Moral Responsibility Matrix

4.3 Issue Based Understanding

This approach is based on the various kinds of ethical issues faced by the business houses from time to time. Based on the contemporary developments, certain issues occupy a place of prominence, relegating those in such place till that time, to the background. Take a look at the issues of the following nature:

- Child labour and child rights
- Violence against women.
- Equal pay for Equal work.
- Minimum wages.
- Safety and security of employees.
- Insider Trading.
- Environmental considerations and pollution of diverse kinds.
- Contract/outsourced Labour.
- Working conditions and work life.

- Non-performing Assets.
- Frauds/Scams.
- Consumer Protection.
- Tax Evasion & Black Money.

Every issue of the above kind has ethical dimension. The business entities face situations of fair play in every aspect. Law may only specify certain things; whereas ethics orients the thinking of managers to be more humane. These principles apply equally to the members of the society; because business has an obligation to the society which gives it the freedom to conduct its activities.

5. ETHICAL DILEMMAS

Dilemma is a situation in which it is very difficult to decide what to do, because all the choices seem equally good or equally bad. In the pursuit of ethics, business houses face a situation of choosing one among the competing claims or interests. Sometimes, all those choices may be unethical. The nature of these satisfy all stakeholders. At the company level, if the objective of business is interpreted as 'profit maximisation', every employee in the organisation would face a situation of doing anything that contributes to the phenomenon. In the pursuit of profit maximization, anything like low quality inputs, low wages, higher prices, more working hours, evasion of taxation, etc., may happen; impinging on the moral standards of the company.

Sometimes, the very production of the product may not be ethical, like the soft drinks. It has been revealed through the study in India by the Centre for Science and Environment (CSE) that there are pesticide residues present in many of the soft drink brands like Pepsi, Coke, Sprite, etc. The revealation also led to the banning of the sale of drinks at the Government establislunents, Univcrsities, etc What would be more ethical is the stopping of production of such goods. Similarly, many health drinks do not contribute to the health of the individual. But they are advertised in a large scale. The point here is that the fact is already known to the producer. Still the production and sale of the items goes on and on. The case of steroids used by many Athletes and Sports Persons is still worse. While it is not so certain whether they really contribute to the improvement in the performance, they certainly add to the travails of the persons at the later stages of their life in terms various physical and psychological disorders. The production of these stimulants is going on world over unabated.

The advertising scenario for product sale is too worse. Knowing fully well of the facts, an advertisement is drafted and released with all untrue statements. Unfortunately, it is known to both, the advertiser and the advertising agency. The advertising agency further aggravates the unethical stand of the advertiser by designing the Ad with words, captions that are attractive and unreal, if not unnatural. Perhaps, it is for this reason the advertising company is retained. The repealed Monopolies and Restrictive Trade Practices Act, 1969 had contained many provisions to contain the misleading practices of both. The Competition Act, 2002, which replaced the former MRTP Act, had contained no provisions relating to this aspect; but sought to be protected under Consumer Protection Act, 1986.

Today's companies are spending about 10-20 per cent of their sales turnover on promotion of their goods and services. Much of the same is in the form of TV commercials and print Ads. It has become quite common that the corporates engage famous celebrities as their Brand Ambassadors. The Companies engage them to create a positive impact on the minds of the prospective consumers and finally lure them to buy their goods or services. Though it is not very clear as to the impact of such endorsements on the consumers and the consequent raise in the sales turnover, the TV networks thrive vastly on the revenues generated by this process.

But what is important is the responsibility cast on the celebrities endorsing such goods or services. It appears, sometimes, quite unbelievable whether the endorsing celebrity even uses the good or hires the services. It may not be much serious and detrimental, if the celebrity is endorsing goods that are not harmful to the users. But there may be products like health drinks, fitness products, cosmetics, that may cause damage to the consumers. The endorsers need to be careful and concerned about such endorsements. Unfortunately, the Ad business has become so mighty and the revenues involved are frightening. In their eagerness to make money, endorsers may lose their wisdom and discretion.

Therefore, it is high time that some responsibility is cast on the celebrities endorsing such goods or services, as of the following:

(a) That the endorser shall have used the product for at least a year or two and there shall be a certification to that effect.
(b) That the endorser shall also share the compensation for the damage caused by the use of such product or service.

It is also important to note that the 'referent power' of the celebrities will be significant among the consuming public. It will not be fair on their part to encash on their 'Charisma', in utter disregard of the impact of the goods or services they intend to endorse. Business organisations do face several of these situations and the decision they take at the appropriate time and manner decides their future and the future of the people in the society.

5.1 Where do These Dilemmas Arise?

Studies[12] have shown that there are basically four levels from which ethical dilemmas are arising, as of the following:

A. Individual or Professional Level
B. Company or organizational Level
C. Industry Level
D. Global Level

At the **Individual level**, a person experiences pressures from conflicting demands or circumstances that require a decision. Ethical dilemmas at this level can occur as a result of workplace pressures or from personal circumstances or motivations not related to work.

At the **Organizational level**, firms that engage in questionable practices and activities face possible dilemmas with their stakeholders and/or stockholders. For example, American Airlines had to ground 1,000 flights in April of 2008 in order to inspect and 'ion some cases reattach wiring bundles in the wheel wells of its 300 – plane fleet of MD – 80s'. In fact, one technician had inspected the wiring bundles and thought it had the problem fixed two weeks ago. But the FAA (Federal Aviation Administration), upon looking at the planes earlier found some bundles were wrapped and attached to the wheel wells incorrectly, and ordered them to be redone. This was the largest airline grounding in American's history; thousands of passengers were potentially put at high risk with unsafe and low quality of services – in this case, the risk of physical harm or even death'.

In Dukes vs Walmart, 'The largest sexual discrimination lawsuit in U.S. history was brought against Walmart when a federal appeals court approved class-action status for seven women who claim that the retailer was biased in pay and promotions'. Plaintiffs in the case estimated that 1.5 million women who had worked for Walmart in the U.S. stores since 1998 were eligible to join that suit. Walmart's reputation and image will not be easily repaired from this and other lawsuits that have recently been brought against the largest retailer. Going forward, Walmart's officers must decide whether or not this type of possible discrimination is worth from the stand point of legal, social, and media fall-out for the company and its stakeholders.

At the **industry level**, company officers, managers, and professionals may be influenced by and contribute to specific business practices in the industry. In the case of industry practices one can inquire about contract negotiation practices and expectations in the industry, but still one needs to examine organisation's, profession's, and individual ethics with regard to the instructions given. Not all business practices that occur in an industry are ethical – or even legal. The 'subprime lending' crisis illustrates how different organizations across industries violated ethical standards.

At the **societal, international and global level**, industry, organistional, professional and personal ethics may clash with the social, global, and international levels. For example, while tipping and paying money to government and other business officials in some countries may meet customary practices, such offerings may also be illegal bribes in other countries (like the U.S. and Europe). In some countries Tip is included in the bill.

A Research Study conducted by Ethics Resource Centre, USA during 2007 under the title 'National Business Ethics Survey' has made an attempt to list types of risks associated with these dilemmas; so that each of the interested parties can take appropriate measures to make thing more ethical.[13] The three types of risks listed by the organisation are:

(i) Severe risks (happen frequently and usually go unreported)
(ii) High risks (happen often and often, but go unreported)
(iii) Guarded risks (happen less frequently and may go unreported)

The above types of risks are shown in the following Figure 3.5.

Types of Ethical Risks

Severe Risks	High Risks	Guarded Risks
Putting own interest ahead of organization	Stealing/internet abuse	Environmental violations
Lying to employees	Misreporting hours worked	Misuse of confidential organisation information
Abusive behaviour	Lying to stakeholders	Alteration of Documents
	Discrimination	Alteration of financial records
	Safety violations	Using competitors' inside information
	Improper hiring practices	
	Sexual harassment	
	Provision of low quality good and services	

Source: Ethics Resource Centre's Report on 'National Business Ethics Survey, 2007.

Figure 3.5: Type of Ethical Risks

5.2 How to Resolve these Ethical Dilemmas?

Ethics has occupied the Centre stage of public policy in the recent past. Look at the following News appeared in the Media.

(a) 'Not an Absconder' says Mallya as Enforcement Directorate issues summons; an inadvertent error, says CBI; Rajya Sabha Ethics Panel to probe Mallya Issue. (All these captions dated 12-03-2016 in The Hindu).

According to a CBI spokesperson, the agency had *suo motu* registered a criminal conspiracy, cheating and corruption case against Mr. Mallya, Kingfisher Airlines and others on July 29, 2015. The agency, however, conducted searches on October 10 last year when Mr. Mallya was abroad. 'Two days later, the CBI sent a letter to the Bureau of immigration stating that the accused was wanted for questioning. A form seeking issuance of the lookout circular was also sent. But, inadvertently, an official at the Mumbai office ticked the opinion for detention of Mr. Mallya and its intimation to the CBI', said the spokesperson. 'The circular for detention can be issued only when a non-bailable warrant is pending' an official said.

The Enforcement Directorate (ED) issued summons to businessman, Vijay Mallya, in connection with the money laundering case registered against him, while two of his former employees were quizzed by the agency. He has been asked to present himself before the investigating team on March 18, 2016. Refuting the allegations that he was evading the law, Mr. Mallya defended himself on the microblogging site, Twitter. 'I am an international businessman. I travel to and from India frequently. I did not flee from India and neither am I an absconder. Rubbish,' he said, adding that as an Indian MP, he fully respected and would comply with the law of the land.

The Ethics Committee of the Rajya Sabha will be looking into whether an act of impropriety has been committed by Vijay Mallya as a Member of Parliament after he left the country. In the meantime, Indian Banks moved the Supreme Court for recovery of their dues to the extent of about Rs.9,000 crore. This event raised a hue and cry in the Rajya Sabha accusing the government of letting off Mr. Mallya. The Committee, which oversees the moral and ethical conduct of members, is likely to look into the matter pertaining to Mr. Mallya on Monday after members raised the matter with the Deputy Chairperson. The panel examines cases related to alleged breach of code of conduct or ethical misconduct by members.

(b) Spurt in corporate bad loans: Is the problem much bigger for Indian Banks than it originally appeared? (www.firstpost.com, dated March 12, 2016).

The news is about the large NPAs turning bad in recovery, endangering the profitability and survival of some of the state run banks. It is reported that the total corporate bad loans on the books of banks stood at Rs 2.6 lakh crore, more than twice the amount that was due in 2012-13. This puts the ratio of gross non-performing assets (GNPAs) of scheduled commercial banks at 6.78 per cent of the gross advances to the corporate sector by December 2015, the highest in four years, going by the information presented by Minister of State for Finance Jayant Sinha in Lok Sabha.

This means, the amount banks need to set aside to cover such loans in the form of provisions, too have grown significantly, in turn, impacting their profitability. Most banks have begun to aggressively report their bad loans for the December quarter after the Reserve Bank of India (RBI) set a deadline of March, 2017 for banks to clean up their balance sheets. The figure of gross NPAs given above is a measure of the gross bad loans that banks have extended to the corporate sector. What makes this figure worrisome is the steady rise in the percentage of bad loans. The total advances that became bad in 2012-13 were much less at 3.22 per cent. This percentage has soared to 4.55 per cent and 5.34 per cent in the subsequent two years before settling at 6.78 per cent by December 31, 2015.

Besides the worries related to the general economic slowdown, part of the corporate bad loans are also on account of cases of wilful defaults. One instance is the ongoing tussle between banks and the liquor-baron Vijay Mallya, whose grounded airline Kingfisher owes Rs 9,000 crore to banks. Kingfisher is only one instance, and there are several cases of large corporate defaults, where banks are struggling for recovery.

(c) **CBI case against businessman (The Hindu dt.22-02-2016):** The Central Bureau of Investigation has registered a case against the Managing Director of a Chennai-based company for allegedly defaulting on a Rs.124 crore loan following a complaint from the Central Bank of India. CBI sources said that a case was registered against K. Srinivas Kalyan Rao, who is the Managing Director of Chennai-based Best and Crompton Engineering Projects Ltd., under IPC sections related to criminal conspiracy, cheating and forgery, among others. It has been alleged that the company had borrowed Rs.304 crore from a consortium of banks comprising Central Bank of India, Andhra Bank and Corporation Bank by way of fund-based and non-fund-based limits. The CBI reportedly conducted simultaneous searches on the house and company of Mr. Srinivas Kalyan Rao, son of a former CBI Director, in Hyderabad and Chennai in connection with the multicrore bank fraud case. During scrutiny it was found that the accused had allegedly furnished forged documents in support of the purchases. The account was declared as non-performing.

In all the cases cited above, it is the morality that is at stake. There is no case for dilemma as long as you keep in mind the welfare of your fellow citizen. The issue sprouts only when self interest rules the roost. The most sought after question in this regard is: Is there a solution to this problem of declining ethics? The following may be considered for the time being:

1. To make punishments severe for those not adhering to the law of the land. Though law talks of 'proportion' in punishment, it does not seem to be working in the Indian context. Therefore action may be taken to modify/amend the existing laws in this direction.
2. Stepping up the publicity to the effect that it shall turn out to be a 'social sanction' on those contributing to the ethical crisis. For example, list of defaulters of Banks

Loans being put on wide publicity in the media and at every public place may act as a deterrent. The existing laws have limited provisions for these.

3. The third most important factor is to reform our legal system, so as to award punishment in the utmost speedy manner. Since, there is a long pendency of cases; nobody is serious about any law. Besides, the implementation mechanism conceived within the law itself is not commensurate to the task involved in many cases. This needs to be looked into.

It is in this context, the Centre for Ethics and Business, USA, offered a 'three-step strategy' to address the issue.[14]

Step-1: Analyse the Consequences: Assuming that the resolution to the ethical dilemma is to be found within the confines of law–ethical dilemmas that arise in business should be resolved at least within the bare minimum of law and legal framework as otherwise it will lead to a sort of mafia business. One has to look at the consequences that would follow one's proposed actions. And when one has several options to choose from, there will be an array of consequences connected with each of such options, both positive and negative. Before one acts, answers to the following question will help find the type of action that can be contemplated:

1. Who are the beneficiaries of the action?
2. Who are likely to be harmed by the action?
3. What is the nature of the 'benefits' and 'harms'?
4. How long or how fleetingly are these benefits and harms likely to exist?

After finding answers for each of the questions, one may identify the best mix of benefits or harms.

Step–2: Analyse the Actions: Once you identified the best possible option, concentrate on the actions. Find out how your proposed actions measure against moral principles such as 'honesty, fairness, equality, respect for the dignity and rights of others, and recognition of the vulnerability of people who are weak. Then there could be questions of basic decency and general ethical principles involving the rights and choices of people for a better course of action. After considering all these possible factors in the various options, it is sensible to choose the one which is the least problematic.

Step–3: Make a Decision: Having considered all factors that lead to choices among various options, analyse them carefully and then take a rational decision. The Three-step strategy should give one at least some basic understanding to resolve an ethical dilemma.

References

1. www.slideshare.net
2. www.preservearticles.com
3. www.ucadia.com
4. www.forbes.com
5. www.businessinsider.com
6. www.globalpolicy.com
7. www.makewealthhistory.org
8. Velasquez, Manuel G., *Business Ethics : Concepts and Cases*, New Delhi, PHI learning, 2009, p. 29.
9. Ibid., p. 40.
10. Alex C. Michalos, *'A pragmatic Approach to Business Ethics' Thousand oaks', Sage Publications, 1995.*
11. *Milton Friedman, 'The Social Responsibility of Business is to increase its profile'*, The New York Times Magazine, September 13, 1970.
12. (a) Weiss, Joseph W., *Business Ethics: Concepts and Cases"* New Delhi, Cengage Learning, 2009.
    (b) Keith Davis and William C. Frederick, 'Business and Society, Management, Public Policy, Ethics, New York, McGraw-Hill, 1983.
13. Ethics Resource Centre, 'National Business Ethics Survey – 2007', USA, (www.ethics.org)
14. www.cba.lmu.edu (Loyola Marymount University, Los Angeles, California, USA).

Appendix – I

List of 100 Largest Companies of the World, 2015

(Rs. in US $ Billions)

Rank	Company	Country	Sales	Profits	Assets	Market Value
1.	ICBC	China	166.8	44.8	3,322	278.3
2.	China Construction Bank	China	130.5	37	2,698.9	212.9
3.	Agricultural Bank of China	China	129.2	29.1	2,574.8	189.9

Contd.

Rank	Company	Country	Sales	Profits	Assets	Market Value
4.	Bank of China	China	120.3	27.5	2,458.3	199.1
5.	Berkshire Hathaway	United States	194.7	19.9	534.6	354.8
6.	JPMorgan Chase	United States	97.8	21.2	2,593.6	225.5
7.	Exxon Mobil	United States	376.2	32.5	349.5	357.1
8.	Petro China	China	333.4	17.4	387.7	334.6
9.	General Electric	United States	148.5	15.2	648.3	253.5
10.	Wells Fargo	United States	90.4	23.1	1,701.4	278.3
11.	Toyota Motor	Japan	252.2	19.1	389.7	239
12.	Apple	United States	199.4	44.5	261.9	741.8
13.	Royal Dutch Shell	Netherlands	420.4	14.9	353.1	195.4
14.	Volkswagen Group	Germany	268.5	14.4	425	126
15.	HSBC Holdings	United Kingdom	81.1	13.5	2,634.1	167.7
16.	Chevron	United States	191.8	19.2	266	201
17.	Wal-Mart Stores	United States	485.7	16.4	203.7	261.3
18.	Samsung Electronics	South Korea	195.9	21.9	209.6	199.4
19.	Citigroup	United States	93.9	7.2	1,846	156.7
20.	China Mobile	China	104 1	17.7	209	271.5
21.	Allianz	Germany	128.4	8.3	979	82
22.	Verizon Communications	United States	127.1	9.6	232.7	202.5
23.	Bank of America	United States	97	4.8	2,114.1	163.2
24.	Sinopec	China	427.	7.7	233.9	121
25.	Microsoft	United States	93.3	20.7	174.8	340.8
26.	Daimler	Germany	172.3	9.2	229.5	103.3
27.	AT&T	United States	132.4	6.2	292.8	173
28.	Gazprom	Russia	158	24.1	356	62.5

Contd.

Rank	Company	Country	Sales	Profits	Assets	Market Value
29.	AXA Group	France	153.8	6.3	1,016.6	64.2
30.	Nestle	Switzerland	100.1	15.8	134.3	247.3
31.	Banco Santander	Spain	56.4	7.7	1,532.3	109.4
32.	Ping An Insurance Group	China	75.3	6.4	645.7	113.8
33.	Mitsubishi UFJ Financial	Japan	49.2	10.6	2,328.5	90.9
34.	Johnson & Johnson	United States	74.2	16.3	131.1	275.7
35.	Total	France	211.4	4.2	229.8	120.2
36.	Procter & Gamble	United States	81.7	9.5	136.3	224.3
37.	China Life Insurance	China	71.4	5.2	362.1	160.5
38.	Bank of Communications	China	53.6	10.7	1,010.4	71.2
39.	Google	United States	66	13.7	131.1	367.6
40.	Vodafone	United Kingdom	66.3	77.4	200.5	88
41.	BP	United Kingdom	352.	3.5	284.3	120.8
42.	American International Group	United States	67.5	7.6	515.6	75
43.	Itaú Unibanco Holding	Brazil	76.6	9.2	424	63.7
44.	IBM	United States	93.4	12	117.5	160.2
45.	BMW Group	Germany	106.6	7.7	187.3	81.4
46.	Comcast	United States	68.8	8.4	159.3B	147.8
47.	Commonwealth Bank	Australia	39.6	8.1	696.2	117.1
48.	Pfizer	United States	49.6	9.1	169.3	211.7
49.	Goldman Sachs Group	United States	40.1	8.5	856.2	86.5
50.	BHP Billiton	Australia	63.1	10	146.1	119.5
51.	MetLife	United States	70.5	6.3	902.3	57.3
52.	Novartis	Switzerland	53.6	10.1	125.8	272.6
53.	Royal Bank of Canada	Canada	38.9	8.3	857	89.3

Contd.

Rank	Company	Country	Sales	Profits	Assets	Market Value
54.	Siemens	Germany	97.4	6.7	131.6	97.7
55.	China Merchants Bank	China	45.5	9.1	762.7	64
56.	Prudential	United Kingdom	99	3.6	564.5	64.5
57.	Anheuser-Busch InBev	Belgium	47.1	9.2	144.9	204.6
58.	Nippon Telegraph & Tel	Japan	104.7	5.2	172.2	71.5
59.	Rosneft	Russia	129	9	150	51.1
60.	Westpac Banking Group	Australia	35.6	6.9	674.5	94.2
61.	Banco Bradesco	Brazil	66.7	6.5	403.1	51.4
62.	Softbank	Japan	80.6	5.8	168.8	70.3
63.	Honda Motor	Japan	117.1	5.6	148.7	61.4
64.	General Motors	United States	155.9	3.9	177.7	59
65.	UnitedHealth Group	United States	130.5	5.6	86.4	112
66.	TD Bank Group	Canada	32.7	7	851.9	80.4
67.	Intel	United States	55.9	11.7	92	147.2
68.	EDF	France	96.7	4.7	324.3	46.3
69.	Ford Motor	United States	144.1	3.2	208.5	63.6
70.	Deutsche Telekom	Germany	83.1	3.9	156.5	85
71.	BASF	Germany	98.6	6.8	90.2	93.5
72.	Boeing	United States	90.8	5.4	99.2	105.6
73.	Industrial Bank	China	39.4	7.6	650.8	57.9
74.	UBS	Switzerland	39.8	3.9	1,069.3	74.7
75.	ANZ	Australia	32.6	6.7	676.7	77.6
76.	Cisco Systems	United States	48.1	8.7	104.9	139
77.	Sumitomo Mitsui Financial	Japan	34.8	7.7	1,465.4	54.8
78.	Zurich Insurance Group	Switzerland	73	3.9	390	51.8

Contd.

Rank	Company	Country	Sales	Profits	Assets	Market Value
79.	China Minsheng Banking	China	40	7.2	647.2	51.7
80.	Merck & Co	United States	42.2	11.9	98.3	162.3
81.	Roche Holding	Switzerland	51.8	10.2	76.1	240.4
82.	Citic Pacific	Hong Kong	51.9	5.1	767	44.3
83.	National Australia Bank	Australia	33.4	4.9	772.9	71.7
84.	Shanghai Pudong Development	China	38.2	7.6	676.3	49.2
85.	Walt Disney	United States	49.8	7.8	87	179.5
86.	CVS Health	United States	139.4	4.6	74.3	117.4
87.	Telefónica	Spain	66.8	4	148	72.3
88.	Oracle	United States	38.8	10.8	98.8	187.6
89.	ConocoPhillips	United States	52	6.9	116.5	80.5
90.	Sanofi	France	44.8	5.8	117.8	136
91.	United Technologies	United States	65.2	6.2	91.3	107.1
92.	ING Group	Netherlands	65.7	2.6	1,195.7	58.9
93.	Coca-Cola	United States	45.9	7.1	92	179.9
94.	China Citi Bank	China	38.3	6.6	667.1	49.7
95.	Morgan Stanley	United States	39	3.5	803.1	70.8
96.	Hewlett-Packard	United States	109.8	5	100.9	57.9
97.	Nissan Motor	Japan	106.7	4.3	138.9	45.9
98.	GDF SUEZ	France	99.1	3.2	200	49.5
99.	PepsiCo	United States	66.7	6.5	70.5	143
100.	Lloyds Banking Group	United Kingdom	65.6	1.9	1,333	84.4

Source: www.forbes.com

Appendix – II

List of 100 Largest Governments and Corporations by Revenue

Rank	Nation/Corporation	Revenues (US $ Billions)
1.	United States	3,029
2.	China	2,285
3.	Germany	1,680
4.	Japan	1,512
5.	France	1,507
6.	Italy	991
7.	United Kingdom	936
8.	Brazil	861
9.	Canada	675
10.	Spain	530
11.	Australia	493
12.	Wal-Mart Stores	486
13.	Sinopec	428
14.	Royal Dutch Shell	420
15.	Russia	417
16.	Netherlands	414
17.	Exxon Mobil	376
18.	BP	353
19.	South Korea	351
20.	State Grid	334
21.	PetroChina	333
22.	Mexico	301
23.	Norway	294
24.	Sweden	291
25.	Saudi Arabia	279
26.	Volkswagen Group	269
27.	Belgium	268
28.	Toyota Motor	252
29.	Switzerland	228
30.	Glencore International	221
31.	Austria	218

Contd.

Rank	Nation/Corporation	Revenues (US $ Billions)
32.	Total	211
33.	Apple	199
34.	Samsung Electronics	196
35.	Berkshire Hathaway	195
36.	Denmark	193
37.	Chevron	192
38.	Turkey	190
39.	India	186
40.	McKesson	174
41.	Daimler	172
42.	ICBC	167
43.	EXOR	158
44.	Gazprom	158
45.	General Motors	156
46.	AXA Group	154
47.	Phillips 66	150
48.	General Electric	149
49.	E.ON	148
50.	Finland	146
51.	Eni	146
52.	Ford Motor	144
53.	Petrobras	144
54.	Venezuela	143
55.	United Arab Emirates	141
56.	China State Construction Bank	140
57.	CVS Caremark	139
58.	Hon Hai Precision	139
59.	Indonesia	135
60.	At & T	132
61.	Valero Energy	131
62.	United Health Group	131
63.	China Construction Bank	131
64.	Agricultural Bank of China	129
65.	Rosneft	129

Contd.

Rank	Nation/Corporation	Revenues (US $ Billions)
66.	Allianz	128
67.	Verizon	127
68.	Kuwait	125
69.	BNP Paribas	125
70.	Amerisource Bergen	124
71.	Fannie Mae	122
72.	LukOil	121
73.	Bank of China	121
74.	Greece	120
75.	Honda Motor	117
76.	Argentina	117
77.	Costco Wholesale	116
78.	Colombia	114
79.	General Group	112
80.	JX Holdings	111
81.	Hewlett-Packard	110
82.	Kroger	109
83.	JP Morgan Chase	102
84.	Iraq	101
85.	Express Scripts Holding	101
86.	Portugal	100
87.	Nestle	100
88.	Bank of America	95
89.	IBM	94
90.	Poland	93
91.	Marathon Petroleum	91
92.	Cardinal Health	91
93.	Citigroup	91
94.	Boeing	90
95.	Amazon	89
96.	Well Fargo	88
97.	South Africa	87
98.	Microsoft	87
99.	–	–
100.	–	–

Source: www.corporationsandhealth.org.

Appendix – III

List of Top 25 Companies in India in Terms of Net Profit

(Rs. in Crore)

Rank	Company Name	Last Price	Change	% Change	Net Profit
1.	Reliance	1,025.20	9.65	0.95	22,719.00
2.	TCS	2,427.25	81.15	3.46	19,256.96
3.	ONGC	214.55	2.00	0.94	17,732.95
4.	Coal India	297.65	3.30	1.12	13,383.39
5.	Bharti Airtel	344.65	3.10	0.91	13,200.50
6.	SBI	191.05	4.90	2.63	13,101.57
7.	Infosys	1,190.20	30.00	2.59	12,164.00
8.	ICICI Bank	230.35	2.80	1.23	11,175.35
9.	NTPC	127.40	0.60	0.47	10,290.86
10.	HDFC Bank	1,028.65	10.80	1.06	10,215.92
11.	ITC	325.00	1.00	0.31	9,607.73
12.	Wipro	546.65	8.40	1.56	8,193.10
13.	Hind Zinc	171.55	2.60	1.54	8,178.00
14.	Axis Bank	435.95	8.00	1.87	7,357.82
15.	Tata Steel	302.00	6.20	2.10	6,439.12
16.	NMDC	98.10	2.15	2.24	6,421.86
17.	HCL Tech	824.05	9.40	1.15	6,345.95
18.	HDFC	1,127.65	17.95	1.62	5,990.14
19.	Power Finance	169.80	0.05	0.03	5,959.33
20.	IOC	391.90	−6.85	−1.72	5,273.03
21.	REC	168.90	0.50	0.30	5,259.87
22.	BPCL	855.65	−7.00	−0.81	5,084.51
23.	Larsen	1,199.25	5.45	0.46	5,056.18
24.	Power Grid Corp	136.80	0.20	0.15	4,979.17
25.	HUL	846.05	0.05	0.01	4,315.26

Source: www.moneycontrol.com

4
CHAPTER

Functional Areas of Business and Ethics

1. INTRODUCTION

We have observed in the previous chapter that ethics is applicable to everyone in the society. Business being the most significant constituent of the society, there is every responsibility on the persons doing business to follow the principles of ethics. In defining business, Peter F. Drucker has identified eight 'key result areas', of business in setting management objectives.[1] Drucker believed that the survival of the company was at risk when managers emphasized only on the profit objective; because this single objective emphasis may encourage managers to take actions that will make money today with little regard for how a profit will be made tomorrow. Eight key areas in which managers should set management system objectives are:

1. *Market Standing*: Management should set objectives indicating where it would like to be in relation to its competitors.
2. *Innovation*: Management should set objectives outlining its commitment to the development of new methods of operation.
3. *Productivity*: Management should set objectives outlining the target levels of production.
4. *Physical and Financial Resources*: Management should set objectives regarding the use, acquisition, and maintenance of capital and monetary resources.
5. *Profitability*: Management should set objectives that specify the profit the company would like to generate.
6. *Managerial Performance and Development*: Management should set objectives that specify rates of managerial productivity as well as desirable attitudes for their superior performance.

7. *Worker Performance and Attitude*: Management should set objectives that specify rates of worker productivity as well as desirable attitudes for workers to possess.
8. *Public Responsibility*: Management should set objectives that indicate the company's responsibilities to its customers and society and the extent to which the company intends to live up to those responsibilities.

It is evident from the above that business operations have multiple dimensions and an effective combination and coordination of the same would enhance the value of the corporation. In so doing, businesses need to be conscious about what is wrong and what is right. There must also be a realization that businesses not just about buying and selling. It is to be realized that business is an assortment of functions, technologies, transactions, activities, people and institutions. Ethical principles need to permeate all these constituents and then only businesses remain sustainable and long lasting institutions in the society. Following are the key issues concerning ethics in every functional area of business.

2. ETHICAL ISSUES IN PRODUCTION

In case of manufacturing industries, the production related matters may pertain to:

(a) Technology
(b) Inputs
(c) Production processes
(d) Safety and security of workers
(e) Quality of the products
(f) Pollution and other aspects of environment

2.1 Technology

The choice of relevant technology has an ethical issue. It is a fact that there would be a variety of technologies available for producing a particular product. The choice of appropriate and suitable technology rests with the promoter. In doing so, he may many a time, be guided by the costs involved shunning away the aspects of safety and pollution. There is also the issue of 'technical optimum' as E. A. G. Robinson has called in his Book the 'Optimum Firm'.[2] Promoters may not make right decisions in choosing the relevant technology consistent with the interests of the workers, consumers and society. In such context, ethics becomes a causality.

There is now loud talk about the 'Green Technologies', encompassing the techniques for generating energy to non-toxic products. The focus of these technologies is in achieving objectives such as: (1) sustainability, (ii) cradle to cradle design, (iii) source reduction, (iv) innovation, and (v) viability. Sustainability involves meeting the needs of the society in ways that can continue indefinitely into the future without damaging or depleting natural resources. In short, meeting the present needs without compromising the ability of future generations to meet their own needs is the focus .of this technology aspect.[3]

Sustainability implies the long-term positive effects of any product, process or technology. It also involves use and reuse of the material/inputs. In these days, economies are moving towards sustainable development. Development that is having long-term positive results.

"Cradle to cradle" design is about the manufacturing of products by introducing technology that can be fully reclaimed or reused.

Source reduction implies the reduction of waste and pollution by changing the patterns of production and consumption. Innovation is the key to development. Technology develops and survives only through innovation. The focus could be on products, processes and inputs. So far there is not much of attention focused on cost reducing and pollution-free technologies.

Viability is creating a center of economic activity around technologies and products that benefit the environment, speeding their implementation and creating new careers that truly protect the planet are also necessary.

Examples of green technology are very wide and far. They may extend to the fields such as **energy** – which covers alternative fuels, new means of generating energy and energy efficiency; green construction with the choice of building materials, use of environment-friendly inputs like the products whose contents and methods of production have the smallest possible impact on the environment; green chemistry and green nano-technology which involves the use of non-hazardous chemicals and manipulation of materials at the scale of the nanometers — one billionth of a meter. The entire world is no trying to move towards the application of green chemistry and green engineering principles in the development of new products and new processes. The day appears to be not too far, when a new miniature world will be created. All these developments have implications to ethics.

Another dimension of the issue of technology pertains to the rapid spread of Internet and its applications. The use of Net is turning an issue. There is a contention on the issue of 'privacy' in the use of Net. Whole gamut of misuse led to the enactment of cyber laws in many countries. The one that is significant passed by the US Government relates to the US Computer Fraud and Abuse Act (CFAA), 1984. The act is used to prosecute those who transmit 'a programme, information, code, or command to a computer or computer system with the intent to cause damage to the computer or information in the computer or prevent the use of the system without the knowledge or the authorization of the owner of the computer. In addition, the law made it a crime to act with reckless disregard of a substantial and unjustifiable risk of damage or loss. This CFAA is also popularly known in USA as 18 USC Section 1030. Later, the National Information Infrastructure Act (NIIA) was passed in 1996 to expand the scope of CFAA to encompass unauthorised access to a protected computer in excess of the parties' authorization. This was considered necessary because, before NIIA, only if the criminal had acted on commercial gain could he be charged under CFAA. After NIIA was passed, it became illegal to even view information on a computer without authorization.

In the Indian context, these are addressed under the Information Technology Act, 2000. The law in India in this regard is scheduled to address two issues: (i) using computer to attack other computer for such activities as hacking, virus/worm attacks, DOS attack, etc.; (ii) using computer as a weapon to commit real-world crimes like cyber terrorism, IPR violations, cerotic and frauds, electronic funds transfer frauds, money laundering, pornography, etc. Even with a simple e-mail service, there could be multiple crimes committed like the following:

- ✓ Originating the e-mail from one source; when it was actually sent from another source (e-mail spoofing).
- ✓ Sending e-mails to thousands and thousands of users to jam the network (e-mail spamming).
- ✓ Sending malicious codes through mail.
- ✓ Use the mails to send viruses.
- ✓ Sending the mail repeatedly to a ponticual address (e-mail bombing).
- ✓ Sending threatening, defamatory mails, etc.

Therefore, while technology is a boon and can be used for gainful purposes in business, the same has also the chance of being misused with mala fide intentions. The solution under such conditions would be to prevail on the users with more conscience.

2.2 Inputs

Another important aspect in the production function is the one relating to the use of inputs. As the economists have often remarked, economics is the science of allocating scarce resources among competing uses. This advocates the use of resources in the most judicious manner and one should go by the assessment of 'opportunity costs'. The following issues assume significance in terms of the use of inputs in the production process:

- ✓ Quantity and productive use of input materials.
- ✓ Exploration of alternative uses and the choice of the most productive input.

- ✓ Least hazardeous to the user/consumer.
- ✓ Quality of the inputs.
- ✓ Reduction of wastage.
- ✓ Reuse/recycling.
- ✓ Taking all precautions to reduce, if not eliminate pollution.

As discussed earlier, technology has advanced so much that there is lot of research in using finer materials (like nano-materials) to improve the efficiency and reduce wastage. There is also focus on the reuse and recycling of materials. Firms to be ethical in this regard are required to continuously research into the substitution of one with the other having multiple advantages.

This subject assumes further significance in case of business involved in the extraction/mining of natural resources. Everyone is aware that there is no scope for replenishing the extracted natural resources. There is also the case of pollution associated with this activity. Hence, firms of this nature need to be highly responsible and ethical in their operations.

2.3 Production Processes

To a great extent, these depend on the selection of the technology. To the extent possible, firms are supposed to choose cleaner technologies. For instance, in case of production of Cement, there is choice of 'wet and dry' processes. Now that the 'wet' process has got outdated and obsolete, firms are required to replace the same with new processes. Even with this, firms need to allow the processes to take their own course and not to meddle with. This is essential in case of pharmaceutical companies. Drug discovery, dosage, method of administration are all important from the point of view of the patient. In case of polluting industries like jute, leather, mining, processes adopted make a huge difference to the environment.

2.4 Safety and Security of Workers

This is yet another significant and sensitive issue. It is the bounded duty of the business to ensure safety and security of the employees. Risk is imminent to the people working in industries. The industry is required to take all necessary measures to ensure their safety in terms of putting in place signboards, guards to the machinery, and to see that the machines are in good condition. Licenses are issued to the businesses only after they have taken necessary measures in this regard. As far as the Indian Industry is concerned, Factories Act, 1948 and Workmen Compensation Act, 1923 are highly relevant. According to Factories Act, 1948, the following are the important measures that every occupier should undertake. [4]

- There should be proper arrangement of lighting in factories. The premises should be well equipped with lighting arrangement either by natural sources or artificial sources.
- Machines must be properly secured and fenced to ensure safety of the workers.
- As per the Act, employment of young persons and women on dangerous machines is prohibited. If it necessary or compulsory, they may be employed under the supervision of trained personnel.
- Adequate precaution must be taken in respect of electricity arrangements. Every factory should have special devices for cutting off of power in emergencies from running machinery. Suitable striking gear appliances should be provided and maintained for moving belts.
- There are also certain restrictions on the employment of women and children on specific machinery. For example, women and children should not be placed for any part of factory working on cotton pressing.
- It is also the responsibility of the employer to construct and maintain buildings, floors, passages properly and to see that there are no chances of slips or fall.
- Enough care shall also be taken to see that no person is employed to lift, carry or move any load so heavy that might cause an injury. The employer shall abide by the rules and regulations specified in this regard by the concerned authority.
- Special care is to be taken for the protection of eyes of workers. Based on the need, the factory should provide specific goggles or screens to the workers who are involved in manufacturing work that may cause injury to the eyes.
- No worker shall be compelled or forced to enter any chamber, tank, vat, pit, pipe, flue or other confined space; which may cause damage to his health, due to fumes, dust, gases or any other material.
- There should be proper precautionary measures taken to ensure fire safety. There should be safe means to escape in case of fire, and arrangement also shall be put in place to extinguish the same, as quickly as possible.
- It is also the duty of the employer to maintain a fully equipped first-aid box or cupboard with the prescribed contents as per the specifications of the Act.

Similarly, certain diseases are said to be common for those working in certain industrial units, because of their continuous exposure to a different environment. Such industries included cotton, cement, leather, tobacco, beedi, sugar, pulverizing units, mines, oils and lubricants, etc. Even with modern technologies and workplaces, exposure of workers to various kinds of hazardous substances of the following variety could not be contained:[5]

- Fine particles such as asbestos (causes asbestosis)
- Cotton dust (Byssinosis)

- Heavy metals such as lead, cadmium and beryllium
- Gases including chlorine, ozone, SO_2, carbon monoxide, hydrogen sulphide, hydrogen cyanide (damages the lungs and cause neurological problems)
- Solvents such as benzene, carbontetrachloride carbondisulphide
- Certain classes of chemicals like phenols, ketones, and epoxies
- Pesticides (serious threat to agricultural workers)
- Radiation (an occupational hazard to x-ray technicians and workers in the nuclear industry).

In this regard, the Workmen's Compensation Act, 1923 makes it obligatory to every employer to pay compensation to workmen involved in accidents arising out of and during the course of their employment. The Constitution of India also guarantees the protection to life under Article 21. Wherein the Supreme Court of India has upheld this right to life and health. In the case of Consumer Education Research Centre Vs. Union of India, the Supreme Court held that 'occupational accidents and diseases are the most appalling human tragedy of modern industry. Elaborating further, the court observed that the right to health, medical aid to protect health and vigor to a worker while in service or post-retirement is a fundamental right under Article – 21.

2.5 Quality Products

It is the responsibility of every business organization to supply quality products to the consumers. It is no doubt that it is the manufacturer, who knows entirely about the quality of the output turned out by him. It may relate to the use of substandard material, unreliable processes, adulteration and less weight and many other areas. The manufacturers have the duty to adhere to the quality norms as prescribed by statutory organizations. It is gratifying to note that many companies are voluntarlly following the national and international standards like ISO. ISO's quality certification is taken as authentic by many in the industry circles and consumers. International standards organization (ISO) Geneva, Switzerland is an independent, non-governmental international organization with a membership of 162 national standards bodies, established in 1947. The major mission of the organization is to ensure that products and services are safe, reliable and of good quality. For business enterprises, ISO tenders advice to reduce costs, by minimizing waste and errors and increasing productivity. ISO certification helps businesses to access new markets, provide level playing field for developing countries and facilitate free and fair global trade. So far the organization has published more than 19,000 International Standards and related documents covering almost every industry, from technology to food safety, to agriculture and healthcare.

Similar organization was also floated in India in 1986 under the name Bureau of Indian Standards (BIS) (formerly called the Indian Standards Institution (ISI). The

Board is entrusted with the duty to attend all the matters concerning stadardisation, certification and quality. Under the Act, the Bureau establishes standards in relation to any article or process and amends, revises or cancels the standards so established as many be necessary. The Bureau has so far developed over 19,000 Indian standards, covering various products, methods of test, codes of practices, etc.

The organization also issued the BIS (certification) Regulations, 1988, making it obligatory on the part of the companies to take license to use the Standard Mark (called the ISI/BIS Mark). As per these regulations, every licensee shall maintain a system of control to keep up the quality of his production or process by means of a scheme of testing and inspection, so as to ensure that the article/process complies with the relevant Indian standards. In spite of about 19,000 products/ services given certification, there are still standards not available in certain products like soft drinks, mineral water, pharma products, etc. Hallmarking for gold and jewellery has just begun. The unfortunate story in the Indian market is that the consumers are not serious about the issue and they also do not insist on the laying down of standards and their compliance.

2.6 Pollution Control

Pollution is another contentious issue in the industry. It is to be accepted that pollution is imminent in certain manufacturing processes. The better way is to control such pollution, when we cannot eliminate it completely. Different kinds of pollution are generated by the industrial units. Mining and extraction units pollute the air and environment. Certain forging and metallurgical industries pollute by virtue of heavy sound they produce. Water pollution is common resulting from the chemical and paint companies. Cases of pollution in India are quite large and even the Parliament has to discuss and formulate a policy. Huge amounts of allocation for clearing River Ganga is a stunning example for the extent of pollution caused by the industrial units located on the banks of Ganga. The Government has constituted the 'National Ganga River Basin Authority' and has been making significant allocations in the Central Budget. For example, the Cabinet has approved the flagship programme titled 'Namami Ganga' at an estimated outlay of Rs. 20,000 crore for the next five years, beginning 2015-16. It was reported that the amount earmarked was a fourfold increase over the expenditure allocated to the task of cleaning the Ganga River over the past 30 years. This clearly speaks of the severity and depth of the issue.

While we take a look at the extent of pollution, India is also worst hit by the carbon emissions. As per the report of the World Health Organisation (WHO), India is home to 13 out of 20 most polluted cities in the world with deteriorating air pollution levels in the past decade, particularly in North India. Greenpeace (an NGO) has revealed that as many as 15 out of 17 cities in India showed levels of air pollution that far exceeded the prescribed Indian Standards. Again, the report revealed that 23 out of 32 stations across India are showing more than 70 per cent exceedance of the national standards, putting public health at risk. Besides, air pollution, water pollution, noise pollution and land pollution are the major areas of concern. In case of water pollution, the gravity of the situation is that even the groundwater is polluted in some areas to such an extent that it remained unsafe for drinking at Pattancheruvu in A.P. is a standing example. River water pollution is rampart across India. There is no control on the noise pollution is quite evident in India. Automobile horn pollution is so irritating that speaks of the total lack of control on automobile companies and users as well. Open defecation is a common scene in India. Governments are now (after 67 years independence) speaking loudly on '**Swatcha Bharat**' and the construction of hygienic toilets; where the modesty of women also being at sake. Something needs to be done by the industry also on this account. There is no big thing than voluntary involvement and action.

As a matter of fact, there are Pollution Control Boards at the Central and State levels in India. Central Pollution Control Board in India was established in 1974 under Water (Prevention and Control of Pollution) Act, 1974. The Board is expected to save as a field formation and also provide technical services to the Ministry of Environment and Forests of the provisions of the Environment (Protection) Act, 1986. Principal Functions of the CPCB, as spelt out in the Water (Prevention and Control of Pollution) Act, 1974, and the Air (Prevention and Control of Pollution) Act, 1981 are: (i) to promote cleanliness of streams and wells in different areas of the States by prevention, control and abatement of water pollution, and (ii) to improve the quality of air and to prevent, control or abate air pollution in the country. [6]

Air Quality Monitoring is an important part of the air quality management. The National Air Monitoring Programme (NAMP) has been established with the objective of determining the present source to meet the air quality standards. It also provides background air quality data needed for industrial location and town planning. Besides this, CPCB has an automatic monitoring station at ITO intersection in New Delhi. At this station, Resirable Suspended Particulate Matter (RSPM), Carbon Monoxide (CO), Ozone (O_3), Sulphur Dioxide (SO_2), Nitrogen Dioxide (NO_2) and Suspended Particulate Matter (SPM) are being monitored regularly. This information on Air Quality at ITO is updated every week.

Fresh water monitoring is also undertaken on a regular basis. It is a fact that India has many rivers flowing across. It has 14 major rivers, 44 medium rivers and 55 minor rivers besides numerous lakes, ponds and wells. All these are used as primary source of drinking water even without treatment. Most of the rivers are fed by monsoon rains. 'Save water' is the slogan of the nation today. Keeping the above in view, the Parliament of India has enacted the Water (Prevention and Control of Pollution) Act, 1974 with a view to maintaining and restoring wholesomeness of our waterbodies of the country. The mandate for the CPCB is to collect, collate and disseminate technical and statistical data relating to water pollution happening in the country and suggest suitable measures for checking pollution and make it useable.

3. ETHICAL ISSUES IN FINANCE

Of the four factors of production, capital is one of the prime requirements. Businesses come into existence with the capital brought in by the promoters. Finance, if defined, as the science of money; companies are interested in the mobilization and utilization of funds. In both the areas of activity, businesses need to be ethical.

3.1 Mobilisation of Funds

Companies raise funds from various sources such as the promoters, investors, banks, financial institutions, etc. In doing so, there is the need to be honest in raising capital and follow the principles of ethics, as of the following:

- Making adequate disclosures relating to the promoters, activities of the business, directors, finances, etc.
- Following the conditions stipulated by the stock exchanges, as per the Listing Agreement.
- Preparing and publishing Financial Statements as per the legal requirements and complying with Accounting and Auditing Standards.
- Putting in place adequate 'Internal Control' measures to ensure proper use of funds.
- Taking all the necessary measures for reducing the 'cost of capital'.
- Following the guidelines in raising inter-corporate loans, floating various kinds of bonds, debentures, public deposits, etc.

In spite of the elaborate guidelines framed by the Ministry of Corporate Affairs (MCA), Securities and Exchange Board of India (SEBI) and various stock exchanges, there were many instances of foul play creeping in on the front of mobilisation of funds. Mobilization of funds through IPOs with many wrong disclosures is common. The raising of deposits from public is rampant without following any guidelines. This is happening on two counts: one, some businesses accept deposits from public without any permission from RBI. Two, some companies raise deposits beyond the permitted levels and through means not permitted by the RBI. We have seen Sahara and Agri-Gold Group of Companies involved in the cases of illegal mobilisation of money through deposits and not being able to repay at the time of maturity. In both the above cases, the promoters are facing criminal charges and are under custody. The case of Sahara is presented in the case study section. Similarly, there were instances like the imbroglio of Satyam Computers, Maytas, raising funds from market, banks, etc. and finally ending as a corporate failure. These incidents dampen the investment climate. Already, because of many drawbacks and foul play, small investors have shyed away from the stock market and choosing the route of Mutual Funds. This is not a healthy sign for corporate growth.

3.2 Bank Loans and Non-Performing Assets

The attention of the entire world is now drawn towards misuse of bank loans and plundering of public money. More than the banks in the west, Banks in India are suffering from heavy doses of Non-Performing Assets (NPAs). As per the recent news (dated February 10, 2016), the total NPAs of Indian Banks stood at Rs. 3,41,641 crore; which is 5.08 per cent of total loans. There is also extended enthusiasm among banks to write off these bad loans. During the last three years (2012-14), it was reported, that an amount of Rs. 1.14 lakh crore was written off by the 29 state owned banks. What a colossal misuse of public money! As one goes deep into the issue, there are cases of dishonesty usurping and turning into a curse to the Indian banking system.

It will be interesting to trace the story of growing NPAs of all the Scheduled Commercial Banks. These NPAs stood at only 38,385.18 crore in 1994 and they grew up to Rs. 2,64,195.50 crore by 2014 (a sevenfold increase over a decade).[7] Similar trend could be observed in the Net NPAs also. During 1994, Net NPAs stood at 17,366.64 crore only and rose to Rs. 1,42,657 crore (about eightfold). Banks have been claiming that they are able to reduce NPAs in terms their percentages to total advances. It is true that in relative terms, there had been significant improvement in the reduction of Gross NPAs from 19.45 per cent in 1994 to 4.70 per cent in 2014. Similarly, Net NPAs also have come down from 10.67 per cent to 3.10 per cent. There was, once impression created in the banking circles that the Indian banks are heading towards zero tolerance. But the euphoria has vanished in a short period of two/three years.

A synoptic view of the position obtainable from individual banks reveals many interesting aspects. While the Gross NPAs of SBI alone stood at Rs. 61,605.4 crore, SBH is following with Rs. 5,824.2 crore. Among the other nationalized banks, Punjab National Bank is topping the list with Rs. 18,880.1 crore outstanding as on 31st March 2014. As usual, private banks are cautious in their approach. Excepting ICICI Bank (Rs. 10,505.8 crore), many other banks have Gross NPAs less than Rs.1000 crore. Whereas Foreign banks do not have the problem of NPAs at all. There is thus, need to relook into the methodologies of sanctioning advances by the public sector banks especially.

The factors attributed for the cause of NPA may be divided into internal and external factors. Internal factors which lead to increase/rise in NPAs and being internal in nature and controllable by the banks are: defective lending processes, or poor lending decisions, inappropriate technology, improper SWOT analysis, poor credit appraisal system, managerial deficiencies, absence of regular industrial visits, re-loaning process, etc.

External factors which lead to increase/rise in NPAs and non-controllable by banks include ineffective statutory recovery procedures, willful defaults, natural calamities, industrial sickness, lack of demand, changes in government policies, etc. One of the main causes of NPAs into banking sector is the directed loans system under which commercial banks are required to provide a prescribed percentage of their credit (40%) to priority sectors. As of today, nearly 7 per cent of Gross NPAs are locked up in 'hard-core' doubtful and loss assets, accumulated over the years due to the budgetary targets.

1. Poor credit appraisal system.
2. Lack of proper monitoring.
3. Reckless advances to achieve the budgetary targets.
4. Change in economic policies/environment.
5. No transparent accounting policy and poor auditing practices.
6. Lack of co-ordination between banks.
7. Directed lending to certain sectors.
8. Failure on the part of the promoters to bring their portion of equity from their own source or public issue due to market turning lukewarm.

What is worse is that the Government of India had to press CBI into service for making a detailed investigation. Having sensed foul play in the sanction of loans by certain public sector banks, the Government of India ordered an enquiry by the CBI of the top 30 accounts of borrowers from the banking system. The results of the investigation are not yet made public. A cursory look at the website of the CBI clearly indicates numerous incidents of misuse/malfeasance in the sanction of credit by banking officials to unscrupulous and unworthy borrowers. The site has displayed a recent case (Dt.5-3-2015) registered against the then Chief Manager and three other officials of SBI for causing an alleged loss of Rs. 5.73 crore to the Bank. It was alleged that during the period from 2011 to 2013 , the Ex-MP/Ex-Minister resident of Narsapur, West Godavari District had connived with the then Chief Manager, and three field officers, all of State Bank of India, Narsapur Branch and availed 22 Fish Tank Loans under KCC (Kissan Credit Card) for Pisciculture in various names of himself and his family members. During the process, it is reported that the borrower submitted fake documents and routed the entire sanctioned amount to his Savings Bank Account maintained with State Bank of India, Narasapur Branch. He allegedly misused the same for his personal use and not for which it was sanctioned. In spite of all this going on, there was no proper enquiry from the bank. The surprising fact is that the pre-sanction/post-sanction inspection was also not conducted properly.

As a matter of continuation, the Bombay High Court has issued notice to the RBI in connection with a Public Interest Litigation (PIL) filed by a Social Activist – Ketan Tirodkar. The petitioner attempted to bring to the notice of the Hon'ble Court that the nationalised banks are not taking proper care in sanctioning loans and thus the NPAs are swelling up in large measure. He has only quoted data referring to the NPAs from March 2008 (Rs. 455 crore) to March 2012 (9,190 crore). As a matter of fact, the RBI's Annual Report for 2013-14 estimated that the NPAs amounted to Rs. 2.8 lakh crore, which are about 4.7 per cent of gross advances. Justices A. S. Oka and G. S. Kulkarni, while acting on the PIL directed the RBI to register a case with CBI to probe into the 'fraudulent sanctions' leading to such huge NPAs.

3.3 Corporate Debt Restructuring (CDR)

This is another scheme being operated by the commercial banks in India. The objective of CDR framework is to ensure timely and transparent mechanism for restructuring the corporate debts of viable entities facing problems, outside the purview of BIFR, DRT and other legal proceedings, for the benefit of all concerned. In particular, the framework will aim at preserving viable corporates that are affected by certain internal and external factors and minimize the losses to the creditors and other stakeholders through an orderly and coordinated restructuring programme.

The most interesting aspect of the CDR is the amount involved. Ever since the mechanism came into operation in 2001, the information is being compiled by the CDR Cell from time to time.[8] As per the latest Progress Report (as on December 31, 2014), the total number of references made to the cell stood at 647 involving aggregate debt amount of Rs. 4,52,940 crore. The number of cases rejected before admission or approval stood at 122 with an aggregate debt amount of Rs. 65,925 crore. Keeping aside the cases still under consideration of the Empowered Group (No. 5, with a debt amount of Rs. 130 crore), the total cases approved for restructuring numbered 520 with the aggregate debt amount of Rs. 3,80,885 crore.

Industry-wise classification of the cases referred to the CDR Cell reveals the fact that a majority of the cases (together with amounts involved) pertain to five industries covering infrastructure, iron & steel, power, textiles and construction. Of the 288 live cases under consideration of the CDR Cell involving an amount of Rs. 2,72,099 crore, the above 5 industries account for 157 cases (54.5 per cent). In terms of the amount involved, these five industries accounted for Rs. 1,73,824 crore, coming to 63.9 per cent of the total amount. This advocates the bankers and the government to make an in depth analysis of the reasons for such a huge number of cases being referred from the five industries alone. As a matter of fact, these are the industries that are on the rise. The demand for the products is growing high, particularly in the sectors of infrastructure and power.

CDR has turned out to be on issue of great concern for the reason that the hard earned money of the people of the nation pooled as Deposits by the Banks is reported to be swindled by the unscrupulous, and dishonest corporates. As long as sanctioning and recovery of loans is a matter between the lender and borrower, no one need to raise eyebrows. It turns out to be an issue when loan sanctioning authority is only an employee and trustee of the money deposited and uses his discretion indiscriminately to make pecuniary gains from the borrower, or unable to judge the mala fide intentions of the borrower. While the CDR is said to be a useful tool which allows the borrowing organisation to reorganize its outstanding obligations, the tool is said to be misused to extend undue benefit to the borrower from being categorized as NPA.

The reports of the print and electronic media are frightening. Some of the companies like Eastern Silk, Moser Baer, Nakoda Ltd., Mowna Sugar, Sujana Metal have higher stakes in the system. A jolt is given to the banks, particularly to PSBs, by the Coal Block Case, several steel companies and a few power sector companies, which were allotted 'coal blocks' have started making a bee-line for CDR, after the Supreme Court cancelled allotment of 214 blocks. Already, companies including Abhishek Industries, Surana Corporation, Damodar Valley, Electrosteel Castings and Electrotherm Industries that were allotted coal blocks have been referred to the CDR Cell by banks. As per one estimate, banks are attempting to restructure about Rs. 40,783 crore loans (which form about 16.1 per cent) taken by such iron and steel companies. In addition, power companies are expected to add another Rs. 20,253 crore. By now, it is estimated that about Rs. 7 lakh crore of debt outstanding for clearance by corporate bodies would fall into the category of restructuring, thus endangering the very banking system.

A new dimension in the episode is that the banks are lenient towards curbing this menace and even the RBI's control is considered negligible. Interestingly, in May of 2014, the All India Bank Employees Association (AIBEA) pulled out a list of 400 top bank loan defaulters of state run banks as on March 2013. What is more worrying is the allegation that banks are considering borrowers, whose financials are not really proper. A case in point quoted pertains to the Hyderabad based companies, namely, Sujana Towers Ltd. and Sujana Universal India Ltd. Going by the list, both companies in the Sujana group together had defaulted loans worth Rs. 920 crore to two public sector banks, viz., Central Bank of India and Bank of India. Besides the two companies, the Sujana Group also runs another company - Sunjana Metal Products. All the three are listed on Indian bourses.

Over the last few years, the Sujana group of companies were not in a good financial position as reflected through their balance sheets and share prices. These companies were either making losses or managing single digit profits for several quarters. For the financial year ended March 2014, Sujana Metals posted a loss of Rs. 38 core, Sujana Universal, a loss of Rs. 6.3 crore and Sujana Towers logged a net profit of Rs. 1.8 crore.

Between the fiscal years 2011 and 2014, the debt burden on the books of Sujana Towers grew to Rs. 1750 crore from Rs. 565 crore and market capitalization declined to Rs. 37 crore from Rs. 1534 crore. Shares of Sujana Towers eroded almost 94 per cent of their value of 2007. Interestingly, banks continued to lend to the company even though the stress on its balance sheet was evident. Worse still, most of the loan exposure of banks to this company had become bad. If such is the complacency of the banks and if RBI remains only a spectator, CDR ends up as an abuse and fraud on the nation.

3.4 Failure of Lehman Brothers

The one incident that shook the entire world is the failure of Lehman Brothers, USA. The corporate world was taken aback, when the said firm filed for bankruptcy petition on September 15, 2008. This was reported to be the biggest filing in the corporate history of USA. Lehmans' demise also made it the largest victim of the U.S.[9] **'The subprime mortgage-induced financial crisis'** had swept through global financial markets in 2008. Lehman's collapse was a seminal event that greatly intensified the 2008 crisis and contributed to the erosion of close to $10 trillion in market capitalization from global equity markets.

History of Lehman Brothers: Lehman Brothers had humble origins, tracing its roots back to a small general store that was founded by a German immigrant Henry Lehman in Montgomery, Alabama in 1844. In 1850, Henry Lehman and his brothers, Emanuel and Mayer, founded Lehman Brothers. While the firm prospered over the following decades as the U.S. economy grew into an international powerhouse. In 2003 and 2004, when there was boom in Housing Sector, Lehman acquired five mortgage lenders, including subprime lender BNC Mortgage and Aurora Loan Services. The firm securitized $146 billion of mortgages in 2006, a 10% increase from 2005. Lehman reported record profits every year from 2005 to 2007. In 2007, the firm reported net income of a record $4.2 billion on revenue of $19.3 billion. Consequently, its stock price soared to an all time high. Later there were troubles in the US Housing market leading to failure in the mortgages. As a consequence, the stock price had gone down significantly affecting its profitability.

Since then, there was no opportunity available to the company to recover. Moreso, its huge portfolio of mortgage securities made it increasingly vulnerable to deteriorating market conditions. All this led to the fall in the value of assets (mortgaged loans) leading to its final failure. These developments led to a 42% plunge in the value of the stock. This created ripples in the corporate circles of many countries, except India for the reason that there is no much integration of the Indian banking system with that of the world and also due to the fact that banks in India are accustomed to traditional lending methods. Nevertheless, we have cases of dishonesty in terms of NPA and debt restructuring.

3.5 Insider Trading

This has emerged as a menace in the developed and developing countries. As a matter of fact, it is the Securities Exchange Commission (SEC) of USA that made an attempt to frame guidelines for containing this problem. As far as India is concerned, it is the SEBI that started taking action as the stock market regulator. It has issued comprehensive guidelines using the powers conferred on it [SEBI Act, 1992] in the name of SEBI (Prohibition of Insider Trading) Regulations, 2015.

3.5.1 Definition of an Insider

According to these regulations, an 'insider' is a person who is: (i) a connected person; or (ii) in possession of or having access to unpublished price sensitive information. The connected person could be any person who is a director the company, or is deemed to be a director of that company and an officer or an employee of the company holding substantial position and having business relationship between himself and the company. The other important condition is that trading should have taken place using such sensitive information. Depending on the urgency, SEBI has the power to order for an investigation into the matter.

3.5.2 Code of Fair Disclosure

In order to ensure availability of information to all the stakeholders particularly to all traders in the Stock Exchanges, SEBI has formulated 'Code of Fair Disclosure and Conduct' for compliance by all the listed companies. As per the code, the board of directors of every company shall formulate and publish on its official website, a code of practices and procedures for fair disclosure of unpublished price sensitive information. This code of practices needs to cover all significant aspects that can cause variations in the prices of stocks, such as dividend declarations, stock options, issue of securities, contracts, growth trends, collaborations, and many other important matters. The crucial issue in this regard is that the information suppressed shall have some relation with the stock price movements. Further, it is also obligatory on the part of the company to inform the concerned Exchange all changes or amendments made to this code.

3.5.3 Code of Conduct

Yet another requirement for ensuring fair trading in the securities of listed companies is that every listed company and market intermediary shall formulate a code of conduct to regulate, monitor and report trading by its employees and other connected persons. It shall be insisted that every company adopts the code to ensure best practices. It is the duty of every employee or the concerned person to handle unpublished price sensitive information in the course of business operations for the purpose of the company. He is not supposed to utilize the same and take undue advantage by buying or selling shares in the stock market. The same also applies to every market intermediary like the merchant bankers, registrars to the issue, bankers to the issue, lenders, creditors, etc. These entities may also include professional firms such as auditors, accountancy firms, law firms, analysts, consultants, etc., assisting or advising listed companies, market intermediaries and other capital market participants. Even entities that normally operate outside the capital market may handle unpublished price-sensitive information. This provision would mandate all of them to formulate a code of conduct. It is also the duty of the listed company to designate a compliance officer to administer the code of conduct and other requirements under these regulations.

In spite of a host of regulations by the Stock Exchanges, and provisions in various legislations, the insider trading cases are increasing unabated. The following are a few examples in this regard:

- Rajat Gupta, former Director of Goldman Sachs was held responsible for insider trading (2012) and was convicted for that. Recently (5-2-2016), the US second circuit court of Appeals in Manhattan agreed to revisit its rejection appeal.
- Polaris promoter, Arun Jain was penalized in the insider trading case and SEBI ordered seizing of Rs.2 crore gain secured by him.
- In Satyam case, SEBI ordered its promoter, Ramalinga Raju, to return Rs. 1800 crore.
- Two Indian-origin entrepreneurs (Amit Kanodia of Massachusetts and Iftikar Ahmed of Connecticut) were charged by the US authorities for insider trading for making over a million dollars in illegal profits through the proposed acquisition of Cooper Tyre and Rubber Company, USA by India's Apollo Tyres. All these examples emphasize the need to make the law more stringent or take the phenomenon as an indication for changing the behavior and uphold morality.

4. ETHICAL ISSUES IN MARKETING

The ultimate objective of any company is to reach the consumer. As the saying in marketing goes that 'it is not just adequate to manufacture a better mousetrap, the manufacturer should be also able to convince the customer that it really catches mice'. Therefore, unless the production reaches the hands of the consumers, there is no existence for the business. The significant ingredients of marketing are: product, price, promotion and place. In every aspect, the manufacture is required to be ethical. In case of product, as it is already pointed out, the businessman has the bounded duty to sell only good quality products. Besides, while introducing new products, they shall be real new products in terms of satisfying the customer. Mere changes in terms of size, colour, packaging, do not help the consumer. In the marketing terminology, a product is defined as a 'bundle of utilities'. Therefore, there shall be additional utility present in the new product. But in majority of the cases, there is no additional utility, but the new products are introduced only as a marketing strategy. There is thus ethics involved in this ingredient.

4.1 Pricing of Goods and Services

The other issue relates to the pricing of products. Consumers expect that the price shall be reasonable and only reasonable profit be added to the cost of production. The fact is that there are many pricing strategies followed by the businesses and sometimes, the price fixed for a product or service may not have even an iota of relation with the cost of production. While cost of production say is Re 1; the company may sell it at any price as Rs. 10, Rs. 20 or even higher. There is no stipulation at least in India that the companies shall disclose the cost of production of a good or service and the profit percentage (also called mark up) to be added to the base cost. Thus, depending on their own logic, prices are fixed and goods/services are sold. It is a known fact in economics that demand is a function of price and the balance between supply and demand determines the price. Hence, firms have a tendency to create artificial scarcities and take advantage of the people's anxiety for products and sell them at exorbitant prices. We also hear of 'black marketing' done in times of short supply of goods. The other issues pertaining to lesser quantities, weights and supply of defective goods. There are also cases of actual supply not tallying with the 'sample' shown.

Discriminatory pricing is the most common method followed by the businesses. Selling the same product at different prices to different consumers is taken as an usual business practice. But morality cannot accept this. There is the law to check these practices in many countries. The Federal Trade Committee (FTC) Act, 1914 and the Robinson - Patman Act, 1936 are the popular legislations in USA. There was similar Act called Monopolies and Restrictive Trade Practices Act, 1969 in India, till was replaced with Competition Act, 2002. The MRTP Act attempted to check different kinds of monopolistic, restrictive and unfair trade practices and served the public in checking many of these unethical practices.

4.2 Competition Act, 2002

The Competition Act, 2002 seeks to promote and sustain competition in markets, protect the interests of consumers, to ensure freedom of trade for all participants in India and to thwart anti-competition practices. The new Act takes into account the modern issues of globalization and WTO besides the shortcomings of the now repealed MRTP Act, 1969. But the success of the Act depends on the identification and determination of anti-competitive agreements.[10]

According to Section-3 of the Act, no enterprise or association of enterprises shall enter into any agreement in respect of production, supply, distribution, storage, acquisition or control of goods or provision of services, which cause or likely to cause an appreciable adverse effect on competition within India. The key aspect in the implementation of the provision of this section is the identification of situation involving adverse effect on competition. The Act has identified the following types of arrangements/agreements that are likely to cause adverse effect on competition:

(i) Determining sale price or purchase price directly or indirectly.
(ii) Limiting or controlling production, supply, markets, technical development or investment.
(iii) Sharing markets or sources of supply by territory, type, size or in any other manner.
(iv) Bid rigging or collusive bidding.
(v) Tie-in arrangement.
(vi) Exclusive supply agreement.
(vii) Exclusive distribution agreement.
(viii) Refusal to deal.
(ix) Resale price maintenance.

According to Section-4 of the Act, no enterprise shall abuse its dominant position. An abuse of dominant position is said to occur, when an enterprise:

(a) Directly or indirectly imposes unfair or discriminatory purchase of selling prices on condition, including predatory prices.
(b) Limits production, markets or technical development to the prejudice of consumers.
(c) Indulges in action resulting in denial of market access.
(d) Makes the conclusion of contracts subject to acceptance by other parties.
(e) Uses dominance in one market to move into or protect other markets.

For the purpose of determining whether an enterprise enjoys dominant position or otherwise, one or more of the following factors may be taken into account:

(a) Market share
(b) Size and resources of the enterprise
(c) Size and importance of the competitors
(d) Economic power of the enterprise
(e) Technical advantages enjoyed by firm
(f) Dependence on consumers

(g) Monopoly status
(h) Entry barriers
(i) Countervailing buying power
(j) Market structure and size
(k) Any other factor which the commission considers to be relevant.

The organ created under the Act, the Competition Commission of India has been looking into the cases of anti-competition agreements made by the industry. The recent case which attracted the attention of the corporate circles pertains to the anti-competitive aggrements entered by Air travel carriers, pharmaceutical companies, insurance agencies and cement companies. Suprisingly, those that resorted to such anti-competitive practices included public sector companies also.

4.3 Misleading and Deceptive Advertisements

The major part of unfair trade practices of businesses belongs to the category of false and misleading advertisements. These may pertain to false representation relating to:[11]

(a) product features, implying that the goods are of a particular standard, quality, quantity, composition, style or model;
(b) utility of the products containing the need for, or the usefulness;
(c) sponsorships that the seller or the supplier has a sponsorship or approval or affiliation, which he does not have;
(d) warranties and guarantees relating to the performance, efficacy, length of life, etc., that are not based on an adequate test;
(e) price at which the goods or services are ordinarily sold or provided; and
(f) sales promotion and other practices, concerning bargain price, offering gifts, prizes, etc.

In all these, consumers have the opportunity to make a complaint and seek compensation in the event of suffering damage or loss. As per Section-14(f), the District Forum can direct the opposite party to discontinue the UTP or the RTP and not to repeat the same.

Under the repealed MRTP Act, the MRTP Commission also used to pass '**cease and desist**' orders. But such orders proved to be ineffective, because the commission used to accept the 'undertakings' given by the traders that they would not indulge in such practices in future. By then the trader could have reaped the benefit by such unscrupulous trade practices. Many studies have proved that there were a spate of misleading advertisements that lured the consumers public and whisked away with simple 'sorry'. Later through the 1984 amendment, the commission was empowered to award compensation for the loss or damage caused due to such UTP or RTP or MTP. Similar remedy is provided in the CP Act also.

The moot point is that the CP Act seeks to provide relief to a consumer by virtue of his suffering the loss due to the act of the trader. The consumer can bring to the notice of the redressal forum that the goods bought by him suffer from certain defects or there is deficiency in the service and hence he needs to be compensated. The extent of loss suffered by the consumer needs to be assessed and the consumer has to make his own estimate and seek an appropriate remedy. The Forum on examination of the complaint and after giving opportunity to the respondent may order for the removal of the defect noticed in the goods purchased or replace the old one with a new one. As per the amendment made to the Act in 2002, the Forum also has the power now to grant punitive damages in such circumstances as it deems fit. In case of restrictive and unfair trade practices, the Forum may order for discontinuing such practices.

Alternatively, false and misleading advertisements are sought to be regulated through the provisions of the existing legislations:

- The Indian Penal Code, 1860.
- The Indian Contracts Act, 1872.
- The Code of Civil Procedure, 1908.
- The Sale of Goods Act, 19300.
- The Agriculture Produce (Grading and Marketing) Act, 1937.
- The Drugs and Cosmetics Act, 1940.
- The Drugs and Magic Remedies (Objectionable Advertisement) Act, 1954.

Some other principal legislations include:

- The Cable Television Networks (Regulation Act, 1955).
- The Press Council of India Act, 1978.
- The Indecent Representation of Women (Prohibition) Act, 1986.

Each of the above legislations was intended to achieve a limited objective in ensuring protection to consumers.

The establishment of Advertising Standards Council of India (ASCI) in 1985 is a noteworthy development in the pursuit of regulating false and misleading advertisements. The ASCI is a self-regulating, non-statutory tribunal for ensuring ethical advertising practices. Nevertheless, the Government through a separate notification has made the ASCI code compulsory for T.V. Advertisements.

Under the ASCI code, complaints against the advertisements can be made by any person who considers them to be false, misleading, offensive, or unfair. The complaints are evaluated by an independent Consumer Complaints Council (CCC) which has 21 members – 12 from general public and 9 from advertising professionals. There are three types of complaints handled by ASCI: (a) complaints from the general public including government officials, consumer groups, etc., (b) *suo motu* complaints from the member of the ASCI Board, CCC, or the secretariat and , (c) intra-industry, i.e., complaints from one advertiser against another.

On receipt of a complaint, the secretariat acknowledges the complaint and requests the advertiser or agency to provide comments in respect of the complaint. The CCC usually decides upon the complaints within a period of 4 or 6 weeks, once the party concerned is afforded an opportunity of presenting its case. If the complaint is upheld, then the advertiser and its agency are informed of the CCC decision within 5 working days. The advertiser is given 2 weeks to comply with the CCC decision. Non-complaint advertisements are published in ASCI's Media quarterly which is released on an all India basis.

Similar to the ASCI Code, section-6 of the Cable Television Networks (Regulation) Act prohibits the transmission or retransmission of any advertisement through a cable service, unless they are in conformity with the ASCI Code. Further, Rule 7 postulates that any advertisement which derides any race, caste and tends to incite people to crime, causes disorder or are indecent or vulgar are prohibited under the ASCI Code. Section-16 of the Act prescribes punishment to the advertisers as well. However, the punishments are not usual, but the warnings against the advertisers are issued by the authorized officers for the display of advertisements which violates any of the provisions of the Act and the Rules.

4.4 Consumer Protection

Consumerism is the hallmark of capitalism. The movement led by Ralph Nadar (an Advocate by Profession) during 1960s in USA added a new dimension to the history of social movements. There were many other movements across many countries, necessitating governments to make a specific law that can address the issue of ill-treatment of consumers of diverse nature at the hands of business and ensure adequate protection. The significant legislation in the Indian context is the Consumer Protection Act, 1986. The Act seeks to provide better protection of the interests of consumers, which include the following:

(a) the rights to be protected against the marketing of goods which are hazardous to life and property;
(b) the right to be informed about the quality, quantity, potency, purity, standard and price of goods to protect the consumer against unfair trade practices;
(c) the right to be assured, wherever possible, access to variety of goods at competitive prices;
(d) the right to be heard and to be assured that consumers' interests will receive due consideration at appropriate forums;

(e) the right to seek redressal against unfair trade practices or unscrupulous exploitation of consumers; and

(f) right to consumer education.

The Act has undergone amendments in 1991, 1993 and 2002. Of the three attempts in the amendments made 1993 and 2002 are significant. The 1993 amendment intends to enlarge the scope of the Act in terms of the following:

(i) to enable the consumers to file class action complaints where such consumers have a common interest and to file complaints relating to restrictive trade practices adopted by a trader;

(ii) to enable the consumers who are self-employed to file complaints before the redressal agencies where goods bought by them exclusively for earning their livelihood, suffer from any defect;

(iii) to add 'services' relating to housing constructions;

(iv) to enable filing of class action complaints on behalf of groups of consumers having the same interest;

(v) to provide for the constitution of selection committees for the selection of non-judicial members of various redressal agencies;

(vi) to increase the monetary jurisdiction of District Forum/State Commissions/ National Commission;

(vii) to confer additional powers on the rederessal agencies by way of awarding costs to the parties, for ordering removal of defects or deficiency from the services, and for emplowering to recall of goods likely to endanger the safety of the public, etc.;

(viii) to impose punishment on the complainant in cases of frivolous or vexatious complaints; and

(ix) to provide for a limitation period of one year for filing complaints.

Besides, the amendments made to the Act during 2002 are also significant in view of the fact that the Government wanted to pass the Competition Act, 2002 and repeal the MRTP Act, 1969. Those issues that could not find a better treatment in the Competition Act were dealt with through the Consumer Protection Act.

An important dimension of these amendments is the extended focus on Consumer Protection Councils. A three-tier structure has been contemplated at the Central, State and District levels. The respective authorities shall establish these councils in their areas of jurisdiction to protect the rights of the consumers such as the following:

(a) the right to be protected against the marketing of goods (and services) which are hazardous to life and property;

(b) the right to be informed about the quality, quantity, potency, purity, standards and price of goods (or services, as the case may be) so as to protect the consumer against unfair trade practices;

(c) the right to be assured, wherever possible, access to a variety of goods (and services) at competitive prices;

(d) the right to be heard and to be assured that consumers' interests will receive due consideration at appropriate forums;

(e) the right to seek redressal against unfair trade practices (or restrictive trade practices) or unscrupulous exploitation of consumers; and

(f) right to consumer education.

In spite of all these elaborate arrangements, consumer protection remained elusive for the reason of ethics. It is to be accepted as a fact that law can guide and regulate unethical practices to some extent only. The remaining part depends on the voluntary action of the party (individual or institution) concerned. In the context of ethics in practice, it is this voluntary action that transforms the society.

5. ETHICAL ISSUES IN HRM

Human resources are considered invaluable in building sustainable ethical organizations. Ever since Elton Mayo and other management thinkers have proposed the human relations approach to management thought, organizations have started revisiting their concepts and beliefs regarding human resources. Of the two propositions of Douglas McGregor (Theory X and Theory Y); Theory 'Y' is believed to be the one, operationally feasible. The philosophy of development changed the world over rich endowment of natural resources is not considered so essential for development, but for the presence of quality human resources. Knowledge creation and management are being considered *sine qua non* for development. It is for this reason, intellectual property rights (IPRs) are gaining prominence across the world. Under these circumstances, management of human resources in an organisation becomes highly significant. In the field of HRM, the following issues are considered crucial having ethical considerations.

- ✓ Fair and unbiased recruitment.
- ✓ Fair wages.
- ✓ Equal pay for equal work.
- ✓ Ensuring job satisfaction.
- ✓ Providing good quality of work life.
- ✓ Eliminating gender discrimination and harassment of women.
- ✓ Not to impose unjustified layoffs, retrenchments and downsizing.
- ✓ Contributing to the industrial harmony.
- ✓ Planning for the career growth and opportunities of employees working in the organization.

5.1 Recruitment Methods and Injustice

It is nothing but natural that every organization works for recruiting quality work force. In the scenario of large scale unemployment, what is ethical is to devise a proper method of recruitment, that is fair, reasonable and that which provides 'equal opportunity' for job seekers. India, known for providing good amount of job security is slipping into anarchical methods of recruitment. 'Hire and fire' (the concept of the West) is being imported slowly into India. Added to this, private and public sector organizations are filling positions on 'contract basis'. Contract labour has emerged as a big chunk in the Indian industry. As per one estimate (www.livemint.com), contract employees are accounting for 34 per cent of the total workforce in Indian Companies. A survey of 82 companies in India (which accounted for 64 per cent of market capitalization and 46 per cent of revenue of all listed companies) revealed that these companies employed 1.08 million contract labourers as against 2.12 million regular employees. It is also indicated in the case study on Maruti Suzuki that the portion of contract labour is significant in its Manesar plant, Haryana. As against 5500 permanent employees, there was 3200 contract and 2800 temporary workforce as on September 29, 2015. There is a legislation called 'The Contract Labour (Regulations Prohibition) Act, 1970, which specifies the rights of labour and the responsibility of the principal employer.

In spite of the fact that India is a 'pro-labour' country, industry is able to reduce the component of permanent work force to avoid legal rights and benefits. Besides, many companies and government departments are 'outsourcing' a large number of activities to reduce the burden of labour and avoid compliance to many legal provisions. To establish morality and order in the society, there must be security to an employee and others in the society. Lest, social tensions lead to chaos and make the life of every one unpleasant. A practice followed by Japanese companies like the 'life-time employment' need to be adopted in Indian corporate sector also.

5.2 Payment of Low Wages

The other important issue pertains to the payment of wages. In India, there is the Minimum Wages Act, 1948 which provides for fixing minimum rates of wages in certain employments and every employer is bound to pay minimum wages. As a matter of fact, these minimum wages are so low that, no one can make a decent and respectable living with them. More so, the difference between the minimum wages and the wages in regular employment, is so huge that nobody is satisfied about these wages. That is why, the supporters of labour argue in favour of 'fair wages' and not minimum wages. Fair wages include a living wage, while complying with the national wage regulations, adjustments made to recognize the skills and competencies. In effect, fair wages include more than the minimum wages taking into account such factors as : the capacity of the industry to pay, prevailing wage rates in the locality or similar firms, productivity of labour, per capita income, etc.

There is one more ethical issue that is often raised in the Courts of Law pertaining to the equality in the payment of wages. There are several cases in India of differential pays, even though the nature work is same or similar. Ethics is that there shall be equity in treatment and in the payment of wages. There is a legislation in India called the 'Equal Remuneration Act, 1976'; according to which there cannot be different pay scales for different employees carrying out the work of a similar nature. Relying on the Article 14 and 16 of the Constitution of India, Hon'ble courts have categorically declared that there cannot be any discrimination in the pay scales on account of irrational classification of the employees and pay different scale by the same employer.

5.3 Lay-off, Retrenchment and Downsizing

One of the consequences of liberalistion, privatization and globalization world over is the reduction of labour. The labour have a considered feeling that these policies have worked out to their disadvantage. The direct consequence being downsizing, lay-off and retrenchment. A phenomenon of nineties across the globe is the tendency of the business to downsize the operations through reduction of workforce. The single act which created furore in USA during 1995 was the layoff of 40,000 workers by AT & T at one stroke, that too just before Christmas. Imagine how dampening the act would have been on the social and moral fabric of the labour. It was published that the company was implementing drive towards cutting costs and boosting revenues. The surprising fact is that the stock of AT& T, which was ruling at $65 per share then plummeted to $50 over a period of a year. Thus, there is no truth in the belief that downsizing or layoff would enhance the value of the company.[12]

Kenneth W. Johnson[13] has succinctly explained the factors that need to be taken into consideration and the ethical situation of those retrenched and those remaining in terms of such value factors as: empathy, patience, integrity and courage and thus coined the acronym, EPIC.

A. *Those who must Leave*

Empathy – The act of dismissal can be unempathetic, since it negatively affects those who are forced to leave their jobs. This will be naturally very painful.

Patience – Downsizing or cost cutting shall not be resorted as faddish response to the competitive pressures. It must be a well planned and well thought of activity.

Integrity – The decision to lay off the workers also impinges on the workforce. In spite of their best commitment and loyalty, if they are forced to leave, they feel that the management lacks integrity.

Courage – The company involved in the process of downsizing need to be courageous and accept the blame for that.

B. Those who Remain

Empathy – Those remain are forced to share more work, which is unfair. Such organizations put terrible pressures on their surviving employees, and that often affects their families as well. This may also lead to strife between the employees and employer resulting in conflict. This needs to be avoided at any cost.

Patience – Organisations adopting downsizing practices face the situation of more work, less people. This makes the workers lose the interest in the job/duty performed by them.

Integrity – There is also situation that downsizing may lead to extra compensation for extra work. Those who were forced to leave believe that those remained hatched a conspiracy against them. This creates unrest in the employment segment first and later in the society.

Courage – Those remained shall have the courage to stand up for the cause of those that were forced to leave. Such situations improve upon the morality and solidarity among the workforce. That is what is expected to happen in any civilized industrial country.

In the Indian context, there is an elaborate procedure to resort to any of the above practices. The Industrial Disputes Act, 1947 is the seminal legislation that specifies a procedure to lay-off or retrench workers working in the factories. According to section-2(00) of the ID Act, 1947,[14] retrenchment is defined as the termination by the employer of the service of a workman for any reason whatsoever, otherwise than as a punishment inflicted by way of disciplinary action, but does not include: (a) voluntary retirement of the workman, or (b) retirement of the workman on reaching the age of superannuation, if the contract of employment between the employer and the workman concerned contains a stipulation in that behalf; or (c) termination of the service of the workman as a result of the non-removal of the contract of employment between the employer and the workman concerned on its expiry or of such contract being terminated under a stipulation in that behalf contained therein; or (d) termination of the service of a workman on the ground of continued ill-health. There were many cases fought in the courts to decide on whether a particular removal comes under the ambit of retrenchment. The courts have finally held that the following are the four essential ingredients of retrenchment:

1. There must be a termination of the service of a workman.
2. The termination must be by the employer,
3. For any reason whatsoever, and
4. Otherwise than as by way of punishment inflicted by way of disciplinary action.

In this regard Sections-25(F) and Section-25(N) laid down certain conditions to be fulfilled by the employer to retrench employees. According to Section-25(F) the employer must satisfy the following conditions before retrenching an employee employed for a period of continuous period of not less than one year:

(a) That the workman was given sufficient notice of retrenchment, together with the reasons for such retrenchment.
(b) The workman was paid in view of such notice, if it could not be served.
(c) That the workman has been paid compensation which shall be equivalent to fifteen days' average pay.
(d) That notice is also served to the appropriate government, regarding the action proposed.

Further, Section-25N lays down the conditions precedent for retrenchment to take place:

(a) the worker should have been given at least three months' notice in writing indicating the reasons for retrenchment and in view of notice, he is paid wages for the said period of notice;
(b) the establishment has obtained prior permission from the appropriate government for retrenchment;
(c) the establishment has clearly explained to the appropriate authority the reasons for retrenchment;
(d) the appropriate government after thorough enquiry only came to a conclusion that the retrenchment is justified and issued orders accordingly; and
(e) the appropriate government has within the stipulated time of 60 days communicated its decision of acceptance or rejection of the request of the employer to both the parties.

5.4 Gender Discrimination and Cases of Sexual Harassment

Gender discrimination is a reality. The entire world is replete with instances of discrimination of various kinds. Economic, social, cultural and political discrimination is widespread across several countries. It is not surprising to find cases of unequal pay in corporate employment even in USA. The Wall Street Journal (May 27, 2014) has reported that Female CEOs are making strides, but pay gap is persisting.[15] The fact is that fewer women than men are becoming executive mangers; leave alone joining board rooms. As per the survey of McKinsey on 'Global Gender Gap Report 2015', women in corporate boards are too low worldwide. Taking the case of India, of the total directors on corporate boards, only 5 per cent are women; whereas in Norway 34 per cent of the total directors are women (this is the highest percentage). Even in countries like UK (17 per cent), USA (16 per cent), the percentage is low. Very surprisingly, only 2 per cent of directors are women in Japanese companies. They earn less and hold only junior level positions. Therefore, gender pay gap and job rank differences have become real. After all, in the case of Wimbledon, French Open or US Open; the prize money of the women players is far below than that of men. Do we require any other example for glaring discrimination than this!

Discrimination is more pronounced in developing countries like India and turned out to be a social taboo. For a girl child in India, unequal treatment starts at home with less privileged treatment in terms of provision of food, education, facilities and even parental love and care. Low literacy, malnutrition, undernourishment, anemia, stunting are more common with girl children in India. Female foeticide and sex selective abortion are widespread in Indian states, leading to an unfavourable sex ratio. As per the 2011 Census, during the last decade, the number of female children to male children in the youngest age group (0-6 years) fell sharply from 945 per 1000 males to 927 per 1000 males. Time has come in India, that unless corrective steps are taken, this would emerge as a 'social threat', leading to increased atrocities on women. One such corrective scheme recently launched by the Government of India is the 'Beti Bachao, Beti Padavo'. Under the scheme, parents are provided with a facility to open 'Sukanya Samriddhi Account' in any bank, earning a higher rate of interest at 9.2 per cent per annum. Such realisation should also come from diverse state governments as to ensure balance in the composition of population.

As is evident from reports and research, gender discrimination is also widespread in corporate employment. Added to this, the cases of sexual harassment at workplaces has emerged as a new limiting factor. There are two categories of harassment reported in this regard. One, *quid pro quo* arrangement or hostile environment. Under the first one, a superior may offer an employment related benefit in exchange for a sexual favour. In the second, the superior may refuse to give the women employee the deserved benefit, unless she extends the favour. However, it is very difficult to define the expression 'hostile environment'.

5.4.1 Sexual Harassment at Workplaces

Unfortunately, harassment of women at workplaces has been growing world over. Unwelcome sexual advances, requests for sexual favours, verbal or physical conduct of sexual nature, coercion, and intimidation are becoming increasingly evident. As per the information of Equal Employment Opportunity Commission (EEOC) USA, there were 15,836 cases of sexual harassment filed with itself or the state agencies in 2000 with $ 54.6 million paid in monetary benefits. In USA, both state and federal laws protect employees from sexual harassment at work. The Civil Right Act of 1964 is a relevant legislation. Under Title-VII of the Act, there are two recognized types of harassment: (1) *Quid Pro Quo,* and (2) hostile work environment.

Under the *quid pro quo* form, a person in authority, usually superior, demands that sub-ordinates tolerate harassment as a condition to getting or keeping a job or job benefit, including promotions and raises. Even a single instance of harassment is sufficient to sustain a *quid pro quo* claim. Whereas the hostile work environment sufficient for taking legal action is based on the conduct that is unwelcome, based on sex, and severe or pervasive enough to create an abusive or offensive working environment. The other important matters in these cases pertain to:

- Whether the conduct was verbal, physical or both.
- Frequency of the conduct.
- Whether the conduct was hostile or patently offensive.
- Whether the alleged harasser was a co-worker or superior.
- Whether others joined in perpetrating the harassment, and
- Whether the harassment was directed at more than one individual singling out the victim.

The Indian Government has taken the bold initiative of passing a legislation in the name of 'Sexual Harassment of Women at Workplace (Prevention, Prohibition and Redressal) Act, 2013 (Act of 14 of 2013) to provide protection against sexual harassment of women at workplaces and the matters connected thereto. The Act has defined the term as inclusive of the following acts:

(i) Physical contact and advances.
(ii) A demand of request for sexual favours.
(iii) Making sexually coloured remarks.
(iv) Showing pornography sites, pictures.
(v) Any other unwelcome physical, verbal or non-verbal conduct of sexual nature.

What is more relevant in the present context is that the Act has clearly specified the duties of the employer in respect of containing this problem. Such measures include:

(a) providing a safe working environment to ensure safety of women at workplace;
(b) displaying at the appropriate places the consequences of harassment and abuse;
(c) exhibiting the names of the Members of the Internal Committee entrusted with the task of looking into such complaints;
(d) organising workshops and awareness programmes at regular intervals for sensitising the employees;
(e) providing necessary facilities to the Committee members to carry on their work and help in the process of conducting an inquiry;
(f) making available all the information the Internal Committee to enquire into the cases to the best of their ability;
(g) providing assistance to the woman, if she so chooses, to file a complaint in relation to the offence under the Indian Penal Code or any other law for the time being in force;

(h) Initiating action, under the Indian Penal Code or any other law for the time being in force, against the wrong doer.

(i) Treating sexual harassment as a misconduct under the service rules and initiate action for such misconduct.

(j) Monitoring the situation prevailing in the company on the issue from time to time and take suitable corrective action.

In spite of the utmost care and attention being bestowed, the cases of harassment are also reported in India. In a written reply to Lok Sabha, the Women and Child Welfare Minister, Menaka Gandhi informed that 57 cases were reported at office premises and 469 cases were registered at other places related to work during 2014. Surprisingly, the Minister had admitted that though the Act casts a responsibility on the appropriate government to monitor the implementation of the Act and maintain relevant data, on number of cases filed and disposed, there is no centralized mechanism to collect such data. There is thus a need to coordinate with police, industry and employee organizations to check this menace.

6. ETHICAL ISSUES PERTAINING TO INFORMATION TECHNOLOGY AND ITS SERVICES

After the Information and Communication Technology (ICT) revolution, a new world is created in terms of inter-personal relationships and the world has got converged as the digital world. Flow of information has become rapid and information highways and super-highways have come for use by the individuals and companies. Speaking of ethics in this area, the following issues are coming to the fore:

1. Piracy of information and software programmes.
2. Hacking and virus circulation.
3. Privacy and confidentiality of the information and even creation of pseudo networks.
4. Internet freedom.

6.1 Piracy of Information and Software

This has emerged as the most common problem in the IT sector. Infringement of IT Rights is noticed across the globe. Since the computers work and exchange information, stealing and copying such information has grown out of proportions. Microsoft's Windows is said to be the worst sufferer in this regard. As per one study sponsored by them during early nineties, it was found that more than 80 per cent of the software used in Germany, Italy and Spain was illegally copied. In Japan, it was found to be at 90 per cent. Piracy is a big problem for the entertainment world. In the context of a movie costing about 300-400 core in the present-day environment, imagine the loss the producer may have to suffer, if copy CDs are available everywhere. This has emerged as a menace. It is becoming difficult to check these unethical practices. While computers are suffering from all kinds of piracy, it has also been found that companies themselves are indulging in producing pirated versions to face competition in the market.

6.2 Hacking and Virus Circulation

The present-day menace in the computer world are hacking and spreading virus. Hacking is a way of using a computer to get into someone else's computer system without permission. This is a crime committed by the people for making gain or sometimes for fun. In the age of information revolution, information has a prime place and significance. If business is about sharing information, what other businesses are doing becomes highly relevant. When knowledge is centered around 'data bases', peeping into others information is truly unethical. Because of the growth in the internet and promotion of business through e-commerce, data banks have turned very crucial. 'Big data' is now a business. Storing, processing and generating reports are the prime concerns of the business now. Imagine an e-commerce site like Amazon or Flipkart, their entire business is based on the data bases, they create and deal with. Any intrusion into such data bases proves fatal to the organisation. In the times of office administration moving towards 'paperless mode'; every bit of information is stored in the computer or in the form of some input device. Imagine the chaos that may be created, if the 'shareholder register' is hacked and information in the Register is distorted; just before a notice is to be forwarded to the members regarding the ensuring 'Annual General Meeting'. There could be several such incidents to work with.

Hacking turns out to be still a worse crime, if it is related to the 'health research' and 'genetics'. Now after the several breakthroughs and advances in the life sciences research, 'bio-informatics' are the critical inputs in leading the research and even finding a solution to a given 'health disorder'. 'Gene sequencing' is helping scientists to formulate new drugs and develop new therapies. There are many cases of hacking, being tried in several countries. Names like Mathew Keys, Aaron Swartz, Andrew Auernheimer, Fidel Salinas, Lori Drew, David Nosal and Sergei Alleynikob have become notorious on the net world. There are also cases of hacking in India. The case of Ankit Fadia has been in news during 2012, the first of its kind in India. The most controversial issue of hacking has been the activity of Julian Assange, the founder of wiki leaks (a website which collects and posts highly classified documents and videos). Julian Paul Assange is an Australian computer programmer, publisher and journalist. He is the editor-in-chief of the publishing organistion wiki leaks, which he founded in 2006. He was wanted by Sweden and there is a search warrant against him. He has been taking asylum in Ecuadorian Embassy in London for the past three years. The Geneva-based United Nations working Group is arguing in favour of Assange and trying to mobilise opinion against his detention and termed his detention as 'deprivation of liberty'.

Another hurdle created to the computer users is the creation and spread of viruses. A virus is a computer programme that interfers with the working of the computer and disrupts its normal functioning; just as a biological virus causing disease by disrupting the normal operations of living cells in a human body. Normally, the virus attaches itself to the host programme or data and travels anywhere that the host programme or piece of data travels. The harmful spreading of virus may include such activities as stealing the hard disc space or CPU time, accessing private information, corrupting data, displaying political or humorous messages on the user's screen, spamming the contracts, logging key strokes, or rendering the computer useless. Unfortunately, these viruses are causing voluminous damage to the systems and computer time worth several billion dollars each year.

As a response to this menace, computer specialists have come out with free and open source anti-virus tools. Still, anti-virus programmes are pinching the purse of individuals and corporates alike. Many websites run by antivirus software companies provide free online virus scanning, with limited cleaning facilities (the purpose of the sites is to sell antivirus products).[16] Some websites—like Google subsidiary VirusTotal.com—allow users to upload one or more suspicious files to be scanned and checked by one or more antivirus programs in one operation.] Additionally, several capable antivirus software programs are available for free download from the Internet (usually restricted to non-commercial use). Microsoft offers an optional free antivirus utility called Microsoft Security Essentials, a Windows Malicious Software Removal Tool that is updated as part of the regular Windows update regime, and an older optional anti-malware (malware removal) tool Windows Defender that has been upgraded to an antivirus product in Windows 8. There is a saying in Indian languages that: 'why to get dirt and then attempt to clean it'. There shall be realization on the business to check this and many other devious practices for the healthy growth of the software industry and for the widespread benefit of the society.

6.3 Privacy and Confidentiality of the Information

As the number of individuals using internet is increasing, business operations are also slowly being oriented towards using information through the net. With the phenomenal growth of social networking and social media users, information flow has become rapid. This has given rise to privacy issues in this Internet age. Since every individual is also a consumer, business started focusing on getting data about their preferences, likes, dislikes, habits, culture, etc. Some companies offer discounts for sharing personalized information. But still some cautious consumers do not share such information. Offers on e-mail became a growing threat to the public. Unsolicited offers and announcement of winning prizes, lotteries are all flooding the mail boxes of net users. These mails are generally forwarded through others mails.

The major threat to the Net users today is that the companies are sharing (not known whether for a price or free) the information with many businesses. It is the general experience of the mobile consumers that so many unsolicited messages/mails flood the mobile. Perhaps, this could be possible only when the service provider shares the information with others. Thus, privacy is now a global problem.

Another dimension of the issue of privacy pertains to the employees working in the companies. The challenge thus is meeting the business needs; while protecting employees' desire for privacy. The increased use of electronic communications in the workplace and technological advances that permit employee monitoring and surveillance have provided companies with new opportunities to obtain data about employees. From computer monitoring and telephone tapping to video surveillance and GPS satellite tracking, employers are using technology to manage their productivity and protect their resources. The invasion of privacy can be divided into the following three categories:

- ✓ companies snooping on employees,
- ✓ employees peeking into company records and data using the information for their own purposes, and
- ✓ employees peeking into each other's correspondences (through insecure filing systems, for instance).

Owing to these and several other problems, employers were required to frame and establish policies governing personal e-mail use, personal Internet use, personal instant messenger use, personal blogs, and operation of personal websites on company time. A proper understanding between the employer and the employees only can ensure proper use of the personal information of the employees and the company data. The Computer Professionals for Social Responsibility (CPSR), a global organization for promoting the responsible use of computer technology at Seattle, USA has formulated Ten Commandments on 'Computer Ethics'. They are listed here:[17]

1. Thou shalt not use a computer to harm other people.
2. Thou shalt not interfere with other people's computer work.
3. Thou shalt not snoop around in other people's computer files.
4. Thou shalt not use a computer to steal.
5. Thou shalt not use a computer to bear false witness.
6. Thou shalt not copy or use proprietary software for which you have not paid.

7. Thou shalt not use other people's computer resources without authorization or proper compensation.
8. Thou shalt not appropriate other people's intellectual output.
9. Thou shalt think about the social consequences of the program you are writing or the system you are designing.
10. Thou shalt always use a computer in ways that ensure consideration and respect for your fellow humans.

6.4 Internet Freedom

After industrial revolution, the one that has produced profound influence on the people in the society is the information revolution. With the advent of Internet facility, use of websites has become an essential requirement. Not only for knowing things, but also for getting essential services. In today's environment, many services offered by the various government departments are through Net only. Therefore, every citizen is now has no other option except to use internet. The issue now is the availability of the facility to common man. The open Net is central to people's freedom to communicate, share, advocate and innovate. But powerful interests want to censor free speech, block the sharing of information, dampen innovation and control how Net users get online. The contention is that people in the power are making decisions behind closed doors about how the internet should operate. The experts in the computer discipline opine that it is feasible to 'censor content' made available through Net. The methods generally followed include the following:

- ✓ Internet protocol (IP) address blocking.
- ✓ Domain Name System (DNS) filtering and redirection.
- ✓ Uniform resource locator filtering.
- ✓ Connection reset.
- ✓ Network disconnection.
- ✓ Portal censorship and search result removal.
- ✓ Computer network attacks.

There are many cases of violation of internet freedom by companies and governments. It has been reported that companies in the USA, Finland, France, Germany, Britain, Canada and South Africa are in part responsible for the increasing sophistication of online content filtering worldwide.[18] While off-the shelf filtering software sold by internet security companies are primarily marketed to businesses and individuals seeking to protect themselves and their employees and families, they are also used by the governments to block what they consider sensitive content.[19] Even major web ports include in their terms to reserve the right to remove or pre-screen any content, without giving any reason. The phrases like 'at our sole discretion', without prior notice and 'for other reasons' have become quite common under this arrangement, Web companies are trying to interfer into the freedom of 'netizens'.

6.4.1 Net Neutrality Debate

Of late, a major concern has been raised pertaining to internet freedom and equality in treatment. Net neutrality is the principle that internet service providers and governments should treat all data on the internet, the same, not discriminating or charging differently by user, content, site, platform, application, type of attached equipment or mode of communication. The issue of net neutrality has come to light with the violation of neutrality principles by the service provider, M/s Comcast, by slowing uploads from peer-to-peer file sharing applications using forged packets. This has become a big issue during 2007. Since then many governments started taking measures to regulate broadband internet services as a 'Public Utility', similar to electricity, gas, and water supply. Many countries like the Brazil, Canada, Chili, Netherlands, Singapore, Slovenia, USA, UK, and some countries in Europe have framed rules to regulate this aspect.

Looking into the measures initiated in India, it is only in March 2015, the Telecome Regulating Authority of India (TRAI) issued a consultation paper for the 'Unified Access Service' license to promote net neutrality. This paper has generated lot of heat and debate and over a million e-mails were sent to TRAI demanding net neutrality.

6.4.2 Free Basics of Facebook

While there is a heated debate going on the subject, Facebook's Free-basics issue has come up for consideration. Free Basics Programme of Facebook is a non-profit making initiative that aims to bring internet connectivity to the underprivileged in developing regions. This includes a range of services free of cost. Facebook claims that it has been providing such service in 15 countries, including India. It is in this regard, many activists and civil society members felt that the Free Basics Programme of Facebook is nothing but a violation of the principle of 'net neutrality'.

Taking into consideration, the viewpoint of many of the citizen, the TRAI on 8th February 2016, issued an order banning differential pricing of data services by any company. The said ruling prohibits any service provider from offering or charging discriminatory tariffs for data services on the basis of content provider and also prohibits any agreement or contract which might have effect of discriminatory tariffs for data services or may assist the service provider in any manner to evade the regulation. It also specified the financial disincentives for contravention of regulation. However, the ruling does not provide a blanket ban on differential pricing and provides an exception in case of public emergency or for providing emergency services.

7. ENVIRONMENTAL ISSUES IN BUSINESS

There is a great realization that the planet Earth is slowly becoming unhabitable. The temparatures on the earth are continuously rising by about 2-3 degrees a year, since the past decade. There is alround sensitization concerning the 'global warming'. The Rio Conference of the developed and developing nations is a step towards this realization. The deliberations at the conference have contributed to develop an 'action plan' for reducing this growing warming to the level permissible. The recently concluded Ministerial Conference on Environmental Issues as part of WTO negotiations is a welcome sign. At the Paris Climate Conference (COP 21) in December, 2015, 195 countries adopted the first-ever universal, legally binding global climate deal. The agreement sets out a global action plan to put the world on track to avoid dangerous climate change by limiting global warming to well below 2°C. The agreement is due to enter into force in 2020. The Paris Agreement is said to bridge the gap between today's policies and climate – neutrality before the end of the century. The crucial clauses in the Agreement include the following:[20]

1. **Mitigation: Reducing Emissions:** Governments agreed:
   - to set a long-term goal of keeping the increase in global average temperature to **well below 2°C** above pre-industrial levels;
   - to aim to limit the increase to **1.5°C**, since this would significantly reduce risks and the impacts of climate change;
   - to undertake **rapid reductions thereafter** in accordance with the best available science; and
   - to call for **national climate action plans** consistent with the above objectives.
2. **Transparency and Global Stocktake:** Governments agreed to:
   - meet together every 5 years once to **set more ambitious targets** as required by science;
   - **report** to each other and the public on how well they are doing to implement their targets; and
   - track progress towards the long-term goal through a robust **transparency and accountability** system.
3. **Adaptation:** Governments agreed to:
   - strengthen societies' ability to **deal with the impacts** of climate change; and
   - provide continued **support** for adaptation **to developing countries**.
4. **Loss and Damage:** The agreement also:
   - recognises the importance of averting, minimising and addressing **loss and damage** associated with the adverse effects of climate change;

- acknowledges the need to **cooperate** and enhance the **understanding, action and support** in different areas such as early warning systems, emergency preparedness and risk insurance.

The major contributor for environmental degradation is ascribed to the industry. Emissions from industry and pollution of various kinds are identified to be the serious concerns of the economies. Pollution of seas by way of oil sleeks (a great danger created in 1970s), river pollution through dumping of waste, chemicals and all kinds of pollutants and drying of ground water, have become quite evident at all levels and in many countries. Cases of Chernobyl (Russian Nuclear Power Plant explosion), Bhopal (Union Carbide gas leak) Sevaso (the Italian dioxin crisis), the 1952 London smog disaster, Spanish wastewater spill and the Love canal chemical waste dump are examples for the deepening crises. Let us take a look at the news reported on certain incidents that could challenge the environment world over.

✓ For several years, a Du Pont plant in West Virginia had been dumping 10,000 tons of chemical wastes each month into the Gulf of Mexico until it was forced to stop. The waters of the Gulf provided a free dumping site for whose damages Du Pont did not have to pay.

✓ In June 1990, the environmentalists successfully petitioned the US Fish and Wildlife Service to ban the timber industry from logging potentially lucrative old-growth forests of northern California to save the habitat of the spotted owl, an endangered species.

✓ The Environmental Protection Agency (EPA) of USA has found Volkswagan, the automobile manufacturer, prima facie guilty of tampering emission standards.

✓ Oil spill of Union Oil's occurred in 1977, led to the pollution of the Santa Barbara Channel on the California coast and the total costs estimated to be around $16,400,000 (including the costs of cleanup, containment, administration, damage to tourism, fishing and loss of marine life) and in fact the company paid $10,4000, 000 voluntarily.

✓ A report of the United Nations has estimated that the world's 3000 biggest companies lose one-third of their profits, if they have to pay for the use, loss and damage of the environment.[21]

✓ Another study conducted by a London based consultancy firm, Trucost, found that the estimated combined damage was worth US $2.2 trillion in 2008 – a figure bigger than the national economies of all, but seven countries of the world.

✓ There have been about a thousand recorded incidents of pollution from the Agip oil company in the past year. The Governor of the Bayelsa State in Nigeria, Henry Seriake Dixon, recently (March 16, 2016) called for strict regulation on oil companies.[22]

- ✓ The Environmental Protection Index (EPI) providing air quality ranking placed India at 174 out of 178 countries on the basis of the population exposure to particulate matter (PM 2.5).[23]

7.1 Environment Protection Movement

Protection of the environment is the concern of everyone on the earth. There were social movements world over to protect the natural resource endowments like forests, waterbodies, minerals and Ghats. Maintenance of 'ecological balance' is considered an essential duty of the present generation to the future generations. The Lumber Movement (1990s) led in USA had been one great awareness campaign that could stop destruction of forests in northern California to save the rich biodiversity for future generations, in spite of the fact that there was the loss of 36,000 jobs associated with this activity. In another incident, the members of the sea shepherd conservation society have sabotaged 'whale processing plants', sunk several ships and otherwise imposed costs on the whaling industry. These incidents go to show the extent of concern of the people in the society for protection of environment.

There have been movements in India also like the 'Chipko Andolan'. This was primarily a forest conservation movement, beginning in the early 18th century in the State of Rajasthan. One Ms. Amrita Devi with 84 villagers risked their lives to protect the forest trees from being felled on the order of the maharaja. This struggle continued till the recent past and the prominent leader Sunderlal Bahuguna took a 5000 km long march in 1981-83 to sensitise the people against felling of trees. Following this, there were many such movements in other states of India also.

Narmada Bachao Andolan (NBA) is next in the series of such agitations in India. This movement led by residents of the area (across Narmada River spreading the areas in the states of Madhya Pradesh and Gujarat), farmers, adivasls, environmentalists and human right activists was against the construction of large dams across the Narmada River'. Following the settlement of the interstate water dispute (relating to the sharing of water of Narmada), the Narmada Water Disputes Tribunal permitted the states to go ahead with the construction of 30 major, 135 medium and 3000 small dams, including the raising of the height of the **'Sardar Sarovar Dam'**. This aroused the feelings of the people of the area as to the damage to the environment of the area and also displacement of the advasis and others living in that area. Medha Patkar and her colleagues raised an issue on this and led the movement, courting arrests and other actions. World Bank, which assisted the project at the beginning, finally withdrew from the project. Besides the success in stopping the Government of India and the concerned state governments not to go ahead with the stated programme, the movement rendered a yeoman's service to the people of the country, by creating a great awareness about the environmental issues involved in such projects.

Cleaning of the Ganga is a hot topic for discussion among environmentalists. Pollution of the waters of the river is a typical example of the situation prevailing in India and speaks volumes about the scant respect of the industry toward ecology and the lethargy of the governments in implementing the environmental laws. Ganga is the most prominent river in India in terms of geography and culture. The river covers 118 towns and cities and considered the most 'sacred'. The Government of India has established a National Mission for Clean Ganga, the wing associated with the National Ganga River Basin Authority in 2011. The Government also approved a budget of Rs. 20,000 crore for this programme to be spent over in a period of five years. The Central Government also promised that it would provide 100 per cent funding for the activities associated with this project up to the next ten years.

Similar ecological threat is created to the biodiversity present in the Eastern and Western Ghats. The Kasturirangan Report on Western Ghats presents unique opportunity for the governments to enforce discipline and save degradation of forest cover in these Ghats. There is a threat posed to both the Ghats for want of implementing various excavation, mining, dam construction projects. Several issues are raised by environmentalists in Maharashtra, Karnataka, Andhra Pradesh regarding the illegal mining activities going on in these areas. There is thus an urgent need to protect the flora and fauna available in this region. There are many non-government organizations like Greens Alliance for Conservation of Eastern Ghats (GrACE), a Hyderabad based agency, working for the protection of the organisms present in these Ghats and the ecology of the area.

7.2 Depleting Resources and the Obligation towards Future Generations

There is a general argument that the present generation has an obligation to conserve the resources endowed by the nature, which are deplatable, for the future generations. It is a fact that what we call natural resources are limited and if used, they cannot be replenished. There is also an argument by some that there is nothing like future generation and hence there is no justification in this argument. However, John Rawls[24] proposes a blanced view by supporting both the arguments. He maintains that it is unjust to impose disproportionately heavy burdens on the present generation for the sake of future generations and it is also unjust for the present generation to leave nothing for future generation. Therefore, Rawls suggested that the members of each generation should put themselves in the 'original position'. Rawals claims that this method of ascertaining what earlier generations' injustice owe to later generations will lead to the conclusion that what justice demands of us is merely that we hand to the next generation a situation no worse than we received from the generation before us. Thus justice requires that we hand over immediate successors a world that is not in worse condition than the one we received from our ancestors. This principle is also interpreted to mean that the present generation must leave for future generations a world whose output capacity is no loss than that we received from our generations. Thus, each generation must leave the world no less productive than it was given to it.

Viewed philosophically, what is the next generation. It is our children and their children. Can anybody support the argument that the parents have no duty to their children? Societies exist and thrive only because of the love and affection, the members of the society have on each other. If there is no belief in the next generation, there should not be any belief on the civilization itself. But unfortunately, the depletion has gained the added momentum, that certain rare endowments are getting exhausted within the lifetime of the present generation. For example, the International Energy Agency (IEA) believes that oil will peak between 2013 and 2037 and Saudi Arabia, Kuwait, Iraq and Iran (the four countries with much of the world's known reserves) report little, if any depletion of reserves. The world holds enough proved reserves for 40 years of supply of oil and at least 60 years of gas supply at current consumption rates.[25] That is the reason why the focus has now been shifted to the exploration of 'renewable sources of energy'. In India, a separate Ministry has been created to address the issue. The major initiatives include the following:

- Solar cities.
- Solar rooftop grid connected programme.
- Grid connected power.
- Development of wind power, bio-power, small hydro power and solar power.
- Off-grid power activities including bio-mass based heating systems.
- Developing new technologies.
- Promoting research and development.

8. INTERNATIONALISATION OF BUSINESS

After the initiation of measures for encouraging free trade among nations, corporations have spread their operations to various countries thus are becoming global in their outlook and action. Steps taken by many countries, including India, towards liberalization and privatization have triggered the globalization effort so that companies outside the country could extend their business operations to other countries. The signing of General Agreement on Tariffs and Trade (GAAT) in 1947 remained a landmark step in the promotion of trade among nations. This was further reinforced with the founding of World Trade Organisation (WTO) in 1995. WTO is now an international trade body with 162 member countries. The WTO deals with the regulation of trade between participating countries by providing a framework for negotiating trade agreements and a dispute resolution mechanism to make participating countries to adhere to a code. WTO has been taking interest to organize negations among the member countries to facilitate trade across nations.

In the process, it has been organizing several rounds of discussions, significant among them starting with the Uruguay Round (between1986-1994) and now the Doha Development Round (beginning from 2001 – still continuing). As a coordinating body at the global level for promoting 'international trade', is focusing on the following five principles.

1. Non-discrimination
2. Reciprocity
3. Binding and enforceable commitments
4. Transparency
5. Safety Valves

In respect of non-discrimination, it has two major components, viz.,[26] the most favoured nation (MFN) rule, and the national treatment policy. Both are embedded in the main WTO rules on goods, services, and intellectual property, but their precise scope and nature differ across these areas. The MFN rule requires that a WTO member must apply the same conditions on all trades with other WTO members, i.e., a WTO member has to grant the most favourable conditions under which it allows trade in a certain product type to all other WTO members. "Grant someone a special favour and you have to do the same for all other WTO members." National treatment means that imported goods should be treated no less favourably than domestically produced goods (at least after the foreign goods have entered the market) and introduced non-tariff barriers to trade (e.g. technical standards, security standards, etc., discriminating against imported goods).

Reciprocity reflects both a desire to limit the scope of free-riding that may arise because of the MFN rule, and a desire to obtain better access to foreign markets. A related point is that for a nation to negotiate, it is necessary that the gain from doing so be greater than the gain available from unilateral liberalization; reciprocal concessions intend to ensure that such gains materialise.

Binding and enforceable commitments made by WTO members in a multilateral trade negotiation and on accession are enumerated in a schedule (list) of concessions. These schedules establish "ceiling bindings": a country can change its bindings, but only after negotiating with its trading partners, which could mean compensating them for loss of trade. If unsatisfied, the complaining country may invoke the WTO dispute settlement procedures.

Transparency The WTO members are required to publish their trade regulations, to maintain institutions allowing for the review of administrative decisions affecting trade, to respond to requests for information by other members, and to notify changes in trade policies to the WTO. These internal transparency requirements are supplemented and facilitated by periodic country-specific reports (trade policy reviews) through the trade policy review mechanism (TPRM). The WTO system tries also to improve predictability and stability, discouraging the use of quotas and other measures used to set limits on quantities of imports. **Safety volves**, include governments to restrict trade. The WTO's agreements permit members to take measures to protect not only the environment but also public health, animal health and plant health.

There are three types of provisions in this direction:

- Articles allowing for the use of trade measures to attain non-economic objectives.
- Articles aimed at ensuring "fair competition"; members must not use environmental protection measures as a means of disguising protectionist policies.
- Provisions permitting intervention in trade for economic reasons.

Exceptions to the MFN principle also allow for preferential treatment of developing countries, regional free trade areas and customs unions. In spite of the deadlock continuing on the conclusion of Doha Round of Negotiations, member countries are coming forward with their own liberal free trade policies, establishing a solid ground for international business. We have observed in the previous chapter that business firms have grown mighty to such an extent that their revenues are higher than the GDPs of their own nations and by multiple times of small nations. Such has been the power of multinational companies. For instance Wal-Mart, the retail gaint, established in 1962 operates 11,528 stores across 27 countries. Similarly, the General Electric Company (GE) operates in 24 countries. Together Motor Corporation of Japan (founded in 1937) has factories in most parts of the world, manufacturing or assembling vehicles for local markets in Japan, Australia, India, etc., almost having to satisfy customers of 140 countries. As far as the Indian situation is concerned, the top 10 MNCs are present in India including Microsoft, IBM, Nestle, P & G, Coca-Cola, Pepsico, Citi Group, Hewlett Packard and Apple Inc.

In the context of business turning global, their practices are closely scanned under the lense of ethics. The companies have to realize and respect the local norms, customs, and cultures and tailor their practices to suit such conditions. Otherwise, it becomes difficult for them to carry on the business. Not only respecting the culture, but also they need to follow the laws of the land and take every care to protect their land, people and environment. The people of India are not able to ignore the scar on their face left by the then Union Carbide (Bhopal Gas Tragedy). The disaster occurred on 03-12-1984 in one of its subsidiary plants located in the city of Bhopal releasing about 42 tones of toxic MIC gas, exposing more than 5 lakh people to toxic gases. Consequently, between

3500 and 25,000 persons died and about 4.5 lakh people injured. The matter prolonged in the courts of law in India and led to the payment of compensation of 470 million US dollars. Still the people of the city are not able to forget the incident; such had been the devastation, ignoring all the norms of environmental protection.

Similarly, the entry of Wal-Mart into India is being opposed by several thousands of retailers, as it is feared that it would impact their livelihood. After a prolonged deal with M/s Bharti Enterprises and later deciding to go on its own, could open its first store after about four years. Then again, it involved in a great controversy of extending bribes in small measure to officers at lower level to get clearances. These are a few examples from India. Across the world, there are many such incidents calling in question the ethical standards and practices of these transnational companies.

The issue of ethics in respect of these MNCs surrounds the following crucial aspects.

1. That many MNCs operate on global scale without significant ties to any one nation or region.
2. That the size and power of MNCs creates ethical issues involving the exploitation of both natural and human resources.
3. There are cases of raising issues on unfair competition and abuse of monopoly power.
4. Sexual and racial discrimination in providing pay and facilities and in the very treatment.
5. Violation of human rights.
6. Price discrimination as a marketing strategy; even lack of information about the cost of production and pricing strategies.
7. Corruption among government institutions.
8. Production of harmful and hazardous goods, ignoring the health norms.
9. Damage to the environment, both flora and fauna.
10. Illegal transfer of funds and involvement in money laundering.

In all the issues raised above, many big and well known MNCs are involved. The recent examples of Microsoft facing anti-competition case, Facebook on Net Neutrality (Free Basics), Volkswagen on tampering of emission norms, Amway on money laundering go to amplify the ethical issues involved. Therefore, there is a need to agree upon certain 'Code of Ethics', to be followed by these transnational companies.

8.1 Ethical Code of UNO for Transnational Corporations

It is a matter of gratification that the United Nations has focused her attention on this very important aspect and formulated a code titled 'UN Code of Conduct on Transnational

Corporations' in 1983. The code is said to be having universal applicability to states and business enterprises. The major issues covered through the code include the following:

- ✓ Respect for national sovereignty and observance of domestic laws, regulations and administrative practices.
- ✓ Adherence to economic goals and development objectives, policies and priorities.
- ✓ Review and renegotiation of contracts, subject to the changing laws of the host country and follow international legal principles.
- ✓ Adherence to socio-cultural objectives and values.
- ✓ Respect for human rights and fundamental freedoms.
- ✓ Non-collaboration by transnational corporations with racist minority regime in southern Africa.
- ✓ Non-interference in intergovernmental relations.
- ✓ Abstention from corrupt practices.
- ✓ Contribute to the economic, financial and social ownership and control of the countries in which they operate.
- ✓ Contribute to the allevation of pressing problems of balance of payment and finance of such countries.
- ✓ Not to use pricing policies not based on the relevant market prices.
- ✓ Comply with the taxation laws of the host country.
- ✓ Promote competition and not to follow restrictive trade practices.
- ✓ Transfer the technology as per the terms of the agreement.
- ✓ Ensure consumer protection.
- ✓ Not to contribute to the degradation of environment of the host country and take all necessary measures, as it can, to protect the environment.
- ✓ Ensure adequate disclosure of all material information and follow the rules of the game of the host country.

In all, there are 46 clauses which detail the obligations of the companies operating across several countries. The code also made the specific mention of the obligations of the countries in which TNCs operate. They included:

- ✓ Extension of fair and equitable (non-discriminatory) treatment to the domestic and TNCs.
- ✓ Payment of compensation in case of nationalisation of the entity or business.
- ✓ Specify the legal jurisdiction of the TNCs for dispute settlement.
- ✓ Extend all cooperation to carry out the business by the centre and states.

In spite of the fact that there are elaborate codes and guidelines, there are many unethical practices coming to light of the nature of limiting competition, restrictive trade practices, discriminatory practices, abuse of natural resources, damage to the environment, low wages, etc. Cases on companies like Microsoft, Bell Atlantic and Monsanto under of Anti-Trust legislation of USA is a standing example of unethical practices prevailing both in advanced and developing countries.

9. TRIPS AND TRIMS

With the resumption of trade negotiations among countries and the consequent founding of WTO, gave rise to a new era of global business. In order to promote trade among nations in an orderly manner, there arose the need to protect the intellectual property rights (IPRs) generated through painstaking research efforts. Companies carrying on business across several countries were severely hit by the infringement of patent rights, trademarks and other contraband activities. There arose a need to devise a mechanism by which the intellectual property is adequately safeguarded and protected. Thus, Trade Related Intellectual Property Rights (TRIPS) have emerged an important aspect of the WTO terms.

As per the terms of agreement among member countries, intellectual property includes the rights relating to the following:[27]

- literary, artistic and scientific works;
- performances of performing artists, phonograms, and broadcasts; inventions in all fields of human endeavor;
- scientific discoveries;
- industrial designs;
- trademarks, service marks, and commercial names and designations;
- protection against unfair competition; and
- all other rights resulting from intellectual activity in the industrial, scientific, literary or artistic fields.

IPRs are the legal rights given to creators of intellectual property. IPRs usually give the creator of intellectual property, the right to exclude others from exploiting the creation for a defined period of time. Intellectual property laws provide incentives that foster innovation and creativity, and strive to ensure that the competitive struggle is fought within certain bounds of fairness. The protection of IPRs contributes significantly to technological progress, competitiveness of businesses and well-being of countries.

As a matter of fact, TRIPS, was one of the difficult issues in the Uruguay Round agenda, both politically and technically.[28] The issues were not merely new to GATT, but they involved a north-south confrontation. Industrialized countries led by the US, sought ambitious and comprehensive agreement and standards for protection of intellectual property. They pleaded for negotiation to consider a wide range of intellectual property issues and suggested enforcement thereof through WTO dispute resolving system as well as through forum founded on domestic laws and customs. This was opposed by developing countries notably by India, Brazil, Egypt, Argentina and Yugoslavia, which were in favour of framing of rules on trade in counterfeit goods, but were against those on TRIPS in general. They feared that monopoly power of multinational companies may adversely affect the poor by increasing the price of food and medicine. There is truth in these fears and India has to toil a lot to protect its products and processes.

The significant issues relating to TRIPS agreement are of the following:

1. The TRIPS agreement includes nuclear energy, methods of agricultural and horticulture and biological processes and products for patentability (both process and products).
2. It provides for granting product patent to food, medicine, drugs and chemical products.
3. The duration of patents will be 20 years of both for product patents and process patents.
4. There is no specific provisions for licences of right or revocation of patents.
5. There is a provision for protection of plant variety by individual countries and to have an effective *sui generis* system of their own.

In sum, the WTO framework requires member countries (mostly developing countries) to accord adequate protection to the intellectual rights of the other members (mostly developed countries). As far as India is concerned, decks were already cleared for the fulfilment of obligations arising out of these commitments. The Indian Patents Act, 1970 was amended in 1999, and also the law for providing protection of geographical indications of goods had been passed. The legislation relating to industrial designs has been under consideration. Further, amendments to Patents Act to meet the next phase of obligations is also under consideration of the Parliament.

A close examination of developments indicates that developing economies like India are more sincere than expected and are paving the way for imports of developed countries. Whereas the developing economies are required to wait for getting the reciprocal treatment. Further, the patent offices of the west are granting patents ignoring the geographical indications clause and disregarding biodiversity. It is becoming a Herculean task for the developing nations to prove that the provisions pertaining to geographical indications and *sui generis* system apply to them. The patent rights granted by European Patent office (EPO) to the US Department of Agriculture and the chemical gaint W.R. Grace is an instance in point. As a matter of fact, there are several such instances involving grant of patents to the west and western MNCs on the products and processes that are specific to the developing nations. This is rising concern for many companies in India.

9.1 Trade Related Investment Measures (TRIMs)

The objective of TRIMs is to promote expansion and progressive liberalization of the world and to facilitate investment across international frontiers, so as to ensure free competition. From the beginning, there was controversy among developed and developing countries that TRIMs are beyond the scope of GATT. However, there was consensus as to the inclusion of certain provisions in the WTO agreements. It is agreed that all trade distorting TRIMs and those inconsistent with GATT provisions need to be discouraged. Following the above framework, a list of TRIMs has been prepared with items that are considered to be inconsistent with the GATT provisions. There are 5 measures in this list. They are:

1. The purchase or use by an enterprise of products of domestic sign or from any domestic source (local content requirement).
2. That an enterprise purchases or uses imported products be limited to an amount related to the volume or value of local products that it exports (trade balancing requirement),
3. The importation by an enterprise is related to the volume of value of local production that it exports.
4. The importation by an enterprise of products used in or related to its local production by restricting its access to foreign exchange.
5. The exportation or sale for export by an enterprise of products is fixed in relation to its local production or sale. The developing countries are viewing this list as rather restrictive in nature, whereas, similar practices by developed countries (like predatory pricing) are going scot free.

References

1. Drucker, Peter F., 'Practice of Management', originally published by M/s Harper Collins, 1954. Indian Edition published by Allied Publishers, 1975.
2. E. A. G. Robinson
3. http://googleweblght.com/greenTechnology/
4. Health and Safety Provisions as per Factories Act, 1948.
5. C.S.V. Murthy,' *Business Ethics*, Himalaya Publishing House, New Delhi, 2006, pp. 324 -325.

6. www.cpcb.nic.in.
7. K.V. Rao, *'Public Policy and Inclusive Growth in India'*, SSDN Publishers and Distributors, New Delhi, 2015, pp. 129 – 132.
8. Ibid., pp. 120, 126 – 127.
9. Case Study: The Collapse of Lehman Brothers (www.investopedia.com)
10. K.V. Rao & B. Radha, "Competition Act, 2002 – A Critical Analysis", *The Chartered Accountant*, Vol. 53, No. 3, September, 2004, pp. 281 -283.
11. K.V. Rao, 'The Mirage of Consumer Protection', Lecture delivered on the eve of 25 Years Celebrations of District Consumers' Information Centre, Guntur, pp. 1- 13.
12. William Lutz, *The New Double Speak*, New York, Harper Collins, 1996.
13. Hartman, Laura P., *Perspectives in Business Ethics*, Tata McGraw Hill Publishing Company Ltd., New Delhi, 2003, pp. 393-394.
14. Laws relating to Retrenchment under Industrial Dispute Act, 1947.
15. www.wsj.com.
16. Anti-virus, recovery strategies and methods.
17. www.cpsr.org
18. Chadwick, Andrew, *Handbook of Internet Politics*, Routledge International Books, 2009.
19. Evgeny Morzov, 'Political Repression', Net York Times, September 1, 2011.
20. www.ec.europa.eu.
21. www.theguuardian.com.
22. www.forcechange.com.
23. www.fairobserver.com.
24. John Rawls, *A Theory of Justice*, Cambridge MA, Harvard University Press, 1971.
25. www.theguardian.com.
26. http: / / wikipedia / mostfavourednation /
27. Overview of Intellectual Property Rights and the TRIPs Agreement.
28. K.V. Rao, 'WTO – Its Impact on Indian Economy', *Chartered Secretary*, Vol. XXXII, December 2002, pp. 539-540.

5
CHAPTER

Corporate Governance Abroad

1. INTRODUCTION

Unfortunately, governance emerged as an issue of focus on a negative note with the failure of many corporations in USA during 1900s. This was also exactly the reason for focus on the infrequent happenings in the life of corporations like the promotion, merger, buyout and finally winding up. This, in fact, led to the development of principles of "Corporation Finance" by authors such as Thomas L. Green[1], Arthur Dewing,[2] Mead[3] and Mallot,[4] focusing their attention on these issues. It all started with the incorporation of companies till their closure due to bankruptcy. In spite of its significant contributions, corporate financial theory prior to the 1950s was interpreted as riddled with logical inconsistencies and was totally prescriptive, that is, normatively oriented[5]. The major concerns of the field were optimal investment, financing, and dividend policies, but little consideration was given to the effect on these policies of individual incentives, or to the nature of equilibrium in financial markets.

From the last decades of the nineteenth century, the United States experienced a managerial revolution in its industrial organisation. The emergence of a global market, linked by a worldwide network of communications system with millions of consumers created vast business opportunities for businesses. This produced a great spurt in the entrepreneurship. Entrepreneurs had to invest in a large measure in recruiting administrative and technical personnel. With growth in the economic operations there emerged a new phase in the management of corporations in the form of ownership being diverse from management. There appeared on the industrial front two classes of people, viz., owners and managers.[6] Owners invest in the business and managers manage. Thus, ownership is segregated from management in this new setting. The rise of managers to positions of power over corporate resource allocation made it clear that the separation of asset ownership and managerial control was the defining characteristic of the 20th century industrial corporation. The foundations of managerial power lay in the cohesive managerial organizations of technical and professionals that had developed within these companies.

The boom of the US economy in the 1920s turned into the Great Depression of the 1930s. Companies started falling on the stock market. The Great Crash that began in October 1929 precipitated a downward spiral in real economic activity that plunged the US economy, and indeed the whole world, into depression. This prompted the Banks in USA to withdraw funds from the smaller financial institutions that served the nation's farmers and other small businesses. The resultant crisis of small enterprise quickly became transformed into lack of effective demand for the products of industrial corporations. As a consequence, the corporations began laying off large number of employees, especially less skilled production operatives. During the early 1930s the lowest levels of capacity utilization were in the capital-intensive industries for consumer durables and capital goods, and in the industries that major industrial corporations dominated.

The outstanding achievement of the US companies in the Post-World War II is that they were able to introduce many new products, new processes, new management techniques that inspired many including their counterparts in UK and Europe. One more distinctive development during this phase is that the US company management systems were able to distance ownership from management, thus paving the way for professionalism in running the industrial enterprises. This phenomenon led to the need for strengthening the governing practices with a special focus on the interests of diverse stakeholders.

Large scale production in these years also required support of stock markets to raise funds in such a large measure. Thus, there arose the need to ensure safety of investing public by virtue of a slew of measures; including the establishment of Securities Exchange Commission, listing agreement, guidelines on making public issues, etc. It is in this context, businesses needed a code of conduct to disseminate genuine information about the operations of the companies. It is expected that the code would clarify the stakeholders' growing need for information at least in part. The code of conduct clarifies to stakeholders inside and outside about the strategic and other decisions. This kind of awareness generated alround created interest among the researchers and public leading to many studies in this area of governance. The *Fortune* magazine has analysed the operations of one hundred companies from the United States, to verify the importance that companies attributed to the communication of their corporate governance[7]. The study revealed the presence of communications that were able to qualify the ways in which companies establish their relations with the external environment. The findings are as follows:

1. in 65% of the websites analysed, there is an *'about corporate'* link,
2. in 12% an *'investor relations'* link,
3. in 7% a *'corporate social responsibility'* link,
4. in 9% a *'citizenship'* link,

5. in 9% a *'corporate governance'* link,
6. in 6% an *'environment'* link,
7. in 9% some other link (*'host community'*, *'sustainability'*, *'our values'*, etc.).

Interestingly, the *'about corporate'* link, provided information to investors, about the company, directors, promoters, investors, creditors and various other entities connected with the company. It is also revealed through the study that in about 58% of the cases, a code existed (of conduct or ethics) and the same was incorporated into the corporate governance structure.

This was followed by the *'corporate social report'* (15%), the *'corporate citizenship report'* (14%), the *'sustainability report'* (9%) and the *'environmental report'* (3%). The percentage for *'other'* (45%) is high because this comprises numerous tools, which are neither reports, nor codes, but generally tend to describe the activities performed by the company. It also includes 13% percentage referred to cases where a charitable foundation, usually created to finance scientific research or to protect Third World children. It is also interesting to note that often, in the cases analysed, there is no single communication tool but several, usually the code together with a report. This could indicate that most companies prefer to concentrate on a specific tool which provides information about the company's core responsibilities.

A few limitations identified through the studies pertain to the following:

1. The coverage of communication through websites is not so wide, as generally believed; since a vast majority of the people do not have access to the Internet.
2. There is no specific distinction between priority and non-priority areas of communication.
3. The generic and partial nature of information made available through public sources is not highly appreciated by the stakeholders.
4. In the context of changing responses from the stakeholders, there is every need to transform the style of corporate functioning and reporting.

2. UK'S EXPERIENCE

Discussions on Corporate Governance, world over, centred around the experience of the United Kingdom. It all started with the constitution of the Committee by the Government of UK in May 1991 under Chairmanship of Sir Adrian Cadbury, CEO of the Cadbury Confectionery Company. The Committee also included the senior industry executives, financial specialists and academicians. The broad mandate of the Committee was to address the financial aspects of corporate governance. After a thorough study, the committee submitted its report in December 1992.

2.1 Cadbury Committee

It would be interesting to know the backdrop of the constitution of the Committee by the UK Government, i.e., the environment surrounding the establishment of the committee. For one reason, that was the time when several companies collapsed including the bigger ones like Ferranti, Colorol, Pollypeck, Maxwell, and Bank of Credit and Commerce International. These failures were then termed 'scandalous' and proved to be the result of weak governance. It was observed that the executive directors (EDs) have heavily dominated the Boards of Companies. As per the data of the *Financial Times* (1998) for 500 companies, it is only in case of 21 companies, outside directors comprise the majority in the Boards. This means that the Boards are heavily oriented towards executives working with the company. Furthermore, a single individual jointly held the positions of Chief Executive Officer (CEO) and Chairman of the Board (COB) for 349 of the Fortune 500 and 328 of the FT 400. These findings motivated the Government of UK to study the problem in its entirety and thus appointed this committee.

2.1.1 Code of Best Practice

As indicated earlier, the Cadbury Committee submitted its report in December 1992 with a set of recommendations on the structure and responsibilities of the Boards, directors, institutional investors, auditors, etc. The significant aspect of the recommendations of the Committee pertains to its promulgation of the "Code of Best Practice" with 19 clauses, as detailed below. This code was accepted and incorporated into the Listing Rules by the London Stock Exchange (LSE).

A. Compliance with the Code of Best Practice

1 As per the code all listed companies registered in the UK should comply with the Code of Best Practice.
2. The companies are also required to make a statement about their compliance with the code in the annual report and accounts. The reasons for non-compliance, if any, should be indicated.
3. Auditors of the company shall review the compliance statement of the company. If there is any shortcoming, the same shall be brought to the notice of the company and also to the Auditing Practices Board.
4. All the stakeholders shall cooperate with the company in the implementation of the code. Not only cooperation, but they are also required to use their influence through associations to put the code in practice.

B. *Keeping the Code up to Date*

5. It is also the duty of the companies to update the code to broad base the matters and also to take into account the changing business situations and the government.

C. *Directors' Service Contracts*

6. It is the responsibility of the state to amend the relevant company legislations to make them fall in line with the code. It is the duty of company to record all service contracts with the directors of the company.

D. *Interim Reporting*

7. The interim reports of the company may include balance sheet and cash flows and income statement. The interim reports should be reviewed by the auditors and the Auditing Practices Board should develop appropriate guidance. The Accounting Standards Board in conjunction with the London Stock Exchange should clarify the accounting rules which companies should follow in preparing interim reports.

E. *Enhancing the Perceived Objectivity of the Audit*

8. It is also the obligation of the listed companies to declare the remuneration paid to the auditors for audit and non-audit services separately. There is a criticism that the auditors of the company are paid several times more for non-audit services than for audit services; which is the primary duty.
9. It is also advised to formulate separate guidelines for the rotation of auditors.

F. *Enhancing the Effectiveness of the Audit*

10. It has been realized that there shall be an effective system of internal control put in place by the company. It is the duty of the accountants to draw up criteria for assessing effective systems of internal control and guidance for companies and auditors.
11. The accounts of the company are to be prepared keeping in view the conventions and practices. The accounting bodies are supposed to prepare standards for better reporting and compliance.
12. It is also the responsibility of the companies to prepare and submit reports on internal control systems and their utility.
13. The government should take all the necessary measures to protect the auditors while they report mismanagement of funds or fraud happening in the company. If necessary, the government can make a law in this regard.
14. The accountancy profession together with the legal profession should consider the question of illegal acts if any other than fraud.

15. It is also the duty of the accountants to improve the standards of the profession by virtue of good practices.
16. **Institutional investors** shall disclose their policies on the use of voting rights vested in them to ensure transparency and fair dealing.

G. Endorsement of Work by Others

17. The reporting practices also need to be brought to the notice of the workers of the company for promoting congenial relationship between the employer and the employee.
18. To the extent desired, the auditors of the company are expected to submit an expanded report giving all the pertinent details.
19. The code also recognized the role shareholders in setting good practices and for the improvement of the code.[8]

2.2 Greenbury Committee

While the Cadbury Committee focused its attention on the financial reporting, this Committee was asked to focus its attention on Directors' Remuneration. The committee submitted its report in 1995, recommending the "Code of Best Practice" in respect of directors' remuneration. The important clauses are mentioned below for better understanding.

1. It has been realized that companies do have an obligation to declare the policy and practice in fixing remuneration to directors.
2. It is recommended to the London Stock Exchange to make the following obligations to the listed companies:
   - To include in their annual remuneration committee reports to shareholders or their annual reports together with areas of non-compliance.
   - To comply with the provisions of the code with respect to changes of working which may be desirable for legal or technical reasons.
3. To set up remuneration committees of non-executive directors to determine on their behalf, and on behalf of the shareholders and to request the committees to frame policy regarding the remuneration packages for each of the executive directors, including pension rights and any compensation payments.
4. The chairmen of the committees shall be responsible to shareholders through the means specified in this code for the decisions their committees take.
5. To take enough care to see that these committees are formed with non-executive directors having no personal financial interest other than as shareholders. Measures shall also be taken to see that there is no conflict of interest among directors.

6. To ensure determination of remuneration of the non-executive directors, including members of the remuneration committee, within the limits set in the Articles of Association.
7. To make a report each year to the shareholders on behalf of the Board regarding the payment of remuneration to the directors.
8. To approve all new long-term incentive schemes (including stock options) whether payable in cash or shares.
9. To fix the remuneration to the directors in such a way that it will be attractive to retain and motivate them of the quality required but should avoid paying more than necessary for this purpose.
10. The performance-related elements of remuneration should be designed to align the interests of directors and shareholders and to give directors keen incentives to perform at the highest levels.
11. The Remuneration Committee should also keep a watch on the performance of the directors, so as to reward for better performance and punish for unsatisfactory performance.
12. The compensation packages designed by the committee shall be such that there is no scope for directors making money through other methods.[9]

2.3 Hampel Committee

This is the third committee constituted by a cross section of companies and associations of UK with the objective of improving upon the corporate governance. The committee was chaired by Sir Ronald Hampel, the Chairman of ICI PLC and included a chief executive, a financial director, a lawer, an accountant, an actuary, a fund manager and a stock broker. The main task of the committee was to make suitable recommendations to promote high standards of corporate governance in the interest of investor protection and in order to preserve and enhance the standing of the companies listed on the LSE. More specifically, the committee was asked to:

- review the operation of the Cadbury Committee's *Code of Best Practice* and make recommendations for changes if necessary;
- review the role of executive and non-executive directors;
- review the *Code of Best practice* developed by the Greenbury Committee;
- specify the role of shareholders in corporate governance;
- specify the role of auditors in corporate governance; and
- deal with any other relevant matters.

Keeping in view the terms of reference, the committee focused on a document consisting of the following:

(a) a set of principles of corporate governance;
(b) a code of good corporate governance practice.

Basing on the above, the principles set out in the report are as detailed below:

A. Directors Board

I. **The Board:** Every listed company should be headed by an effective board which should lead and control the company.

II. **Chairman and Chief Executive Officer:** There are two key tasks at the top of every public company – the running of the Board and the executive responsibility for the running of the company's business. A decision to combine these roles in one individual should be publicly explained.

III. **Board Balance:** The Board should include a balance of executive directors and non-executive directors (including independent non-executives).

IV. **Supply of Information:** The board should be supplied in a timely fashion with information in a form and a quality appropriate to enable it to discharge its duties.

V. **Appointments to the Board:** There should be a formal and transparent procedure for the appointment of new directors to the board.

VI. **Re-election:** All directors should be required to submit themselves for re-election at regular intervals and at least every three years.

B. Directors' Remuneration

I. **The Level and Make-up of Remuneration:** Levels of remuneration should be sufficient to attract and retain the directors needed to run the company successfully. There shall also be adequate provision to link rewards to corporate and individual performance.

II. **Procedure:** Companies should establish a formal and transparent procedure for developing policy on executive remuneration and for fixing the remuneration packages.

III. **Disclosure:** The company's annual report should contain a statement of remuneration policy and details of the remuneration of each director.

C. Shareholders

I. **Shareholder Voting:** Institutional shareholders shall have a responsibility to make considered use of their votes.

II. **Dialogue between Companies and Investors:** Companies and institutional shareholders should enter into a dialogue based on the mutual understanding of objectives of the company.

III. **Evaluation of Governance Disclosures:** Due weightage shall be given to the matters such as board structure and composition, institutional investors and their advisers in making disclosures by the company.

IV. **The AGM:** AGM should be used as a means to communicate with all the stakeholders of the company.

D. Accountability and Audit

I. **Financial Reporting:** The Board should present a report on the position of the company and its future prospects.

II. **Internal Control:** The Board should maintain a sound system of internal control to safeguard shareholders' investment and the company's assets.

III. **Relationship with the Auditors:** The Board should establish formal and transparent arrangements for maintaining an appropriate relationship with the company's auditors.

IV. **External Auditors:** Necessary arrangements shall make to enable the external auditors to report to shareholders in accordance with statutory and professional requirements. It is also necessary to ensure 'independence of the auditors' to enable them to make free and fair reporting.[10]

3. USA'S EXPERIENCE

The passing up of the Securities Exchange Act, 1934 by the US Congress can be said to be the first logical step towards corporate governance in USA. It paved the way for the creation of the US Securities and Exchange Commission (SEC). The Act empowers the SEC to require periodic reporting of information by companies with publicly traded securities. Companies with more than $10 million in assets and whose securities are held by more than 500 owners must file annual and other periodic reports with the SEC, and make such reports available publicly. The Exchange Act also makes it condition to solicit shareholders' votes in annual or special meetings held for the election of directors and the approval of other corporate action. Arrangements shall also be made to exercise proxy voting. The Act specifically prohibits the fraudulent activity of any kind in connection with the offer, purchase or sale of securities, including insider trading.[11]

In spite of the fact that the SE Act contain certain provisions to ensure compliance to certain norms by the companies, the issue did not get the momentum until the failure of major corporations like Adelphi, Enron, Tyco, and Worldcom at the beginning of the present century. There was a great pressure mounted on the US Government to do something about the responsive mechanism; since many directors, investors and managers were directly involved in hatching up the failures. Consequent upon its public pressure, the US Congress has passed the Sarbanes – Oxley Act on July 25, 2002 and the President George Bush signed it into law on July 30, 2002. The Act was sponsored by the US Senator Paul Sarbanes and US Representative Michael Oxley; hence the Sarbanes-Oxley Act.

3.1 Sarbanes – Oxley Act, 2002

Thus, SOX (short form of the Act) was the most significant piece of financial legislation having a profound effect on the corporate affairs. The Act also impacted the accounting profession, auditing, and financial reporting of public companies. SOX is considered significant in respect of the following:

1. SOX is the legislation that focused on the reporting practices. Through this Act, a quasi-governmental organization called Public Company Accounting Oversight Board (PCAOB) was charged with the responsibility of regulating the accounting profession. The PCAOB was directed to work in collaboration with the Securities and Exchange Commission (SEC) to oversee all public accounting firms and public companies. PCAOB is designed to operate under the same jurisdiction as the SEC. It has the legislated authority to discipline any violators of SOX. The Act also empowered the Board to issue standards on its own volition or it may adopt standards issued by other groups or organizations for the purposes of regulating accounting and auditing practices.
2. There are also several sections that directly impact the interaction and scope of services rendered by auditing firms. This is provided in section 201 of the Act. Traditional bookkeeping services, accounting information system design and implementation, actuarial services are a few such services that were included in the prohibited list. The only exception in this case was tax services. Further, the audit committee of the Board has to approve all audit and non-audit services requested to be provided by the auditors. Rotation of auditing was also first provided in this Act. This has now become a law in India through the Companies Act, 2013.
3. Section 302, of the Act also made it compulsory for the CEO and CFO to take personal responsibility by personally certifying both the quarterly and the annual financial statements and disclosures.
4. It is also obligatory on the part of the companies to bring to the notice of the shareholders all the material off-balance sheet transactions and relationships

with unconsolidated entities. Similarly, transactions involving management or principal stockholders need to be disclosed immediately.

5. The most contentious part of the Act pertains to the statement to be made by the company on its responsibility for and its current assessment of (a) the company's internal control structure, and (b) the effectiveness of those controls. The auditor of the company also has the responsibility to attest and make an assessment of management's report regarding the effectiveness of financial reporting.
6. The Act has proved to be highly useful in reporting disclosure timetables on information pertaining to material changes in the company's operations and financial conditions. The Act also made it mandatory to disclose information that was not previously required for improving the accuracy and the completeness of the financial information.
7. The jurisdiction of the Act has been extended to all registered foreign companies and all non-public companies whose debt securities are publicly traded and whose equity or debt securities are registered under the Securities Exchange Act.[12]

Numerous empirical studies and surveys have indicated that SOX has improved the reliability of financial reporting, effectiveness of governance and provided liquidity to companies. In a way, it can also be observed that there is a significant gap in the corporate failures after Enron and Worldcom. Though it may not be entirely ascribed to the strict adherence to rules which arrested the failure phenomenon, but the Act could produce some positive effects.

There is also criticism of the Act in terms of different costs that the industry was expected to bear; by virtue of the compliance requirements. As per the estimate of the SEC (revised in June 2003), each company was required to spend 383 manhours additionally to comply with the requirements of SOX, at a dollar value of 91,000 per company (or US $1.24 billion in the aggregate). Industry had been complaining that this estimate is unrealistically low. The survey of the Financial Executives Institute (Spring, 2005) stated that the cost to companies was 48 times of the SEC's average estimate. There is a feeling among the companies that the explicit costs are but the tip of the iceberg and there is also the impact of implicit costs in terms of distraction of managers, employees and auditors. The fear is that these persons/agencies may stay focused on the rules/regulations, than their professional/value judgements.

3.2 Blue Ribbon Committee

The SEC set up this committee in 1998 under the Chairmanship of John C. Whitehead[13]. The committee published its report in February 1999 recommending the following:

1. To extend the applicability of the audit committee to all the listed companies with a market capitalization above $200 million. Members of the audit committee shall be independent and shall not have any relationship to the corporation that may interfere with the exercise of their independence.
2. In addition to adopting and complying with the definition of independence set forth above, the audit committee shall consist of only independent directors.
3. In respect of the number, it is recommended to have an audit committee comprised of a minimum of three directors, each of whom is financially literate and further that at least one member of the audit committee have accounting or related financial management expertise.
4. It is also obligatory for each listed company to adopt a formal written charter that is approved by the full board of directors including structure, processes, and membership requirements. The company shall also review and reassess the adequacy of the audit committee charter on an annual basis.
5. The Securities and Exchange Commission (SEC) is supposed to promulgate rules that require the audit committee for each reporting company to disclose in the company's proxy statement relating to the satisfaction of responsibilities during the previous year in compliance with its charter. The committee further recommended that the SEC shall adopt the practice of disclosing all the relevant information.
6. It is to be specified clearly that the outside auditor is ultimately accountable to the board of directors and the audit committee regarding the disclosures and other financial information.
7. It is also necessary that the audit committee specify that it is responsible for ensuring a report from the outside auditors of a formal written statement delineating all relationships between the auditor and the company, consistent with Independence Standards Board Standard 1. The audit committee is also responsible for engaging in a dialogue to ensure objectivity and independence in the disclosure of information.
8. The committee also recommended that the outside auditor discusses with the audit committee the auditor's judgments about the quality and practices in case of financial reporting. The outside auditor is expected to comment on the degree of aggressiveness or conservatism of the company's accounting principles and underlying estimates and other significant decisions made by management in preparing the financial statements.
9. Reporting companies are also required to include a letter from the audit committee in the company's annual report to shareholders disclosing whether or not the management has reviewed the audited financial statements with the audit committee about the quality of the accounting principles and the outside auditors have discussed with the audit committee, the outside auditors' judgments of the

quality of those principles. Both the audit committee and the outside auditors are responsible in this regard.

10. It is also obligatory on the part of the outside auditor to conduct a financial review prior to the company's filing of its Form 10-Q. The auditor shall also discuss with the audit committee, all important matters including significant adjustments, management decisions and accounting estimates, new accounting policies, and disagreements with the management.

4. EXPERIENCE OF CANADA

Unlike the situation prevailing in UK and USA, securities regulation has been the responsibility of the provincial and territorial governments. Canada has 10 provinces that can pass individual legislations. Compared to other provinces, Ontario and Quebec have additional rules designed to ensure fair treatment of minority shareholders in connection with certain types of transactions involving related parties. In order to have a coordinated approach to address the issue of governance, all the provinces have a forum, called Canadian Securities Administrators (CSA). Thus, CSA has been identified as the agency to review applications and ensure compliance. Since the largest number of companies are listed on the Toronto Stock Exchange (TSX), the Ontario Securities Commission is therefore the lead securities regulator in Canada. The companies that are smaller in size are listed on TSX Venture Exchange. The Canadian approach to governance is influenced by the following characteristics:

- the relatively small size of the Canadian capital markets;
- the large number of small-cap Canadian public companies;
- the concentration of share ownership; and
- the privileged access that eligible Canadian public companies have to the US capital markets.

CSA being the agency entrusted with the responsibility of framing rules, has issued guidelines, so far, on the following matters:

- approval of audit and non-audit services, audit partner and cooling-off periods for hiring employees of external auditors;
- certification with respect to the accuracy of public disclosure and filings like the annual reports, financial statements, internal control mechanisms, etc.;
- composition of audit committees, their duties, responsibilities, and fixing a charter to cover some of the following aspects:
    - appointing the external auditors and setting their compensation;
    - overseeing the work of the external auditors, including the resolution of disagreements between management and the external auditors;

  - approving audit and non-audit services;
  - reviewing all public disclosure of financial information; and
  - establishing procedures for dealing with complaints with respect to accounting or auditing matters, and for whistleblowing;
- disclosure obligations, including earlier filing of interim and annual financial statements,and
- disclosure of corporate governance practices, including disclosure of best practices recommended by the CSA, which may include:
  - appointing majority of independent directors;
  - appointing a chair who is an independent director;
  - formulating for the members of the Board and a charter to fix its procedures;
  - adopting a written code of business conduct and ethics; and
  - establishing nomination and remuneration committees composed entirely of independent directors.[14]

There is lot of literature comparing the governance rules of Canada with USA; though they vary significantly between the two countries. It is highlighted that the governance rules of Canada are based on the USA's SOX Act. But the practices of the two countries differ in terms of their imposition of penalties. In US, as seen earlier, the cost of compliance and penalties are heavy. Whereas, Canadian response has been reactive and fragmented. While the Ontario Government has amended the securities laws to increase the maximum penalties for securities law offences. The principal difference between Canadian and US requirements is the non-prescriptive nature of many of the Canadian requirements. This difference is not simply a matter of philosophy. Rather, it is the result of a deliberate cost/benefit analysis based on the fundamental differences between the Canadian and US capital markets.

5. CORPORATE GOVERNANCE IN AUSTRALIA

Focus on corporate governance is of recent origin in Australia. The effort started with the setting of SOX Corporate Governance Council in 2002. This Council is formed with the representatives of the Association of Superannuation Funds of Australia Ltd, Australasian Investor Relations Association, Australian Council of Superannuation Investors, Australian Financial Markets Association, Australian Institute of Company Directors, Australian Institute of Superannuation Trustees, Australian Shareholders' Association, ASX Group, Business Council of Australia, Chartered Secretaries Australia, CPA Australia Ltd, Financial Services Institute of Australasia, Group of 100, Institute of Actuaries of Australia, the Institute of Chartered Accountants in Australia, Institute of Internal Auditors Australia, Financial Services Council, Law Council of Australia, National Institute of Accountants, Property Council of Australia, and Stockbrokers Association of Australia.

The Council has developed a set of principles to evolve a code for companies in Australia. These principles cover a wide variety of issues such as the role and responsibility of the Board, auditors, non-executive directors, managerial staff and the right of the shareholders. The following is the list of such principles:

It is the responsibility of the companies to establish and disclose the respective roles and responsibilities of the Board and management:

- To declare the functions reserved to the board and those delegated to senior executives and disclose those functions.
- To disclose the process for evaluating the performance of senior executives.
- To provide the information indicated in the code from time to time.
- To decide on the effective composition, size of the Board to adequately discharge its responsibilities and duties.
- To fix majority of the board to be independent directors.
- To fix the chair to be an independent director.
- To see that the chair and chief executive officer are not one and the same individual.
- To have a nomination committee.
- To disclose the process for evaluating the performance of the board, its committees and individual directors.
- To maintain confidence in the company's integrity
- To take into account their legal obligations and reasonable expectations of their stakeholders
- To investigate into the cases of unethical practices.
- To establish a policy concerning gender diversity and disclose the policy of the company in achieving the same.
- To lay down measurable objectives achievement by the directors.
- To disclose in each annual report, the proportion of women employees in the whole organisation, women in senior executive positions and women on the board.
- To constitute an audit committee, which:
  - consists only of non-executive directors
  - consists of a majority of independent directors
  - is chaired by an independent chair, who is not chair of the board
  - has at least three members.
- To promote timely and balanced disclosure of all material matters concerning the company.
- To make companies prepare written policies designed to ensure compliance with Listing Rules, disclosure requirements and to ensure accountability at a senior executive level for that compliance.

- To respect the rights of shareholders and facilitate the effective exercise of those rights.
- To design a communications policy for promoting effective communication with shareholders and encouraging their participation at general meetings and disclose their policy or a summary of that policy.
- To establish a sound system of risk oversight and internal control mechanism.
- To design and implement the risk management and internal control system to manage the company's material business risks and report to it on whether those risks are being managed effectively.
- To disclose whether it has received assurance from the chief executive officer (or equivalent) and the chief financial officer (or equivalent) that the declaration provided in accordance with the law is founded on a sound system of risk management and internal control and that the system is operating effectively in all material respects in relation to financial reporting risks.
- To ensure that the level and composition of remuneration is sufficient and reasonable and that its relationship to performance is clear.
- To structure the remuneration committee in such a way that it:
    - consists of a majority of independent directors
    - is chaired by an independent director
    - has at least three members.[15]

6. CODE OF OECD

Organisation for Economic Cooperation and Development (OECD) is a forum of 30 democratic countries, mostly of Europe, working together to address the issues of economy, society and governance. The OECD grew out of the Organisation for European Economic Co-operation (OEEC), which was set up in 1948 with support from the United States and Canada to co-ordinate the Marshall Plan for the reconstruction of Europe after World War II.Created as an economic counterpart to NATO, the OECD took over from the OEEC in 1961 and, since then, its mission has been to help governments achieve sustainable economic growth and employment and rising standards of living in member countries while maintaining financial stability, so contributing to the development of the world economy. Its founding convention also calls on the OECD to assist sound economic expansion in member countries and other countries in the process of economic development, and to contribute to growth in world trade on a multilateral, non-discriminatory basis. In recent years, the OECD has moved beyond a focus on its 30 member countries to offer its analytical expertise and accumulated experience to more than 100 developing and emerging market economies.

At the G8 Summit held in Heiligendamm in June 2007, the G8 Heads of State and Government decided to embark on an active dialogue with the emerging economies (Brazil, China, India, Mexico and South Africa). The OECD was asked by the G8 to provide the platform for this dialogue process. The OECD is funded by its 30 member countries.

The OECD provides a setting for reflection and discussion, based on policy research and analysis that helps governments shape policy that may lead to a formal agreement among member governments. Unlike the World Bank or the International Monetary Fund, the OECD does not dispense money. The OECD's way of working consists of a highly effective process that begins with data collection and analysis and moves on to collective discussion of policy, then decision-making and implementation.[16]

As a coordinating body, OECD also has worked on the principles of corporate governance. This has widely come to be known as OECD Code. The OECD principles of Corporate Governance were endorsed by many countries and have since become an international benchmark. They have advanced the corporate governance agenda and provided specific guidance for legislative and regulatory initiatives in both OECD and non-OECD countries. The Financial Stability Forum has designated the *Principles* as one of the 12 key standards for sound financial systems. The *Principles* also provide the basis for an extensive programme of cooperation between OECD and non-OECD countries and underpin the corporate governance component of World Bank/IMF Reports on the Observance of Standards and Codes (ROSC). These principles being originally developed in April 1998 came for approval and implementation in 2014, after thorough discussion and deliberation. The following are the key areas of attention under the OECD code.

A. The corporate governance framework should be developed with a view to ensure overall economic performance and market integrity. The focus shall be on efficient stock markets.
B. The legal and regulatory requirements shall be consistent with the rule of law, transparent and enforceable.
C. The division of duties and responsibilities among different authorities shall be clearly articulated and the same communicated among them properly.
D. All the authorities connected with the company shall fulfill their duties in a professional and objective manner. Their rulings should be timely, transparent and fully detailed without any ambiguity.
E. Companies should uphold the basic rights of the shareholders in respect of methods of ownership registration; transfer shares; supply of relevant and material information; voting in general shareholder meetings; and to elect and remove members of the board.

F. Shareholders also have the right to participate and know sufficiently in advance amendments to the statutes, or articles of incorporation or similar governing documents of the company;

G. All shares belonging to a particular class should carry the same rights. All investors should be able to obtain information about the rights attached to all series and classes of shares before they purchase.

H. Minority shareholders should be protected from abusive actions of the controlling shareholders and they should have an effective means of redressal.

I. Insider trading and abusive self-dealing should be prohibited.

J. Members of the board are required to disclose to the board material interest in any transaction or matter directly or indirectly affecting the corporation.

K. Stakeholder interests are to be protected by law. Therefore, there should be an opportunity for them to obtain effective redress for violation of their rights.

L. When stakeholders are required to participate in the corporate governance process, they should have the access to all relevant and reliable information on a timely and regular basis.

M. All the stakeholders, including employees and their representative bodies, should be able to freely communicate their concerns about illegal or unethical practices to the Board.

N. The corporate governance framework should be complemented by an effective, efficient insolvency framework and by effective enforcement of creditor rights.

O. Disclosures to be made by the company should cover many other areas, apart from financial information. These may include company objectives, major share ownership and voting rights, remuneration policy, qualifications of the directors, selection process, related party transactions, foreseeable risk factors, and governance structures and policies.

P. Board of Directors should act on a fully informed basis, in good faith, with due diligence and in the best interest of the company.

Q. The board should apply high ethical standards and shall take into account the interests of all stakeholders.

R. The board should fulfill all key functions, which include reviewing and guiding corporate strategy, major plans of action, risk policy, annual budgets and business plans; setting performance objectives; monitoring implementation and corporate performance; and overseeing major capital expenditures, acquisitions and divestitures.

In addition, the OECD also developed a code that is applicable to the state owned enterprises. Writing the foreword to the report Donald Johnson, Secretary General observed that corporate governance of State-owned enterprises is a major challenge in many economies. For, there has not been any international benchmark to help governments to assess and improve the way they exercise ownership of these enterprises. This code was released by the OECD in 2004. The code has basically focused attention on the following six areas of reform:

1. Ensuring an effective legal and regulatory framework for state owned enterprises [SOEs].
2. The state acting as an owner.
3. Equitable treatment of shareholders.
4. Relations with stakeholders.
5. Transparency and disclosure.
6. Responsibilities of the Boards of State owned enterprises.

Within each area of focus, the code has made specific observations and recommendations. Significant of them are given below for a better appreciation of the task of the organization.

1. There should be a clear separation between the state's ownership function and other state functions that may influence the conditions for state owned enterprises. The organization is of the view that SOEs need to be exempted from the application of general laws and regulations. But this is not true across nations. There are countries that have put in place laws applicable to private and public enterprises alike.
2. It is to be noticed that OECD has made it very clear regarding the involvement of the government in the day-to-day management of SOEs. It said that SOEs should be allowed full operational autonomy to achieve their defined objectives.
3. SOEs are expected to observe a high degree of transparency towards all shareholders. SOEs should develop an active policy of communication and consultation with all shareholders.
4. Like every other enterprise, SOEs also should recognise and respect stakeholders' rights established by law or through mutual agreements.
5. Like the private companies, SOEs should develop efficient internal audit procedures and establish an internal audit mechanism consistent with the size of the operations.
6. Like the private companies, SOEs also are responsible for the company's performance. The board should be fully accountable to the owners and act in the best interest of the company.[17]

7. KING COMMITTEE OF SOUTH AFRICA

The Institute of Directors has taken the initiative in South Africa to put in place the code of Governance. The King of the country appointed a committee on corporate governance in 1992. The report submitted by the committee came to be known as the 'King Report, 1994'. This committee adopted a broader perspective and went beyond the financial and regulatory aspects of corporate governance in advocating an integrated approach to good governance in the interests of a wide range of stakeholders having regard to the fundamental principles of good financial, social, ethical and environmental practice. In adopting a participative corporate governance system of enterprise with integrity, the King Committee in 1994 successfully formalised the need for companies to recognise that they no longer act independently from the societies and the environment in which they operate.

While appreciating the good work by the first committee, the second committee realized that there were many more factors that necessitated a fresh look at the issue of governance. First, a number of far-reaching recommendations contained in the King Report, 1994 had been superseded by the changes in the laws of the land. Many new legislations like the Labour Relations Act (No. 66 of 1995), Basic Conditions of Employment Act (No. 75 of 1997), Employment Equity Act (No. 55 of 1998) and the National Environmental Management Act (No. 107 of 1998) amongst a number of others. The intervening period has also seen the listings requirements of the JSE Securities Exchange South Africa (formerly Johannesburg Stock Exchange) ("JSE") comprehensively revised in 1995 and again in 2000 to ensure that they remain current with international best practices. At the same time, some of the recommendations for statutory amendments to the Companies Act (No. 61 of 1973) ("Companies Act") contained in the King Report 1994 were promulgated thereby permitting companies to obtain liability insurance cover indemnifying their directors and officers. The appointment of the company secretary is also made mandatory for public companies with a share capital. The proliferation of accessible communication networks via Internet also facilitated the exchange of information on a real time basis. Many countries in the world got affected by the currency and financial crises occurred during 1990s. The Asian currency crisis was the biggest example of the time.

Keeping all this in view, the committee designed its approach based on the following seven characteristics of good corporate governance:

(i) Discipline
(ii) Transparency
(iii) Independence
(iv) Accountability
(v) Responsibility

(vi) Fairness

(vii) Social responsibility

The committee commenced its work by constituting the following task teams to undertake a detailed review of the areas of corporate governance in their own sphere:

(a) Boards and directors

(b) Accounting and auditing

(c) International audit, control and risk management

(d) Integrated sustainability reporting

(e) Compliance and enforcement

These task teams, comprising of some 50 or so individuals, representing a cross section of South Africa business and society drawn from both private and public sectors. After a painstaking review and analysis, the committee submitted its report, underlining the basic philosophy that: Corporate governance is about leadership. It felt that successful governance in the world of the 21st century requires companies to adopt **an inclusive and not an exclusive approach**. The company must be open to institutional activism and there must be greater emphasis on the sustainable and non-financial aspects of its performance. Boards must apply the tests of fairness, accountability, responsibility and transparency to all acts and be responsive and responsible towards the company's identified stakeholders. It has been realized that there is a greater need for striking a balance between conformance with governance principles and performance in an entrepreneurial market economy.

Like the first committee of 1992, this committee also has brought out a "Code of Corporate Practices and Conduct" with focus on the following aspects:

1. The board is the focal point of the corporate governance system. It is ultimately accountable and responsible for the performance and affairs of the company. Delegating authority to board committees or management does not in any way mitigate or dissipate the discharge by the board and its directors of their duties and responsibilities.
2. The board must give strategic direction to the company, appoint the chief executive officer and ensure that succession is planned.
3. Companies should be headed by an effective Board to take lead and control the company. The board should comprise a balance of executive and non-executive directors. An obvious consideration for South African companies would be to consider the demographics in relation to the composition of the board. This is considered a special feature of the nation.
4. There should be a clear division of responsibilities at the head of the company, to ensure a balance of power and authority. There should not be any scope for unfettered authority.

5. The Board should ensure that there is an appropriate balance of power and authority on the board, such that no one individual or block of individuals can dominate the Board's decision taking.
6. It is also obligatory for the companies should appoint a remuneration committee consisting entirely or mainly of independent non-executive directors. This committee is expected to make recommendations to the board within agreed terms of reference on the company's framework of executive remuneration and to determine specific remuneration packages for each of the executive directors. It is recommended that this committee must be chaired by an independent non-executive director. The CEO may attend the meetings of this committee by invitation; but not participate indecision making.
7. There shall be meetings of the Board on a regular basis at least once a quarter. This information shall be disclosed in the annual report together with the details of attendance of each director.
8. A comprehensive system of control to be established by the Board to ensure that risks are mitigated and that the company's objectives are attained. The environment of the company should also be tailored to follow the principles of ethics, based on the philosophy of the company and cover ethical values, management's philosophy and the competence of employees.
9. There shall be an effective internal audit function to ensure proper working of the company. If for any reason, the company decides not to establish an internal audit function, the same shall be disclosed in the annual report and at the company meetings.
10. Every company is obliged to report at least annually on the nature and extent of its social, transformation, ethical, safety, health and environmental management policies and practices. Care shall be taken to report to the society of the activities of the company in this regard.
11. The code of ethics of the company shall also consist of information on the following:
    - systems and procedures to introduce, monitor and enforce its ethical code;
    - the details of individuals designated to oversee compliance to the ethical code;
    - selection and promotion procedures of the new appointers;
    - delegation of discretionary authority;
    - training of employees regarding enterprise values, standards and compliance procedures;
    - care taken to ensure safe systems for reporting of unethical or risky behaviour;

- Exercise of appropriate discipline with consistency; and
- offences and preventing re-occurrence of such offences.

Later in 2009, the Institute of Directors has taken the initiative to constitute another committee to go into the issue; this came to be known as the third committee (King-III). The institute felt that there arose a necessity for the third committee due to the passing up of new Companies Act (No.71 of 2008) and also to take into consideration of the changes in the international governance practices. Methodology similar to the earlier ones was adopted by the committee; which included the constitution of various sub-committees and probing into the international best practices.[18]

The key aspects of the report revolved around leadership, sustainability and corporate citizenship, as of the following:

1. Good governance is essentially described as the *leadership*. Leaders are expected to rise to the challenges of governance. Ethical values of responsibility, accountability, fairness and transparency are identified as central to the leadership. Performance is also sought to be measured from the point of view of the following these ethical standards.
2. Businesses are deemed to be sustainable. Sustainability implies proper understanding of the nature of business, society and the external environment. It is suggested to be creative rather than focusing on the routine mundane affairs. The focus is on a fundamental shift in the way companies and directors act and organise themselves.
3. The concept of *corporate citizenship* in the country of South Africa which flows from the fact that is emphasizing on the basic issues like the inclusivity, innovation, fairness, collaboration and social transformation. It is important to note that the constitution of the country imposes such responsibilities on the corporate sector. In a nutshall, *inclusivity* of stakeholders is essential for achieving sustainability and this must be taken into account in decision-making and designing strategy.
    - *Innovation, fairness, and collaboration* are key aspects of any transition to sustainability. Companies shall always try to introduce new ways of doing things. As Management gurus talk about, the key is 'doing things differently and not doing different things'.
    - *In the* context of African society, social transformation is considered highly relevant and essential, since the country suffered from the problem of Apartheid for long. It should be realized that social transformation in a strategic and coherent manner will give rise to greater opportunities, efficiencies, and benefits, for both the company and society.

The report also explicitly made a mention that the companies are required to implement the practice of *sustainability reporting* as a core aspect of corporate governance. This has become a widely accepted practice and South Africa is an emerging market leader in the field of industrial activity. The committee also suggested the Stock Exchanges and the companies to construct a Social Responsibility Index (SRI).[19] The committee is also critical that this shall be an integral part of financial reporting.

8. A COMMENT

It is evident from the survey of the practices followed by various countries that corporate governance is of a recent origin, nineties of the twentieth century. Almost prior to 1990, there is not much focus; albeit there were legislations to regulate the activities of corporates and Stock Exchanges. The Companies Acts of UK, India could be cited as examples for a kind of regulation of the activities of Joint Stock Companies even from the nineteenth century. Ensuring adequate protection to the investors is implicit in any legislation. But the kind of special focus on the issues of governance has begun only during the beginning of the present century. Even though the Securities Exchange Act of 1934 of USA was deemed to have served only limited purpose. It was the passing up of SOX Act in 2002 that changed the very face of governance in USA, Canada and in many European countries. In the context of India, the Companies Amendment Act of 2000 can be considered a step in the direction of reforming the governance practices. Whereas, section 292A make it mandatory for the companies to constitute Audit Committees. The effort got concretised with the passing up the New Companies Act in 2013, replacing the old Companies Act of 1956.

The review of the practices also reveals the fact that there appears near unanimity in terms of the practices followed like the:

(a) Audit committee
(b) Independent directors
(c) Listing agreement

The above three appear to be the dominant forms through which governance is sought to be ensured. The Listing Agreement of BSE, in case of Indian companies, makes it compulsory to incorporate a special report on the corporate governance practices adopted by the company under clause 49.

In spite of all these attempts, the issue remains that to what extent the reporting practices have really improved the accountability, transparency and integrity. The effectiveness of the existing mechanisms is already under focus. Researches have shown that there is a vast amount of diversity. Things need to improve over a period of time. Yet, it is time to think beyond the existing mechanisms in view of their limited scope of operation in terms of precept and practice.

References

1. Thomas L. Green, 'Corporation Finance', Political Science Quarterly, Vol.12, No.3, September 1897, pp. 529-531 (www.jstor.org).
2. A. Arthur S. Dewing, 'Corporation Finance', University of California Libraries, 1922.

   B. The Financial Policy of Corporations, New York, The Ronald Press & Co., 1953.
3. Mead, Edward Sherwood, 'Corporation Finance', D. Apleton & Co., New York, 1910.
4. D. W. Mallot, Banker J C., 'Introduction to Corporate Finance', McGraw Hill, New York, 1936.
5. Jensen, Michael C., and Smith, Clifford W., 'The Theory of Corporate Finance – A Historical Overview', in the Book entitled 'The Modern Theory of Corporate Finance', New York, McGraw Hill Inc., 1984, pp. 2-20.
6. William Lazonick, 'American Corporate Economy – Critical Perspectives on Business and Management', Routledge (Taylor & Francis Group), London and New York, 2002, p. 36.
7. Elisa Arrigo, 'Code of Conduct and Corporate Governance', Symphonya Emerging Issues in Management, n.1, 2006.
8. Adrian Cadbury, "Report of the Committee on 'The Financial Aspects of Corporate Governance', London, 1st December, 1992.
9. RecommendationsofGreenbury Committee.
10. G.P. Stapledon, 'The Hampel Report on Corporate Governance', Centre for Corporate Law and Securities Regulation, The University of Melbourne.
11. 'Existing U.S. Corporate Governance Requirements', National Association of Insurance Commissioners, 2012, p. 16.
12. Yousef Jahmani & William A. Dowling, 'The Impact of Sarbanes-Oxley Act', Journal of Business & Economics Research, October 2008, pp. 58-59.
13. Blue Ribbon Committee on improving the effectiveness of Corporate audit Committees, New York Stock Exchange and the National Association of Securities Dealers, New York, 1999.
14. Robert McDermott and Sean Farrell, 'Corporate governance in Canada', McMillan Binch LLP, Canada, 2004.
15. Eric Mayne, 'Corporate Governance in Australia', Corporate Governance Principles and Recommendations with 2010 Amendments, 2nd Edition, *ASX Corporate Governance Council*, August 2007.

16. www.oecd.org.
17. Donald Johnston (Secretary General), 'OECD Guidelines on Corporate Governance of State-owned Enterprises', OECE, 2005.
18. Executive Summary of the King Report 2002, King Committee on Corporate Governance, Institute of Directors in Southern Africa, South Africa, March 2002.
19. King Code of Governance for South Africa 2009, Institute of Directors, South Africa.

6

CHAPTER

Corporate Governance in India: An Overview

1. ORIGIN

We have noted in the previous chapter that the need for corporate governance arose in the context of large scale corporate failures world over. Beginning with the restructuring of companies on a large scale in the United States and European countries, the phenomenon got reinforced with the onslaught of 'depression' of the 1930s. Again, the corporate failures that occurred during the recent past at the global level have drawn the attention of the stakeholders towards governance; since many of them are ascribed to be man-made hatch-up scams. India was no exception to the happenings taking place at the global level. Failure of companies like Satyam, deposit scams of Sahara, Agrigold, Deccan Chronicle are raising the eyebrows of the people in the society and leaving questions as to their management. Constitution of Board of Directors and their conflict of interests are increasingly under scanner these days. On the other hand, the demand for disclosures is mounting up, necessitating the corporates to devise fair and effective systems to deal with the issue of governance.

2. CONCEPT OF CORPORATE GOVERNANCE

The traditional definition of corporate governance refers to relations between a company's senior management, its board of directors, its shareholders and other stakeholders, such as employees and their representatives. It also determines the structure used to define a company's objectives, as well as the means of achieving them and of monitoring the results obtained. Due to the nature of the activities and interdependencies within the financial system, the bankruptcy of a financial institution, produces a cascading effect leading to the bankruptcy of many other financial institutions. This may jeopardize the very financial base of the country and precipitate into an economic crisis; which is avoidable; provided enough care is bestowed on the governance practices of the institutions. This systemic risk led governments and other regulators to be cautious in permitting the companies in the use of public money.[1] As a result, taxpayers are inevitably stakeholders in the running of financial institutions, with the goal of financial stability and long-term economic growth. Furthermore, the interests of the suppliers of funds like the depositors, policy holders or beneficiaries of pension schemes and various saving schemes are associated with the prudent management of the companies. Shareholders' interests get promoted only when the company makes reasonable profit and grows over a period of time in net worth.

This is true of not only the financial institutions; but of every other business entity. The long-term viability of the institution shall be regarded as the ultimate goal. It is for these reasons most financial institutions are strictly regulated and supervised. In a more formal manner, let us go through the interpretations of experts, committees and organizations.

In the words of N R Narayana Murthy, corporate governance is about maximizing the shareholder value in a corporation; while ensuring fairness to all stakeholders. These may include customers, employees, investors, vendors, the government and the society-at-large. He emphasized on a specific aspect that corporate governance is about transparency and raising the trust and confidence of stakeholders in the way the company is run. It is about the trust between management and the stakeholders. While making such observations, he has referred to the 'Trusteeship principles' of Mahatma Gandhi.

The retired **Chief Justice of the Supreme Court, Justice Venkatachalaiah** observed that "Corporate governance is a new pass word in corporate jargon dispensing with the mental fancies and one has to exactly sense what is Corporate Governance". This emphasizes more on the practice than precept. In the foreword to the **Report of Rahul Bajaj Committee on Corporate Governance In India, Sekhar Datta** observed that it implies transparency of the management systems in business and industry. Just as industry seeks the transparency in governance policies and procedures of the government; so also the government and stakeholders seek the transparency in the corporate sector. According to **Standing Committee on Public Enterprises (SCOPE) of India,** corporate governance aims at evolving a control system that helps in good decision making process to ensure transparency and accountability.

According to **Sir ADRAIN CADBURY** Committee, corporate governance is the system by which companies are directed and controlled. It encompasses commitment to values and to ethical business conduct. It is about maximizing shareholder value on a sustainable basis while ensuring fairness to all stake holders. In the opinion of the International Chamber of Commerce, corporate governance is the relationship between corporate managers, directors and the providers of equity. It said that it is the board of directors that is accountable for the pursuit of corporate objectives consistent with the law and regulations. According to **Robert I .Tricker** (who coined the term corporate governance in 1984), governance is as simple as running the business unit properly. The main difference being doing things right and doing right things.

The Cadbury Committee (1992) put forth its contention in very clear terms stating that the country's economy depends on the drive and efficiency of its companies. Thus, the effectiveness with which their boards discharge their responsibilities determines the competitive position of companies. It is about the freedom of companies exercise in carrying about their activities. The essence of governance is said to be hovering around 'accountability'. According to the **Organisation for Economic Cooperation and Development (OECD),** corporate governance involves a set of relationships between the company's management, its board, its shareholders, and other stakeholders. It is also about the structure through which the objectives of a company are set, and attained. This also includes the measurement and monitoring of the performance. According to **Shleifer and Vishny (1997)**, "Corporate governance relates to the ways in which suppliers of finance to corporations assure themselves of getting a return on their investment". This reflects the true profit orientation.

Nevertheless, good corporate governance is not just about prescribing particular corporate structures and complying with a number of hard and fast rules. It is about compliance and action. The corporate sector needs to get convinced of the philosophy and then plunge into action. It is for this reason, the Cadbury and Greenbury committees laid much emphasis on implementation of their recommendations. It implies, on the one hand, that companies should be prepared to review and explain their governance policies, including any special circumstances which in their view justify departure from generally accepted best practices. The stakeholders also are required to understand and participate in the well-being of the company.

3. CHRONOLOGY OF CORPORATE GOVERNANCE IN INDIA

In the context of evolving corporate governance and reforms in the Indian backdrop, it would be interesting to chronicle the developments in this area in a sequential manner.

3.1 Corporate Governance before Independence

Going back to the pre-independence on this issue is an adventure. Still, out of curiosity, an attempt has been made to survey a few important enactments to understand the line of thinking. Ever since the East India Company set on its voyage in 1600, there had been one sided commercial interest of promoting British business interests, against the local Indians. Queen Elizabeth I granted the exclusive right to trade with all countries to the east of the Cape of Good Hope. Corporations at this time would essentially act on the government's behalf, bringing in revenue from its exploits abroad. Subsequently, the company became increasingly integrated with British military and colonial policy. At this time, most of the UK corporations were dependent on the British navy's ability to control trade routes on the high seas. Speaking in the context, Adam Smith observed that 'the directors of such companies have carried out activities that thrive on the capabilities of the military.[2] In addition, this is considered quite unreasonable. What should have been reasonable is the fair treatment to all those in the trade and industry at the relevant point of time. There used to be several restrictions on the establishment of companies in the colonial countries ruled by them till 1825. A new chapter started only during 1844 with the enactment of Joint Stock Companies Act, 1844 providing for a simple procedure of registration of companies.

But this did not help corporates in India due to low key of operations by Indian businessmen. This continued almost unabated till India got independence. The intentions of the British Government were truly reflected in an important piece of legislation – the Government of India Act, 1935 – which was considered a landmark enactment that cleared decks for India to secure freedom. Under the Act, British citizens resident in the UK and British companies registered in the UK must be treated on the same basis as Indian citizens and Indian registered companies, unless UK law denies reciprocal treatment. The unfairness of this arrangement is clear when one considers the dominant position of British capital in much of the Indian modern sector and the complete dominance, maintained through unfair commercial practices. The often cited example is the shipping business of UK across the continents. At that time, there was no investment of Indians in the shipping industry of Britain. This helped the British industry to exploit all routes of the Indian oceans. There are detailed provisions requiring the Viceroy to intervene if, in her unappealable view, any Indian law or regulation is intended to, or will in fact, discriminate against UK resident British subjects, British registered companies and, particularly, British shipping interests. Thus, there was not much discussion about the Indian companies and their governance practices.

3.2 Corporate Governance after Independence

The landmark legislation that set the tone for company management can be identified to be the Companies Act, 1956; which repealed all the previous legislations on this subject, including the Indian Companies Act, 1866, 1882 and 1913. It may be noted that all the legislations prior to the Act of 1956 were modeled on the counterpart legislation prevailed in U.K. Companies Act, 1956 was thus considered the basic law that governed the creation, continuation, the winding up of companies and also the relationships between the shareholders, the company, the public and the Government. Coupled with other legislations dealing with the corporate world, this was undoubtedly an important piece of legislation. Till this was thoroughly amended in 2013, remained significant in guiding, controlling and monitoring the corporate affairs in India. There were also a few other important legislations like the Capital Issues (Control) Act, 1947, Securities Contracts (Regulation) Act, 1956 and Monopolies and Restrictive Trade

Practices Act, 1969 that sought to regulate the activities of the corporates and thus enhance corporate responsibility towards transparency and accountability. In due course, the Capital Issues (control) Act and the MRTP Act were also repealed. A new Act called Competition Act, 2002 was passed (in place of the old MRTP Act) with a different objective and methodology.

3.3 Phase of Economic Reforms

Economic reforms initiated since 1991 saw a new trend in the corporate relationships. Several amendments were proposed to the economic and corporate law, paving the way for liberal operations in the corporate domain. Securities and Exchange Board of India, which was established as a non-statutory body, was given legal status and powers through the enactment of SEBI Act, 1992. Utilizing the powers granted to it under the legislation, SEBI started issuing several regulations and guidelines to reform and strengthen the corporate functioning. There included the Guidelines on Corporate Disclosures and Investor Protection, functioning of the Boards, meetings, etc. A new dimension was added with the insistence by SEBI of the incorporation and amendment of clause 49 in the Listing Agreement by all the listed companies. As per this, now companies are required to prepare a detailed report on corporate governance in their companies.

SEBI also appointed various committees to improve upon the governance practices. The first in the series was headed by Kumar Mangalam Birla (1999). The Birla Committee's recommendations primarily focused on two fundamental goals, viz., improving the function and structure of company boards and increasing disclosure to shareholders. With respect to company boards, the committee made specific recommendations regarding board representation and independence that have persisted to date in Clause 49. The committee also recognized the importance of audit committees and made many recommendations regarding the functions and constitution of boards and audit committees. The Birla Committee also made several recommendations regarding disclosure and transparency issues, in particular with respect to information provided to shareholders. Among other recommendations, the Committee stated that a company's annual report to shareholders should contain a Management Discussion and Analysis section, and that companies should transmit certain information, such as quarterly reports and analyst presentations, to shareholders. SEBI implemented the committee's proposals in February 2000. At that time, SEBI revised its Listing Agreement to incorporate the recommendations of the country's new code on corporate governance. A new section of the Listing Agreement took effect in phases between 2000 and 2003. The reforms applied first to newly listed and large companies, then to smaller companies, and eventually to the vast majority of listed companies.[3]

Following the same, SEBI constituted another committee under the Chairmanship of N.R. Narayana Murthy.[4] Murthy Committee's work is significant in terms of the following:

1. **Audit committees:** In respect of the functioning of audit committee, the committee made the following recommendations:
   A. Audit committees of publicly listed companies should be required to review the following information mandatorily:
      - financial statements and draft audit report, including quarterly / half-yearly financial information;
      - analysis of financial condition and results of operations;
      - reports relating to compliance with laws and the risk management practices;
      - internal control mechanisms; and
      - issues relating to related party transactions.

   B. The Committee wanted all the members of the Audit Committee to be financially literate.
2. **Audit Reports and Audit Qualifications:** The committee noted that the onus of selecting accounting policies should be placed on management to explain why they believe such treatment is more effective. The auditor's responsibility is to express a qualification in case he disagrees with the explanation given by the company's management. It shall not be the responsibility of the auditor to justify departures from an accounting standard. It shall be the duty of the Board to explain deviations, if any. The auditor may draw reference to this in the footnote without necessarily making it the subject matter of an audit qualification, if he so prefers.
3. **Related Party Transactions:** This is one of the biggest maladies of the Indian corporate world. Families, owning more than one company, generally tend to influence the stakeholders of the company. These transactions are to be viewed seriously as they may pertain to the individuals related to the directors and top management officials. The one example quoted quite often in the recent past is the transactions between Satyam and Maytas. As the name itself is suggesting, the transactions also topsy-turvied. The two questions, one should raise in this context are:
   1. Who is a related party?
   2. What is the arm's length principle?

   In respect of the first one, the Murthy Committee recommended that the term 'related party' shall have the same meaning as contained in Accounting Standard

18 issued by the Institution of Chartered Accountants of India. The standard said that a related party is one who can influence the decision making.

Second, in identifying related party transactions, the meaning ascribed to the 'arm's length' principle is very significant. The Murthy Committee noted that a reference may be made of this principle in the report given by the Directors. Such statement may relate to all transactions with related parties including their occurrence. If any transaction is not on an arm's length basis, management should provide an explanation to the audit committee justifying the same.

4. **Risk Management:** This is the issue that is gaining the attention of stakeholders, of late, in the discussions on corporate governance. As a matter of fact, risk management is an issue concerned with the management, since risk is associated with the business operations. After all, business is risk taking. The Murthy Committee believed that it is important for corporate Boards to be fully aware of the risks facing the business and that it is important for shareholders to know about the process by which companies manage their business risks; which may include company-specific risks, industry, economic, and political risks. In the context of globalization of operations, risks attending to these activities have also to be dealt with effectively.

   As a measure of making the stakeholders aware of the risks involved, the committee has made the following recommendations:

   1. Procedures should be in place to inform the Board members about the risk assessment and minimization procedures. These procedures should be periodically reviewed to ensure that executive management controls risk through means of a properly defined framework. Management should place a report before the Board of Directors the details regarding various business risks faced by the company in the recent past. It has to also submit a strategy as to how such risks can be attended to.
   2. It is necessary that every company shall train their Board members in the business model of the company as well as the risk profile of the business parameters of the company.

5. **Initial Public Offerings (IPOs):** IPOs are the means by which investors and companies are connected. Significant disclosures are expected to be made through these IPOs. Market sentiment is strongly associated with the number and volume of IPOs. This is a matter which the Naresh Chandra Committee did not touch upon. The Murthy Committee strongly believed that IPOs are an avenue to test the adequacy or otherwise of the disclosure practices being followed by a company. In this regard, the recommendation of the Committee is that the companies raising money through an Initial Public Offering should disclose to the Audit Committee, the purposes for which the funds raised are put to use.

The company shall prepare a statement of funds utilised for purposes other than those stated in the offer document/prospectus. This statement should be certified by the independent auditors of the company. The audit committee should make appropriate recommendations to the Board in this regard.

6. **Code of Conduct for Board of Directors:** This is yet another issue which the Narayana Murthy Committee has touched upon. Naresh Chandra has presumed the role of Board to be genuine. Going a step further the Kumar Mangalam Birla Committee defined the role and responsibilities of the management. It also felt that there is a need to define a 'code of conduct' for the BoD. The present committee also felt that it should be obligatory for the Board of a company to lay down the code of conduct for all Board members and the senior management of the company. This code of conduct shall be posted on the website of the company.

7. **Role of Nominee, non-Executive, and Independent Directors:** The following are the key recommendations in respect of the role of various kinds of directors:
    1. Where an institution wishes to appoint a director on the Board, such appointment should be made by the shareholders. An institutional director can be appointed by the sponsoring institution; but hold the same liabilities as any other director. Nominee of the Government on public sector companies shall also be similarly elected and shall be subject to the same responsibilities and liabilities as other directors.
    2. All compensation to be paid to the non-executive directors be fixed by the Board of Directors and approved by the shareholders in general meeting. Limits should be set for the maximum number of stock options that can be granted to non-executive directors in any financial year and in aggregate. The stock options granted to the non-executive directors shall vest after a period of at least one year from the date such non-executive directors have retired from the Board of the Company. Companies should publish their compensation philosophy and statement of entitled compensation in respect of non-executive directors in their annual report. Alternatively, this may be put up on the company's website and reference drawn thereto in the annual report. Companies should disclose on an annual basis, details of shares held by non-executive directors. These directors should be required to disclose their stock holding in the listed company in which they are proposed to be appointed as directors. These details should accompany their notices of appointment also.
    3. The Committee has put in a special effort in respect of independent directors. The very definition has been made very comprehensive. The Committee felt that an ID shall be one who:

- except from receiving director's remuneration, does not have any material pecuniary relationships or transactions with the company, its promoters, its senior management or its holding company, its subsidiaries and associated companies;
- is not related to promoters or the management at the board level or at one level below the board;
- has not been an executive of the company in the immediately preceding three financial years;
- is not a partner or an executive of the statutory audit firm or the internal audit firm that is associated with the company. This will also apply to legal firms and consulting firms that have a material association with the entity;
- is not a supplier, service provider or customer of the company. This should include lessor-lessee type relationships also;
- is not a substantial shareholder of the company, i.e., owning two percent or more of the block of voting shares; and
- the considerations as regards remuneration paid to an independent director shall be the same as those applied to a non-executive director.

8. **Whistle Blowing:** Whistle blowing is now an accepted practice even in the public administration. The Companies Act has entrusted this job to the Audit Committee to ensure the establishment of 'vigil mechanism'. The Companies Act makes it obligatory for every company to establish a vigil mechanism. The requirements as per the provisions of the Act are:
   - every listed company shall establish a vigil mechanism for directors and employees to report genuine concerns; and
   - such vigil mechanism shall also provide for adequate safeguards against victimization of persons who use such mechanism and make provision for direct access to the chairperson of the audit committee in appropriate or exceptional cases.

9. **Other Recommendations:** The Committee also focused its attention on some other significant aspects, which included the following:
   - in the case of associate companies, the requirements specified above may be made applicable to subsidiary companies also;
   - the Central Government shall amend the Companies Act, 1956 to exclude common directorships in the holding and subsidiary companies, in computing the limits on directorships that an individual may hold;
   - the provisions relating to the composition of the Board of Directors of the holding company shall also be made applicable to the composition of the Board of Directors of subsidiary companies;

- at least one-third of the Board of Directors of the subsidiary company shall be non-executive directors of the parent company;
- the Audit Committee of the parent company shall also review the financial statements of the subsidiary company;
- the minutes of the Board meeting of the subsidiary company shall be placed for review at the Board meeting of the parent company; and
- the Board report of the parent company should state that they have reviewed the affairs of the subsidiary company also.

Again, an appreciable initiative was taken by the Confederation of Indian Industry (CII), (an industry association) to appoint a task force under the leadership of Naresh Chandra.[5] This task force made many sweeping recommendations that had gone a long way in amending finally the Companies Act, 1956. Significant among them are as follows:

I. Role of the Board of Directors

I.1. Non-Executive and Independent Directors

In respect of Non-Executive Directors (NEDs) and Independent Directors (IDs), the Task Force (TF) has touched upon the following aspects:

(i) Appointment
(ii) Duties and Liabilities
(iii) Remuneration.

As regards the appointment of NEDs or IDs, the TF has recommended that all the listed companies have Nominations Committee, comprising a majority of independent directors, including its chairman. This Committee's task should be to:

- search for, evaluate, shortlist and recommend appropriate independent directors and NEDs, subject to the broad directions of the full Board; and
- design processes for evaluating the effectiveness of individual directors as well as the Board as a whole.

The Nomination Committee should also be the body that evaluates and recommends the appointment of executive directors.

A separate section in the chapter on corporate governance in the annual reports of listed companies could outline the work done by the Nomination Committee during the year under consideration.

Second, the TF has done an elaborate exercise in designing the format and recommended that a Letter of Appointment be issued to every NED or ID, just as it is done in case of appointing employees and executive directors. The letter is supposed to address the following aspects:

- specify the expectation of the Board from the appointed director;
- the Board-level committee (s) in which the director is expected to serve and its tasks;
- the fiduciary duties that come with such an appointment;
- the term of the appointment;
- the Code of Business Ethics that the company expects its directors and employees to follow;
- the list of actions that a director cannot do in the company;
- the liabilities that accompany such a fiduciary position, including whether the concerned director is covered by any Directors and Officers (D&O) insurance; and
- the remuneration, including sitting fees and stock options, if any.

The letter stating the terms and conditions of appointment of any NED or independent director should form a part of the disclosure to shareholders at the time of the ratification of his/her appointment or re-appointment to the Board. This issue was not addressed by the New Companies Act, 2013.

Third, in respect of payment of compensation to the NEDs and IDs for their services, the TF has made the following recommendations.

A. Fixed Contractual Remuneration

The Task Force recommended that the Companies Act, 1956, be amended so that companies have the option of giving a fixed contractual remuneration to NEDs and independent directors, which is not linked to the net profit or lack of it. Therefore, companies should be given the option to choose between:

(a) paying a fixed contractual remuneration to its NEDs and IDs, subject to an appropriate ceiling depending on the size of the company; or
(b) continuing with the existing practice of paying out up to 1% (or 3%) of the net profits of the standalone entity as defined in the Companies Act, 1956.

For any company, the choice should be uniform for all NEDs and independent directors, i.e., some cannot be paid a commission of profits; while others are paid a fixed amount. If the option chosen is (a) above, then the NEDs and independent directors will not be eligible for any commission on profits. The current limits and constraints on sitting fees and stock options or restricted stock may remain unchanged. If stock options are granted as a form of payment to NEDs and independent directors, then these must be held by the concerned director until one year of his exit from the Board.

Constitution of Committees of the Board

Having examined thoroughly the practices prevailing then in the corporate world, the TF has recommended to the Government to constitute the following two committees:

1. Remuneration Committee.
2. Audit Committee.

In addition, the TF has also indicated the structure and other issues to be taken into account in constitution. The following recommendations of the TF are significant in this regard.

1. Remunerations Committee
2. Audit Committee
3. Separation of offices of Chairman & Chief Executive Officer
4. Board meetings through teleconferencing
5. Executive Sessions

As against the above recommendations of the TF, the Companies Act, 2013 has provided for the constitution of (1) Nomination and Remuneration Committee; (2) Audit Committee; and (3) Stakeholders Relationship Committee. The last one is the addition made to the New Act.

Related Party Transactions

This has emerged an important issue in the company management, because of the fact that there are risks associated with such transactions to the company, besides impacting the independence of a director. Hence, the TF has made the recommendation that Audit Committee should pre-approve all related party transactions which are not in the ordinary course of business or not on "arms length basis". All other related party transactions should be placed before the Committee for its reference.

II. Role of Auditors

In the field of company management, the role of the auditor is paramount. An auditor is the linking pin between the company and the outsiders. He is the person who can present an impartial and dispassionate view of the affairs of the company. For this reason, the TF and the Act have placed much value on the role of the auditor in ensuring smooth and responsible industrial economy. Let us now take a look at the recommendations of the TF in this regard.

A. **Appointment of Auditors:** The Audit Committee of the board of directors shall be the first point of reference regarding the appointment of auditors. The Audit Committee should have regard to the entire profile of the audit firm. It is responsible for audit partner, his or her previous experience of handling audit for similar sized companies. The assistants deployed by the audit form in the name of audit clerks understudy chartered accountants or paralegal persons should also have a minimum number of years of study of accounting principles and have minimum prior experience as audit clerks.

B. **Certificate of Independence:** Every company must obtain a certificate from the auditor certifying the firm's independence and arm's length relationship with the client company. The Certificate of Independence should certify that the firm, together with its consulting and specialised services affiliates, subsidiaries and associated companies or network or group entities has not undertaken any prohibited non-audit assignments for the company.

C. **Rotation of Audit Partners:** The partners handling the audit assignment of a listed company should be rotated after every six years. The partners and at least 50% of the audit team responsible for the audit should be rotated every six years, but this should be staggered so that on any given day there isn't a change in partner or engagement manager. A cooling off period of 3 years should elapse before a partner can resume the same audit assignment.

D. **Auditors Revenue from the Audit Client:** There is a stipulation that the revenues of an audit firm singly or taken together with its subsidiaries of a company should not form more than 10 per cent of its total income.

E. **Auditor and the Company Relationship:** The report of the Naresh Chandra Committee on corporate audit and governance had suggested that the auditors should refrain from providing non-audit services to their clients. It also recommended an explicit list of prohibited non-audit services. This recommendation was in fact considered by the Ministry of Corporate Affairs and included the same in Companies Bill, 2009. Finally, this could find a place in the 2013 Act in Section – 144.

   The Task Force concurred with the recommendation that legislation should expressly prohibit auditors from rendering certain services to their audit clients. Audit firms should have to mandatorily disclose network agreements between audit firms and non-audit companies, pecuniary interests exceeding 2% between the audit firm and its affiliate non-audit service firm or company and measures of Chinese walls and data protection/confidentiality that are in place between them. The Task Force noted the existing practice in this regard. And found it to be sufficient.

F. **Auditor's Liability:** The firm, as a statutory auditor or internal auditor, has to confidentially disclose its net worth to the listed company appointing it. Each member of the audit firm is liable to an unlimited extent unless they have formed a limited liability partnership firm or company for professional services as permitted to be incorporated by the relevant professional disciplinary body (ICAI). Even in the case of a limited liability firm undertaking audit in the future, under the new law, the individual auditor responsible for dereliction of duty shall have unlimited liability and the firm and its partners shall have liability limited to the extent of their paid-in capital and free or undistributed reserves.

G. **Qualifications in Auditor's Report:** There is great confusion regarding the quality of audit reports and the qualification remarks made in the report. Realizing the fact that there is a need to standardize the formats, including the language; the committee recommended that the ICAI should appoint a committee to standardise the language of disclaimers or qualifications permissible to audit firms. Anything beyond the scope of such permitted language should require the auditor to provide sufficient explanation.

H. **Whistle Blowing Mechanism:** The Task Force recommended the institution of a mechanism for employees to report concerns about unethical behaviour, actual or suspected fraud, or violation of the company's code of conduct or ethics policy. It should also provide for adequate safeguards against victimization of employees who avail of the mechanism, and also allow direct access to the Chairperson of the audit committee in exceptional cases.

I. **Risk Management:** The committee suggested that the Board of Directors, management and the audits committee shall collectively identify the risks impacting the company's business. Attempt shall also be made to identify and minimize risks attendant with the business of the company. The Board should also affirm that it has put in place adequate risk management mechanism across the company. The same shall also be monitored from time to time. It is to be appreciated that the government has almost incorporated majority of the suggestions in the New Companies Act, 2013 under sections 139–148. The entire Chapter X was devoted to discuss the issues pertaining to the role of auditor.

III. Role of Regulatory Mechanisms

Beginning with the Registrar of Companies, there has been an elaborate mechanism created to ensure smooth and effective working of companies in India. The entire Companies Act is devoted for this purpose. While the Central Government has the general power of supervision and authority to prescribe standards under the Companies Act, it has created many other institutional mechanisms to deal with the specific situations as of the following:

1. Constitution of National Financial Reporting Authority (NFRA) under section 132.
2. Establishment of Serious Fraud Investigation Office (SFIO) under section 212.
3. Constitution of National Company Law Tribunal (NCLT) under section 408.
4. Constitution of Appellate Tribunal (AT) under section 410.
5. Establishment of Special Courts under section 435.

In addition to the above, the Securities and Exchange Board of India (SEBI), diverse Stock Exchanges (through their listing agreements) are issuing various guidelines for the proper and effective functioning of the companies in India.

4. THE COMPANIES ACT, 2013

In terms of corporate governance, the new Companies Act is considered a path-breaking attempt in ensuring strict compliance by the companies in India. The old Companies Act, which was enacted with the objective of promoting the orderly growth of corporate sector in India was in force for about fifty-five years. During this long period of operation, the Act underwent several changes; keeping in view of the contemporary developments. In view of several amendments, a need was felt to enact a new law to meet the changed national and international economic environment and to further accelerate the expansion and growth of the economy. For this purpose, the Companies Bill, 2009 was introduced in the Parliament. Subsequent to its introduction, the Central Government received several suggestions for amendments in the said Bill. The Parliament Standing Committee on Finance also made numerous recommendations. In view of the new proposed amendments to the Companies Bill, 2009 arising out of the recommendations of the Parliament Standing Committee on Finance and suggestions of various stakeholders, the Central Government withdrew the Companies Bill, 2009. Incorporating the recommendations of the Parliament Standing Committee on Finance and suggestions of all stakeholders the Companies Bill, 2012 was introduced in the Parliament.

The New Act is quite significant from the point of view of corporate governance. There are several new dimensions incorporated in the Act such as enhanced accountability on the part of the companies, additional disclosure norms, audit accountability, investor protection, appointment of women directors and steps to introduce e-governance systems in the company management. The following are the salient provisions that were inserted/amended in the New Act for ensuring effective and ethical corporate governance.

- Internal Audit by CAs/CWAs/such other professionals as may be decided by the Board has been made mandatory for prescribed classes of companies (Section-138).
- Mandatory rotation of auditors for listed companies and other prescribed classes of companies after five years in case of auditor who is an individual CA and after ten years for auditors which is a CA firm (section 139).
- Audit Report to be made in authorized accounting and auditing standards (section 143).
- Auditors not to render certain services (section 144).
- Every company to have atleast one director, who has stayed in India for a total period of not less than 182 days in the previous calendar year (section 149).
- Every listed company and other prescribed classes of companies to have independent directors (section 149).
- Mandatory presence or ratification of the decisions of the Board by the Independent Director (section 173).

- Every listed company or such class/classes of companies to establish a vigilance mechanism for directors and employees (section 177).
- Mandatory constitution of the following committees (sections 177 & 178):
  - (i) Audit Committee.
  - (ii) Nomination and Remuneration Committee.
  - (iii) Stakeholders' Relationship Committee.
- Prohibition of Insider Trading of Securities (section 195).
- Mandatory Secretarial Audit for bigger companies (section 204).
- Investigation into the affairs of companies by Serious Fraud Investigation Office (section 211).
- Prevention of oppression and mismanagement (section 241-246).
- Valuation of property and assets of the company by a person registered as valuer only (section 247).
- Punishment for fraudulently inducing persons to invest money (section 36).
- Damages for fraud in accepting or repaying deposits accepted (section 75).

5. CORPORATE GOVERNANCE MODELS

Discussions on corporate governance are always stuck with the right choice of systems and creation of a suitable environment, called modeling. Theoreticians are always bogged down with the establishment of relations among individuals, functions and stakeholders. It is important to keep in mind the objectives sought to be achieved through the model. As regards corporate governance, the focus shall be on three aspects, viz., accuracy, accountability and transparency. All these are finally desired to culminate into business ethics. Discussions on Corporate Governance Centres around the following thee important models:[6]

1. Anglo – US Model
2. Japanese Model
3. German Model

5.1 The Anglo – US Model

This model is characterized by the share ownership of individual, and institutional investors not affiliated with the corporation (known as outside shareholders or **"outsiders"**). A well-developed legal framework defining the rights and responsibilities of three key players, namely, management, directors and shareholders is considered essential in this model. We are aware of the fact that equity financing is a common method of raising capital for corporations in the US and UK. It is not surprising, therefore, that the US is the largest capital market in the world, and that the London Stock Exchange is the third largest stock exchange in the world (in terms of market capitalization). There is a causal relationship between the importance of equity financing, the size of the capital market and the development of a corporate governance system. The US is both the world's largest capital market and the home of the world's most-developed system of proxy voting and shareholder activism by institutional investors.

Chief constituents in the Anglo-US model include management, directors, shareholders (especially institutional investors), government agencies, stock exchanges, self-regulatory organizations and consulting firms which advise corporations and/or shareholders on corporate governance and proxy voting. Of these, the three major players are management, directors and shareholders. They form what is commonly referred to as the "corporate governance triangle." The interests and interaction of these players may be diagrammed as follows:

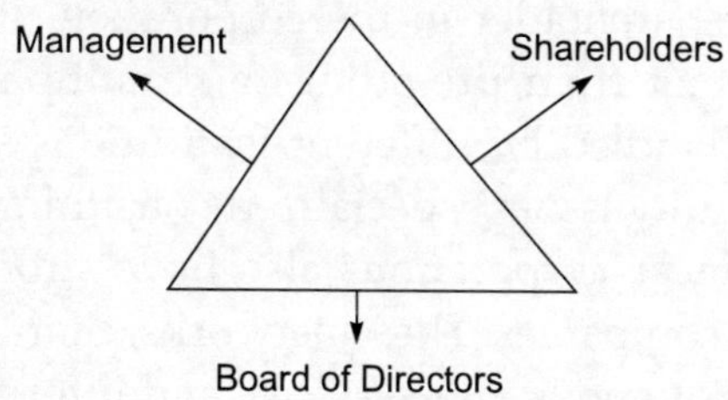

Figure 6.1: Anglo-US Model of Corporate Governance

The Anglo-US model, developed within the context of the free market economy, assumes the separation of ownership and control in most publicly-held corporations. This important legal distinction serves a valuable business and social purpose. It is the practice that the investors contribute capital and maintain ownership in the enterprise, while generally avoiding legal liability for the acts of the corporation. Investors avoid legal liability by ceding to management control of the corporation, and paying management for acting as their agent by undertaking the affairs of the corporation. The cost of this separation of ownership and control was already identified as the problem of **"agency costs"**. The interests of shareholders and management may not always coincide. Laws governing corporations in countries using the Anglo-US model attempt to reconcile this conflict in several ways. Most importantly, they prescribe the election of a board of directors by shareholders and require that boards act as **fiduciaries** for shareholders' interests by overseeing management on behalf of shareholders.

5.2 The Japanese Model

The Japanese model is characterized by a high level of stock ownership by affiliated banks and companies. The most significant feature of the corporate structure in Japan is the participation of banking system. A banking system characterized by strong, long-term links between bank and corporation is the major aspect. Boards of directors are composed almost solely of insiders; and a comparatively low level of input of outside shareholders. Equity financing is important for Japanese corporations. However, insiders and their affiliates are the major shareholders in most Japanese corporations. Consequently, they play a major role in individual corporations and in the system as a whole. Conversely, the interests of outside shareholders are marginal. The percentage of foreign ownership of Japanese stocks is small, but it may become an important factor in making the model more responsive to outside shareholders. The Japanese system of corporate governance is multi-fold concentrating mainly on the network relationship between the bank and the company. The bank system and the industrial network are the two different, yet overlapping and complementary, elements of the Japanese model.

Almost all Japanese corporations have a close relationship with a main bank. The bank provides its corporate client with loans as well as services related to bond issues, equity issues, settlement accounts, and related consulting services. The main bank is generally a major shareholder in the corporation. In the US, anti-monopoly legislation prohibits one bank from providing this multiplicity of services. Instead, these services are usually handled by different institutions such as commercial bank (loans) investment bank (equity issues) specialized consulting firms (proxy voting and other services). Many Japanese corporations also have strong financial relationships with a network of affiliated companies. These networks, characterized by crossholdings of debt and equity, trading of goods and services, and informal business contacts, are known as *keiretsu*.

Government-directed industrial policy also plays a key role in Japanese governance. Since the 1930s, the Japanese government has been pursuing an active industrial policy designed to assist Japanese corporations. This policy included official and unofficial representation on corporate boards in times of financial difficulty. In the Japanese model, the four key players are: main bank (a major inside shareholder), affiliated company or *keiretsu* (a major inside shareholder), management and the government. Note that the interaction among these players serves to link relationships rather than balance powers, as in the case in the Anglo-US model. In contrast with the Anglo-US model, non-affiliated shareholders have little or no voice in Japanese governance. As a result, there are a few truly independent directors, that is, directors representing outside shareholders. The major players and their interrelationships are shown in the following diagram.

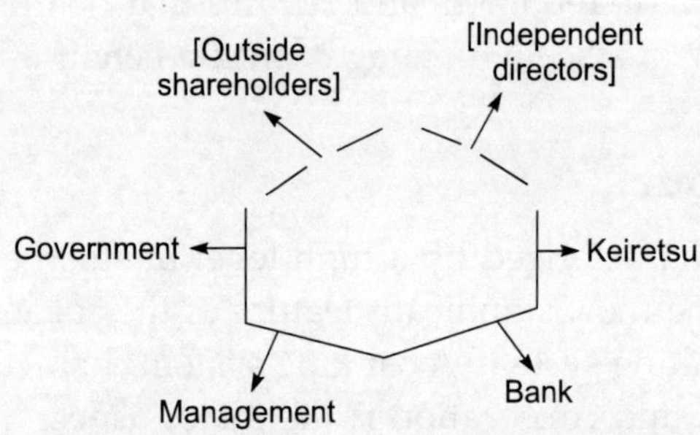

Figure 6.2: Japanese Model of Corporate Governance

As can be seen from the above, the base of the figure, with four connecting lines, represents the linked interests of the four key players: government, management, bank and *keiretsu*. The open lines at the top represent the non-linked interests of non-affiliated shareholders and outside directors, because they play an insignificant role.

5.3 The German Model

This model is mostly found in Germany and Austria. Some elements of the model also apply in the Netherlands and Scandinavian countries. Furthermore, some corporations in France and Belgium have recently introduced some elements of the German model. Under this model, banks hold long-term stakes in German corporations, as in Japan. Bank representatives are elected to the Boards of the companies. However, this representation is constant, unlike the situation in Japan where bank representatives were elected to a corporate board only in times of financial distress. Germany's three largest universal banks play a major role. In some parts of the country, public-sector banks are also the key shareholders.

There are three unique elements of the German model that distinguish it from other models. First, the German model prescribes two boards with separate members. German corporations have a two-tiered board structure consisting of a **management board** (composed entirely of insiders, that is, executives of the corporation) and a **supervisory board** (composed of labor/employee representatives and shareholder representatives). The two boards are completely distinct. Second, the size of the supervisory board is set by law and cannot be changed by shareholders. Third, there are restrictions on the voting rights of the shareholders. These limit a shareholder to voting a certain percentage of the corporation's total share capital, regardless of the share of ownership held by him.

Similar to the Japanese system, banks usually play a multi-faceted role as shareholder, lender, issuer of both equity and debt, depository (custodian bank) and voting agent at AGMs. As of now, the three largest German banks (Deutsche Bank AG, Dresdner Bank AG and Commerzbank AG) held positions on the supervisory boards of 85 of the 100 largest German corporations. This shows the pervading influence of the banking system on the company management.

6. OVERSEEING BODIES

A new development in the framework of corporate governance is the setting up of various monitoring bodies, having specific functions, to contribute to the cause of effective corporate governance. Discussion on the origin and objectives of the following agencies is considered worthwhile to improve the understanding of the corporate governance environment in India. Perhaps, there could be little repetition of a few aspects here and there in the earlier chapters; still it is considered helpful in the present context.

1. National Financial Reporting Authority (NFRA)
2. National Foundation for Corporate Governance (NFCG)
3. National Advisory Committee on Accounting Standards (NACAS)
4. Serious Frauds Investigation Office (SFIO)

6.1 National Financial Reporting Authority (NFRA)

The Standing Committee on Finance (2014-15) (Sixteenth Lok Sabha) of the Ministry of Corporate Affairs has made a significant recommendation that it is urgently required to set up an oversight body *having quasi-judicial authority including suo moto investigation powers in cases of professional misconduct by a Chartered Accountant/firm of Chartered Accountants.* Following this recommendation, the Government of India has incorporated under Section 132 of the Companies Act, 2013, providing for the constitution of National Financial Reporting Authority (NFRA) to make and monitor the work of accounting and auditing firms. However, this Section of the Act is yet to be notified for commencement. The Ministry has informed that a token budget provision of Rs. 13.60 lakh has been made for the National Financial Reporting Authority (NFRA) for the year 2015-16. The draft rules regarding the creation and functioning of this body as well as its Appellate Body, viz., National Financial Reporting Appellate Authority (NFRAA) were prepared and shared with stakeholders for their comments. These rules are yet to be finalized in the light of suggestions made by stakeholders on the draft rules as well as fresh comments received from the Institute of Chartered Accountants of India.

6.2 National Foundation for Corporate Governance (NFCG)

With the objective of promoting better corporate governance practices in India, the Ministry of Corporate Affairs, Government of India, on 1st October 2003 set up the National Foundation for Corporate Governance (NFCG) in partnership with Confederation of Indian Industry (CII), Institute of Company Secretaries of India (ICSI) and Institute of Chartered Accountants of India (ICAI). In the year 2010, the list of stakeholders in NFCG was expanded with the inclusion of the Institute of Cost Accountants of India (ICAI) and National Stock Exchange (NSE). The other objectives sought to be achieved through NFCG are indicated below:

- to foster a culture for promoting good governance, voluntary compliance and facilitate effective participation of different stakeholders;
- to create a framework of best practices, structure, processes and ethics;
- to make significant difference to Indian corporate sector by raising the standard of corporate governance in India towards achieving stability and growth.

In an endeavour to build capabilities in the area of research in corporate governance and to disseminate quality and timely information to concerned stakeholders, NFCG would work to foster partnerships with national as well as international organisations. At the national level, NFCG would work with premier management institutes as well as nationally reputed professional organisations to design and administer Directors Training Programmes. The Foundation would provide **accreditation** to these organisations based on their meeting the stringent eligibility criteria designed along with continuing adherence to the same. On obtaining the accreditation these organisations, with the support of NFCG, would set up National Center for Corporate Governance (NCCG) to provide a training to Directors, conduct research and build capability in the area of corporate governance.

6.3 National Advisory Committee on Accounting Standards (NACAS)

This is a body set-up under section 210A of the Companies Act, 1956 by the Government of India. The main function of the Committee is to advise the Central Government on the formulation and laying down of accounting policy and accounting standards for adoption by companies. The advisory committee shall consist of the following members, namely:

1. A chairperson who shall be a person of eminence well versed in accountancy, finance, business administration, business law, economics or similar discipline.
2. One member each nominated by the chartered accountants of India constituted under the Chartered Accountants Act, 1949, the Institute of Cost and Work Accountants Act, 1959 and the Institute of Company Secretaries of India constituted under the Company Secretaries Act, 1980.
3. One representative each of the Central government, Reserve Bank of India, Comptroller & Auditor General of India to be nominated by it.
4. A person who holds or has held the office of professor in Accountancy, Finance or Business Management in any university or deemed university.
5. The Chairman of the Central Board of Direct Tax (India) constituted under the Central Board of Revenue Act, 1963 (India) or his nominee.
6. Two members to represent the chambers of commerce and industry to be nominated by the Central Government of India.
7. One representative of the Security and Exchange Board of India to be nominated by it. Further, Institute of Chartered Accountants of India (ICAI) has the responsibility of preparing the accounting standards and recommend them to NACAS.

Main Objective of NACAS: To **advise the Central Government** on the formulation and laying down of accounting policies and accounting standards for adoption by companies or class of companies under this Act but at the same time **NACAS does not have any regulatory powers** to regulate the above issues. In effect the role of NACAS was only restricted to the advisory.

6.4 Serious Frauds Investigation Office (SFIO)

The SFIO is a multi-disciplinary organization under the Ministry of Corporate Affairs, consisting of experts in the field of accountancy, forensic auditing, law, information technology, investigation, company law, capital market and taxation to detect the cases of fraud and recommend for prosecution of those involved. The SFIO will normally take up for investigation only such cases, which are characterized by:

- complexity and having inter-departmental and multi-disciplinary ramifications;
- substantial involvement of public interest to be judged by size, either in terms of monetary misappropriation or in terms of persons affected; and
- the possibility of investigation leading to or contributing towards a clear improvement in systems, laws or procedures. The SFIO shall investigate serious cases of fraud received from the department of company affairs.

It may be noted that SFIO does not initiate any investigation on its own, based on any complaints/documents received from any source. The cases are taken up for investigation as are ordered for investigation by the Government, i.e., Ministry of Corporate Affairs under section 235, 237, 239 and 247 of the Companies Act, 1956. (The same are incorporated in the New Companies Act, 2013 under section 210, 213, 219 and 216.)

7. EASE OF DOING BUSINESS

Corporate growth presupposes sensible rules and regulations to be in operation in the country. In order that the businesses are to be carried in a free and fair manner, governments are required to create a hassle-free environment. It is in this context, the World Bank Group has conducted a survey titled 'Doing Business 2015 – Going Beyond Efficiency', comparing business regulations for domestic firms in 189 economies, the bank developed rankings. The report surveyed regulations affecting the business of the corporations. The group considered the following ten areas as significant in ensuring smoothness in business dealings:

(i) Starting a business
(ii) Dealing with construction permits
(iii) Getting electricity
(iv) Registering property
(v) Getting credit
(vi) Protecting minority investors
(vii) Paying taxes
(viii) Trading across borders

(ix) Enforcing contracts

(x) Resolving insolvency.

The significance of this report to the issue of governance is due to the fact that these rules and regulations set boundaries for the operation of the business. Acting within the limits becomes ethical and going beyond the frame turns out to be unethical. The following Table 6.1, details the key areas within each of the ten factors considered focal to the theme.

Table 6.1: 11 Key areas of Business Regulations

I.	**Complexity and Cost of Regulatory Processes**	
	Starting a business	Procedures, time, cost and paid-in minimum capital to start a limited liability company
	Dealing with construction permits	Procedures, time and cost to complete all formalities to build a warehouse
	Getting electricity	Procedures, time and cost to get connected to the electrical grid
	Registering property	Procedures, time and cost to transfer a property
	Paying taxes	Procedures, time and total tax rate for a firm to comply with all tax regulations
	Trading across borders	Documents, time and cost to export and import by seaport/air
II.	**Strength of Legal Institutions**	
	Getting credit	Movable collateral laws and credit information systems
	Protecting minority investors	Minority shareholders' rights in related-party transactions and in corporate governance
	Enforcing contracts	Procedures, time and cost to resolve a commercial dispute
	Resolving insolvency	Time, cost, outcome and recovery rate for a commercial insolvency and the strength of the insolvency legal framework
	Labour market regulation	Flexibility in employment regulation, benefits for workers and labour dispute resolution

Source: Report of the World Bank on 'Doing Business 2015 – Going Beyond Efficiency', p. 16.

7.1 Ranking of Countries

According to the above survey, India ranked 142 out of 189 countries in 2015 on the 'ease of doing business, below its ranking of 140 in 2014. While India is almost at the bottom of the ranking on account of 'dealing with construction permits' and 'enforcing contracts', it ranks 7th in the world in terms of 'protecting minority investors'. (Table 6.2)

Table 6.2: India's Rank' in 'Ease of Doing Business' and other Indicators

Year	Ease of Doing Business Rank	Starting a Business	Dealing with Construction Permits	Getting Electricity	Registering Property	Getting Credit	Protecting Minority Investors	Paying Taxes	Trading Across Borders	Enforcing Contracts	Resolving Insolvency
2014	140	156	183	134	115	30	21	154	122	186	135
2015	142	158	184	137	121	36	7	156	126	186	137

Source: Report of the World Bank on 'Doing Business 2015 – Going Beyond Efficiency', p. 192.

Table 6.3: Country-wise Ranking in terms of Protecting Investors

Parameters	India	China	Brazil	Russia	USA	UK
Protecting minority investors (rank)	7	132	35	100	25	4
Extent of disclosure Index (0-10)	7	10	5	6	7.4	10
Extent of director liability index (0-10)	6	1	8	2	8.6	7
Ease of shareholder suits index (0-10)	7	4	4	7	9	8
Extent of conflict of interest regulation index (0-10)	6.7	5	5.7	5	8.3	8.3
Extent of shareholder rights index (0-10.5)	9	3	7.5	7.5	5.1	8
Strength of governance structure index (0-10.5)	6	2	5.5	3	2.9	6
Extent of corporate transparency index (0-9)	8.5	7	7.5	5	6.5	8
Extent of shareholder governance index (0-10)	7.8	4	6.8	5.2	4.8	7.3
Strength of minority investor protection index (0-10)	7.3	4.5	6.3	5.1	6.6	7.8

Source: Report of the World Bank on 'Doing Business 2015 – Going Beyond Efficiency', p. 192.

'Protecting minority investors' is considered an important indicator of corporate governance. India has fared better than China, Brazil and Russia (Table 6.3). It may be noted that India has been outperforming other BRICS countries persistently over the past 6 years. On the 'strength of minority investor protection index', with an overall score of 7.3 out of 10, India beats the South Asia average of 5.3 and OECD average of 6.3.

7.2 Ranking by Asian Corporate Governance Association (ACGA)

The Asian Corporate Governance Association (ACGA) is an independent, non-profit membership organisation dedicated to working with investors, companies and regulators in the implementation of effective corporate governance practices throughout Asia. ACGA was founded in 1999 with the belief that corporate governance is fundamental to the long-term development of Asian economies and capital markets.

ACGA's scope of work covers the following three areas:

1. **Research:** Tracking corporate governance developments across 11 markets in Asia and producing independent analyses of new laws and regulations, investor activism and corporate practices.
2. **Advocacy:** Engaging in a constructive dialogue with financial regulators, stock exchanges, institutional investors and companies on practical issues affecting the regulatory environment for ensuring better corporate governance practices in Asia.
3. **Education:** Organising conferences and seminars to foster a deeper understanding of the issues involved in corporate governance and ways to implement better methods of corporate governance.

ACGA is funded by a network of sponsors and corporate members, including leading pension and investment funds, financial institutions, listed companies, multinational corporations, professional firms and educational institutions. It is incorporated under the laws of Hong Kong and is managed by a secretariat based there. Its governing council comprises directors from around Asia.[7]

As a part of its job, the Association conducted a survey on the status of corporate governance in the Asian continent, covering about 500 companies. The survey found that the systemic changes in corporate governance in Asia over the past two years are more positive than negative. It is reflected in the fact that seven of eleven markets increased in score in 2012 compared to 2010. The main findings of the latest biannual survey were:

- Markets are on the rise mostly in Southeast and South Asia, including Singapore, Thailand, Malaysia, India, and the Philippines.
- Markets are falling mostly in North Asia, including: Japan, Taiwan and China.
- Hong Kong market rose slightly, but remained second in the ranking after Singapore.

- Korean market rebounded from its low base.
- Indonesia slipped back to the bottom of the survey.

8. THE ROAD AHEAD: FUTURE PERSPECTIVE

It is a fact that corporate governance in India is evolving. Though younger in the adoption of practices, it is appreciable that the Indian corporate system exhibited enough maturity. The failures in the Indian context are not so comparable in terms of their sweep or impact as has happened in the global context. The failure of M/s Satyam Computers remained the lone and biggest ever, exhorting the regulating agencies to put in place adequate safety measures. The record of RBI, SEBI, EDI are creditable in imposing strict discipline in the financial matters. For instance, it is the SEBI, which has identified the inbreeding prevailing in the M/s Sahara Group by denying access to the capital market in 2008. Similarly, in the same case, the Reserve Bank (the Central Bank of the country) did not register two of its financial outfits for allowing them to accept deposits from the public (more details of the same were presented as a case study in this book).

What is required in the present context is that the Indian corporate sector is to instill confidence among the investing public. Stock indices shall be a matter of solace to reflect upon the mood of the investors. It is true that the BSE sensex had crossed many a milestone by rising index from just about 4000 during seventies to about 26,000 now. But the sorry state of affairs is that the individuals are scared of participating in the IPOs and feel comfortable to approach the stock market through Mutual Funds only. This cannot be allowed to continue any longer. The buoyancy which prevailed during 1970s when MNCs were permitted to dilute their equities and thus resulting in the phenomenal increase of small investors, shall return to the market.

Ipso facto, the corporates have to move a step ahead by their 'actions taken upon own volition' in making as many disclosures as they think appropriate. It is not as though, the regulator or stock Exchange insists upon such disclosures through their clauses in the 'listing agreement'. Let the Indian corporate sector adopt the most common adage that 'honesty is the best policy'.

References

1. Green Paper, 'Corporate governance in Financial Institutions and Remuneration Policies', European Commission, Brussels, 2010.
2. Adam Smith, 'An Inquiry into the Nature and Causes of the Wealth of Nations, 1779. (http://en.wikisource.org)

3. Afra Afsharipour, 'A Brief Overview of Corporate Governance Reforms in India', The Conference Board, December 2010 (www.conferenceboard.org).
4. N. R Narayana Murthy, *Report of the Committee on Corporate Governance*, SEBI, Mumbai, February 8, 2003.
5. Naresh Chandra, 'Report of the CII Task Force on Corporate Governance', Confederation of Indian Industry, November 2009.
6. Lectures on 'Corporate Governance - Three Models of Corporate Governance', December 2005 (*www.emergingmarketsesg.net).*
7. Jamie Allen, 'CG Watch 2014 – Market Rankings', Asian Corporate Governance Association (ACGA), Hong Kong.

7

CHAPTER

SEBI's First Committee on Corporate Governance

[Shri Kumar Mangalam Birla Committee]

1. INTRODUCTION

Securities and Exchange Board of India (SEBI) is the agency that has been pursuing vigourously the issue of corporate governance. It is a well recognized fact that the quality of corporate governance shapes the growth and future of capital market and thus the economy. As a regulator, it is the responsibility of the institution to see that proper systems are put in place to retain the investors' confidence. As a matter of fact, the very mandate of the SEBI is to protect the interests of investors in securities and to promote the development and to regulate the securities market and for matters connected therewith or incidental thereto.

2. CONSTITUTION OF THE COMMITTEE

SEBI as a regulator has noticed that there were some companies, which voluntarily established high standards of corporate governance, but there are many more, whose practices are a matter of concern. There is also an increasing concern about standards of financial reporting and accountability, especially after losses suffered by investors and lenders in the recent past, which could have been avoided, with better and more transparent reporting practices. Investors have suffered on account of unscrupulous management of the companies, which have raised capital from the market at high valuation and have performed much worse than the past reported figures, leave alone the future projections at the time of raising money. Another example of bad governance has been the allotment of promoter's shares, on preferential basis at preferential prices, disproportionate to market valuation of shares, leading to further dilution of wealth of minority shareholders.

There are also many companies, which are not paying adequate attention to the basic procedures for shareholders' service; for example, many of these companies do not pay adequate attention to redress investors' grievances such as delay in transfer of shares, delay in despatch of share certificates and dividend warrants and non-receipt of dividend warrants; companies also do not pay sufficient attention to timelydissemination of information to investors as also to the quality of such information. SEBI has been regularly receiving large number of complaints on these matters. While enough laws exist to take care of many of these grievances, the implementation and inadequacy of penal provisions leave a lot to be desired.

It is in this context, SEBI constituted its first committee on Corporate Governance on May 7, 1999 under the Chairmanship of Shri Kumar Mangalam Birla, Member SEBI Board; who is also the CMD of Aditya Birla Group.

The other members of the committee were:

1. Shri Rohit Bhagat, Country Head, Boston Consulting Group.
2. Dr. J Bhagwati, Jt. Secretary, Ministry of Finance.
3. Shri Samir Biswas, Regional Director, Western Region, Department of Company Affairs, Government of India.
4. Shri S.P. Chhajed, President of Institute of Chartered Accountants of India.
5. Shri Virender Ganda, Ex-President of Institute of Company Secretaries of India.
6. Dr. Sumantra Ghoshal, Professor of Strategic Management, London Business School.
7. Shri Vijay Kalantri, President, All India Association of Industries.
8. Shri Pratip Kar, Executive Director, SEBI — Member Secretary.
9. Shri Y. H. Malegam, Managing Partner, S.B. Billimoria & Co.
10. Shri N. R. Narayana Murthy, Chairman and Managing Director, Infosys Technologies Ltd.
11. Shri A K Narayanan, President of Tamil Nadu Investor Association.
12. Shri Kamal Parekh, Ex-President, Calcutta Stock Exchange (Shri J M Chaudhary –President Calcutta Stock Exchange)
13. Dr. R. H. Patil, Managing Director, National Stock Exchange Ltd.
14. Shri Anand Rathi, President of the Stock Exchange, Mumbai.
15. Ms D.N. Raval, Executive Director, SEBI.
16. Shri Rajesh Shah, Former President of Confederation of Indian Industries.
17. Shri L K Singhvi, Sr. Executive Director, SEBI.
18. Shri S. S. Sodhi, Executive Director, Delhi Stock Exchange.

3. THE TERMS OF REFERENCE

The terms of reference set out to the Committee were as follows:

1. to suggest suitable amendments to the listing agreement executed by the stock exchanges with the companies and any other measures to improve the standards of corporate governance in the listed companies, in areas such as continuous disclosure of material information, both financial and non-financial, manner and frequency of such disclosures, responsibilities of independent and outside directors;
2. to draft a code of corporate best practices; and
3. to suggest safeguards to be instituted within the companies to deal with insider information and insider trading.

4. THE APPROACH OF THE COMMITTEE

It is appreciable that the Birla Committee has started its work in the right earnest. It has fairly taken into account the prevailing environment during that time at the national and international level. It has valued the reports of the following important committees that have studied the subject of corporate governance:

International

1. Cadbury Committee (May 1991)
2. Greenbury Committee (1995)
3. Combined Code of the London Stock Exchange (1998)
4. Code of the OECD on Corporate Governance (2004)
5. Blue Ribbon Committee (1998)

National

1. Code on Corporate Governance Published by the Confederation of Indian Industry (CII)

In addition, the Committee also took note of the various steps already taken by the SEBI for strengthening the Corporate Governance, which included the following:

- strengthening of disclosure norms for Initial Public Offers following the recommendations of the Committee set up by SEBI under the Chairmanship of Shri Y H Malegam;
- providing information in directors' reports for utilisation of funds and variation between projected and actual use of funds according to the requirements of

the Companies Act; inclusion of cash flow and funds flow statement in annual reports;
- declaration of quarterly results;
- mandatory appointment of compliance officer for monitoring the share transfer process and ensuring compliance with various rules and regulations;
- timely disclosure of material and price sensitive information including details of all material events having a bearing on the performance of the company;
- despatch of one copy of complete balance sheet to every household and abridged balance sheet to all shareholders;
- issue of guidelines for preferential allotment at market related prices; and
- issue of regulations providing for a fair and transparent framework for takeovers and substantial acquisitions.

5. KEY AREAS AND RECOMMENDATIONS

Having examined the issues involved in corporate governance and after reviewing the prevailing environment then, the committee came to the conclusion that the following are the three key constituents:

- Shareholders
- Board of Directors
- Management

Fundamental to the above, the committee has identified the following three key aspects as crucial to corporate governance:

- Accountability
- Transparency
- Equality of Treatment

It goes without saying that the committee has very aptly identified the issues pertinent at hand. It was also aware of the fact that this is the first formal and comprehensive attempt to evolve a **'code of corporate governance'**. While making the recommendations, the committee had also been mindful that any code of corporate governance must be dynamic, evolving and should change with changing context and times. It would therefore be necessary that this code also is reviewed from time to time, keeping pace with the changing expectations of the investors, shareholders, and other stakeholders and with increasing sophistication achieved in capital markets. It is, thus, the tone and tenor of the committee has become quite evident. Keeping this at the backdrop, the committee made the following recommendations:

1. The Committee recognized the fact that enhancement of shareholder value is crucial to any business. In spite of this, the companies were advised to emulate honesty as a way of life.
2. Like many other committees abroad, K. M. Birla Committee also divided its list of recommendations into mandatory and non-mandatory categories. The Committee thus felt that companies would bestow adequate attention on the priority items and moderate attention on the non-mandatory issues. It is to be highlighted here that the Committee never expressed the opinion that non-mandatory means non-important. It is only in the context of fulfilling legal obligations, such division is considered helpful.
3. The Committee was very particular relating to the role of Independent Directors (IDs). It wanted the IDs not to have any pecuniary relationship with the promoters or any other stakeholder. Further, all such relationships if any should be disclosed in the annual report.
4. The Committee was of the view that the non-executive directors shall also hold responsibility for the deliberations taking place at the Board meetings, especially on issues of strategy, performance, management of conflicts and standards of conduct. Therefore emphasis is laid on the calibre of the non-executive directors, especially of the independent directors.
5. It is the desire of the Committee that the board of a company has an optimum combination of executive and non-executive directors with not less than fifty percent of the board comprising the non-executive directors. It shall also depend on the nature of the Chairman of the board. In case a company has a non-executive Chairman, at least one-third of the board should comprise independent directors; and in case a company has an executive Chairman, at least half of board should be independent.
6. Keeping in view of the role of the Chairman of the company, it is suggested that the non-executive Chairman should be entitled to maintain an office at the company's expense and also be allowed reimbursement of expenses incurred in performance of his/her duties.
7. The Committee was particular that there shall be constituted an 'Audit Committee' with responsible directors as members, to ensure credibility of the financial dealings of the company.
8. The intention of the Committee is that there shall be proper constitution of the Audit Committee with atleast three non-executive directors, and the majority being independent directors. It is also desirable that the Chairman of the Committee should be an independent director. The Audit Committee should invite such of the executives, as it considers necessary to participate in the deliberations of the meetings. It is also felt desirable to involve auditors of the company and other officials dealing with the financial matters of the company.

9. The Committee wanted that there should be proper regularity for the meetings of the Committee and shall meet at least thrice a year. At least one meeting shall be devoted to discuss the annual accounts, before they are finalised.
10. In order to make the deliberations of the Committee meaningful, it is recommended that there shall be adequate attendance at the meetings in the form of minimum quorum of two independent directors.
11. The Committee desired to entrust the following powers to the Audit Committee:
    - To investigate any activity within its terms of reference.
    - To seek information from any employee.
    - To obtain outside legal or other professional advice.
    - To secure attendance of outsiders with relevant expertise, if it considers necessary.
12. The Committee very aptly recognized the fact that there shall be proper coordination among the Board, external auditors and internal auditors in the following matters of importance.
    - Financial reporting process and the disclosure of its financial information.
    - The appointment and removal of external auditor, fixation of audit fee and payment for any other services.
    - Accounting policies and practices covering major accounting entries based on exercise of judgement by management, qualifications in draft audit report, significant adjustments arising out of audit, and related party transactions.
    - The adequacy of internal control systems and the adequacy of internal audit function, including the structure of the internal audit department, staffing and seniority of the official heading the department, reporting structure, coverage and frequency of internal audit.
    - The Audit Committee shall also be vigilant over the suspected fraud or irregularity or a failure of internal control systems of a material nature and to report such matters to the board.
    - Also post-audit discussion to ascertain any area of concern.
    - Risk management policies of the company.
    - Defaults in the payments to the depositors, and other creditors.
13. The other important issues discussed by the Committee pertains to the remuneration of the directors. It is very much true that there are many apprehensions about the amount/percentage of remuneration drawn by the members of the Board. In order to tackle this problem, the Committee suggested the constitution of a 'Remunerations Committee'. This committee is supposed to be entrusted with the responsibility of fixing remuneration of all the directors.

14. The Committee also felt that there shall proper disclosure norms followed by every company in the matters of:
    - remuneration package of all the directors, i.e., salary, benefits, bonuses, stock options, pension, etc.;
    - performance linked incentives, along with the performance criteria;
    - service contracts, notice period, severance fees; and
    - stock option details, if any.
15. The Committee is also critical about the meetings of the BoD. It felt that these shall be held periodically in a proper environment to discuss the important matters of the company. It said that there shall be at least four meetings in a year and the gap between two meetings shall not be more than four months. Further, the Birla Committee is conscious of the pressure of time on the Board members. Keeping this in view, the Committee recommended that a director should not be a member in more than 10 committees or act as Chairman of more than five committees across all companies in which he is a director.
16. The Birla Committee also took note of the recommendations of the SEBI on accounting standards and thus suggested to keep an eye on the following:
    - ➢ The companies are required to give consolidated accounts in respect of all its subsidiaries in which they hold 51 % or more of the share capital.
    - ➢ In cases of companies with several businesses, it is important that financial reporting in respect of each product segment should be available to shareholders and the market to obtain a complete financial picture of the company.
    - ➢ It is again important to ensure adequate disclosure and treatment of related party transactions. Hence, the Committee advised the ICAI to issue adequate accounting standards in this regard.
17. It is gratifying to note that the Birla Committee came out with a novel idea of having a "Management Discussion and Analysis Report (MDAR)", which should form part of the annual report to the shareholders. There is also a specific mention by the Committee of the matters that are needed to be included in this MDAR, as of the following:
    - Industry structure and developments.
    - Opportunities and threats.
    - Segment-wise or product-wise performance.
    - Outlook.
    - Risks and concerns.
    - Internal control systems and their adequacy.

- Discussion on financial performance with respect to operational performance.
- Material developments in human resources/industrial relations.

18. Matters having personal interest of the Directors also need to be brought to the notice of the stakeholders.
19. It is considered necessary that the shareholders have the requisite information regarding the appointment of a new director, such as the profile of the proposed director, nature of his expertise in specific functional areas; and the names of companies in which the person also holds the directorship and the membership of committees of the board.
20. It is also suggested to share all the material information such as quarterly results, presentation made by companies to analysts with the stock exchange concerned as part of the listing agreement. It is also necessary that the half-yearly declaration of financial performance including summary of the significant events in last six-months, should be sent to each of the shareholders.
21. It is also suggested to have a Grievance Redressal Committee to look into the grievances of shareholders on the matters like the transfer of shares, non-receipt of balance sheet, non-receipt of declared dividends, etc. The Committee believed that the formation of such a committee will help focus the attention of the company on shareholders' grievances and sensitise the management to the redressal of their grievances.
22. It is also felt necessary that the companies shall delegate the power of share transfer to an officer, or a committee or to the registrar and share transfer agents. The delegated authority should attend to share transfer formalities at least once in a fortnight.
23. The Birla Committee is highly responsive to the compliance requirements. It wanted all the companies to comply with the provisions of not only Listing Agreement (LA), but also many other requirements generated through the law.
24. One of the very crucial and significant recommendations of the Birla Committee pertains to the strengthening of the Listing Agreement. It wished the Exchanges to make the LA more and more comprehensive and stringent; so that they can ensure proper compliance of code of corporate governance. On the issue of imposing penalties for non-compliance, the Committee is very categorical that they shall be more severe and not to be hesitant even to go to the extent of filing an affidavit for winding up.
25. Yet another significant recommendation of the Birla Committee pertains to the inclusion of a separate report on corporate governance as part of the Annual Report. This could be in the form of a separate section. By virtue of this, it is felt that there will be opportunity to the stakeholders to know the extent of compliance made by the company. This would also enable the market players

to assess for themselves the standards of corporate governance followed by the company. The Committee has put in a painstaking effort to detail the items that should form part of the said 'Governance Report".

(i) A brief statement on company's philosophy on the code of governance.

(ii) Board of Directors, together with the composition and category of directors, their attendance at the meetings of the BoD, and the details pertaining to the number of meetings and dates of such meetings.

(iii) In respect of Audit Committee, details like the terms of reference, composition, name of members and Chairperson, and meetings and attendance during the year.

(iv) In respect of Remuneration Committee, the composition, name of members and Chairperson, attendance during the year, remuneration policy and actual remunerations paid.

(v) In respect of Shareholders Committee, names and designations given to directors and other officers of the company, the details of the meetings held and the matters discussed with particular focus on the number of pending share transfers.

(vi) General Body meetings shall highlight the aspects covering:
- Location and time
- Whether special resolutions
  - Were put through postal ballot last year, details of voting pattern
  - Person who conducted the postal ballot exercise
  - Are proposed to be conducted through postal ballot
  - Procedure for postal ballot

(vii) Disclosures shall pertain to all the material transactions, more specifically those carried with its promoters, the directors or the management, their subsidiaries or relatives, etc. Disclosures also shall pertain to the non-compliance by the company, penalties, imposed and strictures passed by the SEBI and Judiciary, if existing.

(viii) Means of communication shall cover:
- Half-yearly report sent to each household of shareholders.
- Quarterly results
  - Which newspapers normally published in
  - Any website, where displayed
  - Whether it also displays official news releases
  - The presentations made to institutional investors or to the analysts.
- Whether MDAR is a part of annual report or not.

(ix) General shareholder information shall consist of the details relating to AGM, company calendar of events/activities, dates of dividend declarations/ payments, share codes, share transfers, etc.

26. The Committee also recommended that every company should arrange to obtain a certificate from the auditors of the company regarding compliance of mandatory recommendations, and annex the certificate to that effect.

6. APPLICABILITY OF THE RECOMMENDATIONS

The Committee was of the opinion that the recommendations should be made applicable to the listed companies, their directors, management, employees and professionals associated with such companies, in accordance with a given time frame. Compliance with the code should be both in letter and spirit and should always be in a manner that gives precedence to substance over form. The ultimate responsibility for putting the recommendations into practice is placed with the board of directors and the management of the company.

The recommendations will apply to all the listed private and public sector companies, in accordance with the schedule of implementation. As for listed entities, which are not companies, but body corporates (e.g. private and public sector banks, financial institutions, insurance companies, etc.) incorporated under other statutes, the recommendations will apply to the extent that they do not violate their respective statutes, and guidelines or directives issued by the relevant regulatory authorities.

Besides the applicability, the Committee also debated the question of voluntary versus mandatory compliance of its recommendations. As indicated earlier, the Committee was of the firm view that mandatory compliance of the recommendations at least in respect of the essential recommendations would be most appropriate in the Indian context. The Committee also noted that in most of the countries where standards of corporate governance are high, the stock exchanges have enforced some form of compliance through their listing agreements.

The Committee felt that some of the recommendations are absolutely essential for the framework of corporate governance and virtually form its core, while others could be considered desirable. Besides, some of the recommendations may also need change in the statutes, such as the Companies Act, for their enforcement. In the case of others, enforcement would be possible by amending the Securities Contracts (Regulation) Rules, 1957 and by amending the listing agreement of the stock exchanges under the direction of SEBI. **The Committee therefore felt that the recommendations should be divided into mandatory and non-mandatory categories** and those recommendations which are absolutely essential for corporate governance, can be defined with precision and which can be enforced through the amendment of the listing agreement could be classified as mandatory. Others, which are either desirable or which may require change of laws, may, for the time being, be classified as non-mandatory.

As a matter of fact, this methodology was also followed by the Naryana Murthy Committee later. It may be understood that non-mandatory recommendations would pave the way for a congenial atmosphere in meeting the three objectives, i.e., accountability, transparency and equality of treatment.

7. SCHEDULE OF IMPLEMENTATION

One more appreciable aspect of the recommendations of the Committee is that it has emphasized on the 'time frame' for implementation as indicated below:

- All entities seeking listing for the first time shall comply at the time of listing itself.
- In case of others, the time limit fixed is the Financial Year 2000-2001, but not later than March 31, 2001. It shall be open to the companies to comply with the recommendations, much in advance also, and not to wait till they become the law. It is hoped that companies having about 80 per cent of the market capitalization would be covered under this frame.
- All the other entities which are presently listed, with paid up share capital of Rs. 10 crore and above, or net worth of Rs 25 crore or more any time in the history of the company shall fulfil these obligations before 31st March, 2002.
- Finally, all the entities which are presently listed, with paid up share capital of Rs 3 crore and above shall fall in line before 31st March, 2003.

8. FOLLOW-UP ON THE RECOMMENDATIONS

As discussed in the previous pages, the Committee made significant recommendations for improving upon the governance practices of companies in India. It being the first Committee constituted by the SEBI, after the Committee appointed by the CII, the Committee has gone into the issues in the required depth. Later to this, the second Committee constituted by the SEBI under the Chairmanship of N.R. Narayana Murthy has also valued the recommendations of the Birla committee. The recommendations of these Committees and the suggestions of many other stakeholders were considered by the Government of India and thus were incorporated as provisions in the New Companies Act, 2013. Let us now examine as how the recommendations of the Birla Committee could find a place in the Companies Act, 2013.

1. The recommendations of the Committee in respect of non-executive directors, independent directors, their manner of appointment, and remuneration were considered and suitable changes were incorporated through section 149 to 172. While the Committee recommended that the Board of a company to have an optimum number of executive and non-executive directors with not less than fifty

per cent of the Board comprising of the non-executive directors. The Act specified minimum number of independent directors to by appointed by every company. Further, the Act has noted the minimum and maximum number of directorships that a company can have. It is appreciable that the Act has detailed in clear terms the manner of selection of independent directors under section 150; as also the appointment of additional directors, alternate directors and nominee directors under section 161. This can be understood as an attempt to contain the unethical practices adopted by the companies in appointing persons related to them to the Board and thus concentrate power in the hands of a few individuals.

2. The recommendations of the Committee in respect of audit committees were also valued. The Committee has recommended to constitute audit committee with a minimum of three members and all being non-executive directors and majority of them to be independent, and with at least one director having financial and accounting knowledge. This recommendation in the same format was incorporated in the Act under section 177. The powers and functions given to the Audit Committee were based on the recommendations of the Birla Committee.
3. Similarly, the recommendations of the Committee in respect of internal and external auditors and also the internal control mechanisms were examined with the required attention and were incorporated in the new Act.
4. In respect of the role of the Board of Directors, the Committee made suggestions relating to the number of meetings, remuneration and the very functioning of the Board. Many of these suggestions were taken note of in section 173 of the Act and also has taken suggestion relating to the gaps between two consecutive meetings; i.e., it shall be not more than 120 days. Similarly, fresh attention was paid to the issues pertaining to quorum, passing of resolutions by circulation, etc.
5. One of the most significant recommendations of the Committee that could add strength to the efforts of improving corporate governance is the one relating to the creation of a "specific section on corporate governance" in the annual report of the company covering many a significant aspect. In addition, the Committee also recommended to add to the directors' report a part on 'Management Discussion and Analysis' report to improve upon the disclosure requirements. As a matter of response to this suggestion, the Government has incorporated clause (3) to section 134, making it obligatory to the Board to submit a report at the general meeting a report containing statements on the following matters:
    (a) the extract of the annual return as provided under sub-section (3) of section 92;
    (b) number of meetings of the Board;
    (c) Directors' Responsibility Statement;

(d) a statement on declaration given by independent directors under sub-section (6) of section 149;

(e) in case of a company covered under sub-section (1) of section 178, company's policy on directors' appointment and remuneration including criteria for determining qualifications, positive attributes, independence of a director and other matters provided under sub-section (3) of section 178;

(f) explanations or comments by the Board on every qualification, reservation or adverse remark or disclaimer made—

  (i) by the auditor in his report; and

  (ii) by the company secretary in practice in his secretarial audit report;

(g) particulars of loans, guarantees or investments under section 186;

(h) particulars of contracts or arrangements with related parties referred to in sub-section (*1*) of section 188 in the prescribed form;

(i) the state of the company's affairs;

(j) the amounts, if any, which it proposes to carry to any reserves;

(k) the amount, if any, which it recommends should be paid by way of dividend;

(l) material changes and commitments, if any, affecting the financial position of the company which have occurred between the end of the financial year of the company to which the financial statements relate and the date of the report;

(m) the conservation of energy, technology absorption, foreign exchange earnings and outgo, in such manner as may be prescribed;

(n) a statement indicating development and implementation of a risk management policy for the company including identification therein of elements of risk, if any, which in the opinion of the Board may threaten the existence of the company;

(o) the details about the policy developed and implemented by the company on corporate social responsibility initiatives taken during the year;

(p) in case of a listed company and every other public company having such paid-up share capital as may be prescribed, a statement indicating the manner in which formal annual evaluation has been made by the Board of its own performance and that of its committees and individual directors; and

(q) such other matters as may be prescribed.

6. The Committee also made crucial observations in respect of the listing conditions and listing agreement. Basing on the suggestions of the Committee, the clauses in the Listing Agreement were modified and broad based by the BSE. A separate section was created in the Listing Agreement to understand the state of affairs of corporate governance at the company level. The SEBI is also putting constant

watch on these matters. These issues were discussed in separate chapters of this book.

7. In order to make the listing agreement very powerful, the Committee recommended that the Securities Contracts (Regulation) Act, 1956 be amended to empower SEBI and the Stock Exchange to take deterrent action in case of violation of the Listing Agreement. Accordingly, the Securities Contracts Act was amended in 2004 to include the following two clauses under section (23A) by way of penalty for failure to furnish information, return, etc.
   (a) to furnish any information, document, books, returns or report to a recognized stock exchange, fails to furnish the same within the time specified therefor in the listing agreement or conditions or bye-laws of the recognised stock exchange, shall be liable to a penalty [which shall not be less than one lakh rupees but which may extend to one lakh rupees for each day during which such failure continues subject to a maximum of one crore rupees] for each such failure; and
   (b) to maintain books of account or records, as per the listing agreement or conditions, or bye-laws of a recognised stock exchange, fails to maintain the same, shall be liable to a penalty [which shall not be less than one lakh rupees but which may extend to one lakh rupees for each day during which such failure continues subject to a maximum of one crore rupees.]

8

CHAPTER

SEBI's Second Committee on Corporate Governance [Shri N.R. Narayana Murthy Committee]

1. INTRODUCTION

In furtherance of its efforts towards improving the standards of corporate governance, the Securities and Exchange Board of India [SEBI] constituted another committee in 2002 under the Chairmanship of Shri N.R. Narayana Murthy, Chairman and Chief Mentor of Infosys Technologies Limited. The other members of the Committee were:

1. Shri Y H Malegam, Managing Partner, S B Billimoria & Co.
2. Shri Ravi Narain, Managing Director, NSE
3. Shri A C Muthiah, President, FICCI
4. Shri R K Somany, President, ASSOCHAM
5. Shri Ashok Soota, President, CII
6. Shri M K Doogar, Representative, PHDCCI
7. Shri Sumit Mazumder, President, BCCI
8. Shri Kamlesh S. Vikamsey, Member – Central Council, ICAI
9. Shri S Gangopadhyay, President, ICSI
10. Shri T. R. Ramaswami, CEO, AMBI
11. Dr. Manoj Vaish, Executive Director, BSE
12. Shri A K Narayan, President, Tamil Nadu Investors Association
13. Shri Nitin Shingala, Investors Grievances Forum

14. Prof. Manubhai Shah, Managing Trustee, CERC
15. Shri Omkar Goswami, Chief Economist, CII
16. Ms Sucheta Dalal, Consulting Editor, Financial Express
17. Shri R Gopalakrishnan, Executive Director, Tata Sons Ltd.
18. Shri D M Satwalekar, M D & CEO, HDFC Standard Life Insurance
19. Shri M K Chouhan, Chairman, Mahendra & Young Knowledge Foundation
20. Ms. D N Raval, Executive Director, SEBI
21. Shri Pratip Kar, Executive Director, SEBI
22. Shri P K Bindlish, General Manager, SEBI, Member Secretary

2. TERMS OF REFERENCE

The terms of reference for the Committee were set out as below:

1. to review the performance of corporate governance; and
2. to determine the role of companies in responding to rumour and other price-sensitive information circulating in the market, in order to enhance the transparency and integrity of the market. .

The Committee met thrice on December 7, 2002, January 7, 2003 and February 8, 2003 to deliberate on the issues pertaining to the above two terms of reference and make suitable recommendations.

3. METHODOLOGY ADOPTED

The Committee designed its own methodology, which is quite interesting. To begin with, the Committee deliberated upon the issues and prepared draft recommendations. Those recommendations were circulated to the members. They were asked to rate the recommendations on a scale of 1(least) through 10 (most) across the following seven parameters:

(i) Importance – How important is the recommendation to the member?

(ii) Fairness – Does the recommendation enhance fairness to all stakeholders, by minimizing asymmetry of benefits?

(iii) Accountability – Does the recommendation make corporate management more accountable?

(iv) Transparency – Does the recommendation enhance transparency?

(v) Ease of implementation – Is the recommendation easy to implement?

(vi) Verification – Is the recommendation objectively verifiable?

(vii) Enforcement – Can the recommendation be effectively enforced?

The ratings received from members were first aggregated across recommendations and tabulated. Recommendations whose ratings were 7 and above were then aggregated, on each of the seven parameters set out above. The rating score for each such recommendation was aggregated. The recommendations were then sorted out in descending order of importance. The top 20 recommendations were presented to the Committee for their views. These recommendations were discussed in detail by the members to form the basis for the final recommendations of the Committee. Certain recommendations that were not part of the top 20 recommendations were also presented to the Committee. This was because of the significance of the issues. Certain recommendations that were already contained in the Report of the Naresh Chandra Committee on Corporate Audit and Governance (the "Naresh Chandra Committee") were taken into consideration by this Committee. The members of the Committee agreed in principle on some of the recommendations given by the Naresh Chandra Committee that have a direct bearing on the governance practices. Like the earlier committees, Narayana Murthy Committee also categorized the recommendations into mandatory and non-mandatory classes and accordingly advised SEBI to take necessary action. The Committee also suggested to instruct Stock Exchanges to modify the Listing Agreement, to keep in line with the recommendations of the Committee. The Committee has taken every care to incorporate the view points of the members, based on their responses to the questionnaire. Care is also taken to record the qualitative opinions of the members; where it became difficult to assign numerical weights.

4. RECOMMENDATIONS OF THE COMMITTEE

Basing on the methodology adopted, the Committee attempted to categorise the recommendations as mandatory and non-mandatory. This speaks of the priority of the issues and the urgency in taking action. The recommendations are listed on the basis of the key issues:

1. **Audit Committees:** In respect of the functioning of audit committee, the Committee made the following recommendations:
    - to examine the financial statements and draft audit report, including quarterly/half-yearly financial information;
    - to hold discussions with the Management on the financial condition and results of operations;
    - to seek compliance report on the adherence to the laws and risk management practices;
    - to verify the notings and letters issued by the auditors;
    - to examine the records of related party transactions; and

- To ensure that the members of the audit committee are financially literate to know the ins and outs of the financial matters. What is considered important is the ability to read and understand financial statements. It is considered desirable to have membership in a professional organization, or experience in finance and accounting.

2. **Audit Reports and Audit Qualifications:** The Committee noted that accounting policies and principles were selected by a company's management. Consequently, the onus rests on the management to explain the different ways of reporting business transactions. It is the responsibility of the auditor to qualify the report in case he disagrees with the explanation given by the company's management. In no case, the auditor shall justify the departure from an accounting standard. It is the responsibility of the auditor to express his opinion clearly and to agree or disagree with the management's viewpoint. If he so desires, the auditor may make references in the footnotes of such matters of agreement or disagreement.
3. **Related Party Transactions:** This is one of the biggest maladies of the Indian corporate world. Families, owning more than one company, generally tend to influence the shareholders, auditors, creditors for ignoring these inter-company transactions, e.g., transactions between Satyam and Maytas. As the name itself is suggesting, the transactions also topsy-turvied.

   The following two aspects are very important for understanding the issues involved:

   1. Who is a related party?
   2. What is the arm's length principle?

In respect of the first one, the Murthy Committee has recommended that the term 'related party' shall have the same meaning as contained in Accounting Standard 18 (titled Related Party Transactions) issued by the Institution of Chartered Accountants of India. The AS – 18 has defined the term as follows:

"Parties are considered to be related if at any time during the reporting period one party has the ability to control the other party or exercise significant influence over the other party in making financial and/or operating decisions. A transfer of resources or obligations between related parties, regardless of whether or not a price is charged."

Second, in identifying related party transactions, the meaning ascribed to the 'arm's length' principle is very significant. The present Committee, giving credence to this principle, noted that a reference may be made to the report of the Department of Company Affairs' Expert Group on Transfer Pricing Guidelines for a suitable definition. The committee held the view that all related party transactions must be placed before the audit committee. If any transaction violates the principle of arm's length, the management should provide justification of the same.

As a matter of fact, this issue was discussed at length by the Naresh Chandra Committee and felt that the audit committee should discuss all related party transactions which are not in the ordinary course of business or not on "arms length" basis and, in approving or rejecting the transactions shall consider all relevant facts and circumstances including risks, costs and benefits to the company; director's independence, and the availability of other sources for comparable services or products - and shall approve only those transactions that are in the best interests of the company.

5. RISK MANAGEMENT

This is the issue that is gaining the attention of stakeholders, of late, in the discussions on corporate governance. As a matter of fact, risk management is an issue concerned with the management, since risk is associated with the business operations. After all, business is risk taking. The Murthy Committee believed that it is important for Corporate Boards to be fully aware of the risks facing the business and that it is important for shareholders to know about the process by which companies manage their business risks; which may include company-specific risks, industry, economic, and political risks. In the context of globalization of operations, risks attend to these activities have also to be dealt with effectively.

As a measure of making the stakeholders aware of the risks involved, the committee has made the following recommendations:

1. Board has to take proper care in the risk assessment and minimization procedures. These procedures should be periodically reviewed, so as to modify the strategies from time to time.

   The company management should bring to the notice of the Board from time to time all the changes and attendant risks in the form of a report. This document should be formally approved by the Board.
2. It is also considered necessary to train Board members in the business model of the company and the risk profile of the business. It is the duty of the directors to know the risk complexion of the business and strategies designed and employed to mitigate such risks.

6. INITIAL PUBLIC OFFERINGS (IPOs)

Investors and companies are connected through the public offerings. Significant disclosures are expected to be made through the IPOs. Market sentiment is very strongly associated with the number and volume of IPOs. This is a matter which the Naresh Chandra Committee has not touched upon. The Murthy Committee strongly believed that IPOs is an avenue to test the adequacy or otherwise of the disclosure practices being followed by a company. In this regard, the recommendation of the Committee is that the companies shall disclose all the necessary information about the company's sales, revenue, assets, capital, etc. It is also necessary that the company shall prepare a statement of funds utilised for purposes other than those stated in the offer document/prospectus. This will be considered a big deviation by the market. Hence, both the auditor and audit committee shall have complete information on this.

7. CODE OF CONDUCT FOR BOARD OF DIRECTORS (BOD)

This is yet another issue which the Narayana Murthy Committee has touched upon. Naresh Chandra presumed the role of Board to be genuine. Going a step further the Kumar Mangalam Birla Committee defined the role and responsibilities of management. It also felt that there is a need to define a 'code of conduct' for the BOD. The present committee also felt that it should be obligatory for the Board of a company to lay down the code of conduct for all Board members and senior management of a company. This code of conduct shall be posted on the website of the company.

It is the duty of the Board members to comply with this code and make a part of the annual report of the company. The committee in this regard insisted that the CEO and COO make a statement of compliance in this regard.

8. ROLE OF NOMINEE, NON-EXECUTIVE, AND INDEPENDENT DIRECTORS

The following are the key recommendations in respect of the role of various kinds of directors:

1. The appointment of a director on the Board should be made by the shareholders. An institutional director, so appointed, shall have the same responsibilities and shall be subject to the same liabilities as any other director. The same principle shall apply to the nominee directors also.
2. Compensation to be paid to the executive and non-executive directors shall be decided by the Board with the approval of shareholders in general meeting. Limits shall also be fixed on the maximum number of stock options that can be granted to the executive and non-executive directors.
3. Companies should also publish their compensation philosophy and statement of entitled compensation in respect of non-executive directors in their annual report. All this information shall also be hosted on the website of the company. It is also obligatory on the part of the non-executive directors to disclose their stock holding in the listed company in which they are proposed to be appointed as directors.

4. The Committee preferred to define the non-executive director as the person, who:
    - does not have any material pecuniary relationships or transactions with the company, and any other person connected with the company in any capacity;
    - is not related to promoters or management at the board level or at one level below the board;
    - has not been an executive of the company in the immediately preceding three financial years;
    - is not a partner or an executive of the statutory audit firm;
    - is not a supplier, service provider or customer of the company;
    - is not a substantial shareholder of the company, i.e., owning two percent or more of the block of voting shares.

9. WHISTLE BLOWING

Whistle blowing is now accepted to be a practice even in the public administration. The Companies Act has entrusted this job to the Audit Committee to ensure the establishment of 'vigil mechanism'. Clauses 9 and 10 of section 177 of the Act, 2013 make it obligatory for every company to establish a vigil mechanism. The clauses make it obligatory for every listed company to:

- establish a vigil mechanism for directors and employees to report genuine concerns in such manner as may be prescribed; and
- provide for adequate safeguards against victimization of persons who use such mechanism.

In the light of the wider acceptance of the concept, the committee made the following recommendations to take advantage of this tool.

- ➢ to enable such persons to have approach to the audit committee without necessarily informing their supervisors;
- ➢ to ensure that this right of access is communicated to all employees through means of internal circulars; and
- ➢ to provide assurance that such persons will not be victimized.

It is appreciable that the Committee and the Act are conscious of the protection that is required to be extended to the 'whistle blowers'; whether they be employees, directors, or other stakeholders. As a matter of fact, the New Act seeks to extend protection through section 218 to the employees participating in the investigation taken up under sections 210, 212, 213 or 219. Similar protection also needs to be extended to those helping contain malfeasance or misfeasance under section 177 of the Act.

10. OTHER RECOMMENDATIONS

The Committee has also focused its attention on some other significant aspects, which included the following:

1. The Committee noted the following additional suggestions relating to the following aspects:
    - review of investments made by the company;
    - review the number of directorships that can be held by an individual;
    - review of the provisions relating to the composition of the Board of Directors of the holding and subsidiary companies;
    - to ensure that at least one-third of the Board of Directors of the subsidiary company shall be non-executive directors of the parent company;
    - review the financial statements of the subsidiary company by the parent company; and
    - review of minutes of the meetings of the subsidiary company by the parent company.
2. The Committee recommended that the performance of the non-executive directors should be done by a peer group comprising the entire Board of Directors.
3. The Committee also wanted SEBI to makes certain rules relating to disclosure in the report issued by a security analyst.

11. NARAYANA MURTHY COMMITTEE VS THE OTHER TWO COMMITTEES

In the previous chapter, it was highlighted that the issue of Corporate Governance was examined in many a detail by two other committees, viz., Naresh Chandra Committee (1999) and Kumar Mangalam Birla Committee (May 7, 1999). The Narayana Murthy Committee has gone into the recommendations of the above committees and felt that certain recommendations of Naresh Chandra Committee are still valid and hence reiterated them in its own way in the following words:

1. The management shall provide a clear description of the material contingent liabilities and the risks associated with it. It is also necessary to get the comments of the auditor on these liabilities. This should be highlighted significantly in the annual report. The committee felt there may be some significant risk factors that could adversely affect the company's future financial condition and results of operations.
2. The CEO and CFO shall certify that:

- they have reviewed the balance sheet and profit and loss account and all its schedules and notes on accounts, as well as the cash flow statements and the Directors' Report;
- these statements do not contain any material untrue statement or omit any material fact; and there are no misleading statements in the reports;
- these statements present a true and fair view of the company, as per the existing accounting and auditing standards and applicable laws;
- the company has established internal controls and they have evaluated the effectiveness of internal control systems of the company;
- they have brought to the notice of the auditors and the Audit Committee deficiencies noticed by them; internal control, if any, and what they have done or propose to do to rectify these;
- they have also focused their attention on the instances of significant fraud, if any, that involves management or employees having a significant role in the company's internal control systems; and the same is brought to the notice of the auditors and the audit committee; and
- they have indicated to the auditors and the Audit Committee all the significant changes in internal control and/or of accounting policies during the year.

3. Narayana Murthy Committee has made a far reaching recommendation to the Government in respect of non-executive and independent directors relating to the exemption these directors from civil and criminal liabilities. It suggested to the SEBI to recommend that such exemptions need to be specifically spelt out for the relevant laws by the relevant departments of the Government and independent regulators, as the case may be.

12. THE END NOTE

The Committee at the end made a valid observation stating that there is no "one size fits all" structure for corporate governance. The Committee was categorical in expressing themselves that the governance issues are based on the prevailing environment. Governance extends beyond law. Mere compliance only goes to the extent of satisfying the legal obligations. Ideal governance shall permeat all boundaries to care for the welfare of all the stakeholders.

13. PROVISIONS IN COMPANIES ACT, 2013 AS FOLLOW-UP OF THE RECOMMENDATIONS

It will be interesting to the readers and the policy makers to examine to what extent the recommendations of the Narayana Murthy Committee could find place in the Companies Act, 2013.

1. In respect of the constitution and functioning Audit Committee, the Narayana Murthy Committee recommended to constitute the same with persons having understanding of the financial statements, etc. and also to review the financial position, etc. This recommendation was considered by the Government and incorporated the same in section 177 of the Act.
2. In respect of audit reports and audit qualifications, the Committee has put the onus on the management to explain the deviations in the accounting policies and principles. In such a context, the auditor has the responsibility to express a qualification, in case he disagrees with the explanation given by the management. This was incorporated through section 145 of the Act stating that the auditor of the company shall sign the auditor's report or sign and certify any other document of the company in accordance with the provisions of sub-section (2) of section 141. He is also under an obligation to qualify the report, if there are any adverse effects on the functioning of the company mentioned in the auditor's report.
3. Relating to the third party transactions, the Act has incorporated provisions in a more comprehensive manner, than what was suggested by the Committee. Section 188 dealt with this subject.

   As per the same, the Board of Directors of the company shall not enter into any contract or arrangement with a related party unless, there is a specific approval. Such transactions may relate to:

   (a) sale, purchase or supply of any goods or materials;
   (b) selling or otherwise disposing of, or buying, property of any kind;
   (c) leasing of property of any kind;
   (d) availing or rendering of any services;
   (e) appointment of any agent for purchase or sale of goods or other items of property;
   (f) such transactions relating to any subsidiary or associated company; and
   (g) underwriting the subscription of any securities or derivatives of the company.

   However, there could be exceptions in case of small companies having low paid up capital. Similarly no member of the company shall vote on such special resolution, if he is a related party:
4. All contracts signed by the company shall be reported through the report of the Board of directors along with the justification for entering into such contract or arrangement.
5. If such contracts are signed without obtaining the consent of the Board, the same may be reported at the meeting of the shareholders within three months from the date on which such contract or arrangement was entered into.

6. It is open to the company to proceed against a director or any other employee who had entered into such contract without the express approval of the Board and later by the shareholders.
7. Any director or any other employee of a company, who enters into contracts without any authorization is punishable with imprisonment for a term which may extend to one year or with fine.

The Committee is categorical about the code of conduct for the Board of Directors. Through the provisions incorporated in sections 149 to 172, the Companies Act, 2013 has provided for many measures that can ensure the desired conduct. Specific mention may be made of section 166, which indicated the duties of the directors. According to this section, every director of the company:

(i) shall act in accordance with the articles of the company;
(ii) shall act in good faith in order to promote the objects of the company;
(iii) shall exercise his duties with due and reasonable care, skill and diligence;
(iv) shall not involve in a situation affecting the interest of the company;
(v) shall not achieve any undue gain or advantage either to himself or to his relatives and others connected to him; and
(vi) shall not assign his office to any other person.

If a director of the company contravenes the provisions of this section such director shall be punishable with fine which shall not be less than one lakh rupees but which may extend to five lakh rupees.

The Act is also clear in terms of the qualifications, manner of appointment and the powers and duties of additional directors, alternate directors, nominee directors and independent directors. If these provisions are implemented in letter and spirit, there will be a sea-change in the company's Management.

9

CHAPTER

CII's Task Force on Corporate Governances

1. INTRODUCTION

It is highly appreciable that an industry association like the Confederation of Indian Industry (CII) volunteering to prescribe standards for corporate conduct.[1] It has spearheaded the movement by releasing the first Task Force Report entitled "Desirable Corporate Governance – A Code", which outlined a series of voluntary recommendations regarding best-in-class practices of corporate governance for listed companies. It is worth noting that most of the CII Code was subsequently incorporated in SEBI's Kumar Mangalam Birla Committee Report and thereafter in Clause 49 of the Listing Agreement. Moreover, the CII Code was the first and probably a unique instance where an industry association took the lead in prescribing corporate governance standards for listed companies.

Realizing the fact that the corporate misconduct has continued unabated even in India and also due to the fact that there is a greater necessity to reform the governance norms still further, the CII set up another Task Force under the Chairmanship or Mr. Naresh Chandra, retired Civil Servant of Government of India in February 2009 to recommend ways of further improving the corporate governance standards and practices both in letter and spirit. Writing the Foreword to the Report of the Task Force, Mr. Venu Srinivasan, the then President of CII has made the most pertinent observation as follows:

"It needs to be recognised that while the superstructure of corporate governance is built on laws and regulations, these cannot be anything more than a basic framework. Much of the best-in-class corporate governance is voluntary – of companies taking conscious decisions of going beyond the mere letter of law. The spirit of this Task Force Report is to encourage better practices through voluntary adoption - based on a firm conviction that good corporate governance not only comes from within but also generates significantly greater reputational and stakeholder value when perceived to go beyond the rubric of law."

The Task Force consisted of the following:

1. Mr. Naresh Chandra, Chairman, Task Force on Corporate Governance, CII.
2. Dr. J J Irani, Director, Tata Sons Ltd.
3. Mr. Uday S Kotak, Chairman, CII Corporate Governance Council & Executive Vice-Chairman and Managing Director, Kotak Mahindra Bank Limited.
4. Mr. Y H Malegam, Chairman Emeritus, S B Billimoria & Co.
5. Dr. Omkar Goswami, Chairman, CERG Advisory Pvt. Ltd.
6. Mr. Deepak M Satwalekar, Independent Director.
7. Mr. Shardul Shroff, Managing Partner, Amarchand & Mangaldas & Suresh A Shroff & Co.
8. Mr. Amal Ganguli, Independent Director.
9. Mr. Ajay Bahl, Partner, AZB & Partners.

2. TERMS OF REFERENCE

It is customary that the agency constituting the Task Force, or the Committee or the Study Group sets that the terms of reference, which the Task Force should address to. In the case of the present Task Force, the matters to be examined are given in the form of certain issues to be considered for further study and recommendation. They are as follows:

1. Appointment of Independent Directors.
2. Duties, liabilities and remuneration of Independent Directors.
3. Remuneration of Committee of the Board.
4. Audit Committee of the Board.
5. Separation of the offices of the Chairman and the Chief Executive Officer (CEO).
6. Attending the Board and Committee meetings through teleconferencing and videoconferencing.
7. Executive sessions of the independent directors.
8. The role of the Board and the shareholders in the related party transactions.
9. Auditor-company relationship.
10. Independence of auditors.
11. Certificate of Independence.
12. Audit Partner Rotation.

13. Auditor Liability.
14. Appointment of Auditors.
15. Qualifications introduced by Statutory Auditors or Internal Auditors in their Reports, Tax Audit Report or CARO Reports.
16. Whistle Blowing Policy.
17. Risk Management Framework.
18. The Legal and Regulatory Standards.
19. The Capability of Regulatory Agencies – Ensuring quality in audit process.
20. Effective and Credible Enforcement.
21. Confiscation of Shares.
22. Personal Liability.
23. Role of External Institutions.
    (a) Institutional Investors.
    (b) The Press.

3. THE WORK OF THE TASK FORCE

As has already been pointed out, CII holds the view that "while Law may need to be strengthened when occasions so demand, there are fundamental limits to using legislative and regulatory instruments to enforce better corporate governance. The report has attempted to suggest certain voluntary recommendations for industry to adopt. The report was thus structured according to the different elements of corporate governance as detailed below:

I. The Board of Directors
   - Non-Executive and Independent Directors
   - Committees of the Board
   - Significant related party transactions

II. Auditors
   - Independence of Auditors
   - Rotation of Audit Partners

III. Regulatory Agencies
   - Legal and Regulatory Standards
   - Effective and Credible Enforcement

IV. External Institutions
   - Institutional Investors
   - The Press

4. RECOMMENDATIONS OF THE TASK FORCE

After a detailed and thorough study of the issues concerning the corporate governance, the Task Force made altogether 25 recommendations. It is commendable that the work of the Committee has remained a landmark for the reason that the recommendations of the Task Force were taken into account by the Government, Stock Exchanges and the external agencies too. They have, as a matter of fact, served as the basis for amending the Companies Act and the Listing Agreement. Attempt has been made in the following pages to highlight the major recommendations of the Task Force and also indicate whether and to what extent the individual recommendations were given effect to.

4.1 Non-Executive and Independent Directors

In respect of Non-Executive Directors (NEDs) and Independent Directors (IDs), the Task Force (TF) touched upon the following aspects:

(i) Appointment;
(ii) Duties and liabilities; and
(iii) Remuneration.

As regards the appointment of NEDs or IDs, the TF has recommended that all the listed companies have Nominations Committee, comprising a majority of independent directors, including its chairman. This committee's task should be to:

- search for, evaluate, shortlist and recommend appropriate independent directors and NEDs, subject to the broad directions of the full Board; and
- design processes for evaluating the effectiveness of individual directors as well as the Board as a whole.

The Nomination Committee should also be the body that evaluates and recommends the appointment of executive directors. A separate section in the chapter on corporate governance in the annual reports of listed companies could outline the work done by the Nomination Committee during the year under consideration.

Sections 149 and 150 of the Companies Act, 2013 deal with the appointment, qualifications and manner of selection of Independent Directors and maintenance of data base for appointing IDs. In respect of the composition, qualifications, and other matters, clauses (4) to (13) of Section 149 have detailed the issues. As per these clauses;

- Every company shall have at least one director staying in India for a total period of not less than one hundred and eighty-two days in the previous calendar year.
- Every listed public company shall have at least one-third of the total number of directors as independent directors. It is within the domain of the Central

Government to prescribe such minimum number. All companies to which these provisions are applicable shall comply with them within a period of one year.

- The Act has also elaborated on the concept of 'Independent Director (ID) under clause-6. As per the Act, ID is one who is a person of integrity and possesses relevant expertise and experience.
- He shall also be such a person who is not a promoter and having any relation with the promoters or directors of the company. It is important to note that such a person shall not have any pecuniary relationship with the company, or its associates.
- Further, the person, who is supposed to be appointed as Independent Director, shall make a declaration that he is fully qualified to hold the position. Later on, it shall be the responsibility of the person and the company to abide by the rules and regulations, as specified in the Act.
- The Act is very specific in providing compensation to the Independent Directors. They will be eligible to receive sitting allowance and shall not be entitled to any stock option and may receive remuneration by way of fee provided under sub-section (5) of section 197 and reimbursement of expenses for participation in the Board and other meetings and profit related commission as may be approved by the members.
- Further, an independent director shall hold office for a term up to five consecutive years on the Board of a company, and be eligible for reappointment. However, the independent director cannot hold office for more than two consecutive terms. Nevertheless, he may prefer to be appointed again after the expiration of three years of ceasing to become an independent director.
- As per the provisions of the Act, the independent director, shall be held liable, only in respect of such acts of omission or commission by a company which had occurred with his knowledge.

It is evident from the above that the Companies Act, 2013 has dealt at length with the issue of IDs. While the Task Force (TF) has not made any recommendation as to the number of IDs, the Act has prescribed a minimum of one-third of the total number of directors on the Board.

Second, the TF has done an elaborate exercise in designing the format and recommended that a 'Letter of Appointment' be issued to every NED or ID, just as it is done in case of appointing employees and Executive Directors. The letter is supposed to address the following aspects:

- specify the expectation of the Board from the appointed director;
- the Board-level committee(s) in which the director is expected to serve and its tasks;

- the fiduciary duties that come with such an appointment;
- the term of the appointment;
- the Code of Business Ethics that the company expects its directors and employees to follow;
- the list of actions that a director cannot do in the company;
- the liabilities that accompany such a fiduciary position, including whether the concerned director is covered by any Directors and Officers (D&O) insurance; and
- the remuneration, including sitting fees and stock options, if any.

The letter stating the terms and conditions of appointment of any NED or independent director should form a part of the disclosure to shareholders at the time of the ratification of his/her appointment or re-appointment to the Board. This issue was not addressed by the New Companies Act, 2013.

Third, in respect of payment of compensation to the NEDs and IDs for their services, the TF has made the following recommendations.

4.2 Fixed Contractual Remuneration

The Task Force recommended that the Companies Act, 1956, be amended so that companies have the option of giving a fixed contractual remuneration to NEDs and independent directors, which is not linked to the net profit or lack of it. Therefore, companies should be given the option to choose between:

(a) paying a fixed contractual remuneration to its NEDs and IDs, subject to an appropriate ceiling depending on the size of the company; or

(b) continuing with the existing practice of paying out up to 1% (or 3%) of the net profits of the standalone entity as defined in the Companies Act, 1956

For any company, the choice should be uniform for all NEDs and independent directors, i.e. some cannot be paid a commission of profits; while others are paid a fixed amount. If the option chosen is (a) above, then the NEDs and independent directors will not be eligible for any commission on profits. The current limits and constraints on sitting fees and stock options or restricted stock may remain unchanged. If stock options are granted as a form of payment to NEDs and independent directors, then these must be held by the concerned director until one year of his exit from the Board.

4.3 Structure of Compensation to NEDs

The Task Force recommended that listed companies use the following template in structuring their remuneration to NEDs and independent directors

- *Fixed component*: This should be fixed at relatively low level, so as to align NEDs and independent directors to have a greater share of variable pay. Ideally, these should not be more than 30% of the total cash remuneration package.
- *Variable Component*: This shall depend on the attendance at the Board and Committee meetings.
- Additional payment for being the chairman of the Board, especially if he/she is a non-executive chairman.
- Additional payment for being the chairman of the Audit Committee.
- Additional payment for being the chairman of other committees of the Board.
- Additional payment for being members of Board committees: Audit, Shareholder Grievance, Remuneration, Nomination, etc.

The Task Force is particular that any structure of remuneration adopted by the Board should be disclosed to the shareholders in the annual report of the company.

4.4 Remuneration Committee

The Task Force recommended that listed companies should have a Remuneration Committee of the Board, comprising at least three members, majority of whom should be independent directors. The Committee shall be entrusted with the responsibility for setting the remuneration for all executive directors and the executive chairman, including any compensation payments, such as retiral benefits or stock options. It should also recommend and monitor the level and structure of pay for senior management, i.e., one level below the Board. It is also to be ensured that the terms of reference, its role, the authority delegated to it by the Board, and what it has done for the year under review are to be brought to the notice of the shareholders in a separate section or chapter on corporate governance in the annual report.

In spite of the painstaking effort put in by the committee, this particular recommendation was not accepted by the Government and there was no mention of any fixed or contractual remuneration. The New Act has only reiterated its old stand in making a mention that the payment of remuneration to the IDs will be by way of fees as provided under sub-section (5) of Section 197, reimbursement of expenses for participation in the Board and other meetings and profit related commission as may be approved by the members.

4.5 Constitution of Committees of the Board

Having examined thoroughly the practices prevailing then in the corporate world, the TF has recommended to the Government to constitute the following two committees:

1. Remuneration Committee.
2. Audit Committee.

In addition, the TF has also indicated the structure and other issues to be taken into account in constitution. The following recommendations of the TF are significant in this regard.

1. Remunerations Committee
2. Audit Committee
3. Separation of offices of Chairman & Chief Executive Officer
4. Board Meetings through Tele-Conferencing
5. Executive Sessions

As against the above recommendations of the TF, the Companies Act, 2013 has provided for the constitution of (1) Nomination and Remuneration Committee; (2) Audit Committee; and (3) Stakeholders Relationship Committee. The last one is the addition made to the Act. The relevant sections of the Act provided for the following:

- As per section 178 of the Act, it is mandatory for every listed company to constitute the Nomination and Remuneration Committee consisting of three or more non-executive directors; out of which not less than one-half shall be independent directors.
- If the company desires that the chairperson of the company shall be appointed as a member of the Nomination and Remuneration Committee; but shall not chair such Committee.
- While constituting the Committee, the Board shall identify persons who can serve as members on this Committee.
- Since this is an important committee, generally senior persons in the administration are chosen to be in the committee. Keeping in view of the responsibility cast on the members of the committee, they are supposed to first formulate criteria for determining qualifications, positive attributes and independence of a director and recommend to the Board.
- It is also the duty of the Committee to lay down a policy of remuneration to the key managerial personnel, keeping in view of the provisions of the Companies Act.

The general guidelines that the Committee need to follow while recommending a suitable compensation package are stated as follows:

(a) the level and composition of remuneration is reasonable and sufficient to attract, retain and motivate directors of the quality required to run the company successfully;

(b) relationship of remuneration to performance is clear and meets appropriate performance benchmarks; and

(c) remuneration to directors, key managerial personnel and senior management involves a balance between fixed and incentive pay reflecting short and long-term performance objectives appropriate to the working of the company and its goals:

4.6 Stakeholders Relationship Committee

It is also necessary as per the New Companies Act to constitute a committee with the name 'Stakeholders Relationship Committee' to consider and resolve the grievances of security holders of the company. The meetings of the Committee are also required to be held periodically and the status informed to the shareholders of the company. In case of any failure to comply with this provision, the company shall be punishable with fine which shall not be less than one lakh rupees but which may extend to five lakh rupees and every officer of the company who is in default shall be punishable with imprisonment for a term which may extend to one year or with fine which shall not be less than twenty-five thousand rupees but which may extend to one lakh rupees, or with both.

4.7 Constitution of Audit Committee

One of the crucial recommendations of the Task Force pertains to the constitution of an Audit Committee. The same was taken into consideration and the Government incorporated the relevant provisions under section 177 of the Act. Accordingly, every listed company shall constitute an Audit Committee with a minimum of three directors with independent directors forming a majority. The Chairperson shall be one having ability to read and understand, the financial statements. In case there is already such Committee existing, the same shall be reconstituted in accordance with the provisions of the new Act. One interesting aspect of this provision is that the Government has clearly laid down the duties of the Audit Committee, which are as follows:

- to suggest appointment, remuneration and terms of appointment of auditors of the company;
- to review and monitor the auditor's independence and performance, and effectiveness of audit process;
- to examine the financial statement and the auditors' report thereon;
- to review the transactions pertaining to the related parties.
- to scrutinise the grant of inter-corporate loans and investments;
- to undertake valuation of assets of the company, wherever it is necessary;

- to check and evaluate internal financial controls and risk management systems;
- to monitor the end use of funds raised through public offers and related matters.

In addition to the above, the Audit Committee is also required to call for the comments of the auditors about internal control systems, the scope of audit, including the observations of the auditors and review of financial statement before their submission to the Board. Basing on the review, the Committee may make recommendations to the BOD for better functioning of the company. While discharging the duties, the Committee also can investigate into any matter referred to it by the Board and for this purpose shall have power to obtain professional advice from external sources and have full access to information contained in the records of the company. Further, it is the responsibility of the Committee to disclose the matter where the Board had not accepted any recommendation of the Audit Committee together with the reasons therefor. It is also imminent for every listed company to establish a vigil mechanism for directors and employees to report genuine concerns in such manner as may be prescribed. The vigil mechanism shall provide for adequate safeguards against victimisation of persons who use such mechanism and make provision for direct access to the chairperson of the Audit Committee in appropriate or exceptional cases.

4.8 Related Party Transactions

This has emerged an important issue in company management, because of the fact that there are risks associated with such transactions to the company, besides impacting the independence of a director. Hence, the TF has made the recommendation that the Audit Committee should pre-approve all related party transactions which are not in the ordinary course of business or not on "arms length basis" or any amendment of such related party transactions. This measure is expected to strengthen the transparency mechanism of the company.

5. ROLE OF AUDITORS

In the field of company management, the role of the auditor is very paramount. An auditor is the linking pin between the company and the outsiders. He is the person who can present an impartial and dispassionate view of the affairs of the company. For this reason, the TF and the Act have placed much value on the role of the auditor in ensuring smooth and responsible industrial economy. Let us now take a look at the recommendations of the TF in this regard.

A. **Appointment of Auditors:** The Audit Committee of the Board of Directors shall be the first point of reference regarding the appointment of auditors. The Audit Committee should have regard to the entire profile of the audit firm, its responsible audit partner, his or her previous experience of handling audit for similar sized companies and the firm and the audit partner's assurance that the audit clerks and/or understudy chartered accountants or paralegals appointed for discharge of the task for the listed company shall have done a minimum number of years of study of accounting principles and have minimum prior experience as audit clerks.

B. **Certificate of Independence:** Every company must obtain a certificate from the auditor certifying the firm's independence and arm's length relationship with the client company. The Certificate of Independence should certify that the firm, together with its consulting and specialised services affiliates, subsidiaries and associated companies or network or group entities have not / has not undertaken any prohibited non-audit assignments for the company and are independent vis-à-vis the client company, by reason of revenues earned and the independence test are observed.

C. **Rotation of Audit Partners:** The partners handling the audit assignment of a listed company should be rotated after every six years. The partners and at least 50% of the audit engagement team responsible for the audit should be rotated every six years, but this should be staggered so that on any given day there is not a change in partner and engagement manager. A cooling off period of 3 years should elapse before a partner can resume the same audit assignment.

D. **Auditors Revenue from the Audit Client:** No more than 10% of the revenues of an audit firm singly or taken together with its subsidiaries, associates or affiliated entities, should come from a single corporate client or group with whom there is also an audit engagement.

E. **Auditor and the Company Relationship:** The report of the Naresh Chandra Committee on Corporate Audit and Governance suggested that auditors should refrain from providing non-audit services to their audit and recommended an explicit list of prohibited non-audit services. The Task Force, noted that the recommendation was endorsed by the Ministry of Corporate Affairs and has also been proposed under the Companies Bill, 2009. The Task Force concurred with the recommendation that legislation should expressly prohibit auditors from rendering certain services to their audit clients. Audit firms should have to mandatorily disclose network agreements between the audit firms and non-audit companies, pecuniary interests exceeding 2% between the audit firm and its affiliate non-audit service firm or company and measures of Chinese walls and data protection/confidentiality that are in place between them. The Task Force noted the existing practice in this regard. And found it to be sufficient.

F. **Auditor's Liability:** The firm, as a statutory auditor or internal auditor, has to confidentially disclose its net worth to the listed company appointing it. Each member of the audit firm is liable to an unlimited extent unless they have formed a limited liability partnership firm or company for professional services as permitted to be incorporated by the relevant professional disciplinary body (ICAI). Even in the case of a limited liability firm undertaking audit in the future, under the new law, the individual auditor responsible for dereliction of duty shall have unlimited liability and the firm and its partners shall have liability limited to the extent of their paid-in capital and free or undistributed reserves.

G. **Qualifications in Auditor's Report:** ICAI should appoint a committee to standardise the language of disclaimers or qualifications permissible to audit firms. Anything beyond the scope of such permitted language should require the auditor to provide sufficient explanation.

H. **Whistle Blowing Mechanism:** The Task Force recommended to institute of a mechanism for employees to report concerns about unethical behaviour, actual or suspected fraud, or violation of the company's code of conduct or ethics policy. It should also provide for adequate safeguards against victimization of employees who avail of the mechanism, and also allows direct access to the Chairperson of the audit committee in exceptional cases.

I. **Risk Management:** The Board, its audit committee and its executive management must collectively identify the risks impacting the company's business and document their process of risk identification, risk minimisation, risk optimization as a part of a risk management policy or strategy. The Board should also affirm that it has put in place critical risk management framework across the company, which is overseen once every six months by the Board.

It is to be appreciated that the Government has almost incorporated majority of the suggestions in the new Companies Act, 2013 under Sections 139 through 148. The entire Chapter-XIV is devoted to the issues pertaining to the role of the auditor. Therefore, the discussion of the above aspects with particular reference to the provisions incorporated in the Companies Act, 2013 was avoided.

6. ROLE OF REGULATORY MECHANISMS

Beginning with the Registrar of Companies, there has been an elaborate mechanism created to ensure smooth and effective working of companies in India. The entire Companies Act is devoted to this purpose. While the Central Government has the general power of supervision and authority to prescribe standards under the Companies Act, it has created many other institutional mechanisms to deal with the specific situations, as of the following:

1. Constitution of National Financial Reporting Authority (NFRA) under section 132.

2. Establishment of Serious Fraud Investigation Office (SFIO) under section 212.
3. Constitution of National Company Law Tribunal (NCLT) under section 408.
4. Constitution of Appellate Tribunal (AT) under section 410.
5. Establishment of Special Courts under section 435.

In addition to the above, the Securities and Exchange Board of India (SEBI), diverse Stock Exchanges (through their listing agreements) are issuing various guidelines for the proper and effective functioning of the companies in India.

Against this background, let us take a look at the recommendations of the TF, as given below:

Harmonization of Corporate Governance Standards: The Task Force suggested that the Government and the SEBI, at as a market Regulators are required to ensure standards in the corporate governance practices that are deemed desirable for listed companies.

Audit Oversight Mechanism: In the interest of investors, the general public and the auditors, the Task Force recommended that the Government intervenes to strengthen the ICAI Quality Review Board and facilitates its functioning of ensuring the quality of the audit process through an oversight mechanism on the lines of Public Company Accounting Oversight Board (PCAOB) of the United States.

Effective and Credible Enforcement: The Task Force recommended that the instances of investigations of serious corporate fraud must be coordinated and jointly investigated. Joint investigations/interrogation by the regulators for example, the SFIO and the CBI should be conducted in tandem. On the lines of the recommendations of the Naresh Chandra Committee Report on Corporate Audit and Governance, a Task Force should be constituted for each case under a designated team leader and in the interest of adequate control and efficiency. A committee headed by the Cabinet Secretary should directly oversee the appointments to, and the functioning of this office. There shall be effective mechanism also to coordinate the work of concerned department and agencies. Civil recovery for acts of misfeasance, malfeasance, nonfeasance and recovery from the wrongdoers and criminal offences and penalties and punishments should be adjudicated appropriately. It is also suggested to have a fixed time frame for settlement of the cases.

Cancellation of Fraudulent Securities: It is also suggested that there is an urgent need to incorporate a provision for confiscation and cancellation of securities of a person who perpetrates a securities fraud on the company. It would also be in the fitness of things to prescribe suitable penalties/punishments.

Liability of Directors and Employees: It is recommended that there shall be personal penalties on directors and employees who seek unjust enrichment and commit offence with such intentions. Such punishments should be commensurate with the wrongful act and be imposed in addition to disgorgement of wrongful gains. Further, non-executive directors cannot be made to undergo the ordeal of a trial for offence of non-compliance with a statutory provision unless it can be established prima facie that they were liable for the failure on part of the company.

These recommendations of the Task Force were considered well to a great extent. The Central Government and the SEBI are involving in drawing detailed guidelines for implementation by the companies. One good example is the recent notification dated 10-04-2015 by the Central Government in respect to matters to be included in the Auditor's Report under section 143(2) of the Act, 2013. Similarly, the Act has paved the way for the constitution of NFRA which is entrusted with the responsibility of monitoring and enforcing compliance with accounting and auditing standards in such manner as may be prescribed.

7. ROLE OF EXTERNAL INSTITUTIONS

It is quite laudable that the CII's Task Force has recognized the role of external institutions like the media. After all, public opinion is the basis for existence in the society. No individual or corporation can function in vacuum without people. It is for this reason Peter F. Drucker in his book entitled 'The End of Economic Man: The Origins of Totalitarianism' has very rightly observed that "the more the masses need the belief in the leader, the more they feel the strain which this belief imposes and its danger of sudden collapse. This collapse will come as soon as there is an alternative to the belief in the demonic nature of the leader, that is, as soon as there is a new order and a new creed; and that is the mainspring of totalitarian success and strength. It cannot come otherwise. There can be no doubt that the masses in their great majority will continue to worship their self invented demon out of sheer despair as long as the only alterative is the vacuum."[2] It is in this context, the TF has proposed the following course of action.

A. **Shareholder Activism:** Long-term institutional investors, pension funds or infrastructure funds can help to develop a vibrant state of shareholder activism in the country. There is a greater need to design and implement 'model codes' for proper exercise of their votes in the interest of the company. It is needless to mention that it is the shareholder who can analyze and review corporate actions proactively and assume responsible roles in monitoring corporate governance and promoting good management of companies in which he invests. In view of the growing literacy (including financial literacy) there is no reason for companies to be complacent on the activities and sharing of information.

B. **Media as a Stakeholder:** The Task Force recommended that media, especially in the financial analytics and reporting business, should invest more in analytical, financial and legal rigour to highlight the issues of corporate world. It is needless to state that the press and the civil society have become active in mobilizing the public opinion. Civil society has been widely recognized as an essential 'third sector'. Its strength can have a positive influence on the state and the market.[3] Therefore, civil society is seen as an increasingly important agent for promoting good governance like transparency, effectiveness, openness, responsiveness and accountability. Civil society can further ensure good governance, by policy analysis and advocacy; second, by regulation and monitoring of state performance and thus can influence the behavior of public officials. Media can also build social capital and enable citizens to identify and articulate their values, beliefs, civic norms and democratic practices. It has the strength to mobilise particular constituencies, especially the vulnerable and marginalized sectors of masses, to participate more fully in politics and public affairs. The ultimate objective of development being 'well-being of the masses', the affairs of the companies are required to be conducted in the most transparent manner. For these reasons, civil society is considered a sphere of social interaction between the household (family) and the state. The same is manifested in the norms of community cooperative structures of voluntary association and networks of public communication. Civil society, being the force of its own, is destined to play a larger role by the United Nations in achieving the Millennium Development Goals. Even in the context of India, the role of civil society has been emerging paramount. The influence of the civil society was glaring in shaping the public policy in the context of Lok Pal of India. Similarly, the crusade of the civil society is considerable in waging war against corruption, atrocities on women, children, etc. The situation, as at present, is such that no sensible corporation can afford to ignore the clarion call.

Notes and References

1. Confederation of Indian Industry (CII) is a Non-Government, not-for-profit, industry led and industry managed organization founded in 1895. It is the India's premier business association having about 7400 members from private as well as public sectors. It has an indirect membership over 100,000 enterprises from around 250 national and regional sectoral industry bodies. CII assists industry to identify and execute corporate citizenship programmes; collaborates with civil society organistions for integrated and inclusive development. CII is serving as a reference point for Indian industry and the international business community.
2. Drucker, Peter F., 'The End of Economic Man : The Origins of Totalitarianism", Transaction Publishers, Rutgers, New Jersy, 1995, pp. 234&235.
3. Aisha Ghaus – Pasha, 'Role of Civil Society Organisations in Governance', Paper Presented at the 6th Global Forum on Reinvesting Government Towards Participatory and Transparent Governance, 24 – 27 May, 2005, Seoul, Republic of Korea.

10

CHAPTER

Clause-49 of Listing Agreement of BSE

1. WHAT IS LISTING?

Listing means admission of securities of an issuer to trading privileges (dealings) on a Stock Exchange through a formal agreement. The prime objective of admission to dealings on the exchange is to provide liquidity and marketability to securities, as also to provide a mechanism for effective control and supervision of trading. In the normal course of things, it is the issuing company that applies for listing. But in some countries, the exchange may list a company because its stock is already being traded actively via informal channels. Initial listing requirement may include the history of the company, financial position, details of share capital, etc. In this regard, the Securities and Exchange Board of India (SEBI) requires a company, desirous of listing its securities on the Exchange, to file an application, in the prescribed form. This could be before the company wishes to issue securities to the public. Alternatively, an existing company, even not intending to go for public issue, can also list its securities on the exchange. The companies intending to be listed are requested to follow all the requirements as specified in the Companies Act and the listing norms issued by SEBI from time to time. The Bye-laws of the Exchanges become crucial in this regard. It is the prerogative of the exchange to specify the conditions, rules and regulations to be followed by applicants willing to be listed. The issuer shall submit an application for admission of its securities to dealings on the Exchange in such form, as may be prescribed by the Exchange. The Exchange would scrutinize the application for compliance in respect of the existing laws such as the Contracts (Regulation) Act, 1956, Companies Act, 2013 and the Rules, Regulations and norms as may be issued by SEBI/Exchange from time to time.

1.1 Listing Conditions and Requirements

The following are some of the general conditions stipulated by the Stock Exchanges in India when companies approach them for listing. There could be specific compliance requirements by the individual Exchanges. It is completely within their domain; subject to the applicable laws of India.

- Exchanges are not supposed to grant admission to dealings on the Exchange to a security of an issuer; unless the issuer complies with the listing conditions.
- The Exchanges are required to ensure that the company (issuer) has not failed in the dispatch of physical share certificates to, and/or credit of demat shares to the accounts of all the security-holders, maintained with the depositories.
- The Exchange is required to inform the Depository of the Basis of allotment and also permission given to the issuer for carrying on dealings on the Exchange.
- The company whose securities are permitted to be listed shall execute a Listing Agreement, in the prescribed form with the Exchange. SEBI being the regulator has the necessary power to suggest modification or amendments to the agreement; which shall be complied with.
- In the case of a new issue or further issue by the already listed company, Relevant Authority may grant permission for trading in any security at the Exchange.

Whereas, the guidelines for listing of securities at the Bombay Stock Exchange stipulate that the company intending to have its securities listed on the Exchange to comply with the requirements specified by it. Some such important requirements are noted below:

1.2 Minimum Listing Requirements for New Companies

The following eligibility criteria have been prescribed for listing of companies on BSE, through Initial Public Offerings (IPOs) & Follow-on Public Offerings (FPOs):

- The minimum post-issue paid-up capital of the applicant company shall be Rs. 10 crore for IPOs & Rs.3 crore for FPOs.
- The minimum issue size shall be Rs. 10 crore.
- The minimum market capitalization of the Company shall be Rs. 25 crore, calculated on the basis of the issue price.
- All the issuers are required to include a disclaimer clause, forming part of the offer document with a condition that in the event of the market capitalization stipulation not being fulfilled the securities of the issuer would not be listed on BSE.
- The issuer is not in default in compliance of the listing agreement.

- It is to be noted that all these stipulations are in addition to the conditions prescribed by the SEBI under (Issue of Capital & Disclosure Requirements) Regulations, 2009.
- There is a specific mention of the list of legislations, whose provisions are to be complied with on a mandatory basis; which included the following:
    - Securities Contracts (Regulations) Act 1956.
    - Securities Contracts (Regulation) Rules 1957.
    - Securities and Exchange Board of India Act 1992.
    - And any other circular, clarifications, guidelines issued by the appropriate authority.
    - Companies Act, 2013.

1.3 Submission of Letter of Application

As per Section 73 of the Companies Act, 1956, a company seeking listing of its securities on BSE is required to submit a Letter of Application to all the stock exchanges; where it proposes to have its securities listed before filing the prospectus with the Registrar of Companies.

1.4 Allotment of Securities

As per the Listing Agreement, a company is required to complete the allotment of securities offered to the public within 30 days of the date of closure of the subscription list and approach the Designated Stock Exchange for approval of the basis of allotment. In case of Book Building issues, allotment shall be made not later than 15 days from the closure of the issue, failing which interest at the rate of 15% shall be paid to the investors.

1.5 Trading Permission

As per SEBI Guidelines, an issuer company should complete the formalities for trading at all the stock exchanges where the securities are proposed to be listed within 7 working days of finalization of the basis of allotment. A company should scrupulously adhere to the time limit specified in SEBI (Disclosure and Investor Protection) Guidelines 2000 for allotment of all securities and dispatch of allotment letters/share certificates/credit in depository accounts and refund orders and for obtaining the listing permissions of all the exchanges. In the event of listing permission to a company being denied by any stock exchange; the company cannot proceed with the allotment of shares. However, the company may file an appeal before SEBI under Section 22 of the Securities Contracts (Regulation) Act, 1956.

1.6 Requirement of 1% Security

Companies making public/rights issues are required to deposit 1% of the issue amount with the Designated Stock Exchange before the issue opens. This amount is liable to be forfeited in the event of the company not resolving the complaints of investors regarding delay in sending refund orders/share certificates, non-payment of commission to underwriters, brokers, etc.

1.7 Payment of Listing Fees

All companies listed on BSE are required to pay to BSE the Annual Listing Fees by 30th April of every financial year as per the Schedule of Listing Fees prescribed from time to time.

1.8 Compliance with the Listing Agreement

Companies desirous of getting their securities listed at BSE are required to enter into an agreement with BSE called the Listing Agreement (LA), under which they are required to make certain disclosures and perform certain acts, failing which the company may face disciplinary action, including suspension/delisting of securities.

As such, the Listing Agreement is of great importance and is executed under the common seal of a company. Under the Listing Agreement, a company undertakes, amongst other things, to provide facilities for prompt transfer, registration, sub-division and consolidation of securities. The company is also required to undertake to give proper notice of closure of transfer books and record dates. It is obligatory on the part of the company to submit copies of the Balance Sheets and Profit and Loss Accounts to BSE.It is also necessary to file shareholding patterns and financial results on a quarterly basis. It is the duty of the companies to inform the Exchange all important happenings in the company; which may have the chance of affecting the financial performance of the Company and its stock prices. The Listing Department of BSE monitors the compliance by the companies with the provisions of the Listing Agreement from time to time. Care is taken by the Exchange to see that all the conditions of the Agreement are properly honoured. It is within the powers of the Exchange to take Penal action against the defaulting companies.

2. WHAT IS LISTING AGREEMENT? WHAT DOES IT CONTAIN?

Listing Agreement (LA) is an agreement between a company, which wants to list its shares on the Stock Exchange for the purpose of trading by the investors. This is a primary requirement to be executed by the company as a first step to enter the trading platform. Every Stock Exchange will have its own format of agreement to suit its own requirements and conditions that need to be agreed upon by a prospective company. As far as corporate governance is concerned, the listing agreement of the Bombay Stock Exchange (BSE) is prominent documents widely cited and referred. Thus, BSE deserves all appreciation for its efforts and drafting the listing agreement so comprehensive that every committee constituted on Corporate Governance had a reference in more than one occasion. The Committees have also suggested certain modifications to the LA, and the BSE has promptly responded.

The agreement between the company and the exchange gives rise to contractual obligations under the Indian Contracts Act, 1872. Whereby, under section 37 of the Act, the parties to a contract must either perform or offer to perform their respective promises, unless such performance is dispensed with or excused under the provisions of this Act or any other law. The LA of BSE (as per its website on 20.7.2015) is a document of 80 pages containing 55 clauses. Of these, clauses 45 and 51 were deleted. The important matters that are covered in the LA include the following:

- Procedure to be followed for the issue of Letters of Allotment for public offerings, Rights issues and other securities.
- Issues of share certificates.
- Voting rights on different kinds of securities.
- Maintenance of Registers/Records pertaining to various kinds of issues.
- Procedure to be followed for transfer of shares and other securities.
- Closure of Transfer Books for the purpose of declaration of dividend or the issue of securities.
- Intimation to the Exchange about the Buyback of Securities, declaration/ recommendation of dividend/Rights or issue of debentures, etc.
- Redemption of shares/debentures.
- Intimation to the Exchange of the changes in the Board of Directors, Managing Director, Managing Agents, Secretaries, Treasures, Auditors, etc.
- Forwarding of the Annual Reports (audited and unaudited) in the prescribed formats.
- Disclosure of particulars relating to Loans and Advances, Accounting Standards, Related Party Transactions, etc.
- Submission of statement showing shareholding pattern.
- Agreeing to follow all the guidelines of SEBI and other bodies in case of Employee Benefit Schemes.
- Keeping the Exchange informed of the events such as strikes, lock-outs, closure on account of power cuts, etc.
- Agreeing to comply with the requirements of Securities Contracts (Regulation) Rules, 1957 in respect of minimum level of public shareholding.

- Preparation and submission of Financial Results.
- Details pertaining to the use of issue proceeds.
- Corporate governance.
- Corporate filing and discrimination system.
- Dissemination of all important information through the website.
- Submission of Business Responsibility Reports describing the initiatives taken by them from an environmental, social and governance perspective in the prescribed format.

3. CLAUSE 49 OF THE LISTING AGREEMENT ON CORPORATE GOVERNANCE

The most significant aspect of the LA of BSE is its detailed and comprehensive statement on the subject of 'Corporate Governance'. This clause makes the companies (willing to get their securities listed on the exchange) agree to comply with the provisions of clause-49, which shall be implemented in a manner, so as to achieve the objectives of the principles mentioned hereunder:

I. Protection to Shareholders

A. The Rights of Shareholders

1. The company has the obligation to protect the rights of the shareholders in terms of the following:
    (a) to participate in the decisions concerning fundamental corporate changes and to be informed of such decisions, much in advance;
    (b) to participate effectively and vote in general meetings of the shareholders;
    (c) to inform, of the rules, including voting procedures that govern general shareholder meetings;
    (d) to provide an opportunity to ask questions on the items placed on the agenda of general meetings, and to propose resolutions, subject to reasonable limitations;
    (e) to facilitate participation in the nomination and election of board members;
    (f) to facilitate the exercise of ownership rights by all shareholders, including institutional investors;
    (g) to institute a suitable mechanism to address the grievances of the shareholders; and
    (h) to ensure adequate protection of the rights of minority shareholders and also create a suitable mechanism for the redressal of their grievances.

2. The company should provide adequate and timely information to the shareholders regarding:
   (a) date, location and agenda of general meetings, as well as full and timely information regarding the issues to be discussed at the meeting.
   (b) capital structures and arrangements that enable certain shareholders to obtain a degree of control disproportionate to their equity ownership should be disclosed.
   (c) information about the rights attached to all series and classes of shares before they are purchased.
3. The company should ensure equitable treatment of all shareholders, including minority and foreign shareholders in that:
   (a) all shareholders of the same series of a class should be treated equally;
   (b) effective shareholder participation in key corporate governance decisions, such as the nomination and election of board members, should be facilitated;
   (c) exercise of voting rights by foreign shareholders should be facilitated;
   (d) the company should devise a framework to avoid Insider trading and abusive self-dealing;
   (e) equitable treatment of all shareholders; and
   (f) not to make it unduly difficult or expensive to cast votes at the meetings.

B. Role of Stakeholders in Corporate Governance

It is the duty of the company to recognise the rights of all stakeholders and encourage cooperation between company and the stakeholders. The nature of cooperation may relate to any of the following issues, such as:

(a) Respecting the rights of stakeholders that are established by law or through mutual agreements.
(b) Creating opportunity to obtain effective redressal for violation of their rights.
(c) Encouraging mechanisms for employee participation.
(d) Providing access to relevant, sufficient and reliable information on a timely and regular basis.
(e) Devising an effective whistle blower mechanism enabling stakeholders, including individual employees and their representative bodies, to freely communicate their concerns about illegal or unethical practices.

C. Disclosure and Transparency

It is also obligatory for the companies to ensure timely and accurate disclosure on all material matters including the financial situation, performance, ownership, and governance of the company. Such obligations may relate to:

(a) submission of information in accordance with the prescribed standards of accounting, financial and non-financial disclosure;
(b) disseminating information timely and with less cost;
(c) maintaining the minutes of the meeting explicitly recording dissenting opinions, if any;
(d) implementing the prescribed accounting standards in letter and spirit in the preparation of financial statements; and
(e) conducting audit by the external auditor in a timely manner.

D. Responsibilities of the Board

Every member of the Board is responsible to disclose to the board any material interest he has in the dealings of the company. The Board and top management have the bounded duty to maintain confidentiality of information in order to foster a culture for good decision-making.

1. The key functions of the Board include:
   (a) Reviewing and guiding corporate strategy, preparing major plans of action, annual budgets and business plans; and setting performance objectives; it is also their duty to formulate a risk management policy and implement the same.
   (b) Monitoring the effectiveness of the company's governance practices and making changes as needed.
   (c) Selecting, compensating, monitoring and, when necessary, replacing key executives and overseeing succession planning.
   (d) Aligning key executive and board remuneration with the long-term interests of the company and its shareholders.
   (e) Ensuring a transparent board nomination process with the diversity of thought, experience, knowledge, perspective and gender representation in the Board.
   (f) Monitoring and managing potential conflicts of interest of management, board members with other stakeholders.
   (g) Ensuring the integrity of the company's accounting and financial reporting practices.
   (h) Overseeing the process of disclosure and communications.
   (i) Monitoring and reviewing Board Evaluation framework.
2. Other responsibilities that may be thought of in this connection are:
   (a) To ensure effective monitoring of the management and should be accountable to the company and the shareholders.

(b) to set corporate culture to see that the values as fixed are followed by every executive and employee;
(c) to act on a fully informed basis, in good faith, and with due diligence in the best interest of the company;
(d) to ensure that the Board members are kept up to date relating to the functioning of the company;
(e) to treat all categories of shareholders fairly and cordially;
(f) to follow high ethical standards;
(g) to exercise independent judgement on the corporate affairs;
(h) to consider assigning adequate number of non-executive Board members to the issues where impartial judgement is necessary;
(i) to ensure that the decisions of the Board shall not lead to significant risks;
(j) to assist executive management by providing guidance to formulate appropriate strategies on the key areas of the company;
(k) to commit themselves effectively to their responsibilities at all times;
(l) to ensure the availability and access to accurate, relevant and timely information; and
(m) to facilitate the Independent Directors to perform their role effectively as a Board member and also a member of a committee.

II. Board of Directors

As regards the Board, the LA contains many important clauses which cover the number, composition, functions and responsibilities. The most salient of them are highlighted hereunder.

A. Composition of Board

The Board of Directors of the company shall have an optimum combination of executive and non-executive directors with at least one woman director and not less than fifty percent of the Board of Directors comprising non-executive directors.

Where the Chairman of the Board is a non-executive director, at least one-third of the Board should comprise independent directors. In case the regular non-executive Chairman is a promoter of the company, at least one-half of the Board of the company shall consist of independent directors.

B. Independent Directors

The expression 'independent director' shall mean a non-executive director, other than a nominee director of the company, who in the opinion of the company:

(a) is a person of integrity and possesses relevant expertise and experience;

(b) is not a promoter of the company or its holding, subsidiary or associate company; nor is related to any of them;

(c) has no material pecuniary relationship with the company, or any of its directors;

(d) has no pecuniary relationship or transaction with the company or their promoters, or directors, amounting to two per cent or more of its gross turnover or total income subject to such other limits;

(e) who does not hold or has not held the position of a key managerial personnel on the company in any of the three financial years immediately preceding the financial year in which he is proposed to be appointed;

(f) who is not an employee or proprietor or a partner, in any of the three financial years immediately preceding the financial year in which he is proposed to be appointed, as a firm of a auditors or company secretaries in practice or cost auditors of the company. This will also apply to a law firm which is extending legal services to the company;

(g) does not hold together with his relatives two per cent or more of the total voting power of the company;

(h) receives twenty-five per cent or more of its receipts from the company; and

(i) is a material supplier, service provider or customer or a lessor or lessee of the company.

1. Limit on Number of Directorships

(a) A person shall not serve as an independent director in more than seven listed companies.

(b) Any person who is serving as a whole time director in any listed company shall serve as an independent director in not more than three listed companies.

2. Maximum Tenure of Independent Directors

The maximum tenure of Independent Directors shall be in accordance with the provisions of the Companies Act, 2013. As per section 149 (10) of the Act, an independent director will hold the office for a term of 5 years. He is, however, eligible to be reappointed for another term of 5 years; but not beyond two consecutive terms of five years each. Nevertheless, he will be eligible to be reappointed after the expiration of three years.

3. Formal Letter of Appointment to Independent Directors

(a) The company shall issue a formal letter of appointment to independent directors in the manner as provided in the Companies Act, 2013.

(b) The terms and conditions of appointment shall also be disclosed on the website of the company.

4. **Performance Evaluation of Independent Directors**
   (a) The Nomination Committee shall lay down the evaluation criteria for performance evaluation of independent directors.
   (b) The company shall disclose the criteria for performance evaluation, as laid down by the Nomination Committee, in its Annual Report.
   (c) The performance evaluation of independent directors shall be done by the entire Board of Directors.
   (d) It is only on the basis of the performance, a decision is to be taken on his continuation or reappointment.
5. **Separate Meetings of the Independent Directors**
   (a) The independent directors of the company shall hold at least one meeting in a year, without the attendance of non-independent directors and members of management. All the independent directors of the company shall strive to be present at such meeting.
   (b) The independent directors in the meeting shall, inter-alia:
      (i) review the performance of non-independent directors and the Board as a whole;
      (ii) review the performance of the Chairperson of the company, taking into account the views of executive directors and non-executive directors; and
      (iii) assess the quality, quantity and timeliness of flow of information between the company management and the Board of Directors and among other stakeholders also.
6. **Familiarisation Programme for Independent Directors**
   (a) Every company shall organize a familiarization programme for Independent Directors with the company in respect of their roles, rights, responsibilities in the company. It is implicit that they are exposed to the nature of the business, competitors and general environment in industry.
   (b) The details of such familiarisation programmes shall be disclosed on the company's website and a web link thereto shall also be given in the Annual Report.

C. Non-Executive Directors' Compensation and Disclosures

In respect of compensation to the non-executive directors, including independent directors, shall be fixed by the Board of Directors and shall require previous approval of shareholders in General Meeting. The resolution shall also specify the limits for the maximum number of stock options that can be granted to non-executive directors, in any financial year. However, prior approval is not necessary in case of the payment of sitting fees to non-executive directors, provided the same is as per the provisions of the Companies Act, 2013.

D. *Other Provisions as to Board and Committees*

1. The meetings of the Board must be held at least four times a year, with a maximum time gap of one hundred and twenty days between any two meetings. Care shall also be taken to see that adequate information within the time is made available to all the members.
2. It is stipulated as per the Act that the Director shall not be a member in more than ten committees or act as Chairman of more than five committees across all companies in which he is a director. Furthermore, every director shall inform the company about the committee positions he occupies in other companies and notify changes as and when they take place. This information shall also form part of the Annual Report and the Director's Report.
3. The Board shall periodically review compliance reports of all laws applicable to the company, along with the steps taken by the company to rectify instances of non-compliances.
4. The vacancy of an independent director shall be filled at the earliest, but not later than the immediate next Board meeting or three months from the date of such vacancy, whichever is later. This is to ensure that there is no gap in the continuity of the Board. However, if such vacancy does not lead to the reduction in the number of independent directors as per the Companies Act, the same may be left unfilled as per the decision of the Board.
5. The Board of Directors is also required to ensure that there is proper succession of persons in such capacity as directors, respecting the seniority of the persons.

E. *Code of Conduct*

1. The Board shall lay down a code of conduct for all Board members and senior management of the company. The code of conduct shall be posted on the website of the company.
2. All Board members and senior management personnel shall affirm compliance with the code on an annual basis. The Annual Report of the company shall contain a declaration to this effect signed by the CEO.
3. The Code of Conduct shall suitably incorporate the duties of Independent Directors as laid down in the Companies Act, 2013.
4. The independent directors shall be held liable, from the acts that had taken place only with their knowledge. There must be proper evidence to prove that such director or directors have collided with the officers of the company or others connected with the company.

F. Whistle Blower Policy

Whistle mechanism is given a prime place in the new environment. In view of many companies resorting to unethical practices, it is felt necessary to put in place such a mechanism. Few things to be done are:

1. The company shall establish a vigil mechanism for directors and employees to report concerns about unethical behaviour which is in violation of the company's code of conduct or ethics policy of the company.
2. This mechanism should also provide for adequate safeguards against victimization of director(s)/employee(s) who avail of the mechanism and also provide for direct access to the Chairman of the Audit Committee in exceptional cases.
3. The details of establishment of such mechanism shall be disclosed by the company on its website and in the Board's report. All this arrangement is required to be made consistent with the provisions of the Companies Act.

III. Audit Committee

A. Qualified and Independent Audit Committee

Every company shall constitute an independent audit committee with all the qualified staff, and entrust the duties as per the companies requirements and as per the provisions of the law. In this regard, it is to be ensured that:

1. The audit committee shall have minimum three directors as members. Two-thirds of the members of audit committee shall be independent directors.
2. All members of audit committee shall be financially literate and at least one member shall have accounting or related financial management expertise.
3. The Chairman of the Audit Committee shall be an independent director.
4. The Chairman of the Audit Committee shall be present at Annual General Meeting to answer shareholder queries.
5. The Audit Committee may invite such of the executives, as it considers appropriate (and particularly the head of the finance function) to be present at the meetings of the committee, to provide deeper insight into the issues or help in the process of examining the issues in detail.
6. The Company Secretary of the company shall act as the Secretary to the Committee.

B. Meeting of Audit Committee

In view of the significance of the role and responsibility, the Audit Committee should meet at least four times a year and not more than four months shall elapse between two meetings. The quorum shall be either two members or one third of the members of the audit committee whichever is greater. However, there shall be presence of at least two members of the Committee.

C. Powers of Audit Committee

The powers of the Audit Committee shall be as follows. The same may be enhanced by the Central Government, keeping in view of the prudent management of the corporate sector.

1. To investigate into any activity within its terms of reference.
2. To seek information from any employee.
3. To obtain outside legal or other professional advice.
4. To secure attendance of outsiders, if necessary.

D. Role of Audit Committee

The role of the Audit Committee is specified as follows:

1. to ensure that the financial statements are correct, sufficient and credible; and there are adequate disclosures;
2. to recommend the appointment, remuneration and terms of appointment of auditors to the company;
3. to approve payment to statutory auditors for non-audit services;
4. to review the annual financial statements and auditor's report thereon for onward submission to the Board. Also to focus attention on the issues to be included in the Director's Responsibility which is a requirement under the Act;
5. to review the changes, if any, in accounting policies and practices and reasons for the same;
6. to examine the major transactions involving personal judgement by the Management;
7. to review the findings of the audit and suggest suitable corrective action;
8. to ensure compliance with listing and other legal requirements relating to financial statements;
9. to ensure disclosure of any related party transactions and review the draft audit report for any qualifications;
10. to review the quarterly financial statements before submission to the board for approval;
11. to review the sources and uses of funds position from time to time, with a particular focus on the public issues and the use of such collected funds;
12. to review and monitor the auditor's independence and performance, and effectiveness of audit process;
13. to review the transactions of the company with related parties;
14. to scrutinize the dealings relating to inter-corporate loans and investments;

15. to be vigilant over the valuation of undertakings or assets of the company, wherever it is done;
16. to evaluate the internal financial controls and risk management systems;
17. to examine the adequacy of internal audit function in terms of its structure, staffing and seniority of the official heading the department, reporting structure, coverage and frequency of internal audit;
18. to alalyse the findings of any internal investigation of the matters where there is suspected fraud or irregularity due to the failure of internal control systems;
19. to hold discussion with statutory auditors before the audit commences, about the nature and scope of audit as well as post-audit discussion to ascertain any area of concern;
20. to look into the reasons for substantial defaults in the payment to the depositors, debenture holders, shareholders and creditors;
21. to review the functioning of the whistle blower mechanism;
22. to look into the appointment of CFO in terms of his qualifications and suitability to the post; and
23. to carry out any other function as directed by the BOD and as per the Act.

E. Review of Information by Audit Committee

The Audit Committee shall mandatorily review the following information:

1. management discussion and analysis of financial condition and results of operations;
2. statement of significant related party transactions;
3. correspondence that took place between the Management and auditors;
4. internal audit reports relating to internal control weaknesses; and
5. the appointment, removal and terms of remuneration of the Chief internal auditor.

IV. Nomination and Remuneration Committee

As per the Act, every company shall constitute the nomination and remuneration committee consisting of at least three non-executive directors and half of them being independent directors. Chairman of the committee shall be an independent director.

The functions of the Committee shall include:

1. formulation of the criteria for determining qualifications, positive attributes and independence of a director;
2. recommendation to the Board regarding remuneration of the directors, key managerial personnel and other employees;

3. formulation of criteria for evaluation of the efficiency of Independent Directors and the Board;
4. to recommend on the diversity in composition of the Board;
5. identifying persons qualified to become directors and who may be appointed in senior management in accordance with the criteria laid down; and
6. attending Annual General Meeting to answer the shareholders' queries. Generally, it is the Chairman who is supposed to attend such meetings.

V. Subsidiary Companies

In case of subsidiary companies, the following precautions should be taken:

(a) At least one independent director on the Board of Directors of the holding company shall be a director on the Board of Directors of the unlisted subsidiary company.

(b) The Audit Committee of the listed holding company shall also review the financial statements, and the investments made by the unlisted subsidiary company.

(c) The minutes of the Board meetings of the unlisted subsidiary company shall be placed at the Board meeting of the listed holding company.

(d) The company shall declare the list of subsidiaries owned by the listed company and the holding company shall maintain a web link of all such subsidiaries.

(e) The definition of a 'material subsidiary' is clarified in terms of percentage of investment and income. If the listed holding company invests 20 or more per cent of the net worth or if the subsidiary generates 20 per cent or more of the income of the holding company, it becomes a material subsidiary company.

(f) A special resolution in its General Meeting is required to be passed to dispose of the shares in the material subsidiaries; except by an order of the Court/ Tribunal.

(g) Similarly, a special resolution is also required to sell or dispose of or lease assets amounting to more than twenty percent of the assets of the material subsidiary on an aggregate basis during a financial year and it also requires the prior approval of shareholders.

VI. Risk Management

The principles that apply in case of risk management are as follows:

(a) The company shall lay down procedures to inform Board members about the risk assessment and minimization procedures.

(b) The Board shall be responsible for framing, implementing and monitoring the risk management plan for the company.

(c) The company shall constitute a Risk Management Committee to look after the implementation of the risk management policies and strategies.

(d) The Risk Management Committee shall consist of members of the Board of Directors in majority.

(e) The Chairman of the Committee shall be a member of the Board of Directors and other members may be drawn from the executives of the company.

VII. Related Party Transactions

Every listed company is required to be clear about the related party transactions.

A. At the outset, the related party transactions shall be identified as the one involving services or obligations between a company and a related party, regardless of whether a price is charged.

B. The following parameters may be applied to decide on the relatedness of a party:

  (i) such entity is a related party under Section 2(76) of the Companies Act, 2013; or

  (ii) such entity is a related party under the applicable accounting standards.

C. The company shall formulate a clear policy on the significance of Related Party transactions and also on dealing with Related Party transactions.

D. All Related Party transactions shall require prior approval of the Audit Committee. However, the Audit Committee may grant omnibus approval for Related Party transactions proposed to be entered into by the company subject to the following conditions:

  (a) That the transactions are already approved and are repetitive in nature and hence no special focus is necessary and there is the omnibus approval already.

  (b) The Audit Committee has satisfying itself of the need for such omnibus approval and that such approval is in the interest of the company.

  (c) Such omnibus approval shall specify (i) the name/s of the related party, nature of transaction, period of transaction, maximum amount of transaction that can be entered into; (ii) the indicative base price or contracted price, and (iii) such other conditions as the Audit Committee may deem fit.

  (d) There is a review by the Audit Committee atleast on a quarterly basis, the details of RPTs entered into by the company pursuant to each of the omnibus approval given.

  (e) That such omnibus approvals are valid for a period not exceeding one year only and fresh approval is sought after the expiry of such period.

E. All material Related Party transactions shall require approval of the shareholders through special resolution and the related parties shall abstain from voting on such resolutions. Sub-clauses 49 (VII) (D) and (E) of the LA are crucial in this regard. They specify that the following two kinds of transactions need the approval of the shareholders at the general meeting:
   (i) Transactions entered into between two government companies.
   (ii) Transactions entered into between a holding company and its wholly owned subsidiary.

VIII. Disclosures

Disclosures to be made by the listed companies are very important. For, corporate governance depends upon the edifice of information exchange. The following are some of the crucial matters on which adequate disclosures are to be made by every listed company.

A. Related Party Transactions

1. Details of all material transactions with related parties shall be disclosed quarterly along with the compliance report on corporate governance.
2. The company shall disclose the policy on dealing with Related Party Transactions on its website and a web link thereto shall be provided in the Annual Report.

B. Disclosure of Accounting Treatment

In respect of the preparation of financial statements all the accounting conventions and practices are to be disclosed. In case a treatment different from that prescribed in an accounting standard has been followed, the fact shall be disclosed in the financial statements, together with the management's explanation as to why it believes such alternative treatment is considered appropriate. In any case, the accounting practices adopted shall reflect the true and fair view of the accounts of the company.

C. Remuneration of Directors

1. All pecuniary relationship or transactions of the non-executive directors vis-à-vis the company shall be disclosed in the Annual Report.
2. In addition to the disclosures required under the Companies Act, 2013, the following are also made mandatory:
   (a) All elements of remuneration package of individual directors summarized under major groups, such as salary, benefits, bonuses, stock options, pension, etc.
   (b) Details of fixed component and performance linked incentives, along with the performance criteria.

(c) Service contracts, notice period, severance fees.

(d) Stock option details, if any – extended to directors of the board.

3. The company shall publish its criteria of making payments to non-executive directors in its annual report. Alternatively, this may be put up on the company's website and reference drawn thereto in the annual report.
4. The company shall disclose the number of shares and convertible instruments held by nonexecutive directors in the annual report.
5. Non-executive directors shall be required to disclose their shareholding in the listed company before and after they are appointed. These details must also be brought to the notice of the shareholders in the General Meeting.

D. Management

1. Management Discussion and Analysis report should form part of the Annual Report to the shareholders. This report should cover information on all important matters of the company including:

   (i) Industry structure and developments.

   (ii) Opportunities and threats.

   (iii) Segment–wise or product-wise performance.

   (iv) Outlook

   (v) Risks and concerns.

   (vi) Internal control systems.

   (vii) Financial performance and operational performance.

   (viii) Human resources.

   (ix) Industrial relations, etc.

   There shall be disclosure pertaining to all material financial and commercial transactions that may have a potential conflict with the interest of the directors, senior management and the company.

2. The Code of Conduct for the Board of Directors and the senior management shall be disclosed on the website of the company.

E. Shareholders

In all fairness the shareholders must be provided with the following information with respect to the appointment of a Director to the Board:

(a) A brief resume of the Director.

(b) Nature of his expertise in specific functional areas.

(c) Names of companies in which the person also holds the directorship and the membership of Committees of the Board.

(d) Shareholding of the proposed person.

- The notice of appointment of a director shall be intimated to the concerned Stock Exchange also.
- The Quarterly results and presentations made by the company to analysts shall be put on company's web-site, and also sent to the exchange on which the company is listed to put it on its own website.
- A committee under the Chairmanship of a non-executive director shall be formed to specifically look into the redressal of grievances of shareholders, debenture holders and other security holders. This Committee shall be designated as 'Stakeholders Relationship Committee' and shall consider and resolve the grievances of the security holders of the company including complaints related to transfer of shares, non-receipt of balance sheet, non-receipt of declared dividends.
- The company shall also take measures to expedite the process of share transfers. The Board of the company may delegate the power of share transfer to an officer or a committee or to the registrar and share transfer agents. The delegated authority shall attend to share transfer formalities at least once in a fortnight.

I. Proceeds from public issues, rights issue, preferential issues, etc.: When money is raised through an issue including public issues, rights issues or preferential issues, the company shall disclose the activities for which the funds are going to be utilized. It may be for capital expenditure, sales and marketing or working capital. Such details are required to be provided on a quarterly basis as a part of the financial results to the Audit Committee. Further, the company shall also prepare a statement of funds utilized for purposes other than those stated in the offer document/prospectus. Another precaution in this regard is that the details of utilization of funds shall be certified by the statutory auditors of the company. Furthermore, where the company has appointed a monitoring agency to monitor the utilisation of proceeds, it shall place before the Audit Committee, the monitoring report of such agency. Basing the report, the audit committee may make appropriate recommendations to the Board to take follow up action.

IX. CEO/CFO Certification

After many incidents happening in the corporate sector, leading to mis-utilisation of funds and mis-information on the financial position of the company, the Companies Act had made a rule to make CEO and CFO responsible for correct reporting. Both of them are required to certify that:

(a) they have reviewed financial statements and the cash flow statement for the year and to the best of their knowledge and belief those statements do not contain any materially untrue statements or omissions. Further to state that the financial statements present a true and fair view of the company's affairs and are in compliance with existing accounting standards, applicable laws and regulations.

(b) there are no transactions entered into by the company during the year which are fraudulent, illegal or violative of the company's code of conduct.

(c) they accept responsibility for establishing and maintaining internal controls for financial reporting and that they have evaluated the effectiveness of internal control systems of the company pertaining to financial reporting. They also have to state that they have informed the auditors and the Audit Committee of the deficiencies in the design or operation of such internal controls. They are also required to inform to the audit the measures they have taken or proposed to take for correcting such deviations.

(d) they have indicated to the auditors and the Audit Committee regarding the significant changes in internal control over financial reporting during the year and also significant changes in accounting policies during the year. Similarly, instances of significant fraud of which they have become aware shall also be brought to the notice of the shareholders, auditor and audit committee.

X. Report on Corporate Governance

A new and significant feature of the LA is the one pertaining to the reporting on the corporate governance. There shall be a separate section on corporate governance in the Annual Reports. A detailed compliance report on corporate governance shall be appended to the report and same shall be hosted on the website of the company. Non-compliance of any mandatory requirement should be specifically highlighted. The suggested list of items to be included in this report is given in **Annexure XII** of the Agreement and list of non-mandatory requirements is given in **Annexure XIII.**

Companies are required to submit a quarterly compliance report to the Stock Exchanges within 15 days from the close of quarter as per the format given in **Annexure XI**. The report shall be signed either by the Compliance Officer or the Chief Executive Officer of the company. All these measures are expected to impose specific discipline on the company.

XI. Compliance

The company shall obtain a certificate from either the auditors or practicing company secretaries regarding compliance of conditions of corporate governance as stipulated in the Agreement and annex the certificate with the Directors' report. The same shall also be sent annually to all the shareholders of the company. The same certificate shall also be sent to the Stock Exchanges along with the annual report filed by the company. The non-mandatory requirements as given in Annexure XIII may be implemented as per the discretion of the company. However, the disclosures of the compliance with mandatory requirements and adoption of the non-mandatory requirements shall be made in the section on corporate governance of the Annual Report.

For the purpose of ensuring the submission of information in as much detail as possible, the LA also provided for the submission of the following statements by the listed companies.

Annexure X	:	Format for submission of information to be placed before Board of Directors.
Annexure XI	:	Format of quarterly compliance report on corporate governance.
Annexure XII	:	Format for submission of suggested list of items to be included in the report on corporate governance in the Annual Reports of companies.
Annexure XIII	:	Format for submission of information pertaining to non-mandatory requirements.

4. OTHER CLAUSES OF SIGNIFICANCE

Though clause 49 is specific on corporate governance, there are two other clauses that can be considered significant in ensuring transparency and accountability of the company management.

A. Clause 41

This clause is about the preparation and submission of financial results. One of the serious issues complained of in the corporate failures/scams is the misreporting or under-reporting of the financial data. In order to ensure that the companies share authentic information with the stakeholders, this clause is being pressed into service by the BSE. The clause has contained details as to the kind of information that is needed to be submitted to the exchange for onward sharing in terms of the following heads:

I. Preparation and Submission of Financial Results

(a) The financial statements of the company are to be prepared on the basis of accrual accounting policy and in accordance with uniform accounting practices adopted for all the periods.

(b) The company shall submit its quarterly and yearly financial results to the stock exchange in the manner prescribed in this clause.

(c) The company has an option either to submit audited or unaudited quarterly and yearly financial results to the stock exchange within forty-five days of the end of each quarter.

(d) The company shall submit audited financial results for the entire financial year, within sixty days of the end of the financial year. The company shall also submit the audited financial results in respect of the last quarter along with the results for the entire financial year.

(e) If the company has subsidiaries : It also becomes mandatory:

  (i) to submit quarterly and year to date stand-alone financial results to the stock exchange within forty-five days of the end of the quarter, also submit quarterly and year to date consolidated financial results within forty-five days from the end of the quarter; and

  (ii) it shall also submit annual audited consolidated financial results to the stock exchange within sixty days from the end of the financial year.

  (iii) the company shall also submit by way of a note, a statement of assets and liabilities as at the end of the half-year.

(f) The financial results covered under this sub-clause shall be submitted to the stock exchange within fifteen minutes of conclusion of the meeting of the Board or Committee in which they were approved in the mode specified by the stock exchange.

(g) In case, the company has subsidiaries and it opts to submit consolidated financial results, it may submit the consolidated financials as per the International Financial Reporting Standards (IFRS) notified by the International Accounting Standards Board.

(h) The company shall also ensure that the limited review/audit reports submitted to the Stock Exchanges on a quarterly/annual basis shall be given only by an auditor who has subjected himself to the peer review process of Institute of Chartered Accountants of India (ICAI) and holds a valid certificate issued by the Peer Review Board of the ICAI.

II. Manner of Approval and Authentication of the Financial Results

(a) As per the procedure laid down in this clause, every listed company: shall submit quarterly financial results as approved by the Board of Directors of the company or by a committee thereof, other than the audit committee.

(b) The Committee shall consist of not less than one third of the directors and shall include the Managing Director and at least one Independent Director.

(c) The financial results submitted to the Stock Exchange shall be signed by the Chairman or Managing Director, or a Whole Time Director. In the absence of all of them, they may be signed by any person who is duly authorized by the Board to sign the financial results.

(d) The report mentioned above shall be placed before the Board of Directors or the Committee and after approval, the same shall be submitted to the Stock Exchange where the variation between unaudited financials and financials amended pursuant to limited review for the same period, exceeds 10%.

(e) The annual audited financial results shall be approved by the Board of Directors of the company and shall be signed in the manner as specified.

III. Intimation of Board Meeting

In case of Board meetings, the company shall give prior intimation of the date and purpose of meetings of the Board or Committee in which the financial results will be considered. There shall be a notice of seven clear calendar days prior to the meeting. The company shall also simultaneously issue a public notice in at least in one English daily newspaper circulating in the whole or substantially the whole of India and in one daily newspaper published in the language of the region, where the registered office of the company is situated.

IV. Other Requirements as to Financial Results

The other important requirements to be complied with by the listed companies are as follows:

(a) Where there is a variation between the unaudited quarterly or yearly financial results and the results amended pursuant to limited review for the same period to the extent of 10% or Rs.10 lakh, whichever is higher; the company shall submit to the stock exchange an explanation of the reasons for such variations. The explanation of variations so submitted shall also be approved by the Board of Directors.

(b) If the auditor has expressed any qualification or other reservation in respect of audited financial results already submitted or published, the company shall disclose such qualification or other reservation and impact of the same on the profit or loss.

(c) If the auditor has expressed any qualification or other reservation in his audit report or limited review report in respect of the financial results of any previous financial year or quarter which has an impact on the profit or loss of the reportable period, the company shall include a note to the financial results regarding the reasons and impact of such qualification.

(d) If the company has changed its name suggesting any new line of business, it shall disclose the net sales or income, expenditure and net profit or loss after tax figures pertaining to the said new line of business separately and shall continue to make such disclosures for the three years succeeding the date of change in the name.

(e) If the company had not commenced commercial production or commercial operations during the reportable period, the company shall, disclose the details regarding the funds mobilized, the amounts utilized and the remaining unutilized funds. In the same way, information relating to the status of the project, the time taken to the competition and the expected date of commencement of commercial production or commercial operations is to be shared.

(f) The financial information is to be prepared in accordance with the principles laid down in Accounting Standard 25 (AS 25 – Interim Financial Reporting) issued by the Institute of Chartered Accountants of India.

(g) All items of income and expenditure arising out of transactions of exceptional nature shall be disclosed.

(h) Extraordinary items, if any, shall be disclosed in accordance with Accounting Standard 5 (AS 5 – Net Profit or Loss for the Period, Prior Period Items and Changes in Accounting Policies) issued by ICAI.

(i) Changes in accounting policies, if any, shall be disclosed in accordance with Accounting Standard 5 issued by ICAI.

(j) Seasonal variations in the activities of the business are to be disclosed. In addition, they may supplement their financial results with information for the current and preceding years on a rolling basis.

(k) The company shall also disclose any event that occurred during the relevant period that affects the expansion or diversification programmes, strikes and lock-outs, change in management and change in capital structure. The company shall also disclose similar material events or transactions that take place subsequent to the relevant period.

(l) The company shall disclose the following in respect of dividends paid or recommended for the year, including interim dividends:

  (i) amount of dividend distributed or proposed for distribution per share; the amounts in respect of different classes of shares shall be distinguished and the nominal values of shares shall also be indicated; and

  (ii) where dividend is paid or proposed to be paid on pro-rata basis for shares allotted during the year and the number of shares allotted, pro-rata amount of dividend per share and the aggregate amount of dividend paid or proposed to be paid on pro-rata basis.

(m) The company shall disclose the effect on the financial results of material changes in the composition of the company, if any, including the business combinations, acquisitions or disposal of subsidiaries.

(n) The company shall also disclose the number of investor complaints pending at the beginning of the quarter, those received and disposed of during the quarter and those remaining unresolved at the end of the quarter.

V. Formats

In order to ensure proper submission of information by the companies, the LA contained several formats, as applicable to the diverse types of companies and situations and enclosed as annexues to the LA. There are nine such formats appended to this clause.

VI. Publication of Financial Results in Newspapers

(a) The company shall, within 48 hours of conclusion of the Board or Committee meeting at which the financial results were approved, publish a copy of the financial results and inform the stock exchange in at least in one English daily newspaper and one daily newspaper published in the language of the region.

(b) Where the company has submitted consolidated financial results in addition to stand-alone financial results, it shall publish consolidated financial results along with the items on a stand-alone basis, as a footnote. These items shall include: (a) turnover (b) profit before tax (c) profit after tax. Such declarations are subject to the following conditions:

   (i) It shall intimate to the Stock Exchange in the first quarter of the financial year or within the period as specified by the SEBI in this regard and shall not change the same during the financial year.

   (ii) In case the company changes its option in any subsequent year, it shall furnish comparable figures for the previous year in accordance with the option exercised for the current year.

   (iii) It shall give a reference in the newspaper publication about the location of the company, its website and other crucial details.

   (iv) Companies that are required to prepare consolidated financial results for the first time are to indicate the same and take measures accordingly.

B. Clause-55

This clause is about the submission of Business Responsibility Reports (BRRs) describing the initiatives taken by them from an environmental, social and governance perspective in the prescribed format. This clause was inserted on the directions of the Government in 2012, making it applicable to the top 100 listed companies. The suggested formats in which information is to be submitted by the listed companies covers details about the company financial and other details. It also extends to the details about Directors, company policies, employees, contractors, group companies, joint ventures, etc.

The General Information about the Company to be Covered in Section (A) of the Format Covers the Details Regarding

1. Name of the Company.
2. Corporate Identity Number (CIN).

3. Registered address.
4. Website.
5. E-mail ID.
6. Financial Year for which information is submitted.
7. The prime industrial activity of the company.
8. Key products/services produced by the company.
9. Total number of locations where business activity is undertaken by the Company, together with details on International Locations and Number of National Locations.
10. Geographical area of the market of the company.

Section (B) Covers the Financial Details of the Company which Include

1. Paid up Capital in Rupees.
2. Total Turnover in Rupees.
3. Total profit after taxes in Rupees.
4. Total Spending on Corporate Social Responsibility (CSR) as percentage of profit after tax (%).
5. List of activities undertaken as part of CSR.

In Section (C), Information is to be Provided on the Following Matters

1. Does the Company have any Subsidiary Company/ Companies?
2. Do the Subsidiary Company/Companies participate in the BR Initiatives of the parent company?
3. Do any other entity/entities (e.g. suppliers, distributors etc.) that the Company does business with. If yes, then indicate the percentage of such entity/entities?

Section (D) is About the Business Responsibility of the Directors: Which include details of the Director/Directors responsible for implementation of the BR policy/ policies; such as:

- DIN Number
- Name
- Designation and Details of the BR head
- Frequency of Assessment of performance of the company
- Details about the publication of the BR Report.

Section (E) is very important in exacting compliance from the listed companies. This is in the form of a Questionnaire to which the listed companies are required to provide authentic answers. It is stated in the form of nine principles as detailed below:

Principle 1

1. Does the policy relating to ethics, bribery and corruption cover only the company? Yes/No.

   Does it extend to the Group/Joint Ventures/Suppliers/Contractors/NGOs/ Others? Yes/No.
2. How many stakeholder complaints have been received in the past financial year and what percentage was satisfactorily resolved by the management? To give details.

Principle 2

1. List up to 3 of your products or services whose design has incorporated social or environmental concerns, risks and opportunities.
2. Provide the details in respect of resource use like energy, water, raw material, etc. per unit of product produced.
3. Does the company have procedures in place for sustainable sourcing of the above materials? What is the extent of indigenization?
4. Has the company taken any steps to procure goods and services from local & small producers, including communities surrounding their place of work? If yes, what steps have been taken to improve their capacity and capability of local and small vendors?
5. Does the company have a mechanism to recycle products and waste? Give details.

Principle 3

1. Please indicate the Total number of employees.
2. Please indicate the Total number of employees hired on temporary/contractual/ casual basis.
3. Please indicate the Number of permanent women employees.
4. Please indicate the Number of permanent employees with disabilities
5. Do you have an employee association that is recognized by the Management.
6. What percentage of your permanent employees is members of this recognized employee association?
7. Please indicate the Number of complaints relating to child labour, forced labour, involuntary labour, sexual harassment in the last financial year and how they were addressed.
8. What percentage of your under mentioned employees were given safety and skill upgradation training in the last year?

- Permanent Employees
- Permanent Women Employees
- Casual/Temporary/Contractual Employees
- Employees with Disabilities

Principle 4

1. Has the company mapped its internal and external stakeholders? Yes/No
2. Out of the above, has the company identified the disadvantaged, vulnerable & marginalized stakeholders.
3. Are there any special initiatives taken by the company to engage with the above kinds of employees. Provide details.

Principle 5

1. Does the policy of the company on human rights cover only the company or extend to the Group/Joint Ventures/Suppliers/Contractors/NGOs/Others?
2. How many stakeholder complaints have been received in the past financial year and how they were dealt with?

Principle 6

1. Does the policy related to environmental issues covers only the company or extends to all other stakeholders.
2. What initiatives did the company take to address global environmental issues such as climate change, global warming, etc? Give details.
3. Does the company identify and assess potential environmental risks? Y/N
4. Does the company have any project related to Clean Development Mechanism? If so, provide details thereof. Also, if Yes, whether any environmental compliance report is filed?
5. Has the company undertaken any other initiatives with respect to clean technology, energy efficiency, renewable energy, etc? Y/N. Give details.
6. Are the equipment put in place to check the emission levels?
7. What are the cases filed against the company in respect of pollution? What is their present status?

Principle 7

1. Is the company a member of any trade and chamber or association? If Yes, name only those major ones that your business deals with:

2. What steps were taken to improve social service? Give the details regarding the areas of intervention like Governance and Administration, Economic Reforms, Inclusive Development Policies, Energy security, Water, Food Security, Sustainable Business Principles, etc.

Principle 8

1. Does the company have collaborative arrangements with any Non-Governmental Organization? If yes details thereof.
2. What are the programmes/projects undertaken with their collaboration?
3. Has the company done any impact assessment of such initiatives?
4. What is the company's direct contribution to community development projects? Specify the nature of contribution.
5. What are the steps taken to ensure that the community development initiative is successfully adopted by the people in the area? Explain.

Principle 9

1. What percentage of customer complaints/consumer cases are pending as on the end of financial year.
2. Does the company display product information on the product label, and follows the legal provisions in this regard?
3. Is there any case filed by any stakeholder against the company regarding unfair trade practices, irresponsible advertising and/or anti-competitive behaviour during the last five years and any case is pending? Give details.
4. Has the company carried out any consumer survey/ consumer satisfaction trends? Give details.

5. LISTING AGREEMENT (LA) AND THE RECOMMENDATIONS OF THE COMMITTEES

It has been well accepted that the Listing Agreement of the BSE had been very comprehensive. All the Committees (Naresh Chandra, Kumar Mangalam Birla and Narayana Murthy), while acknowledging the good work done by the BSE, have made the following recommendations to make it more meaningful and pointed.

1. The Naresh Chandra Committee made the comment that clause-49 of the LA, though contained mandatory provisions for the Audit Committee of the Board, it has pointed out one correction with respect to Non-Executive Directors. In the earlier version of the clause-49, only Non-Executive Directors (NEDs) could be

members of the Audit Committee, the revised clause omitted this requirement. Under the present dispensation, two-thirds of the members of the Audit Committee must be independent directors, as must the Chairman, but the rest may be either NEDs or executive directors. This was felt by the Committee a mistake and believed that it would run counter to the fundamental operating principle of good corporate governance. Therefore, the Committee recommended that the listed companies have at least a three-member Audit Committee comprising entirely of NEDs with independent directors constituting the majority.

2. Clause – 49 insists that companies should establish a mechanism for employees to report to the management concerns about unethical behaviour, actual or suspected fraud or violation of the company's code of conduct or ethics. Even though companies have adopted and communicated the existence of a whistle-blowing policy, there has not been any success on this front in corporate India. The Task Force pondered over what organisations can do to create an environment which helps employees to prevent undesirable practices. It was felt that adoption and encouragement of the policy should be made mandatory for all listed companies. This is bound to send a positive signal to employees that the management is willing and able to prevent any illegal activity and also ensure that there is a process by which the individuals can expose the problem to the appropriate authority who can take action. The employees would need to be oriented towards the company's ethics policy.

   HR Department can play an effective role in the process by assigning ombudsmen, providing special telephone numbers and email IDs. Since whistleblowers need to be provided with high degree of protection, the Listing Agreement should consider providing statutory protection from dismissal or wrongful termination for acting as a whistle blower. There are many examples that can be drawn from the experience of other countries. Fostering a culture which promotes and supports institutionalisation of whistle blowing policy shall deter corrupt practices and help in preventing corporate disgrace and debacles. Therefore, the Task Force recommended that there shall be an institutional mechanism for employees to report concerns about unethical behaviour. The company shall also provide for adequate safeguards against victimization of employees who avail of the mechanism.

3. The Kumar Mangalam Birla Committee has also suggested many significant changes in the clause-49 of the LA.

4. The Narayana Murthy Committee suggested that SEBI should work towards harmonizing the provisions of clause-49 of the LA and those of the Companies Act, 1956. The Committee is particular that SEBI should recommend to the Government to change the provisions of the Companies Act, 1956 in line with the requirements of the LA.

6. LISTING AGREEMENT AND THE COMPANIES ACT, 2013

It is evident from the above that all the Committees constituted to look into the issue of Corporate Governance have been suggesting to give credence to the clauses of the LA through the provisions in the Companies Act, so that the governance practices would be more effective. It is a matter of gratification that the New Companies Act has taken care of many of these issues. The following sections of the Companies Act, 2013 are an indication of the action taken by the Government in aligning the Act with the issues in the LA.

1. The LA is very particular about the rights of shareholders. The Companies Act also has detailed elaborate procedures to protect the interests of the shareholders. The provisions relating to the Rights spread at diverse places in the Act. May be in the next edition, all these provisions may be pooled up at one place for a ready reference.
2. In respect of the Board of Directors, the LA has made a specific mention of the following:
   (i) Composition of the Board;
   (ii) Responsibilities of the Board;
   (iii) Role of Independent Directors; and
   (iv) Code of Conduct.

   The Companies Act, 2013 vide sections 149 through 195 has covered many of the salient aspects of the LA. There is near agreement between the clauses incorporated in the LA and the Act in respect of the following:
   (i) Composition of the Board;
   (ii) Duties of the Directors;
   (iii) Appointment of Women Director;
   (iv) Appointment of Independent Directors;
   (v) Limit on the number of directorships; and
   (vi) Performance Assessment and submission of Reports to the shareholders.
3. In respect of Audit Committee, section 177 of the Act has echoed the verbatim of the LA with regard to composition, qualifications, and the functioning of the Committee.
4. As regards the risk management and related party transactions, there is a responsibility cast on the Board to discharge its responsibilities. Sections 166 and 188 are significant in this regard. Section 166 of the Act casts a great responsibility on the director to act only in accordance with the articles of the company. And he shall also act in good faith to promote the objects of the company. Similarly, section 188 of the Act prohibits the following arrangements/contracts without the specific approval of the Board.

(a) sale, purchase or supply of any goods or materials;
(b) selling or otherwise disposing of, or buying, property of any kind;
(c) leasing of property of any kind;
(d) availing or rendering of any services;
(e) appointment of any agent for purchase or sale of goods, materials, services or property;
(f) such related party's appointment to any office or place of profit in the company, its subsidiary company or associate company; and
(g) underwriting the subscription of any securities or derivatives thereof, of the company.

5. The beauty of the LA surely lies in its prescription of the submission of a Report on Corporate Governance, as an annex to the Annual Report of the company. The LA is also particular about the list of items that must be covered in the report on Corporate Governance. This aspect needs to be taken into consideration and it would be better to have a separate section in Companies Act in its next amendment.

11
CHAPTER

Role of Board of Directors

1. INTRODUCTION

There could be no two opinions on the fact that the Board of Directors is the 'heart' to the company system. It is the Board, which can make or mar the future of a company. It is generally believed that being the owner of the company, nobody would dare to cause harm to oneself. If companies are entirely owned by the directors and nobody else's interests are associated with it, there could be no reason for so much of worry. But in the modern corporate world, the stake of the promoters of a company is insignificant; and their actions can bind many who invested in the company. Therefore, it became necessary to safeguard the interests of the investors and promote growth of the economy. Imposing checks and balances on the actions of the directors has, thus, become imminent in the modern corporate world. It is for this reason, in most countries, the directors are subject to periodic re-election by the shareholders. As a matter of fact, the Indian Companies Act made the election/re-election of directors at every General Meeting mandatory.

In this regard, the role of the Board was very succinctly elaborated by a South African report in the following words:[1]

- to define the purpose of the company;
- to define the values by which the company will perform its daily duties;
- to identify the stakeholders relevant to the company;
- to develop a strategy combining these factors; and
- to ensure implementation of this strategy.

The purpose and values of a company are often set down in its constitutional documents, reflecting the objectives of its founders. However, it is sometimes appropriate for the board to consider whether it is in the best interests of those served by the company to modify this or even change it completely. For example, NCR (National Cash Register) Corporation is a US producer of automated teller machines and point-of-sale systems, but its origins lay in mechanical accounting machines. As cash registers would quickly become obsolete with the emergence of microchip technology, the company had to adapt to new methodology rapidly. Whitbread PLC originated as a brewer in the 18th century in the UK, but in the 1990s redefined its mission and objectives completely. It is now a hospitality and leisure provider (its brands include Premier Inn and Costa coffee) and has abandoned brewing completely. The directors thus, must take a long-term perspective of the road that the company must travel. Management writer William Ouchi attributes the enduring success of many Japanese companies to their ability to avoid short-term 'knee-jerk' reactions to immediate issues in favour of consensus over the best direction to take in the long-term[2].

It would also be in the fitness of things to survey the philosophy of companies as to the functioning of Boards. In this context, an attempt has been made to draw inputs from the Annual Reports of a few companies.

1.1 Reliance Industries Limited

The company has put in place an internal governance structure with defined roles and responsibilities of every constituent of the system. The company's shareholders appoint the Board of Directors, which, in turn, governs the company. The Board has established seven committees to discharge its responsibilities in an effective manner. RIL's Company Secretary acts as the Secretary to all the Committees of the Board constituted under the Companies Act, 1956/Companies Act, 2013. The Chairman and Managing Director (CMD) provides overall direction and guidance to the Board. Concurrently, the CMD is responsible for overall implementation. In the operations and functioning of the company, the CMD is assisted by four Executive Directors and a core group of senior level executives.

Board Leadership

A majority of the Board, 7 out of 13, are Independent Directors. The Board of the company attempted to create a culture of leadership to provide a long-term vision and policy approach to improve the quality of governance. The actions and decisions of the Board are aligned with the Company's best interests. The focal theme has been the creation of value to the company. Accordingly the Company has defined guidelines and an established framework for the conduct of the operations of the Board and its committees. Attempt has been made to systematize the decision-making process at the meeting of the Board and Board Committees in an informed and efficient manner.

The Board is entrusted with the responsibility to critically evaluate the Company's strategic direction, management policies and their effectiveness. The agenda for the Board reviews includes strategic review from each of the Board committees, a detailed analysis and review of annual strategic and operating plans and capital allocation and budgets. In addition, the reviews also pertain to related party transactions possible risks and risk mitigation measures. Special focus is bestowed on financial reports from the CFO and business reports from each of the sector heads. Frequent and detailed interaction sets the agenda and provides the strategic roadmap for the company's future growth.

1.2 ITC Limited

The primary role of the Board is designed on the principle of '**trusteeship**' to protect and enhance shareholder value through strategic supervision. As trustees, the Board ensures that the Company has clear goals aligned to shareholder value and its growth. The Board sets strategic goals and seeks accountability for their fulfilment. The Board also provides direction and exercises appropriate control to ensure that the Company is managed in a manner that fulfils stakeholders' aspirations and societal expectations. Constant monitoring and review are made an integral part of the job of the Board.

Corporate Management Committee (CMC)

As key constituent, the company has constituted to take up the responsibility of strategic management on behalf of the Board. The CMC is designed to operate under the strategic supervision and control of the Board.

The Chairman is the Chief Executive of the company. He is the Chairman of the Board and the CMC. His primary role is to provide leadership to the Board and the CMC for realising company's goals in accordance with the charter approved by the Board. The Chairman is responsible, inter alia, for the working of the Board and the CMC, for ensuring that all relevant issues are on the agenda and for ensuring that all Directors and CMC members are enabled and encouraged to play full part in the activities of the Board and the CMC, respectively. The Chairman keeps the Board informed on all matters of importance. He is also responsible for achieving balance in the composition of the Board, subject to Shareholders' approval. The company has also created Divisional Strategic Business Unit Management Committees at the operational level to take care of the operations at the divisional level. These committees are designed to assist the CMC.

The Executive Directors, as members of the CMC, contribute to the strategic management of the company's businesses within Board approved activities. Executive Directors assume overall responsibility for the strategic management including governance processes. In the context of the multi-business character of the company, an Executive Director is in the nature of a Managing Director for those businesses and functions reporting to him. As an Executive Director accountable to the Board for a wholly owned subsidiary he acts as the custodian of ITC's interests and is responsible for its governance in accordance with the charter approved by the Board. The Non-

Executive Directors, including Independent Directors, play a critical role in imparting balance to the Board processes by bringing an independent judgement on issues of strategy, performance, resources, standards of company conduct, etc.

1.3 Infosys

The practice of the company is to have a non-executive chairman of the Board and a Chief Executive Officer (CEO) and Managing Director (MD). The responsibility and authority of these officials are identified as follows by the company.

The non-executive chairman of the Board ('the Chairman') is the leader of the Board. As Chairman, he will be responsible for fostering and promoting the integrity of the Board. He is also entrusted with the responsibility to promote a culture where the Board works harmoniously for the long-term benefit of the Company. It is desired that the Board provides effective governance for the Company. In doing so, the Chairman will preside over the meetings of the Board of the shareholders of the Company.

The Chairman will take a lead role in managing the Board and facilitating effective communication among directors. The Chairman will be responsible for matters pertaining to governance, including the organization and composition of the Board. He also has the responsibility to conduct Board meetings, and improve upon effectiveness of the Board, and of individual directors. He is the person to provide independent leadership to the Board, identify guidelines for the conduct and performance of directors, oversee the management of the Board's administrative activities.

The Chairman will actively work with the nomination and remuneration committee to plan for the composition of the Board and Board committees and plan for the succession of directors and key managerial personnel. The CEO and MD are responsible for corporate strategy, brand equity, external contacts and all management matters. They are also responsible for achieving the annual business targets and acquisitions.

A. Board Membership Criteria

The nomination and remuneration committee works in cooperation with the Board to determine the appropriate characteristics, skills and experience required for the Board. Board members are expected to possess the required qualifications, integrity, expertise and experience for the position. They should also possess expertise and insights into the areas relevant to the company's operations. The company has the policy of not appointing any person who has attained the age of 60 years as Managing Director/Executive Director; and shall not appoint any person who has attained the age of 70 years as independent director. The term of the person holding this position may be extended at the discretion of the committee beyond the permitted age and with the approval of shareholders by passing a special resolution in this regard. Board members are expected to rigorously prepare for, attend and participate in all the Board and applicable committee meetings. Each member is expected to ensure that their other current and planned future commitments do not materially interfere with their responsibilities with us.

B. Selection of New Directors

The Board is responsible for the selection of new directors. This job is entrusted to the nomination and remuneration committee, which consists exclusively of independent directors. The nomination and remuneration committee, in turn, makes recommendations to the Board on the induction of any new directors.

C. Training of Board Members

All new non-executive directors inducted to the Board are required to be introduced to the culture of the company through appropriate orientation sessions. Presentations are made by various executive directors and senior management to provide an overview of the company's operations, and to familiarize the new non-executive directors with the managing team. It is also necessary to introduce them to the services, group structure and subsidiaries. A fair understanding is necessary for a Board member about the activities of the company and its risk complexion.

It is also necessary to have separate meetings regularly with independent directors to update them on all business-related issues and new initiatives. At such meetings, the executive directors and other members of the senior management share points of view and leadership thoughts on relevant issues. Also facilitate the continuing education requirements of the directors. As per the policy of the company each director is entitled to a training fee of US $5,000 per annum. Support is provided for independent directors if they choose to attend educational programs in the areas of corporate governance.

D. Membership Term

The Board constantly evaluates the contribution of the members and periodically shares updates with the shareholders about re-appointment of directors. The law in India mandates that two-thirds of the executive board members are liable to retire by rotation every year. However, they are eligible for re-appointment. Executive directors are appointed by the shareholders for the tenure of a maximum period of five years and are eligible for reappointment on completion of their term. An independent director shall hold office for a term of up to five consecutive years on the Board of the Company and will be eligible for re-appointment on passing of a special resolution by the company.

E. Mechanism for Evaluating Board Members

One of the key functions of the Board is to monitor and review performance of the Board members. The Board along with the nomination and remuneration committee will fix the criteria for the performance evaluation of executive, non-executive and independent directors. Conducting a survey is the key part of the process of reviewing the functioning and effectiveness of the Board. Each Board member is requested to evaluate the effectiveness of the Board in terms of its dynamism, information flow, decision-making relationships with the stakeholders. The effectiveness is sought to be measured on a scale of one to five. Feedback on each director is encouraged to be provided as part of the survey. The results of the survey are communicated to the members for their knowledge and correction.

It is desired that independent directors are required to play three key roles, viz., governance, control and guidance. Some of the performance indicators based on which the independent directors are evaluated include:

- Ability to contribute to and monitor our corporate governance practices
- Ability to contribute by introducing international best practices to address top-management issues
- Active participation in long-term strategic planning
- Commitment to the fulfillment of a director's obligations and fiduciary responsibilities; these include participation in Board and committee meetings.

1.4 Seven Trent PLC

In order to have cross-country experience, the role and responsibilities of the Board and other important officers was verified from the Articles of Association of M/s Seven Trent PLC, which is in the business of treating water and waste water in U.K.[3] As per the same, the following are the diverse roles to be performed by the members in the Board.

A. The Board

Unlike the companies in India, there is a procedure of planned retirement from the board of directors; implemented in a sequential manner. The size of the Board also matters. There is a general preference towards smaller boards, which are expected to enable the company to be more competitive in the management. Consequently, the company reduced the Board size from eleven to eight directors. The changes are expected to support the effectiveness of the board with an appropriate balance of innovation, experience, independence and challenge to ensure effective decision making.

B. Role of the Chairman

The role of the Chairman is identified to be to lead a unified Board, facilitating its members at its meetings, and to be responsible for ensuring that the principles and processes of the Board are maintained in line with the Code of Conduct and Charter of Expectations. The Chairman has the responsibility to fix the Agenda for the board meetings in consultation with the CEO and CFO. He may also take into account the request of any director to include an item in the agenda.

It is the Chairman, who shall demonstrate effective and ethical leadership for the company, and has authority to act and speak for the board at the meetings. The Chairman is the person to report to the Board and other committees on the actions taken between meetings of the board and ensures effective working relations with other group executive committee members. He also meets with the non-executive directors to consider the performance of the executive directors, to maintain the necessary depth and breadth of knowledge and skills to ensure the effectiveness of the board as a team. The Chairman is to maintain effective communication with shareholders and other stakeholders by meeting with them in person and to ensure that the board maintains an understanding of the views of major investors and other key stakeholders; while promoting highest standards of corporate governance.

C. Senior Independent Non-Executive Director

The Senior Independent Director is expected to support the Chairman in the delivery of his objectives and ensure that the views of all major shareholders and stakeholders are conveyed to the directors. He is also required to help develop an understanding of any key issues and concerns. He should be available to all shareholders, if they have any concern regarding the operations of the company.

The Senior Independent Director shall meet the non-executive directors, without the Chairman being present, at least annually to take into account the views of them on the issues pertaining to the ongoing monitoring and evaluation of the performance of the Chairman, including communicating the results of performance. Together with the Nominations Committee, he shall take the responsibility for ensuring that an orderly succession planning process is in place, in relation to both the role of the Chairman and the board in general.

D. Non-Executive Directors

Non-Executive Directors are appointed to the Board to contribute their independent external expertise and experience in areas of significance to the company. Their competencies may include corporate finance, including mergers and acquisitions, general finance, corporate strategy, customer care, property management, environmental issues and technology matters. Such issues may also cover engineering, regulation, general management, transformational change, science, regulatory compliance and supply chain management. It is the duty of these IDs to add challenge and rigour to the board's deliberations and are required to make independent assessments of the group's competencies. The non-executive directors, led by the Senior Independent Non-Executive Director shall meet at least once a year to appraise the Chairman's performance. As part of the review of the effectiveness of the Board. The Board has to review the status of the Non-Executive Directors and consider them all to be independent in character and judgment as defined by the Governance Code.

E. Chief Executive

Responsibility is to be delegated to the CE to develop and implement the group's strategy and overall commercial objectives. The non-executive directors, led by the Chairman, appraise CE's performance annually. CE is empowered to take all decisions and actions that further the company's strategy and policies and which in his judgment are reasonable. He shall also be conscious of the limits set for his role as Chief Executive, as set out in the company's Group Authorisation Arrangements (GAA). CE will ensure a continual dialogue with the Chairman on the strategic issues facing the group including forthcoming complex, contentious or sensitive issues; which may affect the group, of which the Chairman might not be aware of. The Chief Executive is required to promote and conduct the affairs of the group with the highest standards of integrity, probity and corporate governance.

F. Executive Directors

The executive directors support CE in effectively leading the company towards the achievement of its strategic objectives and implement the decisions taken by the board. They are committed to doing this in a responsible manner. They are also required to exhibit their commitment to the Code of Conduct, the long term sustainable and responsible stewardship of the business and the delivery of an outstanding customer experience, and environmental leadership.

2. STRUCTURE OF THE BOARD

There is no convenient formula for defining how many directors a company should have, though in some jurisdictions company law specifies a minimum and/or maximum number of directors for different types of companies. Tesco plc, a large multinational supermarket company, has 13 directors. Swire Pacific Limited, a large Hong Kong conglomerate, has 18 directors. Smaller listed companies generally have fewer directors, typically six to eight. The Board of Directors is made up of **executive directors** and **non-executive directors**.

A. Executive Directors

Are full-time employees of the company and, therefore, have relationships and of duties as applicable to the company. They work for the company in a senior capacity, usually concerned with policy matters or functional business areas of major strategic importance. Large companies tend to have executive directors responsible for finance, personnel, IT/IS, marketing and so on. Executive directors are usually recruited by the board of directors. They are the highest earners in the company, with remuneration packages made up partly of basic pay and fringe benefits and partly performance-related pay. Most large companies now engage their executive directors under fixed term contracts, often rolling over every 12 months. In general, in the corporate world, the Chief Executive Officer (CEO) will be the Executive Director, so also the finance officer/manager. Though there are no hard and fast rules, the general practice is that all the important functionaries at the top level are made executive directors.

B. Non-Executive Directors (NEDs)

NEDs are not employees of the company and are not involved in the day-to-day administration of the company. They usually have full-time jobs elsewhere, or may sometimes be prominent individuals from public life. The non-executive directors usually receive a flat fee for their services, and are engaged under a contract for service; similar to that employed to hire a consultant.

NEDs should provide a balancing influence and help to minimise conflicts of interest among directors, senior management and employees. The Higgs Report, published in 2003, summarised their role as below:[4]

- to contribute to the strategic plan;
- to scrutinise the performance of the executive directors;
- to provide an external perspective on risk management; and
- to deal with people's issues, such as the future shape of the Board and resolution of conflicts.

In most of the countries, corporate practice has been that a majority of non-executive directors are independent. Their independence is judged basing on their business, financial and other commitments and involvement in businesses connected to the company. However, it has been held that holding shares in the company does not necessarily compromise independence. Non-executive directors should have high ethical standards and act with integrity and probity. They should support the executive team and monitor its conduct, demonstrating a willingness to listen, question, debate and challenge.

It is now recognised as the best practice that **a public company should have more non-executive directors than executive directors**. In Tesco plc, there are five executive directors and eight independent non-executive directors. Swire Pacific Limited has eight executive directors and 10 non-executive directors, of which six are independent non-executive directors. In addition, there is also a practice of having a shadow director. A shadow director is a person who controls the activities of a company, or of one or more of its actual directors, indirectly. For example, if a person who is unconnected with a company gives instructions to a person who is a director of the company, then the second person is an actual director while the first person is a shadow director. In some jurisdictions, shadow directors are recognised as being as accountable in law as actual directors.

3. RECOMMENDATIONS OF COMMITTEES REGARDING THE ROLE OF BOARD IN CORPORATE GOVERNANCE

Almost every committee that was appointed on corporate governance made significant recommendations on the crucial role to be played by the Board to ensure good corporate governance. The Kumar Mangalam Birla Committee has gone deep into the subject and made many valid recommendations. Highlighting the importance of the Board to the company management felt that it is the Board which provides leadership and strategic guidance to the company. It also recognized that it is the Board to exercise control over the company, which remains accountable always. The measure of the Board is not simply whether it fulfills its legal requirements but more importantly, the board's attitude and the manner it translates its awareness and understanding of its responsibilities. An effective corporate governance system is one, which allows the Board to perform these dual functions efficiently.

The Committee observed that the composition of the Board is important in as much as it determines the ability of the board to collectively provide the leadership and ensures that no one individual or a group is able to dominate the board. The executive directors (like director-finance, director-personnel) are involved in the day-to-day management of the companies. Whereas, the non-executive directors bring wider perspective and independence to the decision making. Till recently, it has been the practice of most of the companies in India to fill the board with representatives of the promoters of the company, and independent directors if chosen were also handpicked thereby ceasing to be independent. This has undergone a change and increasingly the boards are now comprised of promoter directors, executive and non-executive directors, a part of whom are independent. A conscious distinction has been made by the Committee between two classes of non-executive directors, namely, those who are independent and those who are not. Keeping this in view, the Birla Committee recommended that the Board of a company has an optimum combination of executive and non-executive directors with not less than fifty percent of the board comprising the non-executive directors. The number of independent directors would depend on the nature of the Chairman of the Board. In case a company has a non-executive Chairman, at least one-third of Board should comprise of independent directors and in case a company has an executive chairman, at least half of board should be independent.

Further, the Committee made a significant recommendation in respect of the role of nominee directors. The committee felt that when a nominee of the institutions is appointed as a director of the company, he should have the same responsibility, be subject to the same discipline and be accountable to the shareholders in the same manner as any other director of the company. In particular, if he reports to any department of the institutions on the affairs of the company, the institution should ensure that there exist Chinese walls between such department and other departments which may be dealing in the shares of the company in the stock market.

3.1 N R Narayana Murthy Committee

The Committee focused their attention on the following key issues:

(i) Written code for executive management.
(ii) Exclusion of nominee directors from the definition of independent directors.
(iii) Limits on the compensation paid to the IDs.
(iv) Mechanism for evaluation non-executive board members.

Delving into the issues at length, the Committee made the following recommendations for consideration of the stakeholders and the policy makers.

1. It should be obligatory for the Board of a company to lay down the code of conduct for all Board Members and senior management of a company. This code of conduct shall be posted on the website of the company.
2. As opposed to the recommendation of the Birla Committee, Narayana Murthy Committee felt that there shall be no nominee directors and every one shall be appointed by the shareholders. When appointed as such, he shall have the same responsibilities and liabilities.
3. Executive compensation is yet another ticklish issue that needs attention of every company. Murthy Committee proposed that it is the Board which should decide on the compensation to be paid the non-executive directors, including limits on the stock options.
4. The Committee is critical of the evaluation of the performance of the non-executive directors. It felt that their performance be evaluated by a peer group.

3.2 Naresh Chandra Committee

As indicated earlier, this committee was appointed by an industry association. It is rare that complying entities joining together to express their willingness to abide by the code. The Confederation of Indian Industry (CII) constituted this committee under the name of Task Force to suggest 'desirable corporate governance code'. This effort of the task force is to be really appreciated. For, it has made a serious attempt in reviewing the prevailing situation and exhorting the listed companies to put in place the 'best-in-class' corporate governance practices to be a role model. Discussion of the 'Board of Directors' is one of the four parts of the reports of the task force. The following are the significant recommendations of this task force in respect of the Board.

1. Every company shall first constitute a 'Nominations Committee' to search, evaluate and shortlist candidates for being appointed as IDs. It shall also work for the appointment of Executive Directors (EDs).
2. Every company shall issue a formal letter of appointment to every NED or ID.
3. Every company shall constitute a 'Remunerations Committee' with at least three members and majority of them being independent directors. Option be given to the companies to choose between the fixed and varying remuneration packages.
4. Taking into account the advancement in technology, the task force suggested that the members of the Board be allowed to participate at the meetings through teleconferencing and videoconferencing.

4. CONDITIONS AS PER LISTING AGREEMENT

The Listing Agreement of the Bombay Stock Exchange has emerged as one of the key mechanisms in ensuring effective corporate governance in India. Caluse 49 of the Agreement elaborates on the conditions that must be fulfilled by the companies willing to be listed on the Exchange. These conditions include the following. A more detailed version was provided in the chapter on Listing Agreement.

1. Members of the Board and key executives should be required to disclose to the board whether they, directly, indirectly or on behalf of third parties, have a material interest in any transaction or matter directly affecting the company.
2. The Board and top management should conduct themselves so as to meet the expectations of operational transparency to stakeholders while at the same time maintaining confidentiality of information in order to foster a culture for good decision-making.
3. The Board is expected to fulfill certain key functions covering the review of the activities of the company, preparation of action plans, supervision and control of the personnel and overseeing the communication and disclosure requirements.
4. In respect of the composition, the Agreement only specified that there shall be optimum combination of executive and the Board of Directors of the company shall have an optimum combination of executive and non-executive directors with at least one woman director and not less than fifty percent of the Board of Directors comprising non-executive directors.
5. Where the Chairman of the Board is a non-executive director, at least one-third of the Board should comprise independent directors and in case the company

does not have a regular non-executive Chairman, at least half of the Board should comprise independent directors.

6. The Listing Agreement has put a ceiling on the number of directorship an independent director can hold at any point of time. The number is put at seven. Further, a person serving as a whole time director cannot be an independent director for more than three listed companies.
7. In respect of independent directors (IDs), the agreement is insisting on the following:
   (a) Issue of a formal letter of appointment to independent directors, along with the terms and conditions of appointment.
   (b) Evaluation of the performance of the IDs and submission of a report.
   (c) Holding of separate meeting by the IDs at least once a year without the attendance of non-IDs and members of management.
   (d) Organizing familiarization programme for IDs about the company and its operations, etc.
8. The Board shall meet at least four times a year, with a maximum time gap of one hundred and twenty days between any two meetings. The minimum information to be made available to the Board is also specified.
9. A director shall not be a member in more than ten committees or act as Chairman of more than five committees across all companies in which he is a director. Furthermore, every director shall inform the company about the committee positions he occupies in other companies and notify changes as and when they take place.
10. The Board shall lay down a code of conduct for all Board members and senior management of the company. The code of conduct shall be posted on the website of the company.

5. THE COMPANIES ACT, 2013

Companies Act has been a landmark legislation intended to govern the operations of companies in India. Learning from the experience of the British, the independent India passed the first comprehensive legislation, the Companies Act, 1956 (Act 1 of 1956). Economy has undergone many changes since that time and the country also has moved towards integrating itself with the global economy. Many changes were brought through liberalization, privatization and globalization. The process got further momentum with the phase-I of Economic Reforms undertaken in 1991-92. The effort is continuing unabated.

To keep pace with the changes in the economy, legislations also need to be modified and redrafted. Companies Act, 1956 was one such legislation that had undergone many amendments, necessitating the replacement with a new one. Thus, in order to take care of the changing situations and also to incorporate new concepts into the law, the Government of India drafted the new bill and attempted to get it through the parliament many times earlier. But only in 2013, the modified Companies Act, 2013 (Act 18 of 2013) was passed by the Parliament. While the old Act had 568 sections with 15 schedules, the new Act has 470 sections with 7 schedules only.

The significant provisions in respect of the Board of Directors (their qualifications, appointment, duties, obligations, powers, functions, remuneration, etc.) are detailed below.

5.1 Qualifications, Appointment and Duties of the Directors

Sections 149 to 172 of the Act deal with these aspects. Basing on these provisions, an attempt has been made hereunder to highlight significant requirements.

1. Every company shall have a Board of Directors consisting of at least a minimum number of three directors in the case of a public company, two directors in the case of a private company, and one director in the case of a One Person Company; and the maximum is put at fifteen. If a company so desires to have more than fifteen directors, it can do so by passing a special resolution.
2. Every listed public company shall have at least one-third of the total number of directors as independent directors and the Central Government may prescribe the minimum number of independent directors in case of any class or classes of public companies.
3. The appointment of independent director shall be approved by the company in general meeting as provided in sub-section (2) of section 152 and the explanatory statement annexed to the notice of the general meeting called to consider the said appointment shall indicate the justification for choosing the appointee for appointment as independent director. Further, the Central Government may prescribe the manner and procedure of selection of independent directors who fulfill the qualifications and requirements specified under section 149.
4. Where no provision is made in the Articles of Association of the company for the appointment of the first director, the subscribers to the memorandum who are individuals shall be deemed to be the first directors of the company. In case of a One Person Company, an individual being member shall be deemed to be its first director until the director or directors are duly appointed by the member in accordance with the provisions of the Act.

5. At the first annual general meeting of a public company held next after the date of the general meeting at which the first directors are appointed in accordance with the provisions of the Act, at every subsequent annual general meeting, one-third of such of the directors are liable to retire by rotation.
6. Every individual intending to be appointed as director of a company shall make an application for allotment of Director Identification Number to the Central Government in such form and manner and along with such fees as may be prescribed.
7. As per the provisions of the Act, a person shall not be eligible for appointment as a director of a company, if —
   (a) he is of unsound mind and stands so declared by a competent court;
   (b) he is an undischarged insolvent;
   (c) he has applied to be adjudicated as an insolvent and his application is pending;
   (d) he has been convicted by a court of any offence, whether involving moral turpitude or otherwise, and sentenced in respect thereof to imprisonment for not less than six months and a period of five years has not elapsed from the date of expiry of the sentence:
   (e) an order disqualifying him for appointment as a director has been passed by a court or Tribunal and the order is in force;
   (f) he has not paid any calls in respect of any shares of the company held by him, and six months have elapsed from the last day fixed for the payment of the call;
   (g) he has been convicted of the offence dealing with related party transactions under section 188 at any time during the last preceding five years; or
   (h) he has been the director of a company which has not filed financial statements or annual returns for any continuous period of three financial years or has failed to repay the deposits accepted by it or pay interest thereon. Besides, a private company may by its articles provide for any other disqualifications which it considers appropriate.
8. No person shall hold office as a director, including any alternate directorship, in more than twenty companies at the same time. Similarly, the maximum number of public companies in which a person can be appointed as a director shall not exceed ten.
9. The following are the duties to be performed by a person being appointed as a director:
   - shall act in accordance with the articles of the company;

- shall act in good faith in order to promote the objectives of the company for the benefit of its members as a whole, and in the best interests of the company, and its stakeholders;
- shall exercise his duties with due and reasonable care, skill and diligence and shall exercise independent judgment;
- shall not involve in a situation in which he may have a direct or indirect interest that conflicts, with the interest of the company;
- shall not achieve or attempt to achieve any undue gain or advantage either to himself or to his relatives, partners, or associates; and
- shall not assign his office and any assignment so made shall be void.

The Companies Act is very clear in respect of the duties of a director. If any person, having been appointed as such fails to perform such duties, he will be punishable with fine which shall not be less than one lakh rupees but which may extend to five lakh rupees.

5.2 Meetings and Powers of the Board

Sections 173 to 195 of the Act under Chapter-XII, deal with the procedure to be followed for the conduct of meetings of the Board and also the powers vested by the Act in the hands of the Board.

1. Every company shall hold the first meeting of the Board of Directors within thirty days of the date of its incorporation and thereafter hold a minimum number of four meetings of its Board of Directors every year. There shall not be more than one hundred and twenty days interval between two consecutive meetings of the Board. However, the Central Government has the power to direct that the provisions of this sub-section shall not apply in relation to any class or description of companies.
2. The quorum for a meeting of the Board of Directors of a company shall be one third of its total strength or two directors, whichever is higher. Keeping in view of the advancements in technology, the participation of the directors by videoconferencing or by other audio visual means shall also be counted for the purposes of quorum under this sub-section.
3. The Act specifies that every resolution proposed to be placed at the Board Meeting for approval, shall be circulated in advance together with the necessary papers. Otherwise, the resolution is not deemed to have been approved and hence carries no legal sanction.
4. The Board of Directors of every listed company shall also constitute an Audit Committee consisting of a minimum of three directors with independent directors; forming a majority.

5. The Board of Directors of every listed company shall constitute the Nomination and Remuneration Committee consisting of three or more non-executive directors; out of which not less than one-half shall be independent directors.
6. The Board of Directors of a company shall be entitled to exercise all such powers, and to do all such acts and things, as the company is authorised to exercise and do. However, in exercising such powers the Board shall be subject to the provisions of the Act and those in the memorandum or articles of the company. The Board of Directors of the company can exercise the following powers on behalf of the company by means of resolutions passed at the meetings of the Board.
   (a) to make calls on shareholders in respect of money unpaid on their shares;
   (b) to authorise buy-back of securities;
   (c) to issue securities, including debentures, within India and outside India;
   (d) to borrow monies;
   (e) to invest the funds of the company;
   (f) to grant loans or give guarantee or provide security in respect of loans;
   (g) to approve financial statement and the Board's report;
   (h) to diversify the business of the company;
   (i) to approve amalgamation, merger or reconstruction;
   (j) to take over a company or acquire a controlling or substantial stake in another company; and
   (k) any other matter that the Board considers relevant.

5.3 Appointment and Remuneration of Managerial Personnel

Managerial remuneration has been an issue in India for a variety of reasons. First, there is a cap on the remuneration in the public employment. Second, there shall be parity maintained in the society as a matter of upholding the principle of equity. Third, reduction in the glaring inequalities is considered viable through a restriction imposed on the earnings of the corporate managers. Finally, and above all, directors are not the cent per cent owners of companies. There are people who bought the shares of the company, in good faith of getting a reasonable return. And many a time, the shares are widely held and those shareholders are incapable of putting restrictions on the directors and other managerial personnel. Hence, the legislation might have thought it appropriate to put a ceiling on the remuneration. Section 197 of the Act has specified the overall maximum managerial remuneration thus:

1. The total managerial remuneration payable by a public company, to its directors, including managing director and whole-time director, and its manager in respect of any financial year shall not exceed eleven per cent of the net profits of that

company for that financial year computed in the manner laid down in section 198. Further, the remuneration payable to any one managing director; or whole-time director or manager shall not exceed five per cent of the net profits of the company. If there are more than one such director; remuneration shall not exceed ten per cent of the net profits to all such directors and managers taken together.

2. The remuneration payable to the directors of a company, including any managing or whole-time director or manager, shall be determined subject to the provisions of the Act and the articles of the company. There is also the requirement to pass a special resolution in the general meeting and the remuneration payable to a director determined aforesaid shall be inclusive of the remuneration payable to him for the services rendered by him in any other capacity.
3. The Central Government may, using its authority, fix the remuneration with certain limits when a company has no or inadequate profits. Usually, the Central Government, while fixing such remuneration shall have regard to the following:
   (a) the financial position of the company;
   (b) the remuneration or commission drawn by the individual concerned in any other capacity;
   (c) the remuneration or commission drawn by him from any other company;
   (d) professional qualifications and experience of the individual concerned; and
   (e) such other matters as may be prescribed.

6. EMPIRICAL EVIDENCE

Much has been discussed in the foregoing pages of the role of the Board in ensuring effective corporate governance. Attempt is being made every time to bring about improvement in the procedures, systems and finally the law. Yet, the corporate world is subjected to heavy turmoil, leading into great scams/frauds. Joint study (reported on January 5th 2015) conducted by the ASSOCHAM and Grant Thornton, corporate frauds have risen by over 45 per cent in the last two years. The study pointed out that lack of strong internal audit mechanism, along with overriding powers of the top management in the companies, have resulted in the corporate frauds in India. As per the survey, nearly 52 per cent of the corporate frauds have happened in real estate and infrastructure; while financial services sector recorded 34 per cent of frauds, and Telecom, manufacturing, IT and ITs constituting about 10 per cent. As per the information reported, the amount involved in the top 10 corporate frauds (scams) works out to about Rs. 8,21,300 crore since the Bofors Scandal, which raised many eyebrows during that time (see Table 11.1). The number of 'prosecution cases' filed by the Serious Frauds Investigation Office (SFIO), stood at 1165 as on 31-03-2015. Of which, cases filed before the designated courts for prosecution are 1088; cases filed before ICAI/ICSI and other forums are 61 and those filed before Company Law Board (CLB) are 16.

Table 11.1: Top 10 Corporate Frauds that occurred in India

S. No.	Particulars	Year	Amount Involved (Rs. in crore)
1.	Bofors Scam	1980s & 1990s	100 to 200
2.	Fodder Scam	1990s	1,000
3.	Hawala Scandal	1990-91	100
4.	Harshad Mehta Stock Market Scam	1992	5,000
5.	Telgi Scam	2002	20,000
6.	2G Spectrum Allocation	2008	1,76,000
7.	Satyam Computers	2009	14,000
8.	Commonwealth Games	2010	70,000
9.	Wakf Board Land Allocation	2012	1,50,000 – 2,00,000
10.	Coal Blocks Allocation	2012	1,86,000
	Total		**5,21,300**

As per the information made available by the RBI, during the period 2012-13 alone, there were about 29,653 cases of fraud detected in India's nationalized banks involving an amount of Rs. 24,828 crore. Again, between April to December 2014, Public Sector Banks (PSBs) in India incurred losses to the tune of Rs. 11,022 crore due to 2100 cases of fraud reported. Due to inordinate delay in the legal dispensation, it is difficult to book the culprits and to recover the amounts involved. All the more, a corporate fraud will always have a ripple effect on the overall business of a company. Apart from the financial losses that the victim has to incur, a fraud also makes a dent into the 'Brand Image' and reputation of the company. Corporate wrongdoing inevitably ends up creating a 'vicious circle' that dampens shareholders' value, damages investors' confidence, besides locking up of capital and assets of the company and finally causing wider financial instability. The responsibility of the Board in all these cases of malfeasance and misfeasance cannot be discounted by any means.

6.1 BSE's Directors Database

As a measure of improving upon the corporate governance, the BSE has created this database in 2006. This is considered a single point access to information on the Boards of Directors of listed companies, covering many details relating to age, gender, nationality, number of directorships, qualifications, etc. As per the database, there are 16,179 individuals on the boards of 2,743 listed companies. Of these, 16,179 individuals, profiles of 14,332 persons are filed and all these individuals are occupying a total of 19,910 director positions in 3231 companies listed at national-level stock exchanges and 422 companies listed at regional stock exchanges. Of these 14,332 individuals 11,338 hold only 1 directorship each; 6173 hold only independent directorship positions 339 hold 5 or more than 5 directorships in listed companies, with 2 persons holding 14 directorships. Thus, only 2.3% of the total number of directors whose profiles have been filed, hold directorship in more than 5 listed companies. This reduces the doubts over inefficiency of regulation by the non-executive directors. However, since Independent directors are the most important pillar of corporate governance in a public listed company's board, we must also have a look at independent directorial positions in public listed company.

Further, as per section 149 of the Companies Act, 2013, every company shall have at least one woman director on its Board. Under the companies (Appointment and Qualification of Directors) Rules, 2014 issued on 31-03-2014, the following class of companies shall appoint at least one woman director.

1. every listed company;
2. every other public company having -
   (a) paid–up share capital of one hundred crore rupees or more; or has the
   (b) turnover of three hundred crore rupees or more:

As per the database (cited above), of the 16,179 individuals, only 868 were found to be women, constituting just 5.4 per cent of the total. Of course, realizing the fact that the situation has been brought into force only through the 2013 Act (which become operational w.e.f. 20th August 2013), and the same is to be complied within a period of six months. Now that all the companies stated above are required to follow the rule and appoint women as directors. As per the information presently available (13.07.2015), BSE had slapped fines on 530 listed companies for failing to meet the deadline in appointing a women director and boost the gender diversity. The schedule of fine ranges from Rs. 50,000 to Rs. 1,42,000. There is also an additional fine of Rs. 5000 per day, till the company complied with the condition. It is also informed that NSE also sent letters to 260 listed companies, many of which are also listed on BSE. According to the website of Prime Database, (a market research group) 105 companies listed on NSE, out of 1733 had vacancies for woman directors.

In respect of the number of directorships and the number of meetings, there are many interesting points that can be drawn from the data. Of the 14,332 individuals, who have filed their profiles with the Stock Exchange as per requirement, 11,338 hold only one directorship. About 339 individuals held 5 or more than 5 directorship; with

2 individuals holding 14 directorship. Therefore, it can be inferred that there is no heavy density of directorships among individuals. But there is a problem in respect of putting the required attendance at the meeting of the Board. The law (including the listing agreement) itself stipulates that the director participates in a specified number of meetings and the continuous absence may lead to the loss of membership also.

6.2 Review of Research Studies

In an attempt to find the link between the role of the Board and the performance of the firm, researchers have tested many hypotheses as of the following:

1. Board size and Board independence have significant effect on the firm's performance. This view is called the 'Resource Based or Resource Enrichment Theory'.
2. The number of network connections of the directors in the Board influences the firm's performance.
3. Situations in which the CEO is also the Chairman may enhance the performance of the firm, as there is one responsible and accountable steward. This one person is empowered to make effective and timely decisions. This view, thus, has been called the 'Stewardship Theory'.
4. An autonomous Board can more effectively monitor and supervise management, enhancing shareholder value.

6.2.1 Size vs Performance

The researches in this regard have contesting claims. Studies conducted by Pfeffer, Zara, Kakabadse, and Golden have concluded that the Board size matters much in view of the resources and experience the individuals bring into the Board.[5] This view supports the argument that the members help in the form of (a) advice and counsel, (b) access to information, (c) access to resources, and (d) legitimacy. The study made by Saravanan and Shaw has also concluded that Board size and duality decrease would contribute to the performance; negating the hypothesis of agency theory.[6] Lal C. Chugh and others in their study entitled 'Corporate Governance and Firm Performance : Evidence from India' concluded that Board size and financial performance are positively related, providing evidence for the resource enrichment theory.[7]

In an interesting study conducted by Nadeem Mujtaba covering banks and listed companies across the USA, UK and Europe found that the banks with low (1 executive), medium (2 or 3 executives) and high (4 + executives) representations from the management team were in equal proportion.[8] The exceptions are countries where by law there is a separation between the 'Supervisory Board of Directors' and 'Board of Executive Directors' and where executive members are barred from being included in the Supervisory Board of Directors. However, in these countries, the substantive powers to direct and control the companies lie with the Board of Executive Directors, and the role of the Supervisory Board is substantially more constrained than is common among unitary boards operating in most other parts of the world.

Further, the study revealed the fact that the presence of independent directors on company boards is universal in all developed countries. The proportion of the independent directors compared to executive board members, directors elected by employees, shareholder directors and other non-executive directors varies significantly throughout the world. However, in an overwhelming majority of the cases, independent non-executive directors represent the majority of the board. Looking at the results of the primary research on the top 20 international banks, the significance of independent directors is evident. On a global basis, independent directors represented 70% of the boards of these top 20 banks, compared to only 16% representation from the executive management team. It is noteworthy that shareholder linked board members in these top 20 listed international banks represented a mere 1% of the total number of board members.

The question of structuring of Boards was also examined by Renee Adams and others in their study entitled 'The Role of Board of Directors in Corporate Governance: A Conceptual Framework and Survey' published as a working paper (No:14486) by National Bureau of Economic Research, Cambridge (November 2008).[9] Surveying the practices prevalent at different times among the U.S. companies, the authors pointed out that there is large divergence in the Constitution of Boards. In their study, Fich and Shivdasani (2006) considered a sample of 508 of the largest US corporations between 1989 and 1995. They found that, on average, outsiders make up 55% of directors, insiders 30%, and affiliated directors the remaining 15%. The average board contains twelve directors, each receiving approximately $36,000 in fees (plus stock options), and has 7.5 meetings a year. A number of the directors served on multiple boards; and the outside directors in these firms averaged over three directorships. While these data are for large public firms, Linck et al. (2008) consider a larger sample of 8000 (necessarily) smaller firms, with similar patterns in the data".

While the existence and basic structure of boards have remained relatively constant over time, the way in which they are composed has changed. Lehn (et al.)[10] considered a sample of 81 firms that have survived as public companies from 1935 until 2000. As per their findings, board size appears to have a hump pattern over time; it averaged 11 in 1935, peaked at 15 in 1960 and declined to 11 in 2000. However, board size has become more uniform over time as the standard deviation of board size dropped from 5.5 in 1935 to 2.7 in 2000. These companies' boards thus have become more outsider-dominated. The insider representation dropped from 43% in 1935 to just 13% in 2000. Part of this drop could be explained by the typical life cycle of firms. As founding families exit and firms become more professionally managed, agency problems can become worse as those in control are no longer significant owners. In response, firms attempted to add outside directors to counteract the increased agency problems.

Since 2000, there have been significant changes. Sarbanes-Oxley Act contained a number of requirements that increased the workload of and the demand for outside directors. In addition, the scandals at Enron and Worldcom have led to substantially increased public scrutiny of corporate governance. Consequently, boards have become larger, more independent, have more committees, meet more often, and generally have more responsibility and risk. These changes both increased the demand for directors and decreased the willingness of directors to serve for a given price. It is not surprising, therefore, that director's pay and liability have increased substantially. From the shareholders' perspective, these changes are welcome, as they tend to step up the governance.

6.2.2 Network of Connections and Performance

It is presumed that directors provide resources and information external to the firm and thus reduce environmental dependency. It is also the question as to whether executive directors (who are within the system) or the non-executive (independent directors) are better placed in terms of network of connections. It is believed that if the role of the board is to access the external linkages from the firm's environment, the independent director is said to be placed in a better position. The effectiveness of the BOD in monitoring and in provision of resources depends on the interpersonal and group relationship between the executive and the independent directors determined by the process of accountability within the board. Roberts et al. (2005) found that accountability is realized through a range of behaviours like debating, challenging, questioning, probing, discussing, testing, informing and exploring. In any society, the interaction within an organization is determined by its social-cultural setting.

This aspect has assumed further significance in India where organizations hierarchy determines much of the interactions between different ranks of firms and managers. In Indian society, where it is considered imprudent to question one's authority; it is less expected that the independent director will question or challenge the CEO of a firm. So in the board, the accountability of questioning, probing, exploring, etc., is set by the dependent director.

Thus, from the forgoing discussion, one can conclude that the role of the independent director is significantly associated with the firm's performance than the dependent director. The study conducted by Saravanan and Shaw also proved that the degree centrality of the board, prestige centrality of the board and the proportion of directors from same industry has been statistically significant at 5% level of significance.

6.2.3 CEO Duality vs Stewardship

The issue of the Chairman and CEO being one and same person has also been a matter of debate. It is argued that board autonomy is critical to aligning the interests of owners and managers. An autonomous board can more effectively monitor and supervise management, enhancing shareholder value. Board autonomy is generally measured by proportion of independent/outside/non-executive directors on the board. The proposition is that an autonomous board will help to minimize agency costs and thereby improve financial performance.

However, may studies suggested that the excessive autonomy of the board can hurt a firm's performance. Excessive board autonomy may put the management at career risk with higher management turnover, create higher agency costs for creditors, and generate higher costs to protect the proprietary position of the firm. Therefore, a high percentage of outside directors may result in lower financial performance. In their study on this aspect, L. C. Chug and other have found that CEO duality is negatively correlated with the profit performance.

As regards the issue of CEO – Chairman duality, the study conducted by R. Adams and others made it clear that duality has affected the firm's performance.[11] Even if it is true that combining the titles of CEO and chairman means that an individual has, on average more influence over his firm, it does not follow that mandating separate titles would improve corporate performance. In fact, Adams, et al., find that measures of CEO power are not systematically related to firm's performance. This is consistent with our overarching argument that actual corporate-governance practice needs to be seen as part of the solution to the constrained optimization program. Hence, imposing separate titles would either yield a less optimal solution or lead to a possibly inefficient and work-around situation, leading to the optimal amount of CEO power. Consequently, as with most policy prescriptions in the area of governance, policy makers should be wary of calls for prohibiting the CEO serving as Chairman.

7. ICRA'S CODE OF CONDUCT FOR BOARD OF DIRECTORS

The Investment Information and Credit Rating Agency (ICRA) was established in 1991 by the leading financial/investment institutions, commercial banks and financial services companies as an independent and professional investment information and credit rating agency. ICRA is a public limited company with its shares listed on the BSE and NSE. As a part of its service to the promoters and investors, it has been framing and issuing guidelines on various matters of significance to the stakeholders in the corporate world.

In pursuance of its initiative, ICRA has drafted a separate code of conduct for Board of Directors and issued the same on March 30, 2006. This was later modified on November 12, 2014. As per the code in vogue, the Board members and the senior management personnel shall:

1. act in the best interests of the company and also fulfill their fiduciary obligations to the Company;
2. provide expertise and experience in their areas of specialization and share their learning at meetings of the Board of Directors. After all, persons are invited to be on the board only for their knowledge and wisdom;
3. give careful and independent consideration to the affairs of the company and examine all the documents placed before them to satisfy themselves with the soundness of key decisions taken by the management of the Company and call for additional information, where necessary, for making such judgments;
4. act honestly, fairly, ethically and with integrity;
5. conduct themselves in a professional, courteous and respectful manner and not take improper advantage of their position;
6. deal fairly with all stakeholders;
7. comply with all applicable laws, rules and regulations;
8. act in good faith, with due care, competence and diligence;
9. not use the Company's property for their personal gain;
10. not accept gifts or other benefits not customary in the dealings of the company;
11. not use any information or opportunity received by them in their capacity to the detriment of the Company's interests;
12. protect the Company's assets and ensures their efficient use and that all the assets of the Company are used for legitimate business purposes only;
13. strive to regularly attend meetings of the Board of Directors and of the Board committees;
14. bring an open and independent mind to the meetings of the Board of Directors and not make a decision about a matter before attending and participating in the deliberations of the meeting;
15. act in a manner to enhance and maintain the reputation of the Company;
16. disclose any personal interest he has in any matter that may come before the Board and abstain from discussion in such matter;
17. abstain from discussion, voting or otherwise influencing a decision on any matters that may come before the Board of Directors in which they may have a conflict of interest;
18. respect the confidentiality of information relating to the affairs of the Company acquired in the course of their service as Directors or Senior Management;

19. not use confidential information acquired in the course of their service as Directors or Senior Management Personnel for their personal advantage;
20. help create and maintain a culture of high ethical standards and commitment to compliance;
21. The Independent Directors also perform their duties and shall:
    - (i) undertake appropriate induction and update their skills, knowledge and familiarity with the company;
    - (ii) seek appropriate clarification or amplification of information where necessary, and take appropriate professional advice and opinion of outside experts at the expense of the company;
    - (iii) strive to attend all meetings of the Board of Directors and of the Board committees of which he is a member;
    - (iv) participate constructively and actively in the committees of the Board;
    - (v) strive to attend the general meetings of the company;
    - (vi) ensure that the concerns of the company are addressed by the Board and, to the extent that they are not resolved, insist that their concerns are recorded in the minutes of the Board meeting;
    - (vii) keep themselves well informed about the company and the external environment in which it operates;
    - (viii) not to unfairly obstruct the functioning of an otherwise proper Board or committee of the Board;
    - (ix) pay sufficient attention and ensure that adequate deliberations are held before approving related party transactions and assure themselves that the same are in the interest of the company;
    - (x) ascertain and ensure that the company has an adequate and functional vigil mechanism and to ensure that the interests of a person who uses such mechanism are not prejudicially affected on account of such use;
    - (xi) report concerns about unethical behaviour, actual or suspected fraud or violation of the company's code of conduct or ethics policy;
    - (xii) acting within his authority, assist in protecting the legitimate interests of the company, shareholders and its employees; and
    - (xiii) not disclose confidential information, including commercial secrets, technologies, advertising and sales promotion plans, unpublished price sensitive information, unless such disclosure is expressly approved by the Board or required by law.

All said and done, the code of ICRA is persuasive in nature. It is not like the clauses in the Companies Act or listing agreement. The code of ICRA or any other agency speaks of the ideal situation that should be existing. Perhaps, these would be helpful to compare one's position with the ideal and then initiate measures for improvement or to take corrective action.

7.1 BSE's Code of Conduct for its Directors

As the old and most prestigious Stock Exchange of the country, BSE also has bestowed its attention in framing the code of conduct for Directors of the Exchange. The code assumes significance for the reason that it has the highest number of listed companies and also insisting on the Listing Agreement. Clause 49 of the LA is very crucial in the domain of corporate governance. In this context, every director of the Exchange has the following obligations.

1. to participate in the formulation and execution of strategies in the best interest of the Exchange and contribute towards pro-active decision making at the governing Board of Directors;
2. to give benefit of their experience and expertise to the Exchange and provide assistance in strategic planning and execution of decisions;
3. to endeavour to ensure that the Exchange abides by all the provisions of the Securities Legislations and the Companies Act;
4. to endeavour to ensure compliance at all levels so that the regulatory system does not suffer any breaches;
5. to endeavour to ensure that the Exchange takes steps commensurate to honour the time limit stipulated by Board of Directors for corrective action;
6. not to support any decision in the meeting of the Board of Directors which may adversely affect the interest of investors of the listed companies;
7. to accord highest priority for redressing investor grievances and encouraging fair trade practices;
8. to endeavour to analyse and administer the Exchange issues with professional competence, fairness, impartiality, efficiency and effectiveness;
9. to ensure that the listed companies comply with all the regulatory, and disclosure norms;
10. to maintain confidentiality and not to divulge/disclose any information obtained in the discharge of their duty;
11. to maintain the highest standards of personal integrity, truthfulness, honesty and fortitude in discharge of their duties;
12. to perform the duties in an independent and objective manner and avoid activities that may impair, or may appear to impair, their independence or objectivity or official duties;

13. not to engage in any act involving moral turpitude, dishonesty, fraud, deceit, or misrepresentation or any other act prejudicial to the administration of the Exchange and the listed companies;
14. not to encourage the circulation of agenda papers during the meeting, unless circumstances so require;
15. to endeavour to have the date of next meeting fixed at each meeting of the Board of Directors in consultation with other members of the Board of Directors; and
16. to endeavour to ensure that in case all the items of the agenda of a meeting were not covered for want of time, the next meeting is held within fifteen days for considering the remaining items.

8. JUDICIAL PRONOUNCEMENTS ON THE ROLE OF THE BOARD OF DIRECTORS

It will be very interesting to review the observations of the Judiciary on the role and responsibilities of the Board and individual directors. There were many judgements delivered at the various High Courts and Supreme Court. It is true that the role and responsibility of the Board and directors are guided by the provisions in Articles of Association (AOA) of the company. In addition, the prevailing laws such as Companies Act, SEBI guidelines, guidelines of the Ministry of Corporate Affairs, Rules and Regulations issued from time to time by the Government also are binding on the Board. Further, the listing agreements also have emerged as the contours to set limits to the powers and functions of the Board and directors. It is also true that the Board has a big role to play in the company, since it conducts the day-to-day affairs of the company and it may not be possible for the shareholders or the AGM to give directions from time-to-time. It is also not possible to check compliance on a daily basis. While the mechanisms designed may ensure reasonable compliance in case of public limited companies, it is highly difficult to oversee the operations of the private limited companies.

It is in this context, the observations of the learned Judges become paramount. Examining the role of the Board of Directors in terms of Companies Act, the Hon'ble High Court of Delhi in the case between Raj Travels & Tours Ltd. and others Vs. Destination of the world (subcontinent) Private Limited (CRL M.C. No: 2652 of 2010) observed that: it was a matter of common knowledge that when companies are floated and public issues are brought, big advertisements are issued giving big names as directors and promoters of the company. These names are the names of successful CEOs, or directors who have achieved success in other fields. Due to these names at the very inception and formation of company, there is the chance to promote the wealth of the company. Once money is mopped up from the public, in all those cases where the companies were created only for the purpose of mopping up hard earned money of public or to befool them, it is found that those big names disappear and in almost every litigation those directors who formed part of the core of the company and gave promises that the Company would do roaring business quietly disappear from the scene or take plea that they were not responsible for business of the company. It is well settled that directors, while exercising their powers, do not act as agents for the majority or even all the members and so the members cannot by a resolution passed by a majority of even unanimously, supersede the directors' power and instruct them how they shall exercise their power. The only way in which the General Body of a company can overrule the BOD is altering the Articles and refusing to re-elect the directors. This is rarely done. More so, the shareholders cannot themselves usurp the powers, which by Articles are vested in the directors. Thus the relationship of BOD with the shareholders is more of a federation than that one of subordinate and superior. Therefore, the Board is very crucial in deciding the fate of the shareholders, equity markets and finally the society.

References

1. South African Report (also Known as King Report), The Institute of Directors in South Africa (IODSA), www.iodsa.co.za.

   The Kind Report on Corporate Governance is considered a path-breaking work on the subject. There are three reports issued in 1994 (King-I), 2002 (King-II) and 2009 (King-III). Compliance with the King Report is a requirement for companies listed on the Johannes-burg Stock Exchange.
2. 'Corporate governance: the board of directors and standing committees', SA Technical, Association of Chartered Certified Accountants (ACCA), October 2012, p. 4.
3. Annual Report and Accounts 2015 of Severn Trent PLC, Coventry. (www.seventrent.com)
4. 'Review of the role and effectiveness of non-executive directors', Derek Higgs, January 2003. (www.dti.gov.uk/cld/non_exec_review)
5. Quoted from P. Saravanan and Shaw, "Role of Independent Directors – Enhancing or otherwise of the Shareholders wealth – An Empirical Investigation", Study conducted under the aegis of National Foundation for Corporate Governance, May 2014.
6. Ibid., p. 21.
7. Lal C. Chugh, Joseph W. Meador and Ashwini Shanth Kumar, "Corporate Governance and Firm Performance : Evidence from India", *Journal of Finance and Accountancy*, p. 3.

8. Nadeem Mujtaba, "Corporate Governance and Board Composition – A Comparison of GCC Boards with UK, European and US Boards" Survey commissioned by Hawkamah and DIFC, The Corporate Governance Consultants Directors Counsel, kingdom of Bahrain.
9. Renne Adams, Benjamin E. Hermalin and Michael S. Weisbach, "The Role of Boards of Directors in Corporate Governance: A Conceptual Framework and Survey", working paper – 14486, National Bureau of Economic Research, Cambridge, U.K., November 2008.
10. Lehn et al., Determinants of the size and structure of Corporate Boards, *Financial Management*. 38(4), 747-780.
11. Renne Adams (2008).

12

CHAPTER

Role of Independent Directors

1. THE ORIGIN: THE AGENCY THEORY

The roots for the idea of having independent directors on the Boards can be traced back to the 'Agency Theory' of Financial Management. It had been hypothesized that the separation of Ownership from Management of widely held companies leads to the conflict of interests between the owners and managers; whereby the managers have an incentive to pursue objectives contrary to those of the owners. Jensen and Meckling were the first to develop a comprehensive theory of the firm under agency arrangements.[1] The premise is simple that the objectives of management may differ from those of the shareholders. In large companies, shares are held by many persons/ institutions and they cannot come together even to decide their own objectives. In such a context, it is the management, who would be acting on their behalf to run the company in such a way that their wealth is maximized. This requires incentivizing managers and institution of proper control mechanisms. All these activities involve certain costs, called **'agency costs'**. These agency costs may take several forms like empire building, rent seeking activities leading to extra remuneration, perks, or entrenching themselves so as to avoid getting fired when the firm performs poorly. Therefore, the size, structure and composition of the Boards assume significance in creating, and maximizing the wealth of the shareholders and reduce these agency costs.

It is also hypothesized that the less the ownership percentage of the managers, the less the likelihood that they will behave in a manner consistent with maximizing shareholder wealth and he greater the need for outside shareholders to monitor their activities[2]. Some people suggest that the primary monitoring of managers comes not from the owners but from the managerial labour market. They argue that efficient capital markets provide signals about the value of a company's securities and, thus, about the performance of its mangers. Managers with good performance records should have an easy time finding other employment (if they need to) than managers with poor performance records. Thus, if the managerial labour market is competitive both within and outside the firm, it will tend to discipline managers. In that situation, the signals given by changes in the total market value of the firm's securities become important.

Against this backdrop, it is the US Securities and Exchange Commission that has initially discussed the subject of 'independence of directors' in Boards. It has framed certain rules to guide the operations of the Board. This was followed by the provisions in the Sarbanes – Oxley Act. 2002 and the rules of New York Stock Exchange (NYSE) and National Association of Securities Dealers Automatic Quotation (NASDAQ). These agencies have specified that the independent directors must comprise the majority of the board and must meet in regular intervals.

With the happening of Maxwell and Polly Peck Scandals in UK, the Government also thought that it was time to bring about changes on the Corporate Governance practices. This led to the constitution of various committees headed by corporate experts. The first committee to be established in this regard is the Cadbury Committee. It aimed at reporting on the financial aspects of corporate governance. Later in the year 1995, Greenbury Committee was established and it dealt with a contentious aspect of corporate governance relating to the remuneration of the executives in the company. The Committees' main aim was to identify good practice in determining Directors Remuneration and prepare a code of such practice for use by UK companies. Further, in the year 2003, although substantial improvements in corporate governance had been stimulated in the listed companies of UK, certain areas were identified for further improvements by the Higgs Committee. During the same year, the UK Government had to appoint another Committee under the Chairmanship of Smith, to look into the issue of Governance, as an aftermath of the developments taking place with the Enron Scandal.

2. INDIAN SCENARIO: RECOMMENDATIONS OF COMMITTEES

As far as Indian scenario is concerned, the origin of the idea of Independent Directors can be traced back to the recommendations of the various committees appointed by the SEBI and Government of India which included the Kumar Mangalam Birla Committee (1999), Narayana Murthy Committee (2003) and Naresh Chandra Committee (2009). Taking cue from the recommendations of these committees, SEBI has issued guidelines on corporate governance recommending to amend the Clause 49 of the Listing Agreement to pave way for the appointment of Independent Directors. On the whole, this can be considered a phenomenon of the present 21st century in the context of India Inc.

2.1 Recommendations of the K M Birla Committee (1999)

Reviewing the issue of Corporate Governance in depth, the committee noted that the Board of Directors of the company are required to play a responsible role. The committee observed that the Board of a company provides leadership and strategic guidance. It is also the duty of the Board to exercise control over the company, while remaining at all times accountable to the shareholders. The duty of the board is not simply to fulfill its legal requirements, but more importantly, to create awareness among the stakeholders their roles and responsibilities. It has declared that an effective corporate governance system is the one, that allows the board to perform these dual functions efficiently.

Keeping in view of the above, the committee felt that the composition of the Board is critical to the independent functioning of the Board. The Committee also felt that the very definition of 'independent director' is crucial, so that the definition itself does not become a constraint in the choice of independent directors on the boards of companies. The definition should be based on the touchstone of independence, and shall be sufficiently broad and flexible. It felt that relationships which affect the independence of a director are the 'litmus test' of independence and the board of the company would exercise sufficient degree of maturity when left to itself, to determine whether a director is independent or not. The Committee therefore agreed on the point that Independent directors are directors who apart from receiving director's remuneration do not have any other material pecuniary relationship or transactions with the company, and its other stakeholders. Further, all pecuniary relationships or transactions of the non-executive directors should be disclosed in the annual report.

The Committee was of the view that the non-executive directors, i.e., those who are independent and those who are not, help bring an independent judgement to bear on Board's deliberations especially on issues of strategy, performance, management of conflicts and standards of conduct. The Committee therefore laid emphasis on the calibre of the non-executive directors, especially of the independent directors. It is in this context, the Committee felt that the Board of a company shall have an optimum combination of executive and non-executive directors; with not less than fifty percent of the Board comprising the non-executive directors. The Committee finally left the number of independent directors to be appointed should be based on the nature of the chairman of the Board. In case, the company has a non-executive chairman, at least one-third of Board should comprise of independent directors and in case the company has an executive chairman, at least half of Board should be independent.

2.2 Recommendations of N R Narayana Murthy Committee

This is the second committee appointed by the Securities and Exchange Board of India under the Chairmanship of N R Narayana Murthy. This Committee also made significant recommendations in respect of the role of independent directors. The most significant contribution of the committee in this regard is its attempt to portray vividly the responsibilities of various kinds of directors, viz., nominee, non-executive and independent directors. The following are the key recommendations in respect of the role of various kinds of directors:

1. Any appointment as director should be made by the shareholders. In case of those nominated by the financial institutions like banks, etc., they shall also have the same responsibilities and shall be subject to the same liabilities as any other director. The other important recommendation of the Committee in the appointment of Directors is that the nominees on public sector companies shall also be elected by the shareholders.
2. The compensation intended to be paid to the non-executive directors must be fixed by the Board of Directors and should be approved by shareholders in general meeting. Limits should be set for the maximum number of stock options that can be granted to non-executive directors in any financial year. These options shall vest only after a period of at least one year from the date such non-executive directors have retired from the Board of the Company. This is a crucial suggestion as far as the compensation of directors is concerned. It is the responsibility of the companies to publish their compensation philosophy and statement of entitled compensation in respect of non-executive directors in their annual report.
3. In addition, the same may be hosted on the company's website and reference drawn thereto in the annual report. The details of shares held by non-executive directors, including on an "if-converted" basis shall be disclosed annually. Non-executive directors are also required to disclose their stock holding in the company in which they are proposed to be appointed as directors, prior to their appointment. The notice of appointment shall contain all these details.
4. One of the significant contributions of the Committee pertains to the interpretation given to the concept of 'independent director. Apart from the usual disqualifications, it has broad based the understanding and put many other restrictions. According to the Committee, the following persons are not eligible to be appointed as ID.
    - Persons having material pecuniary relationships or transactions with the company, its promoters, its senior management (including subsidiaries and associates);
    - Persons having relation with promoters or management at the board level or at one level below the board;
    - Who is an executive of the company in the immediately preceding three financial years;
    - Who is a partner or an executive of the statutory audit firm or the internal audit firm that is associated with the company;

- Who is a supplier of service provider or customer of the company. This may also include lessor-lessee type relationships;
- A person who owns more than 2 per cent voting power.

2.3 Recommendations of the Naresh Chandra Committee (2009)

This is the Task Force constituted by the Confederation of Indian Industry (CII) to prescribe certain standards for corporate conduct. Being appointed later to the above mentioned two committees, this committee had the advantage of the wisdom of the earlier two committees and also the heated debate going on then on the role and responsibilities of independent directors. Against such background, the Task Force has touched upon the following three aspects:

(i) Appointment;
(ii) Duties and Liabilities;
(iii) Remuneration.

As regards the appointment of NEDs or IDs, the TF has recommended that all the listed companies have Nominations Committee, comprising a majority of independent directors, including its chairman. This Committee's task should be to:

- search for, evaluate, shortlist and recommend appropriate independent directors and NEDs, subject to the broad directions of the full Board; and
- design processes for evaluating the effectiveness of individual directors as well as the Board as a whole.

The Nomination Committee should also be the body that evaluates and recommends the appointment of executive directors. A separate section in the chapter on corporate governance in the annual reports of listed companies could outline the work done by the Nomination Committee during the year under consideration.

The TF has done an elaborate exercise in designing the format and recommended that a Letter of Appointment be issued to every NED or ID, just as it is done in case of appointing employees and Executive Directors. The letter is supposed to address the following aspects:

- Specify the expectation of the Board from the appointed director.
- The Board-level committee (s) in which the director is expected to serve and its tasks.
- The fiduciary duties that come with such an appointment.
- The term of the appointment.
- The Code of Business Ethics that the company expects its directors and employees to follow.

- The list of actions that a director cannot do in the company.
- The liabilities that accompany such a fiduciary position, including whether the concerned director is covered by any Directors and Officers (D&O) insurance.
- The remuneration, including sitting fees and stock options, if any.

The letter stating the terms and conditions of appointment of any NED or independent director should form a part of the disclosure to shareholders at the time of the ratification of his/her appointment or re-appointment to the Board. This issue was not addressed by the New Companies Act, 2013. In respect of payment of compensation to the NEDs and IDs for their services, the TF has made the following recommendations:

A. Fixed Contractual Remuneration

The Task Force recommended that the Companies Act, 1956, be amended so that companies have the option of giving a fixed contractual remuneration to NEDs and independent directors, which is not linked to the net profit or lack of it. Therefore, companies should be given the option to choose between:

(a) Paying a fixed contractual remuneration to its NEDs and IDs, subject to an appropriate ceiling depending on the size of the company; or
(b) Continuing with the existing practice of paying out upto 1% (or 3%) of the net profits of the stand-alone entity as defined in the Companies Act, 1956.

The Committee felt that the choice should be uniform for all NEDs and independent directors. There shall not be a situation leading to some being paid high and low, in terms of pay or commission or stock options. The Committee was specific that if a person chooses fixed remuneration, he shall not be eligible for any commission on profits. The current limits and constraints on sitting fees and stock options or restricted stock may remain unchanged. If stock options are granted as a form of payment to NEDs and independent directors, then these must be held by the concerned director until one year of his exit from the Board.

B. Structure of Compensation to NEDs

The Task Force recommended that listed companies use the following template in structuring their remuneration to NEDs and independent directors.

- Fixed component: This should be relatively low, so as to align NEDs and independent directors to a greater share of variable pay. Typically, these are not more than 30% of the total cash remuneration package.
- Variable Component: Based on attendance of Board and Committee meetings (at least 70% of all meetings should be an eligibility pre-condition)

- Additional payment for being the chairman of the Board, especially if he/she is a non-executive chairman
- Additional payment for being the chairman of the Audit Committee
- Additional payment for being the chairman of other committees of the Board
- Additional payment for being members of Board committees: Audit, Shareholder Grievance, Remuneration, Nomination, etc.

The Task Force also recommended that if such a structure (or any structure) of remuneration is adopted by the Board, it should be disclosed to the shareholders in the annual report of the company.

C. Remuneration Committee

The Task Force recommended that listed companies should have a Remuneration Committee of the Board.

- The Remuneration Committee should comprise at least three members, majority of whom should be independent directors.
- It should have delegated responsibility for setting the remuneration for all executive directors and the executive chairman, including any compensation payments, such as retiral benefits or stock options. It should also recommend and monitor the level and structure of pay for senior management, i.e., one level below the Board.
- The Remuneration Committee should make available its terms of reference, its role, the authority delegated to it by the Board, and what it has done for the year under review to the shareholders in a separate section of the chapter on corporate governance in the annual report.

The above recommendations were not accepted by the Government and there was no mention of any fixed or contractual remuneration. The new Act has only reiterated its old stand in making a mention that the payment of remuneration to the IDs will be by way of fees as provided under sub-section (5) of Section 197, reimbursement of expenses for participation in the Board and other meetings and profit related commission as may be approved by the members.

2.4 Clause-49 of the Listing Agreement of BSE

Listing Agreement is a significant document specifying the obligations of the company in ensuring fair and transparent governance. In this context, the listing agreement of BSE was found to be comprehensive and significant in respect of corporate governance. The relevant clauses of the agreement with reference to independent directors are narrated below:

A. *The expression 'independent director' shall mean a non-executive director, other than a nominee director of the company*

(a) Who is a person of integrity and possesses relevant expertise and experience;

(b) (i) Who is or was not a promoter of the company or its holding, subsidiary or associate company;

(ii) Who is not related to promoters or directors in the company, its holding, subsidiary or associate company; and

(c) Who has no material pecuniary relationship with the company, its holding, subsidiary or associate company, or their promoters, or directors, during the two immediately preceding financial years or during the current financial year.

(d) The Agreement also specified that those persons to be appointed as IDs shall not be related to any person holding key position in the management of the company. Further, he shall not have been an employee or proprietor or a partner, in any of the three financial years immediately preceding the financial year in which he is proposed to be appointed.

B. *Limit on Number of Directorships*

(a) A person shall not serve as an independent director in more than seven listed companies.

(b) Further, any person who is serving as a whole time director in any listed company shall serve as an independent director in not more than three listed companies.

C. *Maximum Tenure of Independent Directors*

The maximum tenure of Independent Directors shall be in accordance with the Companies Act, 2013 and clarifications/circulars issued by the Ministry of Corporate Affairs, in this regard, from time to time.

D. *Formal Letter of Appointment to Independent Directors*

(a) The company shall issue a formal letter of appointment to independent directors in the manner as provided in the Companies Act, 2013.

(b) The terms and conditions of appointment shall be disclosed on the website of the company.

E. *Performance Evaluation of Independent Directors*

(a) The Nomination Committee shall lay down the evaluation criteria for performance evaluation of independent directors.

(b) The company shall disclose the criteria for performance evaluation, as laid down by the Nomination Committee, in its Annual Report.

(c) The performance evaluation of independent directors shall be done by the entire Board of Directors (excluding the director being evaluated).

(d) On the basis of the report of performance evaluation, it shall be determined whether to extend or continue the terms of appointment of the independent director.

F. Separate Meetings of the Independent Directors

(a) The independent directors of the company shall hold at least one meeting in a year, without the attendance of non-independent directors and members of management. All the independent directors of the company shall strive to be present at such meeting.

(b) The independent directors in the meeting shall, inter-alia:

  (i) review the performance of non-independent directors and the Board as a whole;

  (ii) review the performance of the Chairperson of the company, taking into account the views of executive directors and non-executive directors; and

  (iii) assess the quality, quantity and timeliness of flow of information between the company management and the Board that is necessary for the Board to effectively and reasonably perform their duties.

G. Familiarisation Programme for Independent Directors

(a) The company shall familiarise the independent directors with the company, their roles, rights, responsibilities in the company, nature of the industry in which the company operates, business model of the company, etc., through various programmes.

(b) The details of such familiarisation programmes shall be disclosed on the company's website and a web link thereto shall also be given in the Annual Report.

3. COMPANIES ACT, 2013

Sections 149 and 150 of the Companies Act, 2013 dealt with the appointment, qualifications and matters connected therewith. The following are the relevant clauses in respect of independent directors.

A. As regards the number of IDs, the Act prescribes that every listed public company shall have at least one-third of the total number of directors as independent directors. The Central Government also has the power to prescribe the minimum number of independent directors in case of any class or classes of public companies. As regards the qualification and eligibilities, significant suggestions of all the

Committees were taken into account by the Government. As such, a person to be appointed as the Independent Director, must possess integrity, relevant expertise and experience. The Act also has included many other aspects like the disassociation with the promoters, directors and key managerial personnel. The person to be appointed as the ID must be an expert, not having any relation with the company and its associates. It is also important that he shall not have any pecuniary interest in the affairs of the company. If any person has already had any such association, he should wait for two years to be considered for the appointment.

B. Every independent director at the first meeting of the Board in which he participates shall give a declaration that he meets the criteria of independence as provided in the Act. As per the provisions of sections 197 and 198, an independent director shall not be entitled to any stock option and may receive remuneration by way of fee provided under sub-section (5) of section 197, reimbursement of expenses for participation in the Board and other meetings and profit related commission as may be approved by the members. As per the Act, an independent director shall hold office for a term up to five consecutive years on the Board of a company, but shall be eligible for reappointment on passing of a special resolution by the company and disclosure of such appointment in the Board's report. The ID shall be held liable, only in respect of such acts of omission or commission by a company which had occurred with his knowledge, attributable through Board processes, and with his consent or connivance or where he had not acted diligently.

C. One of the highlights of the new Companies Act is that it had the provision to maintain a separate data bank containing names, addresses and qualifications of persons who are eligible and willing to act as independent directors, maintained by anybody, institute or association, as may be notified by the Central Government. Such institutions need to have adequate expertise in creation and maintenance of such data bank and put on their website for the use by the company making the appointment of such directors. However, the responsibility of selecting a worthy candidate rests only with the company.

D. The appointment of such independent directors shall be approved by the company in general meeting. The note circulated for such appointment shall indicate the justification for choosing the appointee for appointment as independent director. *Ipso facto*, the Central Government may prescribe the manner and procedure of selection of independent directors who fulfill the qualifications and requirements specified under section 149.

In exercise of the powers vested with the Central Government under various provisions of the Act, the Government has issued Companies (Appointment and

Qualification of Directors) Rules, 2014 dated 31-03-2014. As per these rules, the following class or classes of companies shall have atleast two independent directors:

(a) the public companies having paid up share capital of ten crore rupees or more; or

(b) the public companies having turnover of one hundred crore rupees or more; or

(c) the public companies having outstanding loans, debentures and deposits exceeding fifty crore rupees.

An independent director shall possess appropriate skills, experience and knowledge in one or more fields of finance, law, management, sales, marketing, administration, research, corporate governance, technical operations or other disciplines related to the company's business. Similarly, any body, institute or association, which has been authorized in this behalf by the Central Government shall create and maintain a data bank of persons willing and eligible to the appointment as independent director and such data bank shall be placed on the website of the Ministry of Corporate Affairs or on any other website as may be approved or notified by the Central Government.

4. VALUE ADDITION BY THE INDEPENDENT DIRECTORS

It would be pertinent to know whether the Independent Directors have added any value to the firm. Though there had been a good amount of literature available on this aspect, there is no conclusive evidence to show that the composition and quality of membership on the Boards has contributed to the improvement in the firm's performance. Study made by Ajay Kumar Gang[3], has addressed the question: Does the board size and independence really matter in terms of influencing firm's performance? He found that:

- There is an inverse association between board size and firm's performance.
- Different proportions of board independence have dissimilar impact on firm performance.
- The impact of board independence on firm performance is more when the board independence is between 50 and 60 per cent.
- Smaller boards are more efficient than the larger ones, the board size limit of six suggested as the ideal.
- Independent directors have so far failed to perform their monitoring role effectively and improve the performance of the firm.
- The guidelines on corporate governance should take into account the 'cross-board' phenomenon while defining the criteria for eligibility for appointment as an independent director.

- Lack of training to function as independent directors and ignorance of the procedures, tasks, and responsibilities expected of them could be reasons for the independent directors' non-performance.
- A bad performance leads to an increase in board size, which in turn, hampers performance.

Reviewing the evolution of the concept of Independent Directors in various countries and the practices followed by them, Rajan R. felt that the mechanism of IDs is not able to contain the corporate scandals.[4] Quoting the debacle of Satyam and others abroad opined that there is growing need to ascertain precisely the standards of determining the liability of IDs for prevention and detection of fraud, in view of the limited role performed by them in the company. Recognizing the fact that the IDs have become a crucial part of the Indian Company Law, Divesh Goyal observed that the definition of ID is not very clear even now in respect of focusing the attention in defining the 'pecuniary relationship'.[5] He felt that the Government should give precise definition to add clarity to the role of ID.

In a more recent study[6], P. Saravanan and T. S. Shaw analysed whether higher amount of network connections among the independent directors have any impact on the firm's value. The study established the fact that increase in the board size and duality decrease would increase performance respectively. The degree of centrality of the board, and the proportion of directors from same industry has statistically significant positive effect on the firm's performance. The studies also proved that the embeddedness of the firm to its core industry through Board of Directors left significant positive effect on the firm's performance and thus establishing the fact that higher the average number of network connection of the directors in a board, higher is the firm's performance.

Since Independent directors are the most important pillar of corporate governance in a public listed company's board, it is necessary to have a look at independent directorial positions in companies. As per the Director's Database of Bombay Stock Exchange, there are 35 companies where the status of its directors is not known. 37 companies do not have even 1 independent director; 19 companies have only independent directors. The survey has revealed the fact that a total of 7,282 individuals occupied a total of 9,447 independent directorship positions on 2,708 BSE-listed companies. Of these 7,282 individuals, 5,284 held only 1 independent directorship. Thus, of total 2708 BSE listed companies, 1.7% had defaulted on the independent director norm. Of the 7282 independent directors 81% held only independent directorial position and 4% of the independent directors held directorship in more than 5 companies. Thus, the percentage of directors holding multiple directorship isn't very high. However, if we compare it with total no. of directors; of the total 339 directors holding more than 5 directorship position 86% are independent directors. This suggests independent directors tend to hold multiple directorships.

A KPMG poll conducted between late November 2008 and early January 2009 among 90 CEOs, CFOs, independent directors and other leaders from Indian corporate world suggests that 89% of the respondents believed that independent directors merely contribute towards fulfilment of statutory requirements. The poll also showed that while the majority believed that all committees other than audit committee are not effective and even the audit committee requires to be strengthened. There is a general point of view that the Indian boards do not get adequate time and information to discharge their duties. Thus, the problem of multiple directorships should be seriously looked into. There is no value addition or compliance obligation that these boards can be credited for.[7]

The other question pertains to the independence of independent directors. As a matter of fact, these directors are appointed on the board to eliminate the biased outlook which other connected directors may have. However, on the subject of independence of an ID, one must remember that no one is invited to join a board to act as a non-executive director unless he/she is well known to the promoters or the Chairman or the Managing Director. All non-executive directors, whether or not independent, need to support the Promoter Group for their re-election. Hence, independence of director is more of a matter of attitude. An empirical study of 499 publicly traded firms showed that directors with very high equity ownership worked in the interest of the firm; as their interests converged with interests of the shareholders. However, given sufficient equity ownership, board members may become entrenched, whereby their interests do not reflect the interests of the shareholders and the board members have sufficient voting power to suppress sanctions on them including their removal. The study also showed that independent directors show similar reactions to financial incentives as independent directors. Hence, there is a requirement of stronger governance norms irrespective of type of director and corporate governance should not be left solely to independent directors.[8] However, in spite of the fact that there are differences of interest between non-executive directors and shareholders, the fact is that the non-executive directors bring different sets of skills to the company and they help in the process of executive learning. They also help in strategic decision making by bringing in independent opinion and fresh view point.[9]

5. ACTION DESIRED

It is evident from the above discussion that there is every effort being made in diverse countries to ensure independence of directors. As long as the directors are the majority shareholders in the company, independence may not turn out to be an issue. Clash of interests of owners and directors occur when majority shareholders are widely scattered and a few dominant shareholders become directors and lead the company. There was a great debate that went on the "5% syndrome"; meaning that those dominant sections holding just 5% of the shares sit in the boardroom to decide the fate of the 95%. Thus, there is conflict between corporate governance and the proprietary rights of controlling shareholders. A study conducted by Macquarie Equities showed that companies whose directors are substantial shareholders outperform the market.[10] The theory, therefore, is that directors with skin in the game are more motivated to improve the company performance.

The damp squib in the entire issue pertains to the phenomenon of excessive concentration of ownership. It is found that in some Asian countries (including India), it is difficult to have a majority of the independent directors; because many listed companies are family controlled and they want the majority of the board to represent them. Nevertheless, the Companies Act, 2013 makes it obligatory on the part of the companies to ensure that one-third of the board to be independent. As is the case in many other countries, this percentage can be enhanced to 50% in the years to come. It is also worthwhile to frame guidelines that prohibit the appointment of relatives/friends/well-wishers as Independent Directors on the Boards. Though it is very difficult to cull out the relationships among the individuals, reasonable/modest attempt can be done towards this end.

Another feasible solution appears to be maintaining a panel of experts/professionals, who can be considered for being appointed as independent directors; from whom companies can choose. The outfit already created by the Ministry of Corporate Affairs, Government of India in the name and style "National Foundation for Corporate Governance" in partnership with the professional bodies such as ICAI, ICSI, CII and BSE could be entrusted with this responsibility. In addition, the services of Indian Independent Directors' Association may also be solicited, since this is an initiative of the Chamber of Indian Micro, Small and Medium Enterprises. Answering a question whether corporate governance was of the highest standard among the start-up community, Sri Ratan Tata, Chairman Emeritus of Tata Group said that governance must ensure that one obeyed the law of the land. The enforcement should be strict and there is equality in enforcement.[11]

5.1 National Foundation for Corporate Governance

This is an agency set up by the Ministry of Corporate Affairs, Government of India in partnership with Confederation of Indian Industry (CII), Institute of Company Secretaries of India (ICSI), and the Institute of Chartered Accountants of India (ICAI). The Foundation has formulated corporate governance norms for independent directors by appointing a core group under the chairmanship of Prof. N. Balasubrahmanian. The salient aspects of the report were detailed below:

(i) Corporate legislation and regulation should promote effective contribution by independent members of a Company's Board of Directors, and of Board

Committees. Towards this end, the legislative and regulatory framework should provide for appropriate strength of independent directors on the board and board committees.

(ii) Corporate legislation and regulation should specify minimum criteria (positively and negatively) that would qualify or disqualify a person as an independent director.

(iii) Quorum requirements for Board and Key Board Committees (Audit, Compensation, and Nominations Committees) should be prescribed such that participation (in person or by audio-videoconference) by a majority of Independent Directors on the Board/Committees is required.

(iv) It must be laid down that there shall be affirmative vote of a majority of independent directors participating in person or by audio-videoconference in the meeting when a resolution is placed for approval.

(v) Directors having conflict of interest requirements should be excluded in reckoning the qualifying number of Independent Directors required for the quorum or for affirmative voting on resolutions.

(vi) Law should enable independent directors on company boards to obtain, expert advice, wherever necessary, with the costs being borne by the company.

(vii) The shareholders also contribute their mite to take meaningful decisions.

5.2 Indian Independent Directors' Association (IIDA)

This is a forum for knowledge sharing among IDs floated by the Chamber of Indian Micro, Small and Medium Enterprises, New Delhi. The main objectives of the Association are:

(i) to share knowledge and assist skill development of Independent Directors;

(ii) to promote and develop sound and progressive ethics, principles and practices for Independent Directors;

(iii) to propagate and strengthen the initiatives and programs of the Government of India, State Governments and Union Territories related to various Statutory Laws and their compliance;

(iv) to conduct workshops, conferences, training programs on related topics; and

(v) to provide a platform to Government and Independent Directors for the interaction on the issues of mutual interest

The Association provides an opportunity to professionals to register themselves for inclusion of their names in the database maintained. Those seeking appointment as ID can register themselves with the Association by subscribing to the due diligence process. This is a mechanism followed by the Association to weed out individuals who do not conform to the rules notified by the Ministry of Corporate Affairs and to maintain a high standard of excellence to comply with the norms. The information uploaded on the site by individuals will pass through at least the following steps so as to verify the credentials of the candidate.

(i) Verification of PAN from the Income Tax Site
(ii) Verification of DIN from the ROCs office
(iii) Verification of the present/past directorship from respective companies
(iv) References from two known persons who can vouch for their standing.

The above list is just explanatory and not exhaustive. Thus, the final approval of the profile for inclusion in the data base of professionals seeking directorship listing on the website may take about seven days after all the details are furnished and payment is made. It is heartening to note that the Association provides guidelines to the members and companies as well.

6. THE HOPE

At the end, it may be hoped that with all the effort and initiative taken so far, the system of ID would stabilize in the future and the corporate governance practices take a new direction under the stewardship of responsible citizen being appointment as IDs. It is in this context, the Ministry of Corporate Affairs is required to play a great role in identifying suitable persons across the country than simply maintaining a data bank. The Ministry may direct the NFCG to launch a drive of 'Talent Search' for this purpose and take the initiative of providing the required skill and training. After all, capacity building is the *sine qua non* for success in any initiative.

References

1. Jensen, Michael C. and Meckling William H., "Theory of the Firm: Managerial Behaviour, Agency Costs and Ownership Structure", *Journal of Financial Economics*, Vol.3, October 1976, pp. 305-360.
2. Van Horn, James C. and Wachowicz Jr. John M., *"Fundamentals of Financial Management"*, Pearson Education Asia, First Indian Reprint, 2001, p. 5.
3. Ajay Kumar Garg, "Influence of Board Size and Independence on Firm Performance – A Study of Indian Companies", *Vikalpa*, Vol. 32, No. 3, July-September 2007, pp. 36-60.
4. Ranjan R. *"Role of Independent Directors in Corporate Governance"*, Indian Academy of Law & Management : The Chronicle of Advanced Learning, August 21, 2014.

5. Divesh Goyal, "*Independent Directors are now a crucial part of Indian Company Law*": www.taxguru.com.
6. Saravanan, P and Shaw, T.S., "*Role of Independent Directors – Enhancing or otherwise of the shareholders wealth – An Empirical Investigation*", study conducted under the aegis of National Foundation for Corporate Governance, May 2014.
7. Rashmi Aggarwal and Rajinder Kaur, "*Corporate Governance – An Indian Legal Format: A Critique*", International Proceedings of Economics Development and Research, Vol. 39, June 2012, pp. 80-85. (www.ebscohost.com).
8. Pergola, Teresa M. and Joseph, Gilbert W., "Corporate Governance and Board Equity Ownership", *Corporate Governance*, Vol. 11, No. 2, 2011, pp. 200-13.
9. Dechins, David and Others, "*Executive Learning in Entrepreneurial Firms and the Role of External Directors*", MCP University Press, Vol. 42, No. 4 & 5, 2000, pp. 317-25.
10. www.macquarie.com
11. The Hindu, dated 19-06-2015, p. 13.

13

CHAPTER

Role of Audit Committee

1. GENESIS

There has been realization world over that there should be some kind of internal control mechanism to supervise the operations of the Board of Directors, Management, Auditors and those involved in leading the company. This realization has given rise to the constitution of Audit Committees (ACs) in various countries. As far back as in 1940 itself, the Securities and Exchange Commission (SEC) of USA advocated the establishment of ACs[1]. Following this suggestion, the New York Stock Exchange (NYSE) made the constitution of ACs by the listed companies mandatory in 1977. The Cadbury Committee (1992) and the Auditing Practices Board of UK have also made out a strong case for the establishment of AC mechanism. The Blue Ribbon Committee (1999) also suggested to strengthen the mechanism of ACs to ensure accountability, beyond the existing mechanism of statutory auditors[2]. Taking cue from the experiences of these, countries like Canada, Australia and New Zealand have joined the bandwagon. Though there are many variations in the constitution, membership, qualifications and functioning in the ACs among countries, but the system of ACs has got firmly established.

As far as the Indian experience is concerned, the discussion on ACs has started with the recommendations of the Kumar Mangalam Birla Committee (SEBI's first committee on corporate governance) constituted on May 7, 1999. The Committee submitted its report with many significant recommendations. Having reviewed the situation, the Committee felt that strong corporate governance is indispensable to resilient and vibrant capital markets and is an important instrument of investor protection. It is the blood that fills the veins of transparent corporate disclosure and high-quality accounting practices. It is the muscle that moves a viable and accessible financial reporting structure. Without financial reporting premised on sound, honest information, capital markets will collapse upon themselves.

The key observations and recommendations of the Committee in respect of ACs are as follows[3]:

1. A qualified and independent audit committee should be set up by every company. It is considered that this would go a long way in enhancing the credibility of the financial disclosures of a company and in promoting transparency. This is one of the mandatory recommendations of the Committee.
2. Regarding the constitution, the Committee felt that the Audit Committee should have minimum of three members, all being non-executive directors, and majority being independent directors. They are also expected to have sound knowledge in the accounting matters. Going into the details, the chairman of the committee should be an independent director and he should be present at Annual General Meeting to answer shareholders' queries. It shall be within the powers of the audit committee to invite such executives, as it considers appropriate to be present at the meetings of the Committee to brief them on the significant matters of finance and accounting. If required, they may call for the presence of Finance Director and a representative of the external auditor to be present as invitees for the meetings of the audit committee. The Company Secretary should act as the secretary to the committee.
3. It is advised that the Audit Committee shall meet at least thrice a year. One meeting must be held before finalisation of annual accounts and one necessarily every six months. This is identified as a mandatory recommendation.
4. The quorum should be either two members or one-third of the members of the audit committee, whichever is higher and there shall be the presence of a minimum of two independent directors.
5. Being a committee of the board, the audit committee derives its powers from the authorization of the board. In order to enable the audit committee to discharge its functions effectively, the committee recommended to grant the following powers to the audit committee:
    - To investigate any activity within its terms of reference.
    - To seek information from any employee.
    - To obtain outside legal or other professional advice.
    - To secure attendance of outsiders with relevant expertise, if considered necessary.
6. As the audit committee acts as the bridge between the board, the statutory auditors and internal auditors, the Committee recommended that its role shall include the following:
    - Oversight of the company's financial reporting process and the disclosure of its financial information to ensure that the financial statement is correct, sufficient and credible.

- Recommending the appointment and removal of external auditor, fixation of audit fee and also approval for payment for any other services.
- Reviewing with management the annual financial statements before submission to the board, focusing primarily on:
    - ✓ Any changes in accounting policies and practices.
    - ✓ Major accounting entries based on exercise of judgement by management.
    - ✓ Qualifications in draft audit report.
    - ✓ Significant adjustments arising out of audit.
    - ✓ The going concern assumption.
    - ✓ Compliance with accounting standards
    - ✓ Compliance with stock exchange and legal requirements concerning financial statements.
    - ✓ Any related party transactions, i.e., transactions of the company of material nature, with promoters or the management, their subsidiaries or relatives, etc., that may have potential conflict with the interests of company at large.
- Reviewing with the management, external and internal auditors, the adequacy of internal control systems.
- Reviewing the adequacy of internal audit function, including the structure of the internal audit department, staffing and seniority of the official heading the department, reporting structure, coverage and frequency of internal audit.
- Discussion with internal auditors of any significant findings and follow-up thereon.
- Reviewing the findings of any internal investigations by the internal auditors into matters where there is suspected fraud or irregularity or a failure of internal control systems of a material nature and reporting the matter to the board.
- Discussion with external auditors before the audit commences, of the nature and scope of audit. Also post-audit discussion to ascertain any area of concern.
- Reviewing the company's financial and risk management policies.
- Looking into the reasons for substantial defaults in the payments to the depositors, debenture holders, shareholders (in case of non-payment of declared dividends) and creditors. This is a mandatory recommendation

2. COMPANIES (AMENDMENT) ACT, 2000

Following the recommendations of the Birla Committee, the Companies Act, 1956 was amended to include a new section 292A, paving the way for constitution of Audit

Committees by every public company having paid-up capital of not less than five crore of rupees. The section was drafted comprehensively, detailing the constitution, functions and procedure. The section provides for the following[4]:

1. Every Public Company shall constitute an Audit Committee with not less than three directors and such number of other directors as the Board may determine.
2. Every Audit Committee shall act in accordance with terms of reference to be specified in writing by the Board.
3. The members of the Audit Committee shall elect a chairman from amongst themselves.
4. The annual report of the company shall disclose the composition of the Audit Committee.
5. The auditors and the internal auditor of the company can attend and participate at meetings of the Audit Committee, without having voting rights.
6. It is the duty of the members of the Audit Committee to discuss with the auditors periodically about internal control systems. Further, the Audit Committee may also review the half yearly and annual financial statements before submission to the Board and also ensure compliance of internal control systems.
7. The Audit Committee shall have authority to investigate into any matter in relation to the items listed in the Companies Act and those referred to it by the Board of Directors. For this purpose, the members of the Audit Committee shall have full access to information contained in the records of the company.
8. The recommendations of the Audit Committee on any matter relating to financial management including the audit report, shall be made binding on the Board.
9. If the Board does not accept the recommendations of the Audit Committee, it shall record the reasons therefor and communicate such reasons to the shareholder.
10. The chairman of the Audit Committee shall attend the annual general meetings of the company to provide any clarification on matters relating to audit.
11. If a default is made in complying with the provisions of the Act, the company and every officer who is in default, shall be punishable with imprisonment for a term which may extend to one year, with fine which may extend to fifty thousand rupees, or with both.

3. N.R. NARAYANA MURTHY COMMITTEE RECOMMENDATIONS ON ACs

The SEBI constituted its second Committee on Corporate Governance in 2002 under the Chairmanship of N.R. Narayana Murthy. This Committee also made the following significant recommendations for revamping the functioning of the ACs.[5]

1. Audit Committees of publicly listed companies should be required to review the following information mandatorily:
   - financial statements and draft audit report, including quarterly/half-yearly financial information;
   - management discussion and analysis of financial condition and results of operations;
   - reports relating to compliance with laws and to risk management;
   - management letters/letters of internal control weaknesses issued by statutory/internal auditors; and
   - records of related party transactions.
2. All audit committee members should be "financially literate" and at least one member should have accounting or related financial management expertise. The term "financially literate" means the ability to read and understand basic financial statements, i.e., balance sheet, profit and loss account, and statement of cash flows.

4. CLAUSE-49 OF THE LISTING AGREEMENT

The mechanism of ACs is sought to be implemented through the condition imposed in the Listing Agreement. It is nothing but natural that every company wishes to get its shares listed on an exchange. While offering this service, the Exchange would try to exact compliance of the conditions. The Listing Agreement of BSE is quite exhaustive. It was discussed in a separate chapter of this book. As far as the issues pertaining to ACs are concerned, attempt has been made to detail the same hereunder.

A. Qualified and Independent Audit Committee [Clause-49(II)(A)]

As per the directions of the SEBI, every company desirous of listing its shares shall set up a qualified and independent audit committee, adhering to the following norms:

(i) The audit committee shall have minimum three directors as members. Two-thirds of the members of audit committee shall be independent directors.

(ii) All members of audit committee shall be financially literate and at least one member shall have accounting or related financial management expertise.

(iii) The Chairman of the Audit Committee shall be an independent director.

(iv) The Chairman of the Audit Committee shall be present at Annual General Meeting to answer shareholder queries.

(v) The audit committee may invite such of the executives and particularly the head of the finance function to be present at the meetings of the committee. The finance director, head of internal audit and a representative of the statutory auditor may be present as invitees for the meetings of the audit committee. The Company Secretary shall act as the secretary to the committee.

In the opinion of the Exchange, a member will be considered to have accounting or related financial management expertise, if he or she possesses experience in finance or accounting or requisite professional certification in accounting, or any other comparable experience. The individual is also expected to have financial sophistication, including being or having been a chief executive officer, chief financial or other senior officer with financial oversight responsibilities.

B. Meeting of Audit Committee (Clause-49(II)(B))

The audit committee should meet at least four times in a year and not more than four months shall lapse between two meetings. The quorum shall be either two members or one third of the members of the audit committee whichever is greater, but there should be a minimum of two independent members present at the meeting.

C. Powers of Audit Committee (Clause-49(II)(C))

The Audit Committee shall have powers, which should include the following:

1. To investigate any activity within its terms of reference.
2. To seek information from any employee.
3. To obtain outside legal or other professional advice.
4. To secure attendance of outsiders with relevant expertise.

Further, it may be noted that the four powers as mentioned above are only illustrative and not exhaustive. The auditor should check whether the terms of reference of the audit committee have been suitably framed mentioning the above powers. It is mandatory for the above-mentioned four powers to be vested in the Audit Committee. The Board may delegate further powers to the committee.

D. Role of Audit Committee (Clause-49(II)(D))

The role of the audit committee shall include the following:

(a) Oversight of the company's financial reporting process and the disclosure of its financial information to ensure that the financial statement is correct, sufficient and credible.

(b) Recommending the appointment and removal of external auditors, fixation of audit fee and also approval for payment of any other services.

(c) Reviewing with management the annual financial statements before submission to the Board, focusing primarily on:

  (i) any changes in accounting policies/and practices;
  (ii) major accounting entries based on exercise of judgments by management;
  (iii) qualification in draft audit report;
  (iv) significant adjustments arising out of audit;

(v) the going concern assumption;
(vi) compliance with accounting standards;
(vii) compliance with stock exchanges and legal requirement concerning financial statements; and
(viii) any related party transactions.

(d) Reviewing with the management, external and internal auditors, the adequacy of internal control system.
(e) Reviewing the adequacy of internal audit function, if any including the structure of the internal audit department, staffing and seniority of the official heading the department, reporting structure coverage and frequency of internal audit.
(f) Discussion with internal auditors on the significant findings during the course of their audit.
(g) Reviewing the findings of any internal investigation by the internal auditors into matters of fraud or any irregularity. The failure of internal control system shall also be examined.
(h) To discuss with external auditors the nature and scope of audit as well as to have post-audit discussion to ascertain any area of concern.
(i) Reviewing the company's risk management policies.
(j) To look into the reasons for substantial defaults in the payment to the depositors, debenture holders and shareholders.
(k) Any other function as requested by the Board.

E. Functions of the Audit Committee

The Audit Committee performs various important functions like investigating the matters referred by board, discuss internal control system, etc. The requirements under these rules are as detailed below:

(i) The Audit Committee should have discussions with the auditors periodically about internal control systems and the scope of audit including the observations of the auditors. There shall also be review of the half-yearly and annual financial statements before submission to the Board.
(ii) The Audit Committee shall have authority to investigate into any matter in relation to the items referred to it by the Board. In discharging such duties, the AC shall have full access to information contained in the records of the company and external professional advice, if necessary.

F. Review of Information by Audit Committee

The Audit Committee shall mandatorily review the following information as per Clause-49 (II) (E):

1. analysis of financial condition and results of operations;
2. significant related party transactions provided by the management;
3. correspondence and letters of internal control weaknesses identified by the statutory auditors;
4. internal audit reports relating to internal control weaknesses; and
5. the appointment, removal and terms of remuneration of the internal auditor.

The auditor should ascertain from the minutes book of the audit committee and other sources like agenda papers, etc., whether the audit committee has reviewed the above-mentioned information. The auditor should also ascertain management discussion and analysis report forms part of the annual report to the shareholders. The auditor should further ascertain whether the management discussion and analysis includes discussion on the matters stipulated in the Agreement. Where certain deficiencies are noted by the audit committee, the auditor will be required to see that these have been suitably dealt with by the management in the Report on Corporate Governance. The auditor should also ascertain that the information reviewed by the Audit Committee is consistent with the reporting in the financial statements including those drawn up giving segment wise break-up for compliance under AS 17 (Segment Reporting).

5. COMPARISON OF THE CLAUSES IN THE LISTING AGREEMENT AND PROVISIONS OF SECTION 292A OF THE COMPANIES ACT, 1956

As a matter of fact, clause-49 of the Listing Agreement has widened the scope of section 292A in respect of strict implementation of the provisions of Companies Act. A synoptic comparison of the two, given in Table-1, would amply testify the sweep of the clause 49. As can be seen from the table, the following are the matters on which section 292A remained silent:

(i) The audit committee may invite such executives, as it considers appropriate (and particularly head of the finance function) to be present at the meeting of the committee, but on occasions, it may also meet without the presence of any executive of the company.

(ii) The company secretary shall act as secretary to the committee. The audit committee shall meet at least four times in a year. The gap between two meetings should not be more than four months.

(iii) The quorum of the audit committee shall be two members or one-third of the members of the audit committee whichever is higher and minimum of two independent directors are to be present.

(iv) The powers and role of the audit committee are elaborately contained in Clause-49 II(C) & (D).

(v) All members of the audit committee shall be financially literate and at least one member shall have accounting or related financial management expertise.

Table 13.1: The comparative chart showing the requirements under Clause-49 (BSE) and Section 292A of Companies Act, 1956.

Clause-49 of the Listing Agreement	Section 292A of the Companies Act, 1956
1. (a) All Companies seeking listing for the first time, at the time of seeking in principle approval for such listing and (b) All existing listed companies with a paid-up capital of Rs. 3 crore and above or net worth of Rs. 25 crore or more any time in the history of the company are required to set up an audit committee.	1. Every public company having paid-up capital of not less than five crore of rupees shall constitute an audit committee immediately on the commencement of Companies (Amendment) Act, 2000, i.e. with effect from 13th December, 2000.
2. The audit committee shall have minimum three directors as members. Two-third of the members of audit committee shall be independent directors.	2. The audit committee shall have minimum three directors of which two-thirds of the total number of such directors shall be directors other than managing or whole-time directors.
3. All members of audit committee shall be financially literate and at least one member shall have accounting or related financial management expertise.	3. No such reference is contained in the Companies Act, 1956.
4. The chairman of the audit committee shall be "independent" director and shall be present at Annual General Meeting to answer queries of the shareholders.	4. The Members of the audit committee shall elect a chairman from amongst themselves. The Chairman of the Audit Committee shall attend the annual general meetings of the company to provide any clarification on matters relating to audit.
5. A representative of the external auditor when required shall be present as an invitee for the meetings of the audit committee. The audit committee may invite such of the executives to be present at the meetings of the committee. The Finance Director, head of internal audit and a representative of the statutory auditor may be present as invitees for the meetings of the audit committee.	5. The Auditors, the internal auditor, if any, and the director-in-charge of finance shall attend and participate at meetings of the audit committee but shall not have the right to vote.
6. The Company Secretary shall act as Secretary to the audit committee.	6. No such reference is contained in the Companies Act, 1956.

On the contrary, the following are the issues on which Clause 49 was silent:

(i) The audit committee constituted shall act in accordance with terms of reference to be specified in writing by the Board.

(ii) The recommendations of the audit committee on any matter relating to financial management, including the audit report, shall be binding on the Board.

(iii) If the Board does not accept the recommendations of the audit committee, it shall record the reasons thereof and communicate such reasons to the shareholders.

6. COMPANIES ACT, 2013

As if to bridge this gap, the Companies Act, 2013 has modified the section 292A and incorporated the following additional aspects under the new section 177.[6]

(i) The Audit Committee shall consist of a minimum of three directors with independent directors forming a majority. The modification in this regard pertains to the upper hand of Independent directors, being the majority in the committee. This was not the case in the old provision.

(ii) That majority of the members of Audit Committee, including its Chairperson, shall be persons with ability to read and understand the financial statements. This was not the case in the earlier section.

(iii) Every Audit Committee shall act in accordance with the terms of reference specified in writing by the Board which shall *inter alia,* include:

  (a) the recommendation for appointment, remuneration and terms of appointment of auditors of the company;
  (b) review and monitor the auditor's independence and performance, and effectiveness of audit process;
  (c) examination of the financial statements and the auditors' report thereon;
  (d) approval or any subsequent modification of transactions of the company with related parties;
  (e) scrutiny of inter-corporate loans and investments;
  (f) valuation of undertakings or assets of the company, wherever it is necessary;
  (g) evaluation of internal financial controls and risk management systems; and
  (h) monitoring the end use of funds raised through public offers and related matters.

(iv) The Board's Report under sub-section (3) of section 134 shall disclose the composition of an Audit Committee and where the Board had not accepted any recommendation of the Audit Committee, the same shall be disclosed in such report along with the reasons therefor.

(v) Every listed company or such class or classes of companies, as may be prescribed, shall establish a vigil mechanism for directors and employees to report genuine concerns in such manner as may be prescribed.

(vi) The vigil mechanism under sub-section (9) shall provide for adequate safeguards against victimization of persons who use such mechanism and make provision for direct access to the chairperson of the Audit Committee in appropriate or exceptional cases.

A plain reading of the clauses in section 177 clearly establishes the fact that law makers have taken the recommendations of the two committees (Kumara Mangalam Committee and N R Narayana Murthy Committee) and the clauses on the Listing Agreement of BSE. This is really appreciable.

7. REVIEW OF THE EFFECTIVENESS OF THE EFFICIENCY OF ACS

Against the above backdrop, one would be curious to know to what extent Audit Committee experiment has yielded fruitful results in ensuring smooth and effective corporate governance. In this context, the opinion survey conducted by Jawaher AI – Mudhaki and P.L. Joshi of University of Bahrain is worth mentioning.[7] The authors have attempted to capture the effectiveness of the functioning of the Audit Committees in Indian Companies (based on the data compiled by the Centre for Monitoring Indian Economy pertaining to companies whose sales turnover was more than US $25 million in 1999-2000 and whose head offices were located in four metropolitan cities, viz., Mumbai, Delhi, Calcutta and Chennai. After a meaningful application of the methodology, including relevant statistical techniques, the authors have concluded that:

(i) So far only 56.2 per cent of the companies have constituted Audit Committees, despite the fact that it is mandatory.

(ii) Only 14.6 per cent of the companies have independent non-executive directors in the committees; while 90.2 per cent have non-executive directors.

(iii) There is lack of independence in their representation and composition.

(iv) The functions of Audit Committees are varied. The very important functions carried out by the Committees included review of annual audited financial statements, recommendations on the audit fees and review of the effectiveness of internal control mechanisms.

(v) The most important areas of focus are compliance with standards and regulatory bodies, probing material items, and undisclosed liabilities.

(vi) The majority of companies' Audit Committees meetings are held monthly or quarterly.

It is evident from the above that the functioning of the Audit Committees needs to be improved towards ensuring effective governance. There are two limitations in interpreting the results of the above study. First, the study was conducted just after two years when the Companies Act was amended in 2000 to include section 292A making the constitution of Audit Committees mandatory. This can be allowed as a gestation or process period. Second, the study is based on a mailed questionnaire forwarded to 286 companies, received 78 and 73 being found usable. The issue is not about the size of the sample, but about the authenticity of the replies. It is a simple premise that nobody would like to under-rate his performance, however, honest he may be. It is a kind of self-assessment/judgment. One needs to be cautious, hence, in accepting the conclusions *a priori*.

In addition to the above, there are also a few other studies that found inverse relationship between the audit committee independence and earnings management.[8] Despite this, there has been a general consensus regarding the role of the audit committee in finding that the ACs have improved the quality of audit reports and thus contributed to the enhancement of the firms' performance.[9] In a more recent study (January, 2016), Nidhi Bansal and Anil K. Sharma concluded that the independence of AC has significantly contributed to the improvement in earnings of the firms selected for the study.[10]

Between 2000 and 2015 much water has flown. The list of scams/frauds given in is any indication, there is no reason to jump to the conclusion that all is well with the functioning of Audit Committees. The recent fall of companies like Satyam has buzzed an alarm on the role and efficiency of Audit Committees and also the statutory auditors.

The unabated failures of the companies are raising the eyebrows of the investors and other stakeholders interested in the growth of healthy stock market. Studies have pointed out many deficiencies in the role and functioning of the Audit Committees even at present.[11] Some such findings are listed below:

(i) that the independent directors are not really independent, since they are not invited and selected by following a proper procedure;

(ii) that most of the independent directors are either family members or friends or relatives or those having close nexus with the other directors of the company;

(iii) there are evidences to show that even the independent directors and directors on the Boards are negotiated by financial ties between the company and themselves;

(iv) that there are strong ties among the members of the Board and members of the Audit Committees; resulting in compromise of the independence, supposed to be maintained;

(v) that the members of the Committee are paying deaf year even when the external and internal auditors being the same and also when they are providing consultancy services. This is the reason why the amended Act has made certain stringent provisions relating to the auditors, which included: (a) mandatory rotation of auditors; (b) authorization to the Tribunal to change auditors; and (c) auditors not to render certain services including internal audit and management consultancy.

Therefore, the above stated factual situation warrants closer monitoring of the role of Audit Committees in ensuring effective governance.

References

1. Jawahar Al – Mudhaki and P.L. Joshi, "The Role and Functions of Audit Committee in the Indian Corporate Governance: Empirical Findings", *International Journal of Auditing*. 8: 33-47 (2004).
2. Blue Ribbon Committee (1999), Improving the Effectiveness of Corporate Audit Committee, New York.
3. Report of the Kumar Mangalam Birla Committee on Corporate Governance, SEBI, 1999.
4. The Companies Act, 1956, Universal Law Publishing Co., New Delhi, 2011.
5. Report of the N R Narayana Murthy Committee on Corporate Governance, SEBI, February 2003.
6. The Companies Act, 2013 (Act 18 of 2013), Universal Law Publishing Co., New Delhi, 2013.
7. Op. cit. Jawahar Al – Mudhaki and P.L. Joshi, (2004).
8. Abbott, L.J., Parker, S., & Peters, G.F. (2002), 'audit Committee Characteristics and financial misstatement: A Study of the Efficary of certain blue ribbon committee recommendations'. http://dx.doi.prg/10.219/ssrn.319125.
9. Arslan, M., Zaman, R., & Malik, R.K. (2014), 'Impact of CEO Duality and Audit Committee on Firm performance: A Study of Oil & Gas Listed Firms of Pakistan', *Research Journal of Finance and Accounting*, 5(17), 2222-1697. http://dx.doi.org/10.2139/ssrn.2515067.
10. Nidhi Bansal & Anil K. Sharma, 'Audit Committee, Corporate Governance and Firm Performance: Empirical Evidence from India', *International Journal of Economics and Finance*, Vol. 8, No. 3, 2016.
11. (a) Hetal Pandya/Vyas, (2013), 'Corporate Governance: Role of Auditors and Auditing Committee', *IPASJ International Journal of Management*, Vol. 1, Issue 2, July 2013, pp. 1-7.

    (b) M.S. Subhas and Kiran Kumar (2015), 'Role of Audit Committee on Corporate Governance: Audit Committees' Effectiveness Increases the Market Value of Shares', *Indian Journal of Applied Research*, Vol. 5, No. 2, February 2015, pp. 379-381.

14

CHAPTER

Role of the Auditor under the Companies Act, 2013

It is to be admitted that the Companies Act, 1956 itself is comprehensive in defining the role of the Auditor of a company. Sections 224 to 233 of the Act narrate the diverse aspects relating to the appointment, remuneration, removal, qualification and disqualification, powers and duties, and the power of the Central Government to order for special audit in certain cases. In the process of achieving simplification, brevity and clarity, the Act was thoroughly modified to also take into consideration the changing context of corporate world. One should really appreciate the drafting team of the new law for framing the provisions in the **positive note.** The role of the auditor was detailed in Chapter-X of the New Act through Sections 139 to 148. An attempt is made in the following pages to compare the provisions in the old and new Acts in respect of several aspects of Audit of Companies, with a view to highlighting the changes made to the existing provisions.

1. ELIGIBILITY OF PERSONS TO BE APPOINTED AS AUDITOR

Section 226 of the Act, 1956 is also comprehensive in specifying the qualifications required to be appointed as an Auditor of the company. While listing the persons not eligible to be appointed as Auditor, the new Act has identified the following categories of persons also to be ineligible:

(a) any person or firm having business relationship with the company, or any of its associates;

(b) any person who is a relative to any of the directors managing the company or in the employment of the company;

(c) any person who is in full time employment elsewhere or acting as a partner of a firm holding appointment as its auditor, and the said auditing firm is acting as auditor for more than 20 companies;
(d) any person who has been convicted by a court of an offence involving fraud and a period of ten years has not elapsed from the date of such conviction;
(e) any person who is retained to act as a consultant to offer certain specialized services as detailed in section 144 of the Act; and
(f) any person charged with any disqualification as mentioned in sub-section (3) of section 226 of the Act.

A closer examination of the provisions of the Act reveals the fact the government is very careful in fixing the eligibility to be the Auditor to a company. More specifically, the Act is unequivocal on the following three types of situations.

(i) having direct or indirect business relationship;
(ii) conviction by a Court of Law for an offence involving fraud; and
(iii) offering consulting and specialized services (non-audit services).

1.1 Having Business Relationship

It is fair to expect that an auditor is fair, independent, impartial and objective in auditing the accounts of a company and in presenting the "true and fair view" of the company's affairs to the sholders. It is also logical and ethical to expect that the Auditor does not have any business relationship with the firm to which he is appointed as Auditor. Ignoring this 'Common Principle of Trust', many auditors are seeking to associate themselves with the fortunes of the firms by having direct or indirect relationships. Reports on the failure of gaint companies like Enron (USA), WorldCom (and) Parmalat (Italy) have clearly evidenced the unholy nexus between the Management and the Auditor. It has been reported that M/s Anthen Anderson, the auditing firm, has lost its independence and objectivity on account of this. Same thing has come true in case of the Satyam episode.[1]

More significant among the other steps proposed by the SEC include the prohibition of certain relationships between audit firms and the companies they audit, as of the following:

(a) **Employment Relationships:** Any person employed by the company shall remain disassociated with the company for a specific period. This is termed the 'cooling off period'. Only after the completion of this period, a company can hire certain individuals formerly employed by its auditor in a financial reporting oversight role. The audit committee should also focus its attention relating to this aspect and advise the company accordingly.

(b) **Contingent Fees:** It is also important to see that the auditors are not paid anything beyond the approved remuneration. Such remuneration is considered to impair the auditor's independence and may lure the auditor to be biased in his disposition.

(c) **Business Relationships:** Audit firms may not have any direct or indirect business relationships with the company, or with any of its officials. Such relationships are treated as impinging on the fair conduct of the auditor. Audit committee also is required to be vigilant over this aspect.

(d) **Certain Financial Relationships:** It is to be noted that world over certain financial relationships between the company and the independent auditor are prohibited. These include creditor/debtor relationships, banking, broker-dealer, futures commission, merchant accounts, insurance products and interests in investment companies.

1.2 Offence Involving Fraud

The expression "Offence Involving Fraud" is very significant in terms of its interpretation. The more the economies are progressing and institutions evolving, the more prounced has become the succeptibility to fraud and dishonesty. This, speaks of the degrading moral fabric of the humanity; alas! no boundaries, however developed or underdeveloped the economies are!

It is appreciable that the Government of Britain had passed a separate legislation called "The Fraud Act, 2006 (which came into force from 15-01-2007) by repealing certain sections from the Theft Act of 1978. Section (1) of the Fraud Act, 2006 creates a general 'offence of fraud' and introduced the following three ways of committing fraud:[2]

(a) by false representation (Section-2);

(b) by failure to disclose information, where there is legal duty to do so (Section-3); and

(c) by abuse of position (Section-4).

In such of the above cases, the defendant's conduct must be dishonest and intention must be to make a gain; or cause a loss or the risk of a loss to another. Further, if the defendant makes a false representation dishonestly, knowing that the representation was or might be untrue, or misleading; the penalties are also heavy ranging from 12 months to 10 years imprisonment.

As far as the Indian law is concerned, Section 420 of Indian Penal Code, 1860 has the omnibus clause, which covers cheating and dishonesty including delivery of property, attracting punishment for a term which may extend to seven years, and shall also be liable to fine.[3] Still a comprehensive treatment is given through Section (17) of the

Indian Contracts Act, 1872, which defined the term 'fraud' to mean and include any of the following acts committed by a part to a contract or with his connivance, or by his agents, with intent to deceive another party or his agent or to induce him to enter into the contract:[4]

1. Making a statement which he does not believe it to be true.
2. Concealment of a fact, having knowledge or belief of the fact.
3. A promise made without any intention of performing it.
4. Any other act fitted to deceive.
5. Any such act or omission as the law specially declares to be fraudulent.

The Act makes a specific mention that mere silence as to facts likely to affect the willingness of a person to enter into a contract is not fraud. The act to be attracting the provisions of this, must be deliberate and with an intention to suppress facts or to deceive the opposite party.

In respect of the affairs of companies, the New Companies Act, 2013 has provided for a wider coverage of the activities purported to be included under the term 'fraud'. Section 447(1) of the Companies Act, 2013 defines the term 'fraud' in relation to affairs of a company or anybody corporate to include: (a) any act, (b) omission, (c) concealment of any fact, or (d) abuse of position committed by any person or any other person with the connivance in any manner. The seminal test in this regard shall be the intention to deceive the other party and thereby gain an undue advantage. Yet another dimension of the new explanation is that any act carried out with the intention of injuring or damaging the interests of the company or any of its stakeholders also comes under the expression 'fraud'. It can thus be understood that the new law has broad based the very meaning of the term.

As a matter of fact, the new Act casts onerous responsibility on the part of statutory auditor/cost auditor/secretarial auditor to report fraud to the Board and the Central Government. It would mean that even for a small fraud involving say Rs. 1000 in a large multi-locational enterprise would cast responsibility on the part of CA/CMA/CS. This provision has paved the way for reporting of frauds to the Central Government; in addition to their existing responsibilities of reporting requirement to the shareholder/ Board of Company. Clauses 143(12) to 143(15) of the Companies Act, 2013 are very significant in this regard. The Auditor of the company has the responsibility to report fraud to the concerned under the following situations without any fail.

- That the officers or employees of the company have or have been committing any fraud against the company.
- Similarly, the Cost Auditor or the Company Secretary, in discharge of their duties, has the reason to believe that there occurred fraud or mismanagement of the affairs of the company; such fact shall be brought to the notice of the concerned.

In such of the above cases, if the persons do not act as per the provisions of the Act, they shall be punishable with fine which shall not be less than Rs. 1 lakh, but which may extend to Rs. 25 lakh.

1.3 Non-Auditing Services

One of the crucial modifications to the existing Companies Act is in respect of barring auditors from rendering non-auditing services which may include various types of consulting and specialized services. Clause (i) of Section 141 (3) is very categorical in making ineligible, a person whose subsidiary or associate company or any other form of entity, is engaged as on the date of appointment in consulting and specialized services as provided in Section 144. Section 144 has made it clear that an auditor appointed under the Act shall provide to the company only such other services as are approved by the Board of Directors or the audit committee, as the case may be, but which shall not include any of the following services:

(i) accounting and bookkeeping services;
(ii) internal audit;
(iii) design and implementation of any financial information system;
(iv) actuarial services;
(v) investment advisory services;
(vi) investment banking services;
(vii) rendering of outsourced financial services;
(viii) management services; and
(ix) any other kind of services as may be prescribed.

The close nexus between the auditor and the management was got amplified by the acceptance of auditors to render services other than auditing of accounts and thus receive huge sums as fees. This has become evident in the cases of failure of Enron, WorldCom, Parmalat and Satyam.

As a matter of fact, this issue has engaged the attention of several agencies, including the governments. The Securities Exchange Commission, USA had been very categorical about offering non-audit services and prohibited the following:[5]

- Bookkeeping
- Financial information systems design and implementation
- Appraisal or valuation services, fairness opinions, or contribution-in-kind reports
- Actuarial services
- Internal audit outsourcing services
- Management functions or human resources

- Broker-dealer, investment adviser, or investment banking services
- Legal services and expert services unrelated to the audit

The intention of the SEC has got the force of the Law through the Sarbanes – Oxley (SOX) Act, passed in July 2002 in USA.[6] This Act was brought into effect with the express purpose of restoring public confidence in corporate financial statements. Prior to the enactment of SOX, investors suffered significant losses due to corporate failures brought out by financial malfeasance. The provisions of the Act were specific in addressing the issues of accounting fraud and the loss of independence on the part of the auditors.

A comparison of the situation prevailing in countries like USA and India clearly indicates that Section 144 of the Companies Act, 2013 has been drawn taking cue from the guidelines of SEC and the provisions of SOX Act. The Companies Act, 2013 has gone further in also interpreting the term 'directly or indirectly' used in the Section 144; thus:

(i) in case of auditor being an individual, either himself or through his relative or any other person connected, and

(ii) in case of auditor being a firm, either itself or through any of its partners or through its parent, subsidiary or associate entity.

2. APPOINTMENT AND REMOVAL OF AUDITORS

Sections 139 and 140 of the new Act have dealt with the issues pertaining to appointment, removal and resignation of the auditor. In the old Act, Section 224 dealt with the appointment and remuneration of auditors and now in the New Act, there was a separate provision incorporated under Section 142 to deal with the aspect of remuneration.

As regards appointment, the New Act has imposed a limitation period for continuation as auditor of a company. Under the present conditions an auditor, being an individual, cannot be appointed for five more years consecutively. In case, the auditor to be appointed is a firm, the said firm cannot be appointed for more than two terms of five consecutive years. Therefore, through this clause, the Central Government intends to put in place the system of 'rotation of auditors' after every consecutive period of five years.

Further, the new Act is specific in making a special mention of the removal and resignation the auditor. Removal of an auditor under Section 140 requires the passing of a special resolution, after obtaining the prior approval of the Central Government. The new Act has also provided for the resignation of the auditor in between, requiring the auditor to file a statement with the CAG, of the reasons and other facts relevant to his resignation. This gives an opportunity to the auditor to narrate circumstances under which he is resigning or perhaps forced to resign. This may warrant undue influence being exerted by the Directors of the company. This provision was highly acclaimed by the analysts and financial experts for the reason that it ensures 'freedom and independence' to the auditors.

3. POWERS AND DUTIES OF AUDITORS

Section 143 of the Act, 2013 contain a detailed list of powers of an auditor for the effective conduct of the audit. The list includes the following:

(i) right to access the books of account and vouchers at all times;

(ii) to require information or explanation from the officers of the company;

(iii) right to access the records of all subsidiaries in case of a holding company;

(iv) to make a report to the members of the company on the accounts examined by him (i.e., called the Auditor's Report); and

(v) right to attend the General Meeting.

Along with the rights, the Act has clearly laid down the duties of an auditor; which included the matters on which he has an obligation to report to the shareholders on the factual position. These pertained to the following matters:

- Loans and advances made by the company together with details like the security and safety.
- Transactions affecting the interests of the company.
- Selling of assets or securities at a price lower than the price at which they were purchased.
- Circumstances leading to the showing of loans and advances as deposits.
- Charging of personal expenses to the revenue account.
- Allotment of shares for cash and the details of such receipts.

3.1 Responsibilities of the Auditor

In addition to powers and duties, the auditor of a company also has certain responsibilities. The same are clearly indicated in the Act.

(a) Developing a familiarity with the organisation and functions of the unit to be audited.

(b) Pre-planning the audit in accordance with the scope and complexity of the areas under review.

(c) Ensuring that an assessment of risks forms the basis of all audit work planned and performed.

(d) Performing assigned tasks in an independent and self-directed fashion.
(e) Completing assigned tasks in a timely, thorough, accurate and well-documented manner.
(f) Conducting oneself in a professional manner at all times; avoiding those situations that would lead to criticism by the area being audited, or by the general public.
(g) Assuming a friendly and cooperative behavior with the audited area's staff.
(h) Acquainting oneself with the premises, responsible employees, and the location of records early in the audit.
(i) Requesting any files that may be needed.
(j) Returning all files/records to the person or area they were obtained from.
(k) Maintaining all records in the same or better condition than that in which they were found.
(l) Retaining all records on premises — never removing vital documents from the premises.
(m) Accepting responsibility and accountability for the audit work performed on assigned projects.
(n) Managing the audit in relation to time and resource budgets.
(o) Ensuring that audit findings and recommendations made during the course of the audits are promptly communicated to the management.
(p) Ensuring that all worksheets issued are properly constructed, supported, and communicated.
(q) As work papers are completed, ensuring that all objectives have been accomplished and all conclusions are properly supported.
(r) Ensuring that the audit or review is conducted with the least amount of disruption to the audited area as is possible.
(s) Finalizing the audit file (s), and ensuring that all supporting documentation is properly retained.
(t) Performing follow-up work as necessary subsequent to the audit.

A closer examination of the powers, duties and responsibilities of the auditor reveals the fact that the Companies Act has endowed the auditor with all the necessary powers and put him in a responsible and piquant position. The Act expects him to act diligently and report the 'true and fair view' on the financial position of the company. It is emphasized time and again that the duty of the auditor is not just to confine himself/herself to the task of verifying arithmetical accuracy of the accounts, but to ascertain that such accounts reflect the genuine activity of the business. As seen earlier, the Act also has provided for the resignation of the assignment with due reasons and also file a statement with the CAG. This is a big opportunity provided by the legislation to disagree and quit, when the affairs are not properly conducted. It remains to be seen in the future to what extent the auditors would be forthright in expressing themselves.

4. AUDIT REPORT AND AUDITOR'S RESPONSIBILITY

Under Section 143 (2) of the new Act, the auditor shall make a report to the members of the company on the accounts examined by him. He is under an obligation to lay his report before the company in general meeting and he shall state through the report that the accounts are prepared taking into account the accounting and auditing standards and matters which are required to be included in the audit report under the provisions of this Act. Whereupon, the auditor is also required to express his opinion as to the fact that said accounts, financial statements give a true and fair view of the state of the company's affairs as at the end of its financial year. If not, he shall 'qualify the report' with specific comments on the matters that came to his notice during the course of the audit. The beauty of the new Act is that there is a specific and detailed mention of the items on which the auditor is supposed to report. They include the following:

- That he, as an auditor, has received all the relevant books, records and other information, sufficient to express his opinion on the accounts.
- That the company has maintained proper books of account as required by law.
- That the company has made all the arrangements for visit to the branches or made necessary arrangements for the production of such records.
- That the company's balance sheet and profit and loss account are in agreement with the books of account and returns.
- That the financial statements comply with the accounting standards.
- That he has also covered all the financial transactions that may have any adverse effect on the functioning of the company.
- That the directors of the company are properly appointed.
- That the company has adequate internal financial control systems in place.

It is clear from the above that the auditor is required to bestow utmost attention in preparing his report with good faith. He is supposed to act like a **'justice', recording the facts only in the case presented before him'**. The Act is also very clear about complying with the audit standards. Further, the Central Government has the authority to prescribe standards of auditing, basing on the recommendations made by the National Financial Reporting Authority (NFRA).

As a matter of fact, the Central Government utilizing this power (under 227 (4A) of the Old Act), has specified the following matters to be included in the audit report of the auditors in respect of manufacturing and other companies (vide Notification No: GSR 909 (E), dated 07-09-1988).

This order, which was considered landmark then, has set the tone of the situation and the bounded duty of the Auditor. The said order has also recognized the diversity in the nature of operations of the companies and thus issued separate orders for each of those. Accordingly, the order made a distinction among:

(a) manufacturing, mining or processing companies;
(b) service companies;
(c) trading companies; and
(d) finance and investment companies, including the nidhis, chit funds and mutual benefit companies.

The intention of the Central Government is very clear that the Auditor of a company shall not ignore any of the crucial aspects of the operations of the company from scrutiny. A few of the significant aspects (in addition to those discussed earlier) covered in the order are as follows:

- Physical verification of fixed and current assets by the management.
- Disclosure of discrepancies during such physical verification.
- Non-maintenance or non-production of significant records.
- Details on the various types of secured, unsecured loans and the status of such securities offered as on date.
- Details of loans and advances made together with their repayment schedule, including information on the over dues, bad debts, court cases, etc.
- Information on the contracts signed by the company and how many of them are in force and consequences in case of non-performance.
- Internal Audit System.
- Measures taken for safety of the employees, PF, insurance, etc.
- Unsettled cases with tax authorities including, customs, excise, income tax, etc.
- Labour turnover and payment mechanism.
- Loss in transit of goods.

Subsequently, this order was revised in 2013 and in 2015, after the modifying Companies Act, 2013. As per the new order dated 10-04-2015, there are twelve areas of interest indentified, as against twenty in the earlier order of 1988. It is a matter of gratification that the Government of India is keen in ensuring proper and meaningful reporting by the auditors on the affairs of the companies. The failures of so many companies and the allegations pertaining to concealment of vital and essential information, leading to filing of cases against auditors of the company, go to underpin the breach of trust, which the stakeholders have placed on the auditors.

4.1 Matters to be Included in the Auditor's Report

As indicated earlier, this is the latest order issued by the Central Government after the enactment of New Companies Act, 2013. Compared to the earlier orders, this was made more brief and comprehensive. For one thing that this order provides the needed guidance to an auditor. Significant matters included in order may be noted as follows:

- Maintenance of proper records as per the legal requirements.
- Physical verification of assets of the company by the management.
- Physical verification of inventory at reasonable intervals by the management;
- Maintenance of proper records of inventory and whether any material discrepancies were noticed on physical verification and if so, whether the same have been properly dealt with in the books of account.
- Granting of any loans, secured or unsecured to companies, or others and the maintenance of proper records for the same.
- Details pertaining to overdue accounts and steps taken by the company for recovery of the principal and interest.
- Institution of adequate internal control systems commensurate with the size of the company and the nature of its business.
- Details of deposits accepted by the company and to declare whether such acceptance is in conformity with the rules and regulations of RBI. Also details regarding the orders passed by Company Law Board or National Company Law Tribunal or Reserve Bank of India or any court or any other tribunal in this regard.
- Maintenance of proper cost records as per the provisions of the Companies Act, if attracting such provisions.
- Deposits of the undisputed statutory dues including provident fund, employees' state insurance, income-tax, sales-tax, wealth tax, service tax, duty of customs, duty of excise, value added tax, cess and any other statutory dues with the appropriate authorities. Information regarding the pending cases and the purported outcome, if any.
- Transfer of the required amounts for investor education and protection fund in accordance with the relevant provisions of the Companies Act, 1956 and rules made thereunder.
- Details pertaining to the accumulated losses and their impact on the net worth of the company.
- Information on the non-payment of dues to a financial institution or bank or debenture holders; and the extent of default in terms of period and amount.
- Details regarding the guarantees given by the company to banks or financial institutions, and the terms and conditions whereof, if prejudicial to the interest of the company.

- Detailed information on the frauds, if any, noticed or detected by him or by any other agency, having financial implication to the company.

4.2 Qualifications in Auditor's Report

As per the law, the auditor is not under an obligation to give a clean chit to the company. He is free to express his opinion; not only free; but under an obligation to report any unfavourable or adverse aspect, having effect on the financial condition of the company. The notification cited supra (dated 10-04-2015) is very clear in stating that whether in the auditor's report, the answer to any of the questions referred to in paragraph 4 is unfavourable or qualified, the auditor's report shall also state the reasons for such unfavourable or qualified answer, as the case may be. Where the auditor is unable to express any opinion in answer to a particular question, his report shall indicate such fact together with the reasons why it is not possible for him to give an answer to such question.

Utilising this provision, the auditors can submit their report with certain qualifications. While the Act has incorporated this provision with good intention to help the auditors to report as genuinely as they can, this is found to be in great misuse, via the route of 'disclaimers'. The Task Force on Corporate Governance appointed by the Confederation of Indian Industry (CII) under the Chairmanship of Naresh Chandra (later came to be known as Naresh Chandra Committee) has discussed at length the issue of 'extensive disclaimers', which are being introduced time and again by firms of auditors.[7] The auditors have to discharge a significantly important responsibility concerning the accuracy of the accounts and the absence of any systemic fraud due to controls established in the listed company. It is important to provide regular audit information, thereby preventing clubbing of work towards the end of a quarter or near the end of the financial year and audit period before publishing the audited accounts; resulting in hurried and hasty clearance. The auditor has the role of watchdog and **ought not to escape liability for dereliction of duty to stakeholders by introducing qualifications into their reports.** The notes of accounts ought to facilitate the audit committee and analysts by their ease of conversion into financial terms having impact on the accounts presented.

Keeping this in view, the Naresh Chandra Committee felt that there is an urgent need to **standardize the language of disclaimers or qualifications permissible to the audit firms.** Anything beyond the scope of such permitted language should require the auditor to provide a sufficient explanation and should not create **a new escape route for avoiding responsibility for discharging the audit function.** Though criticized by some as stating that this requirement would curtail the 'freedom of expression' of the auditors in discharging their duties, the vast number of cases of fraud reported from time to time in the press are making the public to be convinced about such impositions.

It is in this context, an attempt has been made to review the audit reports of top ten companies in terms of their market capitalization for the financial year 2014-15 (Table 14.1). The following are the interesting observations that emanate from the review:

Table 14.1: List of Top 10 Companies in Terms of Their Market Capitalization

(May 2015)

S. No.	Name of the Company	Market Capitalization (Rs. in Crore)	Year of Audit Report	Auditing Firm
1.	Tata Consultancy Services Limited	5,09,837	2014-15	Deloitte Haskins & Sells (LLP)
2.	Reliance Industries Limited	2,85,052	2014-15	Chaturvedi & Shah
3.	Oil and Natural Gas Corporation Limited	2,78,995	2013-14	M/s S Bhandari & Co., M/s Varma & Varma
4.	HDFC Bank	2,58,158	2014-15	Deloitte Haskins & Sells (LLP)
5.	ITC Limited	2,57,659	2014-15	Deloitte Haskins & Sells (LLP)
6.	Coal India Limited	2,42,138	2013-14	De Chakraborty & Sen
7.	Infosys Limited	2,31,601	2014-15	B S R & Co. LLP
8.	Sun Pharma Limited	2,29,765	2013-14	Deloitte Haskins & Sells (LLP)
9.	State Bank of India	2,10,038	2014-15	S. Venkatram & Co.
10.	Hindustan Unilever Limited	1,83,101	2014-15	B S R & Co. LLP

Source: http://business.mapsof India-company/top-10-companies

(i) The audit reports of the 10 selected companies are written in a standard format; may be sticking to the auditing standard promulgated already by the ICAI, in terms of Section 143 (10) of the Act.

(ii) There is near similarity in the language used and tenor of the text in all the audit reports.

(iii) The reports are prepared in consonance with the Companies (Auditor's) Report Order, 2015 issued recently by the Government of India.

(iv) The reports of all the ten companies are straight and they are not '**qualified**'.

(v) The audit reports have been placing greater responsibility on the Management of the company, i.e., the Board of Directors. It is true that the BOD is the agency which should present a correct picture of the company. But basing solely on the information provided by them without exercising due diligence, leads to incorrect reporting. **It is also true that the auditor is not an investigating agency; yet he should have the capacity to smell the rut.**

(vi) The reports appear to be general approximations on the phenomenon and mostly '**non-committal**'. In one case (Auditor's Report of ONGC Ltd.), the language used in the report appeared to be '**evasive**', perhaps to serve as a '**Disclaimer**'. For instance, the following two statements are quoted:

(a) the company has **generally** maintained proper records showing full particulars, including quantitative details and situation of fixed assets; and

(b) the internal control procedures are **generally** adequate and commensurate with the size of the company and the nature of business with regard to purchases of inventory, fixed assets and sale of goods and services. In the very next sentence, the report states that 'during the course of our audit, we have not observed any continuing failure to correct major weaknesses in internal controls. If this had been a fact, the preceding statement could have been **absolute** and not **general.**

(vii) Among the top ten companies, five were audited by the Deloitte Haskins & Sells (LLP). There is near similarity in the wording of the reports of similar companies.

4.3 Auditing Standards

Realizing the fact that the auditor of the company is entrusted with a great responsibility of presenting the "**true and fair vice of the financial position**"; certain standards of accounting practice were set out. This responsibility at the international level was taken up by the International Federation of Accountants (IFA), being established in 1973.[8] The Federation has thus constituted the International Auditing and Assurance Standards Board (IAASB), replacing International Auditing Practices Committee (IAPC). This Board has been doing its job since then and so far issued 36 Auditing Standards to be pursued by the Member Bodies of IFA.

In the response to the call given by the IFA, the ICAI set up the Auditing and Assurance Standards Board (AASB) in September 1982. The Indian Board has so far issued auditing standards on the following matters of significance (complete list is provided in the Table 14.2).

(i) Basic Principles Governing an Audit.
(ii) Objective and scope of the audit of Financial Statements.
(iii) Quality control for audit work.
(iv) Audit Materiality.
(v) Risk Assessments and Internal control.
(vi) Auditing in a Computer Information Systems Environment
(vii) Audit Sampling.
(viii) Auditor's Report on Financial Statements.
(ix) Audit of Accounting Estimates.
(x) Representations by Managements.

Table 14.2: List of Auditing Standards issued by the AASB of India

S. No.	AAS No.	Title of the AAS
1.	1	Basic Principles Governing an Audit
2.	2	Objectives and Scope of the Audit of Financial Statements.
3.	3	Audit Documentation
4.	4	The Auditor's Responsibility to Consider Fraud and Error in an Audit of Financial Statements
5.	5	Audit Evidence
6.	6	Risk Assessments and Internal Control
7.	7	Relying Upon the work of Internal Auditor
8.	8	Audit Planning
9.	9	Using the Work of an Expert
10.	10	Using the Work of Another Auditor
11.	11	Representations by Management
12.	13	Audit Materiality
13.	14	Analytical Procedures
14.	15	Audit Sampling
15.	16	Going Concern
16.	17	Quality Control for Audit Work
17.	18	Audit of Accounting Estimates
18.	19	Subsequent Events
19.	20	Knowledge of the Business
20.	21	Consideration of Laws and Regulations in an Audit of Financial Statements
21.	22	Initial Engagements – Opening Balances
22.	23	Related Parties
23.	24	Audit Considerations Relating to Entities Using Service Organisations
24.	25	Comparatives
25.	26	Terms of Audit Engagements
26.	27	Communications of Audit Matters with those charged with Governance
27.	28	The Auditor's Report on Financial Statements
28.	29	Auditing in a Computer Information Systems Environment
29.	30	External Confirmations
30.	34	Audit Evidence – Additional Considerations for Specific Items

Source: International Centre for Information Systems and Audit, CAG of India.

The following is the procedure followed by the Board in formulating the standards:

1. The Auditing and Assurance Standards Board identifies the areas where auditing standards need to be formulated and the priority in regard to their selection.
2. In the preparation of the auditing standards, the Board is normally, assisted by study groups comprising a cross section of members of the Institute.
3. On the basis of the work of the study groups, an Exposure Draft of the proposed auditing standard is prepared by the Board and issued for comments of the members.
4. After taking into account the comments received, the draft of the proposed auditing standard is finalised by the Board and submitted to the Council of the Institute.
5. The Council considers the final draft of the proposed auditing standard and, if necessary, modifies the same in consultation with the Board. The auditing standard is then issued under the authority of the Council.

While formulating the auditing standards, the Board also takes into consideration the applicable laws, customs, usages and business environment in the country. In spite of the elaborate procedures being put in place for ensuring effective and foolproof reporting, the cases of malfeasance are continuing unabated. The Satyam crisis raised doubts about the very process of audit and the internal controls put in place. The five member disciplinary committee of the ICAI has found **prima facie** in the works of both internal and external auditors (Price Waterhouse, Kolkata & New Delhi) and found both of them guilty of professional misconduct and failure in carrying out their duties.[9] Prior to this, when the scam was being reported in the press and enquiry was ordered, the Price Waterhouse (Statutory Auditor to Satyam Computers) has issued a statement claiming that the audit of Satyam's Books of account was '**conducted in accordance with the auditing standards.** The press note issued by the Auditing Firm (Ref. ET Bureau, dt. 08-01-2009) in this regard speaks of the stand that every other audit firm involved in such fiasco might take. The note reads as follows:[10]

> "Over the last two days, there have been media reports with regard to alleged irregularities in the accounts of Satyam Computer Services. The audits were conducted by Price Waterhouse in accordance with applicable auditing standards and were supported by appropriate audit evidence," said a statement by Price Waterhouse. "Given our obligations for client confidentiality, it is not possible for us to comment upon the alleged irregularities. Price Waterhouse will fully meet its obligations to cooperate with the regulators and others".

Perhaps, it is exactly for this reason, the New Companies Act, 2013 has provided the establishment of the National Financial Reporting Authority (NFRA).

4.4 National Financial Reporting Authority

By virtue of an amendment to the Companies Act, 1956 made in 1999, Section 210a was inserted with retrospective effect from 31-10-1998 paving the way for constitution of National Advisory Committee on Accounting Standards to advise the Central Government on the formulation and laying down of accounting policies and accounting standards for adoption by companies under the new Act. The scope of this Section was widened to include both accounting and auditing standards, providing for the constitution of "National Financial Reporting authority (NFRA) under Section 132. The primary function of the NFRA is to make recommendations to the Central Government on the formulation and laying down of accounting and auditing policies and standards for adoption by companies. It is also the duty of this agency to ensure implementation of such standards for the healthy growth of the corporate sector. By virtue of the authority vested, it can also oversee the quality of service of the professions associated with ensuring compliance with such standards, and suggest measures required for improvement in quality of service. It is also within the powers of the Agency to cause investigation either *suo moto* or on a reference made to it by the Central Government, for such class of bodies corporate or persons, in such manner as may be prescribed into the matters of professional or other misconduct committed by any member or firm of chartered accountants, registered under the Chartered Accountants Act, 1949. While conducting such investigation, it will have the same powers as are vested in a civil court under the Code of Civil Procedure, 1908; which include:

- Discovery and production of books of account and other documents.
- Summoning and enforcing the attendance of persons and examining them on oath.
- Inspection of any books, registers and other documents of any person referred to above.
- Issuing commissions for examination of witnesses or documents.
- The activities of the National Financial Reporting Authority shall be audited by the Comptroller and Auditor-General of India and a report on the same is forwarded annually to the Central Government.
- It shall be the duty of the Central Government to place this report, along with the comments of the CAG of India before the Parliament for approval.

As a follow-up of this provision, the Central government issued draft rules (dt.22-10-2013) for operationalising the NFRA. This is the third set of draft rules that the Corporate Affairs Ministry has released, besides the release of draft rules for SFIO and on Acceptance of Deposits by Companies. Reacting to the draft rules, the ICAI has cautioned that giving all the powers of framing accounting standards and investigation to NFRA will lead to "**duplication of work and undermine the autonomy of the**

institute, which has been self-regulated so far". The ICAI is particularly against giving investigative power to the NFRA. Assuming the charge as the President of ICAI, in his first Press Conference, Manoj Fadnis remarked that the Centre **"should not rush"** in setting up of the NFRA and some more deliberations are required, in view of the fact that NFRA is supposed to act as a **quasi-judicial body** in overseeing the quality of the work of the auditors.[11] In this context, it remains to be seen, whether the Government would go ahead with the constitution or wait for some more time.

5. HOW TO ADDRESS THE ISSUE

In the context of growing failures of corporates, it is nothing but natural that attention is often drawn towards the obligations of persons endowed with some statutory responsibility. It might not also be the intention of the stakeholders to make the auditor responsible for every happening in the company. But an early warning in the form of an alarm is, perhaps, what is expected of him. A responsible 'vigil' over the affairs of the company is all the more important. Rubbing the shoulders with the Management is the one denounced by everyone. True that the issue is highly sensitive, responsible and the one connected with integrity of an individual. At this juncture, the following suggestions are made as a matter of addressing the issue:

1. The Central Government shall immediately finalise draft rules for operatinalising the NFRA. There is no need to be panicky in this matter. The members of the ICAI will again be the members in the NFRA also. There should not be a feeling that it is a super-body. All said and done, ICAI is only a professional body, not having any judicial powers. Above all, it acts for the benefit of members. But there are many other stakeholders interested in the affairs of a company. The NFRA will address the concerns of such persons.
2. The saying goes thus: 'self assessment is the best assessment'. In the same way 'self-regulation' can be followed by every auditor. An auditor is a better judge of the financial health of the firm, he is auditing. It is his duty to share the information with the stakeholders as and when he gets the opportunity.
3. The idea of incorporating a special provision in the Companies Act, 2013 empowering the auditor to communicate with the shareholders directly, which should be made possible by the Management. The idea is about having a separate channel of communication to two important stakeholders, viz., shareholders (being owners) and the Government (for addressing public concerns).
4. Another idea is of making Audit Reports (ARs) non-stereo type. For a variety of reasons, the ARs are being prepared with very closely/strictly guarded words/ phrases. There is a also a move to almost standardize the language to be used to ensure that there is no 'escape route' employed. But this is making ARs lack

lustre and routine commentaries. The issue needs to be discussed at length and if need be also to fall upon the international practices.

5. The auditor should keep up his independence. He should not let others point fingers towards him in reporting the issues. It is not as though that Audit Committee shall keep a watch on his relationship with the firm. After all, audit committee is not superior, either in terms of professional competence or in terms of 'fiduciary relationship'. There is nothing like 'conflict of interest' between him and the client firm.
6. In the today's circumstances corporate affairs growing complex, the auditor may also solicit the services of other experts like Advocates, Attorneys, Patetent filers, Negotiators, etc. to gain a comprehensive understanding of the issues involved. A specific provision may be made in the Companies Act requiring to permit him to have access to such specialized services and also append their reports to the Audit Report as Addendum. Instead of taking risk in making general approximation, specific observations would enhance the value of the report.
7. The New Companies Act has endowed certain powers to the Central Government in respect of:
   (i) prescribing standards of auditing;
   (ii) specifying the matters which shall be included in the audit report; and
   (iii) getting reports on the offence involving fraud.

The Comptroller and Audit General (CAG) has power to conduct test audit in case of Government companies, or Government sponsored institutions. The idea is that how about extending this power to CAG in case of non-government companies; so that public concerns can be effectively addressed.

Notes and References

1. Amrita Mitra, 'Role of the Auditors in Corporate Governance in the light of Satyam Scam', July 10 2012 (Downloadable from http://ssrn.com/adstract=2125528).
2. The Fraud Act, 2006 of UK (Downloadable from www.cps.gov.uk/legal/d_to_g/fraud_act)
3. Gaur, K.D., Commentary on the Indian Penal Code, 2nd Edition, Universal Law Publishing, New Delhi, 2013. Also available from www.lawnotes.in.
4. The Indian Contract Act, 1872 (Act No. 9 of 1872), The Law Commission of India, Report-13.
5. United States Securities and Exchange Commission, downloadable from www.sec.gov.
6. Sarbanes-Oxley Act of 2002 (www.sox-online.com).

7. Report of the CII Task Force on Corporate Governance (under the Chairmanship of Naresh Chandra), November 2009, Confederation of Indian Industry, New Delhi.
8. International Centre for Information Systems & Audit (ICISA), of the CAG of India (www.icisa.cag.gov.in).
9. E T Bureau, 09-10-2009.
10. E T Bureau, 08-01-2009.
11. The Hindu Business Line, 23-02-2015.

15
CHAPTER

Role of Securities and Exchange Board of India [SEBI]

1. INTRODUCTION

The Securities and Exchange Board of India (SEBI) is one of the prime regulating agencies in the Indian Corporate World. Prior to the establishment of this agency, stock market activity was regulated through the provisions contained in the Defence of India Rules, 1943. These rules were in force till the Government of India passed legislation in the name of Capital Issues (control) Act, 1947. The following were the objectives set for this small piece of legislations.

1. To further the growth of companies with sound capital structure.
2. To avoid undue congestion or overcrowding of public issues in a particular period.
3. To ensure that investment takes place in conformity with the objectives of Five Year Plan.
4. To ensure orderly and healthy growth of capital markets with adequate protection to investors.

In order to realize the above objectives, a machinery was created (as part of the Act) for the setting up of the office of the Controller of Capital Issues (CCI). CCI was made responsible to regulate the various issues of capital made by the companies and particularly to look into the type of the issue, size of the issue, timing and premium, etc. This arrangement continued until the passing up of the two New Acts, viz., (1) Companies Act, 1956 (Act 1 of 1956); and (2) Securities Contracts (Regulation) Act, 1956 (Act 42 of 1956). These two landmark legislations together sought to regulate the operations of the companies in India, including capital issues and trading.

After independence, the economy started making a steady progress. As a sequel of this, corporate sector has also grown and several new companies had come into existence. There was dilution of equity of multinational companies and capital issues had progressed phenomenally. With growth in the size of the capital market, there were also certain problems and malpractices associated with it. The Central Government, being the regulating agency under the above two legislations, to control and regulate the activities in the capital market, felt that it would be better to delegate some of its powers to a designated agency. Thus the Government of India set up the Securities and Exchange Board of India (SEBI) as a non-statutory body on April 12, 1988.

1.1 Objectives of SEBI

According to the preamble of the SEBI Act, the primary objective of the SEBI is to promote healthy and orderly growth of the securities market and secure investor protection. For this purpose, the SEBI monitors the activities of not only stock exchanges but also merchant bankers, etc. The objectives of SEBI are as follows:

1. to protect the interest of investors, so that there is a steady flow of savings into the capital market;
2. to regulate the securities market and ensure fair practices by the issuers of securities so that they can raise resources at minimum cost; and
3. to promote efficient services by brokers, merchant bankers and other intermediaries, so that they become competitive and professional.

1.2 Functions of SEBI

Section 11 of the SEBI Act specifies the functions as follows:

1. **Regulatory Functions**
   - (a) Regulation of stock exchange and self regulatory organizations.
   - (b) Registration and regulation of stock brokers, sub-brokers, registrars to issue, merchant bankers, underwriters, portfolio managers and such other intermediaries who are associated with securities market.
   - (c) Registration and regulation of the working of collective investment schemes including mutual funds.
   - (d) Prohibition of fraudulent and unfair trade practices relating to securities market.
   - (e) Prohibition of insider trading in securities.
   - (f) Regulating substantial acquisitions of shares and takeover of companies.

2. **Developmental Functions**
   (a) Promoting investors' education.
   (b) Training of intermediaries.
   (c) Conducting research and publishing information useful to all market participants.
   (d) Promotion of fair practices. Code of conduct for self-regulatory organizations.
   (e) Promoting self-regulatory organizations.

1.3 Powers given to SEBI

SEBI has been vested with the following powers:

1. Power to call periodical returns from recognized stock exchanges.
2. Power to call any information or explanation from recognized stock exchanges or their members.
3. Power to direct enquiries to be made in relation to affairs of stock exchanges or their members.
4. Power to grant approval to bye-laws of recognized stock exchanges.
5. Power to make or amend bye-laws of recognized stock exchanges.
6. Power to compel listing of securities by public companies.
7. Power to control and regulate stock exchanges.
8. Power to grant registration to market intermediaries.
9. Power to levy fees or other charges for carrying out the purpose of regulation.
10. Power to declare the applicability of Section 17 of the Securities Contract (Regulation) Act to any state or area and to grant licenses to dealers in securities.

2. POWERS GRANTED TO SEBI THROUGH THE SECURITIES CONTRACTS (REGULATION) ACT, 1956 (ACT 42 OF 1956)

After the setting up of the Securities and Exchange Board of India and the passing up of the specific legislation, the SEBI Act, 1992, many of the powers hitherto enjoyed by the Central Government were transferred to SEBI. The following are some such powers granted to SEBI, in the context of corporate governance.

1. Every recognized Stock Exchange shall furnish to the SEBI (earlier the Central Government) such periodical returns relating to its affairs, as may be prescribed under Section 6 (1).
2. Every recognized stock exchange and every member thereof shall maintain and preserve books of account, and other documents as decided by the Central

Government for a period of five years. Further, the Central Government may prescribe such other books of account, and other documents that may be necessary in the interest of the trade and public. These books of accounts and documents are subject to inspection any time.

3. SEBI may also take the following course of action, if it considers necessary in the interest of public.
   (a) call upon a recognized stock exchange or any member thereof to furnish in writing such information or explanation relating to the affairs of the stock exchange or of the member in relation to the stock exchange; or
   (b) appoint one or more persons to make an inquiry in the prescribed manner, in relation to the affairs of the governing body of a stock exchange or the affairs of any of the members of the stock exchange and direct the enquiry officer to submit a report of the result of such inquiry to the (SEBI) within such time as may be specified in the order. In the case of an inquiry in relation to the affairs of any of the members of a stock exchange, it may direct the governing body to make the inquiry and submit its report to the (SEBI).
4. SEBI's prior approval is necessary for any recognized stock exchange to make bye-laws for the regulation and control of contracts under section (9). Further, SEBI was also granted power to make or amend bye-laws under specific circumstances (Section-10).
5. To issue regulations pertaining to the public issue and listing of securities (Section 17A).
6. To impose penalties for non-compliance of the regulations framed by it or by the government.
7. To adjudicate on the matters of imposing penalty under section 23A to 23H and appoint any officer to be the adjudicator.
8. To recommend to grant immunity to a person, alleged to have violated any of the provisions of the SCA or gules made thereunder.
9. To make rules and regulations consistent with the provisions of SEBI Act, 1992.

3. SEBI ACT, 1992 AND THE CORPORATE GOVERNANCE

Realising the fact that there is a need to regulate the activities of the stock exchanges and ensure adequate protection to the investors, the Government of India has passed this legislation to empower the already functioning SEBI with legal powers. This was passed on 4th April, 1992 (Act 15 of 1992) to:

(i) protect the interests of investors in securities;

(ii) promote the development of securities market;

(iii) regulate the securities market and for the matters connected therewith or incidental thereto.

The significant provisions of the Act are sections 11 and 12.

1. According to Section 11(1) of the Act, it shall be the duty of the Board to protect the interests of investors in securities and to promote the development and regulation of the securities market by taking necessary measures, as it deems fit. Such measures may relate to any of the following:
   (a) regulating the business in stock exchanges and any other securities markets;
   (b) registering and regulating the working of stock brokers, sub-brokers, share transfer agents, bankers to an issue, trustees of trust deeds, registrars to an issue, merchant bankers, underwriters, portfolio managers, investment advisers and such other intermediaries who may be associated with securities markets in any manner;
   (c) registering and regulating the working of the depositories, participants, custodians of securities, foreign institutional investors, credit rating agencies and such other intermediaries as the Board may deem necessary;
   (d) registering and regulating the working of venture capital funds and collective investment schemes, including mutual funds;
   (e) promoting and regulating self-regulatory organisations;
   (f) prohibiting fraudulent and unfair trade practices relating to securities markets;
   (g) promoting investors' education and training of intermediaries of securities markets;
   (h) prohibiting insider trading in securities;
   (i) regulating substantial acquisition of shares and takeover of companies;
   (j) calling for information from, undertaking inspection, conducting inquiries and audits of the stock exchanges, mutual funds, other persons associated with the securities market, intermediaries and self-regulatory organisations in the securities market;
   (k) calling for information and records from any person including any bank or corporation constituted under any Central or State Act;
   (l) calling for information from authorities, whether in India or outside India, having functions similar to those of the Board, in the matters relating to the prevention or detection of violations in respect of securities laws;
   (m) performing such other functions under the provisions of the Securities Contracts (Regulation) Act, 1956, as may be delegated to it by the Central Government;

(n) levying fees or other charges for carrying out the purposes of this section;
(o) conducting research for the above purposes; and
(p) performing such other functions as may be prescribed.

2. Without prejudice to the provisions contained in sub-section (2), the Board may take measures to undertake inspection of any book, or register, or other document or record of any listed public company or a public company; when it comes to the notice of the Board, that the said company has been indulging in insider trading or fraudulent and unfair trade practices relating to securities market.
3. In conducting enquiry on the matters specified above, the Board shall have the same powers as are vested in a civil court under the Code of Civil Procedure, 1908 (5 of 1908), while trying a suit, in respect of the following matters, namely:
   (i) the discovery and production of books of account and other documents, at such place and such time as may be specified by the Board;
   (ii) summoning and enforcing the attendance of persons and examining them on oath;
   (iii) inspection of any books, registers and other documents of any person referred to in section 12, at any place;
   (iv) inspection of any book, or register, or other document or record of the company referred to in sub-section (2A);
   (v) issuing commissions for the examination of witnesses or documents.
4. Basing on the materiality and intensity of the findings of any enquiry, the Board may, by an order, for reasons to be recorded in writing, in the interests of investors or securities market, take any of the following measures, pending investigation or inquiry:
   (i) suspend the trading of any security in a recognised stock exchange;
   (ii) restrain persons from accessing the securities market and prohibit any person associated with securities market to buy, sell or deal in securities;
   (iii) suspend any office-bearer of any stock exchange or self-regulatory organisation from holding such position;
   (iv) impound and retain the proceeds or securities in respect of any transaction which is under investigation;
   (v) attach for a period not exceeding one month, one or more bank account or accounts of any intermediary or any person associated with the securities market with the approval of the Judicial Magistrate;
   (vi) direct any intermediary or any person associated with the securities market in any manner not to dispose of or alienate an asset forming part of any transaction which is under investigation;

(vii) The amount disgorged as per the provisions of SEBI Act, or section 12A of the Securities Contracts (Regulation) Act, 1956 or section 19 of the Depositories Act, 1996, as the case may be, shall be credited to the Investor Protection and Education Fund established by the Board. The amount may be utilized by the Board as it deems fit in accordance with the provisions of the Act.

3.1 Board to Regulate or Prohibit Issue of Prospectus, Offer Document or Advertisement Soliciting Money for Issue of Securities

The SEBI also has the duty to protect the interest of investors in relation to:

(i) the matters relating to issue of capital, transfer of securities and other matters incidental thereto; and

(ii) the manner in which such matters shall be disclosed by the companies.

In case of the above matters, if the situation warrants, SEBI can take action to:

(i) prohibit any company from issuing prospectus, any offer document, or advertisement soliciting money from the public for the issue of securities; and

(ii) specify the conditions subject to which the prospectus, such offer document or advertisement, if not prohibited, may be issued.

(2) As per the provisions of Section 21 of the Securities Contracts (Regulation) Act, 1956, the Board may specify the requirements for listing and transfer of securities and other matters incidental thereto. In exercise of the powers granted above, SEBI has issued the following regulations in the pursuance of its objective of ensuring investor protection and capital market regulation from time to time:

A. List of Regulations (As on August 15, 2015)

1. Merchant Bankers Regulations, 1992.
2. Stock-Brokers and Sub-Brokers Regulations, 1992.
3. Debenture Trustee Regulations, 1993.
4. Underwriters Regulations, 1993.
5. Registrars to an Issue and Share Transfer Agents Regulations, 1993.
6. Portfolio Managers Regulations, 1993.
7. Bankers to an Issue Regulations, 1994.
8. Custodian of Securities Regulations, 1996.
9. Mutual Funds Regulations, 1996.
10. Depositories and Participants Regulations 1996.
11. Substantial Acquisition of Shares and Takeovers Regulations, 2011.

12. Buy Back Of Securities Regulations, 1998.
13. Credit Rating Agencies Regulations, 1999.
14. Collective Investment Scheme Regulations, 1999.
15. Foreign Venture Capital Investors Regulations 2000.
16. Employees' Service Regulations, 2001.
17. Procedure for Board Meetings Regulations, 2001.
18. Issue of Sweat Equity Regulations, 2002.
19. Central Database of Market Participants Regulations, 2003.
20. Prohibition of Fraudulent and Unfair Trade Practices relating to Securities Market Regulations, 2003.
21. Ombudsman Regulations, 2003.
22. SEBI Self Regulatory Organizations Regulations, 2004.
23. SEBI Regulatory Fee on Stock Exchanges Regulations, 2006.
24. Certification of Associated Persons in the Securities Markets Regulations, 2007.
25. Issue and Listing of Debt Securities Regulations, 2008.
26. Public Offer and Listing of Securitised Debt Instruments Regulations, 2008.
27. Intermediaries Regulations, 2008.
28. Delisting of Equity Shares Regulations, 2009.
29. Investor Protection and Education Fund Regulations, 2009.
30. Issue of Capital and Disclosure Requirements Regulations, 2009.
31. KYC(Know Your Client) Registration Agency Regulations, 2011.
32. Alternative Investment Funds Regulations, 2012.
33. Stock Exchanges and Clearing Corporations Regulations, 2012.
34. Investment Advisers Regulations, 2013.
35. Issue and Listing of Non-convertible Redeemable Preference Shares Regulations, 2013.
36. Foreign Portfolio Investors Regulations, 2014.
37. Settlement of Administrative and Civil Proceedings Regulations, 2014.
38. Procedure for Search and Seizure Regulations, 2014.
39. Research Analysts Regulations, 2014.
40. Real Estate Investment Trusts Regulations, 2014.
41. Infrastructure Investment Trusts Regulations, 2014.
42. Prohibition of Insider Trading Regulations, 2015.
43. Issue and Listing of Debt Securities by Municipalities Regulations, 2015.

B. List of Guidelines (As on August 15, 2015)

1. Guidelines for Opening of Trading Terminals Abroad.
2. Delisting of Securities) Guidelines, 2003.
3. Informal Guidance) Scheme, 2003.
4. Amendment to the SEBI (Informal Guidance) Scheme, 2003.
5. Guidelines for Anti-money Laundering Measures.
6. Employee Stock Option Scheme and Employee Stock Purchase Scheme) Guidelines, 1999.
7. Disclosure and Investor Protection Guidelines, 2000.
8. Framework for recognition and supervision of stock exchanges/platforms of stock exchanges for small and medium enterprises.
9. DIP Guidelines, 2000.
10. Disclosure and Investor Protection Guidelines 2000.
11. DIP Guidelines updated up to August 20, 2009.
12. DIP Guidelines updated up to July 31, 2009.
13. DIP Guidelines updated up to July 9, 2009.
14. Aid for Legal Proceedings Guidelines, 2009.
15. DIP Guidelines updated up to April 20, 2009.
16. Employee Stock Option Scheme and Employee Stock Purchase Scheme Guidelines, 1999.
17. International Financial Services Centres Guidelines, 2015.

Further, in terms of sections 11B, 11C and 11D, SEBI has been entrusted with the following powers:

Section 11B: Power to issue directions to disgorge an amount equivalent to the wrongful gain made or loss averted by contravention of the provisions of the Act.

Section 11C: Power to investigate the transactions in securities, if believed that they are being dealt with in a manner detrimental to the investors/market. The Board has also the power to investigate any violation by any intermediary or person of the provisions of the Act.

Section 11D: Power to pass cease and desist orders to prevent persons from committing or causing violation of the provisions of the Act.

Whereas **Section 12** of the Act makes it obligatory for every stock broker, sub-broker, share transfer agent, banker to an issue, trustee of trust deed, registrar to an issue, merchant banker, underwriter, portfolio manager, investment advisor and any other intermediary associated with the securities market to register with the Board for undertaking such service. Similarly, every depository participant, custodian of securities, foreign institutional investor, credit rating agency or any other intermediary also to register with the SEBI and follow the conditions stipulated. By virtue of the amendment made to the Act in 2002, by the insertion of section (12A), no person shall directly or indirectly:

(a) use or employ, in connection with the issue, purchase or sale of any securities listed or proposed to be listed on a recognized stock exchange, any manipulative or deceptive device in contravention of the provisions of this Act or the rules or the regulations made thereunder;
(b) employ any device, scheme or artifice to defraud in connection with the dealing in securities;
(c) engage in any act, practice, course of business which operates or would operate as fraud or deceit in connection with the issue, dealing in securities which are listed or proposed to be listed on a recognised stock exchange;
(d) engage in insider trading;
(e) deal in securities while in the possession of material or non-public information; or communicate such information in a manner which is in contravention of the provisions of the Act;
(f) acquire control of any company or securities more than the percentage of equity share capital of a company whose securities are listed or proposed to be listed on a recognized stock exchange in contravention of the regulations made under this Act.

4. DISCLOSURE AND INVESTOR PROTECTION GUIDELINES, 2000

Among the various regulations and guidelines issued, the guidelines on "Disclosure and Investor Protection" stand out as a landmark contribution of the SEBI to ensure protection to the investors. Though SEBI had been working on the issue, ever since it came into being in 1988; its efforts got momentum only after it got the official status through the SEBI Act, 1992. As indicated earlier, SEBI was empowered under section 11 of the Act to issue from time to time regulations and guidelines for implementation by all the stakeholders of the securities market. In exercise of these powers, SEBI has issued these guidelines titled "SEBI (Disclosure and Investors Protection) Guidelines, 2000". These have subsequently undergone many amendments, to fall in line with the changes brought about in the relevant legislations and circulars. The website of SEBI is hosting these guidelines in their full form as updated upto July 31, 2009 only. The write up that follows in the subsequent pages is based on the material/guidelines kept in the website of SEBI.

The guidelines are a voluminous document running up to 384 pages, spread through 17 chapters and 30 schedules. Some significant areas of discussion in these guidelines include the following:

1. Eligibility Norms for companies Issuing Securities.
2. Pricing by companies Issuing Securities.
3. Promoters' contribution and Lock-in requirements.
4. Pre-Issue and Post-Issue obligations.
5. Contents of offer Document.
6. Issue of Indian Depository Receipts.
7. Green Shoe Option.
8. Guidelines on Advertisement calling for subscription.
9. Issue of convertible Debt Instruments.
10. Book Building.
11. Shelf Prospectus.
12. Preferential Issues.
13. Qualified Institutions placement.
14. OTCEI Issues.
15. Bonus Issues.

Salient aspects under each of the above heads is discussed below:

A. Eligibility Norms

In order to prevent companies not worthy enough from tapping the funds from the public, SEBI has initially, started with the specification of conditions for issue of securities. These conditions include the following:

(i) filing of offer documents with the SEBI;
(ii) application for listing of those securities on a Stock Exchange;
(iii) signing of an agreement with a depository for dematerialisation of securities;
(iv) obtaining credit rating to make a public or rights issue of convertible debt instruments;
(v) obtaining grading for the issue by an unlisted company;
(vi) not to have any outstanding warrants or financial instruments which would entitle the existing promoters or shareholders any option to receive equity shares:
(vii) converting partly paid-up shares into fully paid up shares; and
(viii) declaring the means of finance.

B. Pricing of Securities

In the earlier years, there used to be restrictions on the pricing of securities. It was related to the performance of the company. There were complaints also as to the fixation of floor price and premium. In order to overcome all this controversy, SEBI has lifted the ban on pricing of securities. Now that companies can freely price their equity shares or any other security convertible later into equity. The following are the two situations, where differential pricing is permitted:

(a) issue of securities to the applicants in the firm allotment category, provided that the price at which the security is being offered is higher than the price at which securities are offered to the public; and

(b) issue of securities to retail individual investors/shareholders, in which case the price at which the net offer is made to other categories of public is not more than 10 per cent of the price at which securities are offered to the other categories of public. Further, the issuer company can mention a price band of 20 per cent in the offer document and actual price can be determined at a later date before filing of the offer document with the ROC.

C. Promoters' Contribution and Lock-in-requirements

Realising the fact that the stake of the promoters being very low and the sale of the shares immediately after allotment, SEBI has thought it appropriate to specify the minimum requirement and lock-in-period. Accordingly, the promoters' contribution shall not be less than 20 per cent of the post-issue capital in a public issue by unlisted and listed companies. Further, the promoters shall bring in the full amount of their contribution (including premium) at least one day prior to the issue opening date. The Lock-in period for the minimum specified contribution is three years. Anything in excess of the minimum will have the lock-in period of one year.

D. Pre-Issue and Post-Issue Obligations

The following are the pre-issue obligations:

(i) The lead merchant banker shall exercise due diligence in respect of veracity and adequacy of disclosure in the offer documents;

(ii) To pay the requisite fee;

(iii) To submit the following documents:

  (a) MOU between the issuer company and the lead merchant banker.

  (b) Due diligence certificate by the lead merchant banker.

  (c) Certificates signed by the Company Secretary, Chartered Accountant in case of listed companies making further issue of capital.

  (d) An undertaking by the issuer company to the effect that all the transactions in securities by the promoters will be reported to the Stock Exchange concerned within 24 hours of the transactions.

(iv) The lead merchant banker to satisfy himself as to the underwriters ability to discharge his commitments; and

(v) The issuer company shall appoint a compliance officer who shall directly liaise with the Board with regard to compliance with various laws, rules, regulations and other directives issued by the Board and investors complaints.

The post-issue obligations of the issuer company are as follows:

(i) the lead merchant banker (LMB) shall submit the monitoring reports as per the formats specified;

(ii) the LMB shall actively associate himself with post-issue activities, viz., allotment, refund, dispatch, etc., and the LMB also take measures to redress the grievances of the investors;

(iii) the LMB shall be responsible to ensure that the basis of allotment is fair and proper and in accordance with the guidelines; and

(iv) the LMB shall ensure that the net offer to public is at least 10 per cent or 25 per cent as the case may be in terms of Rule 19(2)(b) of the SC(R) Rules, 1957.

E. Contents of Offer Document

The offer document issued by the company shall contain the following:

(a) Prospectus with all material information to enable investors to make informed decision on the investment, as of the following:

  (i) Statement of Risk Factors.

  (ii) General information about the issuer company covering address, Board of Directors, etc.

  (iii) Capital Structure.

  (iv) Objects of Offer.

  (v) Funds requirement and deployment.

  (vi) Industry and business overview and business of the issuer company.

  (vii) Business strategy.

  (viii) Purchase of Property.

  (ix) Corporate Governance.

  (x) Key Management Personnel & Employees.

  (xi) Financial Information (including group companies).

  (xii) Changes in the Accounting Policies in the last three years.

  (xiii) Outstanding litigations and material developments.

  (xiv) Information about the present offer.

(b) Abridged prospectus with all the relevant information.

(c) Letter offer containing all the disclosures as required under the offer document.
(d) Particulars of the listed companies under the same management, which made any capital issue in the last three years.

F. Issue of Indian Depository Receipts

These issues are subjected to the Companies (Issue of Indian Depository Receipts) Rules, 2004. The size of an IDR issue shall not be less than Rs. 50 crore. The issuing company shall receive minimum subscription of 90 per cent of the issued amount. If not received, the entire subscription amount shall be refunded within 60 days from the date of the closure of the issue. The prospectus issued for such purpose shall contain the required information.

G. Green Shoe Option

It means an option of allocating shares in excess of the shares included in the public issue and operating a post-listing price stabilising mechanism through a Stabilizing Agent (SA); who could be one among the merchant bankers or Book Runners. This is a facility provided to the companies for stabilizing the post-listing price of their shares. The company desirous of availing this option shall seek authorization in the general meeting for allotment of further shares to the Stabilizing Agent. The SA has several obligations to be fulfilled to ensure smooth operation of the scheme. The SA shall enter into an agreement with the promoter to borrow shares not exceeding 15 per cent of the total issue size.

H. Guidelines on Advertisement

The advertisement proposed to be issued seeking subscription to securities shall be truthful, fair and clear and shall not contain any statement, which is untrue or misleading. An advertisement shall be considered misleading, if it contains:

(a) Statements made about the performance or activities of the company in the absence of necessary explanatory or qualifying statements, which may give an exaggerated picture of the performance or activities, than what it really is.
(b) An inaccurate portrayal of past performance or its portrayal in a manner which implies that past gains or income will be repeated in the future.

Similarly, the following practices are not permitted:

(a) An advertisement shall be set forth in a clear, concise and understandable language. Extensive use of technical, legal terminology or complex language and the inclusion of excessive details which may distract the investor, shall be avoided.
(b) An issue advertisement shall not contain statements which promise or guarantee rapid increase in profits.

(c) An issue advertisement shall not contain any information that is not contained in the offer document.

(d) No models, celebrities, fictional characters, landmarks or caricatures or the likes shall be displayed on or form part of the offer documents or issue advertisements.

(e) Issue advertisements shall not appear in the form of crawlers (the advertisements which run simultaneously with the programme in a narrow strip at the bottom of the television screen) on television.

(f) No issue advertisement shall be released without giving "Risk Factors" in respect of the concerned issue.

Provided that an issue opening/closing advertisement which does not contain the highlights need not contain risk factors.

I. Issue of Convertible Debt Instruments

A company offering convertible debt instruments through an offer document, shall comply with the following provisions in addition to the relevant provisions contained in these guidelines:

(a) No company shall make a public issue or rights issue of Convertible Debt Instrument, unless credit rating is obtained from at least one credit rating agency registered with the Board and disclosed in the offer document.

(b) Where ratings are obtained from more than one credit rating agencies, all the ratings, including the unaccepted ratings, shall be disclosed in the offer document.

(c) All the credit ratings obtained during the three (3) years preceding the public or rights issue of debt (Convertible Debt Instrument) for any listed security of the issuer company shall be disclosed in the offer document.

(d) No company shall issue a prospectus or a letter of offer to the public for subscription of its debentures, unless the company has appointed one or more debenture trustees for such debentures in accordance with the provisions of the Companies Act, 1956.

(e) For the redemption of the debentures issued, the company shall create debenture redemption reserve (DRR) according to the provisions of the Companies Act, 1956.

(f) Distribution of Dividends:

   (a) In case of the companies which have defaulted in payment of interest on debentures or redemption of debentures or in creation of security as per the terms of issue of the debentures, any distribution of dividend shall require approval of the Debenture Trustees and the Lead Institution, if any.

   (b) In the case of existing companies, prior permission of the lead institution for declaring dividend exceeding 20% or as per the loan covenants is necessary, if the company does not comply with institutional condition regarding interest and debt service coverage ratio.

(c)

(i) Dividends may be distributed out of profit of particular years only after transfer of requisite amount in DRR.

(ii) If residual profits after transfer to DRR are inadequate to distribute reasonable dividends, company may distribute dividend out of general reserve.

(g) The offer document shall specifically state the assets on which security shall be created and shall also state the ranking of the charge/s. In case of second or residual charge or subordinated obligation, the offer document shall clearly state the risks associated with such subsequent charge. The relevant consent for creation of security such as *pari passu letter*, consent of the lessor of the land in case of leasehold land, etc., shall be obtained and submitted to the debenture trustee before opening of issue of debenture.

(h) The offer document shall state the security/asset cover to be maintained. The basis for computation of the security/asset cover, the valuation methods and periodicity of such valuation shall also be disclosed. The security/asset cover shall be arrived at after reduction of the liabilities having a first/prior charge, in case the debentures are secured by a second or subsequent charge.

(i) In case of conversion of instruments (PCDs/FCDs, etc.) into equity capital:

(i) In case, the convertible portion of any instrument such as PCDs, FCDs, etc., issued by a listed company, value of which exceeds Rs. 50 lakh and whose conversion price was not fixed at the time of issue, holders of such instruments shall be given a compulsory option of not converting into equity capital.

(ii) Conversion shall be done only in cases where instrument holders have sent their positive consent and not on the basis of the non-receipt of their negative reply. If issues are made with cap price with justification; it will not be necessary to give option to the instrument holder for converting the instruments into equity capital within the cap price.

(iii) Where an option is to be given to such instrument holders and if any instrument holder does not exercise the option to convert the debentures into equity at a price determined in the general meeting of the shareholders, the company shall redeem that part of debenture at a price which shall not be less than its face value.

(iv) The provision of sub-clause (iii) above, shall not apply if such redemption is to be made in accordance with the terms of the issue originally stated.

J. Book Building

An issuer company proposing to issue capital through book building process shall comply with the following:

In an issue of securities to the public through a prospectus, the option for 75% book building shall be available to the issuer company subject to the following:

(i) The option of book-building shall be available to all body corporates which are otherwise eligible to make an issue of capital to the public.

(ii) The book-building facility shall be available as an alternative to the extent of the percentage of the issue which can be reserved for firm allotment and the issuer company shall have an option of either reserving the securities for firm allotment or issuing the securities through book building process.

(iii) The issue of securities through book-building process shall be separately identified/indicated as 'placement portion category', in the prospectus.

(iv) The securities available to the public shall be separately identified as 'net offer to the public', and the requirement of minimum 25% of the securities to be offered to the public shall also be applicable.

(v) In case the book-building option is availed of, underwriting shall be made mandatory to the extent of the net offer to the public.

(vi) The draft prospectus containing all the information except the information regarding the price at which the securities are offered shall be filed with the Board.

(vii) One of the lead merchant bankers to the issue shall be nominated by the issuer company as a Book Runner and his name shall be mentioned in the prospectus.

(viii) The copy of the draft prospectus filed with the Board may be circulated by the Book Runner to the institutional buyers who are eligible for firm allotment and to the intermediaries eligible to act as underwriters inviting offers for subscribing to the securities. The draft prospectus to be circulated shall indicate the price band within which the securities are being offered for subscription.

(ix) The Book Runner on receipt of the offers shall maintain a record of the names and number of securities ordered and the price at which the institutional buyer or underwriter is willing to subscribe to securities under the placement portion.

(x) The underwriter(s) shall maintain a record of the orders received by him for subscribing to the issue out of the placement portion.

(xi) The underwriter(s) shall aggregate the offers so received and intimate to the Book Runner the aggregate amount of the orders received by him. The same will also apply to the institutional investors.

(xii) The Book Runner and the issuer company shall determine the price at which the securities shall be offered to the public.

(xiii) The issue price for the placement portion and offer to the public shall be the same.

(xiv) The underwriter shall enter into an underwriting agreement with the issuer indicating the number of securities as well as the price at which the underwriter shall subscribe to the securities.

(xv) The prospectus shall be filed with the Registrar of Company by the company after the issue price is decided.

(xvi) The issuer company shall maintain separate accounts for placement portion and public subscription.

(xvii) Book Runner shall collect from the institutional buyers and the underwriters the application forms along with the application moneys to the extent of the securities proposed to be allotted to them/subscribed by them.

(xviii) It is to be ensured that the securities allotted under placement portion and public portion are *pari passu* in all respects.

(xix) All moneys are required to be paid in respect of their underwriting commitment by the eleventh day of the closure of the issue. If done, such shares become eligible for listing.

(xx) The bidding terminals shall contain online graphical display of demand and bid prices updated at periodic intervals, not exceeding 30 minutes. Allotment of securities under the public category shall be eligible to be listed.

(xxi) In case of under-subscription in the net offer to the public, preference shall be given to the individual investors. In case of under subscription in the placement portion, spillover shall be permitted from the net offer to the public to the placement portion.

(xxii) The issuer company may pay interest on the application moneys till the date of allotment or the deemed date of allotment subject to the condition provided that payment of interest is uniformly given to all the applicants.

(xxiii) The Book Runner and other intermediaries associated with the book building process shall maintain records of the book building process. The Board shall have the right to inspect such records.

(xxiv) In case of allotment of shares, the following procedure needs to be adopted:

(i) In case an issuer company makes an issue of 100% of the net offer to public through 100% book building process:

(a) not less than (35%) of the net offer to the public shall be available for allocation to retail individual investors;

(b) not less than (15%) of the net offer to the public shall be available for allocation to non-institutional investors, i.e., investors other than retail individual investors and Qualified Institutional Buyers;

(c) not more than 50% of the net offer to the public shall be available for allocation to Qualified Institutional Buyers.

(ii) In case an issuer company makes an issue of 75% of the net offer to public through book building process and 25% at the price determined through book building:

(a) in the book built portion, not less than 25% of the net offer to the public, shall be available for allocation to non-Qualified Institutional Buyers and not more than 50% of the net offer to the public shall be available for allocation to Qualified Institutional Buyers; and

(b) the balance 25% of the net offer to the public, offered at a price determined through book building, shall be available only to retail individual investors who have either not participated or have not received any allocation, in the book built portion.

K. Shelf Prospectus

This is applicable to the securities issued by public sector banks, scheduled commercial banks and public financial institutions. As per section 31 of the Companies Act, 2013:

1. Any class or classes of companies, as the Securities and Exchange Board may provide through regulations in this behalf, may file a shelf prospectus with the Registrar at the stage of the first offer of securities. Such prospectus shall indicate a period not exceeding one year as the period of validity of such prospectus from the date of opening of the first offer of securities. In respect of a second or subsequent offer of such securities issued during the period of validity of that prospectus, no further prospectus is required.
2. A company filing the shelf prospectus shall be required to file an information memorandum containing all material facts relating to new charges created, changes in the financial position of the company as have occurred between the first offer of securities or the previous offer of securities and the succeeding offer of securities and such other changes as may be prescribed, with the Registrar within the prescribed time. Where a company has received applications for the allotment of securities along with advance payments of subscription before the making of any such change, the company shall intimate the changes to such applicants. In case the applicants express a desire to withdraw their application, the company or other person shall refund all the monies received as subscription within fifteen days thereof.
3. Where an information memorandum is filed, every time an offer of securities is made such memorandum together with the shelf prospectus shall be deemed to be a prospectus.

4. Where a public sector bank, scheduled commercial bank or public financial institution proposing to issue a shelf prospectus, shall file a draft shelf prospectus with the Board.
5. Where a draft shelf prospectus is filed with the Board, the relevant Guidelines on issue of shares shall apply as if it were a draft prospectus filed under relevant clause.
6. The shelf prospectus shall also disclose the aggregate amount proposed to be raised through all the stages of offers of securities made under the shelf prospectus.
7. The observation letter issued by the Board shall be valid for a period of 365 days from the date of issuance.
8. The institution, intending to file the shelf prospectus shall file the same, after incorporating the updations in terms of information memorandum in respect of the second or any subsequent offer of securities with the Board. The shelf prospectus as updated shall be uploaded on the website of SEBI and on the website of the lead manager. The institution is required to open the particular stage of offer of securities after filing the information memorandum/shelf prospectus as updated with the Registrar of Companies and with the Board.

L. Preferential Issues

The preferential issue of equity shares or any other security by a listed company is governed by the following norms:

- The issue shall be made at a price not less than higher of the following:
  - (i) the average of the weekly high and low of the closing prices of the related shares quoted on the Stock Exchange during the six months preceding the relevant date; or
  - (ii) the average of the weekly high and low of the closing prices of the related shares quoted on a stock exchange during the two weeks preceding the relevant date.
- Where the equity shares of a company have been listed on a Stock Exchange for a period of less than six months as on the relevant date, the issue of shares on preferential basis (other than an issue of shares on preferential basis to Qualified Institutional Buyers not exceeding five in number), can be made at a price not less than the higher of the following:
  - (a) the price at which shares were issued by the company in its IPO or the value per share arrived at in a scheme of arrangement under sections 391 to 394 of the Companies Act, 1956, pursuant to which the shares of the company were listed, as the case may be;

    or

(i) the average of the weekly high and low of the closing prices of the related shares quoted on the stock exchange during the period shares have been listed preceding the relevant date;

or

(ii) the average of the weekly high and low of the closing prices of the related shares quoted on a stock exchange during the two weeks preceding the relevant date.

- An issue of shares on preferential basis to Qualified Institutional Buyers not exceeding five in numbers all be made at a price not less than the average of the weekly high and low of the closing prices of the related shares quoted on a stock exchange during the two weeks preceding the relevant date.

M. Placement of Qualified Institutional Buyers (QIBs)

These guidelines are applicable to all kinds of equity and debentures. Those companies/ issuers that intend to make these issues are required to fulfill the following conditions:

- its equity shares of the same class were listed on a stock exchange having nationwide trading terminals for a period of at least one year as on the date of issuance of notice to its shareholders;
- in case the listed company is a transferee company due to merger or amalgamations the period for which the equity shares of the same class of the transferor company were listed on a stock exchange having nationwide trading terminals shall also be considered for the purpose of computation of the period of one year; and
- it is in compliance with the prescribed minimum public shareholding requirements of the listing agreement.

1. **Investors:** In this category, only QIBs shall be eligible for allotment of specified securities. Further, a minimum of 10 per cent of specified securities shall be allotted to mutual funds. If no mutual fund is agreeable to take up the minimum portion as mentioned above, such minimum portion or part thereof may be allotted to other QIBs. Further, no allotment shall be made either directly or indirectly, to any QIB being a promoter or any person related to promoter/s. In the following cases, a person is deemed to be related to the QIB.

   (i) a person who enters into an agreement with promoters or persons related to the promoters;

   (ii) persons having veto rights; or

   (iii) persons with right to appoint any nominee director on the board of the issuer;

   In no case the investors will be allowed to withdraw their bids after the closure of issue.

2. **Pricing:** An issue of specified securities shall be made at a price not less than the average of the weekly high and low of the closing prices of the related shares quoted on the stock exchange during the two weeks preceding the relevant date.

3. **Pricing of Shares on Conversion**
   (a) Where securities which are convertible into or exchangeable with equity shares at a later date are issued pursuant to the guidelines and the issuer shall determine the price of the resultant shares in terms of such guidelines.
   (b) The relevant date for the above purpose may, at the option of the issuer or the date on which the holder of the securities which are convertible into or exchangeable with equity shares at a later date becomes entitled to apply for the said shares.
   (c) The specified securities allotted shall be made fully paid up at the time of their allotment.

4. **Adjustments in Price**
   (a) The prices considered for determination of issue price of specified securities shall be subject to appropriate adjustments; if the issuer company:
      (i) makes an issue of shares by way of capitalization of profits or reserves (other than by way of a dividend on shares);
      (ii) makes an issue of shares on rights basis
      (iii) consolidates its outstanding shares into a smaller number of shares;
      (iv) divides its outstanding shares (including by way of stock split);
      (v) re-classifies any of its shares into other securities of the company;
      (vi) is involved in such other similar events or circumstances, which in the opinion of the concerned Stock Exchange, requires adjustments.

5. **Currency of the Security:** In case of a security which is convertible into or exchangeable with equity shares at a later date, the same may be converted/ exchanged into equity shares at any time after the date of allotment of the security, no later than sixty months from the date of allotment.

6. **Shareholders' Resolution**
   (a) Allotment of specified securities issued shall be completed within twelve months from the date of passing of the resolution by the company in terms of sub-section (1A) of Section 81 of the Companies Act, 1956 or any other applicable provision.
   (b) The resolution passed at the meeting of shareholders shall also specify that the allotment is proposed to be made to QIBs pursuant to the existing guidelines and shall also specify the relevant date on the basis of which price of the resultant shares shall be determined.

(c) The placements made pursuant to authority of the same shareholders' resolution shall be separated by at least six months between each placement.

7. **Placement Document**

(a) Specified securities shall be issued on the basis of a placement document.

(b) The placement document shall contain all material information, including the information specified in the Schedule.

(c) The placement document shall be a private document provided to select investors, through serially numbered copies.

(d) The placement document shall also be placed on the website of the concerned stock exchange and of the issuer with a disclaimer to the effect that it is in connection with an issue to QIBs and that no offer is being made to the public or to any other category of investors.

(e) A copy of the placement document shall be filed with the Board for record purpose within 30 days of the allotment of specified securities.

8. **Number of Allottees:** The minimum number of allottees for each placement of specified securities shall not be less than two, where the issue size is less than or equal to Rs. 250 crore; or five, where the issue size is greater than Rs. 250 crore.

N. OTCEI Issue

The following guidelines are required to be followed in case of the issues proposed to be listed on the Over the Counter Exchange of India (OTCEI).

1. Any company making security convertible at a later date into equity shares and proposing to list them on the OTCEI, is exempted from the eligibility norms on the following two conditions:

   (a) it is sponsored by a member of the OTCEI; and

   (b) has appointed at least two market makers (one compulsory and one additional market maker).

2. Any offer for sale of equity share or any other security convertible at a later date into equity shares resulting out of a Bought out Deal (BOD) registered with the OTCEI is exempted from the eligibility norms; provided that the issuer company which has made issue of capital as above, shall not delist its securities from OTCEI for a minimum period of three years from the date of admission to dealing of such securities on OTCEI..

3. *Pricing Norms*: Similarly, those issues proposed to be listed on the OTCEI are also exempted from the pricing norms subject to the following conditions:

   (i) The promoters after such issue shall retain at least 20% of the total issued capital with the lock-in of three years from the date of the allotment of securities in the proposed issue; and

(ii) At least two market makers (one Compulsory and one additional market maker) are appointed in accordance with the Market Making guidelines stipulated by the OTCEI.

4. *Projections*: In case of securities proposed to be listed on OTCEI, projections based on the appraisal done by the sponsor who undertakes to do market making activity in the securities offered in the proposed issue, can be included in the offer document subject to compliance with other conditions contained in the said clause.

O. Bonus Issues

A listed company proposing to issue bonus shares shall comply with the following:

1. No company can issue any shares by way of bonus unless similar benefit is extended to the holders of such FCDs/PCDs.
2. The bonus issue shall be made out of free reserves built out of the genuine profits or share premium collected in cash only.
3. Reserves created by revaluation of fixed assets are not capitalised.
4. The declaration of bonus issue, in lieu of dividend, is not made.
5. The bonus issue is not made unless the partly-paid shares are made fully paid-up.
6. That the company making bonus issue has not defaulted in payment of interest or principal in respect of fixed deposits and interest on existing debentures. Similarly, it is also to ensure that the said company has no statutory dues of the employees such as contribution to provident fund, gratuity, bonus, etc.
7. The company proposing to announce bonus issue does not require shareholders' approval for capitalisation of profits or reserves for making bonus issue. It shall implement bonus issue within fifteen days from the date of approval of the issue by the board of directors of the company and shall not have the option of changing the decision. In case, the company is required to seek shareholders' approval for capitalisation of profits or reserves for making bonus issue as per the Articles of Association, the bonus issue shall be implemented within two months from the date of the meeting of the board of directors.
8. Further, the Articles of Association of the company shall contain a provision for capitalisation of reserves, etc. If there is no such provision in the Articles, the company shall pass a Resolution at its general body meeting making provisions in the Articles of Associations for capitalisation.
9. In case, the subscribed and paid-up capital exceeds the authorised share capital, a resolution shall be passed by the company at its general body meeting for increasing the authorised capital.
10. A certificate duly signed by the issuer company and counter signed by statutory auditor or by Company Secretary in practice to the effect that the above stipulations.

4.1 Issue of Capital and Disclosure Requirements Regulations, 2009

As a matter of continuation and improvement to the existing 'Disclosure and Investor Protection Guidelines, 2000', SEBI has issued new regulations under the title "SEBI (Issue of Capital and Disclosure Requirements) Regulations, 2009 on 26th August 2009. These guidelines, like the earlier one, are voluminous spanning to 240 pages with 11 chapters and 21 schedules. These regulations are made applicable to all kinds of public issues; including rights, preferential, bonus and depository receipts issues. These regulations make the following obligatory on the part of an issuing company.

(i) Appointment of merchant banker and other intermediaries.
(ii) Filing of offer document.
(iii) Approval from recognized Stock Exchange.
(iv) Underwriting Agreement.
(v) Manner of calls.
(vi) Price fixation and price stabilization through green shoe option.
(vii) Details regarding promoters' contribution.
(viii) Allotment procedure and basis of allotment.
(ix) Details of conversion of debentures into equity shares.

5. OTHER MATTERS OF IMPORTANCE

SEBI wields tremendous influence in terms of ensuring protection of the investors. The disclosure requirements are so vast that everything that is conceivable is included. In addition, the following regulations of the SEBI are also significant to exact compliance and thus improve upon the governance practices.

1. Ombudsman Regulations, 2003.
2. Prohibition of Fraudulent and Unfair Trade Practices relating to Securities Market Regulations, 2003.
3. Prohibition of Insider Trading Regulations, 2015.

5.1 Establishment of the Office of Ombudsman

Proper redressal mechanism is an essential requirement for ensuring good Corporate Governance. Perhaps, it is with this intention, the SEBI has issued specific regulations providing for the establishment of the office of Ombudsman to redress the grievances of the investors dealing in securities. Under these regulations, a person may lodge a complaint on any one or more of the following grounds either to the Board or to the Ombudsman concerned:

(i) non-receipt of refund orders, allotment letters in respect of a public issue of securities of companies or units of mutual funds or collective investments schemes;
(ii) non-receipt of share certificates, unit certificates, debenture certificates, bonus shares;
(iii) non-receipt of dividend by shareholders or unit-holders;
(iv) non-receipt of interest on debentures, redemption amount of debentures or interest on delayed payment of interest on debentures;
(v) non-receipt of interest on delayed refund of application monies;
(vi) non-receipt of annual reports or statements pertaining to the portfolios;
(vii) non-receipt of redemption amount from a mutual fund or returns from collective investment scheme;
(viii) non-transfer of securities by an issuer company, mutual fund, Collective Investment Management Company or depository within the stipulated time;
(ix) non-receipt of letter of offer or consideration in takeover or buy-back offer or delisting;
(x) non-receipt of statement of holding corporate benefits or any grievances in respect of corporate benefits, etc;
(xi) any grievance in respect of public, rights or bonus issue of a listed company;
(xii) any of the matters covered under section 55A of the Companies Act, 1956 (now section 24 of the Act, 2013); and
(xiii) any grievance in respect of issue or dealing in securities against an intermediary or a listed company.

5.1.1 Settlement by Mutual Agreement

As soon as the ombudsman receives a complaint, he shall send a notice to the registered or corporate office of the listed company or office of the intermediary named in the complaint. Thereupon, the ombudsmen shall endeavour to promote a settlement of the complaint by agreement or mediation between the complainant and the listed company or intermediary named in the complaint. If any amicable settlement or friendly agreement is arrived at between the parties, the Ombudsman shall pass an award in terms of such settlement or agreement within one month from the date thereof. Also direct the parties to perform their obligations in accordance with the terms recorded in the award. For the purpose of promoting a settlement of the complaint, the Ombudsman may follow such procedure and take such actions as he may consider appropriate.

5.1.2 Award on Adjudication

In the event the matter is not resolved by mutually acceptable agreement within a period of one month of the receipt of the complaint he shall give his award in writing or pass any other directions or orders as he may consider appropriate. The award on adjudication shall be made by Ombudsman within a period of three months from the date of the filing of the complaint. However, no award shall be invalidated by reason alone of the fact that the award was made beyond the said period of three months. The Ombudsman shall send his award to the parties to the adjudication to perform their obligations under the award.

5.1.3 Cost and Interest

The Ombudsman or the Board, as the case may be, shall be entitled to award reasonable compensation along with interest including future interest till date of satisfaction of the award at a rate which may not exceed one percent per mensem. The Ombudsman in the case of an award, or the Board in the case of order passed in petition for review of the award, as the case may be, may determine the cost of the proceedings in the award and include the same in the award or as the case may be, in the order. The Ombudsman also has the power to impose cost on the complainant for filing a wrong complaint; or frivolous complaint.

5.1.4 Consequences of Non-Implementation of the Award

The nature of the award of the ombudsmen is such that it shall be implemented by the party so directed within one month of receipt of the award or within such time as decided by the SEBI. A person, who does not comply with the award, shall be liable to a penalty under section 15C of the SEBI Act. In addition, he will also be liable for one or more of the following:

(i) an action under Section 11(4) of the SEBI Act; or
(ii) suspension or delisting of securities; or
(iii) being debarred from accessing the securities market; or
(iv) being debarred from dealing in securities; or
(v) an action for suspension or cancellation of certificate of registration; or
(vi) such other action permissible which may be deemed appropriate in the facts and circumstances of the case.

5.2 Prohibition of Fraudulent and Unfair Trade Practices

Ever since the operations in the Stock Exchanges have started, there appeared many cases of fraud and unfair trade practices. The scams that occurred periodically in the Stock Market such as the Harshad Mehta. Ketan Parekh go to testify the dubious means prevalent in the Exchanges. It is no exaggeration to remark that the scams hatched by the sinsters frightened small investors and thus distanced them from the stock market.

And those still interested in equities are choosing the other routes like mutual funds. Therefore it is high time that, the regulators take appropriate measures to promote congenial and fair atmosphere in the markets. The regulations issued by SEBI on 17th July 2003 in this regard can be regarded a step in the right direction. As per the regulations no person shall directly or indirectly:

(a) buy, sell or otherwise deal in securities in a fraudulent manner;
(b) use or employ any manipulative or deceptive device or contrivance in contravention of the provisions of the Act or the rules or the regulations made thereunder;
(c) employ any device, scheme or artifice to defraud in connection with dealing in or issue of securities which are listed or proposed to be listed on a recognized stock exchange;
(d) engage in any act, practice, course of business which operates or would operate as fraud or deceit upon any person in connection with any dealing in or issue of securities which are listed or proposed to be listed on a recognized Stock Exchange in contravention of the provisions of the Act or the rules and the regulations made thereunder.

5.2.1 Practices Deemed Fraudulent

As per the said guidelines, the following dealings/practices are deemed to be fraudulent or unfair:

(a) indulging in an act which creates false or misleading appearance of trading in the securities market;
(b) dealing in a security not intended to effect transfer of beneficial ownership but intended to operate only as a device to inflate, depress or cause fluctuations in the price of such security for wrongful gain or avoidance of loss;
(c) advancing or agreeing to advance any money to any person thereby inducing any other person to offer to buy any security in any issue only with the intention of securing the minimum subscription to such issue;
(d) paying, offering or agreeing to pay or offer, directly or indirectly, to any person any money or money's worth for inducing such person for dealing in any security with the object of inflating, depressing, maintaining or causing fluctuation in the price of such security;
(e) any act or omission amounting to manipulation of the price of a security;
(f) publishing or causing to publish or reporting or causing to report by a person dealing in securities any information which is not true or which he does not believe to be true;
(g) entering into a transaction in securities without intention of performing it or without intention of change of ownership of such security;

(h) selling, dealing or pledging of stolen or counterfeit security whether in physical or dematerialized form;

(i) an intermediary promising a certain price in respect of buying or selling of a security to a client and waiting till a discrepancy arises in the price of such security and retaining the difference in prices as profit for himself;

(j) an intermediary providing his clients with such information relating to a security as cannot be verified by the clients before their dealing in such security;

(k) an advertisement that is misleading or that contains information in a distorted manner and which may influence the decision of the investors;

(l) an intermediary reporting trading transactions to his clients entered into on their behalf in an inflated manner in order to increase his commission and brokerage;

(m) an intermediary not disclosing to his client transactions entered into on his behalf including taking an option position;

(n) circular transactions in respect of a security entered into between intermediaries in order to increase commission;

(o) encouraging the clients by an intermediary to deal in securities solely with the object of enhancing his brokerage or commission;

(p) an intermediary predating or otherwise falsifying records such as contract notes.

(q) an intermediary buying or selling securities in advance of a substantial client order or whereby a futures or option position is taken about an impending transaction in the same or related futures or options contract.

(r) planting false or misleading news which may induce sale or purchase of securities.

(s) mis-selling of units of a mutual fund scheme involving the Fund Manager;

   (i) making a false or misleading statement, or

   (ii) concealing or omitting material facts of the scheme, or

   (iii) concealing the associated risk factors of the scheme, or

   (iv) not taking reasonable care to ensure suitability of the scheme to the buyer; and

(t) illegal mobilization of funds by sponsoring or carrying on or causing to be carried on any collective investment scheme by any person.

5.2.2 Action on the Fraudulent Transactions

The SEBI if it finds that there is truth in the allegation that one or more of the intermediaries are involved in the fraudulent transactions can take the following action:

(a) suspend trading of the security found to be or *prima facie* found to be involved in fraudulent and unfair trade practice in a recognized stock exchange;

(b) restrain persons from accessing the securities market and prohibit any person associated with securities market to buy, sell or deal in securities;

(c) suspend any office-bearer of any stock exchange or self-regulatory organization from holding such position;

(d) impound and retain the proceeds or securities in respect of any transaction which is in violation or *prima facie* in violation of these regulations;

(e) direct the one associated with the securities market in any manner not to dispose of or alienate an asset forming part of a fraudulent and unfair transaction;

(f) require the person concerned to call upon any of its officers, other employees or representatives to refrain from dealing in securities in any particular manner;

(g) prohibit the person concerned from disposing of any of the securities acquired in contravention of these regulations;

(h) direct the person concerned to dispose of any such securities acquired in contravention of these regulations, in such manner it may deem fit.

5.3 Insider Trading

One of the serious maladies affecting the healthy growth of stock markets throughout the world is the trading carried out by the insiders. An sider may be anyone connected with the operations of the company and having access to unpublished price sensitive information. Utilizing this advantage, he may buy or sell the securities to take advantage of the variations in the stock prices. Investors hope that the regulator deal with such elements firmly to ensure fair play and fair treatment equal to al the investors. Though there had been many incidents of insider trading in the Indian Stock Exchanges, it is only on 15th January, 2015, SEBI could issue these regulations, though much belated.

The objective of these regulations is to prevent or restrict insiders to take advantage of their privileged position to their advantage of marketing money. As per the regulations, the following are prohibited:

1. No insider shall communicate, provide, or allow access to any unpublished price sensitive information, relating to a company or securities listed or proposed to be listed, to any person including other insiders except where such communication is in furtherance of legitimate purposes, performance of duties or discharge of legal obligations. This provision is intended to cast an obligation on all insiders who are essentially persons in possession of unpublished price sensitive information. They are supposed to handle such information with care and to deal with the information with them when transacting their business strictly on a need-to-know basis. It is also desired that the organizations develop practices based on need-to-know principles for treatment of information in their possession.
2. No person shall procure from insider of unpublished price sensitive information, relating to a company or securities listed or proposed to be listed, except in furtherance of legitimate purposes. This provision is intended to impose a

prohibition on unlawfully procuring possession of unpublished price sensitive information. Inducement and procurement of unpublished price sensitive information not in furtherance of one's legitimate duties and discharge of obligations would be illegal under this provision.

3. No insider shall trade in securities that are listed or proposed to be listed on a stock exchange. When a person who has traded in securities has been in possession of unpublished price sensitive information, his trades would be presumed to have been motivated by the knowledge and awareness of such information in his possession. The reasons or purposes for which he trades are not relevant in determining whether a person has violated the regulation. It would be open to the insider to prove his innocence by demonstrating the circumstances mentioned in the provisions. Failing which it is presumed that he has violated the rules. The Regulations also provide for disclosures to be made by insiders dealing in securities. These disclosures consist of:

A. *Initial Disclosures*

(i) Every promoter, key managerial personnel and director of every company whose securities are listed on any recognised stock exchange shall disclose his holding of securities of the company as on the date of these regulations taking effect, to the company within thirty days of these regulations taking effect.

(ii) Every person on appointment as a key managerial personnel or a director of the company or upon becoming a promoter shall disclose his holding of securities of the company as on the date of appointment or becoming a promoter, to the company within seven days of such appointment or becoming a promoter.

B. *Continual Disclosures*

(i) Every promoter, employee and director of every company shall disclose to the company, the number of such securities acquired or disposed of within two trading days of such transaction. If the value of the securities traded aggregates to a traded value in excess of ten lakh rupees or such other value as may be specified.

(ii) Every company shall notify the particulars of such trading to the stock exchange on which the securities are listed within two trading days of receipt of the disclosure or from becoming aware of such information.

C. *Disclosures by other Connected Persons*

Any company whose securities are listed on a stock exchange may, at its discretion, require any other connected person or class of connected persons to make disclosures of holdings and trading in securities of the company. This condition is stipulated to monitor compliance with these regulations. This is an enabling provision for listed companies to seek information from those who are in possession of unpublished price sensitive information. This provision confers discretion on any company to seek such information. For example, a listed company may ask that a management consultant who would advise it on corporate strategy and would need to review unpublished price sensitive information and should make disclosures of his trades to the company.

D. Code of Fair Disclosure

The board of directors of every company, whose securities are listed on a stock exchange, shall formulate and publish on its official website, "a code of practices and procedures for fair disclosure" of unpublished price sensitive information. The company has to state that it is adhering to all the principles set out in these regulations, without diluting them in any manner.

16

CHAPTER

Corporate Governance Rating Methodologies

1. INTRODUCTION: NEED FOR RATING

We have noted in the earlier discussion that Corporate Governance is about commitment to values and well-being of the people in the society. Good Corporate Governance is reflected in its conduct and fair treatment of various groups having stake in the operations of the company. Though there are many models to evaluate and predict the business performance in terms of quantitative information generated through various ways, there is not much success in formulating a model that can judge the quality of parameters; particularly relating to the aspects such as behaviour, integrity, commitment, etc. Perhaps, it is somewhat easy to assess to what extent a company is transparent in its actions; but it is difficult to judge the level of commitment towards stakeholders. As a matter of fact, Corporate Governance is defined as a 'set of relationships between a company's management, its board, its shareholders and other stakeholders.[1] It is dubbed as the 'structure' through which the objectives of the company are met. Thus, Corporate Governance matters both at the company level and at the society level. As a structure, it is essential that the businesses are encouraged to make efficient allocation of scare resources. It is not as though governance is essential to ensure a favourable climate to raise resources in the market; it is equally important to become an integral part of the societal system.

2. RATING PROCESS

Every rating agency follows a specified procedure for rating the institution or financial instruments. As is evident, rating has, initially, started with the rating of 'financial instruments'. Keeping in view the contemporary developments, and the expectations of the diverse stakeholders, the necessity for rating has got extended to many other areas including the issues of 'governance'. Basing on the focus of the issue, parameters will be identified and weightages are determined. Whatever be the issue under consideration, the following procedure is generally adopted by the rating agencies.

Step-1 : Identification of Key Indicators

Step-2 : Decomposition of Key Indicators into specific components

Step-3 : Assigning weightages to the Key Indicators and Specific Components

Step-4 : Compilation of the relevant information through various reports and documents

Step-5 : Developing score card, based on the values assigned to the indicators

Step-6 : Fixing rating symbols in the form of alphabets or numerals or both to signify the rank assigned

Step-7 : Validation and publication of ratings

It is indisputable that the quality of the ratings depends on the adoption of a foolproof procedure with due diligence. Identification of key indicators and assignment of weights, in fact, decide the strength of the rating process and thus the efficiency of the rating agency. If the methodology adopted is not proper and systematic, results tend to be unrealistic and meaningless. The ingenuity of the rating agency is reflected in the very process it chooses to adopt for rating.

As a case study, the rating methodology adopted by M/s Solaron, India is detailed below:[2] The methodology adopted by the agency begins with the development of industry specific key performance indicators (known as KPIs) and sub-metrics for each industry specific KPIs. The flow diagram can be seen below:

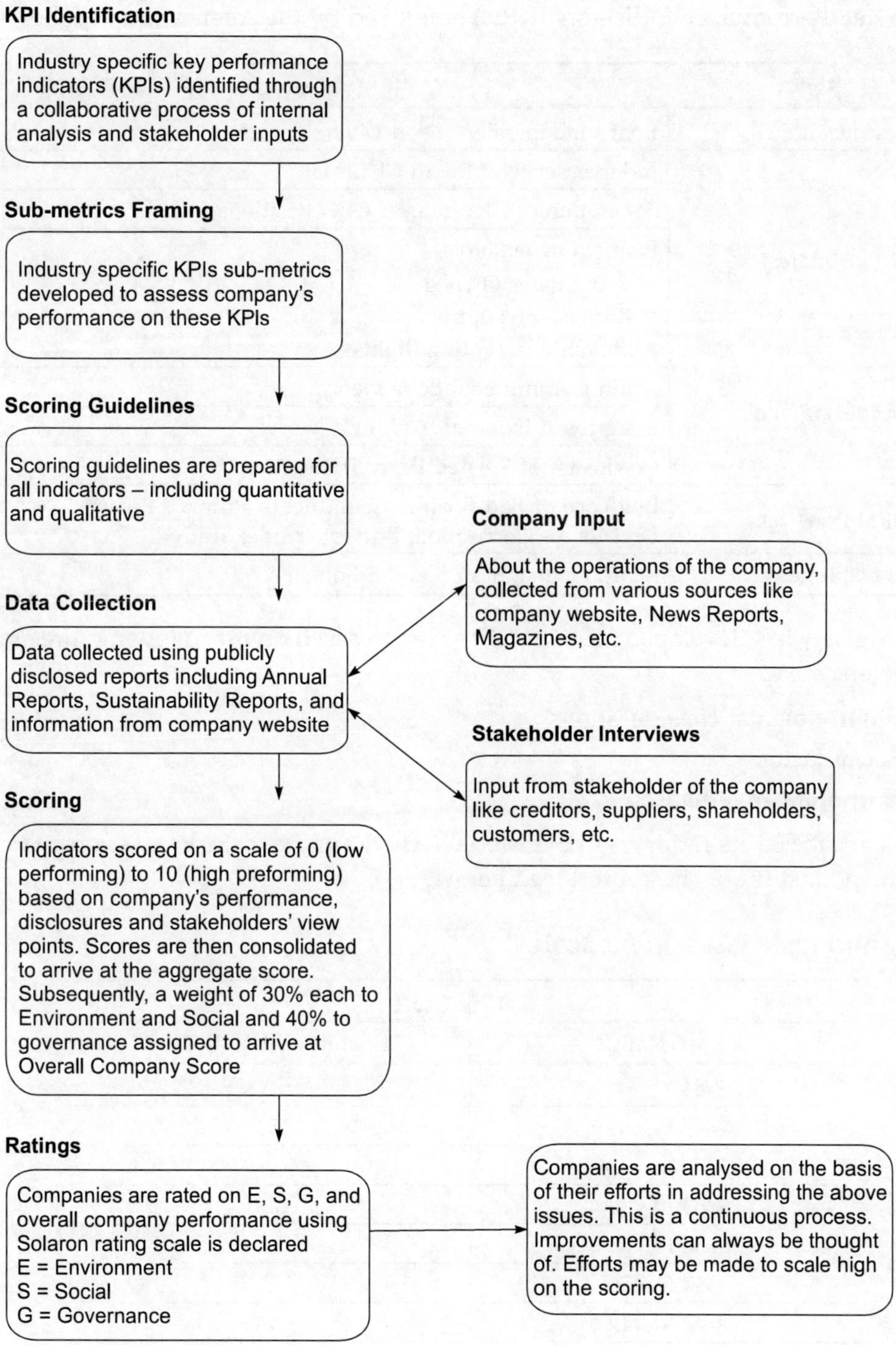
KPI Identification
Industry specific key performance indicators (KPIs) identified through a collaborative process of internal analysis and stakeholder inputs
Sub-metrics Framing
Industry specific KPIs sub-metrics developed to assess company's performance on these KPIs
Scoring Guidelines
Scoring guidelines are prepared for all indicators – including quantitative and qualitative
Company Input
About the operations of the company, collected from various sources like company website, News Reports, Magazines, etc.
Data Collection
Data collected using publicly disclosed reports including Annual Reports, Sustainability Reports, and information from company website
Stakeholder Interviews
Input from stakeholder of the company like creditors, suppliers, shareholders, customers, etc.
Scoring
Indicators scored on a scale of 0 (low performing) to 10 (high preforming) based on company's performance, disclosures and stakeholders' view points. Scores are then consolidated to arrive at the aggregate score. Subsequently, a weight of 30% each to Environment and Social and 40% to governance assigned to arrive at Overall Company Score
Ratings
Companies are rated on E, S, G, and overall company performance using Solaron rating scale is declared
E = Environment
S = Social
G = Governance
Companies are analysed on the basis of their efforts in addressing the above issues. This is a continuous process. Improvements can always be thought of. Efforts may be made to scale high on the scoring.

The Key Performance Indicators (KPIs) employed by the Agency are as follows:

Risk	Indicators
Business Health	Board Independence and Diversity
Conflict of Interest	Independence of Board Chairman
	Separation of Chairman & CEO Positions
	Family Ownership • % of Shares Owned • Exercise of Control • Shareholder Voting Rights
Misappropriation of Assets	Audit Committee Independence
	Integrity of External Auditor
	Disclosure of Related Party Transactions
Unethical Practices	Evidence of Bad Business Conduct in Primary Business or Other Divisions – Corruption, Bribery, Insider Trading
Future Liabilities	Board Oversight of E and S Functions

The Agency has developed sustainability ratings based on the following three major parameters:

1. Environmental considerations
2. Social factors
3. Corporate governance

Thus, it labeled its rating as "ESG Model'. The Rating and Risk Assessment Scales used by the Institution are reproduced below:

Rating and Risk Assessment Scales

Rating Scale	
Score Range	**Sustainability Rating**
>=84	AAA
>=77 to <84	AA
>=70 to <77	A
>=63 to <70	BBB
>=56 to <63	BB
>=49 to <56	B
>=42 to <49	CCC
>=35 to <42	CC
<35	C

Risk Assessment Scale	
Score Range	**Risk Outlook**
0 to <20	Very High
>=20 to <40	High
>=40 to <60	Medium
>=60 to <80	Low
>=80 to <100	Very Low

3. RATING SCALE AND SYMBOLS

As thing stand, there is no hard and fast rule as to the scale and symbols. Rating agencies are devising their own ways to reflect their intentions and methodology. As commented earlier, it has become the prerogative of the agency to imagine whatever the number of grades (notches) and symbols (using alphabets/numerals or both). Since credit rating has started with the rating of financial instruments, there were diverse symbols used to denote differences in the quality of the instrument. For example, CRISIL has been using alphanumeric symbols to convey credit ratings. It assigns credit ratings to debt obligations on three basic scales: (i) the long-term scale, (ii) the short-term scale, and the fixed deposit scale. Given below are the symbols used by the agency.[3] Sometimes, plus and minus symbols are also used to indicate finer distinctions within a rating category. However, the minus symbol associated with ratings has no negative connotations.

Symbol (Rating Category)	Description (with regard to the likelihood of meeting the debt obligations on time)
AAA	Instruments with this rating are considered to have the highest degree of safety regarding timely servicing of financial obligations. Such instruments carry lowest credit risk.
AA	Instruments with this rating are considered to have high degree of safety regarding timely servicing of financial obligations. Such instruments carry very low credit risk.
A	Instruments with this rating are considered to have adequate degree of safety regarding timely servicing of financial obligations. Such instruments carry low credit risk.
BBB	Instruments with this rating are considered to have moderate degree of safety regarding timely servicing of financial obligations. Such instruments carry moderate credit risk.
BB	Instruments with this rating are considered to have moderate risk of default regarding timely servicing of financial obligations.
B	Instruments with this rating are considered to have high risk of default regarding timely servicing of financial obligations.
C	Instruments with this rating are considered to have very high risk of default regarding timely servicing of financial obligations.
D	Instruments with this rating are in default or are expected to be in default soon

Similarly, ICRA has been employing the following symbols for rating the long-term Bonds, NCDs and other debt instruments (excluding public deposits), with original maturity exceeding one year.

Symbol	Description
LAAA	The highest-credit-quality rating assigned by ICRA. The rated instrument carries the lowest credit risk.
LAA	The high-credit-quality rating assigned by ICRA. The rated instrument carries low credit risk.
LA	The adequate-credit-quality rating assigned by ICRA. The rated instrument carries average credit risk.
LBBB	The moderate-credit-quality rating assigned by ICRA. The rated instrument carries higher than average credit risk.
LBB	The inadequate-credit-quality rating assigned by ICRA. The rated instrument carries high credit risk.
LB	The risk-prone-credit-quality rating assigned by ICRA. The rated instrument carries very high credit risk.
LC	The poor-credit-quality rating assigned by ICRA. The rated instrument has limited prospects of recovery.
LD	The lowest-credit-quality rating assigned by ICRA. The rated instrument has very low prospects of recovery.

Whereas, CARE uses Triple 'A' to 'D' for rating the long/medium term instruments like fixed deposits, structured obligations, convertible preference shares, redeemable preference shares, as shown below:

Symbols	Rating Definition
AAA	Instruments with this rating are considered to have the highest degree of safety regarding timely servicing of financial obligations. Such instruments carry lowest credit risk.
AA	Instruments with this rating are considered to have high degree of safety regarding timely servicing of financial obligations. Such instruments carry very low credit risk.
A	Instruments with this rating are considered to have adequate degree of safety regarding timely servicing of financial obligations. Such instruments carry low credit risk.
BBB	Instruments with this rating are considered to have moderate degree of safety regarding timely servicing of financial obligations. Such instruments carry moderate credit risk.
BB	Instruments with this rating are considered to have moderate risk of default regarding timely servicing of financial obligations.
B	Instruments with this rating are considered to have high risk of default regarding timely servicing of financial obligations.
C	Instruments with this rating are considered to have very high risk of default regarding timely servicing of financial obligations.
D	Instruments with this rating are in default or are expected to be in default soon

4. ICRA'S RATING METHODOLOGY

The Information and Credit Rating Agency (ICRA) having been established in 1991, is one of the leading Credit Rating Agencies in India. Apart from rating the financial instruments, the credit rating agencies are also rendering services in other related areas of activity. One such service given by them, upon the request by the SEBI, is the rating of companies in terms of their governance practices. Though many credit rating agencies were involved in this exercise, ICRA's ratings have become popular in the recent past. Therefore, it is necessary to focus our attention on the methodology adapted by ICRA to rate companies on this account.[4]

4.1 Emphasis on Substance over Form

ICRA's ratings are appreciated for the fact that the agency emphasizes on substance over form. It has made it very clear that mere compliance to the legal provisions does not fetch a good ranking. It said that "statutory compliance is only a necessary but not sufficient condition" for a high CGR. Nevertheless, the agency keeps an eye on this aspect, as it verifies the compliance of companies in respect of the following:

- Clauses 49, 47, 41 and 31 of the Listing Agreement.
- Sections 292, 292A, 293, 297, 299, 301, 308 and 372A of the Companies Act, 1956, as amended [now corresponding sections in the new Companies Act, 2013].
- Regulations 7, 8 and 10 of the SEBI's Takeover Code.
- SEBI's Insider Trading Regulations.

4.2 Key Variables in the Rating

ICRA has adopted the definition of OECD for identifying key variables that can guide CG Rating. As indicated earlier, OECD has defined CG in terms of objectives, means and controls. It said that the Governance is a 'system by which business corporations are directed and controlled'. With this background, ICRA has fixed the following criteria for evaluating a company against its performance on CG.

1. Ownership Structure.
2. Governance Structure and Management Processes
3. Board Structure and Processes
4. Stakeholder Relationship
5. Transparency and Disclosures
6. Financial Discipline
7. Ethical Practices

Within each of these key variables, specific guideposts were identified, so that rating methodology could be more robust, meaningful and comprehensive.

A. *Ownership Structure*

The key issues analysed in this regard are:

- Extent to which dominant shareholders are easily identifiable
- Extent of cross-holdings that may compromise minority interest
- Extent of shareholding by the promoter group
- Extent of institutional shareholding
- Pattern of retail shareholding

B. *Governance Structure and Management Processes*

The focus of ICRA's analysis here is on the decision-making process followed within the company being rated, and the quality and nature of information that is presented to its Board. ICRA believes that for a company to be able to respond swiftly to changes in today's dynamic business environment, line managers led by the Chief Executive Officer must be given enough powers to take decisions in the most appropriate manner. However, it needs to be ensured that the powers are exercised in accordance with established procedures and that they are in harmony with the broad policy guidelines and strategic objectives formulated by the Board. Accordingly, the key issues analysed in this regard are:

- Extent to which clearly-defined governance arrangements are present and followed
- Appropriateness of the decision-making process
- Quality of information submitted to the Board

C. *Board Structure and Processes*

The key Board functions of any organisation may be summed up as follows:

- Approving, monitoring and reviewing the strategy proposed by the executive management
- Evaluating the performance of the top management
- Ensuring compliance with legal and statutory requirements
- Balancing the rights and concerns of shareholders and other stakeholders

It is believed that a competent Board of Directors, free of conflict of interest, can help protect stakeholders' interests, ensure compliance with the prevailing laws of the land, and provide strategic guidance to the executive management. However, the full Board may not be able to meet very frequently to devote its close attention to the business of the organisation. Some of the Board functions are therefore performed through specially constituted Board Committees consisting mainly or wholly of Independent Directors. The more important among these committees are the Audit Committee, the

Remuneration Committee, the Appointment Committee and the Investment Committee. Through these Board Committees, organisations seek to strengthen the ability of the Non-Executive Directors to discharge their control functions more effectively.

ICRA's CGR process evaluates the Board Structure and Processes in relation to the following:

- **Structural Aspects, Covering the Areas Like**
  - Size of the Board
  - Proportion of "Independent" Directors
  - Other Directorships held by the Independent Director(s)
  - The mix of skill sets which the "Independent" Directors bring to the Board
- **Effectiveness of the Board as Judged by**
  - Frequency of Board meetings
  - Attendance track record of Directors
  - Quality of agenda papers and extent to which they are circulated in advance
  - Quality of presentations made to the Board
  - Board's role in approving strategy proposed by the executive management
  - Deliberations related to major investments, capital expenditure, and related party transactions
  - Board's role in determining executive compensation
- **Functioning of Board Committees:** It is essential that Boards multiply themselves through the constitution of various sub or mini boards, to look into the specific issues of concern. As a matter of fact, company law in India and in many other countries has made the constitution of sub-committees an essential requirement. Accordingly sub-committees like Audit Committee, Stakeholders Relationship Committee, Social Responsibility Committee have come into existence.

Among the Board Committees, the Audit Committee is clearly the most important in terms of scope of activities. A properly functioning Audit Committee has the potential to improve the quality of financial reporting, strengthen the position of auditors, and ensure that effective internal audit, internal control and management systems are in place. The key aspects relating to the effectiveness of Audit Committees as considered significant by ICRA are:

- Composition of the Audit Committee
- Background, expertise, experience and independence of its members
- Deliberations at Audit Committee meetings with respect to:
  - ✓ compliance with Accounting Standards
  - ✓ qualifications in published accounts

  - ✓ major issues involving the financial reporting process, systems and control, and internal audit coverage
- Role of the Audit Committee in the appointment of statutory auditors, rotation of auditors, extension of non-audit services by the auditors.

➢ **Internal Auditors and Audit Committees:** ICRA feels that it is essential for the Audit Committee to consider the work of internal auditors so as to gain an understanding of the organisation's risk management processes and control systems. It is also the duty of internal auditors to suggest appropriate measures for ensuring effective controls. In the light of the same ICRA focuses on the following:
- Strength and quality of the Internal Audit team
- Internal Audit coverage plan
- Extent of Internal Audit's interaction with the Audit Committee
- Management's responsiveness to issues highlighted by Internal Audit

➢ **Stakeholder Relationship:** The emphasis of ICRA's analysis is on evaluating the extent to which a company goes beyond what is mandatory under law to serve the interests of its stakeholders. The issues of priority include:
- Conduct of Annual/Extraordinary General Meetings (AGMs/EGMs) and the extent of disclosures at such meetings
- Procedures for transfer and registration of shares and payment of dividend
- Company's responsiveness to investor complaints
- Timeliness of release of any market sensitive information
- History of penalties levied for violations of statutory provisions by regulators

➢ **Transparency and Disclosures:** The key parameters used to assess a company's transparency and disclosure standards are:
- Quality of Accounts, Reporting practices, and compliance with the accepted accounting standards and comparison with best practices of the industry
- Changes in accounting policies
- Notes to accounts of materially significant nature
- Quality and level of detail in accounts, especially with respect to item like Loans and Advances, Inter-Corporate Advances and Contingent Liabilities
- Disclosures on transactions with subsidiaries, associates and other related parties
- Additional information to shareholders
- Quality of disclosures in Management Discussion and Analysis (MDA) Report with specific focus on the following:

- ✓ Competitive position of the company's product portfolio and trends in the same
- ✓ Key drivers of the company's operating performance, including sustainability of margins
- ✓ The rate and success of product innovations
- ✓ Risk factors that could have a bearing on the prospects of each business line

➢ **Financial Discipline:** The ultimate objective of Corporate Governance is to create and maximise shareholder value. While the actual shareholder value generated by a company may be dependent on a number of factors that are beyond the control of its management, ICRA believes that maintenance of a certain level of discipline in the conduct of business operations also has an important role to play. ICRA's analysis therefore focuses on factors that are within the company's control, and which would impact the shareholder's value. Such factors may include:

- Major business segments for the company
- Reasons for carrying on multiple businesses
- Return on capital employed in each business compared with the industry average
- History of equity dilution
- Extent of reliance on debt funding
- Dividend policy
- Number of subsidiaries/associates and rationale for the same
- Nature of transactions with subsidiaries

➢ **Ethical Practices:** Corporate Governance, ultimately, is about promoting corporate fairness and transparency. Therefore, a cornerstone of Corporate Governance is a company's commitment to maintain the highest standards of ethical practices in all its transactions. ICRA's analysis thus covers:

- comprehensiveness of code of ethics and integrity;
- steps taken to effectively communicate the principles of corporate ethics;
- extent to which compliance with the codes and guidelines is monitored; and
- extent to which feedback systems have been established to encourage whistle-blowing.

➢ **Miscellaneous Practices:** Although the focus of ICRA's CGR exercise is primarily on a company's financial stakeholders, it also evaluates the company's conduct in relation to its other key stakeholders like employees, customers, suppliers and society at large. Any evidence of unsatisfactory relationship with any of these major stakeholders is factored in negatively. In all, ICRA has identified about 30 variables to judge the performance of a company against the CG Rating Scale.

4.3 Rating Scale

ICRA uses a six-point scale of CGR1 through CGR6. The rating of CGR1 implies that in ICRA's current opinion, the rated company has adopted and follows such practices, conventions and codes as would provide its financial stakeholders, the highest assurance on the quality of Corporate Governance. However, ICRA wants to maintain that its rating is not a certificate of statutory compliance or a comment on the rated company's future financial performance, credit rating or stock price. The following Exhibit indicates the gradation:

Exhibit 16.1: Rating Symbols and their description as employed by ICRA

Scale	Description
CGR1	This implies that the rated company has adopted and follows such practices, conventions and codes as would provide its financial stakeholders 'the highest assurance' on the quality of corporate governance. However, this cannot be taken as a certificate of statutory compliance. Nor, should it be interpreted as a guarantee of the future of the company in terms of growth, its performance and market share or stock price.
CGR2	This implies that the rated company has adopted and follows such practices, conventions and codes as would provide its financial stakeholders 'a high level of assurance' on the quality of corporate governance. However, it is not a certificate of statutory compliance or a comment on the rated company's future financial performance, credit rating or stock price.
CGR3	This implies that the rated company has adopted and follows such practices, conventions and codes as would provide its financial stakeholders 'adequate level of assurance' on the quality of corporate governance. However, this is not a certificate of statutory compliance or a comment on the rated company's future financial performance, credit rating or stock price.
CGR4	This implies that the rated company has adopted and follows such practices, conventions and codes as would provide its financial stakeholders 'moderate level of assurance' on the quality of corporate governance. However, this is not a certificate of statutory compliance or a comment on the rated company's future financial performance, credit rating or stock price.
CGR5	This implies that the rated company has adopted and follows such practices, conventions and codes as would provide its financial stakeholders 'inadequate level of assurance' on the quality of corporate governance. However, this is not a certificate of statutory compliance or a comment on the rated company's future financial performance, credit rating or stock price.
CGR6	This implies that the rated company has adopted and follows such practices, conventions and codes as would provide its financial stakeholders 'low level of assurance' on the quality of corporate governance. However, it is not a certificate of statutory compliance or a comment on the rated company's future financial performance, credit rating or stock price.

5. CRISIL'S RATING CRITERIA

The Credit Rating and Information Services India Ltd. incorporated and promoted by the erstwhile ICICI Ltd, along with UTI and other financial institutions, in January 1987, is the first rating agency in India that has started rating the debt obligations of Indian companies.

5.1 Understanding CRISIL Ratings

Rating agencies assign credit ratings using three rating scales: Global scale, regional scale, and national scale. The essential difference between them is in the form of scope of coverage. While global scale ratings are assigned based on an assessment of the issuer in relation to other issuers globally, and regional scale ratings are based primarily on credit risk comparisons within a specific region, national ratings are based primarily on credit risk comparisons within a domestic context.

CRISIL's credit rating indicates the probability of default on the rated instrument. In other words, the credit rating indicates probability of an investor in rated instruments, or a lender to a rated firm, not receiving interest and principal payments on time and in accordance with the terms of the rated instrument. This probability is reflected in the form of an easily understandable alphanumeric scale. CRISIL uses symbols such as 'CRISIL AAA', 'CRISIL AA', 'CRISIL A', or 'CRISIL A1', 'CRISIL A2', etc. As a matter of fact, credit ratings are only indicative of the following:

1. *Relative measures of default probability, not a guarantee against default:* A credit rating does NOT indicate that payment of interest and principal is completely certain. There are definitive non-zero probabilities of default for any rating category including the highest, 'CRISIL AAA'. The rating indicates that the rated instrument is less likely to default than instruments rated lower.
2. *Not a comment on the issuer's general performance, or potential price of its bonds or equity shares, or suitability to the investor*: A credit rating is an opinion on an issuer's ability and willingness to honour its financial obligations on the rated debt instrument on time. The rating should not be construed as an opinion on the issuer's general performance. Neither is it an opinion on the likely future price of the rated bonds, nor on the potential value of the issuer's equity shares. This rating shall not be taken as a recommendation to buy, sell or hold a rated instrument. Nor is it a comment on the market price or the suitability of a rated instrument in respect of an investor.
3. *Assigned to debt instruments alone and NOT to equity instruments*: Typically, debt instruments such as non-convertible debentures, partially convertible debentures, bonds, fixed deposits, commercial paper, bank loan facilities, short-term debt, and structured debentures, are rated. Firms issuing these instruments can also be rated on their capacity to service their debt obligations on time.

5.2 Governance Rating by CRISIL

CRISIL has titled these ratings as "CRISIL Governance & Value Creation Ratings (CRISIL GVC Ratings)" to make its ratings unique. The two specific aspects of focus of the process adopted by CRISIL relate to: (1) 'management quality, and (2) value creation potential'. Hence, it titled saying that the ratings are not just Governance ratings; but they are also meant to indicate about the **value creation** made by the company. Creation of value rather than profit maximization is said to be the goal of the business. Many companies in the West and in India too have realized that maximizing 'stakeholders' value' is the ultimate focus in the present-day context; which is said to be consistent with every constituent of the company management. Against this philosophy, the rating criteria of CRISIL is based on the following:

(i) **Equitable Treatment of Shareholders:** Ownership structure is a key factor in assessing the treatment given to shareholders. While the presence of a large or majority shareholder is not necessarily a negative governance issue, CRISIL analyses companies with such concentrated shareholding in detail to ascertain the extent to which the majority shareholder acts in the interest of minority shareholders and all other stakeholders. The other issues of significance in this area are the extent of disclosure of shareholding pattern, presence of any disproportionate control and the systems in place to detect and prevent insider trading.

(ii) **Ownership Rights of Shareholders:** The most important aspect examined by the Agency relates to the articulation and protection of shareholder rights. The pertinent questions asked are: to what extent it is complying with the law, and where its practices go beyond laws and regulations to address the spirit of governance. The emphasis is on what a company does, rather than its compliance with the minimum required by the law. It analyses the provisions of the company's charter, viz., memorandum and articles of association for voting rights, classes of shares, presence of anti-takeover provisions, and preferential rights for any section of shareholders. The analysis also focuses on ease and effectiveness of shareholder participation at meetings.

(iii) **Transparency and Disclosure:** Timely and adequate of disclosure of information on the company's operating and financial performance is considered core of the governance. This is expected to help stakeholders to monitor the operation and performance of the management. Good disclosure in a transparent manner is a reflection of the quality of a company's corporate governance practices. It also examines the content of public disclosure for completeness, quality and clarity of reporting. The degree of disclosure in financial statements, on related party transactions, on operational performance, and on governance, is one key aspect that CRISIL looks into. The other aspect of disclosure is the timing whether the company communicates material events and performance in a timely manner to reach the largest possible number of relevant stakeholders.

CRISIL also looks at the independence of the auditor, adequacy of internal audit, and effectiveness of the audit process. The composition and functioning of the audit committee, quality and type of issues discussed at the audit committee, the nature and adequacy of oversight provided with respect to the company's financial statement, and the internal control and risk management functions, are some of the aspects examined under this parameter.

(iv) Composition of Board: Composition of the Board and its sub-committees is another key issue in the governance of a company. Boards should be structured in such a way that the interests of all the shareholders and stakeholders are respected, represented and protected. CRISIL evaluates from the point of view of good balance of independent and executive directors. It looks into whether the Board has the right mix of various capabilities required for governing the company, taking into account the size, industry nature and growth objectives. The analysis also includes aspects like selection process for Board members, succession policies for Board members, processes for ensuring availability of relevant competencies on the Board, and Board compensation.

(v) Functioning of Board: CRISIL examines the functioning of the Board and its sub-committees and assesses the Board's role in providing independent oversight of management performance. Effective Boards are active, engaged, challenging and questioning in attitude, and exhibit true independence in action. CRISIL assesses Board effectiveness in terms of the role the Board has played in directing, articulating and implementing the company's strategy, overseeing the performance of management, and monitoring operational controls and risk management systems. CRISIL also examines the role and contribution of independent directors.

(vi) Management Assessment: It also looks at the reputation, experience, performance and skills of the management personnel. These enable the management to create value for stakeholders. The success of past strategies, proactive nature of management in identifying threats and opportunities in the operating environment, integrity of the senior management, and risk appetite of the management, are some of the key areas CRISIL examines while carrying out a management assessment.

(vii) Value Creation for Various Stakeholders: The strength of a company's relationship with all its stakeholders (including shareholders) is an important determinant of its ability to create economic value on a sustainable basis.

Basing on the above key areas, CRISIL has devised parameters to quantify the delivery of value to each stakeholder. The key parameters that CRISIL considers while analysing the value delivered to various categories of stakeholders are given below [see Exhibit 16.2]:

Exhibit 16.2: Key Parameters of Stakeholders Value

Stakeholder	Key Parameters
Shareholder	Return on invested capital compared to the weighted average cost of capital, dividend track record, and payout ratio
Debt holder	Debt protection measures, credit ratings
Customer	Market share, assessment of customer satisfaction
Employee	Absolute salary levels, adjusted growth in average annual salaries, stock option programmes, attrition rates, and intangible factors like work environment and facilities provided by employer
Supplier	Credit terms, support provided, and transparent dealings
Society	Social projects taken up by the company, care for the environment, taxes paid to Government

The Rating symbols for Governance and value creation (GVC) ratings used by CRISIL are as follows [Exhibit 16.3]:

Exhibit 16.3: Rating Symbols used by CRISIL

S. No.	Rating Symbol	Gradation
1.	CRISIL GVC Level-1	Corporate governance and value creation for all stakeholders is the **Highest**.
2.	CRISIL GVC Level-2	Corporate governance and value creation for all stakeholders is **Very High**.
3.	CRISIL GVC Level-3	Corporate governance and value creation for all stakeholders is **High.**
4.	CRISIL GVC Level-4	Corporate governance and value creation for all stakeholders is **Above Average.**
5.	CRISIL GVC Level-5	Corporate governance and value creation for all stakeholders is **Average**.
6.	CRISIL GVC Level-6	Corporate governance and value creation for all stakeholders is **Below Average.**
7.	CRISIL GVC Level-7	Corporate governance and value creation for all stakeholders is **Low**.
8.	CRISIL GVC Level-8	Corporate governance and value creation for all stakeholders is **the Lowest**.

The following is the list of companies rated by CRISIL in the recent past for CGR purpose; wherein companies like Bharti Airtel, HDGC Bank, Infosys and Mahindra & Mahindra could secure the Highest 'Level-1' rank for their effective governance, as shown below [Exhibit 16.4]:

Exhibit 16.4: Rating of Companies on Corporate Governance Performance

Name of the Company	Areas of Activity	Rating
Bharti Airtel Limited (formerly Bharti Tele-Ventures Limited)	Telecommunication – Services – Equipments/Cable	CRISIL GVC Level 1
HDFC Bank Ltd.	Banks	CRISIL GVC Level 1
Housing Development Finance Corporation Ltd.	Housing Finance Company	CRISIL GVC Level 1
Infosys Technologies Ltd	Computers – Software	CRISIL GVC Level 1
Mahindra and Mahindra Limited	Automobiles 4 wheelers	CRISIL GVC Level 1
Indian Farmers Fertiliser Co-operative Limited	Fertilisers	CRISIL GVC Level 2
Kanoria Chemicals and Industries Ltd.	Chemicals - Inorganic	CRISIL GVC Level 3

6. CARE RATINGS

Credit Analysis and Research Limited (CARE) Mumbai is yet another rating agency floated in India in April 1993, now occupies the position of being the second largest credit rating agency in India. CARE ratings provide the spectrum of credit rating that helps the corporates to raise capital for their various requirements and assist investors to form an informed investment decision based on their own risk-return expectations.[5]

CARE's Corporate Governance Rating (CGR) is an opinion on relative standing of an entity with regard to adoption of corporate governance practices. It provides information to stakeholders about the level of corporate governance practices of the entity. It enables the companies to obtain an independent and credible assessment of the extent of their corporate governance. The rating process would also determine the relative standing of the entity vis-à-vis the best practices followed in the domestic as well as international arena. Companies can also use these ratings as reference and set benchmarks for further improvements. Investors and other stakeholders get benefited as they are able to differentiate companies based on degree of corporate governance.

CARE undertakes perusal of various documents like agenda papers and Minutes of Board and Board Committees, Minutes of the Annual General Meeting and

Extraordinary General Meeting, Annual Return and other documents filed by the company with ROC, SEBI, stock exchanges (domestic and international) and all other regulatory bodies. The evaluating team will interact with the Chairman, MD/CEO and independent directors, key officials of the company, Statutory Auditors, Internal Auditors, Lenders and Institutional/major shareholders. The methodology of rating employed by CARE is based on the following seven key parameters:

- board composition and functioning;
- ownership structure;
- organization structure and Management Information System;
- shareholder relationship;
- disclosure and transparency;
- financial prudence; and,
- statutory and regulatory compliance.

The agency believes that corporate governance helps in ensuring the corporations to take into consideration the interests of a wide range of constituencies, and stakeholders. It aims at value creation for its stakeholders. Evaluation of the extent of value creation and balanced distribution of wealth is undertaken by CARE under its CGV rating exercise. This exercise involves assessment of wealth creation and distribution parameters in addition to the parameters evaluated under CGR. The composite rating designed by CARE is called "Corporate Governance and Value Creation Rating". Wealth creation by a company is based on sound business strategy and practices adopted by its management as also maintaining financial and operational discipline would promote enhancing stakeholder value. The other essential ingredients like the quality of management and its capabilities, corporate strategy and philosophy and succession planning are also examined by CARE to assess the wealth management practices. Creation and distribution of wealth to the stakeholders would be evaluated with reference to the following:

- shareholder;
- employees;
- lenders/creditors;
- suppliers;
- customers; and
- society.

The emphasis will be to assess sustainable value creation and distribution and hence the analysis will not only examine the past but evaluate the future as well.

7. BRICKWORK'S RATINGS ON CORPORATE GOVERNANCE

Brickwork is a Knowledge Process Outsourcing (KPO) company founded in 2005. The company is known for pioneering the concept of Remote Executive Assistance (REA).[6] The idea was to make the benefits of outsourcing available to individuals and small to mid-sized companies, by providing simple to complex business assistance, at an affordable price. This concept found instant worldwide recognition and media attention, including the New York Times best seller 'The World is Flat' by Thomas Friedman. This was followed by several news magazines and TV shows as well. Brickworks India has partnered with more than 15,000 clients in 116 countries, to help them build the foundation.

The company has started 'Brickworks Ratings in 2007 at Bangalore and got registered with SEBI in 2008. Brickwork's Corporate Governance ratings provide an opinion on the general corporate governance quality of the rated entities for all its stakeholders. It is also an eye opener for individual companies to measure themselves against critical benchmarks.

According to the McKinsey survey, foreign investor would pay a premium for well run efficient Indian companies with good governance. Corporate governance rating of Brickworks could be an important signal for such investors. The recent corporate failures witnessed world over have reinforced the importance of corporate governance. Particularly for stakeholders, who have suffered loss at the hands of company's tainted management and board where poor corporate governance practices were adopted to commit and conceal fraud. It is important for stakeholders to differentiate corporates on the basis of Governance principles to identify good from the bad. After the Asian financial crisis of 1997 and the financial turmoils of 2008 and 2014, there have been a number of initiatives to implement governance and disclosures practices in the Indian corporate sector. Undoubtedly, corporate governance is the need of the hour.

Brickworks ratings provide an objective and independent analysis of corporate governance practices and its influence on corporate fairness in dealing with stakeholders. The rating process covers the following five key areas:

1. **Board Composition and Effectiveness:** An effective corporate board is a powerful tool that has the ultimate control over strategy, policies and procedures implemented in the company. Board also plays a crucial role in instituting an effective internal control mechanism. The main task of the Board is to monitor and control executive management on behalf of stakeholders. Separation of the roles of chairman and chief executive officer is expected to ensure clear division of responsibilities at board level; so that no individual director has unrestricted authority with regard to decision-making. The 'board composition and effectiveness' will assess whether all material matters affecting the corporates are appropriately considered and will suggest an appropriate balance to significant decision-making.

2. **Management Transparency:** Transparency is indeed an important aspect in assessing the quality of corporate governance. The intention of the management can make transparency the best practice in the corporate world. Brickwork has considered management transparency as an integral part of corporate governance.
3. **Ownership Structure:** Structure of ownership is a significant factor in determining the success of corporate governance practices. Unlike corporations in the developed countries, which have dispersed ownership, corporations in India have mainly family owned and the control remains in the hands of a few family members. This in fact, turns out as an impediment to the best practices in corporate governance. Only those companies that are widely held can provide a better direction to the company's management to perform efficiently. Brickwork keeps this important aspect in view, while rating companies on governance scale.
4. **Shareholders' Rights:** Shareholder equality is one of the significant and influential principles of Indian company law. It is a fundamental principle of corporate governance. Shareholders' participation in corporate governance is external rather than internal; because they do not take part in the day-to-day business management of the company. Brickworks examines whether the shareholders legal rights/claims have been honored and their grievances addressed timely and appropriately.
5. **Financial Fairness:** Financial fairness is an outcome of internal control mechanisms and it also shows positive results on corporate governance practices. It is evident that companies with better corporate governance have better financial fairness practices than companies with poor corporate governance. This exercise involves companies' policies and practices towards dividend policy, investments, related party transaction, etc.

8. STANDARD AND POOR'S RATINGS

Standard and Poor is yet another agency that examines the matter seriously.[7] Though the agency is thoroughly involved in the credit rating function, it values governance also as an important issue. It has realized that there are times when governance related issues will be a driver in shaping a company's credit quality. There will also be times when governance is not a key determinant of credit quality. Going forward, the links between corporate governance and credit ratings stand to evolve as more research and case studies bring new issues to light. In case of an individual company, the following aspects are considered valuable by standard and poor in rating the companies on governance.

1. ***Ownership Structure and External Influences:*** Understanding the ownership structure of the company is essential; especially when there is a known holder holding majority of the shares. Similarly, the existence of a large number of nominee shareholders will also give an indication to the concentration of share ownership; having an influence on governance practices.

2. ***Transparency of Ownership:*** Key analytical issues are:
   - Breakdown of shareholdings
   - Identification of substantial/majority holders having ownership control
   - Director shareholdings
   - Evidence of indirect shareholdings
   - Management shareholdings

3. ***Concentration and Influence of Ownership and External Stakeholders:*** Key analytical issues included the following:
   - Affiliation among shareholders
   - Commercial arrangements or related party transactions
   - Corporate structure, shareholding and management of key affiliates
   - Terms of key contracts and licenses
   - Internal financial and operational control systems
   - Management shareholding/voting control
   - Contracts with directors or key management personnel
   - Role of institutional investors

4. ***Influence of External Stakeholders:*** Key analytical issues in this category are:
   - Reporting of information on employees, community and environmental activities
   - Evidence of problematic relationships with non-financial stakeholders
   - Proactive programs to address interests of legitimate stakeholder interest groups
   - Undue influence from external stakeholders that detract from shareholder value

5. ***Shareholder Meeting and Voting Procedures:*** Key analytical issues are:
   - Shareholder meeting procedures covering the notices and agenda papers
   - Charter provisions on calling meeting
   - Arrangements for shareholders' participation in meetings
   - Minutes of the previous meeting

- Shareholder information on voting procedures
- Any deposit agreement for overseas listing
- Proxy arrangements
- Charter provisions on voting limits

6. ***Ownership Rights and Takeover Defenses***: Key analytical issues are:
   - Charter provisions on ownership rights
   - Arrangements with registrar to the issue
   - Share structure relating to equity and preference shares
   - Charter provisions relating to shareholders and board authorities
   - Shareholders agreement
   - Dividend history
   - Examples of share repurchases and swaps
7. ***Takeover Defenses:*** Key analytical issues are:
   - Nature of takeovers
   - Related/unrelated diversification
   - Blockholder ownership stakes
   - Multiple voting rights
8. ***Stakeholder Relations:*** The key analytical issues are:
   - Social and environmental reporting
   - Policies of the company in respect of investor and stakeholder interests
   - Evidence of problematic relationships with key non-financial stakeholders and regulators.
9. ***Content of Public Disclosure:*** Key analytical issues in this category are:
   - Accounting standards
   - Financial statements and reports
   - Minority, inter-firm and related party transactions
   - Operating disclosure requirements
   - Governance related disclosure
   - Legal documentation including Memorandum, Articles, bye-laws, etc.
   - Social and environmental reporting
10. ***Timing of, and Access to, Public Disclosure:*** Key analytical issues are:
    - Filing record
    - Access to public information

- Procedures for disclosure of market sensitive information
- Frequency of reporting
- Continuous and fair disclosure
- Presentations to investment community
- Availability of records to all shareholders at the company's headquarters
- Reports to shareholders
- Website and web – based reporting.

11. ***The Audit Process:*** Key analytical issues in this section are:

- Auditor selection
- Non-audit services
- Auditor rotation policy
- Audit committee independence
- Audit committee resources and training
- Audit committee charter
- Audit committee engagement
- Audit committee accountability
- Internal controls
- Risk management

12. ***Board Structure and Independence:*** Key analytical issues are:

- Board size and composition
- Skill mix
- Split of offices regarding CEO & Chairman
- Board committees and leadership
- Director selection
- Director shareholdings
- Independence
- Director tenure

13. ***Role and Effectiveness of the Board*****:** Key analytical issues in this area are:

- Defining the role of the Board
- Agenda papers and their circulation
- Articulation of mission and strategy
- Ethical boundaries
- Internal controls

- External stakeholder relationships
- Self-evaluations
- Succession policies
- Attendance particulars
- Other external directorships
- Meeting frequency
- Training
- Nominations process
- Board change

14. ***Senior Executive and Director Compensation:*** Key analytical issues are:
    - Performance based pay
    - Independence of executive
    - Compensation setting
    - Relationship with compensation consultants
    - Form of compensation
    - Performance evaluation criteria
    - Compensation setting process
    - Grant of stock options
    - Compensation disclosure
    - Executive contracts
    - Compensation plan

9. A COMPARISON OF THE RATING PARAMETERS

It would be quite interesting to make a comparison of the parameters deployed by diverse rating agencies in their attempt to rate the companies in respect of their governance practices. It is to be accepted that corporate governance ratings reflect a broad spectrum of issues than those employed for judging the quality of a financial instrument.[8] After all, it is the basic philosophy and commitment that are more important than the simple credit worthiness. Given the robustness of the methodology employed, corporate governance ratings can pierce through the moral and ethical fabric of the corporates. It is thus corporate governance ratings can be deemed as the 'overall standing/grading' on the quality of management (including BOD) of the company.

Table 16.1: Key Variables Employed by Diverse Rating Agencies for Corporate Governance

ICRA	CRISIL	Care	Brickworks	Standard & Poor
Ownership Structure	Equitable treatment of shareholders	Board composition & functioning	Board Composition and Effectiveness	Ownership structure and external influences
Governance Structure and Management Processes	Ownership rights of shareholders	Ownership structure	Management Transparency	Transparency of Ownership
Board Structure and Processes	Transparency & disclosure	Organization structure and Management Information System	Ownership Structure	Concentration and Influence of Ownership and External Stakeholders
Stakeholder Relationship	Composition of Board	Shareholder relationship	Shareholders' Rights	Influence of External Stakeholders
Transparency and Disclosures	Disclosure & transparency	Financial Fairness	Market for control and ownership base	Shareholder Meeting and Voting Procedures
Financial Discipline	Management assessment	Financial prudence		Ownership Rights and Takeover Defenses
Ethical Practices	Value creation for various stakeholders	Statutory and regulatory compliance		Takeover Defenses
				Stakeholder Relations
				Content of Public Disclosure
				Timing of, and Access to, Public Disclosure
				The Audit Process
				Board Structure and Independence
				Role and effectiveness of the Board
				Senior Executive and Director Compensation

Table 16.1 presents a comparison of the key variables employed by diverse rating agencies in giving their opinion. As is evident from the table, there is a broad agreement on the key parameters employed to rate the companies as to their governance. Minor variations could be seen in the context of sub-metrics. On the whole, the effort of the rating agencies is quite impressive and laudable.

In terms of ratings at the macro level, it is a good news for India that it stands fourth among a group of 25 companies for rankings on the corporate governance policies of the countries. According to a study done by KMPG in Singapore and the Association of Chartered Certified Accountants, the top three highest scoring markets with clear and extensive CG requirements are the UK, the US and Singapore. Australia, India and Malaysia jointly ranked fourth while Hong Kong and Russia tied for the next position, followed by Brazil and Taiwan at 10th position. The study analyzed corporate governance requirements in terms of clarity, degree of enforceability and number and type of instruments used by the 25 markets. The markets with the lowest scores, in descending order, are the Philippines, Indonesia, Canada, China, Cambodia, Japan, Vietnam, Myanmar, Brunei and Laos. It is appreciable that the Indian regulators have taken significant steps to raise the bar on governance in Indian companies by bringing in a paradigm shift in corporate governance requirements, both in the Companies Act 2013 and the recently revised clause 49 of SEBI's listing agreement. In particular, the changes relating to the role and responsibilities of the audit committee, the roles of independent directors, and the codified duties of directors as a whole, are leading to a shift in boardroom dynamics.

10. CAN CORPORATE GOVERNANCE RATING ENSURE BETTER GOVERNANCE?

This is an interesting question for which stakeholders wish to find an answer. There are two contradicting points of view, one, supporting the mechanism that there shall be some kind of mechanism; whereby there would be scope for sharing the information about the company. And that the operations of the company are revealed and the tendency of the entities towards corporate failure becomes evident. It is in this context, many of the corporate failures are attributed to shortcomings in the corporate governance practices. The broad areas of failure are indentified to be:

- Accounting frauds carried out in collusion with statutory auditors.
- Lack of independence of the board with board members having significant financial linkages with the companies.
- Insider trading.
- Disproportionate compensation paid to executive board members and senior management.

- Fiduciary failure by the board to exercise care and diligence in approving proposals, even though all the information was provided by the management.
- Weak internal control mechanisms and lack of supervision corporate governance has thus become a critical area of focus for various market participants and stakeholders.

Therefore, effective governance is presumed to put an end to these practices and ensure healthy corporate world.

On the other hand, there is a feeling expressed by many in the society that ratings do not contribute to the better performance or governance. In a study, Ian Gow and others opined that ratings are not reliable indicators of corporate governance.[9] Focusing on the factors that differentiate the good and the bad factors in rating the corporate governance practices adopted by a company, the authors argued that while the leading ratings firms claim to be "measuring the platonic ideal of good governance, our study suggests that it's far from clear what good governance is, let alone that forcing firms to adopt a checkbox approach to governance will produce good outcomes."

It is for these reasons, Moody's Investors Service (Global Credit Research Firm, New York) in its study published in April 2006, titled "Lessons Learned in Moody's Experience in Evaluating Corporate Governance in Major North American Issuers" pointed out that that governance has been more of a ratings driver for financial institutions (FIs) than for corporates. This trend reflects that FIs are relatively confidence-sensitive and that all of the FIs reviewed were investment grade. However, the firm noted variation by sector within the overall FI universe. The key findings included the following:

- Governance practices were heavily influenced by the ownership structures in each sector. The mutual company structure in the insurance industry, for example, presented governance issues that were different from those associated with the family- ownership control structures, so prevalent in the real estate investment trust (REIT) sector.
- The level of regulatory burden faced by financial institutions varied significantly across sectors, and higher levels tended to support higher quality governance.
- Board composition was characterized by the way the various industries in financial sectors have evolved in the last decade. For example, banks typically still appoint customers and affiliated directors to their boards, even as they grow more complex through acquisitions.[10]

Elaborating further, Moody's has attempted to relate credit rating to governance in one of the following five ways:

- Governance is a credit strength.
- Governance strengths from a creditor standpoint outweigh some weaknesses, but governance is not a ratings driver at this time.
- Corporate governance is neither a positive nor negative factor in our rating at this time.
- Governance weaknesses from a creditor standpoint outweigh strengths, but concern on governance is not a ratings driver at this time.
- Governance is a credit challenge that could constrain future ratings improvements.
- Below, we show the frequency with which we have placed issuers in these categories by sector, and comment on the major factors driving our determinations.

In another interesting study, Mine Ertugrul and Shantaram Hegde (based on the Corporate Governance Ratings provided by three premier U.S. rating agencies, viz. The Corporate Library (TCL), Institutional Shareholder Services (ISS), Governance Metrics International (GMI)) observed that the summary scores are generally poor predictors of primary and secondary measures of future performance. Nevertheless, information on certain key issues provides more positive and reliable evidence of their performance in the context of governance. The study has categorically pointed out that it is extremely difficult to distill all of the complex governance mechanisms into a single integrated, yet informative overall score.[11]

Though governance ratings are not mandatory in India, firms are showing interest in the exercise. More than that, rating agencies are becoming active in publishing scores as a part of their routine. In fact, ITC was the first company in India to have gone for corporate governance rating. It is only now others are following suit. Whether rating or not, companies as per the Listing Agreement have to submit the necessary information. A study posted by **indiacsr** on 10-1-2013 has revealed astonishing results declaring that nearly 200 listed companies have several discrepancies in their quarterly corporate governance reports. Besides, several hundreds of companies were found to be late in submitting these reports. It was reported that the Stock Exchanges are asking these companies to rectify the discrepancies in their reports and to explain the non-submission or late submission. As per the published data of the BSE, (dated 02-01-2013) about 1000 companies have not submitted corporate governance reports and about 500 submitted after the due date (being 30-09-2012).

Therefore, rating reports are to be understood and analysed with a note of caution. It is also to be borne in mind that the places in the rating scale vary from time to time. Few notches up or down should not be viewed as a great sign or indicator of the future of the company. Above all, it is the genuine interest of the management/promoters of the company that shall be held high in the overall process of rating.

References

1. Shleifer, A., & R.W. Vishny, 'A Survey of Corporate Governance', *The Journal of Finance*, Vol. 52, No. 2, 1997.
2. 'Rating Methodology', Solaron: Sustainability Services, Bangalore (www.solaronworld.com).
3. www.crisil.com
4. www.incraindia.com
5. 'Governance Rating', CARE Ratings : Professional Risk Opinion, Mumbai (www.careratings.com).
6. http://www.brickworksratings.com/criteria-corporate-governance.html
7. Standard & Poor's Corporate Governance Scores: Criteria, Methodology and Definitions, *Standard & Poor's Governance Services,* Tata McGrawhill Company Inc., New York, July 2002.
8. Goyal, M.M., 'Corporate Governance Ratings : A Step Towards Better Corporate Governance', *Asia Pacific Journal of Research,* Vol. 1, No. 18, October 2014, pp. 93-100.
9. 'Rating the Raters of Corporate Governance', Kellogg Insight, May 1, 2010.
10. Gregory W. Bauer, 'Assessing Corporate Governance As A Ratings Driver For North American Financial Institutions' Moody's Investors Service (Global Credit Research), April 2006.
11. Mine Ertugrul, Shantaram Hegde, "Corporate Governance Ratings and Firm Performance", Social Science Research Network, Vol. 38, No. 1, Spring 2009, pp. 139.

17

CHAPTER

Reporting Practices of Companies on Corporate Governance: Survey of Annual Reports

1. INTRODUCTION

Keeping in view the specific requirement of the Listing Agreement, every listed company has been submitting separate report on corporate governance as part of the Annual Report. As a measure of examining the practices followed by the listed companies, an attempt has been in this chapter to survey the Corporate Governance Report of 20 companies (chosen on the basis of their market capitalization during 2014-15). The following are the companies, whose Corporate Governance Reports are examined.

S. No.	Name of the Company	Market Capitalization
1.	TCS	497,497.32
2.	Reliance	270,101.14
3.	HDFC Bank	247,665.59
4.	Coal India	213,050.97
5.	ITC	250,250.38
6.	Infosys	243,315.35
7.	ONGC	193,011.86
8.	SBI	167,326.90
9.	HDFC	180,953.46

Contd.

10.	Sun Pharma	201,363.56
11.	HUL	177,327.83
12.	ICICI Bank	144,582.08
13.	Airtel	138,849.69
14.	L & T	140,064.63
15.	Wipro	136,647.48
16.	Axis Bank	107,529.86
17.	Maruti Suzuki	122,585.60
18.	HCL Tech	129,650.21
19.	Tata Motors	109,866.76
20.	Kotak Mahindra	109,139.46

Source: www.moneycontrol.com

Basing on the above, attempt has been made to analyse the salient aspects included in the Corporate Governance Reports by the listed companies.

2. PHILOSOPHY OF COMPANIES ON CODE OF GOVERNANCE

The philosophy of companies has been expressed in the form of certain statements pertaining to the corporate ethics and culture to which they are wedded. It would be quite interesting to anlyse such statements. Narrated below are some statements that may, perhaps, reflect their philosophy towards corporate governance.

1. To oversee business strategies and ensure fiscal accountability, ethical corporate behavior and fairness to all stakeholders comprising regulators, employees, customers, vendors, investors and the society at large (TCS).
2. To encompass a set of systems and practices to ensure that the company's affairs are being managed in a manner which ensures accountability, transparency and fairness in all transactions in the widest sense. In essence, corporate governance is believed to lie in promoting and maintaining integrity, transparency and accountability in the management's higher echelons (Reliance Industries Limited).
3. The cardinal principles such as independence, accountability, responsibility, transparency, fair and timely disclosures, credibility, sustainability, etc., serve as the means for implementing the philosophy of corporate governance in letter and spirit (HDFC Bank).

4. The concept of corporate governance is meant to ensure values, ethical business conduct, transparency, disclosures as per laws, rules and guidelines (Coal of India).
5. The cornerstones of ITC's governance philosophy are trusteeship, transparency, ethical corporate citizenship, empowerment, control and accountability. ITC has defined the corporate governance as a systematic process by which companies are directed and controlled to enhance their wealth generating capacity. ITC believed that the governance process should ensure that the resources of the nation are utilized in a manner that meets stakeholder's aspirations and societal expectations (ITC Ltd.).
6. To manage the business affairs in the most fair and transparent manner with a firm commitment to values. Corporate governance is an ethically driven business process that is committed to values aimed at enhancing the organization's brand and reputation. It is the wish of the company that it always seeks to ensure that the performance is driven by integrity (Infosys).
7. The main objectives that drive corporate governance in ONGC are said to be:
    - A sound system of internal control to mitigate risks associated with achievement of business objectives, both short term and long term.
    - Compliance of laws, rules and regulations.
    - Ensuring corporate success and economic growth.
    - Minimization of wastages, corruption, risks and mismanagement.
    - Adherence to ethical standards for effective management and distribution of wealth and discharge of social responsibility for sustainable development of all stakeholders.
    - Maintains investor's confidence, as a result of which, company can raise capital efficiently and effectively.
    - Clearly defined standards against which performance and responsibilities are measured.
    - Accuracy and transparency in disclosures regarding operations, performance, risk and financial status.
    - A clear delineation of shareholders' rights.
    - Timely and balanced disclosure of all material information to all the stakeholders.
8. SBI is committed to the best practices in the area of corporate governance in letter and spirit. The objectives that were set by the Bank include:
    - Protection and enhancement of shareholder value.
    - Protection of the interest of all other stakeholders such as customers, employees and the society at large.

- Transparency and integrity in communication and to make available full, accurate and clear information to all concerned.
- Accountability for performance and customer service and to achieve excellence at all levels.
- Providing corporate leadership of the highest standard for others to emulate.

9. At HDFC, there has always been a firm commitment to promote, throughout the organization, a culture of integrity, transparency and accountability. This defines the business ethics and core values (HDFC).
10. Sun Pharma has declared to have committed to high levels of transparency, accountability, and consistent value systems. The company has stated that it would try to work for these principles in all its interactions with stakeholders, including shareholders, employees, customers, suppliers and statutory authorities.

It is evident from the above statements that almost all the companies are emphasising on certain aspects like the integrity, honesty, accountability, transparency, credibility and ethics. Every company has stated in clear terms its commitment towards stakeholders. The above discussion covers the statements of ten companies. Notwithstanding the above, distinctive statements made by the other ten companies are highlighted in a nutshell.

(i) Confidentiality of client information

(ii) Prevention of insider trading

(iii) Help to attract financial and human resources in the best possible terms and prevent corporate failure.

(iv) Corporate governance goes beyond the practices enshrined in the laws and is imbibed in the basic business ethics and values that need to be adhered to in letter and spirit.

(v) Intensity to win, acting with sensitivity and unyielding integrity are the three values encapsulated in corporate governance.

(vi) To institutionalize accountability, transparency and equality of treatment for all its stakeholders.

(vii) Where values drive velocity is the slogan of HCL.

(viii) Company's philosophy on corporate governance is founded upon a rich legacy of fair, ethical and transparent governance practices (Tata Motors); where a code of conduct was developed for implementation by group companies.

Going by their philosophical statements, there could be nothing to comment upon. But the spirit shall be evident in practice. After all, practice is more valuable than precept.

3. COMPOSITION OF BOARDS

With respect to composition of the Board, the Companies Act, 2013 has specified the following:

(a) Every company shall have a minimum number of three directors in case of a public company, two in case of private company and one in case of one person company.
(b) Maximum of 15 directors, and can have more than 15 after passing a special resolution.
(c) Certain classes of companies shall have at least one woman director.
(d) Every listed company shall have at least one-third of the total as independent directors.

In the light of the specific provisions of the Companies Act, 2013, it would be interesting to observe the following facts with respect to the composition of Boards of the select companies.

(i) The size of the Board of all the select 20 companies is well within the stipulations of the Companies Act. The Boards of the companies are fairly large and above 10 members. It is only in case of ITC, there are sixteen members on the Board. In terms of the Articles of Association of the company, the strength of the Board shall not be less than five, and not more than eighteen [see Table 17.1].
(ii) The Boards of the select companies are also fairly balanced in terms of the mix of executive, non-executive and independent directors. Yet there are some surprises. The two public sector companies, viz., ONGC and SBI have no independent directors. The reason stated is that they had written to the concerned Ministry and not yet got the names. Similarly, separate details on the number of IDs were not available in case of L & T.
(iii) One more welcome feature of the composition of the Boards is that a majority of them are dominated by the independent directors. In case of Infosys, except the two Executive Directors, all the other eight directors are IDs. Similar is the preference towards IDs by companies like HCL Tech., Wipro and HDFC. All the companies have more than one-third IDs in the Boards, except ONGC and SBI. It is only Maruti Suzuki that has exactly the one-third of the members as the Independent Directors.
(iv) All the companies have also fulfilled the condition relating to the appointment of women directors.
(v) The role of non-executive and non-independent directors is also significant. Among the select companies, SBI has more number of non-executive nominee directors; whereas Infosys has no non-executive director.

Table 17.1: Composition of Board of Directors of Select Companies as per the 2014-15 Annual Reports

S. No.	Name of the Company	Total no. of Directors	Executive Directors	Non-Executive/ Non-Independent Directors	Nominee Directors	Independent Directors
1.	TCS	11	2	3	–	6
2.	Reliance	13	5	1	–	7
3.	HDFC Bank	11	3	3	–	5
4.	Coal India	13	5	–	2	6
5.	ITC	16	4	4	–	8
6.	Infosys	10	2	–	–	8
7.	ONGC	9	6	3	–	–
8.	SBI	14	4	4	6	–
9.	HDFC	12	3	1	–	8
10.	Sun Pharma	9	3	1	–	5
11.	HUL	9	3	1	–	5
12.	ICICI Bank	14	3	6	–	5
13.	Airtel	13	3	3	–	7
14.	L & T	13	5	8 (Inclusive of IDs)	–	–
15.	Wipro	13	3	–	–	10
16.	Axis Bank	13	6	–	–	7
17.	Maruti Suzuki	12	4	4	–	4
18.	HCL Tech	10	1	2	–	7
19.	Tata Motors	11	2	3	–	6
20.	Kotak Mahindra	10	3	2	–	5

Source: Compiled from the Annual Reports of the respective companies.

3.1 Board Membership Criteria

The nomination and remuneration committee works with the entire Board to determine the appropriate characteristics, skills and experience required for the Board as a whole and for individual members. Board members are expected to possess the required qualifications, integrity, expertise and experience for the position. They should also possess deep expertise and insights in sectors/areas relevant to the company, and ability to contribute to the company's growth. Infosys had the policy not to appoint or continue the employment of any person who has attained the age of 60 years as Managing Director/Executive Director and shall not appoint any person who has attained the age of 70 years as independent director. The term of the person holding this position may be extended at the discretion of the committee beyond the age of 60 years/70 years with the approval of shareholders by passing a special resolution. Board members are expected to rigorously prepare for, attend and participate in all Board and applicable committee meetings. Each member is expected to ensure that their other current and planned future commitments do not materially interfere with their responsibilities with the company.

3.2 Familiarisation Programmes for Board Members

It is the general practice with all the companies that the Board members are provided with necessary documents/brochures, reports and internal policies to enable them to familiarise with the company's procedures and practices. Periodic presentations are made at the Board and Board Committee Meetings, on business and performance updates of the company, global business environment, business strategy and risks involved. Detailed presentations on the company's business segments are made at the separate meetings of the Independent Directors held during the year. Quarterly updates on relevant statutory changes and landmark judicial pronouncements encompassing important laws are regularly circulated to the Directors. Site visits to various plant locations are also organized for the Directors to enable them to understand the operations of the Company.

3.3 Mechanism for Evaluating Board Members

One of the key functions of the Board is to monitor and review the board evaluation framework. This is very important in view of the fact that their remuneration and other allowances depend on their contribution. Therefore, the Board works with the nomination and remuneration committee to lay down the evaluation criteria for the performance of executive/non-executive/independent directors through a peer-evaluation excluding the director being evaluated through a Board effectiveness survey. Companies are collecting information through a structured questionnaire for reviewing the functioning and effectiveness of the Board and for identifying possible paths for improvement. Each Board member is requested to evaluate the effectiveness of the Board dynamics and relationships, information flow, decision-making of the directors, relationship to stakeholders, company's performance, company's strategy, and the effectiveness of the whole Board and its various committees on a scale of one to five. Feedback on each director is encouraged to be provided as part of the survey.

Independent directors are primarily evaluated on three key roles, viz., governance, control and guidance. Some of the performance indicators based on which the independent directors are evaluated include:

- Ability to contribute and monitor corporate governance practices.
- Ability to contribute to international best practices to address top-management issues.
- Active participation in long-term strategic planning.
- Commitment to the fulfillment of a director's obligations and fiduciary responsibilities. These may include participation at the Board and other committee meetings.

4. MEETINGS OF THE BOARD

It is a fact that Board is the apex body chosen by shareholders for overseeing the company's overall functioning. The Board provides and evaluates the company's strategic direction, management policies and their effectiveness. It also ensures that the shareholders long term interests are adequately served. Since Board is the agency to lead the company, it shall meet as many times as possible. All the selected companies have fulfilled the norms in respect of meetings to be held by the Board. While companies like ICICI Bank, Airtel, Wipro held just 4 meetings a year, others like ONGC and SBI conducted the highest number of Board meetings. Further, the attendance of the members at the meetings is also impressive, except in case of Infosys (see Table 17.2).

What would be still more interesting is the aspect pertaining to the items/matters that would come for discussion at the meetings. The following is the illustrative list of items slated for discussion at the meetings:

- Annual operating plans of businesses and budgets including capital budgets and any updates
- Quarterly results of the company and its operating divisions or business segments
- Company's annual Financial Results, Financial Statements, Auditors' Report and Board's Report
- Minutes of meetings of the Audit Committee and other committees of the Board
- Show cause, demand, prosecution notices and penalty notices, which are materially important
- Fatal or serious accidents, dangerous occurrences, and any material effluent or pollution problems

Table 17.2: Details Regarding Number of Meetings held by the Board of Directors During 2014-15

S. No.	Name of the Company	No. of Meetings held	% of Attendance by Directors (Average)
1.	TCS	7	94
2.	Reliance	7	96
3.	HDFC Bank	10	90
4.	Coal India	10	87
5.	ITC	7	84.46
6.	Infosys	9	47
7.	ONGC	13	68
8.	SBI	12	74
9.	HDFC	5	87.14
10.	Sun Pharma	5	95
11.	HUL	8	NA
12.	ICICI Bank	4	88.33
13.	Airtel	4	69
14.	L & T	10	90
15.	Wipro	4	NA
16.	Axis Bank	7	83.13
17.	Maruti Suzuki	6	81
18.	HCL Tech	7	74
19.	Tata Motors	10	80
20.	Kotak Mahindra	10	84

Source: Compiled from the Annual Reports of the respective companies.
NA = Not Available.

- Any material default in financial obligations to and by the company, or substantial non-payment for goods sold by the company
- Any issue, which involves possible public or product liability claims of substantial nature, including any judgment or order, which may have passed strictures on the conduct of the company or taken an adverse view regarding another enterprise that can have negative implications on the company

- Details of any joint venture or collaboration agreement
- Transactions that involve substantial payment towards goodwill, brand equity or intellectual property
- Significant labour problems and their proposed solutions. Any significant development in Human Resources/Industrial Relations front like implementation of voluntary retirement scheme, etc.
- Sale of material nature of investments, subsidiaries, assets, which is not in normal course of business.
- Quarterly details of foreign exchange exposures, and steps taken by management to limit risks of adverse exchange rate movement, if material
- Non-compliance of any regulatory, statutory or listing requirements, and shareholders' service, such as dividend non-payment, share transfer delay (if any), among others
- Appointment, remuneration and resignation of Directors
- Formation/reconstitution of Board Committees
- Terms of reference of Board Committees
- Minutes of Board meetings of unlisted subsidiary companies
- Declaration of Independent Directors at the time of appointment/annually
- Disclosure of Directors' interest and their shareholding
- Appointment or removal of the Key Managerial Personnel
- Appointment of Internal Auditors and Secretarial Auditors
- Quarterly/Annual Secretarial Audit reports submitted by Secretarial Auditors
- Dividend declaration
- Quarterly summary of all long-term borrowings made, bank guarantees issued and loans and investments made
- Significant changes in accounting policies and internal controls
- Takeover of a company or acquisition of a controlling or substantial stake in another company
- Statement of significant transactions, related party transactions and arrangements entered by unlisted subsidiary companies
- Issue of securities including debentures
- Recommending appointment of and fixing of remuneration of the Auditors as recommended by the Audit Committee
- Internal Audit findings and External Audit Reports (through the Audit Committee)
- Proposals for major investments, mergers, amalgamations and reconstructions
- Status of business risk exposures, its management and related action plans
- Making of loans and investment of surplus funds

- Borrowing of monies, giving guarantees or providing security in respect of loans
- Buyback of securities by the company
- Diversify the business of the company
- Brief on statutory developments, changes in government policies, among others with impact thereof, Directors' responsibilities arising out of any such developments
- Compliance Certificate certifying compliance with all laws as applicable to the Company
- Reconciliation of Share Capital Audit Report under SEBI (Depositories and Participants) Regulations, 1996
- Brief on information disseminated to the press

5. CONSTITUTION OF VARIOUS COMMITTEES

As per the New Companies Act, 2013 every listed company is required to constitute the following three committees:

1. Audit Committee (Section 177)
2. Nominations and Remunerations Committee (Section 178)
3. Stakeholders Relationship Committee (Section 178)

It is evident from the discussion made in the foregoing pages that every company surveyed is complying with the conditions. In addition, the select companies are also constituting a variety of committees for dealing the specific issues; for instance, TCS constituted the following committee for the year 2014-15.

(i) Bank account committee to oversee the opening and closing of Bank Accounts and to authorize persons to operate such accounts.

(ii) Executive Committee to undertake a detailed review of the matters before they are presented to the Board:
- Business and Strategy Review;
- Long term financial projections and cash flows;
- Capital and Revenue Budgets and Capital Expenditure Programmes;
- Acquisitions, Divestments and business restructuring proposals;
- Senior management succession planning; and
- Any other item as may be decided by the Board.

(iii) Software Technology Parks of India/Special Economic Zones Committee responsible for approval, registration, renewal, etc.

(iv) Risk Management Committee to frame, implement and monitor risk management plan for the company.

(v) Health, Safety and Sustainability Committee to look into these aspects.

(vi) Corporate Social Responsibility (CSR) Committee having the following terms of reference:

- formulate and recommend to the board, a corporate social responsibility (CSR) policy;
- recommend the amount of expenditure to be incurred on the activities referred to above;
- monitor the CSR policy of the company from time to time;
- oversee the company's conduct with regard to its corporate and societal obligations and its reputation as a responsible corporate citizen; and
- oversee activities impacting the quality of life of various stakeholders.

The above narration gives an idea as to different committees constituted by the companies. An attempt has been to locate the effort of the companies to constitute special purpose committees, over and above the compliance requirements. Our survey has revealed the fact that the select companies are going beyond their statutory obligation. The following is the list of some important committees constituted by the corporate world, as a measure of improving upon the governance. Repetition is avoided in the listing.

(a) Credit Approval Committee (HDFC Bank).

(b) Premises Committee (HDFC Bank).

(c) Fraud Monitoring Committee (HDFC Bank).

(d) Customer Service Committee (HDFC Bank).

(e) Review Committee for Willful Defaulters' Identification (HDFC Bank).

(f) Review Committee for Non-Cooperative Borrowers (HDFC Bank).

(g) Foreign Acquisition Committee (Coal India).

(h) Review of Treasury Management Committee (Coal India).

(i) Convergence to IFRS Committee (Coal India).

(j) Human Resource Management Committee (Coal India).

(k) Independent Directors Committee (ITC).

(l) Committee on Dispute Resolution (ONGC).

(m) Research and Development Committee (ONGC).

(n) I.T. Strategy Committee of the Board (ONGC).

(o) Committee for Allotment of Shares under ESOPs (HUL).

(p) Compliance Committee (Wipro).

(q) Committee of Whole-time Directors (Axis Bank).

(r) Special Committee of the Board for Monitoring of Large Value Frauds (Axis Bank).

It is evident from the above that there is lot of vibrancy in managing the affairs of the companies. Corporates are receptive to the new ideas. The survey has made one thing very clear that statutory stipulations and the clauses in the listing agreement have brought about phenomenal change in corporate reporting. Some of the reports of the companies on the corporate governance are so comprehensive that they volunteered to share the information to the maximum extent possible. This is to be viewed as a commitment on the part of the corporates from their side. In one sense, we may understand that the entire annual report is an attempt in sharing every detail about the operations of the company. The Annual Reports of some of the companies are so voluminous that they span to about 400 pages.

6. FUNCTIONING OF THE AUDIT COMMITTEE

As per the existing requirements under section 177 of the Companies Act, 2013 and clause 49 of the Listing Agreement of BSE, every listed company is required to constitute an Audit Committee with a minimum of three Directors , for which, the Chairman of the Committee shall be the independent director. While some of the companies like Infosys, whose shares were quoted outside India at the New York Stock Exchange (NYSE), NYSE Euronext, Paris, and the NYSE Euronext London Stock Exchange, are also following the stipulations of the concerned Exchange. For example, the Blue Ribbon Committee set up by the US SEC recommended that every listed company adopt an audit committee charter. This recommendation being adopted by the NYSE, becomes mandatory for all those companies quoted on the Exchange.

The primary objective of the committee is to monitor and provide an effective supervision of the Management's financial reporting process, and to ensure accurate and timely disclosures. While doing so, it is the responsibility of the committee to maintain the highest levels of transparency, integrity and quality of financial reporting. As part of its duties, the committee oversees the work carried out by the Management in the financial reporting process and work of the internal auditors. It is also required to examine the independent auditors, and notes the processes and safeguards employed by each of them. The committee has the ultimate authority and responsibility to select, evaluate and, where appropriate, replace the independent auditors in accordance with the law. All possible measures must be taken by the committee to ensure objectivity and independence of the independent auditors. The terms of reference usually entrusted to the audit committee included the following:

- Oversight of the company's financial reporting process and the disclosure of its financial information to ensure that the financial statement is correct, sufficient and credible;
- Recommend the appointment, remuneration and terms of appointment of auditors of the company;
- Approval of payment to statutory auditors for any other services rendered by the statutory auditors;
- Reviewing along with the management, Quarterly and Annual financial statements and auditors' report thereon before submission to the Board for approval, with particular reference to:
    - ➢ Matters required being included in the director's responsibility statement
    - ➢ Changes, if any, in accounting policies and practices and reasons for the same
    - ➢ Major accounting entries involving estimates based on the exercise of judgment by management
    - ➢ Significant adjustments made in the financial statements arising out of audit findings
    - ➢ Compliance with listing and other legal requirements relating to financial statements
    - ➢ Disclosure of any related party transactions
    - ➢ Qualifications in the draft audit report
- Reviewing, the position on the case of funds raised through an issue; and also to verify and report on the purposes other than those stated in the offer document. The report submitted by the monitoring agency must also make a statement on the utilisation of proceeds of a public or rights issue, and making appropriate recommendations to the Board to take up steps in this matter depending on the situation;
- Review and monitor the auditors' independence, performance, and effectiveness of audit process;
- Approval or any subsequent modification of transactions of the company with related parties;
- Scrutiny of inter-corporate loans and investments;
- Valuation of undertakings or assets of the company, wherever it is necessary;
- Evaluation of internal financial controls and risk management systems;
- Reviewing, with the management, performance of statutory and internal auditors, and examine the adequacy of the internal control systems;
- Reviewing the adequacy of internal audit function, if any, including the structure of the internal audit department in terms of structure, coverage and frequency of internal audit;

- Discussion with internal auditors of any significant findings and follow up there on;
- Reviewing the findings of any internal investigations by the internal auditors into matters of fraud or irregularity or a failure of internal control systems of a material nature and reporting the matter to the board;
- Discussion with statutory auditors before the audit commences, about the nature and scope of audit as well as post-audit discussion to ascertain any area of concern;
- To look into the reasons for substantial defaults in the payment to the depositors, debenture holders, shareholders and creditors;
- Establish a vigil mechanism for directors and employees to report genuine concerns;
- To review the functioning of whistle blower mechanism.
- Approval of appointment of CFO;
- The audit committee may call for the comments of the auditors about internal control systems, the scope of audit, including the observations of the auditors. It is also the duty of the Audit Committee to review financial statements before their submission to the Board. The same may be discussed with the internal and statutory auditors and the management of the company;
- Carrying out any other function as is mentioned in the terms of reference of the audit committee;
- Oversee financial reporting controls and process for material subsidiaries;
- The Audit Committee is also mandatorily required to review the following information:
  - Management discussion and analysis of financial condition and results of operations;
  - Statement of significant related party transactions (as defined by the audit committee), submitted by management;
  - Management letters/letters of internal control weaknesses issued by the statutory auditors;
  - Internal audit reports relating to internal control weaknesses; and
  - The appointment, removal and terms of remuneration of the chief internal auditor.

The above list of functions appears to be exhaustive. Such a detail is expected to help closer monitoring of the financial affairs of the company. As is evident from the information contained in Table 17.3, there are a good number of meetings held to discuss all the matters of importance from time to time by the companies surveyed by us.

Table 17.3: Composition of Audit Committee of the select companies for the Financial Year 2014-15

S. No.	Name of the Company	Total No. of Members	Independent Members	Non-Independent		Total No. of Meetings Held
				Non-Executive	Executive	
1.	TCS	6	5	1	–	5
2.	Reliance	3	3	–	–	9
3.	HDFC Bank	4	4	–	–	8
4.	Coal India	7	4	3	–	10
5.	ITC	5	4	1	–	8
6.	Infosys	4	4	–	–	4
7.	ONGC	7	–	6	–	13
8.	SBI	8	–	4	4	11
9.	HDFC	3	3	–	–	6
10.	Sun Pharma	4	4	4	–	4
11.	HUL	5	5	–	–	6
12.	ICICI Bank	5	3	1	–	6
13.	Airtel	5	4	1	–	4
14.	L & T	3	3	–	–	9
15.	Wipro	4	4	–	–	6
16.	Axis Bank	4	3	–	1	11
17.	Maruti Suzuki	4	3	–	1	7
18.	HCL Tech	4	4	–	–	8
19.	Tata Motors	4	4	–	–	10
20.	Kotak Mahindra	3	2	1	–	10

Source: Compiled from the Annual Reports of the respective companies.

7. FUNCTIONING OF THE NOMINATION AND REMUNERATION COMMITTEE

Prior to the amendment of clause 49 of the Listing Agreement, companies had committees with diverse nomenclature like Human Resources Committee, Compensation

Committee, etc., to look into the issue of executive compensation. After the amendment, specific titles are given to the committees that are required to look into the aspect of directors remuneration. The major purpose of this committee is to oversee the nomination process for the top level management and the executive remunerative structure. The committee identifies, screens and reviews individuals qualified to serve as executive directors, non-executive directors and independent directors consistent with the criteria approved by the Board and recommends for approval by the Board. It also designs and continuously reviews the compensation program for CEO and senior executives against the achievement of measurable performance. It is also necessary that the compensation so fixed must be competitive in the industry in order to attract and retain the best talent.

The committee makes recommendations to the Board on candidates for (i) nomination for election or re-election by the shareholders; and (ii) any Board vacancies that are to be filled. The committee may act on its own in identifying potential candidates, inside or outside the company. It may also act upon proposals submitted by the Chairman of the Board. The committee shall annually review and approve for the positions of CEO and MD, the executive directors and executive officers. The compensation package may include: (a) annual base salary; (b) annual incentive bonus, including the specific goals and amount; (c) equity compensation; (d) employment agreements, and severance arrangements; and (e) any other benefits, compensation or arrangements.

The basic duties of the Nomination and Remuneration Committee shall relate to the following:

- to identify persons who are qualified to become Directors and who may be appointed in senior management in accordance with the criteria laid down by the Board;
- to carry out evaluation of every Director's performance; To formulate the criteria for determining qualifications, positive attributes and independence of a Director, and recommend to the Board a policy, relating to the remuneration for the Directors, key managerial personnel and other employees;
- to formulate the criteria for evaluation of Independent Directors and the policy on Board diversity;
- to recommend remuneration of the Managing Director(s) and Whole-time Director (s) based on their performance and defined assessment criteria;
- to administer, monitor and formulate detailed terms and conditions of the Employees' Stock Option Scheme including:
    - ➢ the quantum of options to be granted under Employees' Stock Option Scheme per employee and in aggregate;
    - ➢ the conditions under which option vested in employees may lapse in case of termination of employment for misconduct;

- ➢ the exercise period within which the employee should exercise the option, and that the option would lapse on failure to exercise the option within the exercise period;
- ➢ the specified time period within which the employee shall exercise the vested options in the event of termination or resignation of an employee;
- ➢ the right of an employee to exercise all options vested in him at one time or various points of time within the exercise period;
- ➢ the procedure for making a fair and reasonable adjustment to the number of options and to the exercise price in case of corporate actions, such as rights issues, bonus issues, merger, sale of division and others;
- ➢ the granting, vesting and exercising of options in case of employees who are on long leave; and
- ➢ the procedure for cashless exercise of options.

- to carry out any other function as is mandated by the Board from time to time.

In view of the significance attached to this committee, there arose a need to frame a broad structure of constitution of members to the committee, which include executive and non-executive directors (see Table 17.4). An interesting aspect of the constitution is that while some companies are taking independent directors into confidence in this regard, others are found limiting the role of IDs. It may be inferred that the very constitution of the committee reflects the philosophy of the company towards Board constitution and remuneration. One deviation, we could identify is the one pertaining to the public sector companies. Their remuneration policy is guided by the pay structure of the Central Government.

In order to get an idea of the remuneration paid by the corporate world to their managers, attempt has been made to compile (as a case study) information pertaining to the amounts paid to the Chief Executive (may be called Chief Executive Officer or Chairman and Managing Director) during the year 2014-15. This information is provided in Table 17.5. As can be seen from the table, there are wide variations in the payment of remuneration to the CEO. While the least remuneration is paid by the public sector companies like SBI and ONGC, the highest remuneration was drawn by the CEO of L & T (an amount of Rs. 28.41 crore). Companies like Airtel, Reliance, ITC and HCL are in the forefront. Though there has been a provision also to compensate the directors via stock options, only three of the twenty companies (HDFC, ITC and Infosys) utilized this route. Moreover, the amounts paid to the CEOs pertains to the present company and it does not include the remuneration and stock options received by them from their Group Companies.

It may also be noted that this divergence could be seen in the payment of sitting allowance for attending the meetings. While SBI has the policy of paying just Rs. 10,000 for each Board meeting and Rs. 5000 for other Board level Committees; RIL pays about a lakh rupees per each sitting.

Table 17.4: Composition of Nomination and Remuneration Committee of the select companies for the Financial Year 2014-15

S. No.	Name of the Company	Total No. of Members	Independent Members	Non-Independent		Total No. of Meetings Held
				Non-Executive	Executive	
1.	TCS	5	2	3	–	4
2.	Reliance	4	4	–	–	6
3.	HDFC Bank	4	4	–	–	3
4.	Coal India	President of India	–	–	–	Nil
5.	ITC	6	4	2	–	7
6.	Infosys	5	5	–	–	3
7.	ONGC	7	6	6	1	1
8.	SBI	4	–	2	2	–
9.	HDFC	3	3	–	–	3
10.	Sun Pharma	Not formed this committee upto 31.03.2014				
11.	HUL	5	3	1	1	5
12.	ICICI Bank	5	3	2	–	5
13.	Airtel	5	3	2	–	5
14.	L & T	4	–	3	1	7
15.	Wipro	2	2	–	–	4
16.	Axis Bank	4	3	–	1	4
17.	Maruti Suzuki	4	2	2	–	1
18.	HCL Tech	5	4	–	1	5
19.	Tata Motors	4	3	1	–	4
20.	Kotak Mahindra	3	2	1	–	4

Source: Compiled from the Annual Reports of the respective companies.

Table 17.5: Remuneration paid to CMB/CEO of select companies during 2014-15

(Rs. Crore)

S. No.	Name of the Company	Salary	Perquisites and Allowances	Retiral Benefits	Commission	Performance linked Incentive	Total	As % of Total Paid to all Directors
1.	TCS	1.80	3.49	–	16.00	–	–	Nil
2.	Reliance	4.16	0.60	0.83	9.41	–	15.00	Nil
3.	HDFC Bank	2.73	1.82	0.74	–	2.10	7.39	5.20 (lakh)
4.	Coal India	0.18	0.10	–	–	0.28	–	21.39
5.	ITC	4.32	0.89	–	8.64	–	13.85	2.70 (lakh)
6.	Infosys	4.41	–	0.15	–	–	4.56	0.54 (lakh)
7.	ONGC	0.21	0.01	0.37	–	0.02	0.61	–
8.	SBI	0.20	0.04	–	–	–	0.24	–
9.	HDFC	1.60	1.72	–	4.46	–	7.78	–
10.	Sun Pharma	1.92	0.42	0.38	–	–	2.72	–
11.	HUL	6.29	4.69	0.02	0.27	2.92	14.17	–
12.	ICICI Bank							–
13.	Airtel	9.58	0.50	–	–	14.25	24.33	–
14.	L & T	2.88	0.26	5.98	19.29	–	28.41	–
15.	Wipro	0.30	0.13	1.60	7.02	1.18	10.23	–
16.	Axis Bank	2.22	–	1.99	–	–	4.21	–
17.	Maruti Suzuki	2.33	–	–	–	1.02	3.35	–
18.	HCL Tech	1.80	10.05	0.22	–	–	12.07	–
19.	Tata Motors				–			–
20.	Kotak Mahindra	1.53	0.25	0.18	–	0.50	2.46	–

Source: Compiled from the Annual Reports of the respective companies.

Note: The amount shown above is exclusive of the remuneration received by them for acting as the Director/Chairman for other Group Companies.

8. FUNCTIONING OF THE STAKEHOLDERS RELATIONSHIP COMMITTEE

This Committee is meant to establish rapport with the shareholders and others interested in the welfare of the company. Hitherto, there were many such Committees with different names like the Investor Grievance committee, Shareholders Communications Committee, etc. Usually, this committee's job is to approve and monitor transfer, transmission, splitting and consolidation of shares and entertain requests for dematerilisation of shares. Allotment of shares to the employees under stock option scheme are also taken care of by the committee. Not the least, the committee's duty is also to redress the complaints of shareholders on various matters. The list of specific functions may include:

- consider and resolve the grievances of shareholders of the company with respect to transfer of shares, non-receipt of annual report, non-receipt of declared dividend, etc;
- ensure expeditious share transfer process in line with the proceedings of the Share Transfer Committee;
- evaluate performance and service standards of the Registrar and Share Transfer Agent of the Company;
- provide guidance and make recommendations to improve investor service levels for the investors.

As per the details available in Table 17.6, there is a balanced composition of executive and non-executive directors. Nevertheless, there is wide variance in the number of meetings held by the committee from a single meeting to that of 28 in a year. This speaks of the divergence in the kind of interest taken by the companies and the dynamic relationship established between the companies and the stakeholders.

Table 17.6: Composition of shareholders relationship committee of the select companies for the Financial Year 2014-15

S. No.	Name of the Company	Total no. of Members	Independent Members	Non-Independent		Total no. of Meetings Held
				Non-Executive	Executive	
1.	TCS	3	2	3	1	1
2.	Reliance	4	2	–	2	4
3.	HDFC Bank	4	2	2	–	5
4.	Coal India	4	2	2	–	4

Contd.

5.	ITC	4	–	2	2	28
6.	Infosys	3	3	–	–	4
7.	ONGC	7	–	5	2	3
8.	SBI	8	–	6	2	4
9.	HDFC	3	2	–	1	4
10.	Sun Pharma	4	2	–	2	5
11.	HUL	3	2	1	–	1
12.	ICICI Bank	3	1	2	–	1
13.	Airtel	3	–	1	2	7
14.	L & T	3	–	1	2	4
15.	Wipro	3	1	–	2	7
16.	Axis Bank	4	2	–	2	4
17.	Maruti Suzuki	3	1	1	1	1
18.	HCL Tech	3	–	2	1	6
19.	Tata Motors	2	2	–	–	1
20.	Kotak Mahindra	4	1	–	3	2

Source: Compiled from the Annual Reports of the respective companies.

9. SHAREHOLDING PATTERN AMONG THE SELECT COMPANIES

This has been the subject of discussion in the corporate world for a long time. Who owns the company is a crucial question. In the context of Joint Stock Companies being widely held, it will always be interesting to know, who owns them and who manages them. The 'Agency Problem' also is the reflection of the shareholding. Because of separation of ownership from the management, owners are expected to maintain constant vigil on the operations of the company, as a measure of protecting their interests. Further, in order to encourage the managers to work for the company, suitable compensation and incentives are to be provided. Shareholding remains to be an issue as long as the contribution of promoters is meagre.

It is in this context, attempt has been made to compile the details on the shareholding pattern of the select companies to deduce certain conclusions as to the prevailing situation. As can be seen from the data given in Table 17.7, the promoters of the

Table 17.7: Shareholding pattern of select companies as on 31-03-2015

(in per cent)

S. No.	Category	TCS	RIL	HDFC Bank	Coal India (31-3-2014)	ITC	Infosys	ONGC	SBI	HDFC	Sun Pharma (31-3-2014)
1.	Promoter Group	73.89	45.24	21.67	89.65	–	13.08	68.94	58.60	–	63.65
1.a.	Indian Promoters	73.69	45.24	–	–	–	13.08	68.94	58.60	–	63.65
1.b.	Foreign Promoters	–	–	–	–	–	–	–	–	–	–
1.c.	Other entities	0.20	–	–	–	–	–	–	–	–	–
2.	Insurance Companies	3.77	–	2.76	–	21.77	9.74	–	–	7.47	–
3.	Indian Public and Others	3.90	3.23	8.23	1.37	10.56	26.37	1.79	6.00	9.75	5.25
4.	Mutual Fund and UTI	0.88	20.15**	–	0.74	1.68	5.29	0.92	5.34	2.41	1.21
5.	Corporate Bodies	0.45	–	8.63	0.68	3.29	0.81	11.63	2.77	2.47	2.53
6.	Banks, Financial Institutions, State and Central Government	0.05	31.38*	6.96	2.19	11.31	0.06	9.49	13.13	1.80	4.28
7.	Foreign Institutional Investors	14.94	–	32.57	5.34	16.74	37.96	7.18	14.16	75.71	22.51
8.	Foreign Portfolio Investor – CORP	2.01	–	0.29	–	34.10	5.15	–	–	0.21	–
9.	NRI's/OCBs/Foreign Nationals	0.11	–	18.87	0.03	0.55	1.53	0.05	–	0.18	0.57
	Grand Total	**100.00**	**100.00**	**100.00**	**100.00**	**100.00**	**100.00**	**100.00**	**100.00**	**100.00**	**100.00**

* All Institutions put together.

** All Non-Institutions put together.

Contd.

S. No.	Category	Name of the Company									
		HUL	ICICI	Airtel	L & T	Wipro	Axis Bank	Maruti Suzuki	HCL	Tata Motors	Kotak Mahindra
1.	Promoter Group	67.23	–	68.55	–	73.47	–	–	61.64	29.27	40.02
1.a.	Indian Promoters	67.23	–	45.75	–	50.93	–	–	61.64	29.21	39.98
1.b.	Foreign Promoters	–	–	22.80	–	–	–	–	–	–	–
1.c.	Other entities	–	–	–	–	22.54		–	–	0.06	0.04
2.	Insurance Companies	3.39	–	5.34	4.59	1.60	6.12	–	1.22	7.45	–
3.	Indian Public and Others	12.32	–	1.53	33.51	7.94	6.77	2.30	2.81	24.92	10.72
4.	Mutual Fund and UTI	0.40	–	3.19	5.85	1.63	6.56	7.39	2.47	5.72	1.65
5.	Corporate Bodies	1.13	–	4.01	8.03	3.94	1.43	61.11	2.05	0.55	3.30
6.	Banks, Financial Institutions, State and Central Government	0.11	100	0.06	25.65	0.25	27.99	7.30	0.05	0.18	0.21
7.	Foreign Institutional Investors	15.01	–	17.24	16.80	10.13	46.64	21.79	28.85	28.34	36.85
8.	Foreign Portfolio Investor – CORP	0.05	–	–	2.41	–	–	–	0.55	3.19	6.85
9.	NRI's/OCBs/Foreign Nationals	0.36	–	0.08	3.16	1.04	4.49	0.11	0.36	0.38	0.40
	Grand Total	**100.00**	**100.00**	**100.00**	**100.00**	**100.00**	**100.00**	**100.00**	**100.00**	**100.00**	**100.00**

Source: Compiled from the Annual Reports of the respective companies

Table 17.8: Distribution of shareholding according to Size

(in per cent)

S. No.	Name of the Company	No. of Holders					
		1 to 500		501 to 1000		1001 to 5000	
		% in holding	% in Value	% in holding	% in Value	% in holding	% in Value
1.	TCS	96.98	1.90	1.65	0.37	1.05	0.66
2.	RIL	95.68	5.64	2.53	1.55	1.56	2.54
3.	HDFC Bank	–	–	–	–	98.67	4.70
4.	Coal India Limited	–	–	–	–	99.79	1.23
5.	ITC	–	–	–	–	93.21	1.64
6.	Infosys	95.28	1.78	1.61	0.46	1.94	1.64
7.	ONGC	90.14	0.67	4.68	0.22	4.66	0.67
8.	SBI	NA	NA	NA	NA	NA	NA
9.	HDFC	0.81	NA	0.99	NA	3.60	NA
10.	Sun Pharma	–	–	–	–	95.98	1.58
11.	HUL	–	–	–	–	96.17	6.51
12.	ICICI	NA	NA	NA	NA	NA	NA
13.	Airtel	–	–	–	–	97.69	0.71
14.	L & T	91.06	7.17	4.83	3.06	3.43	6.08
15.	Wipro (31.3.2014)	–	–	–	–	97.77	0.92
16.	Axis Bank	–	–	–	–	97.46	2.51
17.	Maruti Suzuki	–	–	–	–	98.57	1.81
18.	HCL	93.89	0.74	1.81	0.17	2.32	0.73
19.	Tata Motors	82.59	1.21	7.06	0.71	8.57	2.47
20.	Kotak Mahinda	79.50	0.64	6.91	0.55	11.48	2.47

Source: Compiled from the Annual Reports of the respective companies.

companies held more than 75 per cent. Analysed individually, the Government of India enterprise (Coal India) has the highest shareholding as the promoter, i.e., the Government of India. Similarly, ONGC also had considerable shareholding to the extent of 68.94 per cent. In contrast, the shareholding of the Government of India in SBI is only 58.60 per cent. Among the private companies, TCS had the highest promoters contribution of 73.89 per cent, followed by Wipro (73.47), Airtel (68.55) and HUL (67.23). Next to promoters, Foreign Institutional Investors (FIIs) have significant holding. The interesting observation is that their share had been the highest at 46.64 in Axis Bank, and 36.85 in Kotak Mahindra. It is usually presumed that banks, financial institutions and Mutual Funds are the substantial investors in companies. The data have shown that this is not true. Another significant fact is that the share of the Indian public is considerable only in 3 out of 19 companies for which information is available. In a majority of the cases, the shareholding of the public is less than 10 per cent; implying that the Indian Corporate Sector is not that widely held. Even considering all the indirect investments through mutual funds, other financial institutions also, their share is less significant.

In continuation of this discussion, attempt has been made to analyse size, i.e., percentage of holding by the small shareholders in terms of their value. These details are given in Table-8. As can be seen from the data given in the table, small shareholders are in a large number, almost above 95 per cent as far as the number of accounts are concerned. But their command on the capital is too limited. In terms of value, their share is less than 5 per cent. This speaks of the insignificant 'say' they would have on the affairs of the company; that too being widely scattered.

10. COMPLIANCE WITH VOLUNTARY CORPORATE GOVERNANCE GUIDELINES OF MINISTRY OF CORPORATE AFFAIRS

In order to improve upon the governance practices and make companies adopt the same on a voluntary basis, the Ministry of Corporate Affairs (MCA), Government of India has published the Corporate Governance Voluntary Guidelines in 2009. These guidelines are in the nature of encouraging companies for the adoption of better practices on voluntary basis; which not only serve as a benchmark for the corporate sector, but also help them in achieving the highest standards of corporate governance. It is also hoped that the adoption of these guidelines will also translate into a much higher level of stakeholders' confidence; which is crucial to ensure the long-term sustainability of the businesses. The focus of these guidelines is on the following important aspects:

(i) issues of formal letters of appointment to Non-Executive Directors and Independent Directors, as is done by them in case of Executive Directors;

(ii) clear demarcation of the roles and responsibilities of the Chairman of the Board and that of the Managing Director/Chief Executive Officer;

(iii) companies to have a Nomination Committee comprising of majority of Independent Directors, including its Chairman;

(iv) independent Directors to have the option and freedom to meet the company management periodically;

(v) to ensure that the level and composition of remuneration of directors is reasonable and sufficient to attract, retain and motivate directors of the quality required to run the company successfully;

(vi) the performance related elements of remuneration should form a significant proportion of the total remuneration package of Executive Directors;

(vii) independent Directors should be paid adequate sitting fees which may depend upon the twin criteria of net worth and turnover of companies. They may not be allowed to be paid stock options or profit based commissions, so that their independence is not compromised;

(viii) the companies should have at least a three member Audit Committee, with Independent Directors constituting the majority. The Chairman of such Committee be the Independent Director.

(ix) the Audit Committee of the Board should be the first point of reference regarding the appointment of auditors;

(x) every company should obtain a certificate from the auditor certifying his/its independence and arm's length relationship with the client company;

(xi) the companies should ensure the institution of mechanism for employees to report concerns about unethical behavior, actual or suspected fraud or violation of the company's code of conduct of ethics policy; and

(xii) the companies should also provide for adequate safeguards against victimisation of employees, who avail of the mechanism and also allow direct access to the Chairperson of the Audit Committee in exemption cases.

As a matter of fact, many of these matters have got included as clauses in the New Companies Act, 2013 and as items under the Listing Agreement. Therefore, what was said to be optional hitherto, has become almost mandatory.

11. WHISTLE BLOWER POLICY OF THE COMPANIES

One of the significant aspects of the Voluntary Guidelines of the Ministry of Corporate Affairs is the institution of a mechanism by the listed companies to encourage employees to become whistle blowers to bring to the notice of the company any unethical, suspected, fraudulent practices to the notice of the competent authority identified by the company in this regard. This practice is expected to keep a constant vigil on the wrong doers in the company. In fact, this clause was made mandatory by the BSE as a part of the Listing

Agreement later under Clause-49. This was later included as Clause (9) of section 177; whereby every listed company shall establish a 'vigil mechanism' for directors and employees to report genuine concerns in such manner as may be prescribed, under clause (10) of section 177. It shall be the duty of the company to provide for adequate safeguards against victimisation of persons, who use such mechanism and make provision for direct access to the Chairperson of the Audit Committee in appropriate or exceptional cases. Further, such details are also required to be kept on the website of the company and in the Board's report. This can be considered an important step in containing corporate frauds, even in a limited measure.

In this context, it would be interesting to review what kind of Whistle Blower Policy, the select companies have framed and implementing. Following is the summary of salient aspects of the policy.

(i) All the companies have put in place a mechanism for reporting illegal or unethical behavior.

(ii) Some companies have constituted Ethical and Compliance Task Forces which operate under the supervision of the Audit Committees.

(iii) Employees were also encouraged to report to the Chairman of the Audit Committee.

(iv) Some companies are also hosting the 'Whistle Blower Policy' on their websites and thus available even to the public.

(v) In case of Government Companies, there are Vigilance Departments headed by an officer, generally on deputation, from the Government of India in the rank of a Joint Secretary or above.

(vi) In a majority of the cases, select companies have formulated a broad policy in the name of 'Code of Ethics/Code of Business Principles', to reflect their value systems. Thus, Ethics is seen in the larger context. The statement of Hindustan Unilever Limited (HUL) in this regard is quite impressive to be quoted thus: "The code reflects the company's commitment to principles of integrity, transparency and fairness. It forms the benchmark against which the world at large is invited to judge the company's activities" (Annual Report of the Company, 2014-15, p. 75).

12. CONCLUSION

The following are the broad conclusions that can be arrived at from the survey:

1. Following the norms in vogue, all the companies under survey have prepared detailed reports on the compliance status of the Corporate Governance practices.
2. The companies have declared in clear terms their philosophy of Ethics and governance as far as their business operations are concerned.

3. The size and composition of the Boards was well within the stipulation of the Companies Act. And there is also a fairly balanced structure followed in constituting the Boards with Executive, Non-Executive and Independent Directors.
4. It is appreciable that the companies are oganising orientation/familiarization programmes for the incoming members of the Board. In a few cases suitable mechanisms were also devised for assessing the performance of the directors.
5. The Agenda for discussion at the Board Meetings is quite exhaustive and covers all the important aspects of the companies' operations.
6. It is also laudable that there had been voluntary compliance over and above the statutory provisions as evidenced by the constitution of various committees and in terms of sharing of information/disclosures.
7. There are wide variations in the payment of remuneration to the CEO of the company. While the least remuneration is paid to the CEOs of public sector companies, the highest amounts are drawn by their counterparts in private companies.
8. Though public limited companies are said to be widely held, it is true only to the extent of number of shareholders; and significantly not in terms of their voting power.
9. In a majority of the cases, select companies have formulated a broad policy in the name of 'code of Ethics/code of Business Principles, so as to reflect their value systems.

18
CHAPTER

Corporate Social Responsibility: Meaning and Scope

1. INTRODUCTION

When it comes to the question of Corporate Social Responsibility (CSR), there are two contradictory points of view. One, negating the very proposition that business has something to do with the society. Nuances of this argument can be found in the discussions of Adam Smith and Milton Friedman. The seminal works of Adam Smith that have a major connection with the concept of CSR are: The "Theory of Moral Sentiments" (1759) and "Lectures in Jurisprudence" (1762). Adam Smith attempted to make a philosophical distinction between justice and beneficence and perfect and imperfect right. The question often raised pertains to how far a company should be expected to go in the pursuit of CSR initiatives. Smith's three main underlying concepts were based on the principle of 'invisible hand'. It is based on the premise that individuals pursuing their own best self-interest would automatically result in the greatest overall good to society. The concept of 'invisible hand' suggests that people decide what is good to them. If people decide that organic food is healthy for them, they buy that only and do not buy genetically modified (GM) or factory-farmed foods or coal-fired energy. This invisible hand concept would guide the production and marketing of those goods and services, in which people have faith. The second notion, that an individual seeking his/her own best self-interest is actually the best thing that the person can do for the society. Given the sufficient motivation for personal gain, each person would work hard, and as a result, society as a whole would benefit with more jobs, more competition, and better quality goods and services. This is something like the theory of aggregation, i.e., the sum of individual elements becomes the total. The third notion effectively put forth is that the Government should stay out of the market, and limit their role to law and order only. Smith is often held up by modern conservatives as a hero of capitalism and free markets. He has highlighted the significance of externalities and other free market breakdowns as significant to the operation of an economy.

Milton Friedman is yet another influential writer in Economics, who championed the Smith's line of thinking. In his own words:

"There is one and only one social responsibility of business — to use its resources and engage in activities designed to increase its profits."

But this line of thinking did not get much acceptance, even among economists; who supported the concept of welfare as the crux of the Economics discipline. Many corporate failures and recession in global economy were ascribed to this illogical idea of CSR. Friedman did eventually go on to add, "So long as it stays within the rules of the game, which is to say, engages in open and free competition without deception or fraud." Friedman also negatived the idea of privatization of jails and openly supportive of the legalization of drugs, which is often overlooked by conservatives.

It is a fact that there may be many evils germinating as side effects from the operation of the business. Such evil consequences need to be tackled properly. For instance, if factory farms using antibiotics for their own gain like faster fattening of animals to bring them to market and causing antibiotic resistant bacteria that has now become a public menace would be the case with the feeding of animals with insects and GM foods. It is the indiscriminate pesticide use that is killing honeybees and causing a decline in pollination for other farmers. It is the coal plants that are producing mercury emissions and causing birth defects and respiratory ailments. There are many industries that were identified to hazardous and dangerous to be the persons working within the factories and to the people of the locality. The list can go on and on.

Joseph Stiglitz, a modern Nobel Prize winning Economist and who also served for a long time for the World Bank, said, "Whenever there are externalities–where the actions of an individual have impacts on others for which they do not pay, or for which they are not compensated markets will not work well."

As opposed to the above, there is a growing demand that corporates need to be socially, ethically and morally responsible for their behaviour. There are at least three grounds that make CSR imminent for a business.

1. A business perspective that recognizes the importance of 'reputation capital' for capturing and sustaining markets. Corporate social responsibility is basically a new business strategy to reduce investment risks and maximize profits by taking all the key stake-holders into confidence.
2. The proponents of this perspective are the new generation of corporations and the new-economy entrepreneurs who created a tremendous amount of wealth in a relatively short span of time. They recognize the fact that social and environmental stability and sustainability are two important prerequisites for the sustainability of the market in the long run.

3. Increased awareness is also shaping the new principles and practices of corporate social responsibility. This is based on the belief that consumers, employees, local communities and shareholders have a right to know about corporations and their businesses.

It is often emphasized that there is a greater need for striking a balance between the company's image and the society's image. An attempt has also been made here to impress upon the readers that what remains in the ultimate is the responsibility and responsiveness of the business to the clarion call of the society; in order that corporates emerge as successful and sustainable entities.

The viewpoint of **Peter F. Drucker** is the one often cited in the Management literature. Drucker categorically differentiated between two types of social responsibilities: those to do with social impacts or what business does to society and those to do with social problems or what business can do for society. Social impacts go beyond the specific contribution of the company, such as providing needed products and services. In effect, Drucker was advocating the philosophy of identification and elimination. The undesirable social impacts of business activities are to be mitigated, if not eliminated, to make business survive in the society. The best thing in this regard would be self-regulation, than allowing Government's intervention. Drucker also viewed social problems as sources of opportunity. Changing complexity of the society throws more opportunities than ever. Society is an institution that transforms and evolves over a period of time. In the process, old traditions, beliefs, practices will give way for new systems. It is this change that needs to be closely watched and taken to the advantage by the business. Opportunity assessment basically involves the awareness to these social issues.

For example, fast food companies certainly appear to have a responsibility to act to eliminate the negative social impacts evident in their contributions to obesity in children. In contrast, the pharmaceutical companies dealing with requests to give away drugs that are harmful to the humans, in terms of their side effects. Companies are responsible for the limited healthcare budgets of developing countries that preclude purchase of drugs at developed country prices, but they might choose to act on the issue of access to essential medicines nonetheless.[1]

Drucker was the one often misunderstood and misquoted for his statement on "Corporate Mission". According to Drucker, the organization's first responsibility must always be to its own mission regardless of other factors. The first "social responsibility" of the business is to make a profit sufficient to cover operational costs in the future. The logic in this is that if the organization failed in its own goals because of misallocation of time, resources, or personnel in attempting to fulfill a particular social responsibility, it would also be prevented from solving any particular social problem. Besides, the business may be wasting the scare resources of the nation. Organizations that fail in this mission, also fail in discharging the basic duty of social responsibility. It is for this basic reason, Drucker, perhaps must have advocated the 'duty first' concept of CSR.[2]

2. CONCEPT OF CSR

CSR has been understood and interpreted in a multi-dimensional context. There emerged many complementary and developing explanations, such as responsiveness, volunteerism, citizenship, charter, ethics, stakeholder management and sustainability. It is nothing but natural that these wide ranging concepts and definitions help in the process of better understanding and comprehension of the issues involved. An attempt has been made in the following pages to capture diverse viewpoints on the concept of CSR.

Definitions

As a term "CSR" is used continually, many complementary and overlapping concepts, such as corporate citizenship, business ethics, stakeholder management and sustainability, have emerged. It is not far to seek that the issue having diverse dimensions needs diverse thought processes also. Therefore, it is highly appreciable that all the agencies having interest in the corporate affairs wish to understand and interpret the concept from their own point of view.

A widely cited definition of CSR in the business and social context has been given by the European Union (EU). It describes CSR as "the concept that an enterprise is accountable for its impact on all relevant stakeholders. It is the continuing commitment by business to behave fairly and responsibly, and contribute to economic development while improving the quality of life of the work force and their families as well as of the local community and society at large..." According to the UNIDO, "Corporate social responsibility is a management concept whereby companies integrate social and environmental concerns in their business operations and interactions with their stakeholders".

It is generally understood as being the way through which a company achieves the desired balance between social, economic and cultural domains. It is to be noted here that CSR is not just philanthropy; it is involvement and a concern expressed by the sponsor. A clear integration of the philanthropy with action would contribute well to the upliftment of the downtrodden in the society. The UNIDO's approach also suggests that CSR needs to go beyond communities and beyond the concept of philanthropy. It will be interesting to observe the ways in which this will translate into action at the ground level, and how the understanding of CSR is set to undergo a change.

In another sense, CSR refers to ensuring the success of the business by inclusion of social and environmental considerations into a company's operations. It is the process of satisfying customers' needs with the expectation of other stakeholders such as employees, suppliers and the community at large. It also implies the aspect of contributing positively to society and managing the organization's environmental impact. As Jeremy Moon (2004) has pointed out, CSR is a difficult concept to pin down.

It overlaps with other such concepts as corporate citizenship, sustainable business and environmental responsibility. Thus, any definition will necessarily be challenged by those who wish to contest the reach and application of any version of CSR. Within the literature there exists three discernible 'schools' of thought and practice about corporate social responsibility. These schools may be characterised as the neoliberal, neo-Keynesian, and radical political economy approaches.

The **neoliberal** writers tended to see it fundamentally as the adoption of a set of voluntary policies, codes or guidelines, initiated and driven by the corporation. This is in fact the present day trend; where many companies are developing and implementing 'codes' at their level with a detailed structures and processes. One of the influential thinkers in this context is the Milton Friedman, who expressed the opinion that there is one and only one social responsibility of business that is to use its resources and engage in activities designed to increase its profits so long as it stays within the rules of the game; and nothing else. This is purely based on the principles of Economic Science, leading to the efficient allocation of scarce resources among competing uses.

Corporate social responsibility is referred to as "corporate citizenship" sometimes and is said to involve incurring short-term costs that do not provide an immediate financial benefit to the company. But it may help in promoting positive social and environmental change. It is in this context, Mallen Baker stated that although there is considerable common ground among various definitions; CSR can be interpreted as that the one about how companies manage the business processes to produce an overall positive impact on society.

The World Business Council for Sustainable Development in its publication *'Making Good Business Sense'* by Lord Holme and Richard Watts, stated that Corporate Social Responsibility is the continuing commitment by business to behave ethically and to contribute to economic development; while improving the quality of life of the workforce and society. Following are a few other interpretations:

1. The European Union (EU) defined CSR as the concept whereby companies integrate social and environmental concerns in their business operations and in their interaction with their stakeholders on a voluntary basis."
2. According to Business for Social Responsibility (USA's largest organization devoted to CSR), corporate social responsibility is "Business decision making linked to ethical values, compliance with legal requirements, and respect for people, communities, and the environment around the world."
3. According to World Bank, "Corporate social responsibility is the commitment of businesses to contribute to sustainable economic development by working with employees, their families, the local community and society at large, to improve their lives in ways that are good for business and for development."

4. According to Khoury G, Rostami J, and Turnbull JP. "Corporate social responsibility is the overall relationship of the corporation with all of its stakeholders. These include customers, employees, communities, owners/investors, Government, suppliers and competitors. Elements of social responsibility include investment in community outreach, employee relations, creation and maintenance of employment, environmental stewardship and financial performance."
5. According to Kotler, P. and Lee, N. "Corporate social responsibility is a commitment to improve community well-being through discretionary business practices and contributions of corporate resources.
6. According to Michael and Hopkins (1998) CSR is concerned with treating the stakeholders of the firm ethically or in a socially responsible manner. The aim of social responsibility is to create higher standards of living, while preserving the profitability of the corporation.
7. An ardent promoter of CSR, Simon Zadek has viewed the development of CSR in terms of three generations: the first generation showed that companies can be responsible in ways that do not interfere with commercial success. During this phase the most prominent changes would include adoption of a strategic approach to philanthropy, expansion of the geographic focus of the corporate, and evolving of measurement tools.

   First Generation: 'Can corporations be responsible in ways that do not detract from, and may add commercial value to their business?'

   Second Generation: Are more responsible companies likely to prosper in the future?

   Third Generation: Is corporate citizenship likely to make a significant contribution to addressing the growing levels of poverty, exclusion and environmental degradation?
8. Henry Ford felt that the purpose of business is to do as much good as we can, everywhere for everybody concerned, and the profit making must be incidental to the conduct of business.
9. Going one step further Kenneth Dayton, former Chairman of Dayton Hudson Corporation has stated that "we are in business to make maximum profit for our shareholders and to serve the society. Profit is our reward for doing it well. If we do not serve society, society will not tolerate our profits or even our existence".[3]
10. A more comprehensive expression of the philosophy of CSR is evident from the Mission statement of Johnson & Johnson, a multi-product company of New Jersey, USA, particularly dealing in baby care; when it stated that the first responsibility is to the customers of the company, and later to every other human being.[4]

3. DIMENSIONS OF CSR

There are six key responsibilities or dimensions of corporate social responsibility identified so far. The following paragraphs describe these dimensions, and give examples of the best practices adopted by companies, and indicate how management attention to these elements can enhance growth and profitability. CSR is said to be hovering around these six responsibilities.

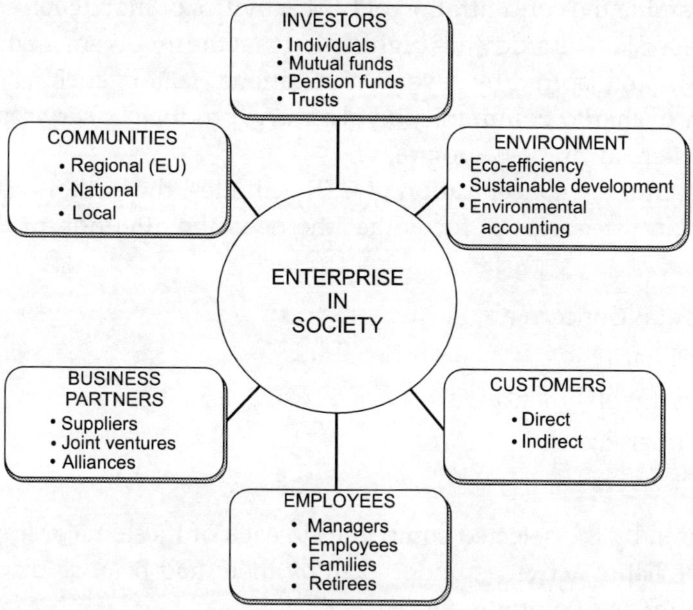

4. FACTORS INFLUENCING INVOLVEMENT OF CORPORATES IN CSR

It is said time and again that the primary role of business is to produce goods and services that society wants and needs. Based on the definition of CSR, CSR behaviors are not constant over time or space. Social expectations and pressure for specific types of CSR have varied over time and are contingent on the nature of the company. A study by Windsor (2001) showed that social responsibility is achieved when the corporation conforms to the prevailing norms and expectations of social performance in a given society.[5] Since CSR behaviors are charitable and discretionary, the likelihood that a specific company will engage in CSR will also depend on the philosophy of the management. A study by Smith (1991) found that heavy manufacturing companies involved in smelting and chemical production are more closely monitored for environmental performance than companies in other industries.

Besides the above, CSR is also said to be influenced by the ethics of the firm. Ethical motivation can guide the business or organization to do the right thing without any external pressure or Governmental constraints. Joyner, Payne & Raiborn (2002) contended that people believe businesses are amoral, when in fact they generally embrace the values of ethics in doing business. They cited several factors that serve to legitimize their position and one of the factors is society, which expects moral behavior of the business when it cries out against immoral labor practices or environmental policies.

In a popular study by Mudamir Bin Mohamed & Norfaiezah Binti Sawandi made an attempt to examine the concentration of CSR activities of mobile telecommunication companies in Malaysia. The study has highlighted that the involvement in CSR activities by the companies are inspired by several motivational factors such as environmental concerns, welfare or charity, community involvement, products or services improvement and natural disasters awareness programs.

While probing into the concentration of CSR activities, the authors have found that there are five main categories of focus that the need the attention of the corporates. They are:

(i) Environmental Concerns
(ii) Welfare or Charity
(iii) Community Involvement
(iv) Products or Services
(v) National Disasters

Activities chosen by the selected companies in each of these major areas were given in Table 18.1. The list of activities undertaken by them had been so diverse, reflecting upon their sincerity and commitment.

Table 18.1: Corporate Social Responsibility Activities by Category

S. No.	Category of CSR involvement	Activities Involved by the Telecommunication Company
1.	Environmental Concerns (E)	1. Pollution control activity over product. 2. Product complies with the environmental condition and the radiation tariff set up by MCMC. 3. Ensures the level of the telecommunication telecast frequency is at the acceptable level. 4. Recycles the unused components of telephone sets that would impact the environment. 5. Collaborates with other government agencies in organizing the 'green' campaign. 6. Develops environmental policy in their organizations to be used at multiple levels of the operation.

Contd.

2.	Welfare or Charity (W)	1. Directly contributes some amount of money for the personal welfare, community welfare and also the welfare of the organization. 2. Involves in developing infrastructure such as buildings, schools, libraries or houses for donation to certain families. 3. Sponsors the treatment for certain types of chronic diseases. 4. Contributes to selected individuals for personnel development in certain areas that could contribute to the development of the industry. 5. Provides counseling and material support to increase motivation amongst the employees. 6. Provides a special bonus plan and reward system to the employees to encourage a positive competition amongst employees. 7. Provides a comprehensive insurance coverage for employees to ensure they are covered in the event of an accident. 8. Establishes a sound placement system for the employee who volunteers to move to another company with valid reasons.
3.	Community Involvement (C)	1. Contributes certain portions of annually allowable donation for R & D in public health concerning radiation exposure. 2. Contributes to the educational institutions in the form of scholarships and research programs in the field of market reaction and customer satisfaction. 3. Supports MCMC with the relevant information on the user coverage and the penetration rate to ensure the country's communication growth policy is well planned. 4. Donates some amount of money to build infrastructure for public use such as bus stops, shades, public toilets and so forth. 5. Jointly sponsors any continual community programs with other institutions. 6. Takes part in exhibitions that promote Malaysia to other countries and encourages the tourism industry. 7. Contributes to games and sports events that are organized by the ministry. 8. Cooperates with police department to organize anti-crime campaigns. 9. Visits some private institutions to promote a healthy and good lifestyle to the students.

Contd.

4.	Products or services (G)	1. Has arrangements to ensure services provided in certain areas would have no health concerning radiation exposure. 2. Ensures the facility used has no effect on the communities' health and tries to minimize the possibility of distraction to the users in long term. 3. Prepares and provides a hotline, control procedure and responsive system to make sure all the registered complaints would be treated as important. 4. Conducts all necessary tests on the radiation frequency interference to reduce disturbance and increase compatibility with technology advancement. 5. Adopts a reasonable, healthiest, technology with the latest innovation set to increase user compatibility. 6. Guarantees that the services in every territory, minutes and destination would be at a 95% satisfactory level. 7. Forms a special team for product or packages offered to respond to any feedback from the market, e.g., subscribers' complaint, rivals promotion strategy and so on.
5.	Natural Disasters (N)	1. Provides services that enable the users to donate to a public fund. Company has arrangement with other private companies to provide the relevant services. 2. Takes action effectively in certain situations by immediately contributing in the form of cash to support the victims. 3. Jointly organizes charitable programs to collect funds for victims of natural disasters directly after determining the amount of funds required. 4. Company's employees also have their own program to make personal contribution for charitable purposes. 5. Keeps on supporting the victims although the charitable program has stopped.

Among all of the factors, companies disclosed that their intention on improving the quality of life of the community was one of the major factors that encouraged them to get involved in CSR activity.

5. MODELS OF CSR

5.1 Carroll's Four Part Model of Corporate Social Responsibility

CSR is a concept whereby companies decide voluntarily to contribute to a better society and a cleaner environment. It is represented by the contributions undertaken by companies to society through their business activities and their social investment. CSR has been making an increasingly prominent impact in the Indian social system by supplementing many developmental projects. It would be really interesting to probe into the exact motivation to delve into the activity of CSR. While one could see it as an economic necessity, the other may treat it only as philanthropy. It is, in fact, very difficult to demarcate the true intentions behind undertaking CSR. Nevertheless, the cost model developed by Carroll and Buchholtz can be seen as having made a sincere effort in this direction. CSR was defined by them as "the economic, legal, ethical and philanthropic expectations placed on organisations by society at a given point in time". The authors made an attempt to classify the motives into the following four categories; as if they organize themselves into a 'pyramid' (see Figure 18.1 below).

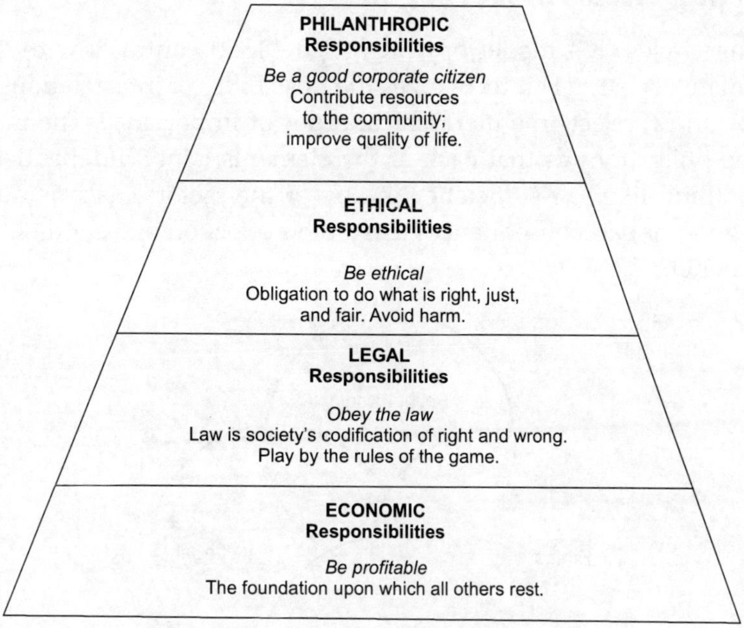

Figure 18.1: Pyramid Structure Model of CSR

1. **Economic Responsibilities:** The first responsibility of the company towards society refers to running the business as an economically health unit. It includes aspects such as return on investment for shareholders, fair employee salaries, and quality products supplied to customers at fair prices; all required by the society.
2. **Legal Responsibilities:** Demands that companies act in accordance with existing legislation and regulatory requirements. The legal framework consequently fosters society's ethical view and all companies attempting to be socially responsible are therefore required by society to follow the law.

3. **Ethical Responsibilities:** It refers to corporation's responsibilities which are not covered by legal or economical requirements, but instead by what could be considered 'right' or 'fair' in the eyes of society. Society therefore expects corporations to act ethically towards their stakeholders.(Crane & Matten, 2004).
4. **Philanthropic Responsibilities:** This involves corporation's willingness to enhance the quality of living for their stakeholders (i.e., employees, local community, and society at large) through charitable donations and organisational support. These corporate decisions are entirely voluntary of less importance than the former three.

5.2 Intersecting Circles model of CSR

The intersecting circles (IC) model of CSR (Figure 18.2) contrasts with the pyramid model in two main aspects: (1) it recognizes the possibility of interrelationships among CSR domains; and (2) rejects the hierarchical order of importance. The major concept underlining the philosophy is that each of the elements is not independent. It is true that there is nothing like self-sufficiency in any of the factors. Each is dependent on the other. The good or bad consequences leave their effect on one another. This is truly an improved model.

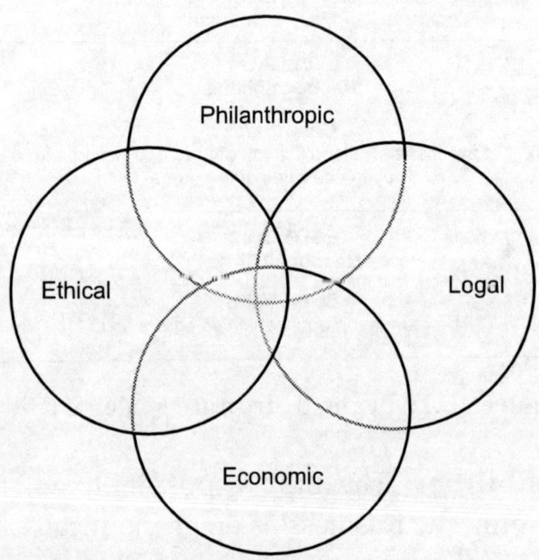

Figure 18.2: Intersecting Circles Model of CSR

5.3 The Concentric Circle Model of CSR

The concentric circle model is similar to the pyramid structure in that it views the economic role of business as its core social responsibility and similar to the intersecting circles (IC) model in that it emphasizes the interrelation among the different corporate social responsibilities. Thus, it can be said as the combination of the two models. While pyramid model defines the corporate economic role in terms of narrow self-interest ("be profitable"), the concentric circle model defines the same role in terms of CSR, namely, the good of the society. In contrast to the pyramid, which scales down the importance of social responsibilities, also allows for no relation among different domains of responsibilities. In such a context, the interrelation among the four could be as follows:[6]

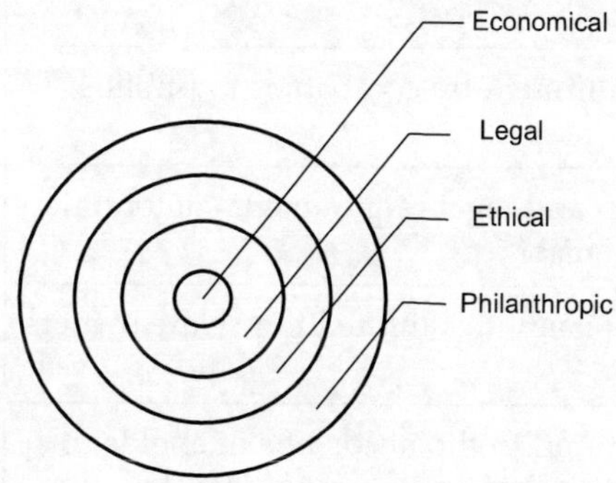

Figure 18.3: Concentric Circle Model of CSR

5.4 Tata Energy Research Institute (TERI) Study

In 2001, TERI conducted an opinion poll regarding the chronological evolution of CSR models and placed them in the following order:

A. **Ethical Model (1930 – 1950):** One significant aspect of this model is the promotion of trusteeship that was revived and reinterpreted by Gandhiji. Under this notion, the businesses were motivated to manage their business entity as a trust held in the interest of the community. The idea prompted many family run businesses to contribute towards socioeconomic development. The efforts of Tata group directed towards the well being of the society are also worth mentioning in this model.

B. **Statist Model (1950 – 1970s):** Under the aegis of Jawaharlal Nehru, this model came into being in the post-independence era. The era was driven by a socialist kind of economy. The important feature of this model was that the state ownership and legal requirements decide the corporate responsibilities.

C. **Liberal Model (1970s – 1990s):** This model is based on the thoughts of Milton Friedman, implying that it is sufficient for business to obey the law and generate wealth, which through taxation and private charitable choices can be directed to social ends.

D. **Stakeholder Model (1990 to till date):** The model came into existence during 1990s as a consequence of realisation that with growing economic profits, businesses also have certain societal roles to fulfill. The model expects companies to perform according to "triple bottom line" (viz., economic, social and environmental) approach. Keeping this in view, the businesses are also focusing on accountability and transparency through several mechanisms.[7] A comparative focus of the four models could be viewed below:

Model	Focus	Champions
Ethical	Voluntary commitment by companies to public welfare.	M.K. Gandhi
Statist	State ownership and legal requirements determine Corporate responsibility.	Jawaharlal Nehru
Liberal	Corporate responsibilities limited to private owners (shareholders).	Milton Friedman
Stakeholder	Companies respond to the needs of stakeholders, i.e., customers, employees, communities, etc.	R. Edward Freeman

6. CHALLENGES OF CSR

Corporate social responsibility is not a new concept in India. However, what is new is the shift in focus from making profits to meeting societal challenges. It is important for CSR strategies to become central to business strategy and part of the long-term planning process. Stakeholders are questioning more on CSR initiatives of the companies today, as of the following.

- **Lack of Community Participation in CSR Activities:** There is a lack of interest of the local community in participating and contributing to CSR activities of companies. This is largely attributable to the fact that there exists little or no knowledge about CSR within the local communities, as no serious efforts have been made to spread awareness about CSR and instill confidence in the local communities about such initiatives. The situation is further aggravated by a lack of communication between the company and the community at the grassroots.
- **Need to Build Local Capacities:** There is a need for capacity building of the local non-governmental organizations, as there is serious dearth of trained and efficient organizations that can effectively contribute to the ongoing CSR activities initiated by companies. This seriously compromises scaling up of CSR initiatives and subsequently limits the scope of such activities.
- **Issues of Transparency:** Lack of transparency is one of the key issues brought forth by many. There is an expression by the companies that there exists lack of

transparency on the part of the local implementing agencies as they do not make adequate efforts to disclose information on their programs, audit issues, impact assessment and utilization of funds. This reported lack of transparency negatively impacts the process of trust building between companies and local communities, which is a key to the success of any CSR initiative at the local level.

- **Non-availability of Well Organized Non-Governmental Organizations:** It is also reported that there is non-availability of well organized non-governmental organizations in remote and rural areas that can assess and identify real needs of the community and work along with companies to ensure successful implementation of CSR activities. This also builds the case for investing in local communities by way of building their capacities to undertake development projects at local levels.
- **Visibility Factor:** The role of media in highlighting good cases of successful CSR initiatives is welcomed as it spreads good stories and sensitizes the local population about various ongoing CSR initiatives of companies. This apparent influence of gaining visibility and branding exercise often leads many non-governmental organizations to involve themselves in event-based programs; in the process, they often miss out on meaningful grassroots interventions.
- **Narrow Perception towards CSR Initiatives:** Non-governmental organizations and government agencies usually possess a narrow outlook towards the CSR initiatives of companies, often defining CSR initiatives more donor-driven than local in approach. As a result, they find it hard to decide whether they should participate in such activities at all in medium and long run.
- **Non-availability of Clear CSR Guidelines:** There are no clear-cut statutory guidelines or policy directives to give a definitive direction to CSR initiatives of companies. It is found that the scale of CSR initiatives of companies should depend upon their business size and profile. In other words, the bigger the company, the bigger is its CSR program. It is appreciable that the Government of India through the Companies Act, 2013 made a sincere effort to relate size of the company to the volume of CSR activity. It is also gratifying that the government made an attempt to outline the nature of activities to be taken by the corporate through Schedule-VII of the Act. These issues were discussed at length in the subsequent chapter.
- **Lack of Consensus on Implementing CSR Issues:** There is a lack of consensus amongst local agencies regarding CSR projects. This lack of consensus often results in duplication of activities by corporate houses in areas of their intervention. This results in a competitive spirit between local implementing agencies rather than building collaborative approaches on issues. This factor limits company's abilities to undertake impact assessment of their initiatives from time to time.[8]

7. SUSTAINABLE CORPORATE STRATEGIES

There is, of late, increased focus by companies on devising strategies towards sustainable development. Increasing evidence is available from the corporate world of the safe and cleaner technologies. Besides, focus is also fixed on poverty alleviation, global warming, water and waste management. It is increasingly realized that the corporation of the present generation need to broad base their horizon on the economic, social and cultural existence. In this context, the experience of Dow Chemical and Xerox are highly reassuring.

Towards Sustainable Strategies

Dimension	Stage one	Stage two	Stage three
Environment	Pollution prevention Continuous effort to reduce waste and pollution	Product stewardship Design for environment and full life cycle Environmental cost accounting	Clean Technology Focus on dvelopment and commercialization of clean technologies
Customers	Driven TQM Customerisation	Focused	Dedicated Process organization
Employees	As costs Fair wages and benefits Working conditions	As assets Employability focus Invest in continuing education and training	As partners Employee ownership Meaningful work Work-family integration
Suppliers	Part of value chain Open bidding		Integration in plants Joint engineering
Communities	Philanthropy Charitablo contributions Sponsorship In-kind giving Employee matched giving Integrity	Community service Employee volunteerism Social investments Cause related marketing Evaluation of impact Job creation	Civic leadership Part of business strategy Local and global strategic partnerships to address societal problems Leadership role, Social reporting and audit
Investors	Arms length Influence governance	Shareholder advocacy	Stakeholder-owned in part or in whole

Source: Mariana Cristina Ganescu, 'Corporate Social Responsibility – A Strategy to Create and Consolidate Sustainable Business', *Journal of Theoretical and Applied Economics* Vol, XIX, No: 11(576), 2012.

8. THE NATIONAL VOLUNTARY GUIDELINES ON SOCIAL, ENVIRONMENTAL AND ECONOMIC RESPONSIBILITIES OF BUSINESS

There is an all-round realization that the adoption of a common set of standards creates an expectation that companies will strive to meet the standards and thus assure public of the safety, security and service. In this regard, the National Voluntary Guidelines (NVGs) on Social, Environmental and Economic Responsibilities of Business, laid down by the Ministry of Corporate Affairs (MCA), Government of India are significant.[9] These are applicable to all businesses, irrespective of size, sector or location. The NVGs were designed with the intent of assisting enterprises to become responsible entities whereby they formulate their financial/business objectives while considering the impact on various diverse stakeholders including society and environment at large.

The nine principles of National Voluntary Guidelines are:

- **Principle 1:** Businesses should conduct and govern themselves with ethics, transparency and accountability.
- **Principle 2:** Businesses should provide goods and services that are safe and contribute to sustainability throughout their life cycle.
- **Principle 3:** Businesses should promote the wellbeing of all employees.
- **Principle 4:** Businesses should respect the interests of, and be responsive toward all stakeholders, especially those who are disadvantaged, vulnerable and marginalized.
- **Principle 5:** Businesses should respect and promote human rights.
- **Principle 6:** Business should respect, protect, and make efforts to restore the environment.
- **Principle 7:** Business, when engaged in influencing public and regulatory policy, should do so in a responsible manner.
- **Principle 8:** Businesses should support inclusive growth and equitable development.
- **Principle 9:** Businesses should engage with and provide value to their customers and consumers in a responsible manner.

9. GUIDELINES OF DOPE ON CSR FOR CENTRAL PSES, APRIL 2010

The Department of Public Enterprises had issued Guidelines on Corporate Social Responsibility (CSR)[10] for CPSEs in March, 2010. Following are the salient features of guidelines on CSR and Sustainability. It is the commitment of the Government enterprises to the public.

- CSR and Sustainability agenda is perceived to be equally applicable to external and internal stakeholders, including the employees of a company, and a company's corporate social responsibility is expected to cover even its routine business operations and activities.

- CSR and sustainable development have been clubbed together in one set of guidelines for CSR and sustainability because of close linkage between the two concepts.
- Public Sector enterprises are required to have a CSR and sustainability policy approved by their respective Boards of Directors. Within the ambit of these guidelines, it is the discretion of the Board of Directors of CPSEs to decide on the CSR and sustainability activities to be undertaken.
- The financial component/budgetary spend on CSR and sustainability will be based on the profitability of the company and shall be determined by the Profit after Tax (PAT) on the company in the previous year.

These guidelines were reviewed in the context of the new provisions in the Companies Act, 2013. All the PSEs are also now required to follow the provisions of the Act. The Department of Public Enterprises (DOPE) may revise these guidelines, whenever it is considered necessary.

10. FUTURE OF CORPORATE SOCIAL RESPONSIBILITY

All of us, being in the society, owe some responsibility towards it. Corporates, which operate in the society and make profits from investments, owe still a greater responsibility. The philosophy permeates, not only helping the society; but also addressing the concerns of the society in terms of social evils and environmental degradation. In a democratic country like ours, there will be more constraints as opportunities. The choice before business and the civil society today is either to join in sharing this responsibility or to suffer as a mute spectator. [11] Therefore, the responsibility of business towards the society needs to be viewed from a wider context as of the following:

- Compliance with the law and statutory provisions in letter and spirit.
- Exploring business at the bottom of the pyramid for helping the poor as well as enriching the business.
- Forming strategic partnership with the stakeholders.
- Taking care of people other than potential consumers.

It is encouraging that the Indian businesses are appreciating the need of the changing times, with most of the companies talking about CSR, some having a CSR policy and a few mobilizing their employees. In India, CSR has evolved to encompass employees, customers, stakeholders and notions of sustainable development and corporate citizenship. The successful implementation of a variety of programmes is the testimony of the commitment of the Indian corporate world. The experiences cited in the following chapter would clearly testify the CSR culture of the Indian companies.

References

1. Craig Smith, 'Drucker on the 'bounded goodness' of corporate social responsibility', The Management Edge, every day, from Knowledge, January 25, 2010.
2. William Cohen, 'Drucker's Surprising View of Corporate Social Responsibility', Process Excellence network, 26-05-2010.
3. A.C. Fernando, "Business Ethics and Corporate Governance", Pearson, New Delhi, 2010, p. 8.4.
4. S. A. Sherlekar, "Ethics in Management", Himalaya Publishing House, 2003, pp. 152-153.
5. Mudamir Bin Mohamed & Norfaiezah Binti Sawandi, "Corporate Social Responsibility (CSR) Activities in Mobile Telecommunication Industry: Case Study of Malaysia", Utusan Malaysia, Dato' Seri Dr Mahathir Mohamed's speech at the Malaysian International Trade Seminar, February 14, 2003.
6. Liangrong Zu, "Corporate Social Responsibility, Corporate Restructuring and Firm's Performance : Empirical Evidence from Chinese Enterprises", Springer, 2009. pp. 24-30.
7. Rajeev Prabhakar and Ms. Sonam Mishra, "A Study of Corporate Social Responsibility in Indian Organisation: An-Introspection", Proceedings of 21st International Business Research Conference, Ryerson University, Toronto, Canada, 10-11 June, 2013.
8. Renu Arora & Richa Garg, "Corporate Social Responsibility - Issues and Challenges in India, International Journal of Research in Finance & Marketing, Vol. 3, Issue. 2, March 201, pp. 4-7.
9. National Voluntary Guidelines on Social, Environmental & Economic Responsibilities of Business, Ministry of Corporate Affairs, Government of India, July 2011.
10. Guidelines on Corporate Social Responsibility for Central Public Sector Enterprises, Department of Public Enterprises, Ministry of Heavy Industries & Public Enterprises, Government of India, March 2010.
11. Naveen Kumar Singh, "CSR (Corporate Social Responsibility) in India and Future Trends with special reference to ITC's CSR Practice", SEEDS, September 23, 2013.

19

CHAPTER

Corporate Social Responsibility in Today's Business Context

1. THE CONTEXT

To begin with, Economists such as Adam Smith and Milton Friedmen opined that the responsibility of a business is to perform its economic function efficiently and provide goods and services to the society and earn maximum profits. It is felt that by doing so, market forces would ensure that business performs its economic functions and leaves the social functions to the Government. This approach has been criticized for a variety of reasons and limitations implied in the market mechanism. It has been proved beyond doubt that there do not exist 'perfect market conditions' except in theory and markets are always irrational.

Then came on the scene, the 'insider-outsider approach', basing on the fact that stakeholders of a business are drawn from insiders – owners (shareholders) and employees and the outsiders—customers, suppliers, creditors, competitors, government and the general public. Under this model, corporations are expected to discharge certain responsibilities towards each group of stakeholders and thus become responsible. A long list of functions had been charted as to how businesses can be responsive to each of the groups, as of the following:

1. *Customers*: Fair price; fair quality; protection; information; and fair trade practices.
2. *Employees*: Meaningful work; fair methods of working; quality implements; fair compensation; security and welfare; training and promotion; and quality work life.
3. *Owners and Creditors*: Fair dividend/interest; fair growth; and continuity.
4. *Govt. and Society*: Optimum utilization of resources; regular payment of taxes; clean environment; employment without discrimination; and community welfare.

There had been another view generated on the foundation that businesses derive their sustenance from the resources owned by the society and hence, they need to be socially responsible. In doing so, they have to deal with social concerns and issues and have to allocate resources for solving social problems. Increasing attention is being paid to the activities undertaken by the companies in this regard. World over, there arose a situation that company can any longer remain detached with the happenings in the society. Though not as saviours, companies are called into service to address the issues of contemporary nature for making the earth a better habitat.

2. COMPANIES ACT, 2013

Which remained voluntary till now has become mandatory with the incorporation of a new section in the New Companies Act, 2013. Section 135 of the Act makes it obligatory on the part of certain category of companies to spend a specific amount on specified activities as listed in schedule-VII of the Act. As per the provisions of the Act:

- Every company having net worth of rupees five hundred crore or more, or turnover of rupees one thousand crore or more or a net profit of rupees five crore or more during any financial year shall constitute a Corporate Social Responsibility Committee of the Board consisting of three or more directors, out of which at least one director shall be an independent director.
- The Report of the Board of Directors shall disclose the composition of the Corporate Social Responsibility Committee.
- Following are the primary responsibilities of the Committee:
  (a) formulate and recommend to the Board, a Corporate Social Responsibility Policy which shall indicate the activities to be undertaken by the company as specified in Schedule VII;
  (b) recommend the amount of expenditure to be incurred on the activities referred to in clause (*a*); and
  (c) monitor the Corporate Social Responsibility Policy of the company from time to time.
- Following the recommendations of the Corporate Social Responsibility Committee, the Board shall formulate the CSR Policy and declare the same through its report and also through the website of the company.
- The policy formulated by the company shall cover the activities proposed to be undertaken in this regard.
- The Board of every company also shall ensure that the company spends, in every financial year, at least two per cent of the average net profits of the company made during the three immediately preceding financial years. While doing so

the company shall give preference to the local area and areas around it where it operates. In case the company could not spend the amount earmarked as per its policy, the company has to specify the reasons for not spending the amount. As could be observed from the experience, there are many companies that have not spent the full amount earmarked for the purpose. The details are provided in this chapter in the succeeding pages.

3. COMPANIES (CSR POLICY) RULES, 2014

The Central Government in exercise of the powers conferred under section 135 (1) and section 464 (2) of the Companies Act, 2013, has issued the Companies (CSR Policy) Rules, 2014 on 27th February, 2014. These rules were meant to detail the policy and activities to be undertaken under this head. There are nine areas of focus including short tile, commencement and definitions. The major issues covered under the rules included the following:

1. Constitution of CSR Committee.
2. Activities covering the CSR policy framed by the company.
3. CSR expenditure which shall include all expenditure.
4. CSR reporting.
5. Display of CSR activities on its website.

At the very outset, every company is supposed to formulate a policy of its own to undertake various activities under CSR. It should list out the CSR programmes. The company shall specify in clear terms the modalities of execution of such projects or programs and implementation schedules for the same; and the monitoring process of such projects. Further, the Board may decide to undertake its CSR activities approved by the CSR Committee, through a registered trust or a registered society or a company established by the company or its holding or subsidiary or associate company under section 8 of the Act. In case the company does not want to establish a Trust or Society, it should have a track record of three years in undertaking similar programs or projects. It is also true that many big companies or groups have already established such outfits and carrying out the CSR programmes. Therefore, in case of such companies, there is no necessity of having one more trust/society.

The companies are required to specify the program to be undertaken through these entities, the modalities of utilization of funds on such projects and programs and the monitoring and reporting mechanism. A company may also collaborate with other companies for undertaking projects or programs or CSR activities in such a manner that the CSR Committees of respective companies are in a position to report separately on such projects or programs in accordance with these rules.

After the notification of these rules, the Ministry of Corporate Affairs (MCA) has received several representations seeking clarifications. Consequently, the MCA has issued clarifications on 18th June, 2014 providing certain examples of CSR activities as detailed below:

A. Promoting Education

1. Educating the masses.
2. Promotion of road safety awareness in all facets of road usage.
3. Safety traffic awareness through print, audio and visual media.
4. Setting up applied Research Training and Innovation Centre (ARTIC) at Nasik (also qualifies under vocational skills and rural development)
5. Consumer education and awareness:
   - Providing effective consumer grievance redressal mechanism
   - Protecting consumer's health and safety, sustainable consumption, consumer service, support and complaint resolution.
   - Consumer protection to be mandated.
   - All consumer protection programmes and activities on the lines of rural development, education, etc.
6. Donations to Indian Institute of Management, Ahmedabad for conservation of buildings and renovation of classrooms.
7. Non-Academic Technopark Technology Business Incubator (approved by Department of Science and Technology, Government of India) not located within an academic institution.
8. Research and studies (or identified specifically under respective items of schedule VIII)

B. Promoting Healthcare including Preventive Healthcare

1. Social business projects such as giving medical and legal aid, treatment to road accident victims.
2. Provisions for aids and appliances to the differently-able persons.
3. Medical aid provided as a disaster relief measure.
4. Trauma care around highways.

C. Vocational Skills

1. Drivers' training, etc.
2. Capacity building for farmers covering best sustainable farm management practices to predominantly benefit rural farming community.
3. Training agriculture labour on skill development to predominantly benefit rural farming community.

D. Eradicating Hunger, Poverty and Malnutrition

1. Food supply as a disaster relief measure.
2. Supplementing government schemes like mid-day meal by corporates through additional nutrition.

E. Ecological Balance

1. Own research for individual crops to identify the most cost optimum and agri-ecological sustainable farm practices.
2. Applied research with a focus on water management

F. Conservation of Natural Resources

Product life cycle analysis from the perspective of soil conservation (also qualify under 'maintaining quality of soil, air and water')

G. Environmental Sustainability, Ecological Balance and Conservation of Natural Resources

Renewable energy projects.

One of the significant aspects of the rules is that they also identified certain activities not coming under CSR. This can be treated as the 'negative list'. Those included the following:

1. Training to enforcement personnel.
2. Capacity building of government officials and elected representatives in the area of public private partnerships and urban infrastructure.
3. Sustainable urban development and urban public transport systems.
4. Programmes providing professional exchange or physicians between India and the United States.

4. CSR POLICY OF THE COMPANIES

It would be interesting, in this context, to quote the CSR policy of a few companies in their own terminology. Let us observe the following statements:

1. The CSR policy of the TCS company is aimed at demonstrating care for the community through its focus on education and skill development, health and wellness and environmental sustainability including biodiversity, energy and water conservation. Also embedded in this objective is the support to the disadvantaged/ marginalized cross section of the society by providing opportunities to improve their quality of life.

2. At Reliance Industries Ltd. (RIL), CSR is embedded into the main line of business priorities. It co-exists with social commitments to drive holistic development of people and communities. The Company's CSR initiatives help elevate the quality of life of millions, especially the disadvantaged sections of the society. It seeks to touch and transform people's lives by promoting healthcare, education and employment opportunities.
3. The CSR policy of ITC has been designed to focus on the creation of significant and sustainable societal value, inspired by a vision to subserve a larger national purpose and abide by the strong value of trusteeship. Care is taken to see that the CSR initiatives embrace the most disadvantaged sections of society, especially in rural India, through economic empowerment based on grassroots capacity building.
4. Being an early adopter of CSR, Infosys concentrates on the sustained economic performance, environmental and social stewardship as a key factor for holistic business growth. The Company works with Infosys Foundation towards removing malnutrition, improving healthcare infrastructure. It is also supporting primary education, rehabilitating abandoned women and children, and preserving Indian art and culture. Over the years, the company has been striving to achieve a fine balance among the economic, environmental and social imperatives. This is adequately integrated to the needs and expectations of internal as well as external stakeholders. The company believes that social responsibility is not limited to philanthropy, but encompasses holistic community development, institution building and sustainability related initiatives.
5. The vision of HUL regarding CSR is that it wants to operate and grow in a socially responsible way. The company's vision is to grow its business, while reducing the environmental impact of its operations. HUL has embraced Unilever Sustainable Living Plan (USLP), which contributes to activities listed in the Schedule VII of Section 135 of the Companies Act, 2013. The USLP has three global goals namely (i) help more than a billion people take action to improve their health and well-being; (ii) halve the environmental footprint of the making and use of the products; and (iii) enhance the livelihoods of millions of people while growing the business.
6. According to the mission statement of ICICI, CSR has been a long standing commitment. The ICICI Group forms an integral part of the activities. The ICICI Group's contribution to social sector development includes several pioneering interventions, and is implemented through the involvement of stakeholders within the Group and the broader community. ICICI Bank established the ICICI Foundation for Inclusive Growth (ICICI Foundation) in 2008 with a view to significantly expand the ICICI Group's activities in the area of CSR. Over the last few years, ICICI Foundation has developed significant projects in specific

areas, and has built capabilities for direct project implementation as opposed to extending financial support to other organisations.

7. Bharti Airtel is focusing on the partners organisations across countries of its operation to foster inclusive growth. The Company is actively pursuing its socio-economic priorities across multiple platforms. Its individual business units, spread across different geographies, have consistently tried to promote social inclusion in an environmentally sustainable manner.
8. L & T has identified a unified focal theme of 'Building India's Social Infrastructure'. Under this scheme, the company has identified a few villages in water-stressed districts around the country. Through its Integrated Community Development programmes, it is partnering with the community to address issues of water, sanitation, education, health and skill-building. Active participation from the community is also sought at every step of the way. Communities are required to pledge their support through 'Shram Daan' or voluntary service. At many places, community people have agreed to partner L&T in implementing projects, and most importantly, assume ownership of the plan. It is expected that this would ensure that the programmes are sustained all the way to success.
9. It is laudable that Wipro has a global outlook in terms of operating on the front of CSR. It believed that the CSR provisions of the Bill may not be the most effective means of getting industry to engage on larger social issues. The company believes that business sustainability plays a critical role in moving the programmes forward and must be included as part of CSR, where appropriate. As a global corporate citizen, the company feels that community programs of all the countries must be united and should not be restricted to India alone.
10. The focus of CSR policy of Maruti Suzuki India Ltd is primarily in the areas of community development, road safety and skill development. The company's approach has been to create a visible unified CSR programmes rather than spreading resources over several projects.

5. CSR ACTIVITIES

Keeping in view the policy framed, select companies are identifying the list of activities that could be taken up. It is appreciable that the coverage is so wide and includes almost every conceivable activity. Schedule-VII of the Companies Act, 2013 has set out a list of ten activities (given below) which may be included by companies in their CSR policies. Plain regarding of the schedule reveals that the list could be considered illustrative and the companies need not limit their activities only to those ten. It is in this context, the practices followed by the companies would tell us the trend involved. Therefore, an attempt has been made to survey the activities of twenty companies to get a feel of the CSR in practice.

(i) eradicating extreme hunger and poverty;
(ii) promotion of education;
(iii) promoting gender equality and empowering women;
(iv) reducing child morality and improving maternal health;
(v) combating human immunodeficiency virus, acquired immune deficiency syndrome, malaria and other diseases;
(vi) ensuring environmental sustainability;
(vii) employment enhancing vocational skills;
(viii) social business projects;
(ix) contribution to the Prime Minister's National Relief Fund or any other fund set up by the Central Government or the State Governments for socio-economic development and relief and funds for the welfare of the Scheduled Castes, the Scheduled Tribes, other backward classes, minorities and women; and
(x) such other matters as may be prescribed by the Central Government.

Apart from the usual areas of health, education, environment, many companies are engaging themselves in the most innovative manner. Such activities included the following:

(i) Rural transformation
(ii) Protection of natural heritage, art and culture
(iii) Disaster response
(iv) Water security and water management
(v) Financial literacy and empowerment
(vi) Skill training and livelihood enhancement
(vii) Social forestry
(viii) Community development
(ix) Energy conservation and management

6. CONSTITUTION OF COMMITTEE ON CSR BY COMPANIES

Social responsibility is high on the agenda of the companies, as evidenced by the constitution of committee with the Directors of the Board. A closer examination of the constitution reveals the fact that all the companies are fulfilling the stipulation under Section 135 of the Act. While the Committee shall be with a minimum of three members, companies like Coal India (7), SBI (7) and HUL (6) are drafting more than the requirement [see Table 19.1]. Interestingly, in majority of the cases, the CEO of the company is the Chairman for this committee. This exhibits the significance of the committee and importance attached to the function of social responsibility. In terms of the number of meetings also, many companies held more than 3 meetings. Whereas big companies like HUL, Maruti Suzuki, TCS could hold only one meeting.

Table 19.1: Composition of the CSR Committee by select companies of India

Sl. No.	Name of the Company	Total No. of Members	Composition			No. of Meetings held during 2014-15
			Executive Director	Non-Executive Director	Independent Director	
1.	TCS	3	1	1	1	1
2.	Reliance	4	1	–	3	4
3.	HDFC Bank	5	3	–	2	4
4.	Coal India	7	2	–	5	4
5.	ITC	5	1	3	1	5
6.	Infosys	4	1	–	3	4
7.	ONGC	3	1	1	1	4
8.	SBI	7	2	5	–	2
9.	HDFC	3	1	1	1	1
10.	Sun Pharma	3	1	1	1	1
11.	HUL	6	2	–	4	1
12.	ICICI Bank	3	–	2	1	2
13.	Airtel	3	1	1	1	4
14.	L & T	3	2	1	–	2
15.	Wipro	3	–	–	3	–
16.	Axis Bank	3	1	1	1	2
17.	Maruti Suzuki	3	1	1	1	1
18.	HCL Tech	3	1	1	1	–
19.	Tata Motors	3	1	–	2	3
20.	Kotak Mahindra	3	2	–	1	3

Source: Annual Reports of respective companies.

7. FUNCTIONS OF CSR COMMITTEE

CSR Committee has the prime responsibility of assisting the Board of Directors in formulating and monitoring the CSR programmes of the company. The terms of reference of the company, though varying from company to company, they normally included the following:

- To formulate and recommend to the Board, a Corporate Social Responsibility (CSR) Policy indicating activities to be undertaken by the Company in compliance with provisions of the Companies Act, 2013 and rules made thereunder.
- To recommend the amount of expenditure to be incurred on the CSR activities.
- To monitor the implementation of the CSR Policy of the Company from time to time.
- To approve the Corporate Sustainability Reports and oversee the implementation of sustainability activities.
- To oversee the implementation of policies contained in the Business Responsibility Policy Manual and to make any changes/modifications, as may be required, from time to time and to review and recommend the Business Responsibility Reports (BRR) to the Board for its approval.
- To observe practices of corporate governance at all levels and to suggest remedial measures wherever necessary.
- To ensure compliance with corporate governance norms prescribed under Listing Agreements with Stock Exchanges, the Companies Act and other statutes or any modification or re-enactment thereof.
- To advise the Board periodically with respect to significant developments in the law and practice of corporate governance and to make recommendations to the Board for appropriate revisions to the Company's Corporate Governance Guidelines.
- To monitor the company's compliance with Corporate Governance Guidelines and applicable laws and regulations and make recommendations to the Board on all such matters and on any corrective action to be taken, as the committee may deem appropriate.
- To review and assess the adequacy of the Company's Corporate Governance Manual, Code of Conduct for Directors and Senior Management, Code of Ethics and other internal policies and guidelines and monitor that principles described therein are being incorporated into the company's culture and business practices.
- To formulate/approve codes and/or policies for better governance.
- To provide correct inputs to the media so as to preserve and protect the company's image and standing.

- To disseminate factually correct information to investors, institutions and the public at large.
- To establish oversight on important corporate communication on behalf of the company with the assistance of consultants/advisors, if necessary.
- To ensure institution of standardised channels of internal communications across the company to facilitate a high level of disciplined participation.
- To carry out any other function as is mandated by the Board from time to time or enforced by any statutory authority.

8. CSR EXPENDITURE

A cursory look at the expenditure incurred by a group of 20 select companies reveals many interesting results.

(i) Of the 20 companies surveyed, two companies, viz., Sun Pharma and Tata Motors have incurred loss on the average computation basis. Hence, they were out of the purview of the legal provision.

(ii) The amounts earmarked for CSR activities are just 2.00 per cent and not beyond; as if the obligation could neither be enhanced nor reduced. It is only Reliance that could earmark the above the statutory limit at 3.35 per cent.

(iii) In terms of absolutes also, Reliance has earmarked and spent substantial amount of Rs. 761 crore during 2014-15; followed by ONGC; which has earmarked Rs. 661 crore and spent Rs. 495 core.

(iv) Not so impressive is the fact at least half of the select companies have not spent the amounts earmarked in full. The extent of spending is much worse in HUL (10.3 per cent only of the amount earmarked), and HDFC (39.8 per cent).

On the whole, the Government of India deserves all appreciation for taking a bold initiative of making CSR expenditure mandatory, though at 2 per cent. This shall be considered a beginning towards sustainable development.

9. VEHICLE USED FOR IMPLEMENTING CSR ACTIVITIES

As per the notification of the MCA on CSR policy, a company may decide to undertake its CSR activities, through a society or a company established by the company or its holding or subsidiary or associate company under section 8 of the Act provided further that:

(i) If such trust, society or company is not established by the company or its holding or subsidiary or associate company, it shall have an established track record of three years in undertaking similar programmes or projects.

(ii) The company has specified the project or programme to be undertaken through these entities, the modalities of utilization of funds on such projects and programmes and the monitoring and reporting mechanism.

(iii) A company may also collaborate with other companies for undertaking projects or programmes or CSR activities in such a manner that the CSR Committees of respective companies are in a position to report separately on such projects or programmes in accordance with these rules.

Therefore, it is clear that there is wider opportunity provided to the companies to choose any means for carrying out the preferred CSR activities. The survey of experience of the select companies reveals the fact they have adopted diverse forms. While some of them are preferring to establish foundations under the Indian Trusts Act, 1882, others are choosing societies and companies. For instance, Infosys company, founded the Infosys Foundation in 1996 as a not for profit trust to conduct social welfare activities. Over the years, it has been striving to achieve a fine balance of economic, environmental and social imperatives, while also paying attention to the needs and expectations of the internal as well as external stakeholders. As a matter of fact, corporate social responsibility is not limited to philanthropy, but encompasses holistic community development, institution building and sustainability related initiatives.

In fiscal 2015, the Foundation's work spanned a wide range of activities such as sponsoring various organizations that promote local arts and culture, funding professorships and scholarships at institutes of higher education, funding community healthcare initiatives in Chennai, Bengaluru and Mumbai, and aiding welfare initiatives in remote rural areas and tribal areas in Arunachal Pradesh and Odisha. The Foundation also sponsored programs providing for the care of the destitutes in several states.

Infosys Foundation USA: The Infosys Foundation USA's ('the Foundation') proposed charter was approved by the CSR Committee of the Board in January 2015 with a focus on bridging the digital divide in the U.S. The trustees of Infosys Foundation USA are Vandana Sikka (Chairperson), Sudha Murty and Sandeep Dadlani. The Foundation is committed to making quality computing education widely and easily accessible to everyone – irrespective of exposure, lack of resources, prior skills or proficiency. From enabling computer education in K-12, to supporting research in computer science, and empowering adults with IT training that enhances their employability; the Foundation is on a mission to catalyze a human revolution. An initial outlay of US $10 million was approved for the Foundation's activities by the CSR committee of the Board. During fiscal 2014-15, the Foundation disbursed US $126,378 towards various CSR activities.

Similarly, Reliance Industries Limited (RIL) has also set up a Reliance Foundation (RF) in 2010 to provide impetus to various philanthropic initiatives of RIL. The efforts of the group have already touched the lives of more than four million people across India, in more than 5500 villages and urban locations. The Foundation has a comprehensive development approach. Its prime objective is to create and support meaningful activities through innovative institutions to address some of India's most pressing developmental challenges. The Foundation lays significant emphasis on leveraging technology for developmental solutions. Following its model of direct engagement, the Foundation directly reaches out to the affected communities through trained professionals. Over the years, Reliance Foundation's initiatives have continued to evolve, while remaining responsive to the ever-changing needs of society.

The Foundation is currently focusing on creating change in areas of Rural Transformation, Health, Education, Sports for Development, Disaster Response, Arts, Heritage & Culture and Urban Renewal. To maximize its reach and improve outcomes, Reliance Foundation has also established strategic partnerships with organizations that have the technical expertise and experience to undertake various programmes in the identified focus areas of operation. Today, Reliance Foundation Bharat India Jodo directly engages with more than 48,000 households in 504 Village Farmer Associations across 12 states of India. It replicates the model from Bharuch in Gujarat to Balangir in Orissa and from Rudraprayag in Uttarakhand to Karaikudi in Tamil Nadu. Furthermore, to facilitate Research and Development, RF BIJ has a Centre of Excellence in Sustainable Agriculture in Mouda, Nagpur.

The Foundation has also started Reliance Foundation Information Services (RFIS) to serve fishermen community. In this regard, Reliance Foundation Information Services (RFIS) provides validated information services to different livelihood information seekers using modern Information and Communication Technologies (ICT). This bridges the gap between lab-derived knowledge and field-based skill. This multi-stakeholder partnership works towards risk reduction by loss aversion, potential additional income per individual and replenishment of natural resources. Since its inception in 2013, the Reliance Foundation Information Services (RF IS) programme aims to provide critical information and linkages using various communication mediums to poor households. Information is disseminated though audio and dial out conferences, local cable TV, All India Radio, print media, voice and text SMS, WhatsApp and field based programmes and training. This enables farmers to make better decisions in areas of livelihood, health and disaster preparedness. Themes covered on broadcasts include agriculture, horticulture, fisheries, health, employment, micro-enterprises and skill building.

Whereas HDFC has opted to establish the HT Parekh Foundation as a not for profit company under section 25 of the Companies Act, 1956. The objective of the foundation was to support and partner socially relevant projects through NGOs, community bodies and organisations in the development space. The foundation will look into the areas of education, child welfare, health and medical, community development, senior citizens and various programmes in the developmental space.

Within the organizations, there are very effective structures created for carrying out the CSR activities. In this context, the experience of the Wipro need to be specially highlighted. The company has constituted an Employee Advocacy Group (EAG) with the Wiproites. EAG is a 120+ member representative group managed by Wiproites to voice employee suggestions. EAG Members are selected amongst employees with the objective to hear out employee ideas and recommendations to improve company policies and processes. The EAG was formed in Sep 2011 with the twin objectives: channelizing feedback on existing policies and practices, and also reviewing new policies before launch, wherever feasible. Since inception, the EAG has received about 5095 suggestions. During 2013-14, 1963 suggestions were received from employees. Themes relating to HR and people processes, recruitment and training account for approximately 50 per cent of the total suggestions received. Suggestions are screened by the EAG team and then by functional SPOCs. The EAG then discusses shortlisted suggestions with Function Heads, and implements them in collaboration with functions. The team has also led specific improvement projects such as a revamp of the performance management system and leave policy.

Further, Wipro BPO launched the Engagement Index (EI) in 2010, to enhance engagement effectiveness for first level and mid-level managers from business across operations. Managers own engagement targets for engagement and retention of talent, reward and recognition and fun-at-work; performance data is tracked and translated into an EI score for each manager. Over the years, EI has been internalized as an integral responsibility of people managers and is linked to their variable pay as well. Engagement Index achievement levels for 2013-14 closed at over 90 per cent, consistent with 2012-13 levels. Given the fundamental axiom that sustainability is about maximizing social and environmental 'good', it requires an engagement template that emphasizes informed advocacy of the underlying issues amongst all stakeholders. Each stakeholder – business, government, academia, civil society – brings a dynamic and energy to the table that is unique and complementary. Wipro thinks that industry's role must go beyond its own boundaries and should be one that seeks to vigorously promote advocacy of sustainability challenges. In doing so, the conscious emphasis must be on the difficult and the long term in preference to the easy and the short term. The areas of focus on policy and advocacy have centered around Clean Energy and Climate Change, Water, e-Waste, Education and Diversity. The company is also working through industry platforms like CII, FICCI, Nasscom as well as with research partners who carry expertise in these domains.

Table 19.2: CSR Expenditure Details of select companies during the Financial Year 2014-15

(Rs. in Crore)

Sl. No.	Name of the Company	Average Net Profit	Amount Earmarked	Amount Spent	Amount Earmarked as % of A.P.	Amount Spend as % of amount Earmarked
1.	TCS	14,250	285	219	2.00	76.8
2.	Reliance	26,648	761	761	3.35	100.0
3.	HDFC Bank	9,856	197	118	2.00	59.9
4.	Coal India	–	472	111	2% of the ANP of Rs. 2 per tonne, whichever is higher	23.5
5.	ITC	10,646	213	214	2.00	100.0
6.	Infosys	12,133	243	210	2.00	98.8
7.	ONGC	33,033	661	495	2.00	74.9
8.	SBI	–	109	116	–	106.4
9.	HDFC	6,131	123	49	2.00	39.8
10.	Sun Pharma	Loss	–	47	–	–
11.	HUL	3,991	798	82	2.1	10.3
12.	ICICI Bank	1,231	25	15	2.00	60.0
13.	Airtel	6,999	140	140	2.00	100.0
14.	L & T	5,056	106	106	2.10	100.0
15.	Wipro	6415	133	133	2.07	100.0
16.	Axis Bank	6689	134	123	2.00	91.8
17.	Maruti Suzuki	2,505	50	37	2.00	74.0
18.	HCL Tech	NA	NA	NA	–	–
19.	Tata Motors	Loss	–	–	–	–
20.	Kotak Mahindra	1960	39	12	2.00	30.8

Source: Annual Reports of respective companies.
*NA = Not Available.

10. AWARDS/DISTINCTIONS/ACCOLADES/RANKINGS

As a measure of appreciation of the good effort taken by the companies, many non-governmental organisations (NGOs), government organisations and public bodies are bestowing various awards and distinctions on the companies that have done well. A glance over the distinctions would reveal the kind of penetration made into the society by the corporates. Across the board, the list of awards included the following:

1. Award for the promotion of National Language – Hindi by the Government of India (SBI).
2. Golden Peacock Award for CSR (SBI).
3. BFSI Environmental Award, Singapore (SBI).
4. CMO Asia Award for Best CSR practices, Mumbai (SBI).
5. Business World Magazine 'Socially Responsible Bank' Award, Mumbai (SBI).
6. Golden Globe Tigers Awards for CSR best Practices & Innovations in CSR. - Kuala Lumpur (SBI).
7. 2012 World Innovation Summit for Education (WISE) Award (Airtel).
8. ICICI Foundation & CNBC TV-18 Inclusive India Award 2012 (Airtel).

Though the list above appears to be limited, many companies have furnished detailed information in this regard.

Table 19.3: India's Top Ten Companies in terms of CSR Expenditure, 2015

2014		2013	
Rank	**Name of the Company**	**Rank**	**Name of the Company**
1.	Mahindra & Mahindra Ltd.	1.	Tata Steel Ltd.
2.	Tata Power Company Ltd.	2.	Tata Chemicals Ltd.
3.	Tata Steel Ltd.	3.	Mahindra & Mahindra Ltd.
4.	Larsen & Toubro Ltd.	4.	Maruti Suzuki India Ltd.
5.	Tata Chemicals Ltd.	5.	Tata Motors Ltd.
6.	Tata Motors Ltd.	6.	Siemens Ltd.
7.	GAIL (India) ltd.	7.	Larsen & Toubro Ltd.
8.	Bharat Petroleum Corporation Ltd.	8.	Coca-Cola India Pvt. Ltd.
9.	Infosys Ltd.	9.	Steel Authority of India Ltd.
10.	Jubilant Life Sciences Ltd.	10.	Infosys Ltd.

Source: www.futurescape.in.

As a matter of fact, the CSR study made by an independent body, viz., 'future scope' reveals the fact that many companies have scaled up operations on CSR activities and considering CSR as a priority function. It made a comparison of the rankings of 2014 over 2013 for the top 10 companies and found that there is keen competition to score high on the rankings [see Table 19.3]. Similarly, the organisation has also published the list of Top 100 companies as per rankings compiled for 2014 [see Table 19.4]. It is evident from the information that companies like Mahindra & Mahindra, Tata Power, Tata Steel, L & T, Tata Chemicals, Tata Motors, GAIL, BPCL, Infosys and Jubilant Life Sciences occupied the first ten places. The last company can be said to be a 'dark horse' in the entire list.

Table 19.4: India's Top 100 Companies in terms of CSR Expenditure, 2015

Rank	Name of the Company
1.	Mahindra & Mahindra Ltd.
2.	Tata Power Company Ltd.
3.	Tata Steel Ltd.
4.	Larsen & Toubro Ltd.
5.	Tata Chemicals Ltd.
6.	Tata Motors Ltd.
7.	GAIL (India) ltd.
8.	Bharat Petroleum Corporation Ltd.
9.	Infosys Ltd.
10.	Jubilant Life Sciences Ltd.
11.	Reliance Industries Ltd.
12.	ACC Ltd.
13.	Shree Cements Ltd.
14.	Maruti Suzuki India Ltd.
15.	Hindustan Unilever Ltd.
16.	Cummins India
17.	Tata Consultancy Services Ltd.
18.	Ultra Tech Cement Ltd.
19.	Indian Oil Corporation Ltd.
20.	Essar Oil Ltd.

Contd.

21.	JSW Steel Ltd.
22.	Steel Authority of India Ltd.
23.	Ambuja Cements Ltd
24.	HDFC Bank Ltd.
25.	Dabur India Ltd.
26.	Cisco Systems India Pvt. Ltd.
27.	Coca-Cola India Pvt. Ltd.
28.	ONGC
29.	Wipro Ltd.
30.	YES Bank Ltd.
31.	Welspun Corp Ltd.
32.	Bharat Electronics Ltd.
33.	Vedanta Limited
34.	Siemens Ltd.
35.	Hindustan Construction Company Ltd.
36.	Rashtriya Chemicals & Fertilizers Ltd.
37.	ITC Ltd.
38.	Bajaj Auto Ltd.
39.	Hindustan Petroleum Corporation Ltd.
40.	Hindalco Industries Ltd.
41.	HCL Technologies Ltd.
42.	Jindal Steel & Power Ltd.
43.	Dr. Reddy's Laboratories Ltd.
44.	Nestle India Ltd.
45.	Bharat Heavy Electricals Ltd.
46.	Chambal Fertilizers & Chemicals Ltd.
47.	NTPC Ltd.
48.	Titan Company Ltd.
49.	Idea Cellular Ltd.
50.	Power Grid Corporation of India Ltd.

Contd.

51.	Jaiprakash Associates Ltd.
52.	Tata Global Beverages Ltd.
53.	National Aluminium Company Ltd.
54.	Genpact
55.	Caim India Ltd.
56.	ABB India Ltd.
57.	Godrej Consumer Products Ltd.
58.	Bosch Ltd.
59.	Neyveli Lignite Corporation Ltd.
60.	Axis Bank Ltd.
61.	Hero MotoCorp Ltd.
62.	Hindustan Zink Ltd.
63.	NMDC Ltd.
64.	Mahindra & Mahindra Financial Services Ltd.
65.	Tata Communications Ltd.
66.	Tech Mahindra Ltd.
67.	Asian Paints Ltd.
68.	Oil India Ltd.
69.	Rural Electrification Corporation Ltd.
70.	Petronet LNG Ltd.
71.	Kotak Mahindra Bank Ltd.
72.	Sun Pharmaceutical Industries Ltd.
73.	Adani Power Ltd.
74.	Lupin Ltd.
75.	DLF Ltd.
76.	Exide Industries Ltd.
77.	Sesa Sterlite Ltd.
78.	Reliance Communications Ltd.
79.	Induslnd Bank Ltd.
80.	ING Vysya Bank Ltd.

Contd.

81.	Bharat Airtel Ltd.
82.	ICICI Bank Ltd.
83.	Coal India Ltd.
84.	IDFC Ltd.
85.	Havells India Ltd.
86.	GMR Infrastructure Ltd.
87.	Union Bank of India
88.	Cipla Ltd.
89.	Container Corporation of India
90.	Aditya Birla Nuvo Ltd.
91.	Bharati Infratel Ltd.
92.	NHPC Ltd.
93.	Mangalore Refinery and Petrochemicals Ltd.
94.	Ranbaxy Laboratories Ltd.
95.	Adani Enterprises Ltd.
96.	Punjab National Bank
97.	Cadila Healthcare Ltd.
98.	Jain Irrigation Systems Ltd.
99.	Reliance Power Ltd.
100.	Citibank

Source: www.futurescape.in.

11. INNOVATIVE AREAS OF CSR

It is quite laudable that many companies are imagining programmes having high innovative value. They can be treated as real pointers to others in the field. For gaining a cursory look at the trend, an attempt has been made below to brief such attempts.

A. **Water Security Programme of RIL:** With the objective of ensuring water security to the farmers spread across multiple agro-ecological regions, RIL has started developing water harvesting structures for the communities living in dry and rain-fed areas. Over the years, the company could create capacities to harvest and store about 203 lakh cubic metres of rainwater in the last one year and in total about 447 lakh cubic metres since inception.

B. **Social Forestry Programmes of ITC:** ITC has taken up a pioneering initiative of wasteland development through Social Forestry Programme (SFP). The project is aimed at covering a huge tract of 67,566 hectares of land in 3,720 villages, impacting 70,000 poor households. This is said to be a part of the social and farm forestry initiative of the company which has together greened mearly 2000,000 hectars to date and generated nearly 90 million person days of employment for rural households. This initiative is also intended to cover food, fodder and wood security to the people of the area.

C. **Solid Waste Management of ITC:** The company's solid waste management programme, named "WoW – Wellbeing out of Waste" is intended to inculcate the habit of source segregation and recycling among school children, housewives and general public as well as industries and business enterprises. As of now, the scheme enjoyed the support of over 3 million citizens, 5 lakh school children, 350 corporates, more than 1000 commercial establishments.

D. **Sangeet Research Academy:** In order to promote the culture of the land, ITC has established in 1977 itself this Academy to promote and endure excellence in 'classical music tradition that adheres to the age-old 'Guru-Shishya Parampara'.

E. **Ankur of HUL:** Ankur is a centre started by the Hindustan Unilever Ltd. for special education of differently abled children at Doom Dooma in Assam. The centre was set up by the company in 1993 and providing educational, vocational and recreational activities to such differently abled children. There are many movies in different languages produced to create awareness about these children in the society.

F. **Making the World Greener of Airtel:** To reduce its carbon footprint, Airtel Africa started converting high OPEX sites to their OPEX-efficient counterparts through a three-way approach:

1. Increasing grid connection percentage, i.e. converting off-grid sites into grid sites
2. Deploying hybrid batteries on bad grid and off-grid sites
3. Deploying green energy solution (solar) on off-grid sites

Till date, over 105 solar sites have been set up in Nigeria, reducing diesel generator usage from 24 hours a day to just three to four hours daily. By 2013, Airtel Africa aims to completely eradicate the constant use of diesel and make its network entirely green power driven. In the last two years, Airtel reduced the diesel consumption by 25% across all sites.

G. **Biodiversity Project of Wipro:** The Biodiversity Project of Wipro takes into account an integrated approach toward the contribution in reducing energy and carbon intensity and improving water retention and harvesting. This project by the company was started in 2011 at its Electronic City in Bangalore and started with an assessment of the existing plant, birds, butterflies, insects, small mammals and other flora and fauna in the campus. The initial study made by the team recommended to increase the diversity of locally adapted species. The project area is divided into four themed parts:

A Butterfly Park: Garden showcasing native butterfly host and nectar plant.

Deccan: Based on the predominant geology of south India using mounds, rocks and natural water body designs.

Medical Circuit: Herbal garden classified by types of healing, i.e., heart and circulation, women's issues, etc.

Wetland Park: Ecosystem sustaining a variety of fish, water birds, insects and amphibians. Also integrating sustainable water management inside the campus.

The first stage of the project, the butterfly park, was completed in March 2013. The park is a witness to hundreds of migratory butterflies who stop over in the park for nearly a month in their 400 km pre-monsoon annual migration from western to the Eastern Ghats in India. The second phase of the project, (wetland park) is conceptualized as a series of five interconnected waterbodies. The company also started biodiversity programs in Pune, with the baseline assessment of biodiversity in the campus. Redesigning and planting work has already started. In all these programs, the company is working closely with expert partners in biodiversity, conservation, ecological design and communications. Building employee connect through expert talks, workshops and field visits to community research centers in forests, is a critical aspect of the program.

12. CONCLUDING OBSERVATIONS

Attempt has been made in this chapter to survey the CSR in practice. It will always be curious to know to what extent corporates have come forward to fulfill their obligations. In this regard, we may note down the following interesting aspects:

1. It is heartening to note that the Government is fully justified in making CSR an integral part of the corporate world. 2014-15 being the first year after the passing up of the new Companies Act, 2013, the survey has brought out the real interest of the companies.
2. The entire exercise can be interpreted as an opportunity to the corporate world to showcase their commitment towards society. This window being actually utilized by many companies.

3. It may be noted that all the select companies included in the survey have complied in total with the rules and regulations put in place in this regard.
4. The CSR policies declared by the companies are astounding and are able to reflect the true spirit of CSR philosophy of the companies.
5. The list of activities undertaken under the CSR programme by the companies is quite impressive and some companies like RIL, TCS, Wipro and Infosys are acting with high innovation in designing the CSR activities.
6. The vehicle used to carry out the CSR activities is adequate to reflect the trend in vogue. Given the focus, some companies may turn out to be international pioneers in this regard.
7. In the context of appreciating the good effort of the companies, Government of India may come out with suitable framework for evaluating the efforts of the companies on the CSR front. The idea of deploying private evaluators, giving scope for rising doubts about their methodology and objectivity is not in the right spirit in the opinion of the authors.

20
CHAPTER

Towards an Ethical and Sustainable Organisation

1. INTRODUCTION

'Better late than never' is the oft-repeated slogan in the Indian context. Though joined the bandwagon of countries taking measures to improve upon the practices of corporate governance late, the Government of India and the corporate sector has realized the need for setting the house right. The turn of the events that had taken place since the constitution of Task Force by the Confederation of Indian Industry have truly deepened the effort of other stakeholders. At this stage, attempt must be made to filip further thinking on the issue and not stop with the few measures like the constitution of Audit Committees and the appointment of Independent Directors. It is to be appreciated that the Government of India has acted by itself and through the organizations such as SEBI in giving shape to many of the recommendations/suggestions made by the committees on corporate governance. As a culmination of the effort, all the significant recommendations could find a place in the new Companies Act, 2013. There had been a mixed reaction regarding the provisions got incorporated in the Act. While many welcomed that the new Act had attempted to plug in many loopholes in several areas, including that of corporate governance, there were also a few having a feeling that the provisions were more severe and stringent, and thus may dampen the very spirit of governance. Nonetheless, the sincere effort of the government deserves all praise.

It is in this context, an attempt has been made in this chapter to set the ball rolling by imagining alternative mechanisms that can shape and improve corporate efficiency and democracy.

One possibility is to dispense with the existing mechanisms and devise newer ones. In such a context, one needs to evaluate the merits and demerits of this alternative. On the positive side, the existing mechanisms got evolved over a period of time; keeping in view the experience within and outside India. It took about two decades to the policy makers to get themselves convinced and finally give credence as a matter of law. Also accepting the fact that these systems are yielding tangible results in the advanced countries like USA, UK, Canada, etc., it may be worthwhile to remove the bottlenecks and inconsistencies, in their design and operation. For instance, it is stipulated that the number of Independent Directors shall be minimum three. Instead, a policy decision may be made to increase their presence in the Board by stipulating that their proportion shall be minimum of 50 per cent. Also to frame guidelines that prohibit the appointment of relatives/friends/well-wishers as Independent Directors on the Boards. Though it is very difficult to cull out the relationships among the individuals, reasonable/modest attempt can be done towards this end.

Another feasible solution appears to be maintaining a panel of experts/professionals, who can be considered for being appointed as Independent Directors; from whom companies can choose. The outfit already created by the Ministry of Corporate Affairs, Government of India in the name and style "National Foundation for Corporate Governance" in partnership with the Professional Bodies such as ICAI, ICSI, CII and BSE could be entrusted with this responsibility. In addition, the services of Indian Independent Directors' Association may also be solicited, since this is an initiative of the Chamber of Indian Micro, Small and Medium Enterprises. Answering a question whether corporate governance was of the highest standard among the start-up community, Sri Ratan Tata, Chairman Emeritus of Tata Group said that governance must ensure that one obeyed the law of the land. The enforcement should be strict and there is equality in enforcement.[1]

2. CONCEPT OF SUSTAINABLE ORGANISATION

Derived from the concept of sustainability, sustainable organizations are expected to integrate themselves with the environment around and convert themselves as ever-lasting. Corporate sustainability is often referred to as the involvement of the companies in the social activities, exhibiting, economic, social and environmental concerns in everything they do. Each company is supposed to choose its own course of action as to how it demonstrates its concern, to reach its ultimate goal of 'maximising its wealth'. The financial Times Lexicon has defined the term 'business sustainability' as managing the triple bottom line – a process by which companies manage their financial, social and environmental risks, obligations and opportunities. The three impacts are sometimes referred to as profits, people and planet.[2] A more robust expression is said to be the one that focuses on the capacity of the firm to survive shocks that are intimately connected to healthy economic, social and environmental systems. In a way, it goes without saying that businesses create economic value and contribute to healthy ecosystems and strong communities.

Sustainable organizations also need to adhere to the principles of 'sustainable development'; which is understood as the development 'that meets the needs of the present without compromising the ability of the future generations to meet their own needs'.[3] Therefore, corporates to be sustainable must address important issues related to economy (like innovation, property, productivity), social issues (like poverty, inequalities in the distribution of income and wealth, equity, health, education, gender discrimination, human rights, etc.) and including the concerns of environment (covering global warming, climate change, water storage, depletion of natural resources, forest cover, etc.). It is only when, corporations as constituents of the society can flourish and get the assent of the society. 'Advocates for Youth', a rights organisation has identified the following seven components of organizational sustainability:[4]

- Organisational identity (covering vision, mission, values, branding, messaging and strong leadership)
- Long range strategic plan (including goals, objectives and benchmarks)
- Annual operating plan (covering objectives, activities, timelines, staffing, programme needs, committed resources)
- Financial and other systems administration (to include budgeting, cash flow analysis, auditing and reporting)
- Long range fund raising plan (focusing on needs, resources, grants, etc.)
- Board development plan (concerning directors, evaluation, recruitment, team building, etc.)
- Staff development and organisational culture (to develop the organization to go with a committed value system)

The above is a broad criteria that every organization needs to follow to make itself sustainable. Under the given circumstances, the Declaration passed at the Rio De Janeiro Earth Summit (2012), Brazil amply explained the true spirit of sustainable development and the role of corporates in the process.[5] The conference has taken the view that sustainable Development meets the needs of the present without compromising the ability of future generations to meet their own needs. This as the guiding principle for long-term global development, focus is laid on the following three pillars:

- Economic development
- Social development
- Environmental protection

These three pillars were called the triple bottom line (TBL). This approach was intended to help companies integrate the above three components of sustainable development into their core operations and to translate 'sustainability theory' into 'management practice'. The focus of sustainable development and the triple bottom line is entirely compatible with the goal of business itself; namely, the creation of long-term shareholder value. The underlying rationale is that those companies emphasizing the economic, social and environmental dimensions of their business will be in a much better position to build 'competitive advantage', generate long-term wealth creation and sustainable profitability than companies that do not.

In this context, the United Nations Agenda for 'Sustainable Development' charted seventeen goals to be attained by 2030 by all the member nations. They are the following:

- End poverty in all its forms everywhere.
- End hunger, achieve food security and improved nutrition and promote sustainable agriculture.
- Ensure healthy lives and promote well-being for all at the ages.
- Ensure inclusive and equitable quality education and promote lifelong learning opportunities.
- Achieve gender equality and empower all women and girls.
- Ensure availability and sustainable management of water and sanitation for all.
- Ensure access to affordable, reliable, sustainable and modern energy for all.
- Promote sustained, inclusive and sustainable economic growth, full and productive employment and decent work for all.
- Build resilient infrastructure, promote inclusive and sustainable industrialization and faster innovation.
- Reduce inequality within and among countries.
- Make cities and human settlements inclusive, safe, resilient and sustainable.
- Ensure sustainable consumption and production patterns.
- Take urgent action to combat climate change and its impacts.
- Conserve and sustainably use oceans, seas and marine resources for sustainable development.
- Protect, restore and promote sustainable use of terrestrial ecosystems, sustainably manage forests, combat desertification, and halt and reverse land degradation and halt biodiversity loss.
- Promote peaceful and inclusive societies for sustainable development, provide access to justice for all and build effective, accountable and inclusive institutions at all levels.
- Strengthen the means of implementation and revitalize the global partnership for sustainable development.

In this context, the observations of Andy Grove (the long time leader of Intel, the world's biggest supplier of microprocessors of Silicon Valley) are very pertinent in understanding the philosophy of sustainability, as it applied to corporations.[6] According to Grove, Silicon Valley was squandering its 'competitive edge in innovation' by failing to propel strong job growth in the United States. He was trying to suggest that hiring workers and building factories outside USA and in Asia may look cheaper; but it masks the high price of off shoring in terms of losing jobs and expertise in USA. He feels that the Silicon Valley has misjudged the severity of those losses and has 'misplaced faith in the power of start-ups to create jobs in USA'. These feelings were pent up Mr. Donald Trump to come to power and become the 45th President of America. It appears that Americans are strongly believing that the exodus of foreign nationals into USA is severely damaging their job opportunities. Hence, they want the Government to limit the number of visas to be granted to outsiders.

Commenting on the free market, he said that there was nothing like unquestioned truism. The belief that 'free market is the best of all economic systems' is flawed, and the principles are not so infallible or immutable. In a job-centric system, job creation would be the nation's No.1 objective; with the governments setting priorities and arraying the forces necessary to achieve the goal and with the businesses operating not only in their **immediate profit interest, but also in the interests of employees and employees yet to be hired.**

The corporations thus, need to have the motive to implement sustainable strategies in every sphere of business activity, be it economy, ecology or law. Michael E. Porter has proposed a three pronged strategy of: (a) product differentiation; and (b) cost leadership, and (c) focus to achieve sustainability in organizations.[7] Porter's competitive strategy is about taking offensive or defensive action to create a defendable position in the industry. In order to gain 'sustainable competitive advantage', Porter suggested action on two aspects, viz., cost leadership and differentiation. Both of these finally culminate into a third viable competitive strategy called 'focus'.

According to Porter, competitive advantage exists when the firm is able to deliver the same benefits as competitors, but at a lower cost (i.e., cost advantage) or deliver benefits that exceed those competing products (differentiation advantage). Thus, the competitive advantage enables the firm to create superior value for its customers and superior profits for itself. According to the 'competitive advantage' model of the Porter, 'distinctive competencies' result from either resources or capabilities. Resources are the firm specific assets useful for creating a cost or differentiation advantage and that a few competitors can acquire easily. Examples of resource specific advantages may include:

- Patents and trademarks
- Proprietary know-how
- Installed customer base
- Reputation of the firm
- Brand equality

While capabilities of the firm refer to the ability to utilize its resources effectively. It may be like the ability to bring the product to market faster than the competitors, innovation, responsiveness and many other factors that can be leveraged to create a cost advantage or a differentiation advantage.

It is thus evident that only those companies that foresee future growth in the societies growth only thrive and sustain. In this context, a few alternative mechanisms are suggested for serious thinking and implementation for the good of the entire mankind.

3. TRUSTEESHIP THEORY OF MAHATMA GANDHI

Gandhiji's views on business have resulted in altogether a new philosophy of business called "Trusteeship Theory". He proposed that "when an individual earns more than his proportion, he becomes a trustee of that portion". Gandhiji viewed industry as a joint enterprise of labour and capital; in which both owners and workers are co-trustees for the society. Trusteeship conceives of no exploitation, black marketing, corruption, hoarding, manipulation of prices, tax evasion and debasement of products, misleading and fraudulent advertisements and unfair trade practices.

Gandhiji believed that this approach to business will reduce and remove inequalities of wealth. If there are no inequalities of wealth, there can be no inequalities of income and vice versa. There can be no peace in society as long as glaring inequalities exist.

The Trusteeship Philosophy of Gandhiji is based on his approach to life and society. It is a philosophy of life and a method of managing interpersonal relationships; where status symbolized by wealth or heredity merges itself with the common man. It envisages a new structure and a system of organization based on non-violence, the welfare of all, and the sharing of responsibilities, fruits of production as well as decision making. Gandhiji believes firmly that there can be no peace in the society, so long as glaring inequalities exist. By the non-violent trusteeship method, he does not seek to destroy the capitalist, he seeks to destroy capitalism. Gandhiji regards capitalist as a trustee for the people in the society for the creation, retention and the growth of his capital.

The Trusteeship theory of Gandhi can be considered a transforming ethics, having the following nuances:[8]

(i) Trusteeship is basically a principle of economic conscience, a dynamic model of the concept of economic organization and moral imperatives.

(ii) It is considered compatible with trust and non-violence. It is imagined that this effective combination would produce such a great power of moral and spiritual energy permeating the philosophies of capitalism and communism.

(iii) Trusteeship is a fraternal partnership between all factors of production, with the aim of achieving larger social benefit rather than working toward a narrow economic objective such as profit.

(iv) Social accountability is implicit in the concept of trusteeship. This also supposes a large number of honest, dedicated and competent technical people. It is not alone regulators that are entrusted with the job of curbing exploitative practices.

(v) Basic education is considered an absolute prerequisite of trusteeship. By basic education, Gandhiji meant a way of life, a method of learning and living and an art that is to be practiced throughout the life.

(vi) Trusteeship is a principle having universal application. All kinds of 'isms' find it convenient and consistent to follow.

It is for this reason, J.D. Sethi in his article entitled "The Awakening" (1978) felt that without proper education, workers participation in management and ownership can become a source of corruption and greed and be easily manipulated.[9] Reforms thus occur only through the growing consciousness of the workers. If the so-called proletarian consciousness has not developed anywhere according to the Marxist model, it is because the proletariat has not been educated about their responsibility as a class to society and the need to resist vested interests within their own ranks and leaders.

People quite naturally get a doubt as to whether there is any one company/group that is keeping faith in this kind of philosophy and running the business. For, the Indian Government never believed in this philosophy and it is said that even Nehru felt that these concepts are practically and politically impossible to follow. And thus the entire trusteeship philosophy was finally lost through the adoption of western industrial practices.

Going by the experience world over, there are many possible manifestations of the trusteeship principle, both in orgnisations and communities. Any of these experiments can be started at any place and at any time. The work in particular of the Intermediate Technology Development Group and the Plunkett Foundation (an agricultural cooperative movement started by Sir Horace Plunkett over 70 years ago) has taken this direction, incorporating a more holistic concern for the land.

The formation of the Scott Bader Commonwealth Ltd. in 1951 was such a manifestation. Founded by Ernest Bader and his family, it comprised the restructuring of an industrial manufacturing company towards the realization of trusteeship principles. Bader was a Swiss emigre who preferred the freedom and wider horizons in England in 1912 and after marrying Dora Scott in 1915 founded Scott Bader Co. Ltd. in 1920 to import Swiss celluloid, later expanding into synthetic resins. Bader had become a Quaker and, as a contributor to making a less violent world, stimulated by the influence of Gandhian non-violence, he and his family gifted the company to a Trusteeship in 1951, forming a cooperative common-ownership company. Two previous attempts to develop a value-driven company had failed, but due in part to the influence of George Goyder, restructuring of the previously privately owned company around the trusteeship concept was successfully accomplished.

The Mondragon Cooperatives in Spain can be considered to be practicing trusteeship principles. Mondragon has been helped by its early schooling through the founder Father Garizmendi, who started a training college. Scott Bader Commonwealth has not set up a formal learning center, but continually attempted to raise the awareness of its members to their responsibilities and common purposes.

Today, institutions are dubbed as 'learning organisations'. This is out of realization that the world around them is so turbulent and dynamic and the organization has to constantly improve upon its thinking and practice. The general orientation is towards the recognition of the stakeholders responsibilities. Realistically the world's resources are the property of all the citizen. Justice prevails only when there s equitable distribution and enjoyment of these resources. That is the reason, why there has been a great debate about ethics in the past and present centuries. Trusteeship provides just such ethics, and it is necessary that those who are aware of Gandhi's principle strive to pursue his unfinished task.

Apart from India, Ethics is being taught in business schools world over. Market economics, currency speculation, soil vitality, air pollution, the destruction of historic social cultures and marginalization of human relationships are all under intense discussion in the media and elsewhere. The continuing violence to the human condition and its environment is being challenged, but often the answer is to apply non-violence as a restraint. Some developments involving the U.N. have been of a trusteeship sort. Treatment of Antarctica as common place is an example of growing realisation. The Law of the Sea Conference was likewise motivated, and there have been proposals that space, atmosphere, and the mineral wealth of the sea bed should be seen as the common heritage of man.

The question in this context would be where will the motivation come from, and how can that motivation become a social force to be able to transform society? The effort should be towards creating passion in life and bring about a more sensible, ethical, and satisfying economic order. It was the intervention of the outsiders like Marx, Engels, Lenin, and others that initially lifted up a mere struggle for better wages and conditions of work to a theory and practice of social revolution of international scale. Lenin himself had pointed out that "the working class left to itself could not have gone beyond trade unionism.

There seems to be no one focuses on the concept of trusteeship. Since the early 1970s environmental awareness has grown so much to save the earth. There are also worldwide summits organisaed for this purpose. The 1992 Earth Summit in Rio highlighted how all our planetary life depends on the sun and the green cells. Awareness is also growing in schools where Agenda 21 and its follow-up involves the development of global thinking in young schoolchildren; almost the kind of basic education Gandhiji had in mind.

3.1 Quotes from the Writings of Gandhiji

People are aware that Gandhiji's principles have not emerged at one go. They were taught and practiced at varying times. It is basing on his own experience that he could declare that "My Life is My Message". Following are some of the quotes that appeared at varying times and places dovetailing his ideas on trusteeship. These are taken from the work compiled by Ravindra Kelkar entitled "Trusteeship" (printed and published by Jitendra T. Desai, Navajivan Mudranalaya, Ahmedabad).[10]

1. **Enjoy the Wealth by Renouncing it:** It is the wish of Gandhiji that the rich should ponder well as to what is their duty today. They who employ mercenaries to guard their wealth may find those very guardians turning on them. The moneyed classes have got to learn how to fight either with arms or with the weapon of non-violence. The best and most effective mantra is to resource wealth. One may earn crores by all means. But understand that the wealth is not yours; it belongs to the people. Take what you require for your legitimate needs, and use the remainder for society". This truth has hitherto not been acted upon; but, if the moneyed classes do not even act on it in these times of stress, they will remain the slaves of their riches and passions and consequently of those who over-power them.

   Gandhiji dreamt of the day of the rule of the poor. He was always preaching to use the force of non-violence. Let it be remembered that physical force is transitory even as the body is transitory. But the power of the spirit is permanent, even as the spirit is everlasting (Harijan, 1-2-1942, p. 20).

2. **Theory of Trusteeship:** "Supposing an individual inherits wealth, either by way of legacy, or by means of trade and industry – he must know that all that wealth does not belong to him. What belongs to him is that portion adequate to lead an honourable livelihood, no better than that enjoyed by millions of others. The rest of the wealth belongs to the community and must be used for the welfare of the community. Gandhiji enunciated this theory when the socialist theory was placed before the country in respect to the possessions held by zamindars and ruling chefs. They could not do away with these privileged classes. Therefore, what is required is to renounce the sense of possession and greed. There shall be a realization that the labourer has to realize that the wealthy man is less owner of his wealth than the labourer is owner of his own, viz., the power to work".

   The question how many can be real trustees according to this definition is not the question. If the theory is true, it is immaterial whether many live up to it or only one man lives up to it. The question is of conviction. If you accept the principle of Ahimsa, you have to strive to live up to it, no matter whether you succeed or fail. There is nothing in this theory which can go beyond the grasp of intellect, though one may consider it difficult to practice, (Harijan, 3-6-1939, p. 145).

3. **Economic Equality:** According to Gandhiji, working for economic equality means abolishing the eternal conflict between capital and labour. It means the leveling down of the few rich in whose hands is concentrated the bulk of the nation's wealth on the one hand, and a leveling up of the semi-starved, naked millions on the other. Gandhiji has realized that a non-violent system of government is clearly an impossibility, so long as the wide gulf between the rich and the hungry millions persists. There shall not be contrast between the palaces of New Delhi and the miserable hovels of the poor laboring class at villages. The poor shall also enjoy the same power as the richest in the land. A violent and bloody revolution is a certainty one day, unless there is a voluntary abdication of riches and the power that riches give and sharing them for the common good. Gandhiji declared that he would adhere to the doctrine of trusteeship in spite of he being ridiculed by his critics. It is true that it is difficult to reach. But we have to make our minds to negotiate that steep ascent. Surely, the effort would worth the wisdom. (Constructive Programme, 1948, pp. 20-21)

   At his tour of Madras, Gandhiji was asked at the Constructive Worker's Conference to explain the concept of economic equality. Then Gandhiji's replied that economic equality of his concept did not mean that everyone would literally have the same amount. It simply meant that everybody should have enough for his or her needs. For instance, the elephant needs a thousand times more food than the ant, but that is not an indication of inequality. So the real meaning of economic equality is the faith in the principle, "To each according to his need". In fact this was the definition of Marx. If a single man demanded as much as a man with wide and four children that would be a violation of economic equality (Harijan, 31-3-1946, p. 63).

4. **Doctrine of Equal Distribution:** In the opinion of Gandhiji, the real implication of equal distribution is that each man shall have the wherewithal to supply all his natural needs and no more. For example, if one man has a weak digestion and requires only a quarter of a pound of flour for his bread and another needs a pound, both should be in a position to satisfy their wants. To bring this ideal into being the entire social order has got to be reconstructed. A society based on non-violence cannot nurture any other ideal. Also, the society may not perhaps be able to realize the goal, if it does not keep in mind and work unceasingly to near it. Then only, there will be contentment and happiness prevailing in the society. That only would bring into being of a non-violent society (Harijan, 25-8-1940, pp. 260-261).

5. **Trusteeship: Not a Legal Fiction:** Gandhiji has stated that love and exclusive possession can never go together. When there is perfect love, there must be perfect non-possession. So a man can only exercise perfect love and be completely

dispossessed, if he is prepared to embrace death and renounce his body for the sake of human service. But that is true in theory only. In actual life, we can hardly exercise perfect love, for the body as a possession will always remain with us. Man will ever remain imperfect, and it will always be his part to try to be perfect. So perfection in love or non-possession will remain an unattainable ideal as long as we are alive, but towards which we must ceaselessly strive (The Modern Review, October 1935, p. 412).

6. **Practical Trusteeship Formula:** The following can be said to be the final principles of trusteeship:
   (i) Trusteeship provides a means of transforming the present capitalist order of society into an egalitarian one. It is not hatred about capitalism or capitalist, but gives the present owning class a chance of reforming itself. It is based on the faith that human nature is never beyond redemption.
   (ii) The concept recognizes the right of private ownership of property only to the extent in so far as it may be permitted by society for its own welfare.
   (iii) It does not exclude legislative regulation of the ownership and use of wealth. As a matter of fact, the Directive principles of the constitution of India contain such provisions. Gandhiji's philosophy is the foundation for framing such principles.
   (iv) Under State-regulated trusteeship, an individual will not be free to hold or use his wealth for selfish satisfaction or in disregard of the interests of society.
   (v) Against this premise, it is necessary to fix a decent minimum living wage and to put a limit on the maximum income that would be allowed to any person in society. The difference between such minimum and maximum incomes should be reasonable and equitable and variable from time to time. The eventual goal is to obliterate such difference.
   (vi) Under the Gandhian economic order, the character of production will be determined by social necessity and not by personal whim or greed. (Harijan, 25-10-1952).

4. THE IDEA OF COMPASSIONATE CAPITALISM

In one of his lectures delivered at the Global Brand Forum, Singapore, N.R. Narayana Murthy outlined this idea of 'Compassionate Capitalism'.[11] It is a fact that capitalism is a system based on the principle of individual rights and responsibilities. The bulk of economic activity is organized through private enterprise operating in a free market. Each person survives and flourishes based on his freedom to use his ability. Individuals and companies are allowed to compete for their own economic gain. Market forces determine the price of goods and services. Such a system is based on the premise of separating the State from the industry. The role of the State being to regulate and protect, each person has a right to the product of his own work and is driven to action by the opportunity to create wealth. Collectively, people create wealth for the society. This results in an efficient and optimum allocation of resources.

The idea of compassionate capitalism is about bringing the power of capitalism to the benefit of large masses. It is about combining the power of mind and heart; the good of capitalism and socialism. The Swedish model that combines private ownership of the means of production with an elaborate welfare mechanism is cited as reflective of the idea of compassionate capitalism. The success of Sweden in improving the economy and quality of life was being cited as the example for achieving "**growth with equity**'.

The benefits of growth have to be distributed widely. We cannot have a situation where there is economic growth for the strong and deprivation for the weak. The resultant social stress will break the very fabric of our economic system. Decades of progress will be reversed. We must remember the works of Adam Smith who said, 'No society can surely be flourishing and happy of which by far the greater part of the members are poor and miserable'. Compassionate capitalism is about fairness, integrity and putting the interest of society ahead of one's own interest. It is about overcoming greed and short-term orientation. It is but creating a community that believes in the concept of "*Vasudhaika Kutumbam*" (the world is one family).

Discussing the concept further, Narayana Murthy has identified the following reasons in support of his claim. First, we have to make it the most accepted model for growth in developing countries like India and other emerging countries. We want the people and leaders in developing countries to become believers in capitalism as the tool for their emancipation. We have to get millions of entrepreneurs excited about the opportunity to create wealth. We need dreamers who see a fire in every spark and an apple in every seed. The idea of prosperity always starts in the minds of men. They have to believe in an economic system which allows them to prosper. However, we cannot have market freedom without a focus on the conditions required to maintain this. We have to redeem people's faith in capitalism as an economic system which believes in the sanctity of private property, the freedom of contract, the power of free trade and the rule of law. Such a system allows them the freedom to experiment, invent and produce.

If we fail to act today, the poor, who have been alienated from economic and social progress, will lose faith in capitalism. Remember that the legitimacy of our economic system is at risk. We will do well to remember the words of John F. Kennedy who said, 'If a society cannot help the many who are poor, it cannot save the few who are rich.' It is our duty to create a mandate for an ideology that we believe in – one which allows unfettered opportunities to create an upward spiral of wealth and prosperity for everyone. This duty is even more vital for us, the business leaders, who have enjoyed the benefits of this system.

Addressing the most important and crucial issue of putting the idea into practice, he advocated the business leaders to take lead in regaining the trust of society and conduct in a more ethical and legal manner. Compassionate capitalism is about putting community interest ahead of private interest in the short term and being a good corporate citizen. It is about civilized behavior and about long-term orientation. It is about making life better for the next generation. This is what civilized societies are about and history has shown that is such civilized societies that have always progressed.

Much before, Peter F. Drucker has attempted to bring to the notice of the world, the limits to capitalism. In one of his writings entitled 'Post-Capitalist Society (1993)" he predicted that every nation tends to reform itself radically in every 200 years of its existence.[12] He was suggesting that there would be a major upheaval in the transition of economies. His predictions were found to be so accurate that the history there was proved that no need to wait for 200 long years for a major transformation to take place and it could even be less, like 75 years as in the case of Soviet Union. The disintegration had produced many lessons leading to a serious debate on the ideological foundations of nations. Furthermore, even without taking sides to capitalism or communism, countries in South Asia such as Singapore, Hong Kong, Malaysia, etc., could register impressive growth rates under 'Mixed Economic System'.[13] Drucker identifies four key transitions in the global economy: in the 1300s, from a feudal, agrarian economy to modern capitalism and the nation-state; in the late 1700s and 1800s, the Industrial Revolution of steam power and factories; in the 20th century, a Productivity Revolution as management of work and processes boosted the productivity of labor, transforming the proletariat class into the middle class; and since the 1990s, the emergence of the Knowledge Economy. In Drucker's analysis, these fast-spreading economic revolutions trigger equally profound political and social dynamics. The dominant social structures that we take for granted – labor and capital, and the nation-state – are not immutable; rather, they are the modern-day equivalent of the late-1200s feudal society that seemed permanent to those who had known nothing else but that was already being dismantled and replaced by the Renaissance-era development of modern capitalism. Drucker thus, feels that one should be a good historian, if one wishes to make a logical and emphatic argumentation in any scientific contribution.

5. THE CONCEPT OF RATIONALITY

It is premised that management is concerned with 'Decision Making Process'. There are diverse view points as to how processes interact with various variables constituting the decision making activity. A new dimension has been added to the process of decision making with the realization of the fact that the whole process is 'Behavioral'. The continuum of decision making behavior begins with Economic Rationality and ends with Social model, as of the following:

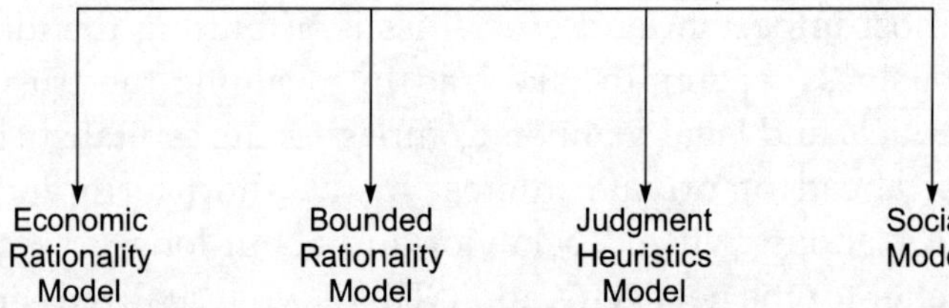

Attempting to find an answer to the question: why does a decision maker choose one alternative over another? There had been several propositions varying from the pure rationality to that of psychological intervention.

Rationality model assumes that a decision maker is completely and perfectly rational in choosing alternatives. Decision making is a means to an end. If appropriate means are chosen to reach the desired ends, the decision is said to be rational. Under this framework, the decision maker always strives to maximize outcomes in the business firm and decisions will be directed to the point of maximum profit where marginal cost equals marginal revenue (MC = MR). Several new techniques such as Activity Based Costing (ABC), Economic Value Added (EVA) and Market Value Added (MVA) are developed basing on this principle to be effective in dealing with the contemporary business phenomenon. Companies like Union Carbide, Hewlett Packard, General Electronics could take advantage of these methods.

Though appeals to the logic, there are several limitations in applying the rationality test. To begin with, it is difficult to separate means from ends, because an apparent end may be only a means for some future end leading to 'means – ends chain'. Authors like Hebert Simon point out that the means-end hierarchy is seldom an integrated and completely connected chain.

Herbert A. Simon proposed the concept of 'Bounded Rationality' as an alternative to Rationality model on the assumption that managers only attempt to satisfy or look for a 'satisfactory' or 'good enough' alternative, rather than focusing only on the alternative of maximum profit. A further extension to this satisfying model has emerged in the form of 'Judgmental Heuristics and Biases' model, which proposes that managers operate on "simple rules of thumb' rather than complex networking, thus saving considerable mental activity and cognitive processing.[14]

On the contrary, a new decision making model has been proposed by like Sigmund Freud. This model views human being as a bundle of feelings, emotions and instincts, with his behavior being guided largely by his unconscious desire, and thus challenging the principle of rationality. Psychologists have a firm belief that decision making is to a great extent irrational, guided by the psychological traits of the manager. Several studies were conducted to prove the point that how irrationality creeps in to the decision making process. Although most contemporary psychologists would take issue with the Freudian description of humans, almost all would agree that social influences have a significant impact on decision making behaviors.

6. FOCUS ON RIGHTS, VIRTUES, VALUES AND JUSTICE

Later to the Doctrine of Utilitarianism, Ethics had been interpreted in several dimensions focusing on rights, morals virtues, values and justice. Immanuel Kant (1724-1804) through his treatise on "Foundations of the Metaphysic of Morals (1785) attempted to show that there are some things that we ought to do and others that we ought not to do, merely by virtue of being rational. Moral obligation thus arises solely from a moral law that is binding on all rational beings. The Rights theory emphasizes on a variety of rights that needed to be extended to human beings as 'entitlements'[15]. It speaks of the legal, moral, general, specific, negative and positive rights, which people are entitled to.

The following choices/actions are treated as reflective of ensuring ethics at corporate places:

1. Equality in the distribution of benefits and burdens.
2. Compensation of persons for wrongs done to them
3. Punishment for wrong doers.
4. Right to basic liberties
5. Principle of equal opportunity
6. Preference to public consumption over private consumption of natural resources
7. Ensuring fair competition at the market place
8. Ensuring employee privacy, consumer privacy and privacy on the Internet
9. Fair disclosure to outsiders
10. Justifying the means used to gather information
11. Eliminating discrimination of all forms based on caste, creed, colour, religion, age, etc., and ensuring equal treatment to all stakeholders.
12. Preventing sexual harassment
13. Principle of comparable worth in terms of job content and productivity.
14. Equal pay for equal work
15. Avoiding unjust dismissal
16. Freedom of contract
17. Acting as model employer
18. Protecting consumer rights in terms of product safety, packaging branding, advertising, etc.
19. Ensuring health and safety of employees
20. Fairness in stock markets.

By no means, the list is exhaustive. Each of the above is a proposition by itself, seeking to emphasize a specific point of view/dimension of corporate ethics.

7. SOCIAL AUDITING VS. GOVERNANCE AUDIT

The notion of 'Social Accounting' or 'Social Audit' emerged during 1950s to make businesses more accountable to the society. World over, the concept has found its application in evaluating the responsive behavior of the corporates towards people in the society; as a measure of understanding the discharge of functions under the scheme of 'Corporate Social Responsibility (CSR)'. One thing has become perceptible that no longer corporates speak only about 'shareholders'; they need to talk about all the 'stakeholders' now. George Goyder (1961), who is believed to have first used the term 'social audit' stated that the roots of the idea lay within the perceived need to make business more accountable to the community and to ensure that the impacts of businesses (both beneficial and non-beneficial) are properly understood by the society.[16] Goyder attempted to link the growing importance of social audit to the need for society to be able to exert the control and influence over corporations as they globalize. It is an approach to reporting a firm's activities which stresses the need for the identification of socially relevant behavior; the determination of those to whom the company is accountable for its social performance and the development of appropriate measures and reporting techniques.[17] Taking cue from these ideas, companies like TISCO, WIPRO, INFOSYS, etc. have shared the information with the public.

The moot point in this context is: can we design and implement a similar mechanism in respect of corporate governance? Under the existing arrangement of Audit Committees and Independent Directors, compliance is verified by the concerned and reported to the Board only. There is no scope for sharing the same with the people in the society. As a step in this direction, it may be good enough to make it mandatory to the companies to publish "Corporate Governance Audit" reports for the information of the public; so that the role of the Audit Committees and the Independent Directors will also come to the notice of the public. This idea can be tried. As a matter of fact, it was quite common in UK for community based organizations to include the commitment to do social accounting and audit within their constitution. This was legalized in 2005 through an Act, whereby a new form of social enterprise structure 'the Community Interest Company' has become popular. The most interesting aspect is that social accounting is being adopted with increasing enthusiasm by private sector orgnisations in UK like Camelot, Shell International, Diageo, United Utilities, Rio Tinto Zinc, etc. This can be considered a step in the direction of "Vigil by the Civil Society'.

8. TOWARDS BUILDING AN ETHICAL ORGANISATION

Ethics shall be construed as old as man himself. Human chains can live and survive only when societies are organized, subject to a 'Code of Ethics'. Indian Epics – Ramayana and Mahabharatha – are a rich treasure in describing the ethical principles of building sustainable societies and organizations. They have enunciated "Principles of Conducting Human Relations". Thus evolved several codes of ethics such as Vyasa, Vidura and Narada. Many other saints later to them also have enunciated their own points of view as to how societies are to be built and how human beings shall establish relations among themselves.

Basing on the broader concept of Social Ethics, Corporate Ethics has been built. Corporate Ethics had evolved as a subject of study with the contributions of Jeremy Bentham (1748-1832) and John Sturat Mill (1806-1873) through their "Doctrine of Utilitarianism". According to Bentham, the Principle of utility means that principle which approves or disapproves of every action whatsoever, according to the tendency which it appears to have to augment or diminish the happiness of the party whose interest is in question; or what is the same thing in other words, to promote or to oppose happiness.[18] The principle requires that consequences be measured in some way so that the pleasure and pain of different individuals can be added together and the results of different courses of action compared. It is assumed that a precise quantitative measurement of pleasure and pain was possible. If this process is repeated for all other individuals whose interests are affected, the resulting sum will show the good or bad tendency of an action for the whole community. Economists have dubbed this as "Social Cost-Benefit Analysis".

In the words of J.S. Mill, utility is the creed which accepts as the foundation of morals, utility or the Greatest Happiness Principle, which hold that actions are right in proportion as they tend to promote happiness, wrong as they tend to produce the reverse of happiness.[19] By happiness is intended pleasure and the absence of pain, by unhappiness, pain and the deprivation of pleasure. In sum, utilitarianism preaches that "an action is right, if and only if it produces the greatest balance of pleasure over pain for everyone. The above Doctrine of Utilitarianism could not be implemented due to the problem of calculating utility in terms of monetary values.

Notes & References

1. The Hindu, Dt.19.06.2015, P.13.
2. Financial Times Lexicon (www.lexicon.ft.com)
3. World Council for Economic Development (WCED)
4. www.advocatesforyouth.org.
5. www.uncsd2012.org.
6. New York Times News Service – published in The Hindu, dated 27.03.2016.
7. Porter, Michael E., 'The Competitive Advantage', Free Press, 1985.
8. Godric Bader, 'Gandhi on Trusteeship: A Transforming Ethics', World Business Academy Perspectives, Vol. 9, No. 4, 1995, Berrett-Kochler Publishers, UK.

9. Sethi, J.D., 'The Awakening', Journal of Lok Sevak Sangh, Vol. I, No. 2, November 1978.
10. Ravindra Kelkar, "Trusteeship", Navajivan Mudranalaya, Ahmedabad, 1996.
11. Narayana Murthy, NR, "A Better India – A Better World", Penguin Books India, 2009, pp. 211-218.
12. Drucker, Peter F., "Post Capitalist Society", Routledge, New York, 2011.
13. Rao, K.V., 'Memorial Lecture on Contribution of Peter F. Drucker to Practice of Management", 2008.
14. Fred Luthans, "Organisational Behaviour", The McGraw Hill Companies, Irwin, 2011.
15. Thomas Paine, 'The Rights of Man', J.S. Jordan, London, 1791.
16. Goyder, G (1961), *The Responsible Company,* Blackwell Publishing Co., U.K.
17. Crowther, D. (2000), *'Social and Environmental Accounting'*, Financial Times – Prentice Hall, London.
18. Jeremy Bentham, *The History of Utilitarianism*, Center for the Study of Language and Information, Stanford University, Stanford, 2014.
19. John Stuart Mill, "*Utilitarianism*", Savill and Edwards Printers, London, 1863.

1

CASE STUDY

The Case of 'Santhara': Salvation or Suicide?

1. THE CONTEXT

The Supreme Court of India on 31-08-2015 passed an order staying the operation of the Judgement of Rajashtan High Court dated 10-08-2015 passed in connection with the practice of Santhara. The High Court had declared the practice of Santhara (also called Sallekhana) i.e., fasting/starving unto death illegal, and an offence punishable under the Indian Penal Code. The High Court, while disposing of the Public Interest Litigation (PIL) filed by a Lawer (Nikhil Soni of Jaipur) in 2006, made the following observations.

1. Article 25 of the Constitution of India guarantees freedom of conscience and free profession, practice and propagation of religion under the heading **"Right to Freedom of Religion"**, subject to public order, morality and health and to the other provisions of this Part, which includes Article 21. No religious practice, whether essential or non-essential or voluntary can permit taking one's own life to be included under Article 25. The right guaranteed for freedom of conscience and the right to freely profess, practice and propagate cannot include the right to take one's life, on the ground that right to life includes the right to end the life. Even in extraordinary circumstances, the voluntary act of taking one's life cannot be permitted as the right to practice and profess the religion under Article 25 of the Constitution of India.
2. The respondents have failed to establish that the Santhara or 'Sallekhana' is an essential religious practice, without which the following of the Jain religion is not permissible. There is no evidence or material to show that the Santhara or Sallekhana has been practiced by the persons professing Jain religion even prior to or after the promulgation of the Constitution of India to protect such right

under Article 25 of the Constitution of India. The over-riding and governing principles of public order, morality and health, conditions the right to freedom of conscience and the right to freely profess, practice and propagate religion. The right under Article 25 is subject to the other provisions of this Part, which includes Article 21. We are unable to accept the submission that the practice of 'Santhara' or 'Sallekhana' as a religious practice is an essential part of the Jain religion, to be saved by Article 25 or Article 26 or Article 29 of the Constitution of India.

3. The writ petition is allowed with directions to the State authorities to stop the practice of 'Santhara' or 'Sallekhana' and to treat it as suicide punishable under section 309 of the Indian Penal Code and its abetment by persons under section 306 of the Indian Penal Code. The State shall stop and abolish the practice of 'Santhara' and 'Sallekhana' in the Jain religion in any form. Any complaint made in this regard shall be registered as a criminal case and investigated by the police, in the light of the recognition of law in the Constitution of India and in accordance with Section 309 or Section 306 IPC, in accordance with law.

2. THE REACTION

Immediately after the judgement by the Rajasthan High Court, there were many meetings and rallies held by the members belonging to the Jain community denouncing the judgement of the High Court. The Jain Associations and individuals openly criticized the judges and called them ignorant and disrespectful of their religious practice. Hence, filed a petition to set aside the order of the High Court. The Bench comprising the Chief Justice H.L. Dattu and Justice Amitava Roy, while staying the order of the High Court, ordered to issue notices to the Centre, Government of Rajasthan and others. There were also many other petitions that came for hearing before the Bench.

3. THE PRACTICE

Santhara (also called pandit-maran, sallekhana and sakham-maran) is a Jain custom practiced by Swetambara Jains of embracing voluntary death. Digambaras call it Sallekhana. To the Jains, santara/sallekhana is an act of supreme renunciation and great piety. It is a practice aimed at self-purification. The vow of santhara is taken when all purposes of life have been served or when the body is unable to serve any purpose of life. It is not the giving up of life, but taking death in their stride.

4. ARGUMENTS IN FAVOUR OF SANTHARA

Even since the PIL was admitted in the Rajasthan High Court and its order on August 10, 2015, there arose a heated debate forcing arguments in favour and against of the practice of Santhara. The following is the gist of such arguments of the experts/ associations supporting santhara as a permissible religious practice and not a crime punishable under IPC.

1. Santhara is an age old practice and is the soul of Janism. Without the same, a Jain sadhak's (practioner) practice is not complete.
2. It is a scientific process, where the body is crushed in a gradual manner. Mostly, only those in the last phase of their life (who are either too old or suffering from serious ailments) starve themselves to death. The vow is carried out in stages, by gradually giving up solid food, and finally, even water. More so, it is to be done under the supervision of a Jain monk. There is also the chance to withdraw from the practice, unlike suicide. The most famous example quoted in this context is that of 'Muni Vidyanand' a Digambar Jain Saint, who withdrew from sallekhana after six years, saying that his body was not yet ready.
3. Jain philosophy believes that 'Body' is the prison of the human soul, unlike the belief in Christianity; where it believes that the body is the God given gift and can be likened to that a of a 'temple of the human soul'. Hence, Jains believe that the soul needs to be liberated by all the sacred means; whereby santhara is one such alternative.
4. Hampa Nagarajaiah, an eminent Kannada scholar on Jainism, speaking in favour of the practice remarked that: "sallekhana is not suicide committed in a fit of anger; it is carried out in a most peaceful way. It has a code of conduct; it has a grammar of its own; a person embracing it first approaches a monk, who administers an oath only after he is convinced that the seeker deserves this form of death'. He says that it has a long unbroken history from 6th century B.C., till the modern times. The roots are deep and has sanctity. The practice denotes a willing submission to death; not out of anger, revenge or hatred.

   He was citing a Book called "Aradhana", written in 2nd century A.D. by a monk named Sivakoti, which can be considered a treatise on death. The book which is written in prakrit language, contained 2500 verses and explained about 48 varieties of death. Of them, 'bala marana' (immature death), is considered the lowest form and pandita marana (matured death) as the highest. Pandita marana is the one called Santhara.
5. Justice (Retired) P.C. Jain calls Santhara as an age old custom and there is lot of difference between Santhara and sati; the latter being of a recent origin and born out of material interests. P.C. Jain was on the bench, which declared 'sati' as illegal on the Deorala case. Perhaps, the incident of Roop Kanvar may be still fresh in the minds of social activists.
6. Kanak Parmar, the General Secretary of the Mumbai based Jain Shakti Foundation believes that Santhara is observed amid festivity and the person concerned is

treated as equivalent of God. The house as a place of pilgrimage. He termed the Judgement as "an assault on the culture of Janism". Similar views were expressed by many Jain associations.

7. The concept of Ichcha Mrityu (voluntary death/death by own choice) is said to be the theme of Hindu culture. It has been described as a rare gift, reserved only for the greatest of souls and those who earned it as the ultimate reward for their righteous karma and dharma. It is cited in Mahabharat that Shantanu when he was happy with his son Devavrata (Bhishma) for the sacrifices he made for him, he blessed the son with Ichcha Mrityu, a right that Bhishma exercised at the end of the war of Mahabharat.

5. ARGUMENTS OPPOSING SANTHARA

1. The practice is not many times voluntary. Many women in India are treated badly and disrespected, if powerless and sent to Vrindavan, a kind of socially imposed prison sentence.
2. Santhara is a glorified suicide and not an essential practice. This is the observation of the Rajasthan High Court and said that there is no dignity whatsoever in the act of fasting. The judges observed that "we do not find in any of the scriptures, preaching's, articles or practices followed by the Jain ascetics, that Santhara has been treated as an essential religious practice, nor is necessarily required for the pursuit of immortality or moksha".
3. Human rights activists allege that old people are made to undertake santhara by their relatives; who do not want to look after them.
4. Nikhil Soni, the petitioner in the PIL at Rajasthan High Court has cited the case of Bimla Devi Bhansali, who was allegedly coerced into santhara by her family and whose cries for help were ignored. Incidentally, Bhansali hails from Churu district of Rajasthan which saw the highest number of santhara cases; as it is a mass hysteria.
5. The petitioner to the case, Mr. Nikhil Soni has described the practice as of Santhara as abhorrent to modern thinking. He submits that no religion howsoever historical, pure or revered, can permit or allow a person to commit death by choice. The fast until death is nothing but a self-destruction in whatever form and belief it may be, and that fundamental right to freedom of religion cannot protect a criminal act as it is subject to public order, morality and health. The guarantee given by the Constitution under Article 25 is that every person in India shall have the freedom of conscience and shall have the right to profess, practice and propagate religion, subject to restrictions imposed by the State on the grounds of: (i) public order, morality and health; (ii) other provisions of the Constitution; (iii) regulation of non-religious activity associated with religious practice;

(iv) social welfare and reform; (v) throwing open of Hindu religious institutions of a public character to all classes of Hindus. No practice or belief or tenet, which is abhorrent to public order, morality and health and violates other provisions of the Part-III, namely, Article 21, can protect the religious practice.

While attempting a synthesis between the beliefs and practices, Shekhar Hattangadi, a Mumbai based Professor of Constitutional Law and an award winning documentary film maker titled "**Santhara : A Challenge to Indian Secularism**" felt that there is a basic difference in the Indian Secularism. We follow the west in legal and economic principles; and keep faith in the Indian traditions. The law being based on the west, naturally ignores Indian religious practices, not known to them.

Question for Debate/Discussion

1. It is said that santhara is practiced by the aged, suffering from illness leading to imminent death, famine or non-availability of food and old age with loss of faculties. The questions that remain unanswered in this context are:
   (i) Can we fix a particular age (say, 60, 70, 80) by which one can be permitted to opt for santhara?
   (ii) Can we identify and list out diseases/illness, so that persons suffering from the same are allowed to practice santhara?
2. Why only the practice is more popular among women, as if men do not wish to have liberation or moksha?
3. How do we distinguish between voluntary and involuntary decisions? Also how to cull out the influence of family members in prompting such practice?
4. In what form and context, santhara distances itself from 'sati'?
5. What comparison can we draw as to the 'samadhi' (burying oneself while alive) practiced by the devotees/followers in Hinduism?
6. How do we compare santhara with the practices like 'Honour Killings" and Mercy Killings, considered illegal?
7. Going by the reaction of the members of the community of the judgement of the Rajasthan High Court in terms of going to the extent of criticizing the judges openly and calling in question their understanding of the practice and terming their attitude as disrespectful, should we need to understand the same as a revolt against judiciary or that judiciary has no business to talk or interpret or comment about the religious practices/dictums?
8. If Ichcha Mrityu (death by own choice) can be accepted as a right bestowed on individuals as per the Hindu Mythology, what wrong would there be in permitting every other religion to choose death?

9. How do we reconcile theological and philosophical beliefs on the one hand and the legal position on the other; in the context that Anglo-Saxon Law is being imposed on the other religions, not being able to understand the very meaning of death?
10. Osho – a spiritual guru – argues that the purpose of Santhara is to cleanse the spirit and prepare it for rebirth and by choosing through this method, become the determiner of the next birth. If Salvation or Moksha is the ultimate goal, where would be the question of rebirth?

2

CASE STUDY

Dadri Incident: It is an Outrage against Freedom of Food?

1. THE INCIDENT

On September 28, a group of people (believed to be right wing Hindu activists) attacked and killed Mohammad Akhlaq Saifi, a resident of Bishahra village in Taluq of Gautam Buddha Nagar district in Uttar Pradesh. They also grievously injured his 20-year old son Damish and misbehaved with his wife. Mr. Akhlaq was a [50 year] Muslim ironsmith living with their Hindu neighbours peacefully for over decades.

2. THE CAUSE/PROVOCATION

The logical question would be: Why was he lynched by the mob. There are different versions as to the cause of lynching. That Akhlaq had kept in his refrigerator meat of beef and the family is consuming the same. Another version is that he had consumed the meat of cow. The PMO's office had asked for a report from the UP Government. The UP Government, accordingly sent a detailed report to the Home Ministry, but did not mention any reason for the murder of Mohammad Akhlaq. Without mentioning the word 'beef or cow slaughter", the state Government has said that there were allegations that the deceased was killed for consuming 'Pratibandhit pashu ka maans (meat of an animal, whose slaughter is banned). The Government said in its report that it was still investigating and had not reached any conclusion yet. Immediately after the incident, the UP Government has airlifted the family to Lucknow and given protection. The Chief of the Air Staff Air Chief Marshal Arup Raha, has come to the rescue of the family and shifted them to a secured military locality. The Air Chief Marshal has commented that "it is very unfortunate that a serving Air Force employee's family has been adversely affected, resulting in death in the family.

3. POLITICISATION OF THE INCIDENT

Because of the sensitivity involved, the incident attracted the attention of diverse political parties/leaders. These persons created heat by their statements, claims and counters. Amid rising tensions in Dadri, BJP leader and MLA from Sardhana Constituency Sangeet Som visited Bishahra on Sunday (one day after the fateful day) and said to have invoked Hindu retaliation during the 2014 Muzaffarnagar riots. He addressed a charged and angry crowd despite Section 144 being imposed in the village. It was reported that his visit had created tension among the residents of the village and they remained completely polarized and divided on religious lines while addressing the crowd, Mr. Som was stated to have declared that a 'heinous crime' like cow slaughter was committed in the village and the Samajwadi Government was acting in a completely one-sided way. The Chief Minister met the family in Lucknow after they were airlifted and announced a financial assistance of Rs. 45 lakh. He said that his party would 'never do politics on such issues'.

The family members of Md. Akhlaq Saifi alleged the possible role of Vishal, son of Sanjay Rana, a local BJP leader inciting the mob. The family had told the local administration that they suspect that it was Vishal who had coerced the priest of the local temple to announce that a cow was slaughtered in Akhlaq's house and that his family was eating beef.

The police altogether arrested eight of the accused (number of accused not known) including Vishal, Shivam and others. With the two high profile visits, first by the Delhi Chief Minister Arvind Kejriwal and later by Rahul Gandhi, the area remained tense. Several hundreds of agitated village women on the streets protested against what they alleged to be 'one-sided media coverage'. Armed with stones, several hundred women took to the streets and abused pressperson and politicians. Literally, the media person were ruthlessly chased away. They also argued with the media that nobody was showing the plight of the family of the accused who were 'wrongly arrested'.

The police have also filed a case against Ritu Rathaur for using social media via Twitter (Twitter handle @ Riturathaur) for spereading sensational and controversial posts. It was said that Ms. Rathaur posted a picture of a sub-inspection's body, alleging that he was mowed down by Muslims, when he stopped a truck carrying beef in Saharanpur. It turned out that the police person was killed not by people carrying beef, but he lost the life when he tried to stop a truck carrying river stones. Ms. Rathaur, who has about 22,300 followers on Twitter, was accused of spreading 'dangerous rumours' on social media against which several Twitter users demanded action. Her post was allegedly well circulated on WhatsApp, Twitter and Facebook. Later, the Sharanpur SP clarified that Ms. Rathaur's allegations were baseless.

Meanwhile a man was beaten to death by a mob at Sirmaur in the Sarahana area of Himachal Pradesh for allegedly trying to smuggle a truckload of cattle to Saharanpur in UP. The five occupants of the truck were beaten up by the mob and one of them Noman (28) who hails from UP died of injuries in hospital. A new sensation was created by the Chief Minister of Haryana, Mr. Manoharlal Khattar by making a comment that all Muslims must give up beef eating, if they wish to stay in India (News reported on 17-10-2015) . This has created an uproar in the political circles regarding the right of the Muslims to stay in India and shadowing questions on their citizenship.

4. THE LEGAL ISSUES

The incident has given rise to many legal issues, including the 'freedom of food'. The questions that sprung included the following:

(i) What freedom do people have in choosing their food?

(ii) Is the right to privacy granted under Article 21 of the Constitution absolute? Can there be restrictions imposed on the same.

(iii) Can one person's religious freedom interfere with another's food preferences?

To begin with Article 21 of the constitution, 'No person shall be deprived of his life or personal liberty except according to procedure established by law'. The right of the person to eat food of his choice has come for discussion before Supreme Court several times. There were conflicting judgements in respect of imposing restrictions for long or short periods. The question came for consideration is what is short and what is long? In the 2008 'judgement in Hinsa Virodhak Sangh Vs. Minzapur Moti Kuresh Jamat and others, the Supreme Court held that the nine day ban on meat consumption in Gujarat is a reasonable restriction; since ban is only for nine days and not for a 'considerable period time'. But the judgement did not define what it meant considerable period of time. This ban was imposed in the States of Maharashtra and Gujarat on the eve of 'penance of the Jain community called Paryushan'.

Earlier in 2004, the Supreme Court has opposed a full year ban on the sale of fish, meat, eggs in Rishikesh, like the one existed in Haridwar and Muniki Reti for many years. On this occasion, the Supreme Court invoked the dietary preferences of pilgrims visiting these towns as sufficient justification for such a ban. But as far as the State Governments' response are concerned, it is mixed. The State of Jammu & Kashmir is the one that had a separate law (J&K Ranbir Penal Code, 1932) which bans the sale and slaughter of bovines. Now there is a more from the opposition seeking to amend this law and pave the way for lifting the ban. While the State legislations in 1950s imposed a complete ban on slaughter of cows and a partial ban on slaughter of bulls, the scope of the ban has increased over the decades. More recent legislations in States like Madhya Pradesh and Maharashtra contain a complete prohibition on the slaughter of cows, bulls and bullocks. Similarly, in a recent petition (news dated 22/9/2015), the Bombay High Court refused to grant an interim stay on the ban on slaughter of bulls and bullocks for Bakrid festival on the ground that it would amount to staying a statutory provision. A section of the Muslim community petitioned that a complete ban is violative of their constitutional rights under Article 25 of the Constitution (i.e., freedom of religion) and requested for lifting of the ban for just three days from 25th to 27th of September, 2015. The petitioners also maintained that slaughter was an essential part of their religious practices. Nevertheless, the High Court has rejected the plea and observed that a detailed investigation was required to decide on the matter as to amending section 5 of the Maharashtra Animal Preservation (Amendment) Act of 1995, which extended ban from cows to bulls and bullocks. During the election time at Bihar (October 6, 2015), senior Congress parliamentarian, Pramod Tiwari claimed that Congress party has imposed ban in 24 of the 29 states, when it was in power. Unfortunately, there are around 36,000 slaughter houses across India.

In the meantime, the Chief Minister of the Government of West Bengal declared that her government had no intention to ban the consumption of meat during the Durga Puja (news dated 22/09/2015). In a similar case of serving or not serving of any food on the days of fasting (during Ramzan), the Government of Kerala issued clear instructions that there shall be no ban on the serving of 'mid-day meal' to the schoolchildren on the Ramzan days. The circular said that meal be served to those who were not on fasting.

5. ROLE OF CULTURAL OUTFITS

Making the matter still complex, right wing activists have started passing dictates to the people of different religions as to the kind of food they shall consume. The outfits included organizations like Shiv Sena, RSS, etc. During the meat ban imposed for 4 days by the Mumbai Municipal Corporation on the occasion of Paryushan (Jain community's annual fasting period), there was lot of hue and cry and the corporation had to withdraw the ban from 4 to 2 days. In this context, Shiv Sena warned the Jain community that it risked being alienated from mainstream Indian society, if it confinued to insist on a ban on meat.

Muslim Rashtriya Manch, an RSS offshoot has released a booklet to persuade Indian Muslims to give up beef. The booklet said that Babur asked his son Humayun not to allow cow slaughter in defence of Hindus' feelings. Even the last Mughal emperor Bahadur Shah Zafar banned cow slaughter. They also advised Muslims that they should avoid consuming diseases in the form of beef.

Meanwhile, RSS claimed that there is scientific basis for cow protection. It identified five products of the cow to be used like the urine, dung, etc. There is a Sangh related Cow Science Research Centre (Gau Vigyan Anusandhan Kendra, Nagpur). Also claimed that cow dung can render hydrogen and atom bombs "ineffective". Radioactivity does not affect a place painted with cow dung or affects it only marginally. It is also reported that cow urine and dung can be used to make better fertilizers, as opposed to chemical fertilizers.

The President of India, while releasing a book about him written by the New Indian Express Editorial Director Prabhu Chawla, Pranab Mukherjee warned against letting go of India's Core Values (News dated 08/10/2015). Shri Mukherjee remarked that 'we cannot allow the core values of our civilization to be wasted. Over the years, this civilization has celebrated diversity, promoted and advocated tolerance, enjoyed plurality'.

Questions for Debate/Discussion

1. Is food an issue of personal nature? Or is it a state subject, requiring the governments to pass a separate legislation?
2. How do we juxtapose Article 21 and Article 25 of the Constitution of India?
3. What are reasonable restrictions that can be imposed in the consumption of animal meat?
4. Do you support the interference of cultural organizations in deciding what to eat and what not to eat?
5. Should the issue be left for political decision or legal interpretation?

3

CASE STUDY

Rigging of Diesel Emission Tests by Volkswagen: A Breach of Trust?

1. THE ALLEGATION

The allegation against the company is that it has used software that deceived regulators measuring toxic emissions. It is said that the company has rigged the emission tests. The issue has come to the fore by virtue of an order passed by the Environmental Protection Agency (EPA) of the United States of America directing the Volkswagen to recall close to half a million (5 lakh) vehicles, accusing the company of fiddling emission tests on diesel-powered vehicles (order dated 18.9.2015).[1] It is also reported in the media that the US Development of Justice has started a criminal probe into the allegations, which may cover several types of vehicles being produced by the company such as Audi – branded diesel models, including the Audi A3, VW Jetta, Beetle, Golf and Passat.

After the revelation by the US Agency, the other governments in Europe, South Korea and Australia also ordered for investigations into the issue. The Germany's Transport Minister is stated to have said that the company has also manipulated with the emission norms in Europe. The Environment Ministry of South Korea has declared that it has ordered a probe into certain types of diesel cars produced by the company like the Jetta, Golf, Audi A3; it may expand the scope of the probe to include all German diesel cars produced by other manufacturers also. At least in the present case, the Korean Ministry is putting the number of vehicles under test at about 5000. Meanwhile the Australia's Department of Infrastructure, said that it is monitoring the situation and also seeking clarification from the Volkswagen company, as to whether vehicles supplied to the Australian market use similar software to that used in the USA.

2. THE COMPANY

Volkswagen is a German car manufacturer headquartered in Wolfsburg, Lower Saxony, Germany. Established in 1946, Volkswagen is the top-selling and namesake marque of the Volkswagen Group, the holding company created in 1975 for the growing company, and is now the second-largest automaker in the world, behind Toyota.

Volkswagen has three cars in the top 10 list of bestselling cars of all time compiled by the website *24/7 Wall St.*: the Volkswagen Golf, the Volkswagen Beetle, and the Volkswagen Passat. With these three cars, Volkswagen has the most cars of any automobile manufacturer in the list that are still being manufactured, which includes model names that span multiple revisions and generations.

Volkswagen was originally created in 1946 by the German Labour Front (*Deutsche Arbeitsfront*). It was originally made by a group of labour. In the early 1930s, the German auto industry was still largely composed of luxury models, and the average German could rarely afford anything more than a motorcycle. As a result, only one German out of 50 owned a car. Seeking a potential new market, some car makers began independent "peoples' car" projects – the Mercedes 170H, Adler AutoBahn, Steyr 55, and Hanomag 1.3L, among others.

Volkswagen partnered with Daimler AG and other companies to market the BlueTec clean diesel technology on cars and trucks from Mercedes-Benz, Volkswagen, and other companies and brands. According to the United States Environmental Protection Agency, four of the ten most fuel-efficient vehicles available for sale in the U.S. are powered by Volkswagen diesel engines. Volkswagen has offered a number of its vehicles with a TDI (Turbocharged Direct Injection) engine, which lends class-leading fuel economy to several models. They were a three-way tie for 8th (TDI Beetle, TDI Golf, TDI Jetta) and ninth, the TDI Jetta Wagon. In addition, all Volkswagen TDI diesel engines produced from 1996 to 2006 can be driven on 100% biodiesel fuel. For the 2007 model year, however, strict U.S. government emissions regulations have forced VW to drop most diesels from their U.S. engine lineup, but a new lineup of diesel engines compatible to U.S. standards returned to the American market starting with Model Year 2009. These post-2009 Clean Diesel engines are limited to running on 5% (B5) biodiesel only to maintain Volkswagen's warranty. Volkswagen long resisted adding a SUV to its lineup, but relented with the introduction of the Touareg, made in partnership with Porsche, while they worked on the Porsche Cayenne and later the Audi Q7. Though acclaimed as a fine handling vehicle, the Touareg has been a modest seller at best, and it has been criticised by auto reviewers for its absence of a third-row seat, the relatively poor fuel economy, and the high vehicle mass. VW set plans to add a compact SUV with styling influences from the "Concept A" vehicle introduced at the 2006 Geneva Auto Show, and on 20 July 2006, VW announced that the new vehicle, called the Tiguan.

In September 2006, Volkswagen began offering the City Golf and City Jetta only for the Canadian market. Both models were originally the Mk4 Golf and Jetta but were later replaced with the Brazilian versions of the Golf Mk4 and Bora. Volkswagen's introduction of such models is seen as a test of the market for a subcompact and, if successful, may be the beginnings of a thriving subcompact market for Volkswagen.

In May 2011, Volkswagen completed Chattanooga Assembly in the US state of Tennessee. The facility has produced Volkswagen cars and SUVs specifically designed for North American markets, beginning with the Passat B7 in 2011. The company recently announced plans to expand further by investing $900 million to add floor space to the factory. The VW XL1 began a limited production run in 2013. The XL1 is a lightweight and fuel efficient two-person vehicle (only 795 kg). The **CrossBlue** (a placeholder name for an as-yet-unnamed large crossover SUV) begins production in late 2016, and aims to help end several years of losses for Volkswagen in the US, the world's second-largest auto market.

3. THE FALL OUT

Immediately after the promulgation of the order dated 18.09.2015 by the US EPA, Martin Wintakorn, the Chief Executive Officer of the company declared on 20.09.2015 that he was deeply sorry that they had broken the trust of customers and the public, making the company to order the investigation by an external agency. The following day, i.e. on 21-09-2015, the shares of the company plummeted by about 20 per cent. It was estimated that the total number of vehicles having this software would be around 11 million throughout the world. Calling them back may be suicidal to the very existence of the company. It is also in the news that the CEO, Martin Winterkorn, may also be sacked.

Regarding the cost of the scandal, it is said that the company has set aside 6.5 billion Euros (equivalent to $ 7.2 billion) to help cover the costs of the scandal. But some analysts think that the final costs could be much more. Immediately after this news, the company's share further tumbled by another 20 per cent (almost to a four year low on 22.09.2015). In this regard, it is worth noting that the company has a robust balance sheet and its cash balances are pretty strong. It is reported that the company had a cash balance of £17.6 billion at the end of Q2 for the financial year 2015-16, and had £15 billion marketable securities. The costs of the Scandal can be met from these cash balances; but the issue is where does it stop?

Adding woes to the company, the credit rating agencies like Moody's, S & P and Fitch have all put negative outlook for the credit worthiness of the company and they may downgrade the rating in the days to come. The fallout has also been felt by some of the Indian companies like Motherson Sumi Systems, New Delhi, the component suppliers to Volkswagen. This company supplies to Volkswagen parts like mirrors, bumpers, dashboards and door trims, not anyway connected to the engines. Still, the shares of the company fell by about 14 per cent during the last week of September 2015. It is also reported that the Indian unit of the Germen car maker (VW) is likely to recall by next month over one lakh diesel cars operating in the country. It is said that the move would affect polo hatewack, polo cross crossover, and vento, Jetta and Passat sedan cars. Meanwhile the Government has directed the Automotive Research Association of India (ARAI), the country's testing agency, to examine the issue and submit a report. Since the issue involves several brands, various models, different engines and gearboxes, it is expected that it would take longer time to come out with a detailed analysis.

Given Volkswagen's extraordinary fall from grace amid the global diesel emissions scandal, it's easy to forget that just a few months ago, it looked quite possible—likely even—that Volkswagen would *lead the world in auto sales* this year. Halfway through 2015, Volkswagen was ahead of Toyota in terms of worldwide sales, with 5.04 million sales for VW versus 5.02 million for Toyota, which has been the global leader for several years.

Starting back in 2007, Volkswagen set the ambitious goal of being the world's top automaker in terms of sales by 2018. The automaker employed many strategies to try to get to the finish line, including cutting base prices for models like the Passat and Jetta, and a big push to sell quote-unquote "clean diesels." Apparently, some within the company decided that it was wise to cut corners with diesel models through the use of "defeat device" software that resulted in false emissions readings.

Martin Winterkorn, who set the 2018 sales goal when he took over as VW CEO in 2007, understandably resigned in the wake of the scandal. Now, with Volkswagen forced to recall millions of diesel automobiles around the globe, and with its reputation reeling, the idea that the automaker could be the worldwide leader in sales is laughable.

Indeed, third-quarter sales results have just been posted, and Toyota has retaken the lead. Through the first nine months of 2015, Toyota sold 7.498 million vehicles, compared to 7.43 million for VW, according to The Detroit Bureau. Considering that VW has halted diesel sales and won't even begin to fix the recall problems until next year, it's a safe bet that the automaker won't be duking it out for the global sales title anytime soon. The other bit of bad—if unsurprising—news for Volkswagen is that prices for those used diesels tarred in the emissions scandals just keep on falling. In the immediate aftermath of the diesel software revelation, consumer trust ratings for VW tanked, and prices for both new and used models fell.

Automotive News is reporting that wholesale auction prices of used diesel VWs have declined week after week since the scandal hit. As of October 12, 2015 for instance, used Jetta TDI (diesel) prices were down 7.9% compared to pre-scandal days, while October 19 prices were down 13.8%, according to Black Book data. The numbers from Kelley Blue Book show a similar trend, with used VW diesel prices falling 13% within two weeks of the emissions scandal, decreasing to a difference of 16% after that. Prices for used VWs powered by traditional gas have inched down "only" by 2.9% over the same time span.

4. THE EMISSION NORMS

EPA of Volkswagen has set standards for vehicle emission and fuel use for cars and light trucks. Presently, Tier 2 standards (finalized in 2000) are in force. The EPA has already issued on 06.10.2015, Tier 3 standards to be effective from 2017, perhaps for the vehicles that might be produced between 2017 and 2025.

For the cars manufactured and operated in Europe, one has to follow the European emission standards. These standards are defined in a series of EU directives staging the progressive introduction of increasingly stringent standards. Starting with the Euro I in 1993 for passenger cars, the EU has progressed the standards now upto Euro VI (promulgated in 2014). EU regulations introduce different emission limits for diesel and petrol vehicles. Diesels have more stringent CO standards, but are allowed higher NOx emissions. A particular number standard (P) or (PN) has been introduced in 2011 with Euro Vb for diesel engines and with Euro VI for petrol engines introduced in 2014. Each country like the US can fix standards to protect its own environment.

As far as the emission norms followed in India are concerned, the Petroleum and Natural Gas Minister Dharmendra Pradhan on 29-10-2015 confirmed that the Government is determined to implement Bharat Stage-IV fuel norms in the country by 2020. As of now BS-III (equivalent to Euro-III) across the country and BS-IV in major cities are in vogue. Speaking to the press, the Minister said that 'while the earlier plan was to implement BS-V by 2020 and BS-VI by 2024, the Ministry is proposing to skip BS-V and directly implement BS-VI standards by 2020.

Questions for Debate/Discussion

1. How do you interpret the Ethical stand of the company?
2. Will it be possible to assess the impact of the moral dilution on the future growth of any business, taking into consideration the present episode?
3. Are the countries justified in fixing individual emission norms? Can we not go for a uniform Global Standard?
4. What lessons do India Car Manufacturers learn from the episode?
5. What kind of policy intervention do you recommend from the Indian Government? Will it be possible for the Government of India to implement BS-VI norms directly, skipping BS-V?

Notes

The United States Environmental Protection Agency (EPA/US EPA) is an agency of the US Federal Government, which was created in December 1970 for the purpose of protecting human health and the environment by writing and enforcing regulations based on laws passed by the Congress. The EPA has its headquarters in Washington, D.C. It has 10 regional offices and 27 laboratories. The agency conducts environmental assessment, research and education. It has the responsibility of maintaining and enforcing national standards under a variety of environmental laws in consultation with the State, tribal and local governments. EPA is enforcement powers include fines, sanctions and other measures.

4

CASE STUDY

Payment of Bribes by Walmart in India

1. THE NEWS

Of late (October 19, 2015), Wall Street Journal (WSJ) published a report stating that the Walmart paid thousands of bribes ranging from \$5 to \$200 to local officials in India to help clear goods through customs or for securing real estate permits. Though the amounts are as small as \$5 to \$200, they totaled millions of dollars (estimated to be around Rs. 13,000 crore in Indian Rupees).

2. THE COMPANY

Walmart is an American multinational retail corporation that operates a chain of discount department stores and warehouses. It has the Headquarters at Bentonville, Arkansas, USA. The company was founded by Sam Walton. The company was started on July 2, 1962. It has over 11,000 stores in 28 countries under a total of 65 banners.

Walmart started its operations in May 2009 with its first store opened in Amritsar, Punjab. The company runs presently 21 Best Price Modern Wholesale stores in cities including Jalandhar, Kota, Bhopal, Ludhiana, Lucknow. In Andhra Pradesh, Walmart has three stores at Vijayawada, Guntur and Rajahmundry and has invested about Rs. 2000 crore by now. It is planning to scale up its business by opening more stores in India; upto about 70 stores in the next five years.

Another turning point in the business strategy proposed to be followed in India has come in the form of a proposed Joint Venture with Sunil Mittal's Bharti Enterprises. As per the latest information, Walmart has decided to go on its own and open 500 stores in India over a period of 10-15 years. Walmart has its corporate office in Gurgoan, Haryana. Mr. Krish Iyer has taken over as the president and CEO of Walmart India since January 20, 2014.

3. THE ANTECEDENTS

Walmart is already facing an enquiry for its bribing activities in Mexico. In December 2011, Walmart disclosed to Securities and Exchange Commission (SEC) through one of its filings stating that it ordered an internal investigation into a potential violation of the provisions of Foreign Corrupt Practices Act, 1977 passed by the US Congress in December 1977. It also informed that the matter is seized by the Justice Department of the US Government. This was a sequel to the news report published by the New York Times (September, 2005) alleging that the company resorted to a 'widespread bribery' in 2005 totaling more than $24 million meant to smoothen the way for the company's rapid expansion in that country. While the report came to light in 2005, the company informed to SEC only in 2011. Similar cases were also unearthed in Brazil, Mexico and China along with India.

4. THE FCP ACT, 1977

The Foreign Corrupt Practices Act of USA is significant in terms of preventing corrupt practices by the multinational companies of US. The FCP Act of 1977 is a federal law aimed at accounting transparency requirements under Securities Exchange Act of 1934 and concerning bribery of foreign officials. The Act was amended in 1988 and 1998.

The idea of the Act is to make all payments made to foreign persons, companies, parties for securing undue advantage as illegal. This also includes payments made to foreign officials for obtaining or retaining business. Going by the information put on the website, Walmart is one of the few cases being tried under the Act.

Violation of the FCPA can result in stiff civil and criminal penalties for both individuals and entities. An entity that violates the anti-bribery provisions may be faced with a criminal fine of up to $2 million per violation. Individuals who violate the provisions may face up to five years in prison, a fine of $250,000, or both. An entity that violates the recordkeeping and internal controls provisions may be assessed criminal fines of up to $25 million. Individuals violating these recordkeeping provisions may be faced with sentences of up to twenty years in prison, fines of up to $5 million, or both. Civil actions brought against individuals and entities by the DOJ under the FCPA are subject to a penalty of $10,000.

The actual calculation of a criminal penalty, whether a fine or a prison sentence, is based on factors enumerated in the advisory of United States Federal Sentencing Guidelines (the "Guidelines") used to determine the culpability of an offending individual or entity. Factors that are particularly relevant to FCPA compliance programs include the history of prior violations, and any steps taken to prevent violations.

When aggregated, these penalties can be overwhelming, even for a large company. Several recent fines have totaled over $400 million. For example, in 2010, BAE Systems pleaded guilty to conspiring to defraud the United States, to make false statements concerning its FCPA compliance efforts, and to violate the Arms Export Control Act and International Traffic in Arms Regulations. As a consequence, BAE Systems was assessed a $400 million criminal fine. In 2008, Siemens paid a combined total of more than $1.6 billion in fines, disgorgement, and other payouts due to anti-corruption charges brought in various countries, which included over $800 million to United States authorities under the FCPA. And in 2011, Lindsey Manufacturing was the first company to be convicted by a jury on FCPA violations. Nevertheless, had the convictions proceeded to sentencing, Lindsey's CEO and CFO, who were also convicted as individuals, would have been "face maximum prison sentences of 30 years."

Loss of Government Contracts: Fines are not the only penalties resulting from FCPA violations by entities. There are significant collateral consequences when the government enforces the FCPA against a company, either through a non-prosecution agreement, a deferred prosecution agreement or an indictment. These include ineligibility to receive export licenses, and suspension and debarment from the securities industry. But for many industries, the most catastrophic of these is suspension or debarment from contracting with the United States government.

Indictment alone can lead to a suspension of doing business with the United States government. Debarment and suspension are technically not penalties for bad conduct; they are supposed to be tools to protect the Government from engaging with irresponsible contractors. Nonetheless, "suspension and debarment are powerful weapons at the Government's disposal." When the government suspends or debars an entity, generally all of the entity's constituent divisions are banned from contracting with the entire executive branch of the government. This can have "devastating consequences" for a company; "some have likened [it] to the death penalty."

Companies should be aware of their dependence on government business when conducting risk calculations regarding FCPA compliance. This is especially true when a company's business plan heavily rely on government work. Some industries are heavily, based on interacting with federal programs such as "the Defense Department procurement programs, the Commodity Futures Trading Commission, and the Overseas Private Investment Corporation." In such cases, any FCPA violation can provide the government with the bludgeon of cutting off business relationships with a company, which may dramatically devalue or even destroy it.

In the instant case, the Wall Street Journal has expressed the doubt that the act of bribery committed by the Walmart may not lead to any penalty on its Indian operations, as these did not yield profit under the provisions of the Act. For, penalties under the Act are often connected to the amount of profit that the alleged misconduct generated. On this basis, it is difficult to decide on the penalty, since bribing is said to have done for gaining entry and for the creation of certain facilities over a period of time. Relating bribing to profit generation is extremely difficult. It is reported that the Indian unit of

Walmart suffered a loss of Rs. 232 crore in 2014 and its revenue had dropped by 32 per cent to Rs. 2,992.7 crore.

In the whole episode, one should understand that it is not the quantum of penalty; but the act of dishonest.

5. THE REACTION OF THE INDIAN GOVERNMENT

After the incident, only on March 11, 2013 an unstarred question (No. 2140) was posed to the Minister for Commerce and Industry with the following querries:

(a) whether the Government has recently appointed an Inquiry Committee to probe into the facts behind reports of Walmart's spending money on lobbying for entering Indian market;

(b) if so, the details thereof including powers and functions of the Committee and the time by which the said Committee is likely to submit its report;

(c) whether the Government had ordered any enquiry into the allegations of violation of Foreign Direct Investment (FDI) and Foreign Exchange Management Act (FEMA) by the promoters of Bharti Group in setting up a company called Cedar Services in which Walmart had invested heavily;

(d) if so, the details thereof and the time frame prescribed by the Government to submit its report;

(e) steps taken by the Government against those companies which have violated the Foreign Corrupt Practices Act; and

(f) whether All India Traders Association have demanded a Central Vigilance Commission enquiry into Walmart bribery case and if so, the details thereof and the reaction of the Government thereto?

In reply to the same, the then Minister of State Dr. S. Jagathrakshakan gave the following reply:

> (a) & (b) The Government has appointed a one-man inquiry committee regarding media reports concerning Walmart (vide resolution dated 31.1.2013). The Committee has been asked to submit its report within three months from issuance of the resolution. The terms of reference of the Committee are as under:
>
> (i) To inquire into recent media reports on disclosures of Walmart before the US Senate regarding their lobbying activities and details thereof.
>
> (ii) Whether Walmart undertook any activities in India in contravention of any Indian law.
>
> (iii) Any other matter relevant or incidental to the above.
>
> (c) & (d) References alleging involvement of Bharti Walmart/Cedar Support Services Limited, in retail trade, in violation of the FDI policy, were received

and forwarded to the Reserve Bank of India, as violation of FDI regulations is covered by the penal provisions of Foreign Exchange Management Act, 1999 (FEMA). The Reserve Bank of India has informed that the matter related to Bharti Walmart/Cedar Support Services Limited has been referred to the Directorate of Enforcement for further investigations. No time frame has been fixed by the Government for conducting the enquiry.

(e) Does not arise, as the Foreign Corrupt Practices Act is not an Indian law.

(f) The Central Vigilance Commission has informed that, as per available information, the Commission has not received any demand from the All India Traders Association to inquire into Walmart bribery case.

Later, on 4-11-2015 the Central Vigilance Commission is stated to have summoned the country head of Walmart, taking a suo-moto cognizance of a media report, which included screening of the documents of the company. It is reported that the official of the company was asked to submit details by November 15, 2015.

On October 19, 2015, the US Government Investigation Agency is said to have found evidence of Walmart paying thousands of small bribes to local officials in India to get customs clearances and obtain real estate permits. While the most interesting question remains as to whether it comes under 'lobbying' or bribery; in view of the fact that lobbying is legal in US and not in India.

Questions for Debate/Discussion

1. How do you interpret the kind of business environment present in India?
2. What kind of law you suggest to curb such practices in India?
3. While India and the various states are scaling significantly on the ladder of 'Ease of Doing Business'; how should we view the present incident?
4. Whether penalty or no penalty, what does India gain out of the US Act?
5. When the incident is reported to have started happening since 2005, how do you perceive the reaction of the Government of India?
6. How does India rank in terms of corruption in business and public life? What precautions do you suggest to contain the problem?
7. How do you perceive the issue of lobbying in corporate sector?

5

CASE STUDY

Coca-Cola and the Water Exploitation: Is the Company Drinking the World Dry?

1. THE CONTEXT

A case has been filed in the court of the Hon'ble Junior Civil Judge, Tenali, Guntur District, Andhra Pradesh under OS. No.:337/2015 requesting the Hon'ble court to declare the resolution passed by the Tenali Municipal Council dated 30-04-2015 proposing to give five million litres of water to Hindustan Coca-Cola Company as null and void and for consequential relief of permanent injunction restraining the authorities of Municipal Administration and the Government of Andhra Pradesh in approving the supply of water to Hindustan Coca-Cola Company located at Atmakur, Mangalagiri Mandal, Guntur District, Andhra Pradesh.

2. THE CAUSE OF ACTION

The suit referred above arose when the Hindustan Coca-Cola Beverages Ltd., wrote a letter to the Municipal Council on 15-04-2015, and the same being endorsed by local MLA on 18-04-2015. It is submitted that the council hurriedly introduced an agenda in the Municipal Council malafidely without having any authority to introduce, making a proposal to give raw water of 5 million litres from out of the Tenali drinking water scheme. It is alleged that the Council passed a resolution without applying its mind and against the interest of general public in Tenali favouring the Hindustan Coca-Cola company without following procedure and standard norms.

3. ALLEGATIONS

The Coca-Cola Company having headquarters at Atlanta in USA, has 58 plants at several places in India. The primary allegations against the plants located in India of the Coca-Cola Company are as follows:

(i) that the company is extracting large quantities of water for its factories from the water bodies located in their vicinity and this is creating shortage of water for the community living around;

(ii) that the company is producing large amounts of waste water, as it uses 3.75 litres of water for producing 1.00 litre of Coke; and discharge of the same into nearby areas including farmlands;

(iii) because of the overexploitation of the groundwater resources by the plants of the company, waterbodies/wells/tanks, etc., are getting dried up in the locality of the plant, thus creating serious shortage drinking water even;

(iv) that the quality of water in the local area is also deteriorating due to pollution by the plants further leading to health hazards;

(v) That the depletion of groundwater is affecting the local residents to raise crops like rice, vegetables and plantations like banana and coconuts;

(vi) that the company is using contaminated water for its Cola products, specially the presence of toxic pesticide residues and insecticides in the water used; which are considered high enough to cause cancer, damage to the nervous and reproductive systems, birth defects and severe disruption of the immune system.

(vii) that the company had not obtained clearance to extract groundwater from the Central Ground Water Authority (CGWA) and stepping up the production capacity ignoring the availability and sustainability of water from the area.

4. OPERATIONS OF THE COMPANY IN INDIA

The Company which has Head Quarters in Atlanta, has many plants located in India. The history of the revival of the presence of the company, dates back to the establishment of its first plant at Agra in October 1993.

The company has a wide portfolio in India, spanning from sparkling drinks, juice, juice drinks, packaged water, energy drinks to tea and coffee. The Indian operations of the company comprise bottling, owned by the company as well as franchises, and contract packaging. The Coca-Cola in India comprises of the following:

A. **Coca-Cola India Pvt. Ltd. (CCIL):** This is a wholly owned subsidiary of the Coca-Cola Company at USA. This company controls the operations of all partners in bottling, suppliers, distributors and other stakeholders.

B. **Hindustan Coca-Cola Beverages Pvt. Ltd. (HCCBL):** This is a part of the Bottling Investments Group of CCIL. This company has 24 bottling plants at strategic locations in various states spread across in India. HCCBL covers approximately 65 per cent of the bottling operations for the Coca-Cola in India. The following is the product portfolio of HCCBL:

- **Sparkling Beverages** – Coca-Cola, Diet Coke, ThumsUp, Sprite, Fanta, Limca, Kinley Soda, Schweppes Tonic Water.
- **Still Beverages** – Maaza, Minute Maid Pulpy Orange, Minute Maid Nimbu Fresh, Minute Maid 100% Juices (Apple, Grapes, Orange, Mixed Fruit), Minute Maid range of fruit flavoured drinks.
- **Water** – Kinley, Bonaqua.

There are many other plants operating under franchisee arrangements. While inaugurating the 58th plant in Chatta region of UP (under franchise arrangement with Brindavan Agro Industries), declared that it has invested around $2 billion in the country between 1993 and 2011 and has plans to invest $5 billion by 2020.

5. CASES OF WATER EXPLOITATION

The company had been in the news in India for a long time. In 1999, HCCBL established a plant in Plachimada, Palakkad District, Kerala. The concerned Perumatty Village Council (PVC) gave licence to the company to commence production in 2000. The company started drawing water from the boreholes and open wells located in the area to the extent of around 5,10,000 litres a day. In 2003, women from Vijayanagarm Colony of Plachimada Village protested stating that their wells got dried up, because of the overexploitation of the groundwater resources by the plant. They also complained that they were forced to walk about 5 km twice a day to fetch water and also that the water was becoming undrinkable.

Consequently, in April 2003 the PVC refused to renew the license. In December 2003, the decision of the PVC was challenged in the High Court of Kerala. The Hon'ble High Court observed that the "State as a trustee is under a legal duty to protect natural resources. It considered that these resources, meant for public use, cannot be converted into private ownership. The residing judge, Justice K Balakrishnan Nair, asserted that the government had a duty to act to "protect against excessive groundwater exploitation and the inaction of the State in this regard was tantamount to infringement of the right to life of the people guaranteed under Article 21 of the Constitution of India." The High Court ordered the plant to stop drawing groundwater within a month, ruling that the amount of water extracted by the plant was illegal. But at the same time, it ordered the Village Council to renew the license and not interfere with the functioning of the company as long as it was not extracting the prohibited ground water. Coca-Cola refuted the accusations of excessive exploitation and pollution and lodged an appeal. The next few years saw a confusing array of legal battle between the Village Council and the company. In 2005, the divisional bench of the High Court granted permission for the company to extract 500,000 litres from the common groundwater per day in the year 2005-2006. The Court also affirmed that the Village Council was not justified in cancelling Coca Cola's license to operate until a full scientific assessment had been made of the facts.

The PVC moved the Supreme Court of India on the orders of the High Court of Kerala and on 4th January 2006, reissued license to the company for three months but laid out thirteen conditions, the first of which is that the company shall not use groundwater from Perumatty Panchayat for industrial purposes, or for producing soft drinks, aerated carbonate beverages or fruit juice. Later, the Government of Kerala and the State Food (Health) Authority, respectively, banned the manufacture and sale of Coca-Cola in the State on the grounds that it was unsafe.

In spite of the fact that the license was revoked with certain conditions, the factory remained closed since 2004. The interesting development in the episode is that the locals are not satisfied with simply closing the factory; they wanted justice for the damage caused to their health and the environment. Reacting to the criticism and charges leveled against it, the Coca-Cola company issued a statement (dated 09-08-2006) detailing the 'safety policy' followed by the company, thus:

"We are completely confident in the safety of our soft drinks in India because they are produced to the same level of purity, regarding pesticides, as the stringent EU criteria for bottled water.

We support the adoption of stringent, science-based rules by the Indian government regarding levels of pesticides in soft drinks. The rules should be based on sound and validated testing methodologies. We continue to work with relevant government bodies, industry associations, non government organizations (NGOs) and the scientific community to develop and finalize criteria and associated testing methods for pesticides in soft drinks.

We have the same uncompromising commitment to product safety and quality in India and everywhere we offer our beverages around the world, and independent third parties regularly audit all plants for compliance. The Coca-Cola Company has stringent criteria for all of the ingredients used in our beverages. These criteria are backed by internationally accepted analytical testing protocols for these ingredients.

Our soft drinks in India have been regularly tested and evaluated by the world renowned and independent Central Science Laboratories (CSL) and all tests show no detectable level of pesticides."

The incident happening in Kerala is not lone and stray. Similar agitations and uprisings had occurred in Tamil Nadu, Uttar Pradesh and in other states, including Andhra Pradesh. For instance in 2003 and then again in 2012, the Uttar Pradesh Pollution Control Board (UPPCB) began an investigation into Coca-Cola's practices. The UPPCB found that Coca-Cola had not obtained proper clearance to extract groundwater from the CGWA, noting that the company had almost doubled production capacity from 20,000 cases per day to 36,000 without the Board's permission and misled authorities about waste discharge quantities. Coca-Cola rejected the decision and announced that it would appeal the case to National Green Tribunal (NGT).

The atrocities (if it can be termed) are not limited to India alone. Similar incidents had happened in countries like Sri Lanka, Mexico, Turkey, Nicaragua, Peru, Russia, Chile, etc. Independent studies conducted by the Research and Non-Government Organisations (NGOs) have revealed facts as to how Coca-Cola has impacted a devastating effect on the water resources of the area, where its plants were located. For instance, the company was accused of exhausting water resources in El Salvador over a 25 year period. In Chiapas, Coca-Cola is positioning itself to take control of the water resources. The Mexican government under Vicente Fox, himself a former President of Coca-Cola Mexico, has given the company concessions to exploit community water resources.

The height of plight is that even the workers of the Coca-Cola Company have been agitating over the practices being adopted by the company. Coca-Cola's own workers have also suffered and the company is being increasingly associated with anti-union activities. The most notable case is in Colombia, where paramilitaries have killed eight Coca-Cola workers since 1990. The main Coca-Cola trade union Sinaltrainal is seeking to hold Coca-Cola liable for using paramilitaries to engage in anti-union violence. Coca-Cola is being sued on behalf of transport workers and their families for its part in the alleged intimidation and torture of trade unionists and their families by special branch police in Turkey. In Nicaragua, workers of the main Coca-Cola union SUTEC have been denied the right to organise and the General Secretary of SUTEC, Daniel Reyes, believes the objective of this ongoing and escalating campaign is to crush the union. Guatemalan workers have been struggling against Coca-Cola since the 1970s. In the years between 1976 and 1985, three general secretaries of the main union were assassinated and members of their families, friends and legal advisers were threatened, arrested, kidnapped, shot, tortured and forced into exile. The violations of workers' rights continue. And Coca-Cola workers and their family members, with ties to unions, have reportedly been subjected to death threats. Elsewhere in countries such as Peru, Russia and Chile, Coca-Cola workers have been protesting against the company's anti-union policies.

6. REPORTS OF INDEPENDENT RESEARCH/GOVERNMENT AGENCIES

Over the years, the practices of the company have attracted the attention of various independent research bodies and certain government/statutory authorities in respect of the products and practices of the company.

1. In 2003, the Centre for Science and Environment (CSE), New Delhi tested Coca-Cola beverages and found levels of pesticides around 30 times higher than European Union standards. Levels of DDT, which is banned in agriculture in India, were nine times higher than the EU limit. In February 2004 Indian MPs who investigated CSE's studies upheld these findings and the Parliament went on to ban Coca-Cola from its cafeterias.
2. The Centre for Global Research on Globalisation, Montreal, Canada in its recent communication titled "The Privatisation of water in India : How Coca-Cola destroys the Aquifer" dated 29-08-2015 has stated that the claim of the company that **'it is close to replenishing all the water"** in India is misleading. It also criticized the statement of the company that it would rebuild its reputation in India by adopting the policy of **'water neutrality'**. The communication has specifically highlighted the crisis faced by the company in India due to its mismanagement of water resources, which included the following:
   - The forced closure of its bottling plant by the Government of Kerala in 2005;
   - The closure of its 15-year-old plant in Varanasi in 2014;
   - The refusal by the Government of Uttar Pradesh to allow a fully built expansion plant to operate in Varanasi in August 2014;
   - Cancellation of a proposed plant in Uttarakhand in April 2014; and
   - Withdrawal of the land allocated to the company for a new bottling plant by the Government of Tamil Nadu in April 2015, due to large scale protests by the local community.
3. The Ecologist (a Magazine published since 1970 focusing on the Environmental Agenda – www.theecologist.org) has published a series of articles on the wrong claims and mismanagement of water in several countries, around the globe. A few of them pertaining to India are suggested here.
   (i) Never mind the green wash – Coca-Cola can never be 'water neutral' by Amit Srivastava, 25th August 2015.
   (ii) Campaigners defeat Coca-Cola plant in South India, 21st April 2015. This news is about the cancellation of land allocated to Coca-Cola Company by the Government of Tamil Nadu for a plant in Perundurai in Erode District.
   (iii) India : Coca-Cola bottling plant shutdown, 19th June 2014. After eleven years of complaining by the local people suffering from water shortages, state authorities have closed the plant at Mehdigans in Uttar Pradesh.

(iv) India: Coca-Cola eviction from 'land-grab' site imminent by Oliver Tickall, 29th January 2014.

(v) Coca-Cola 'misleading' investors over water use in India, 23rd April, 2010.

(vi) Coca-Cola just part of India's water 'free-for-all' by Tom Levitt, 4th December 2009.

4. The India Resource Centre has been campaigning relentlessly to hold Coca-Cola accountable for the depleting water resource in the areas where its plants are located. The severe allegation of the centre is that the company is destroying lives, livelihoods and communities. Water shortages and pollution of groundwater and soil, exposure to toxic waste and pesticides are having impacts of massive proportions in India. In a country where over 70% of the population makes a living related to agriculture, stealing the water and poisoning the water and soil is a sure recipe for disaster. Thousands of farmers in India have been affected by Coca-Cola's practices, and Coca-Cola is guilty of destroying the livelihoods of thousands of people in India. Unfortunately, we do not even know the extent of the damage as a result from exposure to the toxic waste and pesticides as these are long term problems. Most affected are the marginalized communities such as the *Adivasis* (indigenous people) and *Dalits* (formerly untouchables), as well as the low-income communities, landless agricultural workers and women. Coca-Cola is destroying the food security of the people of the land, and by stealing the water and poisoning the water and soil, it is also responsible for ensuring a life of misery for future generations to come. The irony is that most of the impacted community members, who are feeling the brunt of the water shortages and pollution, are unable to afford Coca-Cola. Which may be a good thing given that the product itself is poisonous. But it also raises the larger question of development in India. As is the case with the majority of other commodities in the Indian marketplace, only a fraction of the population are the "beneficiaries" of the current development policies. And unfortunately, the majority are not only left out of the so called "development" process, but they have to pay a high price for it as well.
5. The National Green Tribunal (NGT), a competent authority in India entrusted with the responsibility of looking into the cases of mismanagement and protection of environment, has ordered a Joint Verification by the Central Pollution Control Board (CPCB) and UPPCB) of the correctness of the water user ratio and the present water consumption and actual efficient discharge during operations of the plant located at Mehdiganj, Varanasi, Uttar Pradesh (order dated 21.04.2015).
6. The Central Ground Water Board (CGWB) under the Ministry of Water Resources, River Development and Ganga Rejuvenation, Government of India conducted a study on the use of water resources by Coca-Cola company in 2012 and reported

that the groundwater levels at the Coca-Cola factory of Mehdiganj were the lowest in the area, and the study labeled Coca-Cola's groundwater use as 'excess'.

7. In a recent order (dated April 28, 2015), the Supreme Court of India has denied to intervene in the case where the Nainital High Court had ordered the Uttarakhand government to return about 100 acres of land to Chharba gram panchayat. The details of the case are that the Coca-Cola's plan to set up a bottling plant in Chharba was cancelled, but, SIDCUL was able to receive permission from the gram panchayat to transfer the land to Indian Oil Corporation. The State government decided to give the land to Indian Oil Corporation instead of following the High Court order and it approached the Supreme Court on the case. The Supreme Court said it would not intervene in the Nainital High Court decision. However, the Supreme Court permitted the State government to file a review petition in the Nainital High Court.

Earlier in 2005, the Chharba gram panchayat transferred the land to the State government to set up a university campus, but, the university was never constructed on the acquired land. In April, 2013 a memorandum of understanding (MoU) was signed between the Hindustan Coca-Cola Beverages Private Limited (HCCBPL) and Uttarakhand Government, according to which HCCBPL would set up a Rs. 600 crore bottling plant in 60 acres of land in the village. Chharba, which is around 32 kilometres from Dehradun, has around 70,000 trees. The construction of the bottling plant would result in the cutting of majority of these trees, which would change the area into a dry belt, said Indra Singh Negi, a social-activist associated with the struggle to keep out Coca-Cola from Chharba. She also added that to protect the area from the bottling plant, the villagers took to the streets against the plant; when the news of the MoU was heard. Nitin Pandey, the co-ordinator of Citizens for Green Doon, an organisation working for the protection of environment in the Dehradun area filed a Public Interest Litigation (PIL) in the Nainital High Court for the land to be returned to the gram panchayat. After seven years, the land was transferred to the State Industrial Development Corporation of Uttarakhand Limited (SIDCUL) without the concurrence of the gram panchayat.

Questions for Discussion/Debate

1. Who is the competent authority to make allocation of natural resources like water? Does it vary if it is land, mine or any other natural resource?
2. In the instant case, is a Municipal Council competent to pass a resolution to divert water allocated by another competent authority for consumption by the people of Tenali?
3. In the context of widespread resentment/uprising, do you recommend a complete ban on the use of groundwater for bottling purposes by companies like Coca-Cola, Pepsi, etc?

4. Do you think that the Central Ground Water Board or the National Green Tribunal are discharging their duties in order to protect the environment in India?
5. What role the Central and State Governments are required to play in this regard?
6. Are you convinced that the Coca-Cola Company has misused the water resources of India? If yes, what kind of punitive measures do you suggest? Is there a case for setting up 'Claims Tribunal' for such misdeeds, committed by Foreign and Indian Companies?
7. What kind of advice do you tender to the petitioners of Tenali fighting the case against HCCBL? Make out a case for them.

6

CASE STUDY

Corporate Lobbying: Is it Ethical or Unethical?

1. INTRODUCTION

Offering gift coupons and gifts are considered a marketing drive. In the area of human relations, hosting lunches and dinners is treated as goodwill gesture. If a company sponsors an event to a Government department or organization is taken as a responsibility. Anything committed towards people is considered an exercise in the discharge of social responsibility function. When these things are extended or performed to people in power or to the Government officials dubbed as **gratis**. Drawing a line between gratis and corruption is becoming extremely difficult. One distinction that could be understood is that the former is extended as matter of courtesy or regard; while the latter is demanded and received.

It appears that, in the recent past, similar expressions got new interpretations and words, making the context vey complex and clumsy. Terms like **'lobbying'**, **'quid pro quo'** have come into use with unusual pace. Unfortunately, all of them are treated as having negative connotation. Lobbying and Lobbyists are looked down with suspicion. Though the Dictionary meaning of the term 'Lobbying' does not suggest any foul play, it is treated in the contemporary society as a precursor to corruption. It is in this context that corporate lobbying had become a point of great debate with the media making the issue highly sensational in the case of Niira Radia; roping many a big wig in politics, government, press and industry.

2. PROFILE OF NIIRA RADIA

Radia is a Kenya Born lady. Moved to London from Kenya during 1970s and got schooling at London. Graduated from the University of Warwick and got married to a

UK businessman, Janak Radia, a Gujarati, whom she later divorced and moved to India in the mid-nineties. She started off as Sahara liaison officer and soon became India's representative of Singapore Airlines, KLM, UK Air. It is during this time she forged her contacts in the civil aviation ministry, the government and the media. She tried to float an airline, **Crown Air**, in 2000; but the plan did not take off. In 2001, she set up Vaishnavi Communications, followed by Noesis, Victom and Neucom Consulting. Radia's big-ticket break came when she bagged all 90 Tata group accounts in 2001. Another crowning moment was when Mukesh Ambani's Reliance Industries Limited joined her clients' list in 2008. "She was leveraging the power of her clients who are some of the most powerful businessmen in the country," said Prashant Bhushan, a senior lawyer who filed a public interest litigation seeking the prosecution of Raja on the basis of the taped conversations of Radia. In 2009, she moved from corporate lobbying to allegedly fixing the lucrative telecom ministry, resulting in a scam that depleted the national exchequer by billions of rupees. The suspicious IT department taped her conversations at the time of cabinet formation last year in UPA-II Government. Those tapes have now become part of the national conversation.

3. THE NIIRA RADIA CONTROVERSY

A Kenyan born and London educated suddenly appeared on News Channels for lobbying to get favour from telecom ministry. The Income Tax Department, Government of India recorded the conversations between Niira Radia and the then Telecom Minister A. Raja, senior journalists, politicians and corporate houses. This came to be popular as 'radia tapes story'. The tapes contained conversations between persons leading to accusation of misconduct.

After getting authorisation from the Home Ministry, the Indian Income Tax department tapped Radia's phone lines for 300 days in 2008–2009 as part of their investigations into possible money laundering, restricted financial practices, and tax evasion.

In November 2010, *OPEN magazine* carried a story which reported transcripts of *some* of the telephone conversations of Niira Radia with senior journalists, politicians, and corporate houses, many of whom have denied the allegations. The Central Bureau of Investigation has announced that they have 5851 recordings of phone conversations by Radia, some of which outline Radia's attempts to broker deals in relation to the 2G spectrum sale. The tapes appear to demonstrate how Radia attempted to use some media persons to influence the decision to appoint A. Raja as telecom minister.

In the recorded conversations between Niira Radia and the prominent figures, referred to as the Radia Tapes, several prominent figures are heard in conversation with Radia.

4. NEWS BROADCAST AMONG CHANNELS AND PRINT MEDIA

After the news broke out, there were several claims and counter claims, accusations, retorts regarding the involvement of persons named in the media. While some have commented that the 'authenticity of the transcripts cannot be ascertained, others have commented that the incident painted a 'truer picture of corruption in the country'. Some of the journalists had also filed criminal defamation cases for mentioning their names, roping them into the controversy. Radia, herself served a legal notice on the **The Pioneer** magazine for its title 'Tapped and Trapped' and the related story. The significant fact is that the said tapes became annexures to the petition filed as PIL by Prashant Bhushan, a senior lawyer at the Supreme Court.

5. THE ISSUE OF MAKING CORPORATE LOBBYING LEGAL

Though it sounds absurd and illogical, there were attempts earlier to make lobbying legal. A reference is being made to the effort of the UPA Government, when Mr. Sachin Pilot headed the Ministry of Corporate Affairs to devise a proper framework for lobbying and then to make it legal. It is in this context, the Minister then opined that the term 'Lobbying' needs to be properly defined and should not dubbed as mere 'bribery or corruption'. In the wake of minor and major crackdowns by the Government on 'corporate espionage', involving private sector companies allegedly procuring secret official documents illegally, the ASSOCHAM (an industry body) is pleaded for legalizing the 'act of lobbying' in order to improve upon the transparency in government-industry dealings. The query of the Association is that why should the government decision making concerning policies (which have a bearing on the corporate) should be shrouded in secrecy? It is the desire of the industry that all the policies of the Government be first put up on the website as drafts and let all the conflicting interests debate, deliberate and slug it out by their legitimate arguments and thus the policy be finalized.

As a matter of fact, lobbying is legal and regulated under 'Lobbying Disclosure Act of 1995 in the United States. Subsequently, USA had made another law "Honest Leadership and Open Government Act of 2007"; which provided for mandatory public disclosure of activities and put limits on gifts to the elected public officials among other stringent measures. In effect, lobbying is considered legal and a profession, meant to attract some of the best minds on policy. In the process, a check list is prepared by some to include actions that can be treated right or wrong:

(a) What is Right? The following are considered right:

- Hiring professionals to speak at conferences/meetings.
- Funding research and paying for publication and distribution of books/reports.

- Travelling and staying at hotels to meet and negotiate with decision makers or influencers.
- Asking "independent" professional experts for "voluntary" endorsement.
- Paying for occasional dinners or rounds of golf (sponsoring a vacation would be too much).

(b) What is Wrong? The following are said to be wrong and not legal or ethical:

- Bribe (direct or indirect)
- Paid newspaper articles
- Blackmail
- Conflict of interest (say, my wife does business with the public office that I run)... etc.

Questions for Debate/Discussion

1. What do you think is the connect and legitimate interpretation of the term 'Lobbying'?
2. How do you look at the 'Radia tapes controversy'?
3. Do you think that there is a case for making 'lobbying' legal, as was done in USA?
4. Is it possible in our Indian context to distinguish between 'lobbying' and 'corruption'?
5. What are the various ethical issues involved in the entire episode?

7

CASE STUDY

Clinical Trials by Pharmaceutical Companies: Are Human Beings Used as Guineapigs?

1. INTRODUCTION

Health is an essential requirement for human life. No human being can afford to ignore the same. Though 'prevention is said to be better than cure', the latter becomes necessary for various reasons. Medicines are vital for supporting life of the individuals. In the present context, pharmacy is one of the Sun Rise Industries growing at an annual average of about 30 per cent. The industry is worth about US$ 300 billion world over. Though once dominated by multinational companies, Indian companies are also slowly stabilizing in the industry at the domestic and international markets. Companies like Reddy Labs, Ranbaxy, Cipla and Biocon have made foray into the industry. These companies are able to forge ahead with their new discoveries and new drugs. This is a great success of the Indian industry in the recent past.

In spite of the phenomenal growth, the industry is caught in a controversy for their clinical trials activities. There had been an apprehension that the companies are not following the rules and regulations and conducting trials on poor people, ignoring ethical standards.

2. HOW ARE DRUGS DISCOVERED?

Developing a new medicine begins with understanding the disease or condition as thoroughly as possible. Basic research provides clues about how to treat diseases and potential ways to target the symptoms or underlying causes. Armed with an idea, researchers work to understand biological targets for a potential medicine. A drug target can be a protein, RNA, DNA or other molecule that is somehow involved in the disease. Researchers conduct studies on cells, tissues and animal models to determine whether the target can be influenced by a medicine. Then they look for a lead compound—a promising molecule that could influence the target and, potentially, become a medicine. This is the first step in the discovery and development process, a process that spans from initial research to the delivery of life-saving or life-enhancing new medicine.

3. NEED FOR CLINICAL TRIALS

Before a new drug is actually released into the market for human consumption, its performance in terms of safety, and efficacy is evaluated. There is no case for taking chances or risk. The drug must be fully tested for human consumption. Therefore clinical trials assume a great significance.

A clinical trial is a study that is carefully designed to test the benefits and risks of a specific medical treatment or intervention, such as a new drug or a behavior change (e.g., diet). Every clinical trial is led by a principal investigator, who is usually a medical doctor, and a research team of nurses and others. Because the Food and Drugs Administration (FDA) requires a multi-phase clinical trials process to be completed before deciding if an investigational medicine is safe and effective for a broader patient population, progress in the development of innovative medicines cannot be made without the people who volunteer to participate in clinical trials. Drug and device testing begins with extensive laboratory research which can involve years of experiments on animals and human cells. If the initial laboratory research is successful, researchers send the data to the Food and Drug Administration (FDA) for approval to continue research and testing on humans. Once approved, human testing of experimental drugs and devices can begin and is typically conducted in four phases. Each phase is considered a separate trial and, after completion of a phase, investigators are required to submit their data for approval by the FDA before continuing to the next phase.

Phase I: During this phase, researchers attempt to assess the safety of a drug or device. This the initial phase of testing, which can take several months to complete. It usually includes a small number of healthy volunteers (20 to 100), who are generally paid for participating in the study. The study is designed to determine the effects of the drug or device on humans including how it is absorbed, metabolized, and excreted. This phase is also meant to decide on the side effects that occur as dosage levels are increased.

Phase II: This phase is meant to test the efficacy of a drug or device. This can last from several months to two years, and involves several hundred patients. Most phase II trials are randomized trials where one group of patients receives the experimental drug, while the second "control" group receives a standard treatment or placebo. Often these studies are "blinded" which means that neither the patients, nor the researchers know who has received the experimental drug. This allows investigators to provide the pharmaceutical company and the FDA with comparative information about the relative safety and effectiveness of the new drug. Usually, about one-third of experimental drugs successfully complete both Phase I and Phase II studies.

Phase III: These studies involve randomized and blind testing in several hundred to several thousand patients. This large-scale testing, which can last several years, provides the pharmaceutical company and the FDA with a more thorough understanding of the effectiveness of the drug or device, the benefits and the range of possible adverse reactions. Once Phase III is complete, a pharmaceutical company can request FDA for permission to market the drug.

Phase IV: These are like Post Marketing Surveillance Trials and are conducted after a drug or device has been approved for sale in the market. Pharmaceutical companies use this stage; (1) to compare a drug with other drugs already in the market; (2) to monitor a drug's long-term effectiveness and impact on a patient's quality of life; and (3) to determine the cost-effectiveness of a drug therapy relative to other traditional and new therapies.

4. ROLE OF FDA

In the drug discovery process, FDA review and approval is crucial. If a drug, during trial phases, is found safe and effective, the concerned company has to submit a New Drug Application or Biologics License Application to the FDA. This application includes data from all the stages of testing.

Scientists at the FDA carefully review all the data from all of the studies on the investigational drug and, after weighing the benefits and risks of the potential medicine, decide whether to grant approval. Occasionally, the FDA will ask for additional research before granting approval or convene an independent expert panel to consider data presented by the FDA and the company. The panel will then advise the agency on whether to approve the application and under what conditions.

5. APPROVAL PROCESS FOLLOWED IN INDIA

The approvals in relation to clinical trials and import of study drugs are regulated by Central law and regulations. The approvals for the same are granted by the Drugs Controller General of India (DCGI). The approval process may take 4 – 5 months. Unlike in the US, where a sponsor can proceed with a clinical trial 30 days after submission of an application, if FDA has not commented, in India, the sponsor or its agent in India must receive written approval from the DCGI to proceed with a clinical trial. The shortage of adequate number of skilled staff leads to delays in getting approval from the DCGI's office. This needs to be looked into to hasten the process.

Depending on whether the drug under consideration is categorised as a biologic or a genetically engineered product, additional approvals from other agencies such as the Indian Council of Medical Research (ICMR), the Genetic Engineering Approval Committee (GEAC), and the Department of Biotechnology (DBT) may become necessary. Submission of the proposals to Ethics Committee can be done simultaneously.

The registration of the clinical trial with the Clinical Trials Registry-India (CTRI), has been made mandatory by the DCGI since 15th June 2009. Registration of the trial with CTRI involves declaration and identification of trial investigators, sponsors, interventions, patient population, etc., before the enrollment of the first patient in the clinical trial. Approval by the Ethics committee and DCGI are essential before registration of the trial with CTRI.

5.1 Constitution of Institutional Ethics Committee (IEC)

In the field of pharmacy research, ethics committee plays an important role. According to the guidelines issued by the Indian Council for Medical Research (ICMR), IEC will review and approve all types of research proposals involving human participants with a view to safeguard the dignity, rights, safety and well-being of all actual and potential research participants. The goals of research, however important, should never be permitted to override the health and well-being of the research subjects. The IEC will take care that all the cardinal principles of research ethics, viz., autonomy, beneficence, non-maleficence and justice are taken care of in planning, conducting and reporting of the proposed research. It will review the proposals before start of the study as well as monitor the research throughout the study until and after completion of the study through appropriate well documented procedures for example annual reports, final reports and site visits, etc. The committee will also examine compliance with all regulatory requirements, applicable guidelines and laws.

IEC is a multidisciplinary and multisectoral body with experts drawn from various fields of study. A committee of 7-9 members is considered optimal. The recommended composition is as follows:

1. Chairperson
2. 1-2 basic medical scientists.
3. 1-2 clinicians
4. One legal expert or retired judge
5. One social scientist/representative of non-governmental voluntary agency
6. One philosopher/ethicist/theologian

7. One lay person from the community
8. Member-Secretary

The Ethical Committee at any institution can have as its members, individuals from other institutions or communities if required. There should be adequate representation of age, gender, community, etc., in the Committee to safeguard the interests and welfare of all sections of the community/society. Members should be aware of local, social and cultural norms, as this is the most important social control mechanism. If required, subject experts could be invited to offer their views. For example for drug trials, a pharmacologist, preferably a clinical pharmacologist, should be included. Similarly, based on the requirement of research area, like genetic disorders, etc., specific patient groups may also be represented in the Committee. The membership of IEC will include epidemiologist(s), sociologist(s), lawyer(s), theologian, statistician(s), clinician(s), basic scientists, pharmacist(s)/clinical pharmacologist(s), etc. They should be appointed by the Head of the Institute based on their competency and integrity, and could be drawn from any public or private Institute from anywhere in the country.

6. WHY CLINICAL TRIALS ARE AN ISSUE?

Usually, laboratory tests are conducted on animals like rabbits, mice, etc. Even to conduct the tests on these animals, one (including colleges, institutions, universities) has to follow the norms laid under the Prevention of Cruelty to Animals Act, 1960 ('animal' being defined as any living creature other than human being). While there had been a stated procedure to be followed for trials conducted on animals, trials on human beings require still rigorous procedures to be followed.

Experts in the field have identified the following reasons raising concerns about ethical norms to be observed in conducting these trials:

1. Placebo tests.
2. Care given to patients after trials.
3. Marketing methods used by the pharmaceutical companies.

Placebo tests (or called placebos) are those tests which are conducted on sick persons. In this process, a harmless substance is given to a sick person, instead of medicine, without telling him that it is not real. Placebos are often used in tests in which some people take real medicine and others take a placebo, so that doctors can compare the results to see, if the real medicine works properly. According to the dictionary, a placebo effect is the one that makes the person feel better after taking a placebo; even though it had no effect on his body. The question is that how can one be better without taking any medicine. This is the reason why placebo trials have become controversial. According to Helsinki Declaration (the one adopted by the World Medical Association in 1964), placebo trials can be conducted only in circumstances, where there is no proven treatment available. The Declaration also added that extreme care must be taken to avoid abuse of this option. Unfortunately, neither the FDA of USA or countries in Europe, Canada and South Africa are paying any attention to this growing unethical practice. As a matter of fact, the FDA in 2008 has ruled that the drug companies no longer need to comply with the Helsinki Declaration for the clinical trials conducted outside USA. Imagine how pathetic the situation is!

The second and third reasons have also become controversial due to the unethical practices adopted by the pharmaceutical companies. A large number of cases were reported in India and in Africa of the extremely poor care extended to those persons that participated in the 'trials conducted by the companies'. Youtube is replete with many such video clippings. To cite an example, as to how ridiculous the whole procedure adopted that the persons on whom trial is proposed are required to sign a blank form in a language not known to him. The persons are paid a paultry sum during the tests and are left without any assistance later. Government data show that more than 2600 patients that participated in clinical trials in India, died between 2005 and 2012, and nearly 12,000 suffered serious adverse effects. Of these, 80 deaths and more than 500 serious adverse effects were directly attributed to the drug being trialled. Another sensational trial case that was telecast in the media (2009) pertained to a study aimed to evaluate the cost and feasibility of introducing the human papillomavirus (HPV) vaccine into the country's universal immunisation programme. This was a programme organized by the Programme for Appropriate Technology in Health (PATH), a non-profit organisation based in Seattle in the United States, the Indian Council of Medical Research (ICMR) in New Delhi, and the Indian state governments of Andhra Pradesh and Gujarat. The trial, which involved 24,777 adolescent girls, was halted by the ICMR in April 2010 following media reports of the death of seven participants and a memorandum from 68 human rights and women's groups to the Indian Minister for Health and Family Welfare, opposing the trials of this "unethical" nature.

7. INTERVENTION OF THE SUPREME COURT

It is for these unethical practices adopted by many pharmaceutical companies, the Supreme Court in 2013 directed that all trials for new drugs be put on hold; upon a Public Interest Litigation (PIL) filed by many NGOs. On this, there was a representation from the companies and medical profession, since total ban will not contribute to the growth of the healthcare. Accepting the viewpoint, the Supreme Court directed the Government to put in place a strong mechanism to take care of the situation; while stripping the DCGI of the powers to approve clinical trials. There is a three-tier system now put in place in this regard:

(a) A subject committee of 10-12 members for each therapeutic area.
(b) A technical committee with 20 members.
(c) An apex committee.

Only after the approval by these committees, the application is forwarded to the DCGI for further course of action. The new norms and procedures are termed stringent and cumbersome by the companies. And the consequential effect is that while several hundred clinical trials took place before 2010, there was only one trial that commenced in 2014.

8. CLINICAL TRIALS EMERGING AS A BUSINESS PROPOSITION

It is generally believed that the companies involved in manufacturing medicines would take to the design and development of new formulations. But the situation prevailing at present has given why for a 'Business Model'. Now clinical research is outsourced on a contract basis with what are termed as 'Clinical Research Organisations (CROs)'. In several countries, CROs are permitted to undertake clinical trials on behalf of the company, who is called the 'sponsor'. Now that this contract clinical research being permitted, has emerged as a big business. Many Indian pharmaceutical companies are also outsourcing their 'drug discovery plans' to CROs to conduct trials in other countries; where the rules and regulations are liberal and less stringent. As a matter of fact, it is reported in the press many a time that countries are not focusing their attention properly on this aspect and hence trials are going on unabated. Clinical trials industry, as such, is projected to make a business of about 10 billion US$ in the next few years, up from just 200 million US$.

Therefore, Indian pharmaceutical companies and CROs are suggesting to the Government of India to ease the existing norms, so that drug companies conduct their trials within India and the business will not move outside the country. Let the wisdom of the people and policy makers stay focused in finding a solution to this impasse!

Questions for Discussion/Debate

1. What are the ethical issues involved in the clinical trials? Are we required to think beyond patient-centric issues?
2. To what extent the procedure laid down for conducting trials in India is proper? Is there a case for relaxing those norms?
3. What should be the constitution of various committees associated with the issue of 'clinical trials'?
4. Should we permit 'outsourced research' in clinical trials? If so, what shall be the obligations of the respective parties, viz., the sponsor and the CRO?

5. Do you favour the idea of banning 'placebo tests' and permitting only actual trials?
6. Do you approve the supremacy of FDA of US in drug discovery? If not, what alternative mechanism you have in mind?
7. Finally, should clinical trials be accepted as a business proposition?

8

CASE STUDY

Labour Trouble at Maruti Suzuki's Car Plant in India: Who is at Fault?

1. ORIGIN OF THE TROUBLE

It is reported in the press that the trouble started in the spare parts division of the plant located at Gurgoan, Haryana on July 4, 2015; where a casual worker was manhandled by the Manager. Whereupon the union leader Mr. Janghu intervened in the matter and there was altercation. Following the same, the company suspended Mr. Janghu and thus the trouble started.

Going into the past, the workers were agitating for hike of their average salary from just Rs. 7000 per month fixed in 2009. There was an agreement in 2012 hiking the salary which ranged between Rs. 14,000 and 22,000, based on seniority and experience. The above was made applicable to permanent workers only. The salary levels of contract and other category of workers were too low. The component of temporary workers was about 40 per cent and their salaries were found to be not even half of the regular/ permanent workers. In addition, the pressure to improve productivity and margins got mounted on the workforce due stiff competition in the automobile market. All this led to a strife between workers and management and finally to unrest in the form of workers going to strike on July, 2012. The strike turned violent and riotous. In the scuffle, the HR General Manager died and about 100 other officials and workers got injured.

Again in 2015, the labour unions started negotiating for a revision in the wages, since the old agreement came to close after a lapse of three years period. The management of the Maruti Suzuki India initiated talks with the labour unions for a revised wage agreement. The company announced on September 26, 2015 an average wage settlement of Rs. 16,800 per month to its permanent workforce over three years. The hike in the case of contract and other temporary workers was meager. Temporary workers being the significant component (about 50 per cent by now), about 1000 temporary workers organized a protest in front of the Manesar Plant, Haryana, also led to clashes and series of arrests by the police.

2. FACTORS THAT IGNITED THE TROUBLE

The following are some of the factors that contributed to the trouble.

1. The component of contract labour is high and the wage increases are not on par with the permanent/regular workers and thus the principle of 'equal pay for equal work' is belied.
2. Slowly, Japan (the controlling partner) is increasing its shareholding and removing Indian managers and substituting them with the Japanese. It is also contended that Japanese voice counts and often tends to dominate crucial decisions. Culturally, Indians and Japanese are far apart. Their sense of discipline, punctuality, employee connect are very different.
3. Being a volume player, the only way for Maruti to survive and flourish in the marketplace is to churn out more number of cars. This has resulted into relentless pressure on employees to improve productivity at every level.
4. Particularly at the Haryana Plant, young blue-collar workers have seen dramatic changes around them. Land prices have surged as Gurgaon has become a commercial hub. Overnight, people have become rich and their lives have transformed simply because they sold their lands. Such changes have re-calibrated worker expectation who have seen their sleepy little hamlet transform into a city of high rises and malls in a decade. They are less tolerant and fairly aggressive in their expectations and how they want to achieve it. Poor wage hikes and raging inflation have queered the pitch further, resulting in an impatient, militant workforce, which believes in aggressive posturing. Sonu Gujjar, the leader of the labour unrest at Maruti plant last year, represents that generation. In his 20s, Gujjar organised a concall with analysts to put forth the workers' point of view and made headlines.
5. The persistent deadlock occurred on another issues also, regarding the recognition of their union. While workers want a Union, Maruti Management insisting on a 'Good Conduct Bond'. Both refused to give in and hence the trouble got intensified. As a matter of fact, strikes have become almost common now at Maruti plants.
6. It is contended that neither the management of the company, nor the Government of Haryana, nor the police have taken any measures to contain the impending trouble.

3. CLAIMS OF THE MANAGEMENT

(i) There is already one union and the workers of other plants can join the existing union and there is no need for a union for every factory.

(ii) If the company permits more unions, finally it culminates into politicalisation and 'third party' intervention in the wage negotiations; hence, it does not want to allow any fresh union.

(iii) It is unethical on the part of the union leaders to incite trouble in the company and stop production. It is also unjust to attack executives, leading to the death of a General Manager.

(iv) If a company is to survive in the automobile market characterized by intense competition, it is necessary to increase production and productivity of the plants. It should not be termed 'pressure' on the workers. It is also known to the Government and stakeholders that Maruti Suzuki is a volume player and hence can compete only through the stepping up of production, not to be in the reach of any other competitor.

(v) As a Japanese company, Maruti is fully Justified to follow their own culture and work norms.

4. CLAIMS OF WORKERS

Workers, on the other hand, are arguing on the following:

(i) Wage notiations are improper and the wage enhancements are one-sided.

(ii) The company is hiring vast labour on contract/contingent basis and paying low wages. The wages paid to certain category of workers is not even equal to minimum wages under the 'Minimum Wage Act, 1935'. Also, the working conditions between the permanent and contractual staff differ in many respects. Of the about 2500 workers only 1100 are permanent and the rest are contract, apprenticeship or training.

(iii) Wage differentials are too wide. While a permanent worker gets around Rs. 18,000; a contract worker gets Rs. 7,000; and that of unskilled worker is Rs. 4348; which is said to be below the minimum wages.

(iv) Working conditions are difficult at the Maruti Plants. According to workers, working conditions at the Maruti plant are, in general, 'difficult'. According to workers, the eight-hour shift that they are required to work usually gets extended by an hour. The company provides a 30-minute lunch break, ten minutes of which are spent in travelling to the canteen. A seven-minute break is given for tea and using the bathroom. Going on leave becomes almost impossible as Rs

1500 is deducted for every day on casual leave from their salary. "Last year, we exceeded the targets by working more in the morning and evening. For every hour that we worked extra, we were paid Rs 20. What part did we get of the profit that the company earned by exceeding the targets?" is their question. Therefore, striking for a union was the only option left to them. Maruti Suzuki refutes these allegations and says that its workers are treated fairly.

(v) While the situation being the one as observed above, some of the workers (majority of them apprentices) were jailed for causing disturbances in the plant. The concerned apprentices claim that they are neither permanent workers nor temporary workers and had nothing to do with the union.

5. ABOUT THE COMPANY

Maruti Suzuki was established in 1982 with a plant in Gurgaon, Haryana. The company revolutionized the production of automobiles with the production of Maruti 800. The company has two state of the art manufacturing facilities at Manesar and Gurgaon, Haryana. It also has a Diesel Engine Plant located at Manesar, the first and perhaps the only plant designed to produce world class diesel engines and transmissions for cars. It also has another plant at Bawal, Haryana, which manufactures various types of steel plants for automobiles. It also has plans to set up manufacturing facility in Gujarat. Today, Maruti Suzuki manufactures about 1.5 million cars every year; i.e., one car for every 12 seconds. The company has a nationwide service network spanning over 1454 cities and towns, sales network spanning over 1097 cities. As a matter of fact, the journey of company in India is spectacular.

Questions for Debate/Discussion

1. How do you interpret the labour trouble in Maruti Suzuki in the context of globalisation?
2. Whether Labour Laws of India are applicable to foreign companies? Do you suggest any new law to contain/promote the operations of the company?
3. What are the ethical principles, you think, that the company has floated?
4. Will there be any impact of such labour troubles on the flow of Foreign Direct Investment (FDIs) into India?
5. Going by the claims and counter-claims of management and labour, who do you think is justified?
6. Should India need to implement the law relating to 'equal pay for equal work'? What will be its impact on domestic and foreign companies?

9

CASE STUDY

Deposits Issue of Sahara: Can it be Termed Contagious to the Indian Financial System?

1. THE ISSUE

The issue is about two things. One, raising of deposits by the Sahara from public without permission from the concerned to the extent of about Rs. 24,000 crore from over 30 million investors. Second, non-payment of such deposits even after the due date and forcing of the depositors to shift to the other schemes of group companies.

2. HOW THE MATTER SURFACED

M/s Sahara Prime City Limited (SPCL), a group company of the Sahara filed the draft prospectus for permission to go for Initial Public Offer (IPO) in September 2009. On this, professional group for investor protection, an NGO, made a complaint that the SPCL has made no disclosure about one of the housing companies of the group, viz., Sahara India Real Estate Corporation Limited (SIRECL), which has been raising money from the capital market by issuing convertible bonds for many months.

SEBI after examining the complaint passed an order on November 24, 2010 barring two Sahara Group companies, namely, (1) Sahara India Real Estate Corporation Limited (SIRECL) and (2) Sahara Housing Investment Corporation Limited (SHICL) from mobilizing funds from equity markets or from issuance of any security to the public and also restrained group Chairman, Mr. Subrato Roy from approaching public for raising money. During enquiry, SEBI found that the Sahara Group of entities were raising massive sums of money in the form of 'Optionally Fully Convertible Debentures (OFCD) without following any norm. On perusal of the Balance Sheets of the Sahara

Companies, SEBI team found that they had raised above Rs. 7000 crore by then under this mode. Considering the quantum of money solicited from the market and prima facie violation of many of the provisions of applicable laws, SEBI passed a 34-page order banning the company from tapping resources from the capital market.

Sahara Company (SIRECL) moved the High Court of Allahabad (since the Group Headquarters is located at Lucknow) to stay the order of the SEBI on November 29, 2010. Admitting the petition, the High Court stayed the order of the SEBI, pending investigation (order dated 13-12-2010). On the order of the High Court, SEBI filed a Special Leave Petition (SLP) before the Supreme Court and the Court held that SEBI was entitled to call for any information, which it deems fit, including the names of the investors who have invested in OFCDs of the Sahara Group companies. The Supreme Court also directed the Allahabad High Court to proceed with the hearing of the case on a day-to-day basis from January 12, 2011 without adjourning the case. Further, SEBI and Registrar of Companies (ROC) were directed to file their counter affidavits by January 7, 2011.

In the meantime, Reserve Bank of India (RBI) had issued a public notice dated 18-1-2011 warning investors against money collected in the name of the Sahara Pariwar/ Sahara India Pariwar and cautioned that the public should verify the name of the company, which issues deposit receipt and whether the said company is authorized by the RBI to accept deposits from the public. The Bank also cautioned that it would not guarantee the repayment of deposits accepted by SIFCL or any other company in that Group. Clarifying further, RBI stated that only three companies of the Sahara Group entities got registered with RBI, viz., Sahara India Financial Corporation Limited (SIFCL) and Sahara India Corp. Investment Limited (SICIL) and Sahara India Infrastructure Development Limited (SIIDL). Of these three entities, SIFCL was directed by the RBI to phase out the acceptance of deposits from the public. The remaining two entities, viz., SICIL and SIIDL were not authorized to accept the deposits from public.

3. SERIES OF VIOLATIONS/ALLEGATIONS

There is a long list of violations stated to have been committed by the Sahara Group. Some of them are:

(i) SEBI has alleged that it had submitted prospectus to raise funds from the capital market without providing proper information;

(ii) RBI alleges that no company of the Sahara Group was authorized to accept deposits from public, except SIFCL, and the same was also directed to phase out the scheme;

(iii) Sahara had been attracting large number of small investors into its Time Deposit Scheme through loosely regulated credit cooperative societies; Sahara had floated

Humara India Credit Cooperative Society Ltd. and accepted many time deposits from public.

(iv) That Sahara is forcing investors to convert their maturing deposits into a credit cooperative plan. In this regard, Reuters (a London based International News Agency) conducted interviews with the affected depositors and reported that the company is not allowing depositors to redeem their matured deposits. Also that most of the Deposit Certificates issued by the company do not carry either maturity date or rate of interest.

(v) Sahara has turned their attention to start credit cooperative societies to exploit the weak legal system in the country. The Group has started four credit cooperative societies, viz., (1) Sahara Credit Cooperative Society Ltd., (2) Humara India Credit Cooperative Society), (3) Stars Multipurpose Cooperative Society, (4) Saharayn Multipurpose Society. It is reported that even senior officials of the company were not aware of these societies.

(vi) The Group had been dealing entirely in cash, violating the KYC norms of the banking industry. It had been found that 95% of the transactions in Sahara companies are done in cash and not through cheque.

(vii) There is also an allegation that there are no actual depositors and all of them were held under benami mode and hence it is difficult to identify depositors and pay them.

4. THE PRESENT STATUS OF THE CASE

The case is being presently heard by the Supreme Court and a series of directions have been issued. As it appears, the deposits issue of Sahara has turned very big. As per one estimate, the total money pooled under various deposit schemes through finance companies and credit cooperative societies was estimated to be around $7.5 billion (approximately equivalent to Rs. 49,500 crore). Of this, the Supreme Court has ordered the company to repay to depositors an amount of $5.4 billion (Rs. 35,640 crore). The company is not able to oblige the order of the Supreme Court. Hence, the Chairman, Mr. Subrata Roy was put in jail and had been there for the past one and one-half years. In the recent order, the Supreme Court directed Subrata Roy to deposit Rs. 10,000 crore for paying to the depositors and then get bail. Mr. Roy could not comply with these orders.

While this being the situation, the Enforcement Directorate (ED) of the Government of India conducted searches for almost 20 hours at the Sahara Group headquarters in Lucknow and seized bills, vouchers, records and bank accounts. It is found that the Group had more than 4500 bank accounts across many states in the country. The ED has conducted these searches under the provisions of 'Prevention of Money Laundering Act (PMLA), 2002'. The ED also has stated that it had been in the process of examining the bank accounts to check the amounts deposited and transacted, where the money has gone and how much, and in which period, the transactions took place and who was the signing authority. The focus of the probe of ED was on the allegations that the funds raised were laundered and there were no genuine investors.

During August 2015, when the matter came for hearing, the Supreme Court commented that 'Subrata Roy was in jail by choice' and ordered the 67-year-old Roy to pay Rs. 36,000 crore to the SEBI within 18 months and in nine installments from the date of release. Due to non-response from Roy, the matter is still pending.

5. ABOUT SAHARA GROUP

Sahara India is a major Indian corporate group with diverse business interests that include: Finance, Infrastructure & Housing, Media & Entertainment, Tourism & Hospitality, Consumables, Manufacturing and Services & Trading. The group was founded in 1978 by Subrata Roy, with a capital of Rs. 2000, and today Sahara India has an asset base of over Rs. 50,000 crore.

Business Interests of Sahara India

1. **Finance:** In the field of finance, Sahara Group has interests in parabanking, life insurance, mutual funds, and housing finance.
    - *Parabanking*: Sahara India Financial Corporation Limited is India's largest mobilization company in the private sector with the highest yearly deposit. It is the first RNBC to be granted a certificate of registration by the RBI.
    - *Life Insurance*: Sahara India Life Insurance Company Ltd is the first wholly Indian-owned Life Insurance Company in the private sector.
    - *Mutual Fund*: Sahara Mutual Fund was established in 2005. Presently, it offers 7 schemes: 3 equity schemes & 4 debt schemes.
    - *Housing Finance*: Sahara Housing Finance Corporation Limited was founded in August 2002. It commenced retail lending in May 2004. The company has four regional offices in Kolkata, Lucknow, Hyderabad and Mumbai and a branch each in Kolkata, Asansol, Siliguri, Lucknow, Gorakhpur, Pune, Hyderabad, Vijayawada and Mumbai.
2. **Infrastructure and Housing:** Sahara Infrastructure & Housing is India's largest realtor. It offers broad range of houses, commercial & retail spaces, office spaces and luxurious penthouses & villas. The company is building townships in 217 cities all over India.
3. **Media and Entertainment:** Sahara Group has interests in television, cinema, and newspaper. The group has an entertainment channel called Sahara One and a

news channel by the name of Sahara Samay. Sahara One Motion Pictures is Hindi Cinema Production House with over 50 films in various stages of production. The group also publishes English, Hindi, and Urdu newspapers.

4. **Consumer Products and Retail Chain:** Sahara India offers a range of consumer products and is developing one of the largest retail chains in India under the brand name Sahara Unique. Its product range include: Fashion & Lifestyle Products, Fitness & Leisure Products, Clothing, Jewellery, etc.
5. **Manufacturing:** Sahara India is into jute manufacturing and development of handicraft industry.
6. **Services and Trading:** Sahara has one of the largest V-SAT network called Sahara Net. It has an extensive 6000 strong branch network with 24-hour on-line satellite connectivity. Sahara Care House offers a host of attractive services to the dependants of NRIs in India.

Questions for Debate/Discussion

1. As a student of business ethics, how do you look at the entire episode?
2. How do we combat the situation of accepting deposits from unfortunate small savers and protect their interests from such unscrupulous companies?
3. How do you look at the dimension of accepting deposits from public *via* credit cooperative society route? What kind of regulation RBI shall press into service?
4. Going by the sequence of incidents, do you think that there is any case for booking under Prevention of Money Laundering Act, 2002 and hence there is justification of searches conducted by the ED?
5. Do you think that the Law of India will be able to check such misdeeds? What action is called for preventing such episodes not to recur in future?

10

CASE STUDY

The Gas Dispute between ONGC and Reliance: Is It a Case of Theft?

1. NATURE OF THE DISPUTE

A petition was filed in the Delhi High Court by the Oil and Natural Gas Commission (ONGC), a State owned enterprise and India's biggest explorer of natural gas, petroleum and related reserves in the country, alleging that the Reliance Industries Limited (RIL) and its partners (M/s BP Plc and Niko Resources Ltd.) are drawing out a substantial volume of gas from a 'Block' belonging to ONGC (This news report first appeared on May 15, 2014). This Gas field is located in Krishna – Godavari Basin in the Bay of Bengal. While posting the case for hearing on May 29, 2014, the court has directed the RIL and the Government to submit their responses. Prior to this, the RIL was stated to have slumped the production of gas from about 60 million cubic metres (mcm) a day in 2010 to just 10 mcm in 2015, stating that the reservoir had proved to be more difficult for gas production. Also at the same time, RIL and its partners had issued a notice to Government for arbitration on the increase of gas-price.

The said gas field is located in the Krishna – Godavari Basin (popularly came to be known as KG Basin) in the Bay of Bengal. This Basin was declared by the ONGC as the rich gas field in India and was bid out to RIL in 1999. RIL started production in the field in 2009. In 2013, ONGC reported that RIL had been deliberately drilling wells close to its own block and had been siphoning off a significant amount of gas. RIL countered these claims as baseless, stating that it was technically not possible to draw gas out of an adjoining field. Also claimed that it had been extracting gas as per the Field Development Plan (FDP) approved by the Director General of Hydrocarbons (DGH). On this matter, the ONGC moved the Delhi High Court in May 2015.

2. APPOINTMENT OF CONSULTANT TO FIND FACTS

In order to resolve the dispute and to find facts of the rival claims, the Delhi High Court has appointed De Golyer and Mac Naughton's (D&M), a US based consulting firm with the consent of both ONGC and RIL. The consulting firm had about seven sittings with the officials of RIL and DGH to discuss the matter.

After analyzing the relevant records and data, the D & M has found that RIL had drawn about 58.67 billion cubic metres (bcm) of gas from the wells up to March 31, 2015 and out of which 11.9 bcm may belong to ONGC. This report appeared in press two times once on October 9, 2015 (Rediff.com) and again on 4th January, 2016 (live mint). Because of this news, the share price of RIL has gone down by 2.7 per cent from Rs. 913.85 to 893.40. The present quotation on BSE is Rs. 995.40 (dated 04-01-2016).

Regarding the value of the gas alleged to have drawn by the RIL, ONGC had put it at Rs. 11,000 crore, based on the 2013 market price of $4.2 per cent.

3. EXPECTED OUTCOME OF THE DISPUTE

It has become quite interesting that what will happen to the dispute. Whether RIL would be required to pay compensation for the gas drawn or the Government would lose the case. It may be noted that when the ONGC moved the Delhi High Court, the court disposed of the petition (dated October 10, 2015) asking ONGC to wait for six months for the government to take action on the consultant's report. By now three months have lapsed and there is no response of the Government on the report of D & M. It is reported in the press that the earlier Government (UPA) had not acted properly in the case of NTPC. Similar is said to the situation in case of ONGC also. ONGC, being a government owned company, has no much say to act independently. It can wait for the reaction of the Government alone. It may be noted that the Government took two years to listen to ONGC's demand to raise the issue of gas theft by RIL and appoint an international consultant to verify the claim of the ONGC. Now that the report of the consultant is available, it is for the Government to act and decide the matter.

Questions for Debate/Discussion

1. What lesson of business ethics, we can draw from this incident?
2. Has it anything to do with the public-private partnership models being tried in the country?
3. Do you think that the Government has to revisit its policy on 'Gas Production and Distribution'?
4. Can you think a better model of national resource allocation to the private players?
5. What do you think the action of the Government should be in the present case?

Bibliography

1. Abid Husain, S., *'The National Culture of India'*, New Delhi, National Book Trust, 1978.
2. Acharya Nagarjuna University, *'Endowment Lecture Series, Arts'*, Vol. I, Nagarjuna Nagar, 2012.
3. Adam Smith, *'An Inquiry into the Nature and Causes of the Wealth of Nations'*, William Strahan & Thomas Cadel, 1776 (Reprinted by many publishers).
4. Adam Smith, *'The Theory of Moral Sentiments'*, Edinburg, Strand & A. Kincaid & J. Bell, 1759 (Reprinted by many publishers).
5. Adrian Cadbury, *'Corporate Governance and Chairmanship: A Personal View'*, Oxford University Press, 2003.
6. Alexander Brink, *'Corporate Governance and Business Ethics'*, Springer, New York, 2011.
7. Amartya Sen, *'Inequality Reexamined'*, Delhi, Oxford India, Paperbacks, 1997.
8. Arun Monappa, *'Ethical Attitudes of Indian Managers'*, New Delhi, All Indian Management Association, 1977.
9. Bajaj, P.S. & Raj Agrawal, *'Business Ethics – An Indian Perspective '*, New Delhi, Biztantra, 2004.
10. Baron, Robert A., & Bryrne, Donn, *'Social Psychology'*, Delhi, Pearson Education, 2004.
11. Barry, V., *'Moral Issues in Business'*, Wadsworth, Belmont, 1986.
12. Benerjee, A.M. and K.A. Chandrasekaran, *'Renewing Governance: Issues and Options'*, Tata McGraw-Hill Publication, 1996.
13. Bhandare, S.S. and Others, *'Journey Beyond Liberalization'*, Mumbai, Forum of Free Enterprise, A.D. Shroff Memorial Trust, 2016.
14. Bhatia, S.K., *'Business Ethics and Corporate Governance'*, New Delhi, Deep & Deep Publications Pvt. Ltd., 2007.

15. Cadbury Committee Report, A Report by the Committee on the Financial Aspects of Corporate Governance. The Committee was Chaired by Sri Adrian Cadbury and issued for public comment on 27th May 1992.
16. Chakraborty, S.K., *'Ethics in Management: Vedantic Perspective'*, Oxford University Press, 1995.
17. Chandratre, K.R. and Navare, A.N., *'Corporate Governance – A Practical Handbook'*, Bharat Law House, 2010.
18. Confederation of Indian Industry, Desirable Corporate Governance: A Code, March 1998.
19. Corporate Boards and Governance, edited by N. Balasubramanian, Indian Institute of Management, Bangalore.
20. David Crowther and Lez Rayman-Bacchus, *'Perspectives on Corporate Social Responsibility'*, England, Ashgate Publisher Limited, 2004.
21. Durga Prasad M.K. & Prasad, A.B.K., *'Media Trends and Ethics'*, Mechilipatnam, Krishna University, 2011.
22. Edward Freeman, R., *'Business Ethics'*, New York, Oxford University Press, 1991.
23. Ferando, A.C., *'Corporate Governance: Principles, Policies and Practices'*, New Delhi, Pearson Education, 2006.
24. Fernando, *'Business Ethics and Corporate Governance'*, Delhi, Pearson, 2010.
25. Ferrell, O.C. and Others, *'Business Ethics: A Case Perspective'*, Delhi, Cengage Learning India Pvt. Ltd., 2007.
26. Galbraith, J.K., *'The Affluent Society'*, Boston, Houghton-Mifflin Publishing, 1956.
27. Greenbury Committee Report, 1994, Investigating Board Members Remuneration and Responsibilities.
28. Hakan Altinay, *'Global Civics Responsibilities and Rights in an Independent World'*, Washington D.C., Brookings Institution Press, 2011.
29. Hartman, Laura P., *'Perspectives in Business Ethics'*, New Delhi, Tata McGraw-Hill, Indian Reprint, 2003.
30. ICFAI University, *'Corporate Governance in Emerging Markets'*, Vol. I & II, Hyderabad, 2006.
31. Jagdish Bhagwati, *'Termites in the Trading System: How Preferential Agreements undermine Free Trade'*, New York, Oxford University Press, 2008.
32. John Rawls, *'A Theory of Justice'*, Cambridge, Harvard University Press, 1971.
33. Justice M. N. Rao, *'Readings in Sociology of Law'*, Hyderabad, Administrative Staff College of India, 2013.
34. Kamatchi, P. *'Business Ethics: Foundation for Corporate Social Responsibility and Governance'*, New Delhi, I.K. International Publishing House, 2015.

35. Kanika Datta, *'Table for Two – In Conversation with Power, Fame and Glory'*, New Delhi, B.S. Books, 2012.

36. Kant, Immanuel, *'Fundamentals of the Metaphysics of Morals and What is Enlightenment'*, Indianapolis, Bobbs-Merrill, 1963.

37. Karma Ura and Others, *'An Extensive Analysis of GNH Index'*, Bhutan, The Centre for Bhutan Studies, Thimpu, 2012.

38. Keith Davis and Frederick, William C., *'Business and Society, Management, Public Policy, Ethics'*, New York, McGraw-Hill, 1983.

39. Laeeq Futehally, *'Our Environment'*, National Book Trust, New Delhi, 1988.

40. Laeeq Futehally, *'Our Environment'*, New Delhi, National Book Trust, 1988.

41. Mallin, Christine, A., *'Corporate Governance'*, Indian Edition, New Delhi, Oxford University Press, 2007.

42. Mandal, S.K., *'Ethics in Business and Corporate Governance'*, New Delhi, Tata McGraw-Hill Education Pvt. Ltd., 2010.

43. Mathur, U.G., *'Corporate Governance and Business Ethics'*, New Delhi, McMillan Publishers India Ltd., 2005.

44. Michael Blowfield and Alan Murray, *'Corporate Responsibility'*, United Kingdom, Oxford University Press, 2014.

45. Michales, Alex C., *'A Pragmatic Approach to Business Ethics'*, Thousand Oaks, Sage Publication, 1995.

46. Mira Kamdar, *'Planet India: How the Fastest Growing Democracy is Transforming the World'*, New York, Scribner, 2007.

47. Mitchell, J. M., *'Hinduism – Past and Present'*, Asian Educational Services, 2000.

48. Murthy, C.S.V., *'Business Ethics: Text & Cases'*, Mumbai, Himalaya Publishing House, 2006.

49. Narayana Murthy, N.R., *'A Better India – A Better World'*, New Delhi, Penguin Books, 2009.

50. Panchali, Jinsh N., *'Excellence in Corporate Governance (An Exercise in Assessment of Corporate Governance practices in the Indian Corporate Sector)'*, Indian Institute of Capital Markets.

51. Patterson Report: The Link Between Corporate Governance and Performance, 2001.

52. Principles of Corporate Governance: A Report by OECD Task Force on Corporate Governance, 1999.

53. R.K. Mishra, Punam Singh and Shulagna Sarkar, *'Rethinking Corporate Social Responsibility'*, New Delhi, MacMillan Publisher India Ltd., 2011.

54. Rajagopalan, R., *'Directors and Corporate Governance'*, Chennai, Company Law Institute of India, 2003.

55. Ramakrishna Mission, *'The Cultural Heritage of India'*, Vol. 2, Calcutta, 1957-59.
56. Rebert A.G., Monks and Nell Minow, *'Corporate Governance'*, UK, John Wiley & Sons, Ltd., 2011.
57. Richard De George, *'Business Ethics'*, New York, MacMillan, 1986.
58. Ronald D Francis, and Mukti Mishra, *'Business Ethics: An Indian Perspective'*, Tata McGraw-Hill, 2009.
59. Saharay, H.K., *'Textbook on Competition Law'*, New Delhi, Universal Law Publishing Co., 2012.
60. Sandeep Singh, *'Secularism: From Lab to Field'*, Private Circulation Only, December 2012.
61. Sanjay K. Agarwal, *'Corporate Social Responsibility in India'*, New Delhi, Response Books, 2008.
62. Sarkar, C.R., *'Social Responsibility of Business Enterprises'*, New Delhi, New Century Publications, 2005.
63. Sasidharan, G.K., *'Advaita a Science'*, Kollam (Kerala), Many Worlds Publications, 2014.
64. Scheneider, H.W. (Ed.), *'Adam Smith's Moral and Political Philosophy'*, New York, Harper Torch Book, 1970.
65. Seshadrinath, R., *'Pearls of Wisdom and Stirring Speeches of Dr. S. Radhakrishnan'*, Chennai, Author, 2011.
66. Sherlekar, S.A., *'Ethics in Management'*, Mumbai, Himalaya Publishing House, 2003.
67. Shireen Moosvi, *'Capitalism, Colonialism and Globalization: Studies on Economic Change'*, New Delhi, Tulika Books, 2011.
68. Silverstein, Michael, *'The Environmental Economic Revolution'*, New York, St. Martin Press, 1993.
69. Sngupta, N.K., *'Changing Patterns of Corporate Management'* Delhi, Vikas Publishing House Pvt. Ltd., 1983.
70. Sri Aurobindo, *'The Foundations of Indian Culture '*, Pondicherry, Sri Aurobindo Ashram, 1995.
71. Subhash Chadra Das, *'Corporate Governance in India: An Evaluation'*, New Delhi, PHI Learning Private Limited, 2012.
72. Subhash Sharma, Indian Ethics and Spirit of Development: The VEDA Model of Leadership and Management, Management Perception, 2001 pp. 33-41.
73. The Combined Code of Best Practices in Corporate Governance, The Turnbull Committee Report, 1998.
74. The Committee on Corporate Governance, The Hampel Committee Report, 1998.

75. Thomas Paine, *'The Rights of Man'*, 1791, UK, (Avail in e-books of many publishers).
76. Tulika Saxena and A.P.S. Bhadauria (Eds.), *'Changing Paradigms of Management Dynamics'*, New Delhi, I.K. International Publishing House, 2014.
77. Velasquez, Manuel G., *'Business Ethics: Concepts and Cases'*, New Delhi, PHI Learning Pvt. Ltd., 2009.
78. Viyyanna Rao, K., *'Public Policy and Inclusive Growth in India'*, New Delhi, SSDN Publishers and Distributors, 2015.
79. Vohra, N. N. & Sabyasachi Bhattacharya, *'Looking Back: India in the Twentieth Century'* New Delhi, National Book Trust, 2002.
80. Weis, Joseph W., *'Business Ethics: Concepts and Cases'*, New Delhi, Cengage Learning India Pvt. Ltd., India Edition, 2009.

Index

N

O

P

Q

R

S

T

U

V

W